ECONOMIC TRANSFORMATIONS

Economic Transformations

General Purpose Technologies and Long-Term Economic Growth

RICHARD G. LIPSEY
KENNETH I. CARLAW
CLIFFORD T. BEKAR

OXFORD
UNIVERSITY PRESS

OXFORD

UNIVERSITY PRESS

Great Clarendon Street, Oxford OX2 6DP

Oxford University Press is a department of the University of Oxford.
It furthers the University's objective of excellence in research, scholarship,
and education by publishing worldwide in

Oxford New York

Auckland Cape Town Dar es Salaam Hong Kong Karachi
Kuala Lumpur Madrid Melbourne Mexico City Nairobi
New Delhi Shanghai Taipei Toronto

With offices in

Argentina Austria Brazil Chile Czech Republic France Greece
Guatemala Hungary Italy Japan Poland Portugal Singapore
South Korea Switzerland Thailand Turkey Ukraine Vietnam

Oxford is a registered trade mark of Oxford University Press
in the UK and in certain other countries

Published in the United States
by Oxford University Press Inc., New York

British Library Cataloguing in Publication Data

Data available

Library of Congress Cataloging in Publication Data

Data available

Typeset by SPI Publisher Services, Pondicherry, India
Printed in Great Britain on acid-free paper by
Clays Ltd., St. Ives plc.

0-19-928564-0(hbk)   9780199285648

0-19-929089-x   9780199290895

1

Contents

Contents

List of Figures

List of Tables

List of Boxes

Foreword

THE CANADIAN INSTITUTE FOR ADVANCED
RESEARCH AND THIS BOOK

This book had its beginnings in 1988 when I was asked by the CIAR to set up a research programme on long-term economic growth. I became a Fellow of the Institute in 1989. The programme was accepted by their Research Council soon afterwards and I became its first director. The programme also had an advisory committee chaired by Kenneth Arrow. For several years, Arrow attended our meetings on a fairly regular basis. At the beginning of the second five-year period, Joel Mokyr joined the advisory committee and became almost a de facto member of the group, attending most of our meetings and contributing to much of our debate, especially on matters of the history of technology.[1]

The CIAR's programmes are innovative. Funding is for five years and potentially renewable for another five, after an in-depth peer review. Fellows get full-time relief from university duties and Associates get part-time relief. There is no overarching research design but members are expected to work on related subjects. They meet regularly, present papers, interact, and are encouraged to engage in joint research collaborations, particularly across subdisciplinary borders.

When I set the programme up, I intended to bring together different groups of economists who typically do not interact. I hoped that the sparks this process would inevitably produce would light some interesting research fires. By the end of the first five-year period, our group included growth theorists, labour economists, economic historians, business school economists, and institutionalists. I also wanted to recruit representatives of the evolutionary school, but for various reasons I did not achieve that goal.

When I was first approached by Fraser Mustard, the then president of the CIAR, I was already convinced that technological change lay at the heart of long-term economic growth and that perfect competition was not the right market structure against which to judge the efficiency of dynamic evolving economies. As an undergraduate at the University of British Columbia, I was lucky enough to take part in an

---

[1] The list of those who were members of the programme together with the dates they served follows: Daron Acemoglu (2000–2), Philippe Aghion (2000–2), George Akerlof (1992–2002), John Baldwin (1993–8), Paul Beaudry (1996–2002), B. Curtis Eaton (1991–3), Pierre Fortin (1993–2002), Rick Harris (1993–2002), Elhanan Helpman (1992–2002), Peter Howitt (1994–2002), Richard Lipsey (1989–2002), Huw Loyd-Ellis (1999–2002), David Mowery (1994–8), Kevin Murphy (1994–9), Diego Puga (1999–2002), Craig Riddell (1994–2002), Paul Romer (1991–2002), Nathan Rosenberg (1991–2002), Joanne Roberts (2001–2), Ed Safarian (1991–7), André Schleifer (1991–3), Scott Taylor (1996–8), Manuel Trajtenberg (1997–2002), Daniel Trefler (1997–2002), Eric von Hippel (1994–8), Michael Wolfson (1992–8), and Alwyn Young (1994–2002).

honours seminar run by a young staff member, Bill Merritt, where we read widely in, and reported on, such classic social science authors as Thorston Veblen, H. J. Mencken, Werner Sombart, Vilfredo Pareto, and James Burnham. It was my good fortune to be asked to report on the first few chapters of Schumpeter's *The Theory of Economic Development*. I was profoundly influenced by what I read and the views I formed then were reinforced when as a graduate student at the University of Toronto I studied his *Capitalism, Socialism, and Democracy*. From those readings, I took away several things. First, I developed a mental non-equilibrium model of the circular flow of income that was continually disturbed by new innovations and the cycles that they induced. Throughout my subsequent professional career, I was fond of saying that this model insulated me against the excesses of Hicksian (and Samuelsonian) comparative statics. Second, I rejected the common use of perfect competition as the ideal against which the performance of all other market structures were to be judged. Indeed, the very forces that are seen as undesirable market imperfections in a world of perfectly competitive equilibrium are the driving forces of growth in a dynamic, changing world. Third, I accepted that the main long-term determinant of growth in living standards is technological change, against which the effects of improvements brought about by feasible changes both in economic efficiency and in income distribution are insignificant.

After graduating, I had kept abreast of macro growth theory until the interest in neoclassical growth models petered out in the late 1960s. As editor of the *Review of Economic Studies* in the early 1960s, many of the early growth models had passed over my desk. Also, as a consultant in the early 1960s for the newly formed British National Economic Development Council, popularly known as NEDY, I was made dramatically aware of the gap between theory and policy in the area of economic growth. We were charged with studying obstacles to growth in Britain, and to that end I approached some of those British economists who were most active in the rapidly expanding theoretical literature on growth. I asked: 'What assistance does your work offer to applied economists interested in understanding and improving Britain's poor growth performance?' But, as from the oysters who were foolish enough to walk with the Walrus and the Carpenter, 'answer came there none'.

At the time of my appointment to the CIAR fellowship in 1989, I had not worried much about economic growth for two decades, having spent the 1980s working mainly on trade policy and the 1970s on problems in Industrial Organization and Economic Geography with Curtis Eaton (see Eaton and Lipsey 1997). So I divided my time between the large amount of necessary reading and getting the programme underway. I had already concluded that if technological change was the key to long-term growth, our group needed to know a lot more about technology, invention, and innovation than is normally covered in economics courses, whether on growth or anything else. Early on in my reading, Nathan Rosenberg's *Inside the Black Box* had a profound effect on my thinking about these critical subjects. I also read Freeman and Perez's essay 'Structural Crises of Adjustment: Business Cycles and Investment Behaviour', which got me thinking about how technology was related to the economic and social structure. For some years, I used their concept of a technoeconomic paradigm as my organizing concept. Later, my then co-authors and I replaced it with our concept of a structuralist-evolutionary (S-E) decomposition (see Chapter 4), explaining our reasons in Lipsey and Bekar (1995). Other early readings that had profound effects on my thinking were Rosenberg and Birdzell's *How the West Grew Rich*, and Leonard Dudley's *The Word and The Sword*. The latter led me to realize just how deep the transforming effects of technologies could be. A reading of almost all the chapters of *Technical Change and Economic Theory* by Dosi et al., and a rereading of Nelson and Winter's classic, *An Evolutionary Theory of Economic Change*, put my thinking on an evolutionary track.

In the early days of setting up the programme, Simon Fraser University made me an offer I could not refuse, and my wife and I moved to Vancouver in 1989. In 1991, I began teaching a course called 'Economic Growth and Policy', which laid the foundations for this book. Each year until 1997, fifteen to twenty graduate students and one or two staff members attended. Most confessed to having their minds blown by hearing someone who viewed growth from outside of the neoclassical paradigm, going beyond macro modelling to combine description, history, and theory in one broad view of the growth process.

In the first year, my star pupil was Clifford Bekar, who was particularly interested in the methodological and historical parts of my message. His essay that year, then his MA dissertation, and finally one chapter in his Ph.D. dissertation, looked at the First Industrial Revolution as an illustration of what we then called transforming technologies and later came to call general purpose technologies (GPTs). In the second year of the course, my star pupil was Kenneth Carlaw. He was a theorist at heart and deeply steeped in the neoclassical approach. He fought me tooth and nail every inch of the way. I am not sure what the rest of the class thought, but I soon came to look forward to our twice-weekly battles.

I was impressed enough to recruit both these students as RA's working on many issues, most of which became part of this book. Their work was so impressive that they soon became junior authors of several articles—Lipsey and Bekar (1995) and Lipsey and Carlaw (1996) were the first instances. Finally, their hard work and considerable insight promoted both of them to equal co-authors. Carlaw and Lipsey (2002) and Bekar and Lipsey (forthcoming 2005) were the first papers to signal this change. Because the project that led to this book was initiated by me (in 1990) and the early conceptual work was done mainly by me (during the first half of the 1990s), I have remained the senior author of the book. Over the later years, however, the other two have contributed in big ways to the book's development.

Richard G. Lipsey
Bowen Island, BC
February 2005

Preface

In this preface, I first ask: what distinguishes this book from the many others on technology and on economic growth? I then go on to consider the evolution of the three most important themes of this book.

WHY ANOTHER BOOK ON GROWTH?

While books on long-term growth have always been popular, the last few years have seen a great increase in their number. Readers may wonder if ours is simply another marginal addition to this fast-growing literature. We think not. First, we are interested in the phenomenon of general purpose technologies (GPTs) in themselves and we say much more about them, both descriptively and analytically, than is typical in books on growth. Second, in our work on growth we take up a broader set of themes and employ a larger array of analytical tools than is typical of most books on growth and technological change. While others concentrate on one or another of these techniques, we do not hesitate to use historical analysis, formal modelling, simulation techniques, what Richard Nelson calls appreciative theorizing, and aspects of evolutionary economics.

In Chapter 1, we outline our coverage in detail and note much of what we have to say that is new on each of these topics. Here we merely illustrate the wide scope of our coverage, which, for better or for worse, is one of the distinguishing features of our book. We start by observing that long-term growth is driven mainly by technological change. This leads us to study the nature of technology and how it changes, building on material found in books such as Rosenberg's *Inside the Black Box*. We argue that understanding technological change requires an evolutionary approach, such as was pioneered by Nelson and Winter in *An Evolutionary Theory of Economic Change*. We outline such an approach and contrast it with neoclassical theory. Because over the centuries new technologies radically alter more or less everything in the socio-economic order, doing much more than just increasing output per person, standard neoclassical theory is a relatively poor tool for studying their effects. We argue that one approach that handles these effects well is a combination of institutional and evolutionary economics that we call structuralist-evolutionary (S-E) theory. The contrast between neoclassical and S-E theory leads us to consider two different world views of how the economy works and of what policies are effective in achieving given ends.

We also argue that a full study of growth requires an understanding of quite a bit of the history of technological change as is found in Mokyr's *Lever of Riches*. Here we concentrate on the big shocks caused by GPTs as are discussed in Dudley's *The Word and the Sword* (although he does not use the term 'general purpose technologies'). Big GPT shocks change almost everything in a society and revitalize the growth process by creating an agenda for the creation of new products, new processes, and new organizational forms. To elaborate, we study GPTs through an S-E lens, spending much time developing an S-E theoretical structure in which we situate GPTs. We systematize much more of the knowledge of how GPTs evolve and affect the society than we were able to do in the two chapters that we contributed to Helpman (1998).

We then discuss the nineteenth-century emergence of sustained growth of output in the West, building on the analyses in Rosenberg and Birdzell's *How the West Grew Rich* and in Landes' *The Unbound Prometheus*, but putting much more emphasis on science than is usual. This leads us to ask why sustained growth of output was not generated endogenously outside of the West, where we use much of the analysis found in Toby Huff's *The Rise of Early Modern Science*, and take issue with some of the arguments in Kenneth Pomeranz's *The Great Divergence*. Then we turn to the emergence of the West's sustained per capita growth that happened later in the nineteenth century. This leads to a discussion of population dynamics as is found in Easterlin's *Growth Triumphant*, although, in contrast to his appreciative theorizing, we build our analysis around several simulation models that make use of neoclassical growth theory.

We argue that once sustained growth has been established, we can learn quite a bit about its dynamics from formal models of GPT-driven growth. We develop new ways of theorizing formally about GPTs that allow us to incorporate much more of their richness than was possible in the first-generation models, which were based on crude assumptions needed for theoretical tractability. In doing this, we are taking up the programme that we enunciated at the end of our contribution to the Helpman volume and that we thought would by now have been much further advanced than it is.

Developing satisfactory theories of GPTs is not a task that will be completed quickly or easily. It seems to us that the theoretical research program should be to extend existing models, and/ or to develop new models, to capture more of what we know empirically about GPTs rather than elaborating and generalizing just because we are able to do so. In this program there would be a large payoff to the development of new models that are designed to capture more of the characteristics of GPTs in their assumptions, and then explore the implications of those assumptions. (Lipsey, Bekar, and Carlaw 1998: 217–18)

Finally, we discuss some policy implications of our approach to understanding long-term growth.

Doing all of what we have just outlined requires that we cover a much wider range of topics, using a larger variety of tools, than is found in almost all other books dealing with growth and/or technological change. We hope that we have at least begun the process of integrating these various topics and tools into a coherent analysis of both the causes and the consequences of long-term growth.

EVOLUTION OF THREE IMPORTANT THEMES

Three of the book's most important themes were a long time in gestation: (*a*) the relation between long-term economic growth and general purpose technologies (GPTs); (*b*) the importance of science in the First Industrial Revolution that initiated sustained long-term growth in the West; and (*c*) the relation between the twentieth-century revolution in information and communication technologies (ICTs) on the one hand and the so-called productivity paradox, and the use of total factor productivity (TFP) to measure technological change, on the other hand.

GPTs and Long-Term Growth

Historically, this book began with my investigation into the causes and consequences of long-term growth. I quickly discovered Perez and Freeman's concept of a tech-noeconomic paradigm, which my co-authors and I came to see as a key to understanding the impact of technological change in terms of periodic transformations of the economy. After using the concept for a few years, we developed our own more focused concepts of transforming technologies and the facilitating structure. Later, we discovered that our concept of a transforming technology was more or less the same as that of a GPT that had recently been put forward by Bresnahan and Trajtenberg, so we switched to using that term. Our work then developed into two distinct but interrelated research programmes concerning (*a*) GPTs and (*b*) long-term economic growth.

We sought to understand what GPTs were, how they evolved, and how they impacted on the economy. Since the concept of a GPT was introduced into the literature just over ten years ago, it has received a growing amount of attention with many scholars utilizing it in their research. Unfortunately, on the theoretical side there have been no further advances, either in modelling it or in delineating its extent empirically, since Helpman's 1998 volume (in which the present authors have two chapters). We believe that modelling has not been expanded beyond the crude first-generation models found in Helpman because the standard theoretical maxi mizing techniques applied to GPTs quickly become intractable when elaborations are made in the direction of increasing realism. We sought methods of breaking through the roadblock that was so created. What we regard as a success in this endeavour came when we developed simulation models of GPTs which, although much less elegant than analytical models, are not constrained in the same way and can handle any degree of complexity that is needed to incorporate into formal models a large set of typical GPT characteristics. Some of the many pay-offs to this approach are developed in Chapters 14 and 15.

Unfortunately, on the empirical side there is considerable misunderstanding on just which technologies are and are not GPTs. For example, Moser and Nicholas (2004) argue that electricity, one of the most pervasive GPTs of all time, is not a GPT at all. The questions of what a GPT is and how to identify one are taken up in detail in Chapter 4.

On long-term economic growth, we sought to integrate the concept of GPTs into the historical story of growth and to use our new insights to investigate how the episodic growth that had existed for millennia was transformed in the nineteenth century into sustained growth. In writing the book around the theme of long-term growth, we may have obscured the contributions we seek to make through our research programme to better understand and model GPTs. We hope that this is not so since much of what we say about GPTs, particularly in Chapters 4, 5, and 6, can be divorced from considerations of very long-term growth.

Science and the Industrial Revolution

The second main theme is the importance of mechanistic science in the First Industrial Revolution. No one doubts that science was important in the Second Industrial Revolution and that it grew more important as a driver of invention and innovation as the twentieth century progressed. But the prevailing view in the 1990s seemed to be that, up until the late nineteenth century, empirically based technological advances led science (by, among other things, presenting scientists with such problems as understanding fermentation and heat transference), not the reverse.

I first began thinking about trajectories in the advance of scientific knowledge when I encountered Joseph Needham's argument that, although the Chinese did not have Newtonian mechanics, their holistic approach might have allowed them to jump directly to twentieth-century quantum mechanics. It was clear to me that although he was a great scholar of Chinese technology, Needham could only have held that view if he knew very little about how scientific knowledge grows cumulatively. This led me to think about the place of Western science in the emergence of sustained economic growth at the time of the First Industrial Revolution. Nathan Rosenberg had argued that on balance, up until late in the nineteenth century, technology led science, not vice versa. While arguing with him when I presented some of my preliminary thoughts to the CIAR group (discussed in the Foreword), I had a great insight. He, and many others who argued in a similar vein, were thinking of modern science: great embracing hypotheses from which specific applications were deduced. But this was not the nature of early modern science. At that time, the overarching hypotheses were due to Aristotle, whose science had been fully integrated into Christian theology by the great scholastic philosophers of the Middle Ages. Early modern science can then be seen as a piecemeal testing and gradual refutation of Aristotelian science. Not until Descartes and Newton was Aristotle replaced by new overarching scientific world views.

With these concerns in mind, I reread Mokyr's *The Lever of Riches* and found him dismissive of the importance of science at the pre-industrial stages of technological history. But what caught my attention were his statements that 'Britain did not have a significant scientific advantage that would explain its technological leadership' and that 'Britain had no more science than the Continent, only different science' (Mokyr 1990: 242). That was the clue: it really did matter that only Britain had Newtonian science, while France had Cartesian science, and those outside of the West had neither. Britain had a significant advantage in Newtonian *mechanical* science, which was what mattered for the First Industrial Revolution, and the great eighteenth-century engineering works that preceded it. Two books were critical in my elaboration of this view: Toby Huff's *Rise of Early Modern Science,* and Edward Grant's *The Foundations of Modern Science in the Middle Ages.* Later, Margaret Jacob's *Scientific Culture and the Making of the Industrial West* filled in a missing piece of the puzzle by showing how much Newtonian science permeated the whole of eighteenth-century British thinking. A detailed study of developments in science and technology in the early modern period filled in the remaining blanks.

So, understood as referring to modern science, the statement that technology presented results to be used by science rather than vice versa is correct. (Rosenberg 1982: ch. 7 gives half a dozen examples.) But understood as referring to science as it was in the early modern period, the statement is questionable. This led to a detailed study of the mutual interaction of early modern science and technology. I presented these ideas to our CIAR group in 1997.

Then in 1999, Clifford Bekar and Kenneth Carlaw joined me in preparing a paper on this issue for a conference entitled 'On the Origins of the Modern World: Competitive Perspectives from the Edge of the Millennium' in Davis, California.[2] Stated in a nutshell, our theses were: (*a*) early modern science and technology coevolved without one being the clear leader of the other; (*b*) Newtonian mechanics, the first fully modern, overarching, scientific 'laws' were critical to the First Industrial Revolution, which helped to explain why it occurred where and when it did (in eighteenth-century Britain); (*c*) the absence of Newtonian science solved the puzzle of why China, which was the equal of Europe in so many other ways, failed to generate its own indigenous industrial revolution.

We were roundly attacked by the assembled ranks of Sinologists, who accused us of being hopelessly Eurocentric, but equally encouraged by a group of technology students, who remained silent in open discussion but supported us privately. We wrote these ideas up and had them rejected by three major journals. Nonetheless, we were sure we were onto something because the referees' reports were divided almost equally between those who said the ideas were so commonplace that they should not be published and those who said they were so obviously wrong that they should not be published. Our answers to the Sinologists and our analysis of the importance of science to the Industrial Revolution are mentioned briefly towards the end of Chapter 1 and detailed in Chapters 7 and 8. We were also encouraged by some recent writings in which several authors have increased the importance they accord to science in the First Industrial Revolution.[3]

The Revolution in ICTs, the productivity paradox, and TFP

The third theme is actually a set of interrelated issues concerning ICTs, the productivity paradox, and TFP. Early on, I came to the conclusion that the world was

---

[2] The paper was listed as 'Science, Institutions, and the Industrial Revolution' by Richard G. Lipsey, Clifford Bekar, and Kenneth Carlaw.

[3] Since this Preface was written, we have heard that our paper has finally been accepted by a journal (see Bekar and Lipsey 2005, forthcoming).

experiencing a profound economic, social, and political transformation driven by the revolution centred around the electronic computer. When I first began to express this view in Canadian policy circles in the early 1990s, most economists were dismissive. Typical arguments against my view were:

Technology changes more or less continuously, a little faster sometimes, a little slower at other times, but such change is not interrupted by the kinds of revolutionary events you describe. For conclusive proof look at the growth in total factor productivity, which measures technological change, and which, if anything, has been slowing over the 1980s and early 1990s just when you assert the revolution was occurring.

This conflicting view set in motion three research subprojects within my general study of long-term economic growth. First, Bekar and I set out to study past technological shocks brought about by what we came to call GPTs. We identified twenty or so of these in all of history. (See Lipsey and Bekar 1995 for our first statement of these.) So we had established, contrary to my critics, that such transforming shocks have occurred in the past. This left us with our second project, to study the question: Is the so-called ICT revolution one of these or is it a lesser shock? Studies of its effects first published in Lipsey and Bekar (1995) left us in no doubt that it ranked with the most important of history's transforming GPTs. This led to our third project: to discover what was wrong with the commonly repeated argument that the deceleration in the rate of growth of the Solow residual, now called TFP, indicated a slowdown in technological change rather than a new technological revolution. This set Carlaw and me off on a search that extended over more than half a decade into the meaning and behaviour of TFP. As our understanding of these issues evolved, we presented them in a number of workshops and finally in a massive paper presented at the conference in honour of Nelson and Winter in Aalborg, Denmark (Carlaw and Lipsey 2001). We knew we were onto something when the paper presenting our analysis of TFP was enthusiastically endorsed by students of measurement such as Erwin Diewert and Alice Nakamura, although rejected by a leading journal. The paper has since been published in *The Canadian Journal of Economics* (Lipsey and Carlaw 2004). Our main conclusion in this paper is that since TFP does not measure technological change, there is no paradox in observing high rates of technological change and low rates of TFP growth.

More generally, however, we argue in this book that the whole expectation of an acceleration in productivity growth associated with a new GPT—and the assumption of a paradox when we see the latter but not the former—is a case of the 'Emperor's New Clothes'. The argument concerning why we should not necessarily expect a new GPT to be accompanied by a productivity bonus, as well as an enumeration of changes that make the ICT revolution rank as one of the most important transforming technologies of all time, can be found in Lipsey (2002b). It is substantially repeated here in Chapter 4 under the subheading 'The Myth of the Productivity Paradox'.

Richard G. Lipsey

Acknowledgements

Many people have contributed to this book. First and foremost we wish to thank Fraser Mustard, the then president of the CIAR, who conceived the project on long-term economic growth, recruited Lipsey to be its first director, and took an active part in the further development of the programme. Next, we want to thank all the members of the CIAR Economic Growth and Policy Programme for helping Lipsey to develop his ideas and stimulating him with theirs. Equally important is Joanna Lipsey, the group's administrator from 1989 to 1995 and subsequently Lipsey's personal assistant. She has contributed to this book in ways too numerous and diverse to enumerate. Michele Platje provided valuable research assistance over several years. Alvaro Pereira, who did his dissertation under Lipsey on subjects closely related to this book, has contributed many ideas and much insightful criticism at various stages of the preparation of the manuscript. Peter Howitt, Nathan McLellan, Nathan Rosenberg, Joanna Lipsey, Stan Metcalf, Richard Nelson, Alvaro Pereira, Clyde Reed, Grant Scobic, and Rick Szostak have read some or all of the manuscript and contributed much to its development. Erwin Deiwert, Brian Easton, Kevin Fox, and Les Oxley have provided helpful comments on specific parts of the manuscript. Robyn Wills and Joanna Lipsey coped with volumes of manuscript and patiently deciphered our scrawl, along with Karen Wallace. Rebecca Hurrell kindly aided us with the preparation of our figures for publication. Jack Blaney, the then Vice President of Harbour Centre and Development at Simon Fraser University, offered aid and encouragement at all stages. Karla Carlaw, Maria Bekar, and Diana Lipsey showed amazing patience in putting up with the enormous demands on our time made by this book, particularly in the last years of its development. To these and many more, we offer our thanks and the usual disclaimer: much that is good in what follows has been contributed by them; what is bad or in error is our responsibility alone.

At various times, financial support has been provided by the CIAR, Social Science Research Council of Canada, Royal Society of New Zealand's Marsden Fund, grant number UOC 101, Donner Foundation, and National Research Council of Canada. Simon Fraser University, The University of Canterbury, and Lewis and Clark College generously provided office space and support staff.

Clifford T. Bekar
Kenneth I. Carlaw
Richard G. Lipsey

Part I

Growth, Technological Change, and General Purpose Technologies

1

Technology as Revolution

This book is about two interrelated phenomena: long-term economic growth and the pervasive technologies that occasionally transform a society's entire set of economic, social, and political structures and that have come to be called 'general purpose technologies' (GPTs). In most of the existing literature, these have been treated separately, and indeed much of our discussion of GPTs can be taken on its own, independent of long-term growth. Importantly, however, we seek to relate these phenomena by treating GPTs as one of the main forces that sustain economic growth in the long term.

Largely working through the mechanism of general purpose technologies, economic growth has transformed our economic, social, and political structures over past millennia, and is still doing so. Over the last ten or so millennia since the neolithic agricultural revolution, economic growth has helped to turn us ever so slowly but quite decisively from hunter-gatherers, consuming only what nature provides directly, into people who consciously produce what we consume, often using materials that we ourselves have created. Growth has occurred not by producing more of the same, using static techniques, but by creating new products, new processes, and new forms of organization.

Over the last two and a half centuries, the pace of economic growth has quickened, raising the material living standards of average citizens in industrialized countries to levels previously undreamed of by any of their earlier counterparts and reducing the typical working hours for urban dwellers in industrialized countries from 60–72 hours a week at the beginning of the nineteenth century to 35–40 hours a week at the beginning of the twenty-first century. But this more rapid growth has not benefited everyone, at least in the first instance, since growth is an uneven process that initially yields gains for some and losses for others (although, on average, each generation in the countries that have succeeded in producing sustained growth has been better off materially than all previous generations). This rapid growth has also come at a significant cost by threatening and sometimes destroying many aspects of social and political organizations, cultures, and the environment. There is no question that these side effects exist, although how important they are when set against the beneficial effects of growth is, today, a matter of intense debate.

Because one of our major concerns is to understand how and why growth has both accelerated and become sustained over the last two centuries, we concentrate most of our study of growth on the West—Europe and the former English-speaking British colonies, the USA, Canada, Australia, New Zealand, and, to some extent,

South Africa—since it was there that modern sustained, as opposed to episodic, economic growth emerged sometime in the eighteenth or early nineteenth century. But when we ask why sustained growth did not emerge elsewhere, we need a comparison set and we chose China and the Islamic countries for this purpose.

We argue that all long-term growth is best understood as a *historical* process driven by innovative activity. Indeed, the evolution of technology causes much of the economic, social, and political change that we experience. Consequently, we pay much more attention to both the structure and the evolution of technology than is usual in the writings of most growth theorists (but not those historians who study growth). When studying the early evolution of technology, we take a wider geographical focus than what we now think of as the West. Since the West's technological development can be seen as a continuum of developments that began in the Middle East, particularly the countries of the Tigris–Euphrates Valley and the surrounding uplands, we begin our historical survey with developments in that area. To avoid cumbersome expressions, we use the term 'the West' to refer to the countries of the West listed above plus those middle eastern areas that were the cradle of Western civilization and technology until some time in the second millennium BC when the centre of technological development shifted to the countries that bordered on the Mediterranean. Many of the technologies that we study were innovated independently elsewhere, often in China. In concentrating on the West, we do not mean to imply that these innovations were unique to the West. (Later in the chapter we consider the charge that this focus makes us Eurocentric in some undesirable ways.)

I. PERVASIVE ECONOMIC CHANGE

We live today in a world of rapid economic and social change. Any one change typically causes other changes, which in turn cause others, and so on in a concatenation of linked causes and effects. For example, the invention of the dynamo in 1867 allowed for the practical generation of electricity. The use of electricity allowed a separate power source to be attached to each factory machine (rather than being driven by a central power source through a system of shafts and belts as in the steam-powered factory). The 'unit drive' electric motor allowed the machines in the factory to be rearranged to coincide with the rational flow of production through the factory. In turn, this arrangement allowed Henry Ford to mechanize production with a moving assembly line. In Ford's hands, the assembly line, together with standardized parts (themselves the result of another key invention in the machine tool industry), enabled the mass-produced, affordable automobile. The model T, and its successors, transformed American (and later European) society in myriad ways. It allowed people to move about more quickly and more cheaply than ever before. It provided high-paying work to many immigrants who could not easily converse in English. It helped to create the suburb, the shopping centre, the domestic tourist industry, and the motel. It helped to alter sexual mores (as courting couples were freed from the eyes of parents and chaperons)—to mention only a few of its far-reaching effects.

The Power of Growth

Economists most often focus on economic growth (usually measured by increases in gross domestic product, GDP) rather than economic change. This is understandable since growth in GDP is relatively easy to measure and its cumulative effects are dramatic. An annual growth rate of 3 per cent doubles output every twenty-four years, and then doubles it again, increasing output by just over 15-fold in one century. Even at the modest rate of 1 per cent per year, output doubles in about seventy years and then doubles again to four times the starting point in another seventy years. A further reason for focusing on growth of GDP is that it correlates strongly with many other things that people care about, such as increases in literacy, reductions in absolute levels of poverty, increases in life expectancy, more gender equality, and increased ability and willingness to deal with environmental issues.

We too analyse growth in GDP, but at the core of our analysis is the notion that a full understanding of the *causes* and *consequences* of long-term economic growth also requires an appreciation of the qualitative changes induced by technological innovations—a point stressed by Schumpeter (1934, 1943) many years ago. People living at the beginning of the twenty-first century experience measured real consumption that is over ten times as much as the consumption of those living at the beginning of the twentieth century. But they consume this enormous increment largely in terms of *new commodities* made with *new techniques*. People living in the first decade of the twentieth century did not know modern dental and medical equipment, penicillin, bypass operations, safe births, control of genetically transmitted diseases, personal computers, compact discs, television sets, automobiles, opportunities for fast and cheap worldwide travel, affordable universities, central heating, air conditioning, and food of great variety free from ptomaine and botulism, much less the elimination of endless kitchen drudgery through the use of detergents, washing machines, electric stoves, vacuum cleaners, refrigerators, dishwashers, and a host of other labour-saving household products, which their great-grandchildren take for granted. Nor could our ancestors of 100 years ago have imagined the robot-operated, computer-controlled, modern factories that have largely replaced their noisy, dangerous, factories that spewed coal smoke over the surrounding countryside. Technological change has transformed the quality of our lives. It has removed terrible diseases that maimed, crippled, and killed—plague, tuberculosis, cholera, dysentery, smallpox, and leprosy, to mention only the most common. In 1700, average European life expectancy was about thirty years; in early eighteenth-century France, one in five babies was dead by the end of its first year, and 50 per cent of registered children were dead by age ten.[1] In 1900, death from botulism and ptomaine poisoning from contaminated food was common. Chemical additives virtually eliminated these

---

[1] Many were not registered because they died before their births had been registered or were victims of parental infanticide. (Data in the text and the footnote are from Blum 1982.)

killers and allowed us to live long enough to worry about the long-run cancer-causing effects of some of these additives. Now they are being replaced by safer preservatives.

In summary, technological advance not only increases our incomes but it also transforms our lives through the invention of new, hitherto undreamed of products that are made in new, hitherto undreamed of ways. For all these reasons and more, it is clear that changes in per capita GDP radically understate the impact of economic growth on the average person. Nonetheless, changes in real GDP do convey significant information. They give us information of how much the market value of the nation's total output has grown when measured at constant prices. This tells us, among other things, how much is available for gross investment and consumption in one form or another.

Various Concepts of Growth

Material living standards are not a function of total production and total consumption but of how much is available for each person. So we need to distinguish two types of growth: 'extensive growth'—a simple increase in real GDP; and 'intensive growth'—an increase in GDP per person. Assuming that living standards were not much above subsistence at the beginning of the neolithic agricultural revolution, the growth in the world's population gives a minimum estimate of extensive growth as measured by the rate of growth of total output.[2]

If population is constant, all growth is intensive growth. If population increases at least as fast as GDP, we have only extensive growth. Thus the population dynamics that we study in Chapters 9 and 10 are central to understanding the relations between extensive and intensive growth, which have existed at different times and different places.

Throughout human history, both extensive and intensive growth have sometimes occurred in occasional bursts and at other times have been sustained for long periods. This suggests that two further concepts are needed. The first is 'sustained growth'—a well-defined concept within the context of a formal model, existing when growth never ends. Such growth is usually modelled to occur along a balanced or a stationary equilibrium growth path. But since we can never know what will happen over the indefinite future, that definition has no empirical counterpart. For example, the assertion that some policy would produce sustained growth, or that we are currently living in a regime of sustained growth, could not be shown to be empirically correct. No matter how long growth has continued, it might end in the future. In an empirical context, sustained growth is probably best understood as self-reinforcing growth that is not obviously episodic. So the criteria are first, that it is obviously not a short burst of growth that comes to an end in a few decades or less; and second, that there are reasons to believe that the growth is self-sustaining.

---

[2] It is a minimum because it is what would be needed to keep the growing population on the subsistence level. To the extent that living standards have risen, the rate of growth of total output has *exceeded* the rate of growth of total population.

The second concept is 'sustainable growth', which was made famous by the World Commission on Environment and Development (1987), popularly known as the Brundtland Commission. It refers to growth that continues without causing unsustainable alterations to the environment, or unsustainable depletions in the overall stock of natural resources. For example, a country's growth that is based mainly on cutting down teak forests much faster than they can be regenerated is not sustainable for longer than the stock of trees lasts. World growth that raised global temperature to the extent that various growth-stopping crises developed would also not be sustainable. As these examples show, it is conceivable that one country, or the world as a whole, could engage in a bout of unsustainable growth that continued for a long time, until the problems it caused became insurmountable. We consider the problem of sustainability further in Chapter 13.

Underestimating the Power of Growth and Technical Change

Modern societies are constantly adapting to new technologies. Because not all of these adaptations have been peaceful or trouble-free, technology has a bad name in some circles. Some critics emphasize the destructive aspects of technological change. It destroys specific jobs (while creating others), alters patterns of trade, and even eliminates entire ways of life. The First Industrial Revolution destroyed the livelihood of many craftsmen, while moving work from the villages to the new industrial towns, where the poverty and squalor that had existed for millennia in the countryside became visible to urban onlookers. The automation, restructuring, and downsizing that has resulted from the late twentieth-century revolution in information and communication technologies (ICTs) has destroyed the jobs of many unskilled and semi-skilled factory workers as well as many in middle management. Also, while narrowing the gap between rich and poor through the first seven decades of the twentieth century, technological change has helped to widen that gap dramatically since then. Detractors also stress that new technologies are sometimes environmentally destructive. Modern fishing technologies have caused the near extinction of many previously plentiful sea creatures. Although smoke pollution in industrial cities is much less than it was 100 years ago, global warming, with all its harmful potential, was not then an issue, nor were industrial disasters on the scale of Chernobyl or Bhopal even thinkable.

Although many of the alleged harmful effects of technological change have substance, many others are based on misinformation and misunderstanding. As outlined above, technological change is responsible for all the new products, process, and forms of organization that have raised material living standards 10-fold over the last century. Also, the number of new jobs created by all previous technological changes has far exceeded the number of old jobs destroyed. So, in spite of recurring worries, technological change has not so far been a net destroyer of jobs.

Despite the valid points they make about the many harmful side effects of technological change, few of even the most vociferous critics of the effects of modern technology would be willing to go back to the technologies of 1900, foregoing all twentieth-century products and processes. Because they are never faced with such a stark choice, many of the critics of technological change underassess the power of the growth that it drives. This leads to many misguided policy views, including the belief that past technological change has been harmful on balance and that further growth is undesirable. We mention four of the many reasons for this underassessment of the benefits of growth.

For more than a century most economists paid little attention to the importance of technological change. In spite of Schumpeter's strong criticisms (1943) of the excessive emphasis that economists gave to static efficiency and their relative neglect of the economics of technological change, the profession continued largely to ignore his criticism. Although today there is more interest in economic growth and technological change than there was fifty years ago, the typical introductory economics course still spends far more time on the static theory of market allocation than on economic growth. Furthermore, if students do take a course on growth, it typically starts and ends with mathematical growth models in which technology is hidden in the black box of the neoclassical aggregate production function. As a result, students all too often learn almost nothing about technology and technological change when learning about 'growth'. They can also come away with some serious misconceptions of what has really happened in the history of long-term growth. One common misconception is that the upheavals that have beset the world over the last few decades of the twentieth century, and that are associated with new ICTs are unique. In fact, large economic, social, and political upheavals due to new technologies have occurred episodically ever since humans first abandoned their nomadic hunter-gatherer existence 10,000 or so years ago. 'New economies' are not new to human experience and the changes wrought by the current new economy are in many ways repeats of those wrought by previous 'new economies'. Among other things, our study of technological shocks provides material that may help to guard against some common but mistaken beliefs about the actual record of growth and innovation—some of which are crude misconceptions, while others are quite subtle.

A second reason why many dismiss the importance of technological change is that the majority of young people, naturally enough, take for granted the massive alterations that technology has wrought. It is hard for the youth of any recent generation to imagine the world in which their parents and grandparents grew up, let alone the world of their more distant forebears a century or two ago. An economist beginning his professional life in 1950 would have known no electronic computers and would have done his econometric work on a mechanical calculator, which took ten or more seconds to do one long division. Two or three moderate regressions, done by inverting matrices using the Doolittle method, would have been a good day's work. International phone calls were expensive and difficult. Letters were the main method of communicating hard copy over distances, and they took days or weeks to reach their destination. Travel was expensive and rare, employing two-lane highways, rail, ocean liners, and, only rarely, slow and expensive propeller aircraft. Ballpoint pens were unknown. There were no credit cards or automatic teller machines, and to be caught away from one's hometown without cash on a weekend was a serious matter. Dental work was slow and painful, and medical diagnosis and treatment were rudimentary by today's standards. The point is that those who have not studied social and economic history typically have little idea of how technology has transformed and improved the ordinary person's lot, even over the lifetime of people still alive, and much more so over the centuries.

A third reason why the power of growth is often underassessed is because the growth of 1 or 1.5 per cent per annum changes per capita GDP so slowly that people barely notice its variations from year to year and hence do not regard variations in growth rates (over their normal range) as a big force in their lives. But anyone who was taken back 50 or 100 years would see the enormous power of such growth to alter living standards and to reduce the blight of poverty. Describing how the slow growth that transformed the living standards of working people over the course of the last two-thirds of the nineteenth century[3] went unnoticed for nearly a century, Rosenberg and Birdzell (1986: 6) wrote:

Over a year, or even over a decade, the economic gains [of the late eighteenth and the nineteenth centuries], after allowing for the rise in population, were so little noticeable that it was widely [and incorrectly] believed that the gains were experienced only by the rich, and not by the poor.

A fourth reason for underassessing the power of technical change to raise living standards is that contemporaries pay most of its costs—in terms of such things as lost jobs, lost values of physical and human capital, and environmental effects associated with the teething troubles of new products and processes—while the benefits of the technologies in use (including other technologies that are built on it) are enjoyed by some in the present and all in future generations. We still benefit, for example, from the wheel, much of Greek mechanics, and the dynamo. This temporal asymmetry in costs and benefits tends to skew assessments. Everyone benefits from past technological change and few would want to undo advances that have been made in the past. But not everyone gains from current changes. Some—for example, a fifty-eight-year-old man who loses his job and the full value of the large investment in his now obsolete human capital—might have been better off if technological change had stopped just before it impinged so unfavourably on him. Indeed, it is possible that a self interested contemporary electorate would vote to prevent some proposed new technological advance because the losers outnumbered the gainers, while the same technology would win overwhelming support in a vote taken fifty years hence because most of the losers would then be dead while the gains persisted.

The discussion so far should be sufficient to show that economic growth and increases in a sense of well-being are not necessarily perfectly correlated. In concentrating on economic growth in this book, we do not mean to imply any judgement that all forms of growth increase people's sense of well-being or *necessarily* make

---

[3] Although current research suggests that the living standards of ordinary working people may have fallen in the earlier stages of the Industrial Revolution, there is strong evidence that living standards had risen significantly between 1800 and 1900.

them better off in any demonstrable way. We do believe, however, that growth often makes people better off and improves their sense of well-being.[4] Our discussion of how people are usually unaware of what past growth and technological change has done for them is sufficient reason for saying that making people better off in definable ways does not guarantee that it will increase their sense of well-being.

Causes of Growth

We distinguish three main sources of extensive growth.[5] The first is increases in *market size*. The resulting growth is sometimes called Smithian growth since it was emphasized by Adam Smith in *The Wealth of Nations*. Increasing the size of the market allows for increased gains from trade based on a finer division of labour. It also facilitates the exploitation of scale economies of the sort we discuss in Chapter 12. Further, a growing market may encourage innovation by increasing the pay-off to the introduction of new technologies and products because the costs of making inventions and innovations tend to be independent of the size of the market that they will serve but the potential pay-off is not.

The second source is *investment*. In standard economic analysis, investment in physical and human capital is distinct from technological change. Investment gives each worker more capital to work with and this, according to the neoclassical aggregate production function, increases per capita output. The classical economists stressed the accumulation of capital as a major source of long-term growth, as do many modern economists.

The third source is *technological change*. We consider our definition of technology in some detail in Chapter 3. In the mean time, we adopt the provisional definition that by technological knowledge, technology for short, we mean knowledge of everything—products, processes, and forms of organization—that can create economic value. In the long term, new technologies are potent sources of economic growth, as emphasized by Schumpeter and his followers. In standard growth models, new technologies cause growth by increasing the amount of output that can be produced from a given set of resources. At least as important, however, is that new technologies enable new products, new processes, and new forms of organization.

The three sources of growth typically interact, making it difficult (but not necessarily impossible) to estimate the separate contribution of each. For example, market size and technological change are interrelated. Falling transport costs that increase the size of markets are often driven by technological changes in the transport industry, such as the introduction of the three-masted sailing ship in the fifteenth century, the building of railroads in the nineteenth century, and the replacement of 10,000-ton tankers and freighters by supertankers and large container ships in the 1960s. The resulting expansions in market size, in turn, drive other innovations such as the development of the joint stock company and the legal

---

[4] See Helliwell (2002) for a fascinating analysis of the relation between economic growth, globalization, and people's sense of national well-being, as well as an argument for the importance of institutions.

[5] See Mokyr (1990).

concept of limited liability that helped to finance the sixteenth-century voyages of discovery.

In spite of such interactions, we can still hope to provide a general qualitative answer to the question: How do expansions of the market, capital accumulation, and technological change compare as engines of long-term growth? We reject the most common way of doing this by estimating the contribution of technology to economic growth through the so-called Solow residual. This method uses an aggregate production function fitted to the data for measured inputs and GDP, to account for as much as possible of the increases in GDP by increases in measured inputs, and then assumes that the remainder, the Solow residual or total factor productivity (TFP), measures the contribution of technical change (and a few other lesser influences). We discuss our reasons for rejecting this commonly used measure in the Appendix to Chapter 4, in Carlaw and Lipsey (2003), and Lipsey and Carlaw (2004).

Instead, we use a simple thought experiment that illustrates a conclusion on which economic historians and students of technological change agree: technological change is the most important determinant of long-term economic growth. Consider investment first. Imagine freezing technological knowledge at the levels existing in, say, 1900, while continuing to accumulate more 1900-vintage machines and factories and using them to produce more 1900-vintage goods and services, and training more people longer and more thoroughly in the technological knowledge that was available in 1900. It is obvious that today we would have vastly lower living standards than we now enjoy (and pollution would be a massive problem). The contrast is even more striking if the same thought experiment is used to compare today's knowledge of product and process technologies with those that existed at even earlier times. Similarly, holding technology constant and expanding market size would have some effect, but could not be the source of exponential growth over the centuries. Now hold constant the sizes of the market and of the capital stock (which means positive gross investment but zero net investment), then introduce all the new products, processes, and forms of organization that characterized the twentieth century. As old plant and equipment wore out or became obsolete, they would be replaced with new equipment embodying new technologies to make new goods and services. The effects of these innovations would be much less than if they were accompanied by an increase in the capital stock. But the illustrative list of new products and new processes given above shows that the effects would be substantial. These products and processes have transformed people's standards of living, how and where they work, their social and political ways of life, and even their value systems in ways that mere capital accumulation and expanding markets within the context of unchanging technology could not have done.

We should not, however, conclude that savings and investment do not matter. Most new technology is embodied in new capital equipment whose accumulation is measured as gross investment. Because technological change and investment are two aspects of a single phenomenon—the latter being the vehicle by which the former enters into use—anything that slows the rate of embodiment of new technologies through investment, such as unnecessarily high interest rates, will slow the rate of growth. The resulting strong, short-run relation between growth and investment has erroneously led some observers to conclude that investment is the major determinant of long-term growth. In the very long run, however, it is technological change that has the most important effect on living standards.

Technological Change and General Purpose Technologies

We humans are technological animals. Through many millions of years of biological evolution, technology has helped to make us the physical beings that we are today. Through many thousands of years of economic and social evolution, our adaptations to the technologies that we have created have helped to mould and remould our economic, social, and political institutions and our behavioural patterns.

We can think of technological change as occurring in three stages: invention, innovation, and diffusion. Invention creates new technologies or improves existing ones. Until the nineteenth century, individuals, operating more or less on their own, were responsible for most inventions. In the second half of the nineteenth century, invention became institutionalized by the creation of research laboratories both in firms and in the public sector. Today, a large share of invention is done in government and university research laboratories or in the R&D facilities of large firms, while a much smaller fraction is performed by individuals. 'Innovation' occurs when some agent commercializes an invention by producing something that has economic value. This can itself require much development and supporting inventions before the original invention can be embodied in saleable goods or services (thus blurring the distinction between the two). 'Diffusion' is the spreading of invention and innovation from the place where they first occur to other firms in the same industry, to other industries, and to other countries. As technologies diffuse, they usually require changes to adapt to different situations. So diffusion and innovation are to a great extent intertwined; they are different but closely related activities.

In many contexts, the distinction between invention and innovation is important. For example, many societies have been good at one but not the other. Being able to innovate on the platform of other people's inventions can be socially profitable, while being successful at invention but not at innovation can lead to serious social wastes. In many of the circumstances in which we are interested in this book, however, the distinction is unimportant. At those times we use the two terms interchangeably. Where the distinction matters to our argument, we state clearly to which of these concepts we are referring.

Technological change runs the whole gamut from continuous, small, incremental changes, through discontinuous radical inventions, to occasional new GPTs that evolve to pervade much of the economy. We will define these terms fully in Chapter 4. In the mean time, we merely observe that GPTs share some important common characteristics: they begin as fairly crude technologies with a limited number of uses and they evolve into much more complex technologies with dramatic increases in the range of their use across the economy and in the range of economic outputs that they help to produce. As they diffuse through the economy, their efficiency is steadily improved. As mature technologies, they are widely used for a number of different purposes, and have many complementarities in the sense of cooperating with many other technologies.

Any technological change requires alterations in the structure of the economy that often proceed incrementally, more or less unnoticed. Sometimes, however, major new GPTs cause extensive structural changes to such things as the organization of work, management of firms, skill requirements, location and concentration of industry, and supporting infrastructure. Since not all GPTs require great structural changes to become effective, we distinguish two types. 'Transforming GPTs', such as the ones discussed in Chapters 5 and 6, lead to massive changes in many, sometimes most, characteristics of the economic, social, and political structures. Other GPTs do not. Lasers provide one example of the later type of GPT. They are used widely throughout the economy for multiple purposes: to measure interplanetary distances in astronomy; to read bar codes at retail checkout counters; and to facilitate numerous types of surgery in hospitals. They are instrumental in communications; they cut diamonds; they are used to mill materials in new cutting-edge machine tools; they weld plastics; and in the future, they may facilitate the usage of nano-technology. Lasers, do not, however, qualify as a transforming GPT because they fitted well into then-existing social, economic, and institutional structure, causing no major transformations. Unless we specify otherwise, when we speak of GPTs, we will be referring to transforming GPTs.

We discuss the historical experience of GPTs in some detail in Chapters 5 and 6. All the GPTs we identify there fall into five main classes: materials (e.g. bronze); power (e.g. the steam engine); ICTs (e.g. the computer); transportation (e.g. the railroad); and organizational technologies (e.g. the factory system).

Some economists question whether the concept of GPTs is useful and whether the last few decades have been characterized by events that are typical of the evolution of a new GPT. We discuss this question more fully. in Chapter 4. Here briefly are some of the key points. We first appeal to historical data to show that such transforming shocks have occurred in the past. Call them what you will, but they surely did occur. Once this is agreed, the next question is: Have we been living through such a shock over the past few decades? Much of the debate about this second question has assumed that a GPT must be accompanied by certain observed phenomena such as investment booms, productivity slowdowns, increasing demands for human capital, and so on. Indeed, most of the existing theoretical models of GPTs are engineered to produce such phenomena. Those who wish to answer 'no' to the above question often argue that, since these phenomena have not been systematically observed, there has been no recent GPT-induced shock. In contrast, we argue that the existing theories make such unequivocal predictions only because they are crude first approximations, which omit most of the rich and varied behaviour that characterizes the evolution of real GPTs. We argue that it is wrong to expect all GPTs to be accompanied by a specific set of phenomena such as those just mentioned. Thus our argument for the existence of a GPT shock in recent decades must take us beyond any behaviour that is assumed to accompany *all* GPTs. In Chapter 4, we consider and reject the argument that, because GPTs may or may not be accompanied by any or all of these phenomena, our GPT theory is an untestable rationalization, consistent with any set of observed facts.

The level of 'aggregation' that one employs tends to influence how one sees technology. If, for example, one studies the efficiency of energy production measured as the output of all energy sources (in horsepower) divided by the proportion of the nation's productive resources devoted to producing it, one will see an upward sloping curve that is more or less continuous with some alterations in slope. But if one looks inside the black box of the technologies that produce horsepower, one will see a succession of GPTs, and other technologies, that alter not only the efficiency of producing horsepower but also the technological possibilities facing society. For example, electricity produced power at a lower price than did steam but, much more importantly, it allowed things to be done that were technically impossible with steam. For example, power could now be generated in one place and used in another, and a small, efficient power source could be attached to individual machine tools and individual consumer goods.

History Matters

Chapters 5 and 6 illustrate in detail why and how historical processes matter. Briefly, since new technologies largely result from activities of profit-motivated agents, technological change is significantly endogenous to the economic system. Furthermore, scientific and technological knowledge is cumulative. Today's knowledge could not have been discovered or invented in the absence of many earlier discoveries and inventions. Thus, growth and technological change is a historical process in which there is a clear arrow of time. Outcomes are not reversible: introducing a shock and then removing it will not return the economy to its original, pre-shock position because the reaction to the shock will typically lead to the accumulation of new knowledge that will affect future outcomes. Since agents' behaviour and choice sets are path-dependent, technological change is replete with the possibility of multiple equilibria, lock-ins, and possible 'butterfly effects'. To understand where the system is today, we need to know where it has been in the past. In the study of innovation and economic growth, we need explanations that contain an arrow of time, explanations in which past history does exert an influence on the present— *explanations and theories in which history matters.*

Wright (1997: 1561) argues in a similar vein that the key to understanding the path-dependent evolution of technological knowledge lies in increasing our understanding of how GPTs have impacted societies through history:

The extent of technological opportunity for a particular sector is related to its proximity to what are known as 'general purpose technologies', new schemes or conceptions of broad potential import, such as the steam engine, the electric motor, and semiconductors.... Identifying and tracing the course of general purpose technologies should be central to the research agenda of this sub-field. But the appropriate research will be historical in character, that is to say, specific to the technologies and institutions in question; as such, it will not always look or feel like conventional applied economics.

But since each 'historical tape' is played only once, we may wonder if we can ever hope to do more than tell unverifiable stories to explain historical events. Fortunately, things are not quite that hopeless. Although every event is in some ways unique, so do events also share commonalities. At one extreme, a city's rush-hour traffic problems recur every working day. Although a full history of each day's traffic, including who was driving what car, when, and where, will differ day by day, hypotheses about causes and cures of the overall traffic flow can be stated and then tested by verifiable results. At the other extreme, there was only one First World War and only one First Industrial Revolution. But the First World War was not the only war in history, and for purposes of comparison, all wars share some commonalities and subgroups of wars share more commonalities. Also, useful contrasts are possible with periods when war seemed imminent but did not happen. Similarly, the period of the First Industrial Revolution was not history's only period of profound technological change.

Although there can be no finality to theories of why such one-off events as the Industrial Revolution occurred, the absence of finality does not imply the presence of total uncertainty about explanations. For example, Freeman and Louçã (2001) identify a number of commonalities among the five waves of major technological and organizational change that they identify over the last two and a half centuries. More generally, the theory that event X was a necessary condition for outcome Y can be rejected by showing that X was absent when Y happened, and the theory that event X was sufficient for outcome Y can be rejected by showing that event Y occurred while X did not happen.

Why Is the West So Rich?

The simple answer to the question 'Why is the West so rich?' is that the industrialized countries of the West pioneered the development of the technologies, which raised their material living standards above those of all other civilizations past and present. But why did this happen?

In AD 1000, Europe was technologically backward and uncivilized by the standards of both Islam and China. By 1900, Europe and its offshoots in the English-speaking nations that had been seeded by Europeans were the technological leaders and possessors of the world's dominant civilization. In Chapters 7 and 8, we investigate some of the factors that we believe contributed to the West's success, such as the freedom to innovate; reliance on market rather than political decision-making with respect to new technologies; institutions—particularly private property and patent laws—that allowed successful entrepreneurs to reap large gains; pluralism that weakened the strong links between political and economic activities, which persisted in many other civilizations and allowed vested interests to resist revolutionary technological change; rule of law; and, most importantly, fostering of free scientific enquiry.[6]

---

[6] Most of these points are described in detail in Rosenberg and Birdzell (1986). When we say that these factors contributed to the success of the West, we do not wish to imply that any of them were either

II.   SOME COMMENTS ON PROCEDURE AND METHOD

Much of our concern in the rest of this book is with the *causes* and *consequences* of economic growth over the very long run. As observed at the beginning of this chapter, we concentrate geographically on what is roughly called the West, defined as Europe, the English-speaking former British colonies, and, in preclassical times, the countries of the eastern Mediterranean and the Middle East. For comparative purposes we examine some limited aspects of China and the Islamic countries. Chronologically, we draw our illustrations of technologies from some 11,000 years of human experience, beginning with the neolithic agricultural revolution.

Are We Technological Determinists?

Accepting the importance of technological change as a determinant of long-term growth does not imply technological determinism. In this respect, we accept three propositions, the second and third of which directly conflict with technological determinism:

1.   Major new technologies, particularly transforming GPTs, have important effects on the socio-economic system of any country into which they are introduced.
2.   The same technology introduced into different places, and/or at different times, will have different effects because the rest of the political, social, economic, and institutional structures will differ between the two situations.
3.   Because knowledge builds on previous knowledge in an uncertain, path-dependent, and sometimes discrete process, the introduction of a new technology cannot have unique predetermined results.

Much of the rest of this book is dedicated to demonstrating the first proposition. Because we are interested in the transforming effects of major new technologies, we emphasize these throughout. But nothing that we say on these matters is meant to imply that technology was the sole determinant of the changes that we study or that all important changes are primarily caused by new technologies.

   The second proposition is a generalization from historical experience, and one that we build into our structuralist-evolutionary theory outlined in Chapter 3. For example, consider the effects on political behaviour of the introduction of the television in the USA and UK. Unconstrained by government regulations, American TV ads for political elections became the 10–30-second bursts that encouraged the simplification of issues and *ad hominem* attacks rather than debate over substantial issues. It also vastly raised the cost of fighting a US election, and the need to raise large sums of money has important consequences on who can run and to whom the winners are politically indebted. Although not all successful candidates become the tools of their sponsors, many do (at least sometimes and for some issues). People with money have always had ways of exerting influence on governments, but with

---

necessary or sufficient or that they were absent in all other times and places. Later, however, we do argue that there was one necessary condition present in the West, but absent everywhere else.

the rapid acceleration of the cost of fighting US elections, the distribution, form, and scope of that influence has altered greatly. In the UK, TV stations were originally all owned by the government, and when commercial TV was introduced, it was heavily regulated. Political parties were given allotments of free time in multi-minute slots. Later, they were allowed to buy time but in units that were controlled. Without being differently motivated and without a very different audience, the political appeals had to be much more focused on issues than was possible in short clips common in the USA. As a result, political campaigns are conducted very differently in the USA and UK, and money raised by individual candidates is much less important to British than to American politicians. The technology had big effects in both countries, but the effects were different because the technology was introduced into different institutional settings. This is technology mattering, not technology determining.

The third proposition concerning the absence of unique outcomes is also emphasized in much of what follows. If we could return to some point in history, the same technology introduced under the same conditions could produce different results as different choices were made under uncertain conditions, and as related chance events took different courses.

One of our themes concerning technological change is that it is endogenous to the economic system, responding to such signals as changes in output processes, input costs, and new opportunities. When we say that technological change is 'endogenous', we mean 'responds to economic signals such as prices and profits'; we do *not* mean 'wholly determined by such signals'. All that the theory of endogenous technological change requires is that economic incentives be strong enough influences for innovation to respond to them. Economic incentives are not assumed to be the only determinants of technological change. There is room for pure curiosity and any number of other 'non-economic' variables. The footnote distinguishes formally among endogenous, exogenous, and technologically deterministic theories.[7]

A Question of Focus

Our focus on the West raises the question of whether we are Eurocentric in the pejorative sense of the term. We take the charge of Eurocentrism to include three main issues: (*a*) taking European developments as unique; (*b*) imbuing European cultures with unique, unexplained advantages that created its superior technologies; and (*c*) missing important influences of causes originating elsewhere.

On the first issue, we have already observed that we concentrate on the West because it was there that sustained economic growth first emerged in the nineteenth century to

---

[7] Consider the function: *innovation* $= f(e,s)$, where e is a vector of economic variables such as prices and costs, and s is a vector of non-economic variables, such as social attitudes and political systems. Exogenous theories of technological change say that the partial derivative of f with respect to each variable in e is effectively zero; endogenous theories say that the partial derivative of f with respect to at least one variable in e is significantly non-zero (as also may be many of the partials with respect to items in s). Economic determinists argue that all the partial derivatives of f with respect to all s items are effectively zero. Since we are neither determinists nor believers in exogenous innovation, we have no expectation that *any* of the partials are necessarily zero.

spread elsewhere over the subsequent two centuries. Our discussion of the development of particular technologies in the West is not meant to imply that they were
unique to the West. Often they developed independently, and frequently earlier,
elsewhere. If we occasionally make statements about the West's technological history
that seem to suggest that similar developments did not occur elsewhere, this is a sin
that, in common with many others, we may commit out of ignorance but not, we hope,
out of arrogance. Since some modern scholarship has suggested that parts of China
may have been on the verge of an Industrial Revolution in the eighteenth century, and
since Islam was an acknowledged leader in early scientific and technological developments, we explore both societies and their technological and scientific records.

On the second issue, our view of agents and technological change is that all
humans are innovative creatures. In a non-repressive environment, we expect
all societies to innovate in reaction to the problems, challenges, and opportunities
that they face. If some societies are more innovative than others, this is not due to
anything inherent in their members but to differences in circumstances often in
institutions, many of which arose because of historical accidents.

The third reason is possibly the most important critique of focusing on the West:
we may miss some of the important sources of long-run growth. Pomeranz (2000: 4)
makes the point this way:

> The resemblances between western Europe and other areas that force us to turn from a purely
> comparative approach—one that assumes essentially separate worlds as units of compari-
> son—to one that looks at global conjunctures have another significance as well. They imply
> that we cannot understand pre-1800 global conjunctures in terms of a Europe-centred world
> system; we have, instead, a polycentric world with no dominant center.

But as strong as the resemblances no doubt are, we argue in Chapters 7 and 8 that the
important determinants of the West's nineteenth-century transition to sustained
economic growth were primarily local. We also argue that, contrary to Pomeranz's
view, no other region was ever a serious contender to produce an endogenously
generated Industrial Revolution. Further we argue that the key difference between
the West and China was the former's development of mechanistic science. This
provided the intellectual underpinning of the First Industrial Revolution, as well as
of the great eighteenth-century engineering works that preceded it. This difference is
what really mattered and we need only to look inside the two areas to discover the
presence (or lack) of mechanistic science and the effects that this had on the
technological development of each society. We also seek to explain, not just to
document, this difference. But even if our specific explanations are not the last
word on the subject, that cannot upset the key difference of the presence of
Newtonian mechanics in one society, and its absence in another.

For us, the explanation of this difference lies in institutions, of which two sets were
highly important.[8] The first set comprised the institutions of learning that allowed

---

[8] Jones (1988) notes that while similar events and pressures may be felt by various regions, they may
give rise to vastly different responses. The reasons for these differences arise from the different internal
structures of the regions.

Western science to be cumulative while Chinese science experienced the acquisition of isolated bodies of knowledge, and often the loss and subsequent relearning of such knowledge. The individual pieces of knowledge often rivalled or surpassed Western learning up until sometime in the early modern period, but the Chinese did not build them into an evolving and integrated body of scientific knowledge. Their learning never led to anything resembling Newtonian mechanics. The second set comprised the West's pluralistic institutions that contrasted sharply with the relatively centralized institutions in China.[9] When either secular or ecclesiastical authorities tried to stunt new scientific learning and/or technological developments in Europe and China—as they often did in both regions—the different consequences stemmed from the different internal make-ups of those places. Both these explanations depend on differences in institutions, not on innate European advantages.

Beyond Formal Models

Formal models dominate most books on economic growth written by economists. While we accept that much can be learned from such models—and we do develop some formal models of our own in Parts II and III—we believe that existing theoretical models are unable to capture much of the rich knowledge concerning economic growth and technological change that has been accumulated over the past decades by economic historians and students of technology. For example, after decades of work on innovation, very little of the process has been formalized, and the same holds for theories of knowledge accumulation. (See Mokyr 2002 for more on this.) Some even argue that these sorts of processes will never be formalized. Be that as it may, no one has succeeded in formalizing them yet and to do so is beyond our capabilities. So, whenever such knowledge seems to be needed to deal with some question in which we are interested, we do not hesitate to use techniques other than formal modelling. Furthermore, since much of what we deal with has not yet been adequately measured, we must seek an understanding of both technology and its impact on society in ways that often go beyond quantitative measures.

For these reasons, we spend time reporting and systematizing much of the existing but widely scattered knowledge about technological change. We argue that developing a purely descriptive understanding of long-run growth and innovation can be important, even to those seeking to capture such processes through formal models. But we go further. We generalize this knowledge into a series of stylized facts, which we hope can be used to constrain theories of growth. We then go on to develop what Richard Nelson calls appreciative theories. These are theories that are not expressed in formal mathematical language but are developed rigorously in verbal form. They are the natural complements of formal theories, not substitutes for them.

We would like to deal with all the questions that we think are important for understanding long-term growth by using formal models. But standard growth models do not deal with most of the characteristics of major technological shocks

---

[9] As with our geographical focus, our focus on the relatively high degree of plurality in European institutions as a reason for European growth also strongly echoes Jones (1988).

that we have discussed earlier in this chapter, while the models that attempt to do so, by incorporating some of the characteristics of GPTs, are only in their infancy. These latter models are first approximations that omit many of the rich details that we think are relevant when dealing with some of the key issues related to economic growth. If we want to deal with these, we have no alternative but to provide much descriptive material on the complex and often subtle facts concerning technology and technological change. We then need to theorize about them in an appreciative manner, building formal models only when the questions we are dealing with are simple enough to be handled by existing theoretical models and such extensions of them as we can make. We then go on to develop our own formal models of GPT-driven, long-term growth. This is how we proceed, moving from one approach to another as is required by the problem at hand. We hope that the justification of our unusually eclectic method will be apparent in our results—although we understand that we run the risk that specialists in each of several growth-related fields of study will find in our pages too little of their favourite method and too much of others.

Historical Specificity

When we do build models of growth, they are specific in both time and space. In time, they are specific to the period that began sometime in the nineteenth century when the conditions that made growth self-sustaining were established (as discussed in Chapter 7). They are specific in space to the group of countries that generate their own technological change endogenously, in contrast to catch up economies whose growth is mainly generated by adopting and adapting technologies imported from abroad. Neoclassical models, and those of the newer endogenous growth theories, are relatively unstructured models based on a single aggregate production function. They are thus one-size-fits-all models, applying to all times and places. In contrast, our models are more structured and as such specifically focused on the group of economies, mainly but not exclusively, in the West, whose own technological advances drive much of their long-term growth.

Our view on the specificity of our models is in line with what Hodgson (2002) calls 'historical specificity', an issue that was much discussed in earlier times by both the historical and the institutional schools. Hodgson (2002 : 23) describes it this way.

The problem of historical specificity addresses the limits of explanatory unification in social science: substantially different socio-economic phenomena may require theories that are in some respects different. If different socio-economic systems have features in common, then, to some extent, the different theories required to analyse different systems might reasonably share some common characteristics. But sometimes there will be important differences as well. Concepts and theoretical frameworks appropriate for one real object may not be best suited for another. The problem of historical specificity starts from a recognition of significant underlying differences between different objects of analysis. One theory may not fit all.

Hodgson shows that the question of how far highly general theories could apply, and how much specificity was required for satisfactory theoretical explanations of specific phenomenon, was front and centre in the analyses of the historical and the institutional schools in both Europe and the USA. But times have changed. As Hodgson (2002: 22) goes on to argue: 'The domination of economics and sociology by general theorists, plus a minority of atheoretical empiricists, has excluded this problem.... The methodological discussion of the general and the specific, of sameness and difference, is forgotten.' Most social scientists are, he believes, not even aware of the issue, taking it for granted that the more general a theory is, the better it must be. But this assumption ignores the probability that the more general a theory is, the less empirical content it will have since, by ignoring the specific context in which many problems arise, it becomes impossible to analyse them in depth. In Chapters 14 and 15, we discuss why our more structured theory of GPT-driven, long-term growth cannot apply to all countries at all times. In Chapters 16 and 17, we argue that most useful policy advice must be highly context-specific and not of the generalized sort that follows from much neoclassical policy analysis—remove 'market imperfections' wherever they are found.

Long and Short Term

Most of our study is concerned with the long-term effects of changes in technology, particularly the introduction of new GPTs. For this reason, we make the usual assumption of full employment of the available resources, peculiarly labour. There are many reasons why technical change may be associated with business cycles and unemployment that, even if transitory, can be quite long-lasting. But ours is already a long book and we cannot study in detail everything that is associated with technological change in general and GPTs in particular, so we do not include labour market effects in our formal models, although we do deal with them where they are relevant in our descriptive analyses.

III. A PREVIEW

Our book is divided into four parts: Part I presents descriptive and historical material concerning economic growth and technological change; Part II deals with the emergence in the West of sustained economic growth, both extensive and intensive; Part III models modern GPT-driven sustained growth; and Part IV considers some of the policy implications arising from our theories of the growth process.

Part I

In Part I, we deal mainly with technology and technological change, which is the main engine of long-term economic growth. Most university courses on economic growth concentrate exclusively on formal growth models, but just as one cannot fully understand present international conflicts without knowing their history, we believe that one cannot understand long-term growth without knowing much of the relevant historical and descriptive material about technology and technological change. This is why we believe that, even though it cannot all be reflected completely in our formal modelling, the material in Part I is critical to understanding growth.

Chapter 1 has considered the nature and power of long-term growth as a historical, path-dependent process embedded in irreversible time. Chapter 2 introduces two contrasting views of the workings of the market economy, which we call 'neoclassical' and 'structuralist-evolutionary' (S-E). Although recent developments in economics have blurred this distinction at the margin, it still divides two different ways both of understanding long-term economic growth and of developing policies to influence it. Chapter 3 covers our 'S-E decomposition', designed to get inside the black box of the aggregate production function by distinguishing the technology, facilitating structure, policy, policy structure, inputs, and outputs. It avoids equating technological change with productivity change, an equation that we argue is at the heart of many modern day confusions, including the unjustified concern over the so-called 'productivity paradox'. This decomposition leads us to consider agents and their motivation. Chapter 4 deals with some important characteristics of technology and technological change, introducing the concepts of general purpose technologies (GPTs) and general purpose principles (GPPs). Chapters 5 and 6 provide a tour through the history of the transforming effects of GPTs, starting with the neolithic agricultural revolution and ending with nano-technology. Our S-E decomposition provides a framework for organizing and interpreting these historical data.

Part II

In Part II, we consider the West's transition first to sustained extensive growth and then to sustained intensive growth, asking why, when, and where it happened. Chapter 7 deals with the transition to sustained extensive growth. In contrast with existing formal models of this transition, we argue that it was the result, first, of a specific set of contingent events that culminated in the First Industrial Revolution and, second, of the subsequent institutional changes that endogenized the growth process, thereby making it self-sustaining. We argue that only in Europe could this revolution have happened anywhere near the time that it actually occurred (which is accepted by many), and that within Europe, in the late eighteenth and early nineteenth centuries it could only have happened in Britain (which is more controversial). We deal with the commonly noted important influences that encouraged the revolution, such as Europe's freedom to innovate, its pluralism in government and religion, and its rule of law. However, in contrast with many other explanations, we stress the role of science. We argue that mechanistic science, whose roots lay in the last half of the medieval period, was, by the early modern period, contributing essential inputs to the technological inventions that created the First and Second Industrial Revolutions. Thus, the questions of why the West made the transition to sustained growth, and why most of the rest of the world did not for at least another century, call for country-specific explanations—there is no generic theory of industrial revolutions that applies to all areas of the globe. The difference between Europe and the restzcannot be handled within any of the existing formal models of the transition, all of which predict that sustained growth will emerge when certain very general conditions are fulfilled—conditions that have existed at many times and in many places outside of eighteenth-century Britain. Nor can any existing formal growth model handle them. Historical analysis is necessary.

Chapter 8 asks a related question: Why did the Chinese and Islamic civilizations, both of which were technological leaders well into the medieval period, not develop industrial revolutions of their own? We answer that all non-western parts of the world lacked the necessary condition of formal mechanistic science. Our set of non-western countries includes China, which according to the research of Pomeranz (2000), had most of the other characteristics that are usually associated with the European Industrial Revolution. The failure of China and the Islamic countries to develop anything like modern science was to a great extent due to their lack of the institutions that supported and protected science, allowing its discoveries to accumulate in a path-dependant, progressive advancement of knowledge.

Next we consider the relation between the growth in total output and growth in per capita output. Chapter 9 builds models of population dynamics designed to analyse how the effects of extensive growth are divided between increases in population and increases in living standards (intensive growth). Our main models deal with the 1,000 or so years prior to the Industrial Revolution and are consistent with some sketchy evidence that, although medieval living standards did not rise rapidly by modern standards, they may not have been as stagnant as is often assumed. We find that much insight can be gained by using models that cover more than just the agricultural sector, compared with many other studies that either explicitly or implicitly confine themselves to one sector. We also find that when the constant elasticity of substitution functions, which are commonly used in theoretical formulations, are replaced by a production function, which is more realistic, much of the conventional wisdom about population dynamics ceases to apply.

Chapter 10 considers the demographic revolution, which allowed the sustained growth in total output that was set in motion by the First Industrial Revolution to be increasingly transformed into growth in per capita output. We argue against the view commonly held among economists that the main cause was parents becoming less concerned about the number of children they had and more concerned about the human capital with which they could endow each child. After the demographic revolution, whatever its causes, most extensive growth became intensive growth, at least in the high income countries of the West. This implies that, from that time on, models such as those we develop in Part III to explain extensive growth also explain intensive growth (with only minor corrections).

Part III

In this part, we develop a model of sustained, GPT-driven economic growth in a series of four successive abstractions. Chapter 11 surveys the literature on GPTs and other similar concepts, such as Freeman and Perez's technoeconomic paradigms (1988), and Mokyr's macro inventions (1990). Chapter 12 does further ground clearing by dealing with the important topic of scale effects. We argue that the standard theoretical treatment of scale economies in economic theory is scholastic in purporting to deduce empirical propositions from formalistic theorizing devoid of empirical content. We then go on to consider the important phenomenon of scale economies in economic history. We argue that these historical scale effects cannot be picked up by most conventional studies of scale. We conclude with a discussion of the treatment of scale effects in macro growth models.

Chapter 13 begins our series of abstractions, which take us progressively further away from the rich detail in Part I but closer to a tractable macro model of sustained GPT-driven growth. We make our first abstraction by looking for commonalities among the GPTs that we have discussed in Part I. We find these in each of our structuralist categories since, while no two GPTs are identical, they do share some common characteristics that are useful in theorizing. Our second level of abstraction then divides the evolution of the 'typical' GPT into five phases, which must be broad and flexible enough to accommodate the major differences between the development of various GPTs as well as their common features. Our third level of abstraction divides the evolution of the 'typical' GPT into two categories: the efficiency with which it delivers its services and the range of its applications. We develop an appreciative theory of how each of these phenomena evolves logistically.

Chapters 14 and 15 complete our series of abstractions by building a model of GPT-driven growth in which the logistic formulation of Chapter 13 plays a key part. This gives us a baseline model with which to work. It also gives us a standard of comparison when considering the importance of the various complications, which we introduce sequentially, to make the model evolve in the direction of an S-E approach. As we proceed along this route, we are able to use our theory to develop some specific predictions about GPT-driven growth, and to test the efficacy of various methods of measuring growth-related phenomena. A full evolution in this direction that would include many structuralist and evolutionary characteristics at lower levels of aggregation is a major research programme that we can only begin in this book. We hope, however, that the latter part of Chapter 15 indicates the outlines of, and takes the first steps in, such a potentially fruitful programme.

Part IV

Part IV gives a brief discussion of some of the policy implications of what has gone before. In particular, the absence of a welfare-maximizing equilibrium, when agents are operating under uncertainty (as emphasized by Lipsey and Carlaw 1998*a*, 1998*b*) and when knowledge is non-rivalrous but appropriable (as emphasized by Romer 1993*a*, 1993*b*, 1994), has profound implications for policy recommendations and policy analysis.

Chapter 16 investigates some of these implications and applies them to technology policy. We consider how policies with respect to technological change can be assessed. We also contrast how they are typically assessed when viewed through either neoclassical or S-E lenses. We then go on to outline a package of policies that seems effective from an S-E point of view.

2

Two Views of Economic Processes

Two distinct views of economic processes are contrasted throughout this book: the neoclassical and the structuralist-evolutionary. 'Neoclassical' is our collective term for the well-known body of theory based on rational maximizing agents operating under well-defined exogenous scarcity constraints. It has been an extraordinarily successful theory. It has produced a rich set of predictions about reactions to many types of shocks and its static equilibrium properties (such as the equality of the value of one factor's marginal products everywhere in the economy) are used as maintained assumptions in many measurement exercises. It produces its most general results by focusing on the static equilibrium state of a competitive model that allows micro outcomes to be aggregated to produce unique macro outcomes. Where growth is studied, it is in terms of an aggregate production function with flat (i.e. unstructured) technology. In Solow's version, technological change is exogenous; in the newer versions, it is endogenous. When dealing with the microeconomic issues surrounding innovation and long-run technological change, however, the canonical general equilibrium (GE) version of neoclassical economics due originally to Arrow and Debreu is largely silent.[1]

'Structuralist-evolutionary' (S-E) is our collective term for the body of theories developed explicitly to analyse long-term growth using dynamic evolutionary concepts. Instead of focusing on equilibrium states, these theories seek to capture the processes by which technologies evolve under the impact of a stream of innovations. This requires dealing explicitly with such real-world aspects of innovation as uncertainty and path dependency. It should be noted at the outset that an evolutionary approach does not require dubious biological analogies. Many non-biological systems evolve. Indeed evolution of any system only requires that it be subject to change as a result of disturbances and selection.

We take the pragmatic view that each approach has its own advantages and disadvantages and each has a set of problems for which it is better suited. For most resource allocation issues in which it is safe to take technology as given, neoclassical tools have a proven track record. But S-E tools may be more appropriate for situations where technology can be expected to change endogenously. Because

---

[1] The authors of the first generation of GPT models, such as Aghion and Howitt, and Helpman and Trajtenberg, do not regard their models as neoclassical because they explicitly model technologies as existing in a 'hierarchy' rather than being 'flat'. Nonetheless, they do utilize a number of neoclassical characteristics such as maximizing agents operating under conditions either of perfect foresight or risk but not uncertainty, and they employ a stationary equilibrium concept.

our main interest centres around endogenous technological change, we need to be concerned with the differences between these two approaches. *Nothing critical that we say about neoclassical economics when applied to growth driven by technological change should be taken to deny its enormous value in dealing with many other issues.*[2]

Over the last few years, mainstream economics has begun to analyse situations excluded from the canonical neoclassical GE model. Akerlof (2002) provides an excellent summary of many of these recent developments. Thus, there has been a slow blurring of the sharp contrast that was drawn between these two views in the first five chapters of Nelson and Winter's pathbreaking book (1982) *An Evolutionary Theory of Economic Change* (distinctions that were much clearer at the time). Typically these newer theories still use some key neoclassical assumptions that are not found in evolutionary models. In particular, although they often allow for incomplete and sometimes asymmetric knowledge, they typically assume that people maximize with respect to the knowledge that they do have. The theories also typically analyse end states of the competitive process rather than the dynamic processes themselves.

So in spite of this blurring at the margin, important contrasts remain between S-E theories and the rest. For example, much work in both theoretical and applied economics is based on neoclassical approaches such as the following:

1. The study of reactions to shocks typically uses long-run, static equilibrium models[3] in which there is no arrow of time, and induced technological changes are absent by assumption.
2. Most analyses of situations that depart from perfect knowledge are based on risk rather than uncertainty.
3. Virtually all general equilibrium models are based on large group situations of perfect or monopolistic competition rather than on small group oligopolistic situations.
4. Much microeconomic policy advice is based on removing impediments that would prevent the attainment of an optimal allocation of resources in a static GE world.
5. Virtually all growth models, including those that explicitly allow for GPTs, are based on stationary equilibrium concepts.
6. Many market characteristics that are seen as desirable in neoclassical-type theories may be problematical in their effects when viewed by S-E theory, while many characteristics that create imperfections from a neoclassical viewpoint are the very driving forces of economic growth in S-E theory. (This last point is critical from our point of view and it is taken up more fully in Section II below.)

---

[2] We stress this point because some readers of earlier versions of our manuscript have thought we were dismissing neoclassical economics as useless.

[3] We use 'long run' in Alfred Marshall's sense: a period of time long enough for all adjustments to be made to any exogenous shocks, including altering all components of durable capital, within the context of given and unchanging technology.

Importantly, many mainstream economists take the view, either explicitly or implicitly, that the only way to investigate a problem is to model it. (See Colander 2003 for discussion of this issue.) The result is that many problems related to long-term growth are not investigated by growth theorists because the known historical evidence is too complex to model with existing techniques or, when they are modelled, the necessary simplifications conflict with much of the known evidence[4]. (See Chapters 7 and 8 for examples.) For these and other similar reasons, we believe that the contrasts we draw in Section I are still relevant in spite of being lessened by some modern developments. As long as some of these distinctions between the two views remain relevant, the choice between them is not merely a matter of taste and convenience; it is also a choice between two world views with many divergent implications.

In Section I, we compare and contrast these two approaches in a number of key aspects. In Section II, we discuss how these differences lead to two distinct views on the overall working of the market economy. We also consider arguments advanced by Alchian (1950) and Friedman (1953) that there is no operative distinction between the two.

I. COMPARISONS AND CONTRASTS

In this section, we compare and contrast specific elements of what we call the canonical versions of neoclassical and S-E theory. These are generalizations of the main elements of the two bodies of theory. Although exceptions can be found for each generalization, we believe they do suggest two distinct approaches to understanding the workings of a market economy and, as we point out in Chapters 16 and 17, to different policy advice on such issues as when and how to use public policy to encourage technological change.

Tastes

The treatment of tastes is one of the few areas where the neoclassical and S-E views are similar. Few economists in either camp have tried to model explicitly the formation of tastes. It seems, however, that if one is to understand long-term growth fully, one must accept a substantial endogeneity of tastes—an endogeneity that probably also exists over shorter periods of time but is ignored in the interests of obtaining tractable models. Consumers buy many goods that did not exist in the past and it seems to us unreasonable to assume that they have taste functions defined over the unknown (although some economists insist that they do). For example, could an Egyptian peasant in the second millennium BC have had tastes defined over the range of ethnic foods available in New York in 2005, over the services of a

---

[4] From Baumol (2002: 9) '[T]he growth literature is full of invaluable analyses. But much of it is unsuited to deal directly with the distinction between the growth accomplishments of capitalism and those of other economic systems, because these analyses are preponderantly ahistorical, and all explicit references to the special features of free-market economies have been expunged.'

modern travel agent, and over the range of computer and Internet services available today?[5]

In the context of long-term growth, we believe that endogenous tastes fulfil an important function of preventing what would otherwise be a steep decline in the marginal utility of income as per capita incomes rose under the impact of exponential growth rates. If the technology of consumer goods and services had been held constant at those existing at some earlier time, say 1900, diminishing marginal utility of income would be a reality as consumers wondered what to do with a third and fourth horse and buggy or a tenth steam train excursion to a seaside resort town. Technological changes in consumers' goods constantly present consumers with new consumption possibilities for which they must develop new tastes, and which prevent the marginal utility of income from declining steeply as real income grows exponentially.[6]

Technology and Technological Change

In neoclassical price theory, technology is assumed to be captured by the forms of the relevant production functions that determine the output flows of various goods and services resulting from given input flows. Neoclassical (and most other equilibrium-based) growth theories use the concept of an aggregate production function. Because the details of technology are hidden in the 'black box' of this function, the process and the structure of technological change are observable only by their results when given quantities of all inputs are associated with larger quantities of output.[7] Conceptually, this phenomenon is observed by measuring the amount of the change in output that cannot be statistically associated with a change in the inputs. The

---

[5] Of course, one can argue that Egyptian peasants did have tastes defined over an infinite set, but as prices of non-existent goods were infinite, they did not enter their utility maximizing calculus. There can be no finality about such assertions and it may be convenient to assume such universal tastes in some theories where it is an innocuous assumption. But where it matters, we believe one has to experience new goods and services that were unimaginable before they came into existence before one knows if one will like them or not. For example, one of us used to like batting around in a force 8 gale in his 26-foot sloop, Scalza, while some of his friends who thought they would like it found they were repelled by such an experience once they tried it. They thought their tastes were one thing and learned by experiencing the 'service' that their tastes were something different.

[6] We need to distinguish sharply between cross section and time series comparisons of the marginal utility of income. As people move upwards in the income distribution, they may or may not develop new tastes that mitigate against a decline in the marginal utility of income. But even a cross-sectional marginal utility income that declines at all levels is consistent with a constant or rising marginal utility of income as new tastes are developed under the impact of the new goods and services that accompany growth-inducing technological change.

[7] There are two other ways in which, conceptually at least, technological change may be manifested in the neoclassical aggregate production function. First, some of the values of the parameters in the production function may alter. Second, if physical capital is measured so as to include the value of new, embodied technological change, while human capital is measured so as to include the value of new knowledge, some of the effects of technological change will be observed as increases in measured inputs of physical and human capital. This may happen inadvertently due to measurement conventions or advertently when inputs are measured in efficiency units.

remaining change is referred to as the Solow residual, or TFP, which we discuss in more detail in the Appendix to Chapter 4.

Modern growth theory models technological change as endogenous (although in modern micro theory technological change is commonly treated as exogenous). But since the theory is formulated at the macro level, it makes little contact with the much older strand of micro work on endogenous innovation and technological change that goes back to such writers as Schumpeter (1934), Schmookler (1966), and Rosenberg (1982). So, while it has been influential, it does not have the detailed prescriptions for micro economic policy issues that are implied by both the canonical neoclassical and S-E theories.[8]

In S-E theories, technology is observed through its embodiment in such things as physical and human capital. Technological change is modelled as evolving endogenously. Also, because S-E theories attempt to incorporate many of the awkward facts surrounding the microeconomics of innovation, they often treat the economic, social, and political structure of an economy explicitly. Institutions are seen as co-evolving with technology. Chapter 3 lays out an explicit model of the structure of the economy and Chapter 4 discusses the details of innovation.

In S-E theory the firm is seen as inhabiting a specific point in input space with the possibility of moving to other points, but only in real time, at significant cost, and under conditions of uncertainty. Designing, building, and working up a production facility that uses inputs in a different proportion than they are now being used, even when no 'new' technological knowledge is required, is a costly process with significant uncertainty attached to it. Indeed, the greater the departure from existing input proportions that is envisaged, the more learning the firm is required to do (i.e. the more aspects of the plan are exposed to uncertainty). This stands in stark contrast to the assumptions of the neoclassical model where the firm can make costless choices among a continuum of known alternatives expressed by a production function. The difference, in terms of input spaces and production trajectories, is illustrated in the Appendix to this chapter.

Information and Motivation

In neoclassical models, agents are assumed to have an information set that is sufficient to allow them to make maximizing decisions. This implies that all decisions are made either with perfect foresight or with foresighted rational expectations. For such rational expectations, agents need to know all possible outcomes of their choices and to have well-defined probability distributions about the likelihood

---

[8] While the original endogenous growth models had perfectly competitive behaviour and sustained growth that was achieved by assuming constant returns to the accumulation of broadly defined capital or knowledge, sometimes with externalities, newer models have incorporated imperfect competition, using a constant elasticity of substitution aggregator such as the Dixit–Stiglitz function. These later models demonstrate that sustained growth can occur in models with some forms of imperfect markets. This result takes macro growth theorizing just a little closer to well-known empirical observations about growth and market power, long chronicled in the literature of industrial organization. (There are many references of which Chandler (1977, 1990) are the best.)

of each possible outcome. This implies that when they operate with less than perfect certainty, they do so in situations of 'risk' rather than 'uncertainty'. We use these terms in the senses defined by Knight (1921). A risky situation is one in which the possible outcomes can be delineated and a probability distribution attached to each. An uncertain situation is one in which it is impossible either to delineate all the possible outcomes or to attach probabilities to the outcomes that can be identified. Risk is insurable, uncertainty is not.

Almost all neoclassical models assume that agents maximize over exogenous tastes subject to an exogenous production technology, the equilibrium outcome for which displays no arrow of time. Agents need not learn from experience since all information that is relevant to their decisions is known by them initially. Optimal decisions can be taken by scrutinizing all possible outcomes of any choice, assigning probabilities to each and then choosing the alternative that has the highest expected value associated with its outcome. Two individuals with the same endowments and tastes, faced with the same choice between two alternative courses of action and possessing the same set of relevant information, *are predicted to make the same maximizing choice.*

Of course, exceptions can be found in the literature to each of these points. Many neoclassical-type models have been used to study problems where the information set of the agents is less than perfect (to say nothing of models of pure uncertainty). Examples include studies of habit formation in choice theoretic models, studies of the effects of learning by doing, principal agent problems, moral hazard, transactions costs, and a host of other 'market imperfections'. Industrial organization economists have used partial equilibrium models with many neoclassical characteristics to study oligopolies and 'market imperfections' as well as other sources of non-convexities. Yet all these models typically retain many neoclassical characteristics, such as stationarity in their equilibrium concepts, well-defined choice sets, and optimizing behaviour. More importantly, however, the canonical GE model, on which the policy of removing market imperfections is based, encompasses few if any of these complications.

In S-E theory, innovation is typically seen as endogenously determined by decisions taken by individuals in search of profits. The theory does not endow agents with perfect information or perfect foresight. Instead, agents face genuine uncertainty when making their decisions, particularly those associated with innovation. Since innovation means doing something never done before, there is an element of genuine uncertainty in all innovative activity. The existence of such uncertainties implies that agents may not even be able to enumerate in advance the full set of possible outcomes of a particular line of research, let alone assign probabilities to them in order to conduct risk analysis as conventionally defined. The assumption of rational maximizing behaviour is, therefore, usually replaced by an alternative assumption, such as groping in a purposeful, profit-seeking manner. Bounded rationality is often used to approximate these conditions.[9] Whatever the explicit

---

[9] Many S-E theories also appeal to the substantial body of evidence indicating that, even in well-defined situations involving only statistically measurable risk, agents do not maximize expected values but instead

theory of choice that is used, the key implication of genuine uncertainty is that two individuals with the same endowments and tastes, faced with the same choice between two courses of action, and possessed of the same bounded set of relevant information, *may make different choices*. In effect, each is deciding to back different horses in a race with unknown odds. Given the uncertainty, neither individual's choice can be said to be irrational.[10]

Note, however, that decision-making under uncertainty does not imply totally blind groping. Agents look forward. They consult evidence from past behaviour. They try to anticipate future events from what they know both of public policy and of the normal behaviour of the economy. But because to look forward under conditions of uncertainty involves an irreducible element of personal judgement, what agents cannot do is to arrive at a unique probability distribution of each possible outcome that would be agreed by all rational agents.

Technological Trajectories

In the neoclassical world where agents have sufficient information to make maximizing choices with respect to all their decisions, they are assumed to allocate their R&D expenditures so as to maximize the expected value of the results. This, as we shall see in Part IV, has important consequences for how firms are predicted to respond to policies designed to encourage technological change and on how such policies should be designed.

In an S-E world where firms are groping into an uncertain future in a profit-oriented way, each firm must form its own subjective evaluation of the possible pay-offs of different lines of R&D and decide how to allocate its expenditures. Although it is possible analytically to treat an individual agent's subjective assessment as an objective probability distribution and use risk analysis on it, the agent is still acting under uncertainty. The key difference between risk and uncertainty is so important that it bears repeating in this context: two individuals with the same endowments, tastes, and objectives, faced with the same choice between two alternative courses of action and possessing the same set of relevant information, are predicted to make the *same* maximizing choice when operating under conditions of risk, while they may make *different* choices when operating under conditions of uncertainty, and there is no objective way to determine at the time that the choices are made whether one is more likely to achieve a preferred result than the other.

Thus different firms in similar situations may make different decisions based on the external state of technological developments and their internal capabilities and operating procedures, which Nelson and Winter (1982) call their 'routines' (discussed in Chapter 3). This introduces the possibility of significant amounts of path dependency and inertia in technological choices. To emphasize this, researchers in

display 'loss aversion' or 'endowment effects'. For discussion of these alternatives see, for example, Kahneman and Tversky (1979), Thaler (1980), Knetsch and Sinden (1987), and Tversky and Kahneman (1992).

[10] An economist who has continually emphasized the importance of uncertainty is Nathan Rosenberg. See, for example, Rosenberg (1996).

the area of technological change speak of technological trajectories, the tendency of technological developments to follow distinct lines that are not easy to alter. (Of course, big enough alterations in signals can deflect a trajectory as many agents perceive an advantage in responding more or less in the direction signalled.) This concept is similar to that of a design configuration with scope for development as used by many students of innovation. There are several reasons for the existence of these trajectories, some external and some internal to the firm.

Reasons External to Individual Firms

Certain problems pose clear objectives that seem worth striving to achieve. This is what Rosenberg (1963) calls 'technological imperatives'. Bottlenecks such as short-ages of woven materials in the early 1800s, or obvious weaknesses in a range of products such as metal fatigue and other causes of structural failures, may direct R&D along specific lines. These may persist for long periods as problems are solved successively and as human capital in dealing with this type of problem accumulates relative to human capital directed at dealing with quite different types of problems. Nelson and Winter's 'technological regime' (1982: 258–9) also suggests trajectories. It is a concept that relates to

technicians' beliefs about what is feasible or at least worth attempting. For example, ... the advent of the DC-3 in the 1930s defined a particular technological regime; metal skin, low wing, piston-powered planes. ... For more than two decades innovation in aircraft design essentially involved better exploitation of this potential: improving the engines, enlarging the planes, making them more efficient.

More generally, particular technologies and particular stages of scientific under-standing of related fundamental issues cause particular lines of advance to look most promising. As solutions are developed to specific technological problems and underlying scientific issues, new problems arise and the mutual causation between science and technology is reinforced.

While natural trajectories almost invariably have special elements associated with the particu-lar technology in question, in any era there appear to be certain natural trajectories that are common to a wide range of technologies. Two of these have been relatively well identified in the literature: progressive exploitation of latent economies of scale and increasing mechan-ization of operations that have been done by hand. (Nelson and Winter 1982: 259)

There are fads and fashions in research funding and such funding clearly influences the R&D that does occur. The slow evolution of these fashions imparts a certain stability into actual R&D behaviour.

Reasons Internal to Individual Firms

Internal reasons concern the firm's developing its research capabilities by doing research. Importantly, firms' capabilities to follow various lines of research that may look promising depend to a significant extent on decisions that they have made in the past. For example, one firm's past decision to work on automated production procedures will give it substantial capabilities in that direction. Not only will it be predisposed to look for solutions to current production problems that involve further automation but that may be the least costly thing for it to do because it will use human capital of the type that the firm's past behaviour has created. A second firm that has looked for solutions that involve moving towards lean production methods and away from mass production configurations will be predisposed to look for solutions to problems similar to those facing the first firm by going further in the lean production direction. Again, this may be the least costly procedure for that firm. An important example of an internally driven trajectory of developing knowledge is provided by Chandler (2001: 13–14):

The [US] radio sector, appearing in the 1920s, evolved from the learning acquired in the initial commercializing of modern electrical and telephone equipment in the 1890s. The technical knowledge learned in commercializing the radio, in turn, laid the foundations for the commercializing of television in the 1940s and 1950s. That knowledge, in turn, provided the base for the innovative tape and disk technologies of the 1970s and 1980s.

In summary, trajectories exist because there is path dependence in the development of technologies. This path dependence results from the cumulative nature of knowledge concerning how to deal with problems, and it is accentuated by uncertainty about which is the best technological path to pursue. The result is a tendency to continue along the path already being explored unless the incentives to deviate are strong and persistent. One aspect of path dependence is pursued a little further in the appendix to this chapter, others are touched on in Section IV of Chapter 3.

Equilibrium

Much neoclassical theory is Newtonian in conception. Forces balance each other to produce equilibria that are typically stationary, unique, and rendered stable by negative feedback. Small perturbations are dampened so that the system returns to its initial equilibrium position.

The great contribution of early neoclassical theorists was to show that under conditions of perfectly foresighted, rational, maximizing behaviour, the decisions of agents would result in a unique and optimal equilibrium.[11] In contrast, the groping behaviour, endogenous choice sets, and endogenous technology of S-E theory imply the absence of a unique, welfare-maximizing, and in many cases stationary equilibrium.[12] The innovation process is replete with non-convexities, such as once-for-all costs of developing and acquiring technological knowledge, positive feedbacks from current market success to further R&D efforts, and complementary relations among various technologies.

---

[11] Some modern versions of the neoclassical theory have extended the model (using the mathematics of topology) to versions where uniqueness is no longer a necessary characteristic of the optimal equilibria. However, in most such models all possible equilibria are optimal.

[12] In Chapter 15, we use a non-stationary equilibrium concept to illustrate how the different behavioural assumptions of neoclassical and S-E models can give rise to significant differences in results.

Models with uncertainty and non-convexities display non-linearities and path-dependent processes. Some formulations of the resulting behaviour yield punctuated equilibria: long, stable periods alternating with bursts of change, the timing and substance of which are not predictable in advance. Others yield multiple equilibria, in which historical accidents determine which equilibrium will be reached or approached at any one time. Still others yield only perpetual change. In this case, although theories that employ stationary equilibria are inapplicable, behaviour is still open to theoretical analysis that seeks to understand the system's laws of motion. Considerations such as these put an arrow of time into S-E theories. For example, because people learn from their behaviour, there is no guarantee that the imposition and subsequent removal of an exogenous shock will cause the dependent variables to change and then return to their original values. This is particularly important in the context of technological change.[13]

It also follows, as pointed out by Nelson and Winter (1982), that the clear neoclassical dichotomy between the objective function and the choice set that enables it to produce stationary and unique equilibria is not sustainable in S-E theory. In S-E theory, firms are continually faced with a choice of how much and what type of innovation they should attempt. We know that a firm's current capabilities depend partly on decisions made in the past, so its set of feasible choices evolves endogenously in a path-dependent way. The resulting 'equilibrium' is a dynamic evolving process that must be analysed in terms of the system's laws of motion.

Competition

Neoclassical theory treats competition as the *end state* of the competitive process. There is no ongoing process of rivalrous behaviour. Instead, what is modelled is the static state in which firms are all adjusted to their environment. Under the assumption of perfect competition, firms have no power over the market and so have neither the need nor the ability to engage in rivalrous behaviour vis-à-vis each other. In fact, there is no active competition in the sense that it is used in ordinary language. The use of long-run equilibrium analysis is typically justified as showing the end state towards which dynamic real-world competition is continually tending, even if it is never reached.

The Dixit–Stiglitz version of monopolistic competition drops the assumption of a set of perfectly competitive, price-taking firms in favour of a set of monopolistically competitive firms all producing products that have equal elasticities of substitution with respect to each other. This allows each firm some degree of market power. However, when a new product is introduced, all existing products suffer the same loss of sales. This characteristic is at odds with the observations of how consumers actually behave with respect to differentiated products but is used because it makes

---

[13] Mokyr (1990) was one of the first economic historians to discuss punctuated equilibria in the context of technological change.

the model tractable.[14] This model of differentiated firms in one industry has sometimes been treated as if it described an entire economy. But we know of no GE model that contains several industries in which each firm is monopolistically competitive with all other firms in the same industry but not with any of the firms in other industries. Furthermore, all the other assumptions about foresight and maximizing behaviour that characterize the canonical neoclassical model are found in the Dixit–Stiglitz monopolistically competitive model. It is probably best seen, therefore, as an extension of the neoclassical model rather than as a wholly new paradigm.

S-E theory follows the Austrian tradition in treating competition as a *process* that takes place in real time. In this view:

[F]irms jostle for advantage by price and non-price competition, undercutting and outbidding rivals in the market-place by advertising outlays and promotional expenses, launching new differentiated products, new technical processes, new methods of marketing and new organisational forms, and even new reward structures for their employees, all for the sake of head-start profits that they know will soon be eroded. (Blaug 1997: 255)

Here competition encompasses rivalrous situations among both large and small groups of firms. Simple passive price-taking behaviour is not involved. Rather, behaviour takes the form of active struggling of firm against firm, each seeking a temporary advantage over the others. In this type of competition, technological innovations are a major tool by which firms strive to gain competitive advantages. Since no such advantages are permanent, none will show up in long-run equilibrium. As a result, long-run equilibrium analysis of the competitive process is argued to be not just irrelevant but misleading because firms that are competing through innovations will cause technology to change endogenously long before any long-run tendency based on fixed technology and tastes is manifested in observed behaviour (see, for example, Dosi and Orsinego 1988).

The great problem with this type of theory is that no one knows how to aggregate the behaviour of rivalrous, price-setting firms into a theory of the macro behaviour of the whole economy. We argue, however, that if that is the way the world is, there is no point in pretending otherwise. This difficulty of aggregating known micro behaviour to obtain the aggregate variables and relations that we would like to have for macro analysis is one of the main reasons why we do not base our models in Part III on micro evolutionary theory, but begin instead with an (unorthodox)

---

[14] As we will observe in several places, this mathematical version of Chamberlin's once-famous symmetry assumption is empirically falsified by the observation that all differentiated products of one generic type, such as the range of automobiles available today, are not equal substitutes for each other. Instead, they are linked in a chain of closer and less close substitutes. Thus a new entrant into one part of the product spectrum will not take sales equally from all incumbents, as is required by the symmetry assumption, but will take more sales from close substitutes and less from others further away in the product spectrum. Furthermore, the Dixit–Stiglitz model uses a representative consumer who consumes some of every differentiated version of a single generic product although no one has been able to show that such a consumer can be aggregated from the behaviour of individual consumers, each of whom consumes only one or a small number or the whole range of differentiated versions of one generic product. (See Eaton and Lipsey 1989: Introduction for further discussion.)

aggregate growth model, which we amend incrementally to incorporate S-E behaviour piecemeal.

Structure

The neoclassical view tends to display the world as smooth, subject to incremental alterations, with a featureless technology and homogeneous agents whose behaviour is adequately displayed by that of a single representative for each class of agent. The S-E view tends to display the world as lumpy, subject to discrete alterations, with a structured technology and heterogeneous agents. We will encounter many examples of such contrasts throughout this book and for easy reference we will refer to them as the 'structural contrasts'. Here we briefly foreshadow a few of these contrasts by way of illustration. First, neoclassical economics portrays technology flatly, often by a productivity constant, A, that 'scales up' the relevant production function (e.g. in the aggregate production function that makes GDP a function of inputs of capital services, k, and labour, l: $GDP = Af(k,l)$). In contrast, S-E theorists see individual technologies as characterized by structural hierarchies and linked by a network of complex complementarities and substitutabilities. Second, neoclassical economics tends to see the effects of changes in process technologies as being adequately captured by changes in the input prices that are produced by these technologies, while S-E theory sees new technologies as often creating many new possibilities that were technically unfeasible with previous technologies. Examples of this contrast will occur many times in subsequent chapters. Third, much neoclassical theory makes use of the representative agent so that aggregation is a trivial matter of multiplying any quantity chosen by that agent by the number of such agents. In contrast, S-E theories make diverse agents a centrepiece. The evolution of the economy is driven by differences among agents and it is often the outlier, not the median agent, who drives change.[15]

II. FUNCTIONING OF THE MARKET

As we have seen, the neoclassical market is one in which suitably informed agents acting to maximize their own objective functions subject to well-defined feasibility constraints achieve the optimal market equilibrium. In contrast, the S-E view is one of imperfectly informed agents groping under uncertainty towards outcomes they perceive as better, thus driving a historical, path-dependent process that never settles

---

[15] Eaton and Lipsey (1997: Introduction and ch. 14) argue that the representative consumer in the Dixit–Stiglitz model of monopolistic competition cannot be aggregated from the empirically observed behaviour of heterogeneous consumers, each of whom purchase only a small subset of the available differentiated versions of each generic product. The fiction that it can causes this accepted version of monopolistic competition to have implications that were refuted on empirical grounds in the early debates between Kaldor and Chamberlin. Nonetheless, this empirically refuted model continues to be the one used for virtually all analyses of markets with differentiated products. Many of the predictions derived from this model are in direct conflict with the predictions from a model that allows for heterogeneous agents.

into a stationary equilibrium but is, instead, continually jostled by new, endogenously created innovations. When contrasting these two views of how the market functions, Nelson and Winter referred to the 'hidden hand' and the 'evolutionary hand' views. These have different implications for many matters. Here we stress two of them: the coordinating function of the market and the general justification of the market economy.

Coordination

One of the great issues in economics is to explain why the whole economy behaves in a more or less ordered way although the key decisions are made by many unrelated agents. The economy's coordinated behaviour is an emergent property of group behaviour that cannot be predicted by studying the behaviour of any number of isolated individuals. It is important in this respect not to confuse an ordered structure, which is a generally agreed empirical property, with a theoretical equilibrium, which is not.

Coordination in Traditional Neoclassical Theory

The traditional neoclassical explanation is that the price system produces publicly available signals that reflect relative scarcities. Individuals respond to these in a self-interested manner and, in the process, impart order to the whole system. In this view, agents do most of the work. They have the best information that is available and do the maximizing calculations themselves. Where aggregation is required, markets behave as if they were either perfectly or monopolistically competitive.[16]

Although it is not clear how far the property of optimality relates to real economies, it is clear from experience in places where the operation of the price system has been seriously hampered by heavy-handed government interventions that market-determined prices and quantities do fulfil a major signalling and coordinating function. Without them, decentralized decisions of individual agents would not produce the emergent property of an economy that looks as if it had been consciously coordinated. Little more needs to be said about this since it is well known and well investigated.

Because the coordinated macroeconomy is an emergent characteristic of uncoordinated micro behaviour, macro outcomes that are *unexpected* can emerge (in the sense that the outcomes are not consistent with the objectives of individuals). The most obvious example emphasized by classical and neoclassical economists is that the unconstrained pursuit of maximal profits by individuals operating in a competitive setting ends up reducing their profits to zero. The tragedy of the commons is another example well known to economists.

Coordination in New Classical Economics

Robert Lucas introduced rational expectations in the 1970s and by the mid-1980s this view of the world had come to dominate macroeconomics. A key part of such

---

[16] Where they are monopolistically competitive, they must obey the assumptions of the Dixit–Stiglitz model that we discussed earlier.

models is the representative agent. A representative consumer is blown up to explain the nation's total consumption behaviour and a representative firm is blown up to describe the whole of the nation's production behaviour. If everyone is the same and the macro behaviour of producers and consumers is merely a blow-up of the micro behaviour of representative agents, there can be no coordination problem. As Howitt (2006) puts it: 'When rational expectations was adopted ... the gap between micro and macro became not bridged but papered over.'

Coordination in Evolutionary Economics

The evolutionary hand approach typically employs neither the fiction of the rational maximizer nor the representative agent (although some evolutionary models do make use of these concepts). Agents are assumed to lack the relevant information that would be required to maximize, and further, when agents are operating under uncertainty, it is unclear what maximizing behaviour even means. Also agents are usually assumed to be diverse and so can, and often do, have different expectations about the future state of the market and hence what a good profit-seeking strategy is.

In these sorts of models, the market is much more important as a coordinating mechanism, because there is real work to be done in coordinating the diverse and sometimes inconsistent decisions of heterogeneous agents. Agents do the best they can, often forming mistaken views on underlying processes and often being subject to bandwagon thinking, and various other misdirecting influences. Sometimes they get 'it' right but often they get 'it' wrong. So the job of the market is to direct behaviour towards more value-creating activities by rewarding successes and punishing failures. Those who, by luck or good judgement, get it right are awarded big profits, much larger than the normal return on capital that is all that is needed to direct resources in static perfect competition. Those who get it wrong lose and, if their losses are sufficient, they disappear from the scene.

Compared with the static world of neoclassical welfare economics, the problem of coordination is much more complex in an S-E world of continuous change. How does a system that is continually changing and destroying much of what it has, and that is subject to cumulative causation and increasing returns to scale and a host of non-linear dynamic structures at the micro level, produce relative order at the macro level? Was the Great Depression of the 1930s an example of the poor functioning of the market-coordinating mechanism or just of poor policy that exaggerated what would otherwise have been a normal recession? Some years ago Dosi and Orsenigo (1988: 25) posed the issue of coordination this way:

In standard models coordination among plans and actions of individual agents—and thus the theoretical possibility of economic 'order'—rests on the interaction between a simple behavioural assumption (maximization) and some sort of scarcity constraint. Conversely, the 'core' heuristics of the [S-E] approach ... depends on the interaction between exploitable opportunities, present in non-stationary environments, which are too complex and too volatile to be fully mastered or understood by individual agents, and institutions which, to different degrees, simplify and govern behaviour and interactions. As a consequence, 'order in change' is generated by varying combinations of (a) *learning*, (b) *selection mechanisms* and (c) *institutional structures*.

We briefly consider each of these generating mechanisms. First, technologies develop along relatively structured paths shaped by their technical characteristics, and the cumulative experience that evolves as knowledge is acquired. This is the concept of technological trajectories, discussed earlier and in the Appendix to this chapter (and further in Chapter 4). They help to impart stability to R&D behaviour.

Second, in static states, markets can deliver all the relevant information and even discount future contingencies where risk is involved. However, when technologies are evolving endogenously, markets cannot 'deliver information about or discount the possibility of future states-of-the-world whose occurrence is, to different degrees, the unintentional result of present decisions taken by *heterogeneous agents* characterised by different competencies, beliefs and expectations' (Dosi and Orsenigo 1988: 18). In such situations, the evolutionary hand of the market is the major selection mechanism for choosing which of the possible directions that agents follow will be reinforced by profits and which discouraged by losses. Without this selection mechanism, firms that began on different paths would deviate progressively; with it, firms that deviate too much from paths that turn out *ex post* to be the successful ones are eliminated. This market behaviour is often modified by substantial government intervention that either consciously or inadvertently affects the speed and direction of change.

Third, the uncertainty associated with technological change requires institutions first to shape behaviour and second to organize the interactions of agents. Institutions in both the public and private sectors serve to narrow the possible choice set and impart some stability to decisions in the face of uncertainty. For Dosi and Orsenigo (1988: 19), institutions play a role analogous to that of maximization in the neoclassical model: 'they are factors of *behavioural order* which contribute to explain coordination and consistency in uncertain, complex and changing environments.'

When discussing coordination, we must take note of what is probably the most important appreciative theoretical treatment of long-term economic growth in the S-E tradition that has been published in the last decade—Freeman and Louçã's *As Time Goes By*. The six key themes of their book (which we number for easy reference) are:

Theme 1:   Economic growth is to be understood in terms of five partially independent and partially interacting subsystems: economic, technological, scientific, political, and cultural.

Theme 2:   The historical evolution of these subsystems is coordinated by a process that is not evident at the micro level but emerges at the economy-wide level.

Theme 3:   The incremental evolution of these subsystems is occasionally interrupted by large shocks leading to what in historical terms are discontinuous changes.

Theme 4: These dramatic discontinuities that are important in understanding what is driving growth and change are not typically evident in macro data and so need to be studied at the micro level.

Theme 5: These discontinuities cause 'structural crises of adjustment' because much of the economic, political, and social order needs to be adjusted to the new developments.

Theme 6: This whole historical process causes economic growth to occur in spurts that give rise to long-wave cycles similar, but not identical, to those posited by Kondratieff and Schumpeter.

In developing these themes, they present a treatment of long-term growth that is in some ways similar to ours and we consider their ideas in more detail in Chapter 11.[17] What matters most at this point is to note that they give importance to the issue of the coordination of dynamic evolving systems. Their five subsystems noted in Theme 1 are partly independent of each other and partly interrelated in a complex system of mutual causation. They argue that understanding the historical dynamics of technological change and economic growth requires understanding the process that coordinates the semi-autonomous and semi-interdependent evolutions of these subsystems. This coordination process is not explicit but is an emergent property resulting from the actions of individuals and groups. These actions are based partly on calculations and partly on conventions and they create tensions that integrate conflicts through many different forms of behaviour based on such things as cooperation, competition, power, strategy, and domination. Unfortunately, the authors do not outline this critical mechanism in any detail.

When all the work on this issue is surveyed, it is hard to avoid the conclusion that in spite of the amount of thought that has been devoted to understanding the type of market coordination, which produces stable macro behaviour relative to the individual micro behaviour, which guides decision-making over time in S-E theory, no really coherent appreciative theory has been developed so far. Such a theory would need, first, to show how markets coordinate and produce relative stability in spite of having many micro characteristics that tend towards instability (e.g. positive feedback loops associated with competition in technological change) and, second, to

---

[17] The interrelation of these subsystems, Theme 1, is a major theme of our book and is stressed in Chapters 5, 6, 7, 8, and 13. The issue of coordination, Theme 2, is discussed in the text above. We deal with the confusion caused by different meanings attached to the concept of technological discontinuities in Chapter 4, while the discontinuities themselves are discussed throughout the book since GPTs are our major mechanism for producing such shifts. The difficulty of observing these changes from an inspection of macroeconomic data, Theme 4, and the important confusions of interpretation that this causes, are discussed in Chapters 4, 4A, and 13. Although we do not use the concept of 'structural crises of adjustment', Theme 5, our discussion of the structural changes required by new GPTs is closely related. It is set up in our Chapter 3 and recurs at many subsequent places, particularly in Chapter 13. We do not deal explicitly with long-wave cycles, Theme 6, as our analysis is not affected by the existence or non-existence of such cycles. We believe, however, that Freeman and Louçã have developed a sophisticated theory of the relation between long-term economic growth and long-term cycles that fits much of the empirical data. Those who wish to dismiss such cycles should at least detail the sources of their disagreement with the powerful arguments put forward by these authors.

establish the useful functions of governments and other public bodies in such markets. For this we must await the S-E analogy to the Arrow Debreu model, but one that will be immensely more complex. In the absence of such a theory, we cannot fully understand how well the coordinating system works and what public policies, if any, might improve its functioning.

Coordination in Endogenous Growth Theory

Some endogenous growth theorists who do not work in the new classical paradigm have recently caught up with the evolutionary view of the coordination problem.[18] Much of this work is directed to showing causes of instability in micro processes. The modern work here goes back at least to Brian Arthur who argued throughout the 1980s that many of the processes associated with technological change created positive feedback loops.[19] For example, in the common situation where two or more versions of some basic new technology compete with each other, should one get a temporary advantage, it may generate sufficient profits to finance an increasing flow of R&D that pushes it further ahead of its competitor. Eventually, the pay-off to R&D on the weaker competitor may become so small that further work on it is abandoned. There is no guarantee, however, that such a process will chose what might, with an equal input of R&D over a long period, have turned out to be the superior alternative. Given the uncertainty associated with technological advance, there is no way of showing after the event which one would have been the superior version if sufficient time had been allowed to explore the possibilities of both. In such cases, equilibrium if it exists at all, is not unique and historical accidents matter.

Recently, several other cases of positive feedback loops have been investigated. For example, consider R&D designed to save on a particular factor input. The traditional theory has it that if a factor becomes scarce, its price will rise and so will the pay-off to R&D designed to economize on it. But if large quantities of the factor are not in use, the total pay-off to the R&D may be less than the expected pay-off from economizing on some plentiful factor, which, although its price is low, is widely used. If everyone could do R&D, if there were perfect capital markets available to everyone, and if there were no indivisibilities associated with R&D (no set-up costs, no learning curves, etc.), this would not be a problem, as every potentially profitable possibility would be explored. But given that none of these conditions hold, there is

---

[18] Communication between endogenous growth economists and evolutionary economists (who long ago stressed endogenous growth) is so slight that the rediscovery of the coordination problem among endogenous growth theorists seems to have proceeded without any recognition that these issues have been discussed for more than two decades by evolutionary theorists. Nonetheless, the growth theorists are in the main stream, at least in North America, so it is their rediscovery that will probably serve to revive interest in the coordination problem among the mass of economists.

[19] See Arthur (1994) for a collection of essays reporting on this work. Discussing the difficulty he had in getting his ideas published in mainline journals, Arthur wrote (1994: xvii–xix): 'In looking back on the difficulties in publishing these papers, I realize that I was naïve in expecting they would be welcomed immediately in the journals. The field of economics is notoriously slow to open itself to ideas that are different.'

no general prediction about whether R&D will be directed to saving on the scarce or the plentiful factor.[20]

More generally, Rosenberg and Birdzell (1986) argued that the West grew rich by being willing to accept the upset that is caused by growth, which is driven by technological change. Vested interests lose out and inequalities are often exacerbated as some find themselves well equipped to take advantage of the new technologies while others with human capital invested in the skills required by the older technologies lose out. When technologies are heavy users of human capital, there is a positive feedback loop in that those who win from the new process are better able to educate themselves, and their children, in the skills that command a high market price. Rosenberg and Birdzell argue that, compared with other areas, the West has been tolerant of such disruptions and has gained the benefit of sustained economic growth. Here is a clear case of positive feedback: 'to him (or her) that hath is given'. The West grew because it tolerated the upset of technological change. As it developed the culture of doing so (and the institutions that encouraged that culture), it grew more and more, with the gap between it and the rest increasing through the nineteenth and early twentieth centuries. Only when other nations were willing to accept the consequence of technological change, and to create the conditions that welcomed it, did they begin to grow and narrow the income gap between themselves and the West. In today's world, there is also a clear division within the West of such tolerance, with it being higher in the USA than in Europe.[21]

It is understood that such positive feedback loops can cause growth to be accompanied by disruptions and all sorts of non-equilibrium behaviour. Thus far, endogenous growth theory, in reacting to the neoclassical point of view, has emphasized how and why the market may not perfectly coordinate individual decisions. Much less attention has been devoted to the issues raised long ago by evolutionary economists: How can a system that contains so many micro sources of instability proceed in a more or less coordinated way—not perfectly coordinated, but more stable than chaotic?

The Evolutionary Hand in Action

One situation in which the evolutionary hand of the market is often seen in action is when technological changes require big alterations to the structure of the economy (what in Chapter 3 we call the facilitating structure) and it is not clear to agents what

---

[20] Which way the R&D goes would depend, among other things, on (i) the amount of use of each factor; (ii) the price of each; (iii) the expected relative costs of R&D required to save a unit of each factor; and (iv) the expectations of success in each line of research. For this last consideration, the trajectory of past research, and thus the human capital developed in various kinds of R&D, would be a historically determined influencing factor.

[21] Of course it is not necessary to accept all the social costs that accompany disruptive technological change. The tax-transfer system, working through institutions that do not dampen the incentive to innovate and invest in human capital, can mitigate much of the social costs. However, if policies are adopted that intentionally or unintentionally curtail technological change in the interest of preserving the existing distribution of jobs, wealth, and incomes, growth can be reduced and, in the limit, stifled altogether.

constitutes the best adaptations to the technological shock. For example, firm size is an important element of the facilitating structure, and it was impacted when automated textile machines were developed sufficiently for the movement out of cottages into early factories to begin some time in the late eighteenth century. But, as is typical with an emerging GPT (this time an organizational one), no one was sure what kind of factory was best.[22] There was a wave of investment in factories, some run by water power and some mere sheds containing a number of hand-operated, automated machines. The investment boom proceeded until there were too many factories, many of them too small to be competitive. The evolutionary hand sorted out and preserved those arrangements that worked and eliminated those that did not. For another example, when electricity replaced steam, large-scale operations became efficient in many manufacturing activities, but not all. When petroleum became big business, large-scale production and distribution became efficient in many petroleum-related activities. As a result of these, and other developments, a vogue for bigness led to a wave of US mergers in the 1890s. Some proved efficient and others inefficient. Where they proved efficient, those who brought them about earned large profits; where they proved inefficient, those who brought them about lost heavily as new smaller firms entered and outcompeted their larger opponents. If there had been perfect foresight, one set of mergers would have happened and the other would not. As it was, no one was sure where large was going to prove better than small, and the evolutionary hand had to sort out, reward, and preserve the efficient mergers, while punishing and eliminating the inefficient ones. A somewhat different story needs to be told about the wave of conglomerate mergers that swept the USA in the 1970s, most of which were then undone a decade later. In the other merger waves, there were genuine gains to be reaped but it was not known precisely where they were located. With conglomerate mergers, the idea that diversification was more efficiently produced within conglomerate firms rather than within the portfolios of investors proved to be generally mistaken.

Similar things happen with new products. Chandler (2001: 17–18) illustrates the evolutionary hand operating in the early days of the US electronics industry. In October 1921, the first licence was issued for a US commercial radio station, but at that time no one anticipated the enormous popularity of radios among consumers. Within three years most of the available frequencies had been allocated and the number of broadcasting stations levelled off in the 600–700 range. There was a massive influx of firms to produce the radios that fuelled the expansion of stations. Over 600 radio-producing firms were established during the period 1923–6, but only 18 survived until 1934. By 1934, the evolutionary hand had done what no individual could have done in 1923—to sort out those who had what it took to survive from those who did not. This experience also provides another illustration of path dependence since, as Chandler points out, 'the most successful survivors were

---

[22] There is debate about the sources of the efficiency of factories over cottage production, but the move would not have persisted (although it might have been experimented with) if it were not more efficient than cottage industry in some important dimensions.

existing producers of electrical devices that had built their functional capabilities before the coming of the new radio technologies'. Indeed, there were only two successful start-ups in the list of survivors; the rest had developed their skills previously in such industries as auto batteries, auto ignition systems, telephone equipment, light bulbs, and other electrical equipment. A more recent story of the evolutionary hand in action concerns telecommunications where billions of dollars were invested in the mistaken belief that the public would take to new telecommunications products in volumes that were not forthcoming.

To summarize the evolutionary hand view: because innovation is surrounded by uncertainty, the prospects for new products, new processes, and new forms of organization are hard to assess both absolutely and relatively to other competing products, processes, and forms of organization. Agents often do not have sufficient information to tell which of several choices will turn out to be good ones and which bad. So experimentation takes place and agents learn by making various decisions. The role of prices and profits is to provide some general signals, to motivate people to invest in these uncertain situations, and to sort out the winners from the losers after the investments have taken place. In the neoclassical world of end-state competition, profits above the normal rate of return on capital are rents and serve no social purpose. In the evolutionary and uncertain world, large profits are the needed incentive to motivate not only innovation but also investment in all kinds of related activities, including altering elements of the economy's structure to adapt them rightly or wrongly to new technologies.

The General Justification of the Market Economy

Neoclassical theory provides what can be called a formal justification of the free market system. It is based on a type of reasoning that dates back at least as far as Walras and is currently embodied in the two fundamental theorems of welfare economics. The theory proves that the perfectly competitive idealization of the market economy would lead, in equilibrium, to an *optimum* allocation of resources. Although the proof of the optimality of perfect competition was an intellectual triumph, it raised practical problems. The assumptions of perfect competition are not even remotely related to much of the world in which we live. Nor is static perfect competition an achievable state in our dynamic changing world.[23] Another important limitation is that the formal argument concentrates on static resource allocation and says nothing about economic growth. The static model deals with intertemporal issues by having dated inputs and outputs as well as myriad futures markets. It does not, however, contain the endogenous, path-dependent, technological change that is by far the most important force influencing our living standards over any long period of time.[24] An unfortunate consequence of these limitations is that each

---

[23] In the view of the methodologist, Mark Blaug (1997: 255), 'everyone admits that these beautiful theorems are mental exercises without the slightest possibility of ever being practically relevant'.

[24] See Lipsey (2001) for a fuller discussion of the formal defence and a comparison with what we later call the informal defence.

individual must rely on his or her own intuitive judgement to decide what relevance, if any, these neoclassical welfare theorems have to the functioning of any real economy.

Because there is no concept of optimality in most S-E theories, the formal justification of the price system is irrelevant in the context of these theories. The justification of the market system is provided by what we call the 'informal justification'. It is not laid out in equations leading to a formal, mathematical result. But it does follow from some tight, appreciative theorizing and it has been subjected to searching scrutiny over the years. This informal justification uses four well-known points.

1. The market system is self-organizing. It coordinates economic decisions better than any known alternative—not optimally, just better than the alternatives. But economic self-organization is not a static process; instead it leads to self-transformation, which is a more subtle notion of endogeneity than static theory allows for.
2. Markets tend to accomplish this coordination relatively efficiently by producing prices that are influenced by relative scarcities and that respond to changes in these. Although prices are important signals, given continuing change in the face of uncertainty, there is no way to prove that current prices are an optimal set. But they do usually reflect scarcities sufficiently to induce agents to economize on the use of resources that are scarce and to make lavish use of resources that are plentiful.
3. A well-functioning market economy with the necessary institutional underpinnings tends to decentralize power and to involve less coercion, and fewer opportunities for corruption, than does any centrally administered type of organizing mechanism.
4. The market system is conducive to growth by encouraging the exploration of opportunities for innovation by decentralized, profit-seeking decision-makers who compete against each other using privately owned capital. Market societies are open societies in which no position is free from challenge unless protected by government fiat. It has proved to be a marvellous framework for the kind of business experimentation and discovery that facilitates growth.

Desirable Characteristics

So far we have contrasted many characteristics of market behaviour as seen in the two approaches. We now ask of each view, which of these characteristics are regarded as contributing to, and which detracting from, the efficient functioning of the market.

In the canonical GE version of neoclassical economics, desirable market characteristics include the absence of market power so that price taking is the typical situation; prices are equal to opportunity costs and do not, therefore, allow for any pure profits; rents associated with market power of oligopolies and monopolies or other forms of market power are eliminated; and sources of non-convexities such as scale effects and high entry costs are minimal or non-existent.

In the S-E view, the things that drive the economy towards desirable results are the very characteristics that are undesirable sources of market imperfections in neoclassical economics. Although the special case of an entrenched monopoly that does not innovate is regarded as undesirable, most other market 'imperfections' are the very forces that drive economic development.[25] Perfectly competitive industries rarely innovate. It is rather oligopolies that do the most. One illustrative example is that none of the innovations that have transformed agriculture in the twentieth century has come from price-taking farmers. Instead, they have come from oligopolistic firms producing farm machinery, fertilizers, and other inputs, as well as from publicly funded research laboratories. An innovator knows how to do something his competitors have not yet learned to do; he has market power and can earn profits until competitors learn what he knows. If information were transferred immediately and costlessly (as in the model of perfect competition), there would be no profits of innovation and hence little or no innovation. Innovation creates asymmetric information, which creates market power, which in turn creates the profits that drive the system. Really large profits are the carrot that induces agents to attempt leaps into the unknown and to make many more modest decisions under conditions of uncertainty.[26] Path-dependent evolutions brought about by new technologies are preferable to static equilibria. Non-convexities are a key part of the desirable growth process. Scale effects, rather than being imperfections to be offset, are some of the most desirable results of new technologies. Entry costs for new products and new firms are the accepted costs of innovation and the source of some of the rents that drive such behaviour.

Because they see different market characteristics as desirable, the two theories have radically different implications for economic policy. The main neoclassical advice is to remove all market imperfections and other things that would prevent the attainment of an optimum allocation of resources in such an economy. But, according to S-E theory, the very market imperfections that are seen as impediments to optimality are often important sources of growth in a dynamic economy and are to be encouraged, not suppressed. We pursue this line of enquiry at some length in Chapters 16 and 17.

Is There a Meaningful Difference?

Some economists have argued that there is no operative difference between the two concepts of the market's functions. In practice, they argue, each will produce the maximizing result, whatever the individual micro behaviour that lies behind it. Here we consider the two best known arguments, which are due to Milton Friedman and Armen Alchian.

---

[25] Indeed Baumol (2002) wrote an entire book elaborating on the proposition that it is the profits of imperfect competition that drive the technological arms race, which ultimately ends up generating long-run growth.

[26] It is interesting that in another context, measuring total factor productivity, the returns to innovation are called 'manna from heaven' or 'free gifts' as if they were not the opportunity cost of inducing entrepreneurs to act under uncertainty. See Appendix to Chapter 4 for further discussion of this point.

Friedman (1953) appeals to Darwinian theory to argue that the survival of the fittest guarantees optimal outcomes just as if individuals were choosing the best ways to fit into environmental niches. So, according to this argument, we can use a model of micro maximization even if firms are not maximizers because the market will produce the results that would have occurred if they were maximizers. In other words, the selection mechanism of the evolutionary hand will ensure that in equilibrium the market will be inhabited only by maximizers.

There are at least three problems with this view. First, in a static world, all that competition ensures is that those who survive will all be about as good as each other. If, for example, all engage in behaviour that causes what Leibenstein calls X-inefficiency, the overall result will be X-inefficient. All that the market will ensure is that those who are relatively more X-inefficient will lose out to those who are relatively less X-inefficient.[27] Second, in a dynamic, path-dependent world, a snapshot of an economy full of maximizing firms may look very similar to an economy full of firms groping under uncertainty. For example, when the relative price of some factor rises, both types of firms will use less of that factor (see Appendix to Chapter 3). Even though both may respond qualitatively in the same way to some shocks, the array of practices in firms, and hence their average performance, will be different in the two types of economy. Firms in the groping economy will investigate some lines of enquiry that look unpromising but that occasionally turn out to have very high pay-offs, while maximizing firms would avoid them. Third, in a dynamic world of uncertainty there is nothing in the market selection process to guarantee that *only the fittest* will survive, that *all the fittest* will survive, and that *all others* will be eliminated—as long as 'fittest' is defined independently of survival and not tautologically as 'those who survive'.

Alchian's argument (1950) is a subtler version of Friedman's. Whereas Friedman argued that survival of the fittest ensured that firms would be profit maximizers, Alchian argued only that survival of the fittest produces aggregate results that are qualitatively similar to what would happen if everyone were a maximizer. In other words, the evolutionary hand selection mechanism guarantees that the market outcome will be the same as if the market were inhabited only by maximizing agents.

Alchian starts by saying that when there is risk in which the distribution of probable outcomes for any two actions overlaps, there is no unique way to decide on an optimal choice of action. He then argues that it is not rational to choose the more likely of the two most probable outcomes since there is no reason to ignore higher moments of the probability distributions. This is a much more extreme dismissal of maximization than the argument we have relied on, that maximization is not a definable concept in the face of *uncertainty*. Alchian then goes on to state

---

[27] X-inefficiency covers 'all the elements that could be involved in non-allocative inefficiencies many of which are assumed away in neoclassical maximising theory .... [It] ... is similar to technical inefficiency ... [but is based on the assumption] that there is nothing technical about most of the substantial sources of non-allocative inefficiencies in organisations.' The theory of X-inefficiency predicts significant amounts of non-maximizing behaviour under circumstances such as substantial inertias, incomplete contracts, and significant amounts of discretion in economic decision-making (see Leibenstein 1987: vol. 4, 934–5).

many of the points that we have argued, including that the market selects those who make positive profits only on the basis of relative efficiency, not profit maximization. Only at the end of his article does he reach a conclusion that we do not accept. Having made all the relevant points he (1950: 220–1) concludes:

I have asserted that the economist, using the present analytical tools developed in the analysis of the firm under certainty, can predict the more adoptable or viable types of economic interrelationships that will be induced by environmental change even if individuals themselves are unable to ascertain them. That is, although individual participants may not know their cost and revenue situations, the economist can predict the consequences of higher wage rates, taxes, government policy, etc. Like the biologist, the economist predicts the effect of environmental changes on the surviving class of living organisms; the economist need not assume that each participant is aware of, or acts according to, his cost and demand situation.

This, as Koopmans (1957: 140) points out, leads to a very different theory: 'But if this [evolutionary selection mechanism] is the basis for our belief in profit maximization, then we should postulate that basis itself and not the profit maximization which it implies in certain circumstances.'

To justify Alchian's confidence in the ability of profit maximizing theory to predict the behaviour of the real groping economy, if not that of individual firms, we would need a dynamic theory covering such things as entry, exit, and the altering of decision rules under the accumulation of experience. Some evolutionary models will produce 'good' results from groping, profit-oriented or even random behaviour, but only when the fitness function and the selection procedure work in the right way. There is no guarantee that all evolutionary processes will produce the reactions that the static maximizing model predicts, even as a general tendency. Path dependency, scale effects, and uncertainty imply that the dynamic process can result in situations that would never have been consciously chosen from the vantage point of either the initial or final situation.

The formalization and testing of the Alchian thesis lies in evolutionary or other dynamic formulations of economic change, not in asserting that the results of the static model will be duplicated by any imaginable dynamic process and selection mechanism. As Blaug (1992:102) says, we have two theories here—the neoclassical and Alchian's—not just two small variants of one great, all-embracing, neoclassical theory. What Blaug calls Alchian's theory is a theory of (more correctly a set of assertions about) the dynamic functioning of the market that S-E theory seeks to address. In Chapter 15, we use our own dynamic model of GPT-driven endogenous growth to develop a counter-example that refutes Alchian and Freeman's assertions and illustrates the arguments made by their critics.

Conclusion

In many situations, firms face relatively simple choices made under fairly predictable conditions. In such cases, maximizing behaviour is possible and something like it may well occur. But when firms are making choices about inventing, innovating, and diffusing new technologies, there is an inevitable element of uncertainty. These are the cases that interest us here and for them we need a groping, profit-oriented rather than a maximizing view of the firm and an evolutionary rather than a hidden-hand view of market behaviour.

Does it matter? Understanding long-term growth in S-E rather than neoclassical terms matters in many ways, particularly as relates to policy. An important debate relates to the conditions for creating growth in poorer countries. There is general agreement that a necessary condition is that the economy be market-oriented to a significant extent. Some in the neoclassical tradition argue that establishing completely free markets for goods, services, and capital flows is also sufficient. Free up markets, establish the right rules of the game, and the miracle of the market will do the rest. Others in the S-E tradition argue that the evolutionary hand needs significant amounts of policy assistance. It received such assistance, they argue, in most of the older industrial economies, also in the Asian Tigers, and it is needed in other countries today (see Lipsey 2002*a*).

Another debate concerns technology enhancement policies in advanced countries. Many in the neoclassical tradition are critical of all such policies. They argue that fully informed maximizing firms can do anything the government can do, and do it better. At most, they point to a generalized R&D externality to justify a 'non-distorting' general subsidy or tax relief for all such expenditure. Those in the S-E tradition argue that 'assistance that distorts' is a concept that is related to optimality conditions that are unobtainable and hence irrelevant to a growing economy operating under uncertainty. They argue further that governments should offer, and have offered, aid to specific technologies and that governments that do so are likely to create substantial national innovation leads over those that do not. In this context, they observe that many of the most important new twentieth-century technologies were developed with substantial assistance from public funds—often coming from the Department of Defense in the USA. They also accept that such specific ('distorting') assistance can go wrong in many ways. We consider this debate in some detail in Chapters 16 and 17.

APPENDIX: TECHNOLOGICAL CHOICES AND TRAJECTORIES

Technological trajectories play a large part in both theory and empirical work on technological change. They reflect the inertia provided by agents pursuing innovations in a path-dependent process of knowledge accumulation such that what is decided today with respect to R&D is strongly influenced by what was done in the past. In this appendix, we consider the neoclassical and S-E views on the choices open to firms, paying particular attention to trajectories and their implication of path dependence.

The Neoclassical Formulation

First consider the neoclassical microeconomic production function. A firm produces good X using two inputs, f and g. Its production function

$$X = X(f,g)$$

represents its production choices with a given technology. A level surface, or isoquant, for a given output, X_m

$$g = g(X_m, f)$$

is illustrated in Figure 2A.1.

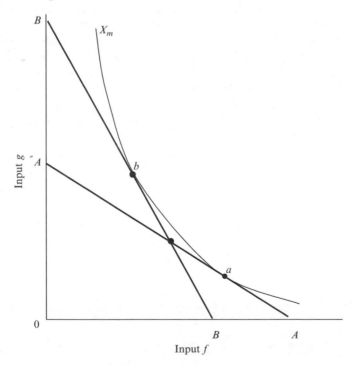

Figure 2A.1. *Substitution along a neoclassical isoquant*

A firm making a long-run decision to build a plant is assumed to be able to choose any point in this factor space. To minimize costs of producing some target output, X_m, the firm will choose point *a* for relative factor prices given by the slope of the line *AA*, and point *b* for relative prices given by the slope of the line *BB*. If the firm is located at *a* and factor prices change from those indicated by the slope of *AA* to *BB*, the firm will shift from point *a* to point *b* when it comes to replace its old plant. This formulation is time-reversible. A new firm can choose to locate at *a* or *b* and a firm at *a* can shift to *b* just as easily as a firm at *b* can shift to *a*.

An S-E Formulation

In the S-E formulation, the firm knows its current and past locations in factor space, but moving to somewhere else in that space involves an uncertain cost and time. Assume (Figure 2A.2) that the firm is currently at point a_3, producing output X_3 with factor inputs f_1 and g_1. The shaded area between the lines $X_3'X_3'$ and $X_3''X_3''$ shows the range of uncertainty about where the isoquant X_3 will turn out to lie *if resources are devoted to* altering the production process so as to use a different ratio of inputs to produce the output X_3. The kinked line $X_3''X_3''$ indicates the least favourable outcome thought 'possible', while $X_3'X_3'$ indicates the most favourable outcome thought 'possible'.

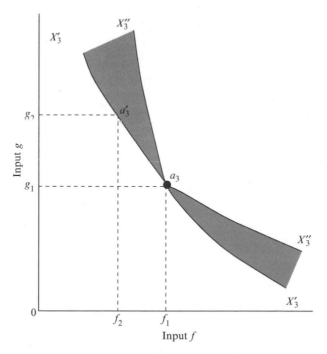

Figure 2A.2. *Changing factor proportions under uncertainty*

This is not the only uncertainty. If the firm targets a move from say a_3 to a'_3, it does not know what the cost of the move will be in terms of designing a plant and getting it operating to full efficiency—as factors go through the inevitable learning by doing and the bugs are worked out of the design in learning by using. Assume that a firm at a_3 tells its engineers to design and set up a plant located at a'_3 in factor space, using input amounts f_2 and g_2 to produce X_3. It then faces three types of uncertainty. First, when the facility is designed and put into practice, it may not turn out to be located at a'_3; instead, it may use the factors in some different proportion. Second, it does not know what the full cost will be of developing and providing a facility that produces at or near a'_3. Third, it does not know precisely what isoquant will pass through a'_3. The facility's capacity output may be somewhat greater or less than X_3.

Now let factor productivity change. First, consider a single firm *having a constant rate of output period by period.* Technological change (embodied in new capital) will impart a trajectory to the firm's location in factor space.[28] The numerical subscripts on Figure 2A.3 now refer to times. The firm's facility (which for convenience is assumed to have a time-invariant, capacity output) is located in input space successively at a_0, then a_1, then a_2 and at times t_0, t_1, t_2, and so on. If the resulting trajectory has a negative slope, as illustrated by arrow (1), the technological change

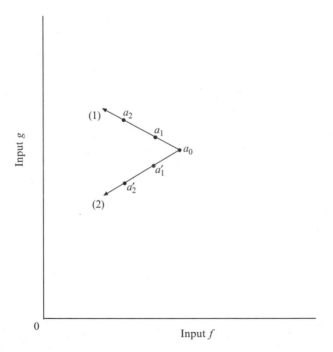

Figure 2A.3. *Two alternative trajectories for technological change*

[28] Here we take 'trajectory' to mean a series of discrete points corresponding to past input combinations.

uses more of one factor (g in the case shown) and less of the other. If the trajectory has a positive slope, the technological change is absolutely factor-saving, using less of all factors to produce a given output. In the case shown by arrow (2), the trajectory is absolutely factor-saving and relatively f-saving, using more g per unit of f.

If the trajectory is of type (1), there is a past history of other blueprints that could become relevant when factor prices changed enough. However, one of the things agreed to by virtually all the writers on technological change is that the typical trajectory is of type (2). In these cases, a firm's past history gives no experience to guide cost-reducing factor substitutions when input prices change.

If the innovations save on all inputs, any new technique will be preferred to all older techniques. In the absence of competition, a firm would encounter buoyant profits as its costs fall along *any* positively sloped trajectory no matter what its precise slope. Consider the firm in Figure 2A.4. It is currently at a_0, having followed the trajectory indicated by the solid arrow. If it continues to follow its present routines (in Nelson and Winter's sense), it will proceed along the trajectory of the broken line, arriving at a_n at time t_n. Now assume that at time zero there is a large fall in the relative price of input f. Let the firm direct those managing its technological change to put effort into biasing that change to be more f-using relative to g.

Now everything depends on the nature and flexibility of the trajectory. To illustrate, define an iso-R&D curve telling us all possible locations in factor-input space that could be occupied by a plant at time n for given expenditures on R&D, including learning by using any new equipment. Such a precise curve implies a

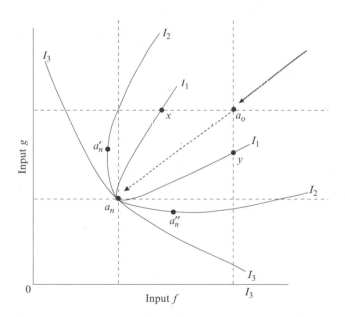

Figure 2A.4. *Alternative iso-R&D curves*

spurious degree of precision in the firm's choice, but the iso-R&D curve is for purposes of illustration only. So let the firm at a_0 decide to spend a given amount on R&D plus 'teething' expenditures *and* then order that effort to be directed at moving along a *specified* factor-ratio trajectory. It can obtain any one desired point on the iso-R&D curve, I_n.

The figure shows three cases. In case 1, the kinked iso-R&D curve I_1 through a_n shows that no deflection of the path is economic. Although some points on the iso-R&D curve I_1 are absolutely efficient compared with a_0 (the segment xa_ny), all but a_n are absolutely inefficient compared with a_n: any attempt to alter the technological trajectory is absolutely costly in all inputs. Iso-R&D curve I_3 is at the other extreme. It looks like a neoclassical isoquant. The firm can chose its point a from a large range of alternatives for a given expenditure on R&D. Curve I_2 is closer than I_3 to what students of technology often find. This trajectory has some flexibility, but not a lot. Variations in the relative factor price, p_g/p_f, between zero and infinity only lead to a deflection of the trajectory between a'_n and a''_n (where the slope of the curve is respectively vertical and horizontal).

What it is at issue here is the extent to which the trajectory of productivity growth can be altered by economic signals and the extent to which it is determined by the internal logic of science and specific technologies (e.g. the period starting in the mid-1880s was the age of electricity, irrespective of specific economic situation, while the late twentieth century was the age of computers and new materials just because science has got to that place).

Attempts by agents to deflect the trajectory may be associated with uncertainties whose number is an increasing function of the angle of deflection that the firm tries to impose on the *input* trajectory that would arise from following existing routines. The logic of a trajectory (e.g. substituting electric for steam power) implies that big alterations of factor ratios from what would have been if previous plans and inertias had been followed, 'go against the grain' of the technology and may be associated with an increasing number of things that become uncertain. Adding an uncertainty cost to the R&D cost increases the curvature of the iso-R&D curve, and could turn a type 2 curve into a type 1 curve.

Contrast the picture of the firm in Figure 2A.4 with the neoclassical version in Figure 2A.1. The neoclassical firm can choose any point in the whole space spanned by the production function and knows the implications of doing so. Each point implies given production costs in terms of known inputs of factor services. There is no cost in moving from one point to another. In Figure 2A.4, all that the firm knows for certain is its past trajectory. It has conjectures about its future trajectory if it follows its current routines, which implies among other things going on doing more of the same type of R&D. It may have some limited conjectures about where it would end up if it decided to shift the slope of the trajectory one way or the other, but this will by no means be certain (i.e. the iso-R&D curve should be an area rather than a line). The firm's present position, and alternatives for the future, depend on its past history and its present location. *For it, history matters.*

3

A Structuralist-Evolutionary Decomposition

In Chapter 2, we contrasted the neoclassical and S-E world views. Here we continue on the same theme with a more detailed focus on the standard neoclassical growth model and our S-E approach. Any study of technological change and its relation to economic growth requires a theoretical framework. Ours, which is presented here, incorporates many elements of the S-E approach and provides an organizing device to guide our study of historical cases of GPTs in Chapters 5 and 6. Its categories help to open our minds to possibilites that are left behind the scenes in all growth models based on aggregate production functions. An illustration of why our decomposition is so important arises in later discussions when the economy's technology, structure, and productivity move in different directions—breaking the equivalence between technological change and various measures of productivity growth that is found in any growth model using an aggregate production function.

The neoclassical aggregate production function, a key element of most growth models, is shown schematically in Figure 3.1. It maps inputs passing through a single aggregate production function to produce the nation's output, as measured by its GDP. Institutions and the structure of technology help to determine the function's form but are hidden inside the 'black box' of this function. Technological change is only observable by its effects on productivity, as measured by such variables as TFP and labour productivity. There are no independent ways of separately measuring changes in technology, economic structure, and productivity. For example, coexistence of rapid technological change and slow productivity growth cannot be observed in this model.

Figure 3.2 summarizes our S-E alternative.[1] Since we use it to break open the black box of the production function, we also call it an 'S-E decomposition'. The

Figure 3.1. *The neoclassical aggregate production function*

---

[1] Our model is not intended as a full description of the economy, but only as a somewhat fuller description than is provided by the aggregate production function. For some purposes, it is necessary to

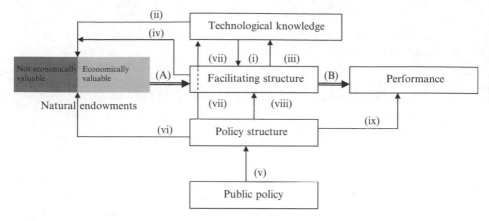

Figure 3.2. *The structuralist-evolutionary decomposition*

Note: The double arrows indicate (A) the flow of natural endowments into the facilitating structure where labour and capital goods are used to produce (B) the flow of income and output that gives rise to the whole spectrum of economic results, which we call performance.

The single arrows indicate the main internal flows of influence:

- changes in **technological knowledge** will (i) induce changes in the facilitating structure and may (ii) move the boundary between valuable and non-valuable natural endowments;
- changes in the **facilitating structure** can (iii) affect the accumulation of technological knowledge, (iv) move the boundary between valuable and non-valuable endowments, and (B) influence performance;
- **public policy** is (v) embedded in the **policy structure** and, operating through that structure, can (vi) move the boundary between valuable and non-valuable endowments, (vii) directly affect the accumulation of new technological knowledge, (viii) influence elements of the facilitating structure, and (ix) directly affect performance.

Examples of each influence are (i) new technological knowledge is embodied in new machines; (ii) new technologies make previously useless materials valuable; (iii) new research laboratories increase the rate of R&D; (iv) a rise in population makes it economical to redeem waste land, (v) a new public policy requires creating a new government department; (vi) a new environmental protection law makes certain mineral deposits no longer profitable to extract; (vii) a new tax incentive policy increases the amount of R&D; (viii) a new anti-monopoly policy alters the concentration and location of industry; and (ix) a new tax policy alters the distribution of income.

decomposition separates technology from the capital goods that embody it, making the latter a part of what we call the economy's 'facilitating structure'. It also separates public policy from the policy structure that gives it effect. Separating changes in technology, changes in structure, and changes in performance opens the possibility that they can change in different directions, or that some will change while others will not.

go further, distinguishing technological and scientific knowledge and allowing for social and other structures that are not included in our facilitating structure.

I. THE S-E DECOMPOSITION

The six main categories of our S-E decomposition are shown in Figure 3.2. Because of the strategy we follow in Part III for developing formal theoretical models— altering macro models incrementally in an S-E direction rather than using micro evolutionary models—we do not need to say as much about the agents who make choices concerning each of our variables as we would have to if we were going to develop formal micro evolutionary models involving explicit assumptions about the behaviour of heterogeneous agents.

Technology

The concept of technology is variously defined and often loosely employed. For some it refers to the knowledge of how to make things; for others it refers to the tools and other artefacts actually used to make these things. For example, the *Cambridge Encyclopaedia* (1990: 1190) defines technology as:

The use of tools, machines, materials, techniques, and sources of power to make work easier and more productive. ... Whereas science is concerned with understanding why things happen, technology deals with making things happen.

The definition is unsatisfactory for several reasons. Technology is not just the tools themselves, nor is it simply their use; it is the ideas or specifications of which the tools are embodiments.[2] Also, making work 'more productive' is ambiguous and might refer only to reducing the costs of producing given products. To cover all aspects of technology, we must expand the meaning of 'more productive' to include the creation of wholly new products and wholly new processes.[3]

We require a definition that has two key characteristics. First, it must clearly differentiate technology from the capital goods that embody it and the humans who retain knowledge of it. People often speak loosely about a capital good, such as a steam engine or an automobile, as being a technology. But such goods are

---

[2] In developing a model of knowledge-led growth, Mokyr (2002: 2–3) makes a distinction similar to ours: 'The term "useful knowledge" was used by Simon Kuznets ... as the source of modern economic growth. One could debate at great length what "useful" means. In what follows, I am motivated by the centrality of technology. Because technology in its widest sense is the manipulation of nature for human material gain, I confine myself to knowledge of natural phenomena that exclude the human mind and social institutions.' We agree with Mokyr that the appropriate focus is on the knowledge base underlying the embodiment of technology.

[3] Some writers distinguish techniques (and crafts) from technology. Cardwell (1995: 4) makes this distinction and says that inventions in the field of techniques and crafts 'do not involve systematic knowledge and are, in a sense, empirical' while inventions deriving from technology 'involve systematic or scientific knowledge'. Yet this distinction seems unsustainable. If it refers to what is intrinsically involved, many inventions that were made on wholly empirical grounds were subsequently found to involve important scientific discoveries. If it refers to the body of knowledge used by the inventor, we do not know how to assess this: for example, is it the body of knowledge the inventor generally had at his or her disposal or what he or she used for this particular invention? (Many discoveries made by highly educated scientists are stumbled on and in this sense are wholly empirical.) In any case, it does not seem useful to make a distinction between various kinds of tools depending on the knowledge used by, or available to, their inventors.

embodiments of technology, not the technology itself. For example, if you knew nothing about cars but were given a set of blueprints for a 1922 Model T Ford, you could build it (acquiring quite a bit of tacit technological knowledge along the way). But if you were given a Model T and no blueprints, you would have to reverse-engineer it to arrive at the technological knowledge that it embodies before you had a chance of building another one.

Second, we want our definition to include all practical knowledge about how to create economic value. This makes it more embracing than is typical. Some things are included that would not commonly be thought of as technology. For example, the knowledge of how to write a best selling novel is technological knowledge since it is knowledge about how to create economic value. Some of it is innate; some is tacit; but some of it can be codified and taught to would-be writers. Similarly, knowledge about how to play professional football is technological knowledge (embodied partly in the capital goods of teaching manuals, and equipment and partly in the human capital of players, referees, and coaches).

These two considerations lead us to the following broad definition:

Technological knowledge, technology for short, is the set of ideas specifying all activities that create economic value. It comprises: (1) knowledge about product technologies, the specifications of everything that is produced; (2) knowledge about process technologies, the specifications of all processes by which goods and services are produced; (3) knowledge about organizational technologies, the specification of how productive activity is organized in productive and administrative units for producing present and future goods and services (which thus includes knowledge about how to conduct R&D).[4]

This definition distinguishes technological knowledge from other types of knowledge, including scientific knowledge. As with all definitions, there are grey areas at the boundaries. In particular, some things are excluded that come close to being what we might think of as technological knowledge. For example, knowledge about some physical process is scientific knowledge until it is put to use to make something of economic value. When that is done, the knowledge that does the job becomes technological knowledge. For example, Newton's laws of motion are scientific knowledge; but when that scientific knowledge was used to make a better waterwheel, which embodied Newton's laws, the knowledge of how to make the wheel was technological.

Since all technology is knowledge, it follows that all economies are knowledge-based.[5] Although all capital goods embody technological knowledge, they are not

---

[4] Our inclusion of organizational knowledge in technology is contentious. But such definitions are matters of convenience and we find it helpful to put all knowledge that assists in the creation of economic value into the one category of technology. In any case, process and organizational technologies shade into each other at the margins. For example, how to organize the productive process (an organizational technology) is close to how to produce it with given instruments (a process technology). For those who do not like to bundle these together, the term 'technological and organizational knowledge' can be substituted in everything that we say about what we call technology.

[5] When people refer to the modern economy as being knowledge-based in contrast to previous economies, they are probably referring to a presumed drastic increase in the ratio of human capital to physical capital.

themselves technology. Although it is humans who know how to construct and operate the things that create economic value, the embodiment of this knowledge in their memory circuits is not technology. Although technology is embodied in both physical and human capital, *it is distinct from both.*

As our definition is a subtle change to some definitions of technology, we offer two illustrations that may help clarify it. The first is a thought experiment that we use several times in this book to distinguish technology from physical capital. Consider increasing capital while holding technology constant at the level that existed at some specific point in time. With physical capital, this would require making more capital goods that were known at that time and were designed to produce the goods and services that were then known. With human capital, it would require increasing the knowledge about how to use the technology that existed at that time to create economic value by embodying it in goods and services of all sorts—more people would be learning more about the technological knowledge that existed at the time.

The second illustration concerns the difference between technological knowledge and its embodiment. The statement that *A embodies B* is different from the statement that *A is B*. For example, let a given blueprint for a machine be used by two different firms in two different places to build the machine. The technology used is identical but the resulting capital good may be different because the embodiment requires a translation from the blueprint to the specific reality in each case. We do not say that there are two different technologies but that the one technology has been embodied slightly differently in the two distinct capital goods. Similarly, when two persons learn the same codifiable piece of technological knowledge about how to construct a capital good, a translation is needed in order to fit this knowledge into their own mental systems. The results of embodying this one bit of technology into two different pieces of human capital residing in two different people may be somewhat different and will show up in how they are able to use their knowledge. As a result, when they each construct the specified capital good, the two may differ somewhat. Again, we do not say that there are two different technologies but that the one technology has been embodied first in two slightly different pieces of human capital and then in two slightly different machines.

When it matters, we distinguish between technology as ideas from the embodiment of technology in physical goods and organizations. But when it does not matter, we follow the common usage of not distinguishing between the ideas and their realizations.

Some technological knowledge is codifiable. It is stored in such things as blueprints and instruction manuals. Other technological knowledge is tacit and can only be acquired by experience. It can only be stored as human capital. All product, process, and organizational technologies have elements of both tacit and codifiable knowledge.[6]

---

[6] In practice, some technologies are more codifiable than others: product and organizational technologies tend to be more codifiable while process technologies typically include relatively more tacit knowledge.

Notice also that technologies typically come in triplets. For every product technology, specifying the make-up of an individual good or service, there is at least one corresponding process technology, specifying how to produce that product, and at least one set of organizational technologies, specifying the organization of all the activities associated with producing, marketing, and improving it.

The agents who develop technological knowledge and commercialize it are scientists, engineers, entrepreneurs, users, and many others who contribute to technological change. They operate mainly within the structures of public and private sector research organizations and of firms, including single proprietorships. When it comes to creating economic value from new technologies, the entrepreneur is key—an opportunist who recognizes the possibilities inherent in new technologies. 'In that sense, the entrepreneur gives life, so to speak, to an implicit demand on the part of the consumers' (Sautet 2000: 60). Because the outcomes of entrepreneurial efforts are uncertain, successful entrepreneurs are adept at coping with uncertainty. Their ability to create economic profit from innovation is one of the most important weapons of competition among entrepreneurial firms.

The Facilitating Structure

We define the facilitating structure as the set of realizations of technological knowledge, by which we mean the actual physical objects, people, and structures in which technological knowledge is embodied. To be useful, most technological knowledge must be embodied in one way or another. Even what is called disembodied technological knowledge in the literature is usually embodied either in the human capital of those who know how to use it or in various forms of organization such as the layout of machines in a factory. The facilitating structure comprises the following broad categories, which of course need subdivision in many practical applications:

- all physical capital;
- consumer durables and residential housing;
- people, who they are, where they live, and all human capital that resides in them and that is related to productive activities, including tacit knowledge of how to operate existing value-creating facilities;
- actual physical organization of production facilities, including labour practices;
- managerial and financial organization of firms;
- geographical location of productive activities;
- industrial concentration;
- all infrastructure;
- all private-sector financial institutions, and financial instruments;
- government-owned industries[7];

---

[7] These are on the borderline between the facilitating structure and the policy structure since although nationalized industries may be run just as private sector firms would be, they can also be used as instruments of public policy. But our policy structure is restricted to those organizations such as the civil service, which are directly under the control of some government and are primarily the instrument for giving effect to public policy. In contrast, nationalized industries are usually run by a board that is

- educational institutions[8]; and
- all research units whether in the public or the private sector.

The agents who take most of the decisions concerning these elements are firms and households, with some input from the public sector, particularly for infrastructure.

We have assigned the stocks of capital and labour that provide the inputs of capital and labour services to the facilitating structure. Capital is a man-made stock that embodies technological knowledge. The analysis of its place in the productive process, and of its slow change in response to new technological knowledge, is best accomplished if we treat it as part of the facilitating structure.

We place labour in the facilitating structure because people are analytically similar to capital. Theories sometimes make the distinction between pure 'unskilled' labour and the human capital that is embodied in labour. But a genuinely unskilled person who embodied absolutely no learnt human capital would be totally unemployable and hence of no economic value. Humans learn from the time of birth, constantly acquiring knowledge that makes them valuable as productive agents. So a labourer can be regarded in exactly the same way as capital. An item of physical capital is made of basic materials that have characteristics and that are formed into shapes that embody the technological knowledge without which the basic materials would be useless. Similarly, a newborn infant has characteristics. The adult worker has acquired a vast amount of human capital, without which he or she would be useless. Thus from our point of view, a worker is as much a produced factor as is a piece of physical capital. The stocks of both adjust with lags when there is a change in the requirements of productive processes.

As with all definitions, the value of these is to be decided on grounds of usefulness, not of right or wrong. The usefulness of these categories depends on the ability to make them operational. It is clear that each of them can be observed and either measured, as with concentration and location, or described fully, as with managerial forms. Historically, it is possible to identify good and poor matches between new technologies and the various elements of the existing structure. For example, the new IC technology required a change in the locations of people and firms, different human capital, and different management structures compared with the older paper-based forms of organization and mass production–based factories. The necessary adjustments took considerable time and caused much strife while they were being made.

So the categories are useful in interpreting historical experience. Because the facilitating structure has the dimension of an array whose elements themselves have many dimensions, it cannot be compressed into a single scalar measure,

---

removed from public policy intervention, although policy may direct its behaviour in broad ways such as to price to maximize profits or to cover average or marginal costs.

[8] Educational institutions are not in the policy structure for similar reason that the nationalized industries are not included. But those that are fully publicly funded and operating at the elementary or secondary levels do respond to public policy. They are also under the general direction of governmental departments of education, which are themselves in the policy structure. But they maintain considerable independence and typically act not unlike privately owned educational institutions.

which can be compared across economies to conclude, for example, that one structure is better, or larger, or different in some other unique way than another. Dealing with the facilitating structure in a formal rather than an appreciative theory is difficult although not, we contend, impossible, and we take a first step at modelling it in Chapter 15.

Natural Endowments

Natural endowments are the basic materials used in producing output (through production processes embedded in the facilitating structure). They are what the classical economists called 'land', which includes physical land and all natural resources. The only truly exogenous inputs are those provided by nature. Agricultural land, forests, fish, all the natural materials, including ores and chemicals, are the basic materials. They are fed into the productive system that is embedded in the facilitating structure and are transformed by the services of capital and labour into outputs, creating what we call performance variables.

Although what is provided by nature is exogenous, the current size and value of stock of many of the items included under land is partly endogenous. Users and public policymakers decide the rate of utilization of both renewable and non-renewable resources. New technologies and new public policies reduce the value of some resources and increase the value of others. We will see many examples of this in Chapters 5 and 6.

Public Policy

Public policy is the set of ideas covering the specification of the objectives of public policy as expressed in legislation, laws, rules, regulations, procedures, and precedents, as well as the specification of the means of achieving them, expressed in the design and command structure of public sector institutions from the police force to government departments to international bodies. In Figure 3.2, policy is shown as an exogeneous variable, although, of course, it reacts to changes in the variables both in all of the other boxes and outside of our schema.

The Policy Structure

The policy structure is the set of realizations that provides the means of achieving public policies. It includes all public sector institutions, parliament, courts, civil services, regulatory bodies, and other government bodies. It also includes humans who staff these organizations and whose human capital embodies the knowledge related to the design and operation of public sector institutions, that is, institutional competence. (Note the parallel with technology and its embodiment in capital goods that are a part of the facilitating structure.[9]) Just as we put nationalized industries into the facilitating structure, so we put public sector research facilities there as well.

---

[9] One interesting group that might seem difficult to categorize is the lobbying industry. Since this is a private sector institution that is designed to influence public policy but cannot make it, we place it in the facilitating structure.

Elected bodies decide on public policy at a high level and make decisions with respect to the policy structure and some aspects of the facillitating structure (such as publicly provided infrastructure). Bureaucrats administer public policy and make lower-level decisions with respect to it.[10] Public policy, operating through such policy structures as the tax department and government research bodies, influence invention and innovation.

Economic Performance

We refer to the system's economic performance rather than just its output since we wish to include more variables than just its GDP. Economic performance includes:

- aggregate GDP, its growth rate, its breakdown among sectors and among such broadly defined groupings as goods production and service production;
- aggregate gross national product (GNP) and its distribution among size and functional classes;
- total employment and unemployment and its distribution among such sub-groups as sectors and skill classes; and
- 'bads' such as pollution and other harmful environmental effects.

Economic performance is determined by the interaction between inputs and the existing facilitating structure. The facilitating structure is in turn influenced by technology and the policy structure, while performance is strongly influenced by the compatibility of technology, policy, and the facilitating structure. It follows that changes in technology typically have no effect on performance until they are embodied in the facilitating structure. Furthermore, the full effects on performance will not be felt until the elements of the structure have been adjusted to fit the newly embodied technology. But as we emphasize in Chapter 13, causation runs in both directions. Not only do changes in technology induce changes in the existing facilitating structure but the existing facilitating structure and changes in it also influence what happens to technology—when and how it changes and how effective any change will be.[11]

Precision of the Concepts

The approach taken in constructing our categories is unusual because we work from empirical observations to definitions of categories that do not necessarily lend themselves to easy measurement. Our variables seem vague to some because they cannot all be measured on a numerical scale in the way that the inputs into the neoclassical production function can be defined and measured as index numbers.

---

[10] Of course, these functions are often blurred in practice. Bureaucrats often make policy decisions and elected persons often meddle in administration.

[11] Freeman and Louçã (2001: 150) emphasize a similar set of ideas when they argue that the speed with which a major new technology becomes dominant 'depends to a considerable extent on the new infrastructures that are needed for its diffusion'. These new structures include, according to them, physical infrastructures, facilities for educating and training people in the skills needed for designing and developing the new range of products and services (we would add processes and organizations) that are enabled by the new technology.

We have two main responses, both of which argue that our concepts are no vaguer than many of those used in standard theories of growth and technological change.

First, the measured values used in applications of neoclassical growth theory are sometimes only vaguely connected to the theoretical concepts that they purport to measure. What, for example, is meant by the concept of a given amount of pure capital when the capital is, in reality, a collection of heterogeneous goods—an issue long debated but never settled by economists at Cambridge, Massachusetts and Cambridge, England. What does it mean to say that we have x per cent more of this pure capital than we had a century ago, when that real capital embodies radically different technologies?[12] One might argue that the meaning is in the definition of the index number that is used to measure this concept. But if we cannot point to a real-world counterpart of the concept of pure capital, we are involved in a vagueness that precise index numbers only conceal.

Second, many of the micro variables that research shows to be important characteristics of technology, and important causes of technological change, are not measurable as simple scalar values (at least given current measurement techniques). Property rights are one important example. The strength of property rights legislation is one determinant of the overall amount of inventive activity, while the intra-economy differences in its enforceability influence the allocation of inventive activity among various lines of endeavour. The strength and enforceability of property rights laws are not easily quantified. Qualitative changes in them are often discernible without being accurately measurable on a cardinal scale. Effective changes in property rights can sometimes be inferred from changes in the number of patents, but this is an imperfect measure since patents are taken out for many purposes, only some of which are affected by the strength and enforceability of property rights. If such problems exist with something so straightforward as property rights, they exist in much stronger form in respect to many of the other determinants of technological change, such as the current state of pure scientific knowledge and the extent to which the applied potential of existing pure knowledge has already been exploited. Yet these things are generally agreed to be important determinants of invention and innovation.

Lines of Influence

The main lines of influence are shown in Figure 3.2 and described, along with an example of each, in the caption. Although we only give one example in each case, changes in both public policy (operating through the policy structure) and technology can affect each one of the elements of the facilitating structure.

Restrictive Modelling Requirements

Formal models require, among other things, the assumptions of unique causality and simplicity of explanation. The uniqueness requires the model not to be over-

---

[12] Of course, there are vintage capital models but in them virtually all of the measurements of growth in output and productivity, as well as of technological change, are made in the context of an aggregate production function in which each generic input is measured as a scalar value.

determined, whereas we have argued that in reality there are often more than enough sufficient causes for some observed result. Simplicity requires that the myriad interrelated variables observable in technological history be represented as a few abstract ones. As a result, many of the important details of history disappear from the explanation. In contrast, appreciative theories in which history matters are not constrained by such assumptions. They are, therefore, potentially productive in analysing the messy history of innovation and growth over the very long term. In our view, both appreciative and formal theorizing are complementary tools for studies such as ours.[13] In Chapters 7 and 11, we argue that some issues, such as the timing and precise location of the emergence of sustained growth in the West, require appreciative theories. In contrast, we use formal theories to deal with population dynamics in Chapter 9 and with GPT-driven growth in Chapters 14 and 15.

II. INCENTIVES AND BEHAVIOUR

To discuss innovation, and to compare innovating and non-innovating societies, we need a theory of the incentives for the various agents who make decisions with respect to the above S-E categories. As discussed in Chapter 2, and again later in this chapter, we see firms as groping into an uncertain future in a profit-oriented manner. We have little to say about households and so are content to see them as utility maximizers, at least over the range of knowledge that they can be expected to have in given situations (see Chapter 14). What matters most for our theorizing is the behaviour of inventors and innovators, because they are the agents who create and commercialize technological knowledge. We approach the issue of their behaviour in a series of steps, starting with the most general ideas relating to innovative behaviour. This first step may seem a digression but it gives rise to our major hypothesis concerning invention and innovation.

The Technological Ape

Homo sapiens share the use of tools with a dozen or so other animals that routinely make use of a few simple tools.[14] What distinguishes us from all others, however, is our routine use of a wide range of tools and our ability to invent new tools consciously and persistently.

Hominids diverged from other apes somewhere between 4 and 8 million years ago. The three main features that evolved to distinguish them from their close ape

---

[13] We do not limit our methods of investigation to these two. We expect that a plurality of approaches to understanding the many linkages posited in our models would be best. In this sense, we are operating in line with Szostak's notion (2003) of scientific diversity.

[14] For most of these other animals the use is instinctive, stereotyped behaviour that does not have to be learnt. For our closest relative, the chimpanzee, culture and learning do seem to play some part in tool use. 'It is only in the human lineage, however, that culture and technology are coupled and fundamental to our existence' (Schick and Toth 1993: 51).

relatives were bipedalism, dependence on toolmaking, and large brains. Of these, bipedalism came first, but dependence on technology was crucial for much of what followed. Looking backwards from the present, the history of human evolution looks inevitable, but like other animals: 'good luck, ill fortune, decline, near extinction, and startling recovery have peppered the story of our evolution. There was nothing predetermined about the human race' (Stringer and McKie 1996: 18).

Although the interpretation of the fossil evidence is subject to debate, the evolution from primitive to modern humans seems to have been characterized by a series of relatively rapid changes in biological make-up, each one followed by a long period of stability. Each of these changes in anatomy was followed by a burst of technological change, after which the technology remained relatively stable for a long period. The probable explanation is that the maximum complexity of the technologies that each type of early hominid could master was in part genetically determined, just as it is today with the other tool-using animals: their brains do not allow them to use more than a few simple tools.

The hominids that made these early tools used them to do things done by many different types of animals, each with their own specialized biological make-up—a process called techno-organic.[15] This line of development gave hominids an increasingly varied diet, allowing them to colonize new environments and putting them into competition with a much wider range of animals than any other species. The use of tools set up a positive feedback loop—the first of many to be found in the history of technological change. Better toolmakers and users were more successful and were selected for survival.[16] The better the tools that were used, the more dependent on them hominids became, and thus the more did the hominid ability at making and using them become a criterion for survival. In short:

[T]echnology is probably *the* most significant element in determining what we are today, not just in forming modern 'civilization,' but in directing the course of our evolution from a distant apelike ancestor. Genetically, anatomically, behaviourally, and socially, we have been shaped through natural selection into tool makers and tool users. This is the net result of more than 2.5 million years of evolutionary forces working upon our biology and behaviour. (Schick and Toth 1993: 17–18)

About 1.7 million years ago, a new larger-brained hominid, called *Homo erectus*, emerged. The associated technology, called Acheulian, was a dramatic improvement

---

[15] See Schick and Toth (1993: 183–4) from whom the following examples are drawn. Clubs and stones allowed smaller animals to be attacked, thus overlapping the niche of smaller specialized carnivores. Cutting tools allowed larger animals to be dismembered and eaten, so that *Homo habilis* could do what larger carnivores did with their meat-shearing teeth or what other animals such as crocodiles could only do after waiting for the meat to be softened by putrefaction. Hammers crushed bones, overlapping the food sources of those animals, which had powerful bone-crushing teeth. Anvils used in conjunction with hammers allowed the crushing of nuts, overlapping with the food supply of birds with specialized nut-breaking teeth. Prying tools allowed access to gums below the tree bark, overlapping a niche occupied by some specialized birds, reptiles, and small mammals.

[16] Although there is debate over this view, we accept the strong evidence in its favour and make it a basic assumption for our analysis of invention and innovation.

on what had gone before. Compared with their predecessors, their tools were larger, more specialized, and more standardized, requiring much more skill and strength to manufacture. Adam Smith's specialization and division of labour was developing within Stone Age technology. At about this time, *Homo erectus* spread out of Africa, taking their technologies with them to all inhabitable parts of the world. What was habitable at any moment in time was technologically determined. For example, colder climates were uninhabitable before the development of fire, clothing, and reasonably sturdy dwellings for shelter, as they are today for most other types of apes and monkeys.

Because of this early colonization, it was long believed that these separate groups all evolved into modern humans in various places with enough interchange to make them biologically as similar as the earth's human inhabitants now are. However, genetic evidence, reinforced by some reinterpretations of other older evidence, now strongly suggests that all modern humans have descended from a small group of relatively modern people, perhaps a couple of hundred, who left Africa sometime in the last 100,000 years. This group spread throughout the world and eventually outcompeted all the hominids that had become established earlier, including Neanderthals in Europe.[17]

There is debate about the last creative evolutionary surge that produced anatomically modern people, but one strong force was undoubtedly the development of the human vocal equipment. Speech gives such enormous advantages of remembering, collating, and coordinating information that once the evolutionary track to better speech was established, a positive feedback mechanism improved it quickly.[18] Such a mechanism appears to have come into play about 100,000 years ago and to have produced modern speech equipment some time before 40,000 BC. It was the last great biologically driven information and communication revolution.

There is no reason to believe that 40,000 years ago the dominant hominids, *Homo sapiens*, were significantly different anatomically from their descendants today. So 40,000 BC can be taken as the beginning of the period of fully modern people equipped biologically with a large brain and full speech. For the first time in human evolution, we can be certain that the technology developed by hominids would not quickly reach limits imposed by brainpower.

Technological Solutions to Material Challenges

We now introduce a basic assumption that is consistent with the evidence of human evolution just discussed:

[17] This story is well told by Stringer and McKie (1996). Although important in many ways, this view of a modern African exodus is not important for our basic story of hominid's long evolutionary connection with technology.

[18] See Diamond (1992) and Howell (1965) for arguments that the development of a modern voice box was the driving force behind this change, which was the last great biologically driven ICT revolution.

Assumption: Humans are inventive creatures. Faced with a challenge that threatens to worsen their situation, or perceiving an opportunity to better it, they will typically seek solutions that involve invention and innovation.

The assumption that humans are inventive and innovative animals could take either of two forms. We could assume that these activities are their own reward; people do them because they are enjoyable and fulfilling. Without denying that this type of behaviour does sometimes exist, particularly among inventors, we make a different assumption:

Assumption: Invention and innovation are risky and costly; people will only engage in these activities if they anticipate a gain that exceeds the expected personal cost.

So we regard the amount of invention and innovation that goes on without being motivated by a search for personal gain as random behaviour that provides a background against which gain-motivated inventive and innovative activity occurs. It should also be noted that the anticipated gain may be purely monetary or may also include such things as prestige and other types of non-monetary rewards. (In the above discussion it was necessary to speak of invention and innovation. From here on, we revert to our procedure of using the term innovation to cover both inventing and innovating, except where the distinction is needed.[19])

III. INNOVATING AND NON-INNOVATING BEHAVIOUR

The decision to innovate depends on the anticipated costs and benefits. Benefits depend on the opportunities that people perceive and the reward that is expected. Perceived opportunities depend on the external environment and the 'world view' with which they interpret that environment. The environment may or may not provide many opportunities, and people may or may not perceive those that are there. Reward depends on many things, such as property rights, taxes, market values, and social approval. For rewards to be adequate to induce innovative behaviour, the innovator need not receive the entire social value of his or her innovation. What is required is that there be some margin of return over the opportunity cost of innovating.[20] Opportunity costs depend on the net benefits of alternative activities and any social disapproval of the activity in question.

---

[19] Some readers have asked us to frame the two assumptions as testable hypotheses. We have two responses. First, formally, assumptions about motivation are required in any theory that involves behaviour. Second, we do not subscribe to the methodological prescription that only predictions of theories should be tested against evidence. Instead, we accept that any empirical statement in a theory, whether cast as an assumption, a prediction, or anything else, should be open to empirical testing and we learn from such testing. For example, if a theory is built on empirically refuted assumptions, it is a good idea to know so. (See Lipsey 2001 on this latter point.)

[20] A large set of extreme assumptions is needed to get the neoclassical result that the optimum amount of innovation occurs only when the innovator is paid the full social value of his or her innovation. In Chapter 16, we explain why we reject this proposition.

Our general assumption implies that we do not need to explain the existence of inventive and innovative behaviour. What requires explanation is why it is sometimes absent, and when present, why it sometimes fails to lead to growth-creating cumulative advances in technology. We deal with this issue in three places. In the next subsection, we mention some broad considerations that are relevant to the issue of non-innovating societies. In the following subsection, we raise the issue of why we see non-innovating behaviour even in very innovative societies. In Chapters 7 and 8, we deal with the issues of innovating and non-innovating societies in some key historical contexts.

Opportunities for Innovation

Innovative opportunities arise in many ways. One way is the challenge of negative changes in the environment, such as worsening weather, the exhaustion of some natural resource, or a new enemy. These undesirable phenomena may present opportunities to overcome them with an innovation—to innovate around the problem. Opportunities may also be presented by some advantageous change in the environment such as climatic warming (e.g. the end of the last ice age), by new techniques of exploiting the environment (e.g. the discovery of bronze), or by a change in non-economic conditions (e.g. the end of hostile invasions by the barbarians who destroyed the Western Roman Empire). Another way is when some new theoretical knowledge creates new opportunities for inventions. For example, the understanding of genetics that followed the discovery of the double helix by Crick and Watson soon presented many opportunities for useful inventions in the area of biotechnology.

Similarly, a new GPT presents a host of new opportunities for developments based on that GPT. The computer opened up many new lines of product and process development. When it was miniaturized, a new set of opportunities arose, including in-ear hearing aids, navigational systems in automobiles, and automatic control of many household gadgets. New opportunities may also arise simply when, for no obvious reason, someone perceives an opportunity to do something new, possibly to make a new product or to make an old one in a new way. Public policy can also create many opportunities for innovation. Sometimes this is done consciously as when governments assist in the development of new basic advances, such as superconductivity, in the hope that they will have commercial applications. At other times, the opportunities are unintended by-products of policies introduced for other reasons. For example, many environmental protection laws have created the incentive for firms to develop new conforming technologies that subsequently turned out to have a wide market.

One can think of the various incentives just outlined as providing the 'carrots' of positive rewards for innovating and the 'sticks' of penalties for not innovating. Agents in social systems that encourage risk-taking, such as the USA, will require smaller potential rewards to act as an effective incentive than agents in societies that regard business failure as a serious social failure, such as Japan and Germany. Of course, risk-taking is a multidimensional concept. For example, some environments encourage short-term risk-taking while others encourage risk over longer periods. In societies that discourage risk-taking and change, people may be satisfied to do as well as their neighbours and Leibenstein's X-inefficiency may abound.[21] A low level of challenge may also induce customary satisficing behaviour while too much challenge can make individuals or whole societies dysfunctional.[22] In Chapters 7 and 8 we illustrate many of these broad points in the context of specific historical situations when innovations were either encouraged or stifled.

The above discussion may sound like a *challenge-response theory of innovation*. If this term is meant to imply that many innovations are made in response to challenges, we accept it. If it is meant to imply that all are made for this reason, we reject it. We illustrate throughout Chapters 5 and 6 that even GPTs, the most important of innovations, have sometimes been developed as responses to quite clear specific challenges and at other times have arisen when no specific challenge can be identified.

Non-Innovating Societies

Why might a society containing many innovative agents fail to innovate the kinds of technological advances that produce economic growth? We note five classes of reasons, with no claim to being exhaustive.

First, the environment may present few if any perceived opportunities or challenges. For example, a society whose production techniques are well adapted to its environment may present few apparent opportunities for the kinds of innovations that would raise its GDP. This is analogous to animals that evolve to become well adapted to some static environmental niche, and then evolve no further. Hunter-gatherer societies in rich areas, such as the Pacific Northwest of North America, were a probable case in point.

Second, people may not perceive opportunities that are in fact present. Given the external environment, what they perceive depends on how they interpret that environment. Faced with a challenge, someone whose world view is mechanical, as was common with Europeans in early modern times, will tend to look for mechanical solutions. Someone whose world view is mystical will tend to look for magical solutions. A change in attitude or approach may reveal opportunities in an unchanged environment that were hidden from previous generations. For this to be a valid explanation, the existence of a 'misleading' world view must not be inferred from the lack of innovation in the face of perceived opportunities. Instead, the world view must be shown to preclude searching in the direction necessary to deal innovatively with an identifiable challenge. For example, faced with military defeat many rulers asked why they had lost the favour of their Gods, while others voiced ritualistic explanations while looking for failures in their military technology and tactics (see Hanson 2001: ch. 1–3).

---

[21] X-inefficiency was briefly introduced on page 47 of Chapter 2.

[22] See, for example, Porter (1990) on the national attitudes that create different incentives to innovate.

Third, people may not be innovative because they do not expect to obtain sufficient personal rewards for taking the necessary risks. Absentee landlords or a rapacious state may confiscate the entire gain. Intellectual property rights may be so inadequate that innovators cannot gain from their innovations. In this respect, it is important to recall that the gain that is required to motivate innovation is only an amount that exceeds the costs and risks of innovating; it is not the whole of the gain that the innovation creates for society. Where the state owns the physical and intellectual property as in many ancient empires and in the USSR of the twentieth century, the innovator may be able to appropriate few of the gains from success, while suffering most of the penalties for failure. The disincentives for innovating are then very strong.

Fourth, human institutions may put various constraints on innovative activity, penalizing it or even outlawing it. Powerful vested interests often have much to lose from innovation. The state, unions, guilds, businesses, and many other institutions may seek to protect their existing rents by stifling innovative activity. Religious doctrines may sometimes condemn and stifle technological and scientific advance. The more the society's institutions concentrate power, the more likely it is that vested interests will be able to stifle innovation. But the relation between the concentration of power and the suppression of inventive and innovative activity is not a simple one. When powerful rulers approve of some activity, they can channel great resources into it and offer great rewards for success. So when the Chinese emperors wished to push some activity, whether mathematics under the Sung dynasty or foreign maritime activities early in the fifteenth century, they were able to do so, as were the Soviet authorities when they sought to push advances in, and applications of, atomic physics and rocketry. But the danger in such centralized decisions is that the interest of the authorities will wane and with it support for the activity and even memory of what had been accomplished. This happened many times in China when at one time or another the imperial court lost interest in activities such as astronomy, clocks, and overseas exploration. Another danger with centralized authority is that some line of activity will run afoul of religious or political dogma, as when the Soviet authorities' support of Lysenko's erroneous theories about the inheritance of acquired characteristics set the USSR's biological science back for decades, along with its many possible applications. One more disadvantage of centralized power is that groups of individuals who are seeking to act in their common interest will be judged and controlled in the interest of the authorities. For all of these reasons, pluralistic institutions that decentralize power provide more fertile ground for invention and innovation in the long run. If one power loses interest, or turns hostile, there is likely to be another that will have its interest aroused, as when the Catholic Church condemned much of early modern science while Anglican clerics embraced it. With many small clusters of power, there is more likelihood that one of them will find it advantageous to support some new innovation. In this way, European cities often encouraged emerging universities in the twelfth and thirteenth centuries for the advantages that they would bring to the city, although a wider authority might have seen little gain or even threat. Pluralistic institutions also tend to create what are called 'autonomous spheres of action' in which groups can pursue lines of investigation that are in their common interest without having the value of their activities judged and possibly controlled by higher authorities, as long as they conform to certain broad norms of group conduct. The pluralistic institutions of the West have done this for at least the last 1,000 years while China's monolithic institutions typically did not.

Fifth, the human propensity for innovative activity itself may be stifled. Endemic debilitating diseases may reduce human energy and initiative to the extent that humans cease to be innovative animals. For example, production that entails long periods of standing in water can produce such effects in a segment of the population.[23] Conditions of survival may be so harsh that no intellectual and emotional effort is available for innovative activity.[24] Some religions have similar effects by channelling energy into non-innovative activities by encouraging 'other-worldliness'. Those that see success in the world as a sign of approval from the Gods tend to encourage innovative activities.[25]

When technological innovation is actively discouraged, or carries an insufficient reward for any of the above reasons, the perception of costs and benefits may channel innovative activity into non-growth-producing activities such as art, sport, or ceremonial activities. In these cases, a society may remain innovative and highly civilized but in the context of static product and process technologies.

Non-Innovation in Innovating Societies

Why is it that in societies that do not suppress innovation existing opportunities often go unexploited? This question leads us to ask another: When dealing with day-to-day issues, and when looking for specific innovative solutions to their problems, how do agents act? There are several reasons why agents are not rational maximizers possessed with full information about the consequences of their actions. We consider two of these: uncertainty and complexity.

First, as discussed in Chapter 2, innovation takes place under uncertainty. So agents can often only learn the consequences of their actions by acting first and then observing what happens. This implies that in many innovative situations, agents make decisions based on conjectures about expected outcomes, groping for profits and learning as they proceed. This behaviour is imposed by the nature of our path-dependent world, where things are learned sequentially as experience accumulates through time.

Second, one can think of what Arthur (1992) calls a 'complexity boundary' that divides situations where maximizing behaviour is possible from those where it is not. On the feasible side of the barrier, agents can behave according to deductive

---

[23] See McNeill (1976: 43–8).

[24] This gets us close to the Leibenstein theory that there is an optimal amount of challenge. Too little encourages satisficing and too much makes people dysfunctional. Such a relation is clearly observable at the individual level. Whether or not it is observable and testable at the level of a whole society is less clear.

[25] This simple statement of tendency does not imply any stand on our part in the debate on the Weber–Tawney hypothesis that religion played *a big part* in the rise of capitalism.

logic. They can enumerate all the consequences of possible actions and then rationally calculate the best alternative course of action. In even moderately complex situations, however, such a procedure is rendered impossible by the vast number of possibilities, even when there is no uncertainty. (One cannot, for example, use the deductive process to deduce the optimal moves of a perfect game of chess.) On the infeasible side of the boundary, problems are ill-defined; agents who grope towards solutions are not acting suboptimally because optimality is not a defined concept in such circumstances.

So how do agents make decisions in the kind of ill-defined situations that occur continually? The key is that people do not just store bits of knowledge; they categorize them by fitting them into representational schemes. Acquiring knowledge is not just acquiring facts; it is finding categories in which to organize and store perceptions. We see how this affects behaviour when we see some outmoded categories being used, such as the mass production mindset. General Motors' misunderstanding of Japanese lean production in the 1980s, leading it to waste several billion dollars on a fully automated factory, is an example of not being able to make sense of observations because they were fitted into the wrong representational scheme.[26] It follows that two agents who have been exposed to different experiences in the past, with resulting differences in the stock of conceptual representations that they have formed, may act upon the same data differently. This kind of learning is one reason for the path dependence that we discussed earlier.

[We] clearly reason, analyse and deduce. But to do so at all we must first have constructed categories, representations, and models. Further, in ill-defined problems, or in complicated ones like Chess, pure deductive reasoning either is not possible or is beyond our abilities and it is applied to only part of the decision process. And so we reason by other, different means. We formulate internal models; we search for and use analogies; we recognize patterns; we transfer experience from other, similar situations. We use these methods to fill the gaps in our understanding so to speak, to allow us to infer from part-information to the whole, to extrapolate from the particular to the general. In other words, in 'knowing' and 'learning'— in gathering and gaining understanding—we operate heavily in the *inductive mode*. In any particular problem, of course, we combine the deduction we *can* carry out with a considerable amount of induction. (Arthur 1992: 10)

When we cross the complexity barrier, intelligent behaviour is forced to use subjective assumptions and temporary hypotheses to reason from incomplete information to a solution. Inductive reasoning then comes into play because people see information and look for sequences or other patterns and generalize from them.[27] The common use of inductive reasoning is also one of the main reasons why people stubbornly persist in believing clearly false things (see Shermer 1997).

---

[26] See Womack et al. (1990).

[27] Arthur quotes a study by Feldman, who gave people sequences of binary numbers [0,1] and asked them to guess the next number and talk aloud about how they were making their guesses. They kept finding patterns, held to them over one or two refutations, and altered hypotheses as old ones were refuted—all this in spite of the fact that all numbers were randomly generated!

Many of the situations in which agents make decisions on innovations are beyond the complexity barrier, both because the consequences of assumed results are too complex to estimate, and because the consequences of R&D are to a great extent unpredictable, being subject to many uncertainties. So we must envisage agents as groping in a profit-oriented way and occasionally interpreting their empirical observations in quite inappropriate ways.

Routine Behaviour

Faced with uncertainty and complexity, most agents rely to some extent on what Nelson and Winter call 'routines' to decrease the degree of uncertainty in decision-making. Routines do several things. They act as the agent's memory. The agent 'remembers by doing', which requires exercising routines and skills frequently. The routine is partly in human memory—specific individuals possess the skills required to operate the routines—and partly in the communication structures of firms and other organizations, which is one reason why the ICT revolution caused such large changes in the internal organization of firms.

Routines also act as a stable truce that reconciles the conflicting pressures and interests within any organization, reducing the costs associated with hostilities. Adoptions of innovations that seem obvious and easy to an outsider may be ignored because they could upset the organization's internal political equilibrium. It 'seems safe to say that fear of breaking the truce is, in general, a powerful force tending to hold organizations on the path of relatively inflexible routine' (Nelson and Winter 1982: 112). Routines also act as controls on behaviour. Things that upset routines, such as loss of a key person or group of persons, or a new product or a radically new production method, can be thought of as mutations. Firms struggle to control against these. Of course, some are advantageous but most are upsetting and better repressed.

The theory of routines can be reconciled with maximizing theory by saying that the apparent non-maximizing behaviour of firms is merely maximizing behaviour in the face of high internal transactions costs. But such a defence of maximizing theory makes it consistent with just about any possible observations of firm behaviour and hence renders it empirically empty. Even if we take that line, it is still necessary to break open the black box of the firm to understand its behaviour as a result of its internal structure, a procedure that the simple maximizing theory of the firm is meant to avoid. Whatever one calls it—non-maximizing routine behaviour or maximizing behaviour under heavy internal transactions costs—routines provide one technique that agents use to cope with the complexity and uncertainties facing them. The theory then explains a number of phenomena that create anomalies for simple maximizing theory. Here we mention a few that are most relevant to understanding technological change.

Restraints on Innovating Behaviour

Although routines are often helpful in allowing firms to proceed without too much internal conflict along established lines, they can inhibit the discovery and adoption of truly innovative solutions to problems. The theory of routines helps to explain why—in spite of our general assumption about the human propensity to invent and innovate—some agents are not as innovative as we would expect them to be if they were fully informed maximizers. For example, new firms with less rigid routines than established firms often have a higher propensity to innovate than established firms.

Slow Diffusion

Routines slow the diffusion of innovations because they affect the ability to replicate behaviour in different locations. It is a standard assumption of much economics that costless replication is possible: if a production facility is built identically to an existing one, both will behave identically. Experience of transferring technology from advanced to developing countries shows that replication is not a costless and instantaneous affair. One major reason is that much of the knowledge on how to operate a productive unit that embodies a particular technology is tacit knowledge. It can only be acquired through experience, through learning by doing. Some of this must be embodied in the human capital of individual workers and managers and some must be embodied in effective routines. Since an established routine is not in any substantial sense 'available as a template', routines are typically much more difficult to copy than specific pieces of capital equipment. (Further reasons for slow diffusion are discussed in Chapter 4.)

Quick Reactions to Large Shocks

In a world of perfect information and maximizing agents, all existing possibilities for new innovations would be investigated and exploited as soon as the expected gain exceeded the expected cost. In an uncertain world, such calculations cannot be made with any precision and the balance between future costs and benefits can at best be only roughly estimated. Also, when agents deal with uncertainty by resorting to routines and other non-maximizing rules of behaviour, opportunities for innovations may often be avoided as long as present courses of action offer acceptable returns.

The result is the existence of a pool of unexploited inventions and improvements (external and internal to the firm) that can be tapped when circumstances change. These opportunities are often only dimly perceived or not located at all for lack of looking until some pressing need focuses attention on unsatisfactory aspects of existing lines of behaviour and technologies. This is one reason why endogenous technological responses to unforeseen shocks, such as unfavourable changes in the exchange rate, increases in competition from new products and processes, or the actions of foreign rivals, are so important and often appear quite rapidly: there is always a pool of innovations that could be made using existing knowledge, but that waits for some new need to focus attention in its direction. The efficient horse collar and the three masted sailing ship are examples from the past of innovations that could have been made much earlier than they were, given the then existing corpus of knowledge. At a later date, there was no technical reason why the major improvements to sailing vessels that were made in the nineteenth century could not have been made a century or more earlier. But they did not occur until after steamships seriously challenged sail.

For a more modern example, there is no technological reason why lean production could not have been invented decades earlier. Yet it was invented only when Japanese automobile producers found that, given the size of their protected home market, they could not produce efficiently using American techniques of mass production. Had the Japanese market been the size of the US market or had US firms been allowed to enter Japan (as they were in Canada), the course of automobile production in Japan would in all likelihood have been very different. (These examples are discussed further in Chapters 5 and 6.) The existence of this pool of unexploited knowledge is one important reason why shocks that threaten the profitability of enterprises are often met by a burst of innovations in excess of what would be feasible if they all had to be based on inventions newly made in response to the shocks.[28]

Notice that all we are saying is that when firms adopt routines, there is likely to be some pool of unexploited innovation possibilities. From this it does *not* follow that the *more* uncertain is the situation facing a firm, the *larger* that pool will be. Routine behaviour is quite consistent, for example, with a positive relation between the complexity of situations and the degree of innovative behaviour—a possibility that we leave uninvestigated here.

The Need for the Evolutionary Hand

The theory of routines presents a view of the functioning of firms (and other organizations) in which innovative behaviour is often inhibited. This raises the question of how the system as a whole acts to obtain innovative solutions to problems. This issue was first raised in Chapter 2 when we compared the hidden hand and the evolutionary hand views of the market economy. We are now able to add three further points to that discussion.

First, successful firms that operate in rapidly changing situations realize that they need to innovate to survive. Therefore, they build some propensity to innovate into their routines. Second, where situations are relatively stable over some period of time, incumbent firms tend to forget the injunction: innovate or die. When established organizations do not react to signals that make change or experimentation profitable, new organizations often do so. If these become profitable, either they grow at the expense of the established firms or they are taken over by them. In either case, the resulting macro behaviour is similar (but of course not identical) to what would have happened if the established organizations had made the changes or conducted the experiments themselves. Third, when the entire array of firms do not adapt overtly to changing circumstances, a large amount of aggregate change can still be brought about solely by selection forces acting on an array of strategies employed by agents, each with its distinct, fairly rigid, mode of behaviour. In the limit, agents might alter their behaviour only randomly, while the price system rewarded

---

[28] Porter (1990) gives many other examples.

behaviour that was accidentally well adapted to new circumstances and punished behaviour that was not. This evolutionary hand mechanism, which can bring about changes that appear purposeful at the macro level, is considered briefly in the Appendix to this chapter.

IV. PATH DEPENDENCE AND THE ARROW OF TIME

Path dependence is implied by much of what we have said up to this point, including the cumulative nature of knowledge, firms groping into an uncertain future in a profit-oriented way, today's choice set with respect to R&D depending on past decisions with respect to R&D, and the evolutionary hand rather than the hidden hand view of the functioning of the market. In Chapter 2, one of our contrasts between the neoclassical and the S-E approaches involved the timeless nature of long-run neoclassical equilibrium theory and the presence of an arrow of time in S-E theory. At that point, we could not explore the full implications of path dependence for our approach since we had not developed enough of the related ideas. We now turn to a more detailed examination of this important topic.

David (1997: 13) defines a path-dependent process as follows:

A negative definition: Processes that are non ergodic, and thus unable to shake free of their history are said to yield path-dependent outcomes.[29]

A positive definition: A path-dependent stochastic process is one whose asymptotic distribution evolves as a consequence (function) of the process' own history.

We focus on three important processes that involve path-dependent issues: the evolution of technology, the embodiment of technological knowledge in the facilitating structure, and economic policy.[30]

Evolution of Technology

New knowledge and new theories build upon existing knowledge and existing theories.[31] One does not, for example, invent the dynamo without an understanding of

[29] Put loosely, 'ergodic' is a mathematical term used to describe a specific class of sequences that are stationary, and in which predicting a variable x at time t does not require any knowledge of any past values of that variable. For a non-ergodic sequence, predicting the value of any x at time t requires some knowledge about how the sequence of xs evolved in the past.

[30] Some have argued that path dependence is primarily tied to network externalities, which in turn relate to issues of product compatibility, which in turn concerns the ability of products in a technology system to work in a complementary fashion, for example, the ability for the users of word processors to share files, or the users of VCRs to share tapes. Katz and Shapiro (1994: 95) identify the key questions relating to network externalities as: (a) technology adoption decisions; (b) product selection decisions; and (c) compatibility decisions. While not disagreeing with much of what they say, we see path dependence as a broader issue than network externalities.

[31] See Mokyr (2002) for a detailed discussion of the cumulative nature of knowledge acquisition. This is one reason why we find so implausible as to be incredible Joseph Needham's argument that Chinese scientists could have jumped from the pre-Newtonian science, which was all they had at the beginning of the 20th century, straight to quantum physics without an intervening stage of Newtonian mechanics. For further discussion see Chapter 8.

magnetism, conductivity, and so on.[32] New GPTs, often called 'signposts' in the literature, establish whole new research trajectories.[33] Practical electricity generation, for example, enabled a vast range of new product, process, and organizational technologies, which took over a century to develop fully. Thus, as argued in Chapter 2, the accumulation of knowledge displays trajectories akin to those of technology, with bottlenecks, reverse salients, focusing devices, and the like.

A related source of path dependence in the development of technology arises because existing ideas and norms condition and constrain what is thought to be worth doing in the immediate future. These ideas also help to guide and shape the search for new knowledge by presenting opportunities in related research activities.[34] Nelson and Winter's technological regime, which we discussed in Chapter 2, is a similar phenomenon. Dosi (1997: 1541) notes that the evolution of R&D projects is most often shaped by 'systematic underestimation of costs, cognitive path dependencies, irresponsiveness to environmental feedbacks, etc.' This behaviour is consistent with path-dependent evolution of what is thought to be worth doing rather than a maximizing assessment based on full information.

The Embodiment of Technology in the Facilitating Structure

The evolution of the facilitating structure displays path dependence. For example, when they are embodied in machines and other capital assets, the engineering nature of new GPTs and many other technologies creates technological complementarities. These constrain and channel the direction of innovations as they are exploited over long periods of time, decades or even centuries.[35] For example, the introduction of the gasoline engine caused an enormous amount of path-dependent change in the facilitating structure, including the creation of a highly complex energy delivery system, highway construction, urban planning, social and cultural changes, as well as numerous reactions to environmental issues. The evolution of these sorts of technology systems are most successfully understood through appreciative theories and historical accounts of the evolution of a specific innovation or a specific body of knowledge.[36]

Policy and the Policy Structure

We have more to say about path dependence in Chapters 16 and 17. For now, we consider two issues: the implications of path dependence in the policy structure on policy decisions; and the possible efficiency implications of path dependence.

---

[32] See Chapter 7 for a list of the steps that led to an understanding of electricity and the development of the dynamo.

[33] See Diamond (1997) and Adams (1996) for more on such signposts.

[34] Such a conception of knowledge plays a role in Mokyr's book (2002) *The Gifts of Athena*.

[35] See the section on spillovers under GPTs in Chapter 4 for a full discussion of these concepts. Our discussion is close to that of Liebowitz and Margolis (1994), who distinguish between pecuniary and technological externalities.

[36] Thus, we go beyond Liebowitz and Margolis' view to argue that fully incorporating notions of path dependence and network externalities into theories regarding the embodiment of technology in the facilitating structure requires much more than a focus on standards, network size, efficiency of standards, or product compatibility. It requires giving up a Newtonian ahistorical view of market processes for a more historical-evolutionary view. See Dosi (1997) for a detailed and persuasive argument on exactly this point.

Path-Dependent Policy

As with new technologies, policy innovations have to be embodied in a structure and made compatible with other, often pre-existing, elements of that structure before they can be enacted and enforced. The policy structure displays complementarities among the various elements of embodied policy that lead to 'durability', which imposes a form of path dependence. Institutional durability differs from that of capital durability in that while capital durability is dictated by engineering relationships, institutions are made durable by the complementarities among a combination of institutional decision-making mechanisms, the workings of interest groups, and the feedback between an existing policy and the further accumulation of knowledge.

Path dependence is clear in the co-evolution of technology and policy in the exploitation of US energy reserves.

The continuing flow of new discoveries was a return on investments in knowledge, public and private. The US Geological Survey and other agencies developed an extensive infrastructure of public knowledge in the location and character of mineral deposits. (Wright 1997: 1563)

To this we could add a whole host of policy decisions that helped accentuate the energy intensive nature of the US economy—an important policy trajectory that is proving costly to alter today.

North (1990) explicitly builds on Arthur (1994), arguing that almost all organizational change displays fundamental path dependencies, which help to determine how different nations or regions will respond to changes in relative prices, new technologies, and other shocks (many of which may offer significant opportunities for growth).

We can now integrate the path-dependent character of the incremental change in institutions with the persistence of patterns of long-run growth or decline. Once a development path is set on a particular course, the network externalities, the learning process of organizations, and the historically derived subjective modeling of the issues reinforce the course. (North 1990: 99)

Path Dependence and Efficiency

One of the deepest divisions in the literature on path dependence concerns efficiency and policy. The theory of path dependence suggests that competition between technologies does not necessarily ensure that the most efficient technology will always triumph. In this context, 'efficient' may have several interpretations. At one extreme is neoclassical optimality while at the other is engineering efficiency. If, for example, the surviving technology used more of all inputs than its defeated alternative, both neoclassical and S-E theorists would agree that the competitive process had yielded an inefficient result. Admitting such possibilities still leaves open the question of whether or not relatively simple changes in policy could improve social welfare by moving economies to new, more efficient technologies.

For Liebowitz and Margolis (1994) efficiency concerns are such an important aspect of path-dependent systems that they make it the defining aspect of such systems—an identification that does not seem productive to us. They define three degrees of path dependence. First- and second-degree path dependence arise when history matters, and events, small or otherwise, determine a path leading to an equilibrium that is not costless to abandon. If such an equilibrium is optimal, this is first-degree path dependence. Second-degree path dependence occurs when, in contrast, the equilibrium is not optimal because agents did not have enough information to foresee the outcome of their decisions.

Third-degree path dependence occurs when a 'sensitive dependence on initial conditions leads to an outcome that is inefficient—but in this case the outcome is also remediable. That is, there exists or existed some feasible arrangements for recognizing and achieving a preferred outcome, but that outcome is not obtained' (Liebowitz and Margolis 1994: 207). They argue that it is this last form of path dependence that dominates the literature. They add that only third-degree path dependence matters to policymakers, since it is only for this type of path dependence that a meaningful policy intervention could be mounted.

They go on to argue that the market is efficient at internalizing externalities, demonstrating that in many models the right network will be selected, and that the network may even be of an efficient size. They also argue that empirical cases of third-degree path dependence are rare (Liebowitz and Margolis 1994: 149). They criticize alleged examples of third-degree path dependence such as Apple versus PC, and VHS versus Beta.

We accept much of their argument. Given the difficulties of comparing relevant technological/institutional alternatives, it is hard to see how policymakers could often improve on the choice of technology systems. But we find it hard to agree that the selection system embedded in market decision-making can be shown to always choose the 'best' technological trajectory. The reason is that we can never know what the efficiency of an abandoned technology might have been if R&D had been directed at improving it over an extended period of time. We cannot even know whether or not we routinely ignore alternatives that might have been better. The steam-powered car of the early twentieth century is clearly dominated by twenty-first-century gasoline-driven cars, but what if the development trajectories had been switched and steam had enjoyed the benefits of a full century of R&D spending? In many cases, path dependence and uncertainty imply that you cannot test Liebowitz and Margolis' belief that markets typically chose the best technological alternatives.

Also, just because the opportunity to shift from one market-determined technological trajectory to an obviously superior one may seldom arise in practice, it does not follow that path dependence presents no opportunities for public policy. One obvious role for public policy is to gather and provide as much information as is possible for agents involved in adoption decisions before particular trajectories become locked in. Another possible role is for the government to delay decisions that might lead to lock-ins. This may be particularly important for government procurement decisions that may influence the evolution of emerging technologies, as have many Department of Defense decisions in the USA. (We consider several such cases in Chapter 16.) In the crucial early period of network formation, governments might try to 'hold the door open' as argued by David (1991a). This would allow systems to evolve, agents to learn, and possible mistakes to be avoided.

Another role is in establishing technological standards as the US Department of Defense did in the emerging US software industry in the 1970s.

What Matters for the S-E Approach

What is the importance of path dependence to S-E theory? That discovering and implementing new technological knowledge implies almost pervasive path dependence seems obvious to any student of history. That some path-dependent effects are important is equally obvious, as when the reaction to a temporary shock involves learning, which persists after the shock is passed; or when specific random events not predictable by any theory influence the system's further development. Importantly, path dependence involves leaving uninvestigated some of the rejected alternatives in the evolution of technological knowledge. This leaves open and unanswerable the question of whether uninvestigated alternatives might have led to preferred situations, through a succession of innovations that cannot even be imagined by those who did not follow the forgone trajectory.

One set of cases that comes under Liebowitz and Margolis' second-degree path dependence is important in technological history. Consider two different trajectories for the evolution of some technology, leading to end states A or B. One set of local circumstances made the first steps in the path leading to an unforeseen A seem best for one set of agents, while a different set of local circumstances made the first steps in the path leading to an unforeseen B seem best for another set of agents. Much later, it becomes clear to everyone that end state A is preferable to end state B. The costs of changing to A are, however, prohibitive for those who are now at B. So one set is at A while the other stays at B, which for each is the best choice given their present situation. But, if they could go back and make earlier decisions knowing what they now know, both would have made choices that led to end state A.

Although there is no room for policy action to improve the situation, the economic system has led one set of agents to a situation that they regret. Examples are those who stayed with driving on the left when the majority of countries ended up driving on the right. When the UK entered the EU in 1975, policymakers seriously considered changing from left- to right-hand drive but studies suggested that the costs of the changeover would exceed the benefits. There was no doubt, however, that UK decision-makers, if returned to 1920 with 1975 knowledge, would have then chosen to move to right-hand drive, as did most other countries.

Another example that we consider in detail in Chapter 5 is phonetic versus ideographic writing. There were many good reasons why some languages evolved phonetic writing while others evolved pictographic and then ideographic forms of writing. Faced with a costless choice in say 1975 and with no existing (path-dependent) literature, most countries with ideographic forms of writing would have chosen to change over to a phonetic system (as a few did in the twentieth century). But the path-dependent process that produced their situation in 1975 made the costs of changeover prohibitive for most countries using alternative systems. A further example concerns the gauge of railways where a few, such as Australia, did not choose what became the 'standard' gauge. They faced large costs of changeover, which would not have existed if policymakers had been able to forecast the future at an earlier time when establishing a common standard gauge would have been a low-cost operation.

Thus in understanding both history and the present state of any economy, path dependence matters, whether or not it leads to situations that can be improved by policy intervention. Although in many actual cases, policy interventions operating under typical informational constraints could not have helped, the evolution led to some situations that are currently inferior to well-defined alternatives so that past decisions are regretted. A timeless theory applied to a comparison of the various current positions could not explain the difference—because costless choice among the various existing alternatives would lead everyone to the same situation. Only a theory that involves a clear arrow of time and path-dependent decisions can explain the current differences. In contrast, because path-dependent processes are not included in standard neoclassical models that use a stable equilibrium concept, these models may be seriously misleading whenever a shock sets in motion reactions that are path-dependent and non-reversible.

APPENDIX: THE EVOLUTIONARY HAND AND FACTOR SUBSTITUTION[37]

In this Appendix, we show the evolutionary hand in operation in the basic situation specified in the Appendix to Chapter 2. All the assumptions made there apply here. In particular, the firms have a constant target level of output and are innovating to reduce the costs of producing that output measured in terms of two inputs, f and g.

For simplicity, let all competing oligopolistic firms start at a_0 at time t_0 with relative factor prices shown by the slope of the line through that point. Now let the firms follow different trajectories as shown in Figure 3A.1. At time t_1, draw a line whose slope conforms with the unchanged factor prices to just touch one firm's location, leaving all others above it. The one firm, a_1 in this case, on this line is the most successful in its innovations. Now draw a parallel dashed line indicating the

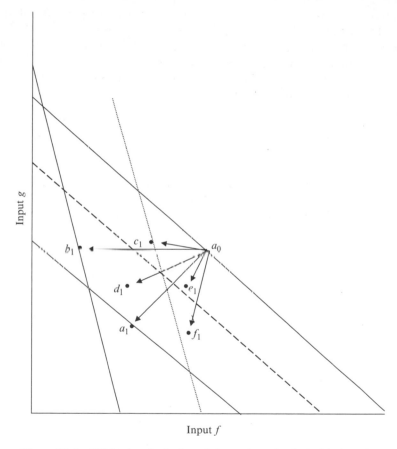

Figure 3A.1. *Hidden hand selection of alternative technological trajectories*

[37] A much more detailed consideration of the topic of this appendix can be found in Nelson and Winter (1982: ch. 7).

highest level of factor costs that will allow a firm to stay in business.[38] Firms whose innovations get them inside the dashed line continue in business. Firms that did not reach that line fail, c_1 and e_1 in this example. Some of the successful firms have innovated in a way that is relatively saving on inputs f and others on inputs g.

Now let factor prices change unexpectedly between time t_0 and t_1 with unchanged behaviour of the firms. Now draw a line in Figure 3A.1 whose slope indicates these new prices so as to just touch one firm's position leaving all others above it. Given the new prices, the firm on the line, b_1 in this case, turns out to be the most successful innovator. Now draw a dotted line parallel to the first, indicating the highest sustainable level of factor costs at the new relative prices.[39] Firms whose innovating activities take them into the area between the two new lines succeed; the others fail—e_1 and f_1 in this example. The evolutionary hand has determined a different set of winners from the situation in which factor prices remained un-changed. In this case, all the winners have innovated in a manner that is relatively saving of the factor whose relative prices have risen.

This illustrates that when prices change, selection will tend to favour those whose innovation is biased towards using relatively more of the factor whose relative price falls. They need smaller absolute gains in input efficiency to be winners than those whose trajectories are biased in the other direction. *This is the operation of the 'evolutionary hand' that makes the overall industry results look as if firms were consciously reacting to altering factor prices even if, as in this case, they did not anticipate the price change.*

---

[38] Drawing this line requires that we solve the short-run, price-output game that the firms will play. We assume this has been done.

[39] See n. 38.

4

Technology and Technological Change

This chapter deals with a variety of issues related to the nature of technology and innovation. We first take up some topics related to the microeconomics of technological change. As well as summarizing matters dealt with earlier, we point out that not only is the development of technology endogenous to the economic system but so also is much of science. We then discuss the distinction between incremental and radical changes in technology, arguing that some confusions in debates about continuity and discontinuity of technological change can be resolved by distinguishing between what we call 'technology radical' and 'use radical'. Next we discuss the many important ways in which individual technologies are integrated into the economy's technology system. A discussion of three types of learning, by design, by doing, and by using, follows and the section concludes with a brief consideration of salients, which illustrate one of the many implications of decisions taken under uncertainty rather than risk.

We then undertake a detailed discussion of the concept of a GPT, which was first introduced in Chapter 1. We consider various possible definitions of GPTs and conclude by defining them as technologies that usually start crudely, then evolve to be used across much of the economy to have multiple uses, and myriad spillovers. After that, we discuss in some detail the spillovers that are associated with new GPTs. We then take up the issue of the usefulness of the concept of a GPT, asking, among other things, how we can identify a new GPT when it emerges. One of the most important parts of this discussion is our argument that the existence of new GPTs, and the 'new economies' that they initiate, cannot be identified by how productivity is changing. Serious confusions follow from the erroneous belief that a new GPT must be accompanied by a 'productivity bonus'. We conclude with a case study of the current ICT revolution that illustrates much of what has been said earlier in the chapter. The Appendix details our argument that TFP does not measure technological change and hence does not allow one to separate the proportion of any output growth that is due to such changes from the proportion that is due to factor accumulation.

I. MICROECONOMICS OF TECHNOLOGICAL CHANGE

In the first section of this chapter, we outline and discuss some relevant facts and empirical relations concerning innovation. These have been established over the years by many researchers.[1] Although we can only touch on these issues, some of

[1] See, for example, Bresnahan and Trajtenberg (1992); Dosi et al. (1988); Freeman and Louçã (2001); Landes (1969); Mokyr (1990); Nelson and Winter (1982); Rogers (1995); and Rosenberg (1976, 1982).

which would require an entire monograph for full exposition, they are important for an understanding of the technological change that drives long-term economic growth. Theories should try to make contact with these facts wherever possible and not contradict them without good cause and full awareness.

Endogenous, Uncertain, Path-Dependent Innovation and Diffusion

We first elaborate on some themes we have alluded to in earlier chapters. Long before endogenous growth became popular in macro growth models, microeconomic research had established pretty conclusively that research, development, and technological change respond to microeconomic incentives (see, for example, Schmookler (1966) and Rosenberg (1982), based on material first published in the 1960s and 1970s). Indeed, an abundance of empirical evidence shows that competition in both product and process technologies is critical in many if not most industries where failing to keep up with one's opponents in developing new technologies is far more serious than choosing a wrong price or an inappropriate capacity.[2]

Everything that is known about the evolution of technology suggests that its course is not merely risky, but uncertain. 'Almost by definition, trying to do a new thing involves the impossibility of knowing what the new thing will look like, what its economic properties will be, what is the best way of doing it and even what are the feasible ways of achieving the result' (Dosi and Orsenigo 1988: 18). Because of such pervasive uncertainties, technologies evolve along trajectories that are path-dependent in the sense that what seems a possible next step in its development depends on the successes and surprises in the previously attempted steps.

Sources of Uncertainty

Uncertainty is involved in more than just making some initial technological breakthrough. We know that many new technologies come into the world in crude form, after which they are slowly developed as their range of applications is expanded in ways that are impossible to predict in advance. Even a technology whose use remains single purpose can improve in quality and cost so much that its sales defy all predictions. For example, the market of cellular phones and email proved to be vastly larger than was originally anticipated. In such cases, the uncertainty is about cost reductions, quality improvements, and customer acceptance.

Another cause of uncertainty is that two or more technologies sometimes prove, to everyone's surprise, to be complementary and to produce much more when operating together than the sum of the parts when they operate independently. For example, the laser and the computer operating together did many things that

---

[2] See Porter (1990) and Dertouzos, Lester, and Solow (1989) for supporting illustrations. As Baumol (2002: viii) puts it: 'My central contention here is that what differentiates the prototype capitalist economy most sharply from all other economic systems is free-market pressures that force firms into a continuing process of innovation, *because it becomes a matter of life and death for many of them*. The static efficiency properties that are stressed by standard welfare economics are emphatically *not* the most important qualities of capitalist economies.'

neither the laser nor the computer could have done operating on its own. In such cases, it is as impossible to predict the outcome as it would be to guess the nature of water from a knowledge of its constituents, hydrogen and oxygen.

Yet another important source of uncertainty concerns those technologies that are seen as likely to become important from a very early stage in their development. For example, as soon as it became possible to alter the genetic structure of living things in the laboratory and as soon as the possibility of building things atom by atom was realized, the potential of biotechnology and nanotechnology was seen to be almost limitless. The uncertainties in such cases concern not the existence of great potential but such things as the costs and timing of development and commercialization, unforeseen and undesirable side effects, and consumer acceptance. For example, probably no one, including the management of Monsanto, anticipated the reaction against their 'Frankenfoods', which were almost universally expected to be accepted as beneficial, as new strains of plants and animals created by selective breeding had been in the past.

There are also uncertainties about how long a technology will continue to be useful before it is replaced by a superior technology. For example, few people visiting London to attend the Great Exhibition of 1851 could have anticipated that steam would be replaced by electricity as the dominant power source within the lifetimes of many of the people then alive.

Diffusion

Similar comments apply to diffusion, which is slow, costly, and often uncertain. Just to discover what is currently in use throughout the world is a daunting task, particularly for small firms.[3] Even if a firm can identify best practice techniques, this (at best) provides it with a blueprint; learning how to produce successfully what is described in a blueprint implies acquiring all the tacit knowledge that goes with adopting something new. It follows that the existing set of technologies does not provide a freely available pool of immediately useful knowledge. Furthermore, adapting technologies in use elsewhere to one's own purpose often requires innovation. As a result, innovation and diffusion shade into each other rather than being clearly distinct activities.

Fixed costs provide strong inertias that also slow diffusion. New technologies will not be embodied in new capital until the full costs of creating and operating with the new technologies is less than the out-of-pocket costs of using existing (already embodied) technologies whose capital costs are largely sunk. Fixed costs also guide current developments because all decisions are what Archibald, Eaton, and Lipsey (1986) call mixed short-run/long-run developments. The empty plain often envisioned by location theorists does not exist in practice. New developments must be fitted into an existing structure, including the location and amount of relevant fixed capital. Although perfectly competitive firms can make simple entry and exit

---

[3] In his classic work on diffusion, Rogers (1995: 397) lists three key aspects of uncertainty as they relate to the acceptance of new technologies: technical uncertainty, financial uncertainty, and social uncertainty.

decisions, most firms are engaged in Austrian-style process competition in which they make strategic decisions. Hence, even if one firm could make what looked like a pure long-run decision, either because it was a new entrant or because all of its capital had worn out at the same moment, it would still have to decide on its new capital in the context of the quantities, ages, and locations of the fixed capital of its suppliers, customers, and competitors. Similarly, the rankings of expected pay-offs to specific investments in R&D will differ depending on the nature of the whole structure of existing technologies and existing embodiments in such things as location, size, and details of existing production facilities. Fixed costs also give a strong element of irreversibility. For example, if circumstances favour the generation of new knowledge, that knowledge will exist even in a new set of circumstances in which it would not have been profitable to incur the fixed cost of learning it. (Knowledge is sometimes lost but not all that easily or quickly.)

The Returns to Investing under Uncertainty

In neoclassical equilibrium theory, all inputs including the services of capital and labour earn the values of their marginal products. Under conditions of risk, the expected net returns in all lines of capital investment are equal. This includes investment to embody existing technologies in new capital goods and investment in R&D to invent and innovate new technologies.

But as we have repeatedly stressed, invention and innovation occur under conditions of uncertainty, not just risk. Many agents lose all they have staked on attempted innovations while a few make large gains, and occasionally massive ones. From a static point of view, the large returns earned by successful innovators look like rents, since they are well in excess of what can be earned by investing in capital that embodies existing technologies. But in dynamic economies, they are the return to innovation. The many uncertainties involved in successful invention and innovation would not be accepted if they offered a return no larger than that of investing in known and proven technologies. As Knight (1921) observed long ago (pure or economic) profits are the return for undertaking uncertainty.

There is an important implication of this analysis that seems to have escaped general notice. When innovation causes the outputs of firms to rise by more than the cost of their inputs, including the R&D costs of innovating, this is not a free gift of nature or manna from heaven; it is the normal, and allocatively necessary, return to innovation. In the Appendix to this chapter, we consider in detail what TFP does measure. In the mean time, we observe that most of those economists who argue that TFP measures the return to innovation that is in excess of all its full costs almost invariably call these returns 'free gifts' or 'manna from heaven', as if they were benefits that agents reaped without sowing. In so far as TFP measures external effects, that is, measures innovations that allow third parties to gain without cost, it is a free gift or 'manna from heaven'. But in so far as TFP measures the increases in output above increases in measured input costs that accrue to the innovators themselves (whether firms or individual agents), it is measuring resource costs—the opportunity cost of inducing the scare resource, the human capital of innovators, to do its job of innovating.[4] It is only because this cost is not associated with a *measured* input that these returns appear as increases in TFP. But free lunch, manna, or reaping without sowing they are not. In their absence, potential innovators would do something else.[5]

Endogenous Science

While it is widely understood that scientific advance influences technological advance, innovation's impact on science is often minimized. Rosenberg (1982: ch. 7) has shown that the advancement of scientific knowledge is strongly influenced by motives similar to those that guide technological advance. This makes scientific research at least partly endogenous to the economic system, just as more applied technological R&D is.

Each line of technological improvement usually has a natural trajectory with a limit. The problems that arise when that limit is approached identify directions for new scientific research having the possibility of a high pay-off. Then, when a major technological breakthrough occurs, it signals not just the culmination of past research but the opening of a new research agenda.[6] Powered flight, the first internal-combustion engine, the first nuclear device, the transistor, and the electric motor all signalled a high potential pay-off in terms of money and prestige from pure and applied research in related directions. Solid-state physics attracted only a few physicists and was not even taught in most universities until the advent of the transistor. As Rosenberg (1982: 159) puts it:

[T]he industrialization process inevitably transforms science into a more and more endogenous activity by increasing its dependence upon technology. Technological considerations, I have argued, are a major determinant of the allocation of scientific resources. Thus, I suggest that a promising model for understanding scientific advances is one that combines the 'logic'

[4] Strictly speaking, only some of this 'super normal return' is a cost. This is the amount needed to encourage the existing volume of inventive and entrepreneurial activity; the rest, if any, is a rent. But determining the amount that is a cost in an evolving uncertain economy is a difficult if not impossible task. It is often alleged, for example, that the few massive gains from innovation are a more important incentive than the average gains. If so, even if those who earned the massive gains might have engaged in their innovative activity for less returns, those gains may be the opportunity cost of encouraging others to engage in their existing amounts of inventive and innovative activity.

[5] Baumol (2002: 29) makes a related point: 'If freedom of entry into the innovation process reduces expected profits to zero, however, higher expected payoff prizes will be offset precisely by the high cost of obtaining a superior invention. So the expected gross earnings from the second prize should exceed those to the third by precisely the incremental cost necessary to advance the firm from being the expected winner of the third prize to winner of the second.' This is fine as far as risk is concerned and the costs should show up mainly as R&D costs, but the cost of inducing entrepreneurs to undertake genuine uncertainty is unlikely to show up in any cost that is measured for TFP calculations. Typically, it shows up as extra profit for the enterprise and hence in TFP, *but it is not a free lunch.*

[6] Scientific advances often follow a technological breakthrough with a long lag. New technologies are often limited in their application (due to cost, range of use, etc.), making the pay-off from pure research directed to its problems small. As the technology matures, the pay-off to scientific R&D typically increases. This is increasing returns to research activity as successive new research discoveries open up possibilities that often expand exponentially. But as with most growth phenomena, this is a transitory experience, not something inherent in a macro production function that links R&D to output growth in some stable way.

[i.e. path dependence] of scientific progress with a consideration of cost and rewards that flow from daily life and are linked to science through technology.

Incremental Versus Radical Innovations

One important distinction concerns the relation between an innovation and existing technologies. An innovation is *incremental* if it is an improvement to an existing technology. (Although each improvement is typically small in its impact, research shows that a significant proportion of aggregate increases in productivity are due to the cumulative effects of these incremental changes.[7]) An innovation is *radical* if it did not evolve through improvements to, and modifications of, existing technologies.

Although this distinction, which is common in the literature of technology, seems obvious enough, it does not distinguish between the evolution of a specific technology and the evolution of the technologies used for specific purposes. In contrast, we distinguish between two different trajectories: that of the technologies used for a specific purpose and that of a specific technology.

Consider first the trajectory of the technologies applied to a specific use, such as reproducing written text. A radical innovation along this type of trajectory is an innovation that could not have emerged out of the technologies that preceded it in that specific use. We call this 'use-radical'. For example, the printing press could never have evolved incrementally out of the quill and ink used in a medieval scriptorium, the technology that it replaced in the reproduction of the written word. It was use-radical.

The second type of trajectory concerns the evolution of a specific technology, such as the printing press. A radical innovation along this type of trajectory is a technology that has no clear technological parents. We call this 'technology-radical'. For example, the printing press itself was largely a collection of long-existing technologies, which had been assembled in a new way and combined with some supporting new developments. Thus it was not technology-radical (see Section II in Chapter 6). Indeed, almost none of the technologies considered in Chapters 5 and 6 were technology-radical, although they were all use-radical.

Interrelations among Technologies

Technologies interact with each other in myriad ways, and these interactions are one of the sources of the complementarities that play, as we argue later, an important part in the economic system's reactions to changes in specific technologies. We have earlier observed that technologies typically come in triplets: a product; a process that makes it; and the organization of all the activities associated with producing, marketing, and improving it. Products and process technologies do not, however, stand in a one-to-one relation to each other. One product can often be made by more than one process.

Different and unrelated products are sometimes made with similar process technologies—a phenomenon that Rosenberg (1976) calls 'technological convergence'.

---

[7] See Rosenberg (1982: ch. 3) for evidence.

This can be the basis of interacting clusters of firms, which seem, judging from their outputs, unrelated to each other. It also facilitates discontinuous jumps in product technologies because each such product may not have to develop its own radically different process technology. For example, early in the twentieth century, the new aircraft industry used process technologies that were already well established in the bicycle and sewing machine industries.[8] Technologies that require radical jumps in both product and process technologies are relatively rare in the history of innovation (although much less rare in the history of failed government attempts to encourage radically new technological developments).

We call the technology that specifies each physically distinct, stand-alone, capital good a 'main technology'. It is the blueprint for a distinct tool or product that is useful by itself, such as a lathe, a bicycle, a dynamo, or a blast furnace. In contrast, a 'subtechnology' is the blueprint for a technology that cooperates with other sub-technologies to make a main technology. For example, the main technology of a commercial airliner is made up of a large number of subtechnologies, including an engine to deliver power, a thrust technology to turn that power into movement, a body, an undercarriage, a navigation system, and an internal control system. Analysis of these subtechnologies shows them to be made up of sub-subtechnologies. For example, an aircraft's navigation system is composed of compasses, gyroscopes, computers, sensing devices, radios, radar, and so on. Analysis of each of these shows them, in turn, to be made up of sub-sub-subtechnologies. Notice that some of the subtechnologies, such as compasses and food warmers, can also be used as stand-alone main technologies while other subtechnologies, such as the aircraft's stabilizer and landing gear, are useful only as part of a specific main technology.

This layered make-up of the aircraft is typical of most capital goods. It is also typical of consumer durables, such as automobiles and refrigerators that deliver services for use in consumption. The interdependence of the subtechnologies is often Leontief in nature: the main technology will not function if you remove one of its subtechnologies. For example, a standard gasoline engine will not run without its spark plugs. Other subtechnologies increase the efficiency of the main technology without being essential. For example, the air filter is not necessary for the internal-combustion engine, but the engine's efficiency is greatly increased by it. Each generic type of subtechnology, such as a spark plug or a tyre, usually comes in several differentiated versions that are close substitutes for each other.

When we look beyond any one main technology, we find that several are often grouped horizontally in a *technology system* that we define as a set of two or more main technologies, which cooperate to produce some range of related goods or

---

[8] For another example, when an existing technology is imported into a country whose labour has little or no experience in operating it (or similar technologies), time must pass before experience with operating it allows the requisite amount of tacit knowledge to be acquired. Having acquired that knowledge, a different imported technology that requires similar skills will take much less time before it can be efficiently operated. This is something that many less developed countries have come to understand. Importing the physical embodiment of a technology is not enough; a path-dependent process of learning by using is required as well.

services. They may cooperate within one firm, among firms within one industry, among firms in closely linked sets of industries, and even across industries that are seemingly unrelated from an engineering point of view (Rosenberg 1976, 1982: ch. 3). Technology systems overlap each other in the sense that a subset of the technologies that are used in activity *A* is used, along with other technologies, to make product *B*, and so on. In some cases, the technology may be used in the process technology that produces the good that embodies it, as when computers are used to manufacture computers. In other cases, some main technologies assist the operations of others without being necessary. For example, much of the value of a computer depends on its cooperation with its peripherals, such as printers, modems, and software. Many of the separate main technologies in some technology systems may simultaneously compete with, as well as complement, each other. Trucks deliver freight to the railhead, making railways more useful and profitable, but they also compete with rail for long-distance haulage.[9]

Most of the technologies covered in our tour of technological history in Chapters 5 and 6 act both as main technologies, subtechnologies, and elements in broader technology systems. There is one class of exceptions: the specifications of how to make and use materials are seldom if ever main technologies; they are subtechnologies that show how to produce or create the materials incorporated in main technologies.

In summary, at any point in time, the economy's technological endowment is a set of interlocking technologies, which are embodied in a set of interrelated capital goods. First, there is the layered set of lower-level subtechnologies, which form any one main technology. Although some of the subcomponents in this engineering structure are necessary, others are important auxiliaries but not essential. Furthermore, each general type of subcomponent often comes in various versions that compete with each other. Second, there is an external structure of interrelations that links several main technologies into technology systems, as when several capital goods cooperate to produce a final product. Third, there are interrelationships across industries, as when the output of one industry is used as an input in another. Fourth, there are process interrelationships as when technologically similar processes produce technologically distinct products. This interlocking nature of an economy's technology system creates myriad spillovers that spread over sectors, geographical space and time when any major new technology is innovated. They lie at the very core of our understanding of the effects of major new technologies on investment and economic growth and they are considered further in the discussion of GPTs in Section II.

Learning

The potential of a new technology is realized through the innovative activities that occur via three learning mechanisms: by design, doing, and using. When a product is

---

[9] Main technologies are also often related vertically when the output of one is used as an input by another, often across industries. Industries producing such material as iron and steel, forest products, and aluminium create inputs used in manufacturing. Industries that produce power and those that produce human capital provide inputs of most other industries.

being designed, much is learned about it and things that were in the specifications of desired performance characteristics often have to be amended. When the product is first being produced, much is learned about how to produce it and efficiency in production rises as described by the usual learning-by-doing curve. Once the product is put into use, further learning occurs as its performance proves to be different from what was expected (in both positive and negative directions) and users learn how they would like the performance characteristics to be altered. All three types of learning imply learning curves and path-dependent, time-irreversible processes. Interestingly, one thing that new technologies often do is to alter the balance between these three types of learning. For example, computer-assisted design (CAD) has reduced the cost of some learning by design that was previously feasible and made other forms of learning by design technically feasible where they were previously impossible.

Salients

Technological evolution with positive feedbacks is typically accompanied by the emergence of efficiency salients that occur because the subtechnologies that compose most main technologies do not all perform at the same level of efficiency. As a result, a given main technology's performance is limited by that of its weakest link, its weakest performing subtechnology, which is said to create a 'reverse salient'. In a world of certainty, R&D would proceed on all subtechnologies until there was no weakest link. But in a world of uncertainty, this does not happen. Reverse salients provide an incentive to direct R&D at improving the operation of the weak subtechnology. But when the improvement comes, it will typically not increase efficiency by just enough to eliminate the reverse salient. Instead, efficiency will typically rise more, making it a salient and creating another reverse salient or weakest-link and an incentive to improve that subtechnology. This whole process creates a positive feedback loop in which improvements in any one subtechnology raise the pay-off to R&D directed at improving the efficiency of some other subtechnology. (Everything said here also applies to technology systems in which several main technologies cooperate to produce some final product.)

II.   GENERAL PURPOSE TECHNOLOGIES[10]

So far we have discussed some key aspects of technology and technological change. For most of the rest of the chapter we focus on a particular type of technology that we briefly introduced in Chapter 1, GPTs. We first consider the concept's definition in some considerable detail. This is necessary because a variety of definitions have been used by others and because, in developing our own definition, we cover a considerable amount of important related material, including the rich set of spillovers that spread from GPTs to the rest of the economy. In the next section, we consider the usefulness of the concept, while in Chapter 11 we survey what others have written

---

[10] Much of the material in this section is a revised and updated version of analyses that we first presented in our two chapters in Helpman (1998).

about GPTs. Note that many of the things we say about GPTs also apply to other technologies. It would be surprising otherwise because the contrary would imply that GPTs were unique in all their characteristics.

What a GPT Is Not

We now move towards our conceptualization of GPTs, first outlining characteristics that are not helpful in defining them and then discussing those that are.

Not Just One Manifestation of a Generic Technology

A GPT is a generic product, or process, or organizational form that, although it evolves over time, is recognizable as one generic thing throughout. For example, although modern PCs differ from the their early ancestors, they, and intervening varieties, are recognizeble as examples of one generic technology—a machine that does calculations electronically. The steam engine, a machine that delivers power through a piston driven by steam, is the generic technology that is the GPT, but not any individual variant. The domestication of animals is a process technology— a specific set of instructions on duplicating animals and improving them by selective breeding. The instructions are used to create many different animals and are refined over time by new instructions such as 'avoid exessive inbreeding', but they are recognizable as a set of generic instructions throughout. If we regard each individual variety of product, or specific set of instructions relating to one animal, as a GPT, we would lose the characteristics that GPTs evolve through different manifestations as their efficiency and range of applications increase.[11]

Not Always Endogenous or Exogenous

In contrast to our position that most innovation is endogenous to economic signals, many other writers have either argued as a matter of fact, or assumed for theoretical convenience, that GPTs are largely exogenous to the economic system.[12] To deal fully with a specific technology's endogeneity to economic forces, two questions need to be considered: To what stage in the technology's evolution are we referring? and Endogenous to what?

Virtually all GPTs are originally introduced in an underdeveloped form—as crude versions of their ultimate selves. The process of refining a technology is a long-drawn-out affair. Even if a technology's original introduction is exogenous to the economic system (itself a rare event), its further development soon becomes driven

---

[11] As with all definitions, there is some ambiguity at the margin. Some would include in the definition of the steam engine GPT its precursors, especially Newcomen's atmospheric engine. We prefer to define the GPT as an engine in which steam is the force that drives a piston, and treat the earlier engines as the kind of precursor that is found for almost all GPTs, but not as an early manifestation of the GPT, the *steam* engine. Another case closer to the borderline is the steam turbine. It uses steam power to turn a turbine rather than to drive a piston. It is a matter of convenience and taste whether one treats such closely related technologies as a single GPT or as two.

[12] For example, Mokyr (1990) has his macro inventions occurring more or less 'out of the blue' and all the GPTs in the Helpman (1998) volume appear exogenously.

largely by economic concerns. Thus, those who talk of the exogenous development of GPTs must be talking about the very earliest stages of that GPT's evolution.

The second question is more complex. The introduction of different GPTs may be endogenous to different influences. For example, if the GPT arises directly due to either a crisis in an existing technology or out of a clearly perceived profitable opportunity, we can conclude that the technology is endogenous to the economic system. The developments of the Savery steam pump and Newcomen's atmospheric engine are clear examples. However, a technology could initially be endogenous to non-economic influences, such as those coming from science or political/military concerns.

A new technology is endogenous to pure science when a scientific research programme rather than economic signals drives its early development. Electricity provides an example of such a technology. Electricity was developed through a research programme with roots going back to the early sixteenth century. (See Chapters 6 and 7 for details.) Early modern research into magnetism was driven by practical problems of navigation when Europeans began to venture into distant oceans where their compasses behaved in surprising ways. Subsequent research into electricity, however, was largely driven by scientific curiosity—although as research continued into the nineteenth century, scientific curiosity was reinforced by the understanding that electricity had economic potential. Nonetheless, its early development was not a direct response to a crisis in steam power, nor to evident profit opportunities; it was rather endogenous to pure science. Even here, however, economic motives became significant long before the dynamo was invented in 1867. The voltaic cell gave electricity some commercial applications, most notably in the telegraph, which became increasingly important as the century progressed.

Historically speaking, governments have often been relatively unconcerned with the direct economic relevance of the technologies they seek to develop for political or military reasons. (This has changed somewhat in more recent times as the goals of government policies have changed.) For example, the electronic computer arose out of efforts in the Second World War to create a calculating machine that could break enemy codes and help to solve the complex equations of ballistics. While the computer was in part developed in the research laboratories of large universities and private companies, the early funding of such research came from government, and the economic applications were limited. Thus, at its earliest stages of development the computer was exogenous to the economic system and endogenous to the political/military system. After the war ended, however, the computer's evolution became increasingly driven by economic concerns.

We conclude that technologies of all sorts and sizes have various origins. For example, the GPTs that we consider in Chapters 5 and 6 include some that developed as endogenous responses to economic signals and others whose development was exogenous to the economic system. But few if any seem to have arrived out of the blue without prior evolutionary origins stretching well back in time. To conform with the awkward facts, therefore, theories should not make the early evolution of technologies in general and GPTs in particular as either always exogenous or always endogenous to economic signals. Once a major technology becomes established, however, its further evolution, which may stretch over centuries, becomes largely endogenous to the economic system.

Not Always Radical

Importantly, our definition of GPTs contains no statement about their being technology-radical. That GPTs are not typically technology-radical matters for at least two reasons. First, Mokyr's widely used concept (1990) of macro inventions creates the impression that discontinuous jumps out of nowhere are common in the development of technologies. This is not correct, although discontinuous jumps in the technology used for specific purposes are common—use-radical not technology radical (as defined above on page 90). Second, it also matters because much futile debate can occur when people confuse the two meanings of radical, producing examples of use-radical change to support claims of the common occurrence of technology-radical changes and vice versa.

GPTs are typically use-radical but not technology-radical. For example, the steam engines that powered the iron steamship had a long evolutionary history stretching back over more than two centuries before they had evolved enough to be used in large ships. The iron steamship was, however, a radical innovation in the transport industry and could not have evolved out of the sailing ship that it replaced.

Cases that are genuinely technology-radical are often accidental discoveries. The discoveries of the control of fire and of the force of static electricity may well have constituted important technology-radical and accidental discoveries. However, the list of technology-radical inventions and innovations that can be described as having no clear technological or scientific antecedents seems a very short one.

In his discussion of 'macro inventions', which are close to our GPTs, Mokyr does not distinguish between the two senses of radical. He does, however, define his macro inventions as appearing 'without clear precedent' and, as he puts it 'more or less ab nihilo' (Mokyr 1990: 13). He adds that these discontinuities in the evolution of technology can, under certain conditions, lead to discontinuities in the growth process. We agree with Mokyr that there are many important discontinuities in the growth process caused by non-incremental innovations that confer big technological shocks on the economy. However, we would add that these shocks are most often caused by innovations that are use-radical, but not technology-radical. This seemingly simple distinction allows us to accept discontinuous technological shocks while avoiding having to defend the position that they are generated by innovations with no clear technological parentage.

To summarize, we take an evolutionary view of the development of individual technologies: the vast majority are not technology-radical; and we take a revolutionary view of the impact of many, if not all, GPTs: the vast majority are use-radical, bringing discontinuous jumps in the technologies used for specific purposes.

Our Definition of GPTs[13]

At the outset, we note two important points about any definition of a GPT. First, what distinguishes GPTs from other technologies is a matter of degree. So there will always be technologies that on our definition are almost, but not quite, GPTs. Second, any definition of a GPT must be historical in nature. Since GPTs are not born in their final form, they often start off as something we would never call a GPT (e.g. Papin's steam engine) and develop into something that transforms an entire economy (e.g. Trevithick's high-pressure steam engine).

Scope for Improvement

Given the way that agents learn about and develop technologies, any technology that ends up being widely used in many different forms will typically go through a process of improvement and evolution. As the technology is developed, its costs of operation in existing uses fall, its value is improved through the inventions of ancillary supporting technologies, and its range and variety of uses increase. This is so for all three aspects of the technology. The technology of the product is improved (e.g. cars became more and more durable), its process technologies are improved (e.g. cars are now produced in high tech computer aided factories), and organizational technologies are improved (e.g. the automobile industry gave rise to mass production and later to lean production). Every GPT displays this evolutionary experience in which the processes of technological change and diffusion are intermingled in time, space, and function.

Range and Variety of Use

A technology's range of use refers to the proportion of the economy in which that technology is used. A process technology may be used in a single industry, as with electrolysis for aluminium, or in many different industries, as when mass production started in the automobile industry and spread to the assembly of many other manufactured products, and eventually to service industries as well. A product technology that is embodied in a capital good can have a range of use that runs the whole gamut from helping to produce one specific product to all the products of one industry to products that spread over the entire economy. For example, a tax software package is used in the production of a single product (a completed tax return); a nail gun is used in a wide range of products that are largely found in a single sector of the economy (construction); computers are used to produce many products across virtually the entire economy.

By *variety of uses*, we refer to the number of distinct uses that are made of a single technology. Notice that having a variety of uses is not the same thing as being widely used. For example, although it is widely used across the economy, an electric light bulb is only used to produce light. In contrast, some technologies have multiple uses.

[13] The papers in Helpman (1998) are seminal with respect to GPTs. We discuss them in detail in Chapter 11. Lipsey, Bekar, and Carlaw's (1998a) had most to say on matters of definition.

Steam power provides an example of a technology that had, at its zenith, a wide variety of uses. In the mid-Victorian 'age of steam', it was used to pump water out of mines, to stabilize the flow of water through locks in canals and over water wheels, to pump bellows in breweries, to force preheated air into blast furnaces, to power factories, to drive railways, steamships, early coaches, automobiles, and steam tractors. The latter brought major changes in farming where they not only replaced horses for pulling ploughs and harrows but provided stationary engines to run, through belt drives, all sorts of machinery such as threshers and saws.

All the technologies that we study in Chapters 5 and 6 fulfil both these conditions of being widely used for a variety of purposes. But technologies vary more or less continually in both these dimensions and can be found with almost every possible combination of them. Thus, there are many technologies that have all the characteristics of a GPT but to a lesser degree. No doubt some of these will be called GPTs in the future and there is probably no harm in some ambiguity at the margin. But to be a GPT, all of these characteristics must be pervasive, and to be a transforming GPT, the effects on the facilitating structure must also be widespread and deep.

Spillovers

Another major characteristic of GPTs concerns *spillovers*. GPTs matter because the complex set of technological interrelationships that characterize the economy of any developed country spreads the effects of any major technological change far beyond those agents that initiate the change. GPTs impact on existing technologies, creating the opportunity, and sometimes the need, to alter many of these. They also create opportunities for profitable investments in a large set of new product, process, and organizational technologies. They expand the space of possible inventions and innovations, creating myriad new opportunities for profitable capital investments. These in turn create other new opportunities, and so on in a chain reaction that stretches over decades, even centuries. An example is the computer, which enabled the development of efficient, precisely controlled robots, which in turn enabled the restructuring of many factories along highly automated lines. We use the term 'spillovers' to cover all such interrelations, and below we define precise measures that cover them.

Necessary and Sufficient Conditions for a GPT

Almost every technology one would care to identify possesses at least some of the characteristics we have just mentioned. Any one of the above characteristics is not sufficient to identify a GPT; a technology must possess all four characteristics to be a GPT. Since each of them exists on a continuum, another defining aspect of GPTs is that they possess each of the four characteristics in abundance.

Definition: A GPT is a single generic technology, recognizable as such over its whole lifetime, that initially has much scope for improvement and eventually comes to be widely used, to have many uses, and to have many spillover effects.

Many non-GPTs have some of these characteristics and some non-GPTs may have one or more in greater measure than some GPTs. For example, gunpowder transformed the Western world but was not a GPT because it had only a limited number of uses.

General Purpose Principles

A general purpose principle (GPP) is a scientific or technological principle that shares many of the characteristics of a GPT, with the important exception that it is not embodied in a distinct generic technology that is recognizable as such over its lifetime. Whereas a GPT provides a set of instructions for some product, process, or form of organization, a GPP is a concept suggesting that certain things might be done, but not a blueprint for doing them—not, that is, the technology for a single generic product, process, or form of organization.

One example is the principle of mechanical advantage—that by altering the nature of the work done, an operator can exert a force that he or she could not exert unaided. In one application, a series of loops through two pulleys can allow an operator to pull in several metres of rope to raise a heavy stone by only one metre, thereby lifting it easily. Levers, pulleys, reduction gears, and worm drives all make use of the principle to do work that humans would find difficult or impossible to do unaided. However, the technologies that make use of this principle are not all one single identifiable technology, nor does the principle itself tell someone how to design any one of these technologies.

Mechanization provides another example. The principle of mechanization, using machines to do what human hands and feet used to do directly, is an enormously powerful concept, but it is not a distinct technology. Nor is it a set of instructions telling someone how to replace humans in some specific activity. The machines that helped to create the Industrial Revolution made use of the principle of mechanization, but each was a distinct machine doing a distinct job at different stages of the process of manufacturing textiles.

A third example is the transforming effects of fire. That fire could transform materials was an important GPP discovered early in technological history. But by itself, this knowledge does not tell one how to transform any particular material or carry out any particular process. The principle was used, however, to create several distinct technologies, including the processes that produce iron, lime plaster, glass, ceramics, terracotta, cement, and pottery.

These considerations lead us to define a new concept:

Definition: a 'general purpose principle' or concept ('GPP') is a principle that shares many of the characteristics of a mature GPT, with the main exception that it is not the specification of a single generic product, process or organizational technology that is identifiable as such over its lifetime. It is a concept that is employed in many different technologies that are widely used across the economy for many purposes and that has many spillover effects.

As well as the similarities, there are many differences between GPTs and GPPs. For one, the evolution of a GPP is typically somewhat different from that of a GPT. It is unlikely to start in crude form and then evolve into something much more sophisticated, although it often starts in one use and then spreads to many others. For another, because it is not embodied in one generic technology recognizable as such over the GPP's lifetime, the GPP cannot be classified specifically as a product, process, or organizational principle. Neither does it have any bounds being, in the limit, found everywhere and always. More usually, however, a GPP, such as mechanization, will be more prevalent in some societies and at some times than others. Although we do not make extensive use of this concept, which many find too vague to be useful, we need to identify it since GPPs, such as mechanical advantage and mechanization, are often confused with GPTs. We will say more about GPPs in Chapter 6.

Spillovers Further Considered[14]

As observed, one of the most important aspects of GPTs is that they rejuvenate the growth process by creating spillovers that go far beyond the concept of measurable externalities. In this section, we deal with these spillovers in more detail. We argue that, as conventionally defined, externalities miss many of the spillovers that are both causes and consequences of new GPTs. To deal with these, we introduce a much wider concept called *technological complementarities*.

Externalities

We begin by considering externalities. The standard textbook treatment takes place in a general equilibrium framework in which tastes and technology are fixed and there is no irreversible 'arrow of time'. One typical case can be written as

$$y_i = A f_i(x_1, \ldots x_n, Z) \qquad (4.1)$$

where y_i is the production of the ith agent, $x_1, \ldots, x_n$ are the amounts of n inputs that it purchases and uses, A is a parameter, while Z is the result of some activity external to agent i. In various applications, Z may be such things as some other agent's output, or one of its inputs, or society's stock of human capital.

Because we will be dealing with growth and change, we need to state the definition of externalities a little more explicitly than is often done:

Definition: Externalities are unpaid-for effects conferred by the *continuing* and *potentially variable* actions of one set of agents (whom we call 'initiating agents') on another set of agents (whom we call 'receiving agents') who are not involved in the initiating agent's activity, and for which the receiving agents would be willing to pay to receive a positive externality and to avoid a negative one.

---

[14] Much of the material in this section is a revised version of material first published in Carlaw and Lipsey (2002: 1305–15). Reproduced by permission of Elsevier N.H. Publishers.

Externalities typically prevent the fulfilment of the general equilibrium optimality conditions in neoclassical analysis since there will be too many of the activities that produce negative externalities and too few of the activities that produce positive externalities. Everything that we require can be established by considering only positive externalities, which we do from now on.

Following Arrow (1962*a*), externality analysis has been extended to a world of changing technology. Technological knowledge is non-rivalrous in the sense that one person's use of it does not preclude others from using it. Hence it confers benefits on many agents beyond the firm, industry, or sector in which it was originally produced. (Of course, it can be made rivalrous by such conventions as intellectual property laws but this does not alter its natural property that it can be used simultaneously by many different agents.) When studying these spillovers, Z in equation (4.1) is usually taken as some measure of R&D expenditure. The externality arises because Z includes the R&D of some agents other than the ith.[15]

To deal with spillovers from technological changes (not just R&D), we distinguish two types of externalities, both of which fit the definition given above.

Definition: *Static externalities* occur when the actions of the initiating agents and the effects on the receiving agents are confined to those that can occur in an Arrow–Debreu-type general equilibrium model with constant tastes and technology.

Definition: *Dynamic externalities* occur when the continuing actions of initiating agents generate technological changes that increase the value of existing technologies and/or create new opportunities for the receiving agents to make further technological changes. A dynamic externality arises from an action that the receiving agents would be willing to pay to have altered (or a social planner would alter on his behalf if it were unfeasible for the individual to do so for any number of reasons such as excessive private transactions costs).

Given a risk-only neoclassical world, both these types of externalities upset the optimum conditions in that too little of the activities that create them will be undertaken by individual maximizing agents. Importantly, these concepts do not cover all the spillovers that arise from technological change. In one common case, the initiating agent's innovation creates an *opportunity* for the receiving agents to conduct further potentially profitable R&D. These spillovers will sometimes give rise to dynamic externalities, but in at least the following three sets of circumstances they will not.

First, the initiating agent may capture all the rents associated with the downstream applications. Dynamic externalities are created only to the extent that the initiating agents are unable to capture all the benefits conferred on the receiving agents. But whatever the extent of the externality, the spillover is there in the sense that

---

[15] Carrying out both the theoretical and empirical analyses of the externalities associated with technological change in terms of R&D rather than the inventions themselves avoids some awkward problems that arise from the fact that inventions and innovations are discrete events. But just as it was necessary to go inside the 'black box' of the production function to understand technological change fully (Rosenberg 1982) and to model it as having some structure (e.g. Helpman 1998), we argue that to understand spillovers fully, it is necessary to go inside the black box of R&D expenditures.

something done by one set of agents is useful to another set, and to the extent that the initiating agents capture the rents, the externality falls short of the spillover.

Second, there may be no rents of innovation. This important case turns up in many situations. Let the initiating agent's original technological advance enable the receiving agent to make an innovation that just covers its R&D costs and yields a rate of return on new capital investment just equal to what would have been yielded by investing in existing technologies. Furthermore, let the receiving agent's innovation enable another receiving agent to make an innovation with a similar pay-off, and so on. In this case, there is technological advance but the cost of making it just covers the opportunity cost of the alternative of investing in existing technologies. There are then no externalities to create rents or 'free lunches' for receiving agents. But there are technological spillovers that provide receiving agents with opportunities that they did not previously have and that are worth taking up. This is the limiting case, but even if some surplus value is created and accrues to downstream innovators, the value of these externalities is less than that of the spillovers.

Third, any action that is completed cannot give rise to a current externality. Yet, there is benefit for anyone who incorporates wheels, screws, electricity, or silicon chips into some newly invented technology that would be more costly or impossible without them. The economic durability of many basic technologies gives rise to an enormous list of such unpaid-for technological interactions. Agents would pay to avoid doing without these public-domain technologies. But these are not externalities since they are not the result of current activity that any current agent would wish to alter. Nor would the set of current beneficiaries, transported back to the time of the innovation and given perfect foresight, want to pay present-day resources to accelerate or otherwise alter the innovative activities before returning to the present—because an alteration in that activity long past would have no appreciable effect on current opportunities.[16]

The existence of spillovers that are not dynamic externalities leads us to look for a broader concept of spillovers. We find this in the concept of complementarities. But since this term is used in many different ways in the literature, it is necessary to consider its meaning in some detail.

Complementarities, Hicksian and Technological

In standard microeconomic theory, complementarities refer to the response of quantities to a change in price. In contrast, when students of technological change speak of complementarities, they are often referring to the impact of a new technology. Furthermore, technological interrelations are often referred to in the litera-

---

[16] Of course, this alteration in historical experience would have had untold further repercussions that we can have no hope of predicting. We use this thought experiment only to heighten the argument that these bygones are not current externalities in any operative sense.

[17] Game theory introduces the concept of 'strategic' complementarities, where the actions of one agent affect the pay-offs of another. In technological competition, the most obvious example is when R&D done by *A* increases the expected value of the R&D done by *B*. This strategic complementarity covers some, but not all, of what we call complementarities.

ture as complementarities, when the intended meaning is often 'closely related', rather than complementarity in the theoretical sense.[17] We are concerned with the response of the system to certain types of technological changes, and distinguish two types of complementarities called 'Hicksian' and 'technological'.

The Hicksian concepts of complementarity and substitutability in production theory refer to the signs of the quantity responses of all other inputs to a change in the price of one input. *Net complementarity* is defined for a constant level of output while *gross complementarity* allows output to change in response to a change in one input price, and thus combines an output effect with a substitution effect.

Hicksian complementarity can result from technological change. For example, an innovation that reduces the cost of an input, x, which is widely used as a service flow in many production processes, will cause substitutions among some inputs. It will also increase the demand for other inputs that prove to be gross complements to x. Where the demands for inputs other than x increase in response either to an actual fall in the price of x or to any other change in the production of x that can be treated as if it were a fall in price, these are Hicksian (gross) complementarities.

To develop our second type of concept, technological complementarity, consider an innovation in one technology whose full benefit cannot be reaped until many of the other technologies that are linked to it are re-engineered, and the make-up of the capital goods that embody them are altered. The most important point about this type of complementarity is a phenomenon we have already discussed in Chapter 2: the effects often cannot be modelled as the consequences of changes in the prices of flows of factor services found in a simple production function. All of the action is taking place in the structure of capital and the consequent changes will typically take the form of new factors of production, new products, and new production functions. For example, the massive set of adjustments in existing and new capital structures that Fordist mass production brought about could not be modelled as resulting from a fall in the price of non-interchangeable parts. Even a zero price of these parts would have had an impact on the automobile industry that was both quantitatively smaller and qualitatively different from the revolution in the organization of production that followed from interchangeability.

This discussion leads us to define a new concept:

Definition: A *technological complementarity* arises in any situation in which the past or present decisions of the initiating agents that alter the technologies under their control (*a*) alters the value of other existing technologies and/or (*b*) creates the opportunity to alter the nature of other existing technologies and/or (*c*) creates opportunities for developing new technologies.

There are two necessary conditions for the existence of technological complementarities. First, technological knowledge must be a path-dependent process in which one new discovery enables others. If each piece of knowledge were independent of every other piece—what Mokyr (2002) calls singleton knowledge—there would be no knowledge spillovers. Second, specific bits of knowledge must have multiple uses. If every output, final or intermediate, had its own unique production process and inputs, new knowledge would be user-specific.

Technological externalities require both of these conditions, plus several others. First, the knowledge must be non-rivalrous. Second, its creator must not be able to appropriate its full benefits. Third, the initiating agent's actions must be continuing and alterable. It follows that the existence of a technological complementarity is a necessary, but not sufficient, condition for the existence of a technological externality.

In summary, let C be the class of all technological complementarities (and C' its negation), and E the class of all externalities (and E' its negation). Then $C' \cap E$ defines standard externalities; $C \cap E$ defines technological externalities; and $C \cap E'$ defines those technological complementarities that do not give rise to externalities and so are not covered by conventional measures of R&D externalities.

Definition of GPTs Elaborated

Earlier in the chapter, we defined GPTs in terms of four characteristics, one of which is the presence of many important spillovers. We can now elaborate on this characteristic by noting that having extensive Hicksian and technological complementarities is a necessary condition for a technology to be a GPT. *Ceteris paribus*, the more pervasive a technology, the more of both types of complementarities it is likely to have with other technologies. Because GPTs provide inputs that enter into virtually all production (materials, power, transport, and ICTs), and because they typically lie at the centre of large technology systems, they are vertically and horizontally linked to many other technologies. For this reason, innovations in GPTs will typically induce major structural changes in many, sometimes even the great majority of, other existing technologies and present myriad opportunities for the development of new ones.[18]

Case Studies

Carlaw and Lipsey (2002) discuss four examples—automobile, railroad, electricity, and the American system of manufactures—where new technologies created technological complementarities that went well beyond any measurable externalities and that permeated most of the economy, taking many decades to be fully exploited. The same can be said of all the GPTs discussed in Chapters 5 and 6. Here we give but one illustration, which concerns an organizational GPT.

The US natural resource base (along with some key forces on the demand side) encouraged the development of technologies, which the nineteenth-century Europeans called 'The American System of Manufactures'.[19] These resource-intensive and labour-saving techniques were based on standardized goods produced by specialized machines. They can be classed as the early stages of the organizational GPT that

[18] Of course, having these complementarities is not sufficient to be a GPT because many other technologies also have them. For example, the modern shipping container has revolutionized cargo handling and had many complementarities, causing adjustments in size of ships, layout and location of ports, handling facilities, labour skills, the design of trucks and railcars, and international location of production. But it is not a GPT because it is a single-purpose technology.

[19] This example is based on Rosenberg (1994: ch. 6).

culminated in Ford's assembly line. While this system developed in the USA through the second half of the nineteenth century, Europe's resource endowments encouraged craft techniques that were labour-intensive and resource-saving.[20] It turned out that the US system was capable of much more technological improvement than the European system. So the US choice of techniques, based on static advantages, accidentally conferred on the USA the dynamic opportunity for much more technological change than did the European choice.

The static choice of techniques that constituted the US system, while creating higher growth and higher incomes in the USA compared with the UK for over 100 years, was not fully reflected in measurable externalities. There was no surplus created for receiving agents separate from the initiating agents, since everyone was an initiating agent in the choice of technique. So no current agent would have wanted to change the choices that created the system.

As this and all the other examples discussed in Carlaw and Lipsey (2002) illustrate, the technological complementarities that follow from a new GPT and that drive growth are too many, too diffuse, and too long-lived to be captured by the concept of externalities. Nor can they be caught by any of the practical methods used to measure the externalities associated with technological advance, all of which depend on relating current costs and current production benefits. This matters because it shows that existing measures of the externalities associated with any new GPT must be radical underestimates of their true spillover effects. These measures give a wholly misleading impression of the importance of new GPTs in generating new growth by creating myriad new opportunities for many agents to invent and innovate throughout the entire economy.[21]

III. IS THERE A TESTABLE GPT THEORY?

On its own, the concept of a GPT is not a theory. Methodologically speaking, it is a subset of the wider category of technology. Those who study technologies and technological change have usually found it useful to distinguish among types of technologies, types of innovation, and different stages of the innovative process. For such definitions to be useful they must refer to something that is identifiable and can be distinguished from other related concepts. We first take up the issue of how to

[20] Freeman and Louçã (2001: 205) quote Musson to the effect that in the mid-nineteenth century the British led in mass production with standardized parts. Be that as it may, the US system was widespread by the latter part of that century and was not used elsewhere over any wide range of products.

[21] Although our discussion is almost exclusively confined to process technologies, similar stories can be told about products. For example, the new radio technology was at first confined to dots-and-dashes transmission. Then amateurs proved the practicality of continuous voice transmission. When the first commercial radio stations were licensed in the USA, neither firms nor anyone else expected continuous voice transmission to outcompete dots and dashes. But within two years, consumers had proved the enormous popularity of voice-receiving radios. Hundreds of firms, most of them new, rushed to produce the new radios and within a few years, all possible frequencies were filled with licensed radio stations. The radio went on, along with the movies, to eliminate vaudeville, transforming the entertainment industry in the process and creating a host of new radio personalities.

identify a GPT, along with some misconceptions in the literature about its identifying features. We then show in Chapters 5 and 6 that we can identify GPTs in
history, finding about two dozen over the last ten millennia. Of course, like all
categories used to distinguish the stages of a continuous variable, there are always
uncertainties at the margin. Although there can be debate about where to draw the
line, what matters is that the typical GPT has a number of characteristic features. We
deal with these in the present chapter and in Chapter 13.

To be useful in theorizing about growth, GPTs need to have a number of
methodological characteristics. First, they need to be identifiable and distinguish-
able from other technologies. Second, their characteristics and their effects need to
be measurable (quantitatively wherever possible but sometimes only qualitatively).
In Chapters 5 and 6, we discuss a selection of the observed characteristics and
effects that have been established by the many researchers who have studied the
GPTs that we identify. Third, it must be possible to develop theories about them.
The models in Helpman (1998) are the first generation of such theories. Although,
as we observe in Chapter 11, these were necessarily relatively simple models; so
were the original formulations of many other theories that subsequently went on to
be highly elaborated and successful. In Chapters 14 and 15, we report on our
attempts to develop a group of second-generation theories, which are capable of
including many of the characteristics that the historical studies reported in Chapters 5 and 6 suggest are important features of GPTs, but that were omitted from the
first-generation models in the interest of building-tractable models. Fourth, the
theories should not just be play things, but should have explanatory power and
yield testable predictions.

The first generation of GPT theories found in Helpman (1998) all produced the
prediction that each new GPT would be accompanied by a temporary slowdown in
the rate of productivity growth. This was a clear prediction but it has not stood up
to careful observation since some GPTs seem to produce such a slowdown while
others do not. In contrast, we argue at length throughout this book that there are
almost no simple predictions that apply to the behaviour of all GPTs treated in
isolation. We argue, for example, that GPTs may or may not be accompanied by
productivity slowdowns, which may or may not be followed by productivity
bonuses. This varied behaviour occurs because the influence of a new GPT depends
not only on characteristics shared by all GPTs (which are just a few quite general
ones) but also on more specific individual characteristics and, more importantly,
on how each new GPT interacts with technologies already in place. For example,
they are typically substitutable for some existing technologies and complementary
to others. In some observed cases, the GPT that was challenged had a great deal of
development potential left in it and a long period of competition ensued between
the challenger and the incumbent. In other cases, the incumbent GPT was quickly
dominated by the new challenger and rapidly retreated into a few specialized
niches.

Some critics see it as a flaw that GPT theories do not yield simple predictions of
the type that new GPTs must always be associated with specific observed phenom-

ena. But it is the complex interactions among GPTs and related technologies that determine what we see in that part of economic growth which is driven by technological change. This makes the theory more difficult to develop and at the same time potentially richer than simple theories, which operate at a very high level of abstraction.[22] Although still in the formative stages, we believe that our second-generation models come much closer to yielding significant testable predictions than did the first-generation ones (which, of course, is neither surprising nor an implied criticism of the first-generation work). We develop some of these in Chapters 14 and 15.

All of this raises the issue of historical specificity that we mentioned briefly in Chapter 1. As that analysis emphasizes, there is a trade-off between generality and content in all theories. The more general a theory, the more detail that distinguishes one situation from another it must omit. Hence, the less detail it can explain. Growth has some very general characteristics and these are appropriately studied by theories that operate at a high level of generality, such as those that model the economy's production technology by a single aggregate production function. But many other issues of growth are dependent on specific contexts. For example, one important set of issues is: (*a*) to identify the conditions needed to start a stagnant, technologically backward economy growing; (*b*) to ask if these are the same for all such economies or if specific local differences make different conditions necessary; and (*c*) to see if these conditions are different from those that are needed to maintain growth in a dynamic economy, which is operating on the technological frontier. Such questions cannot be addressed unless the theory contains enough detail to be able to distinguish among such economies. This issue of historical specificity—generality and wide applicability versus context specificity and more detailed explanatory power—is taken up again briefly in Chapter 14.

In this context, the development of theories concerning GPTs can be seen as part of a research agenda to incorporate into growth theories concepts of technology that are more complex than the flat technology, which gives rise to Harrod or Hicks neutral growth in models based on an aggregate production function. Such models of 'flat technology' have a high degree of generality and hence little context specificity. Models that deal with more complex concepts of technology that mirror more of what students of technological change observe are less general but have more potential to probe deeper into specific issues concerning the significance of different types of technology as drivers of economic growth and relevant economic policies.

---

[22] Consider an analogy. Although a few human characteristics, such as eye colour and the ability to roll one's tongue, seem to be determined by a specific and unique gene, most human characteristics seem to be the result of fairly complex interactions of a number of genes; for example, there is no single gene for intelligence or bad temper. This relative absence of simple predictions about a one–one relation between a gene and a specific human trait does not, however, make gene theory useless. It just makes it more difficult to develop and, at the same time, potentially richer.

Thus there is no one correct way to make the trade-off between generality and context-specific, explanatory power. Each choice must depend on the problem at hand.

IV.   HOW DO WE KNOW A NEW GPT WHEN WE SEE ONE?

Knowledge of the Evolution of the Technology Is Not Sufficient

In Lipsey, Bekar, and Carlaw (1998b: 196) we observed that 'the majority of existing models of GPTs have assumed that their short- and long-term effects are determined by the GPT itself and its predetermined need for supporting technologies'. We went on to argue on the basis of historical evidence that while 'this may be a reasonable place to begin,... the effects are actually determined not only by the new GPT's characteristics but also by how it interacts with other exiting technologies, the facilitating structure, and public policy'.

An illustration of the importance of our warning is provided by Moser and Nicholas (2004, M&N hereafter) who attempt to identify a technology as a GPT by studying the evolution of the technology itself. They use patent data to argue that electricity is not a GPT. They (2004: 392) state that 'without empirical data, the concept of a GPT has been based on anecdotal evidence involving a few extremely general inventions, such as David's dynamo'. We argue that readily available empirical observations outlined in the section on electricity in Chapter 6 show that electricity meets all the criteria that we have laid down for a technology to be a GPT: its production started out crudely and then became very sophisticated; it is widely used throughout the entire economy; it has multiple uses, and it has many technological complementarities—having enabled a vast number of goods and processes that were not possible in the previous era of steam power. When laid out carefully, as we do in Chapter 6, this is the evidence for electricity being a GPT. Similar arguments apply to all the other twenty-four GPTs that we study in Chapters 5 and 6. Readily available evidence—from common observations in the case of modern GPTs to masses of historical studies in the cases of older ones—show that each of these meets the four conditions that we have laid down.[23]

What then do we make of M&N's argument that electricity is not a GPT? Note, first, that nothing is said about patents in our definition of a GPT given above, or in the similar one given originally by Bresnahan and Trajtenberg. So there is clearly a need to consider if these definitions imply anything about patents and, if so, about what kind of patents.

Based on patent data, M&N identify what they call the ten most general inventions. They (2004: 392) then state that 'only two of them, Robert Williamson's

---

[23] Of course, if anyone provides a plausible argument that one or more of the conditions just discussed does not hold, then it becomes necessary to gather evidence more systematically, but it will still in most cases be nothing more than an enumeration of existing evidence.

winding for an electric dynamo and Truman Fuller's invention of an electrical contact ... are electricity inventions'.[24] This statement reveals that they have made what we have warned as one of the most common mistakes about a GPT, which is to associate its effects with one particular sector. For example, the computer-based information and communication revolution (which could not have existed without the complementary technology of electricity) is a process revolution, not a sectoral one. Much can be learnt about it by studying the computer industry in particular and the high-tech sector in general. But this does not get at the impact of the technology, which transformed products and processes throughout the economy.

Consider two examples. First, modern sawmills make much use of ICT. X-rays survey the log and computers decide where to make the first cut, a job that used to be done by experienced sawyers. Second, the computer allowed senior managers to communicate directly with all levels of both management and production personnel, and, as a result, the old hierarchical pyramidal organization of firms, where hoards of middle managers processed information and passed it up and down, gave way to a new, much more decentralized, flatter form of organization (and in the process, many middle-range managers lost their jobs). Neither of these important results of the ICT revolution could have been discovered, or their impacts measured, by studying events in, and patents taken out by, the computer industry, or even the whole high tech sector.

The number of patents in the electricity-generating sector tells us only how many patentable improvements were made in the electricity-generating and -distributing sectors. But just as the full impact of the ICT revolution is not measured by the number of improvements in the computer industry, nor the full impact of the steam engine by the number of improvements in that engine, so the full impact of the development of practical methods for the generation and distribution of electricity is not measured by the improvements in the electricity industry itself. No one who today patents a product or a process that uses electricity needs to cite an invention in the electricity industry as a precursor, even though, without electricity, that product or process could not have been patented. The same is true for products that use the computer or some bio-engineered material.

A relevant patent study would be to discover how many patents were taken out for products and processes that could not have existed without the GPT in question, electricity in this case, or the computer in another example. But what M&N have measured, although interesting in itself, tells us nothing about the importance of electricity as a GPT, or whether or not it fulfils our necessary conditions to be one.

Evidence on the Four Criteria

What is needed to identify a technology as a GPT is to locate a technology identifiable as a single generic product, process, or organizational form over its whole evolution, such as the computer or the steam engine, and then collect evidence that it fulfils the

---

[24] This statement along with their title 'Was Electricity a GPT' reveals their concentration on improvements in the GPT itself rather than in what it enabled. If electricity *was* a GPT and is still widely used it still *is* a GPT.

four necessary conditions that we have identified in our definition. Initially, it must have had much scope for improvement and development, as did the early hard-wired electronic computers that were first introduced during the Second World War. In its mature state, it must have multiple uses and be widely used through much of the economy, as is the case with modern-day electronic computing devices that are found almost everywhere doing a wide range of things. It must also have many technological complementarities and spillovers, as are seen, for example, when computers enable products to be designed in virtual form, facilitate complex calculations in a number of areas of science and technology that were impossible with mechanical calculators, and control robots, which themselves have multiple uses, and so on more or less ad infinitum. In the case of most GPTs, there is a mass of existing material that can be used to establish that each of the four criteria are met. All that is then needed is to gather this material together and classify it into the four categories defined by the definition. This is the evidence. The fact that we do not usually need a host of researchers to gather it, or regression techniques to analyse it, does not make it any less cogent as evidence. We do just this for a case study later in this chapter and for the GPTs that we consider in Chapters 5 and 6.

What Can Be Said about Emerging GPTs?

There is a class of technologies that can be reliably identified as potential GPTs based on their technological characteristics alone. For example, if one is told that a new technology will allow for the rearrangement of matter at the molecular level to enable the construction of almost any type of product or material, whatever its engineering specifics (i.e. a mature nanotechnology), it can be confidently said that the technology has a clear potential to develop into a GPT. No one can predict how such technologies will evolve in detail, or whether they will encounter insurmountable cost obstacles to their commercialization, but they are prime candidates for close attention as potential GPTs.

It is far easier to identify some emerging technologies as potential GPTs than to rule out others. So while we may be able, with some confidence, to put some new technologies into the class of potential GPTs, we cannot with equal confidence assert that all of the remainder have no promise of developing into GPTs.

Even if it cannot be spotted in advance as a potential GPT from its technological characteristics alone, it is often clear that a technology is maturing into a GPT long before it reaches its full potential. For example, the computer's potential to alter the technology of production fundamentally was becoming clear long before the modern desktop computer emerged. The ability to identify a potential GPT even decades after it was first introduced can be useful in helping policymakers understand, facilitate, and smooth out the structural adjustments that accompany the diffusion of a major new GPT.

While there is a good chance of identifying a GPT before it fully matures, there is very little chance of identifying the precise evolutionary path that it will follow. The uncertainties associated with the development of all technologies, especially with a transforming GPT, make their detailed historical evolution impossible to predict in advance. Once the dynamo was invented, it was recognized that electricity was a technology with potentially large economic impacts. But few anticipated the specifics of how electricity would transform our economy.

Despite the difficulties associated with enumerating the set of specific uses and complementarities that a new GPT will develop, it is possible to predict, qualitatively, that the set will be large. For example, while the full potential of the cluster of technologies associated with ICTs was not clear at the outset, some specific developments, such as networking, were predicted well in advance. Further, it became clear to some in the 1980s, and to many in the 1990s, that the world was experiencing a profound transformation associated with this GPT. We take this issue up again in Chapter 13 where we develop an appreciative model of some general characteristics that we expect all GPTs to share.

The Myth of the Productivity Paradox[25]

One of the most common erroneous beliefs is that new GPTs lead sooner or later to a 'productivity bonus'—an acceleration in the rate of productivity growth.[26] Growth economists typically have these expectations because in any model based on an aggregate production function there can be no technological change without productivity growth. The lack of such a bonus until the mid-1990s was often taken as an argument against the existence of an ICT-induced revolution. We reject the expectation of a productivity bonus necessarily accompanying the introduction of every new transforming GPT for several reasons.

First, although a new technology will be instituted whenever it promises to be profitable, there is no guarantee that each new GPT will have larger, or even the same, effects on productivity as the ones that preceded it (however this is measured). As already observed, a new GPT may be conceptualized as a research programme—a programme that itself evolves as the power and efficiency of the GPT is steadily improved. The resulting innovations spread over decades in a process of linked inventions and innovations. There is, however, no reason to expect that the total impact of successive GPTs should stand in any temporal relation to each other. One may introduce a rich programme that brings large changes in products, processes, and organizational arrangements, and perhaps productivity; another may introduce a programme that is less rich. So although the level of productivity will be increased as GPTs follow one another, there is no reason to expect that the average rate of productivity growth will be accelerated from one GPT to the next. Because changes in technology are only observable in neoclassical models by their effects on productivity, economists often assume that big changes in technology must be associated with big changes in productivity, and are puzzled when they are not. But there is no reason to be puzzled. New technologies will replace older ones as long as they promise some gain in profitability. Sometimes the difference between the

---

[25] Much of the discussion in this section is drawn from Lipsey (2002*b*).

[26] In all of our discussions of productivity, we continue with our maintained assumption of full employment of resources so that the shorter-run effects on productivity of changes in unemployment rates are ignored.

productivity of the old and the new is large and at other times it is small. But as the S-E decomposition emphasizes, there is no necessary relation between these variables. Current changes in productivity may or may not be well measured, but there is no paradox in there being major changes in technology with no acceleration in the measured rate of productivity increase.[27]

Second, even if one GPT has a larger impact than its predecessor, it may take longer to work through the economy and thus show smaller gains each year. In this connection, notice that many of the effects of the ICT revolution on new design and production methods that are listed below occurred in the period 1975–90, so that the gain was spread over decades, and occurred long before the 1990s when economists started trying to identify the new GPT by a productivity bonus. Relevant evidence is also produced by Crafts (2003) who demonstrates that the measured contribution to growth of the ICT revolution exceeded that of steam and at least equalled that of electricity. He (2003: 10) concludes: 'Perhaps the true paradox is that so much was expected of ICT.'

Third, the extent to which the new technology comes to pervade the economy and the extent of the induced changes in the facilitating and policy structures bear no necessary relation to the induced changes in productivity or real wages. There is only a paradox when neoclassical growth theory, which cannot distinguish between changes in technology, the facilitating structure, and productivity, is used to interpret what is going on.

Fourth, if no further GPTs were invented to provide new research programmes, the number of derivative technological developments would eventually diminish. There would be further innovations using existing GPTs, but their number and their productivity would be much less than if further GPTs were to become available. Consider, for example, what the range of possibilities for new innovations would now be if the last GPTs to be invented had been the steam engine for power, the iron steamship for transport, steel for materials (no man-made materials), the telegraph for communication (the voltaic cell but no dynamo) and the mid-nineteenth-century factory system for organization. So what new GPTs, such as computers, electricity, and mass production do is to prevent the number of efficiency-increasing innovations from petering out. They prevent a steady decrease in the return on investment and the opportunities for innovations that increase productivity. But there is no reason to believe that each of them will increase the average rate of productivity growth over all previous GPTs. If each did, we would see a secular trend for productivity to rise as each GPT succeeded its predecessor.[28] In summary, new GPTs rejuvenate the growth process; they do not necessarily accelerate it.

Fifth, there are reasons why a new GPT may slow the growth of productivity during the first stages of its introduction below what it will be on average over its

---

[27] Part of the neoclassical confusion about the two phenomena of technological change and productivity change stems from the assumption of perfect information (or risk). In a world of genuine uncertainty, the lack of a tight relation between these two types of change is clearer.

[28] This view of GPTs as research programmes and their relation to productivity growth is discussed and modelled formally, in Carlaw and Lipsey (2001, 2006: forthcoming and in chapters 14 and 15).

lifetime. Very long lags exist because it takes much time for (*a*) the range of a GPT's use and applications to evolve; (*b*) for ancillary technologies to be developed; and (*c*) for changes to be made in all the elements of the facilitating and policy structures that support it. Typically, several decades are required for a GPT to make a major impact—and that impact may then stretch over more than a century as new technologies that are enabled by the GPT are developed. As argued by David (1991*b*, 1997), electricity is a prime example of this trend. Thus, for some GPTs there may be a slowdown in productivity growth in the early stages followed by an acceleration to its average rate after the facilitating structure has been fully adopted but its full potential has not yet been worked out. But this acceleration is not a real productivity bonus, in the sense that the GPT has brought more productivity growth than previous new technologies; it is only a return to whatever underlying rate of growth the particular GPT in question will produce. Neither is it a phenomenon that is necessarily associated with all new GPTs. The possibility of an economy-wide slowdown is problematic because (*a*) at any one time there are likely to be several GPTs, at least one in each of the categories mentioned at the beginning of Chapter 5, and each at various stages of its development; and (*b*) typically, the existing GPT in any one category has not been fully exploited when another challenges it.

Finally, as argued in detail in the Appendix to this chapter, traditional measures of productivity, including TFP, emphatically do not measure technological change in spite of the common opinion to the contrary. One of the many reasons why this is so is that conventional measures of the quantity of capital cause much technological change, which is embodied in new capital equipment to be measured as changes in the quantity of Capital, rather than as changes in technology. Thus, for example, Jorgensen's statement (2002: 30) that 'Capital investment has been the most important source of US economic growth throughout the post-war period' needs to be understood as referring to capital as it is measured, which includes much embodied technological change.

New GPTs Predicted?

After all this analysis, we must wonder if we can identify some actual future GPTs that are emerging on the current technological horizon? As already observed, the characteristics of new technologies do sometimes allow us to identify potential GPTs. Whether or not their potential will be fulfilled, however, depends on many contingencies that cannot all be foreseen. Here are a few cases in point.

Nuclear power was heralded by many as a potential GPT. Technological difficulties and public liability restricted its application to an auxiliary power source, except in a few countries such as France. If it could be developed, low-cost fusion in micro generators would have myriad applications that would make it important. Currently, however, we have no idea if low-cost, trouble-free nuclear power will be developed and widely used or if alternatives such as solar, hydrogen, or geothermal power will dominate.

Superconductivity is another much heralded technology that has not yet lived up to expectations. No one knows if the technical problems will be overcome to make it a major technological revolution, or merely, as it now is, a technology with a limited range of important applications (such as in quantum computing).

As we have already observed hydrogen fuel cells have the potential to transform the economy. They may well become a GPT that generates myriad spillovers transforming existing product, process, and organizational technologies. They also have the potential to greatly influence political relations, since if they come into general use, they will greatly curtail the West's need for petroleum. Whether such fuel cells can be developed to produce power efficiently for its wide range of potential uses is still in the realm of uncertainty. What is clear is that their development has taken much longer and been far more expensive than was anticipated a decade ago.

Robotization is another possibility, one that already has many applications. Computer-operated robots have been used widely for years in manufacturing assembly processes and have spread into many other areas, such as driving trains, performing surgery, and creating lifelike toys. Also in the early development stage are micro machines, minute robots that can be programmed to self-replicate and produce at a very small scale.

Biotechnology is an obviously developing GPT. Many diverse possible uses have already been established and more are being discovered at a rapid pace. Many of their practical applications, however, await further reductions in costs and an assessment of their side effects. Nonetheless, what has happened so far makes us confident that biotechnology is an emerging GPT.

Nanotechnology, the building up of materials and machines atom by atom, is another possible GPT of the future with a large number of potentially valuable applications. These include allowing non-invasive surgical techniques, improved tolerances in material development, and drastically lowering the cost of producing integrated circuits. The potential for a new GPT is clear, while the evolutionary path is as yet uncertain. These last two emerging GPTs are considered in more detail in Chapter 6.

The ICT Revolution: A Case Study

We conclude this chapter with an illustrative case study, the ICT revolution. Like all transforming GPTs, the computer started as a crude, specific-purpose technology and took decades to be improved and diffused through the whole economy. Like all GPTs, this one presented a research programme to improve the GPT itself and to apply it across the whole economy in new processes, new products, new organizational forms, and new political and social relations. Its effects became visible in the 1970s and today we are living through an ongoing and profound transformation of economic, political, and social structures.[29]

The string of technological changes, in products, processes, and organizational forms, enabled by the computer-created ICT revolution had already created a New Economy well before the end of the twentieth century—one that is still evolving. To

---

[29] This is discussed in more detail in Lipsey and Bekar (1995) and Lipsey, Bekar, and Carlaw (1998b).

justify this statement we list a few of the many ICT-driven changes that have occurred since 1970. They are grouped loosely under the headings of process, product, and organizational technologies, and social and political implications, although the categories clearly overlap. Goods (G) are distinguished from services (S) where relevant. As this listing makes clear, the New Economy has had a major impact on services, probably even more than on goods.[30]

Process Technologies

- Computerized robots and related technologies have transformed the modern factory and eliminated most of the high-paying, low-skilled jobs that existed in the old Fordist assembly line factories. (G)
- CAD is revolutionizing the design process and eliminating much of the need to 'learn by using' that was analysed for the aircraft industry by Rosenberg (1982). (G)
- Surgery on hips, knees, and other delicate parts of the body is more and more done by computers, which will soon facilitate distant surgery, permitting specialists working in major urban hospitals to operate on patients in remote parts of the world. (S)
- Instead of flying to meetings and appearances, business persons, lawyers, and other professionals in many outlying cities use teleconferencing, turning a long travelling slog into an effort that takes little more time than the actual appearance. (S)
- Research in everything from economics to astronomy has been changed dramatically by the ability to do complex calculations that were either impossible or prohibitively time-consuming without electronic computers. (S)
- Computer-age crime detection is much more sophisticated than it was in the past. Here the biological and the ICT revolutions complement each other as is so often the case with coexisting GPTs. (S)
- Traffic control in the air and on the ground has been revolutionized in many ways while navigation at sea is now so easy that many lighthouses, the sailor's friend for several millennia, are now being phased out as unnecessary since ships can determine their distance to within yards using satellites and computers. (S)

Organizational Technologies

- The management of firms has been reorganized as direct lines of communication opened up by computers eliminated the need for the old pyramidal structure in which middle managers processed and communicated information. Today's horizontally organized loose structures bear little resemblance to the pyramidal management structures of the 1960s. (G&S)
- Firms are increasingly disintegrating their operations. Virtually no firm in Silicon Valley now produces physical products. In other industries, the main firm is increasingly becoming a coordinator of subcontractors, who do everything from designing products through manufacturing them to distributing them. (G)

---

[30] What follows is a revised version of a list that first appeared in Lipsey (2002*b*).

- The e-lance economy—groups of independent contractors who come together for a single job then disperse—is growing and, incidentally, becoming difficult for authorities to track. (S)
- Just as the First Industrial Revolution took work out of the home, the ICT revolution is putting much of it back, as more and more people find it increasingly convenient to do all sorts of jobs at home rather than 'in the office'. (S)
- ICTs have been central to the globalization of trade in manufactured goods, and of the market for unskilled workers. This has shifted the location of much manufacturing and allowed poorer countries to industrialize. It has created new opportunities and challenges for both developed and developing nations. (G&S)
- Digitalized special effects have changed the movie industry in many ways, for example, by reducing the need for shooting on location and for myriad extras whose presence can often be produced digitally. (S)

Product Technologies

- Many goods now contain chips that allow them to do new things or old things more efficiently. New applications continue to be developed. For example, cars can be equipped with systems that warn the driver of oncoming dangers and take over control if the driver fails to take evasive action. (G)
- Computer- and satellite-linked automated teller machines (ATMs) have enormously facilitated accessing one's bank account and obtaining funds in any currency in almost any part of the world. (S)
- Email has largely replaced conventional mail with a large increase in volume and speed of transmission, from days or weeks in the past, depending on the locations, to seconds today. (S)
- The ability to download music into computers that burn CDs is welcomed by many users while threatening the music recording industry. (G)
- Computerized translation is now a reality and will go from its present crude form to high degrees of sophistication within the lifetimes of most of us. We are witnessing the arrival of Douglas Adam's vision in *The Hitch-Hiker's Guide to the Galaxy*: the ability to hear in one's own language words spoken in any other, and to be understood in any other language while speaking one's own. The only difference is that instead of inserting a fish into one's ear, a small computer needs to be attached to one's body. (S)
- Children do school work by consulting the Internet. Instead of hearing only the received wisdom from their teacher and the proscribed texts, they are now exposed to a battery of diverse knowledge and opinion and will have to learn how to cope at a very early age with more than one view on any subject. (S)
- Distant education is growing by leaps and bounds and many are enrolled in educational courses where they never (or only rarely) set foot inside the institution that they are attending. (S)
- Cars can now receive real-time information on traffic conditions at all points in their projected journey. (S)

- Smart buildings and factories already exist and will grow rapidly in number. Among many other things, power consumption can be adjusted continually in response to real-time price signals sent out by the electricity supply company and calculated in response to current loads. (G&S)
- The electronic book looks like it might do an end run around consumer resistance to reading books on screen. The book's blank pages fill up on demand with any one of a hundred or more books stored in a chip that is housed in its cover. A touch of a button, and one is reading a Physics 101 text on what looks like a conventional book; with only another touch, a Chemistry 202 text replaces the other on the book's leaves. (G)

Social and Political Implications

- The computer-enabled Internet is revolutionizing everything from interpersonal relations to political activity. Chat rooms form the basis for new forms of community, making interpersonal relations possible on a scale never seen before. Non-governmental organizations (NGOs) are able to organize activities to protest against such things as clear-cut logging, World Trade Organization (WTO) efforts to reduce trade barriers, and the push for a Free Trade Area of the Americas (FTAA). Never again will trade negotiations take place in the relative obscurity that they enjoyed from 1945 to the 1990s.
- Dictators find it much harder to cut their subjects off from knowledge of what is going on in the outside world.
- Driven by the Internet, English is becoming a lingua franca for the world and, unlike Latin in the Middle Ages, its use is not limited to the intelligentsia.
- In former times, a physical presence was required from virtually everyone providing a service. With computers, email links, and a host of other ICTs, this link between physical presence and service provision has been broken in many lines with profound social and political effects on such things as place of residence and the ability to regulate and tax many activities.

Two of the dissenters from the view just expressed are Triplett (1999) and Gordon (2000), who make similar criticisms of the importance of the ICT-driven New Economy. In throwing doubt on the revolutionary effects of IC technologies, Gordon observes that they have not given rise to anything like the range of new goods that transformed people's lives in the previous fifty or so years, such as the flush toilet, the automobile, and the range of electric appliances that transformed household work. We agree but point out that, as the above list illustrates, some of the most important changes initiated by the ICT revolution have been in process technologies and in consumer services. There are few goods and services produced today that are not made with the aid of computers at some stage in their production processes. Also the new communications services have transformed peoples' lives in ways possibly just as fundamentally as did electrically powered consumer durables.

In these and many other ways, new ICTs have already revolutionized society and will continue to do so well into the twenty-first century. Some of these are minor while others are transforming, such as globalization and its many ramifications, the dramatic changes in the organization of firms, the end of mass production and its associated labour and management requirements, the alternations in the political power structure, the emergence of the civil society and its effects on the conduct of international negotiations. One cannot help but marvel over how many economists can assert, first, that all of these rich events can be adequately summarized in one series for productivity (usually total factor productivity) and, second, that the existence or non-existence of this entire ICT revolution depends on how this one number is now behaving in comparison with how it behaved over the past couple of decades!

Nonetheless, many growth theorists tend to associate this New Economy, and technological change more generally, with changes in some measure of productivity—either labour productivity or, more often, total factor productivity. Such is the strength of this way of thinking that many American economists were sceptical of the existence of the New Economy until US productivity picked up in the mid-1990s. That scepticism was reactivated when the US economy slowed down in 2001.

In this vein, Gordon (2000) defines a new economy as occurring when the rate of improvement in new products and services is greater than in the past and there is thus an acceleration in the rate of productivity growth. (See Triplett (1999) for a similar argument.) This leads him to date the New Economy as starting sometime in the 1990s and not to be a very dramatic phenomenon. He is able to do this because, as we have earlier observed, growth economists use the aggregate production function in which technological change is visible only by its effects on TFP, thus equating changes in technology with changes in productivity. However, it is precisely the non-separation of these two phenomena that gives rise to productivity puzzles in periods when independent evidence suggests that technology is changing rapidly but productivity is changing only slowly or not at all.

In contrast, many other economists, especially those in the S-E tradition, betray no such doubts that the economy at the beginning of the twenty-first century is substantially different in most aspects from that of the 1970s. They look at the implications for labour, education, the growing inequalities in the distribution of income, taxation, and legal matters of changes that accompany the New Economy. To summarize how we see it, the phenomenon in which we are interested is the full effects on the economic, political, and social systems of the ICT revolution—a revolution that is driven by computers, lasers, satellites, the Internet, and a few other related communication technologies with the computer at the centre. In this view, the ICT revolution concerns an economy-wide process not located in just one high-tech sector. It has its roots in the development of the electronic computer in the Second World War (1939–45) and really began to make its effects felt throughout the economy in the 1970s. Indeed, many of the changes that we listed above were completed by 1990.

We conclude that there may well be an ICT-induced productivity bonus around the corner but there is no guarantee of this. Furthermore, the existence or non-existence of such a bonus tells us nothing about how profound are the current and future transformations to be induced by the ICT revolution. We hasten to add that at the beginning of the twenty-first century, the ICT revolution did seem to be improving (correctly measured) productivity so that the productivity slowdown was being at least partially reversed. Nonetheless, there is no reason either in technology or in economic theory why productivity growth over the next couple of decades should equal or exceed growth during the last period, 1945–75, when GPTs were being exploited within a stable structure that was well adapted to them.

APPENDIX: MEASURING TECHNOLOGICAL CHANGE[31]

In this Appendix, we consider the issue of measuring technological change. We argue that the commonly used TFP does not measure technological change but instead measures only some of what we call the supernormal profits associated with it. It follows that TFP cannot be used to divide the growth in output between what is due to technological change and what is due to additions to the accumulating factors, physical and human capital and labour.

Lipsey and Carlaw (2004) provide quotations from several eminent economists giving mutually incompatible interpretations of TFP, only one of which says that it measures technological change. They group the quotations into three categories: TFP measures technological change; TFP measures only the 'free lunches' associated with technological change; and TFP is at best a measure of our ignorance and at worst a measure of nothing that we can identify. Surely it must be a cause of major concern that a measurement that is relied on for so many purposes in theory, applied work, and policy assessment is so variously interpreted by the experts.

A.I AN OVERVIEW OF TOTAL FACTOR PRODUCTIVITY

The identification of changes in TFP as a measure of technological change originates in Solow's seminal 1956 and 1957 articles. An aggregate production function is used to relate indexes of inputs to an index of output. Growth in output that is not associated with the growth in inputs is interpreted to be the result of changes in technology (and some other causes such as scale economies).[32] Indeed when an aggregate production function is the tool of analysis, changes in technology can only show up as changes in the Solow residual, that is, in TFP. Lipsey and Carlaw (2004) consider three methods of calculating TFP: the growth accounting method, which we rely on here; the index number method, which differs from the growth-accounting method only in non-essential matters; and the distance function method, which they argue is fatally flawed.

---

[31] The material in this Appendix is based on the much more detailed treatment in Lipsey and Carlaw (2004).

[32] The word 'associated' means different things in different contexts. In Solow's model, there is causality running from productivity increases to economic growth. In any purely measuring context, there is no such causality.

Growth-accounting calculations of TFP require the specification of a production function that is both stable across time (regardless of changes in technology) and valid at whatever level of aggregation the calculations are to be made.[33] They typically assume price-taking behaviour to ensure that the marginal equivalences used in TFP calculations will hold.[34]

Consider the simple, but usual aggregate production function:

$$Y = AF(K,L) \tag{4A.1}$$

where Y is output, K is physical capital, and L labour. All that we require can be demonstrated by using the specification of this function as Cobb–Douglas:

$$Y = AK^{\alpha}L^{\beta}; \ \alpha \in (0,1), \ \beta \in (0,1), \ \text{and} \ \alpha + \beta = 1 \tag{4A.2}$$

TFP is calculated as a geometric index in levels:

$$TFP = Y/(L^{\alpha}K^{\beta}) = A \tag{4A.3}$$

and its growth as an arithmetic index in rates of change:

$$\frac{\dot{A}}{A} = \frac{\dot{Y}}{Y} - \alpha\frac{\dot{L}}{L} - \beta\frac{\dot{K}}{K} = \Delta TFP \tag{4A.4}$$

where α and β are equated to their share weights in income. Equation (4A.4) defines

---

[33] Our discussion of such a function simplifies broader concepts of the aggregate production variously provided by Jorgensen and Griliches (1967), Jorgensen (2001), and Barro (1999) that include R&D among the lines of production in the aggregate function. Jorgensen and Griliches (1967) and Jorgensen (2001) treat all lines of production activities, including R&D, as having constant returns to scale, which implies that the part of technological change that involves costly R&D is not measured by TFP. In contrast, Barro (1999) uses production functions that allow R&D to generate increasing returns to the intermediate R&D inputs to production. In Barro's case, TFP measures the exogenous (Hicks' neutral, 'mana from heaven') component of technological change and the endogenous technological change generated from costly R&D. However Barro's endogenous component has the same 'free lunch' characteristics of the unpaid-for 'mana from heaven' benefits that are in Jorgensen and Griliches' model. This is because the endogenous component results from increasing returns to all lines of production activities. All of this leaves open the questions about the meta- or all-encompassing notion of aggregate production and about the appropriate formulation of R&D and knowledge production in that framework.

[34] Lipsey and Carlaw (2004) argue that calculations of TFP using this approach require several dubious assumptions: (*a*) that we can meaningfully measure the inputs of factors over these long periods, and across very different technologies; (*b*) that the production function remains stable, with productivity-increasing changes in technology being registered solely by changes in the productivity factor, *A*; (*c*) that competition among firms be treated as the *end state*, which is perfectly competitive equilibrium, rather than as in the contrasting Austrian view of competition as a dynamic *process*, which takes place in real time; and (*d*) that the markets over which aggregation occurs are all perfectly competitive or monopolistically competitive in the Dixit–Stiglitz sense of that term and do not contain the mixture of monopoly, oligopoly, monopolistic and perfect competition that characterizes real-world industrial structures, even if all firms were in end-state equilibrium.

changes in TFP as the difference between the proportional change in output and the proportional change in a Divisia index of inputs.[35]

A.II TFP AND COSTLY TECHNOLOGICAL CHANGE

We argue that although TFP does not measure technological change it does, ideally, measure the supernormal profits, externalities, and some of the other 'free lunches' associated with such change. Others who have argued something close to this position include Nelson (1964), Jorgensen and Griliches (1967), Rymes (1971), and Hulten (1979, 2000). No one, however, seems to have argued, as we do later in this Appendix, that TFP measures what Knight (1921) called the economic profits that are the return for undertaking uncertainty, and not 'free lunches'.

Virtually all technological change is embodied in one form or another, in new or improved products, in new or improved capital goods, or other forms of production technologies, and in new forms of organization in finance, management, or on the shop floor. Here we use the term capital goods to cover any embodied technology. Although much theory proceeds as if these technological changes appear spontaneously, most are the result of resource-using activities. The costs involved in creating technological changes are more than just conventional R&D costs. They include costs of installation, acquisition of tacit knowledge about the manufacture and operation of the new equipment, learning by doing in making the product, and learning by using it, plus a normal return on the funds invested in development costs. We refer to the sum of these as 'development costs'.

It was the important contribution of Jorgensen and Griliches (1967) to point out that TFP would only measure the gains in output that were over and above their development costs and, therefore, TFP would not measure the full contribution of new technology, but only what they called the externalities or 'free lunches' associated with technological change. They then argued that these gains would, when properly measured, be close to zero. The unfortunate consequence was that the subsequent debate centred on whether or not the measure should approach zero, which obscured their really important point that TFP did not measure the full contribution of the new technology.

A Thought Experiment

To make contact with the standard treatment of TFP, we assume end-state perfect competition under conditions of risk. The important implication for our purposes is equality in the expected marginal returns accruing to all lines of investment, both in

---

[35] Most work on TFP uses a Tornquist index, which is a discrete approximation of the continuous Divisia index. It is a percentage change index that averages base and given years weighted indexes, as does the Fisher Ideal index. For our exposition of conceptual issues surrounding TFP we use the continuous time Divisia index, which weights percentage changes in specific inputs by their share of total cost. Where we specifically wish to measure TFP using real discrete world or simulated data, we use the Tornquist or Fisher indexes.

embodying existing technologies in new capital goods and in developing new technologies through R&D.

Whenever an investment is made in the development of a new technology, the investors must be expecting to recover at least all of their development costs in the selling price of whatever embodies that technology, which for concreteness, we assume is a physical capital good. This implies that the price of the good, and thus the investment that the users must make in buying it, will capitalize all of the development costs.

We use an example in which an existing machine is improved so that it does more work on the same job than did its predecessor, and there are no spillovers affecting agents other than those involved in developing, selling, and purchasing the capital good that embodies the new technology. We first consider this case in broad outline and in a later section we study it at more length by embedding it in a specific production function.

Let the value of the fully perfected new machine's marginal product in the user industry be v. This is the maximum price that users will be willing to pay for each new machine. Given the expected sales, let the development cost per unit of the new machine be w. There are three cases to consider for costly technological development:

1. $w > v$ implies perfectly foresighted firms would not invest in the technology. If they did, the TFP change would be negative.
2. $w = v$ implies the TFP change is zero, because the cost of the new machine is equal to its net addition to output.
3. $w < v$ implies the TFP change is positive.

Because the returns to all lines of investment must be equal in competitive equilibrium characterized by risk (and no uncertainty), only case 2 is possible in equilibrium. In that case, where full development costs are just covered, the returns to investing in the new technology are just equal to the returns to investing in existing technologies. In case 1, the new technology would not have been developed if the outcome had been foreseen. In case 3, there is a return over and above what is needed to recover the development costs that created the innovation. In a perfectly competitive, risk-only economy this extra return must have been unexpected returns. It will be shared between the capital goods producers and the users in a proportion that will depend on the type of market in which the good is sold.[36]

Importantly, there is technological change in all three cases, while under our assumption that there are no externalities, there is a positive change in TFP only in case 3. (If there were realized externalities, TFP would increase by that amount in all cases.) So changes in TFP capture only that portion of technological change that yields returns in excess of full development costs (or below in the case of negative TFP changes). Thus, zero change in TFP does not mean zero technological change. It

---

[36] If we were to allow beneficial spillovers to other agents such that the output rises without any measurable change in their inputs, TFP can be positive in case 2 because although opportunity costs are just met in the innovating sectors, there is an additional pay-off reaped by third parties.

only means that investing in R&D has had the same marginal effect on income as investing in existing technologies (investment with no technological change), and that there are no externalities that show up in increased output elsewhere without corresponding increases in inputs.

Free Lunches and Supernormal Benefits

As noted above, in a perfectly competitive end-state equilibrium in which foresighted individuals invest in new technologies under conditions of risk, the expected returns from all lines of expenditure are equated. Thus, the expected returns to investing in a new technology will just cover the opportunity cost of its full development and will be equal to the return to investing in new capital that embodies existing technologies. Under these conditions, additional returns would then only arise because of externalities (or unexpected events that are not consistent with full equilibrium). For this reason, Jorgensen and Griliches, and many others who followed them, associated TFP with the 'free lunches' of externalities.

In contrast, under the path-dependent process competition that characterizes the real world of technological change in which new technologies are developed under conditions of Knightian uncertainty, investments in new technologies can, and often do, yield returns well above the going rate of return on existing technologies. Much of this extra return is a reward for undertaking the many uncertainties associated with the development, proving, and applying of new technologies. As argued in Chapter 4, *these returns are not free lunches*. Instead, they are the incentives required to persuade entrepreneurs to attempt technological advance in highly uncertain and often capricious environments. The concept of a free lunch can then be associated with externalities and other unpaid-for benefits that accrue to others. In the case of GPTs, these benefits typically spread over much of the whole economy and over long periods of time, because GPTs present a research agenda for applying them in myriad ways to new processes and new products. These benefits are genuine free lunches. They bring gains in terms of new opportunities, which agents typically do not have to pay for. (For example no one has to pay for the opportunity to incorporate electricity or a computer chip into the design of a new product or process.) To allow for this extra return, as well as for genuine free lunch externalities, we define the 'supernormal benefits' associated with technological change as the sum of all associated output increases and cost reductions accruing to anyone in the economy *minus* the new technology's development costs.

These considerations do not alter the measured value of TFP changes, which remain increases in output in excess of measured increases in inputs, but they do suggest an alteration in how we interpret it. As long as one understands that TFP includes that part of the return on innovation that is a reward for undertaking uncertainty, there is no problem in calling it a measure of 'free lunches'. We prefer the term 'supernormal benefits' since it avoids the impression that they are strictly manna from heaven that serve no purpose in the allocation of resources. Certainly, most innovators would be surprised to hear that the amount they earned in excess of what they could have made by investing in a long-established firm making nails with well-known technologies was an unearned free lunch!

We make the distinction between free lunches and supernormal benefits because it is so easy to misinterpret what TFP does measure once it is accepted that it is not a measure of technological change. For example, Hulten (2000: 9, n. 5) writes that the Hicksian shift parameter, A_t, 'captures only *costless* improvements in the way an economy's resources of labor and capital are transformed into real GDP (the proverbial "manna from heaven"). Technological change that results from R&D spending will not be captured by A_t.' In practice, all of the gain from R&D that accrues to the innovators in excess of the 'normal' rate of return on investing in existing technologies is potentially captured. This does not require that the improvement be either disembodied or costless.

Lipsey and Carlaw (2004) go on to argue that TFP is a very imperfect measure of the supernormal benefits associated with technological change for a number of reasons that seriously bias most measurements. These are covered in detail in their text but need not concern us here.

Conclusions

We may now summarize the conclusions that we have reached so far:

- TFP is correctly interpreted as measuring changes in the difference between *measured* outputs and increases in *measured* inputs.
- Changes in TFP do not measure technological changes, since part of the return to innovation reimburses the (widely defined) development costs and thus show up as offsetting input costs.
- Changes in TFP are correctly interpreted as being an imperfect measure of the returns to investing in new technologies that are in excess of the returns to investing in existing technologies, that is, the supernormal gains of technological change. It is conceptually possible, therefore, to have sustained, technologically driven economic growth with zero changes in TFP.
- The returns that TFP does conceptually measure include two distinct things: first, the returns to undertaking uncertainty, which is correctly interpreted as the cost of entrepreneurship; and second, the effects of spillovers that cause outputs to rise or inputs to fall without a corresponding change in the other. The latter is reasonably thought of as manna from heaven but the former is not.

Costly Change Considered in More Detail

To further study the issue of embodied technological change, we assume two industries. The final goods industry produces a constant amount of some final good, Y, whose specifications never change. Its inputs are labour and the services of a capital good that takes the form of a machine delivering an unchanged service. The final goods industry has the following Cobb–Douglas production function:

$$Y = A(mK)^{\alpha}(nL)^{1-\alpha} \qquad (4A.5)$$

where K is capital measured in value of fully employed machines and L is labour measured in physical units, while m and n are efficiency parameters attached to capital and labour respectively. The machines are produced by a capital goods industry. The producers spend money on broadly defined development costs to create new technologies that alter the efficiency of the machine they produce. New machines are sold by their producers at a price that is just sufficient to recover the direct costs of production and the full development costs—the price of the improved capital good capitalizes the development cost that created it. Thus, the capital good producers will register no change in their TFP since their costs change in the same proportion as the value of their output, and any change in TFP will occur only in the user industry.[37] We consider four different types of technological change and one case with no technological change. Whenever possible, we assume that the development cost of the machine, and hence the rise in its price, is just equal to the saving in inputs that it generates so that there is also no TFP gain in the consumer goods industry. We also assume no externalities so that all the gains accrue to the makers and users of the machine.

Case 1

The disembodied technological change in the final goods industry lowers both labour and capital costs by x%.[38]

For purpose of comparison, we first consider a disembodied improvement that lowers operating costs in the machine-using industry. There is no change in the machines that it buys from the capital goods industry.

Now consider two polar cases. First, at the least costly extreme, let the organizational change be costless; it is an isolated stroke of genius with virtually no development costs. Now the value of output is unchanged while the physical quantities of both inputs fall by x%. The industry's TFP will rise by x%.

Second, let the industry's organizational change have positive development costs. These are incurred in period zero and, to set up the most costly extreme case, assume them to be equal to the discounted present value of the cost savings, which begin to accrue at period one. This makes the total development cost equal to

$$\sum_{j=1}^{n} \frac{r}{(1+i)^j}$$

where i is the return to investing in the technology when it is organized in the original way (or the opportunity cost of R&D), r is the old cost minus the new cost

---

[37] We make this assumption purely for heuristic reasons. If we altered the example so that some or all of the gain accrued to the machine producers, the only conclusion that would change would be the *location* of the TFP gains.

[38] The famous productivity-increasing reorganization of the factory that occurred when (unit drive) electric motors succeeded (central drive) steam engines in providing factory power is an example. Although the change was embodied in a new organization of the machine tools on the factory floor so that the flow of goods through the factory could be continuous, there was no need to alter the amount of physical capital or labour inputs. So with unchanged measured inputs, output rose.

per period (or the net cost savings per period),[39] and n is the number of periods over which the new organization is expected to be useful. Because R&D is treated in the national accounts as a current cost with no parallel output, there will be a reduction in the level of TFP when the R&D is being conducted (equal to the present value of the future stream of benefits from R&D). There will be a subsequent increase in the level of TFP from its pre-R&D level, starting when the new organization is in place and extending over its lifetime. (The extra TFP will be r for n periods.) Over the lifetime of the new organization, the extra TFP will just make up for the loss of TFP while the R&D was being conducted (everything appropriately discounted).

Now assume that these disembodied changes are going on continually. If they are costless, there will be a continuous rise in the TFP of the consumer goods industry. If they are costly, so that at each point in time there is a new expenditure on R&D and an accompanying benefit from the past R&D expenditures still generating increases in output, TFP will be constant with no blips as in the once-for-all case.

What these polar cases show is that, contrary to what is often stated in the literature, disembodied technological change does not necessarily raise TFP. What matters is how the discounted present value of the gains due to the fall in direct costs per dollar's worth of output compares with the development cost of creating the disembodied change. We suspect that the contrary presumption in the literature is due to an invalid implicit assumption that disembodied changes are costless.

Case 2

The new embodied technology saves equally on both labour and capital costs.

We now go to our main case in which the efficiency improvement is embodied in a machine produced by the capital goods industry. We first consider the empirically common case in which the capital goods industry develops a new machine that is absolutely saving on both labour and capital. Toyota's new stamping presses discussed in chapter 6 under the heading lean production is one of many examples (see Womack et al. 1990).

Since we are assuming that the new technology saves equally on both labour and capital, we cannot assume a development cost that would leave TFP unchanged. An unchanged TFP would require an increase in the cost of the machine, which would violate the requirement that both costs fall in equal proportion.[40] So we assume that the cost of producing the new machine is $2x\%$ less than the cost of producing the old one. The development costs are just covered when the new machine is sold for $x\%$ less than the old machine. The new machine is also assumed to use $x\%$ less labour to produce the same amount of output as the old machine. Thus, with constant output, inputs of capital and labour both fall by $x\%$ so that the industry's TFP rises by $x\%$. This innovation shows up in equation (A4.1) as an increase in both the efficiency parameters, m and n, by $x\%$.

---

[39] r is related to x in the following way: $r = $ old $-$ new, $x = (r/\text{old}) \times 100\%$.

[40] Let the machine reduce the number of labour and machine-hours required to produce a unit of output by $x\%$. If the cost of labour and machine-hour were unchanged, TFP would rise by $x\%$. For TFP to be unchanged, the cost of a machine-hour would have to rise by $x^{1/\alpha}$, which violates the assumption that capital and labour costs fall by the same amount.

Notice that in equation (A4.1) this change is empirically indistinguishable from an increase in the parameter A by $x\%$. So this type of embodied technological change looks like disembodied change. Note also that the mixed case, in which one efficiency parameter rises by $x\%$ and the other by $y\%$ $(x > y)$, is indistinguishable in the Cobb–Douglas function from an overall increase in A by $y\%$ combined with an increase of $(x - y)\%$ in the efficiency parameter that actually increases by $x\%$.[41]

Case 3

The new embodied technology saves only on labour inputs.

The new machine is assumed to produce $x\%$ more output using the same amount of labour, a type of invention that is common in the history of technological change. We assume that the development cost of the new machine can just be recovered by the capital goods industry if the machine sells for $x\%$ more than the old machine. When the consumer goods industry replaces the old machines with new ones, it uses savings equal to the additional value of the machines. So the industry's capital stock will grow by $y\%$. It will have $y\%$ more measured capital and $x\%$ more output. To get the limiting case in which TFP is zero, y must equal x/α.[42]

Case 4

The new embodied technology saves only on capital inputs.

Now assume that the new machines act *as if* there were $x\%$ more of them than the old machines, making output increase by $\alpha x\%$. Machines increase in efficiency but labour does not. The efficiency parameter on machines grows by $x\%$ and, by assumption, the sale price of each physical machine rises by just enough to cover development costs of $y\%$. To get the limiting case of no TFP change, we assume that the development costs are such that $y = x$. (The percentage change in output minus the weighted percentage change in capital is $\alpha x - \alpha x = 0$.) If development costs exceed this amount, foresighted firms will not develop the machine; if they are less, there will be an TFP gain.

In the discrete once-for-all cases, 2, 3, and 4, there is a fall in TFP when the development costs are incurred and then a subsequent increase in TFP. In the limiting cases, 3 and 4, the present discounted value of the TFP gain is equal to the R&D cost. This blip can be eliminated in either of two ways. First, the R&D can be capitalized and treated as a capital investment in the first period. Then it can be depreciated over the lifetime of the new machines. Thus in the first period there will be an output of R&D capital to match the loss of other outputs and no change in TFP, while in subsequent periods the slightly higher output will be matched by the depreciation of R&D capital, again leaving TFP unchanged throughout. Second, technological improvements may continue period by period. Now there is a constant amount of R&D in each period and there is a fall in costs in the consumer goods industry of the same value in each period, leaving TFP unchanged.

---

[41] The same statement is also true for some specific parameters in the translog function but not for all.

[42] For example, if capital costs are 25 per cent of total costs, then the quantity of capital must increase by four times the increase in output if TFP is to be zero. If development costs would cause a greater increase, the innovation will not be made by foresighted individuals. If it is less than that, there will be some surplus over development costs and some increase in TFP.

Case 5

No technological change.

The assumption that development costs could just be covered by the increased price of the new machine in cases 3 and 4 imply a certain amount of capital investment in the new machine. We now calculate the increase in output that would have occurred if that amount of investment had been made when there was no technological change. In case 3, the measured amount of capital increases by $x/\alpha\%$ and output by $x\%$, giving no change in TFP. Now let capital increase by x/α in equation (A4.1) with no technological change. Output then increases by $x\%$. So the results are the same. In case 4, capital increased by $x\%$ and output by $\alpha x\%$. With constant technology, an $x\%$ increase in K causes output to increase by $\alpha x\%$. So, once again, the results of case 4 with development costs just covered are the same as when an equivalent amount of investment occurs with static technology.

We have now reached a number of conclusions:

- In each of the first four cases, measures of TFP correctly reflect the net increase in output due to technological change, that is, the difference between what the industry's output would be with and without technological change for a given amount of investment.

- This TFP measure is not, however, a measure of technological change per se but only of returns over and above those needed to recover the broadly defined development costs that created the innovation. Thus, zero TFP does not mean zero technological change but only that, at the margin, investing in R&D has the same effect on output as investing in existing technologies (investment with no technological change).

- In theoretical treatments, the distinction between embodied and disembodied technological change is often made in terms of the parameter of the production function that is affected, a shift in A being disembodied technological change, and a shift in either m or n (in equation 4A.1) being embodied change. However, we cannot distinguish empirically, using an aggregate Cobb–Douglas production function, between genuine disembodied technological change and technological change is embodied in a new machine that lowers all input costs in equal proportion (a common case empirically). Both appear in the observed function as Hicks' neutral growth. The empirical observation of Hicks' neutral growth does not, therefore, imply that technological change is not embodied in new capital equipment. Also, even when technological change is biased towards saving one factor more than the other, this is indistinguishable in the Cobb–Douglas function (but not necessarily in a translog function) from a case of Hicks' neutral technological change of an amount equal to the contribution of the factor that is saved in the smaller proportion, combined with a change that saves a smaller amount on the other factor.[43]

---

[43] Specifically, let $0 < \Delta m_a/m_a < \Delta n_a/n_a$. These values are indistinguishable empirically from $\Delta A_c/A_c = \Delta m_a/m_a$, and $\Delta n_c/n_c = \Delta n_a/n_a - \Delta m_a/m_a$, where the subscripts a and c stand for actual and calculated (or measured).

- Chen (1997) argues that the size of the TFP is affected by whether technology is treated as disembodied or embodied, the former always yielding the higher number. In contrast, we argue that it is not whether the technology is embodied that matters but whether or not the gains from the technological change more than cover its development costs. We suspect that Chen is stating a commonly held view and hence that ours is an important point.

A.III   COUNTERFACTUAL MEASURES

If TFP does not measure technological change, we must look for an alternative. Consider case 2 of our earlier thought experiment where the net addition to output from some capital good embodying the new technology just equals its full development costs. The change in TFP is therefore zero. Yet there has been technological change. But where is the benefit in the new technologies when the marginal productivities of investing in new and existing technologies are the same? Carlaw and Lipsey (2002, 2006: forthcoming) argue that the gain under these circumstances is not to be found at any current margin. Instead, it is to be found in the difference between the time path of GDP if technology had remained constant and the path of its actual behaviour as technology changes. If there were no technological change, diminishing returns to capital would result in a declining rate of growth of GDP for any given rate of capital accumulation. Instead, one innovation enables another, as we see from the course of any of the major GPTs discussed in Chapters 5 and 6.

As discussed in Chapter 13, the time path of *cumulative investment opportunities* related to a particular GPT from its inception to its replacement by a superior alternative often resembles a logistic curve, rising slowly at first when the GPT is still in its crude specific use stage; then rising evermore rapidly as each innovation expands the space for further innovations at an increasing rate; and again slowing as the possibilities for new technologies that are enabled by the GPT begin to be exhausted.[44] For simplicity in graphing our relations, we assume here that the cumulative curve has a linear portion at the outset and then eventually flattens as possibilities begin to be exhausted.

Now consider again a continuing rate of technological change that just covers its development costs so that investment in new technologies yields the same rate of return as investment in existing technologies. Capital accumulation does not encounter diminishing returns. The rates of return on investment in old and new technologies hold constant and the growth rate of output does not fall for a given rate of capital accumulation. The gain from technological change is not, therefore, measured by any gap between the returns from investing in the old and new technologies but by the growing gap between the actual time path of output and what the path would have been if technology had been static.

This is illustrated in Figure 4A.1, which gives two time paths for the return on capital. The first is constant along the arrowed curve, R_1, assuming a succession of overlapping GPTs. Along this trajectory, investments in successive innovations are assumed each to earn only their opportunity cost as measured by the return on

---

[44] The analysis of Freeman and Louçã (2001) is built around phenomena of this type of relation.

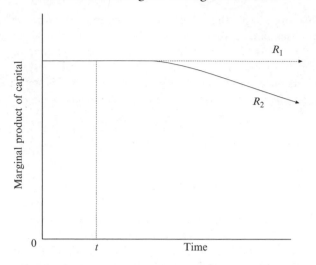

Figure 4A.1. *Alternative time paths for the marginal product of capital*

investment in existing technologies, as in case 2 in an earlier section. Changes in TFP will thus be zero (which is why TFP is emphatically not a measure of technological change). The second curve, R_2, falls on the assumption that no new GPTs are invented after time t so that returns eventually fall as innovation possibilities get used up.

So whether or not there are externalities in the form of technology transfers for which the recipients would have paid more to obtain than they actually did, and whether or not there is a discrepancy between private and social rates of return, the technological complementarities that arise from radically new technologies have been a major (we would say *the* major) source of growth over the last three centuries.

When presenting these ideas at various seminars we have encountered very strong feelings to the effect that if we cannot show how to measure our counterfactual concept of the effect of technological change on output, we should not criticize the methods that are used, specifically TFP. We reject this argument on three grounds. First, if TFP does not measure the output effects of technological change, confusion may result from pretending that it does. Second, if concepts cannot be published and discussed before they can be measured, very few really innovative concepts would ever be developed. Any such concept, or other idea, requires much investigation and developing to refine it before methods of measuring it can be worked out. To ask that a new concept be eventually measurable is not an unreasonable demand; to ask that it be not discussed until it is shown to be measurable is unreasonable. Third, one of us is currently developing measures of the impact of technological change on output, by developing independent measures of technological diffusion, application, and investment, then relating these patterns to actual patterns of TFP change. In another line of measurement development, we are generating data from the model provided in Chapter 14, and comparing what is known from the model where the growth of technology is directly measurable with TFP made under various measurement methodologies.

5

A Survey of GPTs in Western History (Part A): 10,000 BC to AD 1450

We now start a tour through the West's technological history, stopping briefly to consider what we see as the most important transforming GPTs and using our S-E categories (inputs, technology, facilitating structure, policy, policy structure, and performance) to organize the wealth of historical facts. Since books have been written on each of the GPTs covered in this and the next chapter, what we say about them should be taken as illustrative rather than exhaustive. We concentrate more on the broad consequences of new technologies than is typical in the growth literature, illustrating how technological change has the power to transform a society's economic, political, and social institutions. We do not, however, enter into some of the many controversies over the causes of these changes.

This tour provides a base of factual material to guide our subsequent theorizing. It also provides many cautionary tales concerning the wealth of important detail that is omitted in any formal modelling of GPT-based growth. (See Chapter 11 for an overview of such models.) Since it is important for our subsequent theorizing to have at least a basic knowledge of the most important GPTs in history, we put all the material in Chapters 5 and 6 on record. Readers are encouraged, however, to pick and choose those GPTs that most interest them. Any material that is skipped can be referred to later when references to specific GPTs become important.

Starting from the neolithic agricultural revolution, we identify twenty-four transforming GPTs listed in Table 5.1. (We discuss in footnote 1 those classifications that have seemed questionable to some readers.)[1]

Although others might expand or contract our list by a few items, it illustrates several important points. First, the current ICT revolution is not unique; there have

---

[1] The idea of replanting seeds and selecting those that produced the most desired crops is a process technology with a wide variety of applications of product outputs. So is the idea of selecting animals for breeding to create a wide variety of docile and useful animals. Writing is a process technology that produces a wide variety of written materials—although it uses goods as inputs such as clay, a stylus or pen, ink, and paper. The first factory was an organizational innovation in the production of textiles, but later the system spread to the production of a wide variety of other manufactured goods. The same can be said about mass and lean production, which can be regarded as separate GPTs in their own right or as developments of a single GPT, the factory system. Biotechnology is a process technology that is built on three key innovations: how to segment, recombine, and reduplicate sections of DNA. Nanotechnology is likewise a process technology that is built on several innovations concerning how to manipulate individual atoms and molecules, and combine them in almost any way that does not violate the laws of physics.

Table 5.1. *Transforming GPTs*

No.	GPT	Date[2]	Classification
1	Domestication of plants	9000–8000 BC	Pr
2	Domestication of animals	8500–7500 BC[3]	Pr
3	Smelting of ore	8000–7000 BC	Pr
4	Wheel	4000–3000 BC[4]	P
5	Writing	3400–3200 BC	Pr
6	Bronze	2800 BC	P
7	Iron	1200 BC	P
8	Waterwheel	Early medieval period	P
9	Three-masted sailing ship	15th century	P
10	Printing	16th century	Pr
11	Steam engine	Late 18th to early 19th century	P
12	Factory system	Late 18th to early 19th century	O
13	Railway	Mid 19th century	P
14	Iron steamship	Mid 19th century	P
15	Internal combustion engine	Late 19th century	P
16	Electricity	Late 19th century	P
17	Motor vehicle	20th century	P
18	Airplane	20th century	P
19	Mass production, continuous process, factory[5]	20th century	O
20	Computer	20th century	P
21	Lean production	20th century	O
22	Internet	20th century	P
23	Biotechnology	20th century	Pr
24	Nanotechnology[6]	Sometime in the 21st century	Pr

Note: P, product; Pr, process; O, organizational.

been (GPT-driven) 'new economies' in the past. Second, GPTs have not been common in human experience, averaging between two and three per millennium over the last 10,000 years. Third, the rate of innovation of GPTs had been accelerating over the whole period. We start with millennia between GPTs, then centuries.

[2] Many of these dates are approximate and are based on rough estimates of when their use in the West became widespread enough for the technology to be identified as a GPT from contemporary experience, although many were first innovated centuries and even millennia ago.

[3] We include items 1 and 2 but not more modern agricultural developments because the domestication of plants and animals were truly generic developments with many uses that go far beyond food to such things as clothing, containers, shelter, transport, and power (many of which are still being worked out), while later innovations had a much narrower range of mainly agricultural uses.

[4] There is little evidence regarding the origins of the wheel but it was certainly not in use before the agricultural revolution and was in common use by about 3000 BC.

[5] Although continuous process techniques began to evolve with the rationalization that followed the electrification of factories in the late 19th century, we date the emergence of mass production as a GPT at Henry Ford's innovations in the first decade of the 20th century.

[6] Nanotechnology has yet to make its presence felt as a GPT but its potential is so obvious and developing so quickly that we are willing to accept that it is on its way to being one of the most pervasive GPTs of the 21st century.

In the eighteenth century there are two important GPTs, four in the nineteenth century, and seven in the twentieth. The time from first discovery to a fully developed GPT has also accelerated (although not smoothly). Several millennia passed between the discovery of iron and the onset of the Iron Age; hundreds of years passed between the introduction of the waterwheel to Europe in Roman times and its widespread, multipurpose use in the late medieval period; just over a century lay between Papin's first steam engine and the innovation of the high-pressure steam engine that turned a useful technology into a GPT; while from the nineteenth century onwards, the gestation period between first introduction and emergence as a full GPT has typically been measured in a few decades.

These technologies fall into six main classes, with some overlap. Notice that at any one time there may be several GPTs in existence and even more than one in a particular class (e.g. the dynamo and the internal combustion engine).

1. *Materials technologies*: domesticated plants[7]; domesticated animals[8]; bronze; iron; biotechnology.
2. *Power*: domesticated animals; waterwheel; steam engine; internal combustion engine; dynamo.
3. *Information and communications technologies*: writing; printing; computer; Internet.
4. *Tools*[9]: wheel.
5. *Transportation*: domesticated animals; wheel; three-masted sailing ship; railway; iron steamship.
6. *Organization*: factory system; mass production; lean production.

To check that each of these belongs on our list we need to relate each to our fourfold definition of GPTs given in Chapter 4. Stated briefly, a GPT is a technology that initially has much *scope for improvement* and eventually comes to be *widely used*, to have *many uses*, and to have *many spillover effects*. The class of technologies, on our list whose inclusion might be thought to be questionable are transportation technologies, and this only with respect to the criterion of multiple uses. For example, from a very broad perspective ships are for one purpose, to transport people and goods—but this is no different than power technologies, which in the broadest

---

[7] Although their first use was mainly for food, plant products provide many varied materials such as cotton, flax, materials for making baskets, clothing, and small boats, and many other vegetable-based products such as herbal medicines.

[8] Although domestic animals were very probably first used for food, they became a major power source and stayed so for millennia, as well as providing many materials such as leather, feathers, furs, and fertilizer.

[9] Of course there have been many other important tools in the history of technology but most are too specialized to have achieved the status of a transforming GPT. The laser is a tool-GPT but, as mentioned in the text, it fitted too well into the existing facilitating structure to be classed as a *transforming* GPT. As we have argued, the idea of mechanization that is embodied in most factory machinery is a GPP, not a GPT.

perspective only provide power. But just as these provide power for a multiplicity of different uses, so do ships have many uses in addition to transporting people and things, such as to act as gun platforms on warships, landing fields for airplanes (aircraft carriers), harbour tugs, sports vehicles using both power and sail, rescue vessels, entertainment media, geographical and mineral exploration, cable mainten- ance and repair, mapping and surveying, and so on. (Similar comments apply to the other transportation technologies on our list.)

In Chapter 4, we also defined the concept of a GPP. The most important of these for our purposes is the principle of mechanization that was used in the automated textile machines—key components of the First Industrial Revolution. Because it is so important in technological history, we also discuss this GPP along with the above list of GPTs.[10]

I. INITIAL CONDITIONS

As mentioned in Chapter 3, long before the emergence of modern *Homo sapiens*, early hominids had invented technologies that put them into competition with a wider range of creatures than any other animal. This increased the evolutionary pressure to develop better and better tools and skills. It also made possible the move out of Africa, often into climatic conditions that humans could never have tolerated unaided by technology.

The initial conditions on the variables in our S-E model can now be enumerated. They have been discovered by a combination of archaeological exploration and the contemporary study of numerous hunter-gatherer societies that survived up into the nineteenth and early twentieth centuries.[11]

Technology

The technology of 40,000 BC has been outlined earlier. Technological knowledge beyond tool- and weapon-making consisted mainly of accumulated experience of

[10] In various previously published discussions of GPTs, we have sometimes included and sometimes excluded the textile machinery that underlay the Industrial Revolution and/or the more general concept of mechanization as GPTs. The textile machines cannot, however, be regarded as GPTs since each was a single-purpose machine. This raised the question: Was the principle of mechanization not a GPT? However, since it is not embodied in a single generic product, process, or form of organization, but in a vast variety of each, it is not a single technology. The concept of GPP solved our problem. It covers this and a number of other cases in which there were general purpose ideas that were not embodied in a single generic product, process, or form of organization. With GPPs, it is the principle that matters. It lasts forever and may be embodied over millennia in many different technologies, including many GPTs.

[11] 'Recent studies reveal the intimacy of the relationship between hunting man and his natural environment; the relative simplicity of the material culture (only 94 different items exist among the Kung bushmen); the lack of accumulation of individual wealth; the mobility. ... [B]ushman's subsistence requirements are satisfied by only a modest effort—perhaps two or three days' work a week by each adult; they do not have to struggle over food resources; their attitudes towards ownership are flexible and their living groups open. Such features set hunters and gatherers apart from more technologically developed societies whose very survival depends upon their ability to maintain order and to control property' (Barraclough 1978: 35).

hunter-gatherer societies with respect to the nature of edible plants and game animals, the making of protective clothing and means of shelter.

Inputs

One main input in the S-E model is land (which is taken to include all natural resources). The land was still in the grips of the last ice age 40,000 years ago. The climate, at least outside of Africa, was harsh and unsuited to the kinds of plants that were eventually domesticated. Wildlife included many large animals that are now extinct.

Policy Structure

The best available evidence suggests that hunter-gatherer societies were typically non-hierarchical. There was no well-defined private property and many goods were held in common. The most common political unit was the 'band', members of which were mostly close genetic relatives. There was no hereditary leader class and decisions tended to be taken democratically.[12]

Facilitating Structure

Accumulated tools, clothing, and shelter were the main capital stock. The organization of production was hunter-gatherer: humans thus carried on with the form of production that had been used by all the hominids that had gone before them, and by the majority of other animals.[13] There was probably little intergroup specialization in productive activities, although there was much intragroup specialization between the sexes.

Anatomically people of 40,000 BC were identical to modern humans. They differed in what they knew, human capital, but not in their mental or physical capabilities. These *Homo sapiens* were, as we have earlier observed, the end product of millions of years of evolution in a positive feedback loop between human characteristics and technology.

Performance

Standards of living varied with the natural endowments in which different hunter-gatherer groups operated. When they lived in relatively clement conditions, such as were found in the Fertile Crescent during neolithic times, hunter-gatherers could satisfy their material wants with quite modest amounts of work. One common interpretation is that hunter-gatherers typically tailor their wants to their existing resources, and that the unlimited wants assumed by standard economic theory is a post-hunter-gatherer phenomenon.[14] Another interpretation, more congenial to

---

[12] See Wenke (1990: 282–3) for a fuller discussion.

[13] Not all animals are exclusively hunter-gatherers. For example, ants routinely farm aphids, 'milking' them for their honeydew.

[14] Wenke (1990: 280) says that 'people living in complex sedentary communities seem to live in the eternal economic dilemma of unlimited wants and limited means, but simpler societies have adjusted to their limited means by having few wants'.

economists, is that since (*a*) there were only a few commodities available for consumption, (*b*) and these were produced with relatively small amounts of labour (both direct and indirect through produced capital goods) so that (*c*) their marginal utilities declined rapidly with increasing consumption, it follows that the opportunity cost of leisure was low and hence much of it was consumed.

II.   AN EVOLVING HUNTER-GATHERER SOCIETY

Early Opportunities

At the very beginning of the age of modern humans, there was, using Pfeiffer's term (1978), a 'creative explosion' marked by rapid technological innovation and cultural change. This explosion of innovation is associated with the emergence of modern speech. The environment was unchanged, the earth still being in the grip of the most recent ice age. But as with all previous biological jumps, the new hominids perceived opportunities to do better than their predecessors by innovating.

Early Responses

Tools became much more sophisticated. Blades with cutting edges at least twice as long as wide appeared; these were attached to wooden shafts to make harpoons, spears, and arrows. Stone was supplemented with animal bones, antlers, and ivory, as well as wood and hides. Rope was invented and used for lines, nets, and snares, which allowed fish and birds to be added to the diet. Fire was fully mastered, with its advantages for light, heat, flesh softening, and the control of germs in cooked animals. Later it became important to toolmaking itself.[15] By 20,000 BC technological advances included spear throwers, barbed harpoons, and bow and arrow—a vastly more sophisticated set of weapons than anything previously available. Shelters became much more elaborate and widespread, including tents and stone houses. Needles and sewing also appeared, making it possible to produce more sophisticated forms of clothing. Necklaces, bracelets, and other forms of personal adornments, as well as statues and cave paintings made their appearance. The diffusion of ideas is suggested by the emergence of well-defined regional art forms and tools that conform to stylistic patterns common to a region, but varying across regions. The list of innovations goes beyond what was needed to subsist, suggesting the emergence of an aesthetic extending beyond a tool's functionality.

Early Performance

As these new technologies were perfected, economic performance improved dramatically. People became formidable hunters, able to take on any beast, no matter how large or ferocious. Clothed in animal skins and protected from the cold nights by fire, people spread to the most remote parts of the globe. The number of people

[15] How and when fire was first controlled and used is still subject to major debate. It seems, however, that it has not been in common use for much more than 50,000 years.

who could be supported on each acre of land increased as hunting technology improved and land area occupied rose. Human populations grew substantially.

Opportunity from Climatic Change

From 40,000 to 10,000 BC many large species of animals such as the woolly mammoths, mastodons, cave bears, woolly rhinoceros, giant deer, and sabre-toothed tigers became extinct. Others were greatly reduced in numbers. Although there is debate about the causes of some of the extinctions, there is no doubt that human hunters were a major contributing factor.[16]

Between 15,000 and 10,000 BC the climate warmed, average temperatures rising by as much as 10°C to about 1–2° above modern temperatures.[17] The ice receded rapidly and many animals followed the retreating ice line northward. The area from the Mediterranean Sea through to India warmed and developed the climate that we now call Mediterranean. Many new wild plants evolved or spread from other niches into newly fertile valleys.

The Response

Some humans followed the gradual northward migration of cold-climate game. Others stayed behind and learnt to live on plants, smaller animals, and fish. The new diet led to a shift in technologies. Most important were the bow and arrow (to hit smaller game more accurately), and new tools to harvest plants, catch game, and cook this more varied diet: 'Thus, a great diversity of plants and animals was being exploited with varying intensities and technologies in a wide range of climates. Out of this vast mixture of peoples, plants, animals, and places the first domesticates and farmers appeared' (Wenke 1990: 232).

The first major step towards settled agriculture was a split between nomadic hunter-gatherers and what Testart (1982) calls 'storing hunter-gatherer societies'. In the wetter parts of the Fertile Crescent that runs from the mouth of the Tigris–Euphrates river on the Persian Gulf in the east to the eastern shores of the Mediterranean in the west, wild grains were found in profusion. As hunter-gatherers depended increasingly on these grains, they found it advantageous to settle. The abundant fish also encouraged settled life because, unlike so many game animals, they did not migrate: 'by shortly after 10,000 BC an almost sedentary population resided in the caves of the region, from Mt. Carmel in Palestine to the Caspian Sea' (Starr 1991: 15).

New technologies were invented for carrying, storing, grinding, and preserving plant food. These included baskets, bottles, jars, grindstones, and cool cellars. As

---

[16] 'Changes in climate and forest cover were partly responsible for their extinction, but many were tracked down and killed by human hunters with improved skills and hunting equipment' (Scarre 1993: 64). Indeed, the extinct animals were all hunted by neolithic hunter-gatherers and were mostly slow breeders near the top of their food chain, which makes them, like the modern whales and eagles, likely candidates for extinction when hunting is accelerated.

[17] Most geographic and climatic facts of this period are drawn from Roaf (1990).

settled food gathering became established, villages grew up in favoured sites. By 9000 BC one of the earliest known settlements had developed at Jericho, near a good water supply. Settled life led to continual improvement in the technology of shelter. Jericho had houses with walls constructed of sun-dried mud bricks and was surrounded by a stone wall.

III.   THE NEOLITHIC AGRICULTURAL REVOLUTION[18]

The great transformation wrought by the invention of agriculture extended over a period from roughly the ninth to the fifth millennium BC in the Old World and came even later on the American continents. The revolution involved two of the greatest transforming GPTs in all of human history: the domestication of plants and of animals.[19] These gave rise to two distinct clusters of innovations that caused the first two of human history's great technological divides. In each case, the divide separated those societies that made the innovation and went on to further technological advance from those that did not, the latter often becoming technologically stagnant.

The Domestication of Plants

Around 10,000 years ago the domestication of plants turned humans into settled farmers. In settled gatherer societies, unconscious human selection gradually altered the wild plants, making them more amenable to cultivation. For example, a single gene mutation removes the explosive characteristic that is needed to scatter seeds in the wild but that inhibited human harvesting. Over time, more and more of the most desirable types would have been found near the campsite as the useful mutations accumulated.

---

[18]   The facts in Section III are taken largely from Diamond (1997: ch. 4–8). Diamond has been criticized for being a 'geographical determinist'. We do not interpret him as holding such an extreme position. Be that as it may, we argue a position that economists trained in the Heckscher–Ohlin tradition should not find extreme: natural resource endowments are an important determinant of production and trade.

[19]   For our purposes, what matters is that the revolution did happen, not why it happened. So we avoid the ongoing debate on this matter. We merely observe that in many ways revealed by modern archaeological studies, farmers in less lush areas than those where farming first began seem to have been less well off than were hunter-gatherers before the mass extinctions occurred. This does not necessarily imply that the first farmers chose a life style that seemed to them inferior to hunter-gathering. First, they were already settled gatherers who had given up the nomadic life for the easier gathering life where food was readily available. Second, although the standard of living of early farmers may not have compared well with those of hunter-gatherers at earlier times, there is no reason to suggest that it was less than the contemporary alternative after the mass extinctions of the easily hunted animals. Third, the harshness of the farmers' existence no doubt increased when they moved to less lush environments than those where agriculture first began. Fourth, the health hazards of a less varied diet and lack of nomadically induced exercise would not have been apparent to those who made the first agrarian lifestyle choices. Fifth, in a path-dependent trajectory, once agriculture had been developed, the population rose dramatically and the bulk of the population was no longer faced with a viable alternative to farming.

The Innovation

At some point, two great innovations produced the GPT of settled agriculture. First, people realized that they could replant some of their seeds and expect to harvest the resulting crop at the end of the next growing season. Second, they discovered that they could alter the characteristics of the species they were cultivating by selecting for replanting those with the properties they most desired. Less intelligent hominids could have been agents of the unconscious part of this sequence of domestication. Only relatively advanced humans, however, could make the innovative jump to doing the same things consciously and inventing the necessary supporting technologies.[20]

Relatively few places around the world had the conditions that encouraged the critical step of the selective breeding of crops. Other places required the technology and seeds to diffuse from those areas. The crops first domesticated in the Fertile Crescent were easiest to tame and, of those eight 'founder crops', only two, flax and barley, are found in profusion in any area outside the Fertile Crescent and Anatolia (Diamond 1997: 141).[21]

The Domestication of Animals

The second great GPT of the neolithic agricultural revolution was the domestication of animals. As with plants, domestication is not the mere taming of animals, but their genetic alteration to accentuate traits favourable for cohabitation with humans. For example, elephants are sometimes tamed and used by humans but they have not been domesticated, since those that humans use are no different genetically from wild elephants. As with plants, most of the initial developments were almost certainly unconscious.

The Opportunity

Many societies that developed agriculture failed to domesticate animals because they lacked such animals. According to Diamond, there are only about twenty animal types suitable for domestication.[22] In areas such as Africa, where earlier human types

---

[20] Indeed in previous interglacial periods (the penultimate one ended about 110,000 years ago), similar conditions must have arisen and, whatever unconscious selection was made by food-gathering hominids of the time, there is no evidence that the crucial jump to conscious settled agriculture was made.

[21] Food production seems to have evolved independently in at least four areas. It arose in about 8000 BC in the lower Tigris–Euphrates valley and its surrounding uplands in what is called Sumer, and spread throughout the Fertile Crescent. From there it diffused to Greece in about 6000 BC, to Egypt soon after, to central Europe and North Africa by 5400 BC, to southern Spain by 5200 BC, and to Britain around 3500 BC. It spread eastward to India and central Asia. It arose independently in China and spread to tropical South-East Asia, the Philippines, Indonesia, Korea, and Japan. It arose independently in West Africa and spread to East and South Africa. Finally, it arose independently in Meso-America and spread to North America. In all cases, as it diffused, the technology was improved by the addition of local crop variations, animals, and technical practices.

[22] Diamond (1997: ch. 9) argues that to be a prime candidate for domestication, an animal needs several characteristics. It must be vegetarian (ruling out much of the animal kingdom); it must have a fairly rapid growth rate (ruling out such animals as elephants and gorillas); it must not need strict privacy

had existed for millennia, these animals had time to evolve a fear of humans before humans become such effective killers. But in newly settled areas, the very character-istics that made some animals domesticable also made them easy prey for hunters. Archaeological evidence makes it fairly clear that when modern humans with formidable hunting techniques entered such previously uninhabited areas as North and South America, they wiped out the domesticable animals. So the initial conditions that favoured the development of societies based on domesticated ani-mals were millennia of cohabitation of evolving hominids and the existence of potentially domesticable animals. When humans evolved the intellectual capacity of exploiting this opportunity, it was critical that the necessary animals still exist.

The Innovation

The best guess from available evidence is that humans did not select animals to live with them but animals elected to live with humans.[23] At some point a decisive innovation occurred. Humans realized that the camp following animals could be put to use. They could be protected from their predators, raised, and slaughtered only as needed. They could supply milk, meat, and materials (hides, bones, etc.). Over centuries both unconscious and conscious selective breeding has caused these domesticated animals to diverge more and more from their wild ancestors.

Effects on S-E Categories

Technology

As with any major innovation that changed lifestyles, the domestication of plants was followed by a burst of supporting technological developments that greatly increased agricultural productivity. In many cases, these innovations raised living standards by providing such non-food products as better shelter and clothing. A partial list of items found in excavations from the time of the neolithic revolutions includes wooden-handled sickles; rush and grass mats bound with string; baskets of twisted coils coated with bitumen; cord varying from fine string to ropes

---

for mating (ruling out such animals as the cheetah, and the Andean wild camel); it must have a relatively docile disposition (ruling out most of the remaining animals from the grizzly bear to the zebra); its reaction to threat must not be to panic and flee individually but to gather in herds (ruling out the widely distributed gazelle along with a host of other jumpers and runners); it must have a social structure that supports three things: herd rather than individual living (so that in captivity it can be kept in groups), a well-developed dominance hierarchy (which allows humans to become the dominant individual), and group life in overlapping rather than exclusive ranges (strongly territorial animals will fight to death with others who are not of their herd). These conditions rule out most animals and what is left is less than twenty species, which are prime candidates for domestication.

[23] Certain types of animals found it valuable to live near human habitations and feed off their crops and waste products. Mice and houseflies are examples where this domestication had little or no human encouragement. But with larger more useful animals a symbiotic relation was established and cemented by the positive feedback mechanism of genetic adaptation of all of the world's animals of over 100 pounds. Diamond (1997) lists only five—cow, sheep, horse, pig, and goat—that were domesticated and put into widespread use, while another nine were used in limited geographic areas. We would add the wolf, the ancestors of all modern dogs.

10 millimetres thick; carved stone bracelets; containers made of lime plaster and ashes, gypsum plaster, or baked clay; lime house plaster whose manufacture required high-temperature kilns; beads, pins, and tools made of copper (probably the meteoric form of the metal that does not require smelting).[24]

Materials made from natural fibres, rather than animal skins, greatly expanded the uses of fabrics. Pottery first appeared in the Fertile Crescent in the eighth millennium BC. Pots were originally shaped by hand and dried in the sun. Later, it was discovered that higher temperatures hardened clay and made it waterproof. The potter's wheel was invented about the same time. These two inventions turned pottery into one of the most important and flexible technologies of its age.

The plough was a crucial innovation following from the domestication of animals. Without draft animals, ploughing was confined to what humans could scratch with light sticks. The draft ox, pulling a plough, allowed the cultivation of previously unusable tracts, and improved the fertility of existing farmland.

The wheel was an important GPT to follow from domesticated animals. Its first certain use was in Anatolia in the fourth millennium BC. From there it spread east as far as China, and west to the shores of the Atlantic. Although the wheel is useful to all, it is crucial to societies with domesticated animals. One wheeled cart, pulled by a team of oxen, can transport loads two orders of magnitude heavier than a human porter. The wheel and axle have many other applications, such as the waterwheel and machine parts. But their original use seems to have been to enable draft animals to pull loads with increased efficiency. Every society that failed to domesticate animals failed to exploit the wheel and, without the wheel and axle, very few machines are possible.[25]

The leap from rollers under large building stones to wheels and axles seems relatively simple. Subsequent leaps, using water to move a wheel and harnessing that wheel to machinery, occurred independently in many societies using animal power. But going from no wheel at all to waterwheels driving machinery with axles and gears seems to have been too great a leap of the imagination. No society is recorded to have managed it. This emphasizes the importance of two things we have repeatedly stressed: historical accidents, in this case having suitable animals available at the time when conditions favoured their domestication and trajectories, in this case from domestic animals to wheels to machines.[26]

---

[24] The list comes from Roaf (1990: 35).

[25] Extensive research on our part has failed to discover an exception to this statement, and since that was done, Diamond has argued the same point. The ancient Mexicans did use wheels in toys, but the challenge of putting wheels to practical use seems always to have been associated with the need to use animal power for purposes of transportation. Diamond (1997: 248) explains the lack of Mexican exploitation of this invention by their lack of domesticated animals. A wheeled wagon pulled by humans offered little advantage over porters carrying loads on their backs.

[26] The one place where the domestication of animals was not accompanied by the use of the wheel was in the highlands of the Andes where llamas had been domesticated by the beginning of the third millennium BC but wheels never made their appearance, perhaps due to the unsuitable nature of the terrain.

Facilitating Structure

Social organization changed as the nuclear family, living in settlements of 100 or so blood-related people, gradually replaced the hunting and gathering group as a unit of production. These settled areas sometimes grew so large that by about 7000 BC several settlements covered as much as 10 hectares with populations of 1,000 or more. Most sites, however, were about one hectare with populations in the range of 50–100. Houses became much more elaborate and rectangular in structure rather than circular. Stone walls up to 6 feet high surrounded some villages. Although the purpose of these walls is unclear, they were not for protection against organized armies, which did not yet exist.[27]

Sometime after the growth of settled agriculture, specialization as farmers and craftsmen developed. 'The precocious use of metals, public works, craft specialisation, long-distance trade and increasing importance of religion all signalled that these communities of the Aceramic Neolithic period [8500–7000 BC] had taken a major step on the road to civilization' (Roaf 1990: 35). Little if any of this would have been possible had humans remained food gatherers rather than food producers.

Policy Structure

The political structure appears to have evolved first from bands of hunter-gatherers to tribes, which are groups larger than bands and have a nominal leader who makes some key decisions, usually in consultation with others. The leader is in charge of food distribution but has no privileged access to wealth himself. Then tribes evolved into chiefdoms, which have a recognized hierarchy of decision-making and are often based on hereditary principles with the rulers having preferential access to the society's wealth.[28]

Non-food producers, including rulers, priests, and craftspersons, had to be supported by the agricultural surplus and various types of taxation arose to manage this redistribution.

Nomadic hunter-gatherers had a limited number of tools and weapons, typically held in common. Settled agriculture and animal husbandry required a much more elaborate array of tools and the need to invest substantial personal effort in these probably gave rise to the concept of private property.

Performance

The few nomadic hunter-gatherers who survived did so in niches separated from agriculturists by mountains, seas, or deserts. Since nomadic hunter-gatherers cannot transport the kinds of physical materials that are needed if technology is to advance

---

[27] The wall at Tell Maghzaliyeh surrounds a small village that occupied less than one hectare. '[T]he site did not need protection against flooding (unlike Jericho) and the wall was possibly intended as a defence against invaders, *though there is little evidence for warfare at this period*' (Roaf 1990: 33, emphasis added). The evidence suggests that 'marauders' would have been a more accurate word than 'invaders'. Other possible uses for the walls were protection against wild animals and evil spirits.

[28] See Wenke (1990: 282–4) for details.

beyond their own limited tools, their needs continued to be satisfied by a static set of organizational and social arrangements and technological artefacts. The engine of economic growth and technological change came to a halt in their societies— although many continued to develop rich cultures.

Food production increased dramatically when farming replaced gathering over many centuries. Farmers exchanged harder work over longer hours for a more secure and abundant food supply. Agricultural surpluses were redirected from sustaining farmers' leisure to sustaining classes of non-farmers, including artisans and priests. There was a burst of supporting innovations, which increased the agricultural surplus allowing increasing amounts of non-agricultural activity to be maintained.

The domestication of animals also introduced many diseases and plagues hitherto unknown to humans. Many of the worst bacterial and viral diseases that attack humans migrated from domesticated animals.[29] These diseases differed from multi-celled parasites since the human body could develop immunity to them. To become endemic, a disease required a minimum local population, measured in thousands rather than hundreds. Without such a population the diseases tend to die out after the first infestation. Most modern diseases—including the ordinary non-lethal childhood diseases—are thus the products of two developments: the domestication of animals and urbanization. (See McNeill 1976: ch. 2 for details.)

Disease became a potent, if unconscious, weapon of urban civilizations. In rural areas, where animals had been domesticated, critical populations were not reached, which rendered rural areas and towns with populations smaller than 10,000 easy marks for conquest by larger cities. The armies of urban societies, immune to most diseases, could increasingly wipe out the armies of non-urban societies, who remained vulnerable. It often seemed to locals that their gods were inferior to the army's gods who killed them but not the invaders. Weakened physically and psychologically, they easily succumbed. This was one natural reason why city states could extend their sovereignty to rural areas and smaller towns. All that was required was that cities become large enough to develop diseases and that enough time pass to evolve the requisite immunities.

Large parts of the Americas, Australia/New Guinea, and the Pacific Islands had no domesticated animals. When Europeans ventured forth in the age of discovery to trade with, and often conquer, newly discovered lands, they brought their diseases. These had the same effect on local populations as they had had on rural populations in earlier millennia. If the locals had domesticated different animals with different diseases to which they would have evolved some resistance, these people would have equally devastated the Europeans with novel diseases. As it was, having had no long-term, close interaction with domesticated animals, they were unprepared biologically both to resist what Europeans brought with them and to 'fight back' with their own domestic brands of disease.

---

[29] McNeill (1976: 51) lists 264 diseases that human populations share with domesticated animals.

Conclusion

The Fertile Crescent was fortunate in being endowed with both plants and animals suitable for domestication. The techniques developed there diffused and evolved through the entire Euro–Asian belt. Further related technological advances followed. Particularly important were the non-human sources of energy that were provided by domesticated animals. Throughout history, power sources have been critical in economic development. Those societies that mastered cultivated crops but not domesticated animals did not experience the technological evolution that the in-heritors of Fertile Crescent's technologies underwent. Diamond goes so far as to argue that the discrepancies in technologies that characterized the world before European technology spread elsewhere in the modern era were pretty well set in place and accounted for by the technological advances that did or did not occur in the neolithic agricultural revolution. We do not go this far—there were many other pitfalls along the path to the Industrial Revolution—but it is reasonable to argue that the domestication of plants and animals was a necessary condition for a long path of further technological developments. The argument for necessity is in two parts: first, nomads cannot carry with them technological artefacts that might evolve into complex production and consumption technologies; and second, settled gatherers do not develop societies complex enough to require writing as a coordinating device, which is a necessary condition for developing a society able to foster further innovative activities.[30]

IV.　WRITING[31]

Challenges

The earliest development of settled agriculture in the West occurred in the upland areas of the Fertile Crescent, where rainfall permitted the practice of dry farming. To the south, the soil was rich, but the lack of rainfall ruled out dry farming. Settled agriculture diffused slowly, and sometime in the sixth millennium BC, neolithic farmers reached the alluvial plains of the Tigris–Euphrates valley. Although the rivers flooded in the late spring—an inconvenient time from an agricultural point of view—the many seepages and old river channels brought enough water to allow the newcomers to farm with the aid of irrigation.

The early Sumerian settlers rose to the technical challenges of wet farming. Upstream, they brought water to the fertile shelves above the river level by using ditches and aqueducts. Downstream, the challenge was to drain swamps and hold back the waters, which they did by banking drainage canals. One constraint on the size of these early wet-farming communities was the small scale of their irrigation

---

[30] While the food-producing societies of the Americas developed rich cultures, they were technologic-ally backward by the standards of a medieval European or even a citizen of the Roman Empire.

[31] Although the theoretical argument in this section owes a large debt to the work of Dudley (1991), the significant historical events are attested by many writers.

projects. If these communities were to grow, some way had to be found to organize larger-scale irrigation projects. This required an increase in political complexity.[32] Specifically, it required a central political authority that could organize and pay for the irrigation works, which had the characteristics of public goods, since once built it is hard to stop any individual from using them. The absence of stone and other basic resources in the region necessitated its transport from upland sources. This presented another challenge in that a technology was required that could help to facilitate long-distance trade. Finally, for the settlements in Sumer to grow, they had to support an increasingly complex division of labour, with the implied increase in local trade. Most of these activities were organized by the religious authorities based in the temples.

Early Innovations

To deal successfully with the rising complexity of trade and construction projects in Sumerian villages, the central authorities required an information technology that could handle the storage and transmission of a complicated flow of information. The key innovation that facilitated the solution to these problems was writing. This is the first great ICT created deliberately. It was a conscious solution to the problems of coordination that went with larger political units and larger engineering activities, and it allowed a complexity of organization that was previously unimaginable.[33] Large villages grew into cities in Sumer long before they did anywhere else in the Fertile Crescent, while many smaller villages were abandoned.

There is debate about the origins of writing. One view is that writing evolved from tokens and counters used to represent numerical magnitudes that were developed soon after the domestication of plants and animals.[34] While 'simple' or 'plain' tokens had existed from around 8000 BC, sometime around 4000 BC complex counters were developed to account for manufactured and temple goods, distinguishing their use from the largely agricultural plain tokens. According to the research of Schmandt Besserat (1992), the first radical, but single-purpose, innovation that started the evolution of writing was the use of counters placed in bullae (clay containers which somewhat resemble envelopes) to record information.[35] Bullae emerged sometime between 3700 and 3500 BC. Later, marks evolved to show what was included in the bullae without having to break them open and count the contents. Seals were also introduced to allow specific agents to be identified with specific bullae.

---

[32] We address below the issue of whether or not irrigation 'caused' the rise of the city. The literature remains divided on this issue. What cannot be denied, however, is that the increasing scope of Sumerian settlements required a substantial increase in what Dudley calls the internal margin of the state.

[33] Although Sumerian writing influenced languages found in Iran, India, and Crete, writing was invented independently, although much later, in at least three other places: China, Egypt, and Meso-America.

[34] This view of writing evolving slowly out of previous technologies is consistent with the history of most other GPTs.

[35] An alternative to bullae was to place tokens on a string. Collecting tokens in this manner existed alongside bullae—an early example of two competing technologies to produce one result.

Writing evolved over several centuries until around 3100 BC a writing complex enough to record written commands and economic transactions had been developed in Sumer. The economic and social consequences were enormous. In a pattern reminiscent of other GPTs, bullae and counters coexisted with writing until sometime around 2600 BC.

As we have noted earlier, debate about what is a cause and what is a consequence are frequently encountered in the evolution of transforming GPTs, since there is often positive feedback among variables. This was the case with three great Sumerian developments: writing, irrigation, and the increasing complexity of Sumerian institutions. All of these occurred over about the same period. Slightly larger cities led to larger workforces to create better irrigation systems, which increased agricultural output; this allowed cities to grow in size but put pressure on the ability of the temple authorities to continue coordinating economic activity. Better coordination techniques and bigger towns led to larger agricultural surpluses and so on.

Whatever its early origins were, once writing came into common use, its further evolution is traceable because the medium then in use, the baked clay tablet, was durable. In its earliest form, Sumeric writing created an important new system of storing information. First, it was not limited by human memory. Second, it had higher costs of reproduction than oral records—one individual can talk to thousands of others, but a written record must be copied to be dispersed. The high reproduction costs caused the writing-based information system to be more centralized than an oral one (see Dudley 1991: 37–9). Third, access to primary information was restricted to the literate few who had borne the fixed cost of learning to read and write. In contrast, the previous oral information system had been decentralized and accessible to all of the population (Dudley 1991: 38–9).

The earliest writing was pictographic. It evolved over several thousand years to a phonetic form.[36] The Sumerian cuneiform did not abandon pictographs/ideographs totally; it remained a hybrid mixture of these and phonetics called 'logo-syllabic'. But it did make the critical transition from symbols that were associated with a picture and/or a concept in the reader's mind to symbols that were associated with a sound.[37]

Effect on S-E Categories

Technology

The positive feedback loops between irrigation, city size, and bureaucracy reinforced each other. The technology of irrigation systems improved dramatically. The bur-

---

[36] The need to organize large workforces led to the need to record personal names, for which there was no obvious picture. The solution was to select a pictograph to denote names either by association or by using homonyms (soundalikes). This was then extended to other words such as parts of speech that had no obvious pictorial representation. In these cases, the symbols stood for whole words or syllables, not for single consonant sounds. These developments began the transition from purely pictographic representation to ideographs and to phonetics.

[37] See Saggs (1989: ch. 4) for an excellent history of the evolution of writing from Sumerian times to early Greek civilizations.

eaucracy grew and became more specialized. Both architecture and building materials co-evolved. Since stone was not found locally in Sumer, the technology of brick was gradually improved until even very large brick buildings could be erected.

Facilitating Structure

As mentioned, the exact causal relationships among these many disparate technologies remains debated.[38] What seems beyond doubt, however, is that the middle of the fourth millennium BC saw major changes in social organization. Writing permitted a dramatic increase in the scope of coordinated activity and the temple became much more important to the economy of Sumer. Previously, people interacted in small groups, everyone knew everyone, and strangers were likely to be enemies. Kinship ties largely determined local trade patterns. After cities evolved, and many smaller settlements were abandoned, the typical resident would come into contact with many strangers. In the small villages of the pre-writing age, the temple only looked after religious matters and was the home of the local deity. With the increased size of city and tax base, larger-scale irrigation works could be financed and the temple became the centre of economic, commercial, as well as religious activity.[39] Among other things, its officials oversaw the distribution of basic foodstuffs and long-distance trade for wood, metals, and other products not available locally.

Over the next several hundred years after the use of writing became widespread, the typical settlement increased by an order of magnitude from 1,000 people (at most) to more than 10,000. For example, the population of Uruk reached 10,000 around the beginning of the third millennium BC, then continued to grow reaching 30,000–40,000 by 2700 BC—such urban populations had to be supported by a large and growing agricultural surplus. The writing-based bureaucracy had scale effects because, once set up, it could administer a much larger volume of activities over a wider geographic area than could any oral-based administration.

[38] The extent to which irrigation works were 'public goods' is in some doubt. Dudley argues that their public good nature is an important element in the rise of a Sumerian bureaucracy. Adams (1960: 281) argues that 'there is nothing to suggest that the rise of dynastic authority in southern Mesopotamia was linked to the administrative requirements of a major canal system.' The link between city size and writing is also disputed in the literature. Dudley (1991) puts a great deal of weight on the development of writing leading to the growth in cities. The timing of early forms of writing in the archaeological record leads Schmandt-Besserat (1992: 6) to disagree: 'These first documents occur in level IVa of Uruk, lagging far behind the rise of cities and the emergence of the temple institution, which was already well under way some 200 years earlier.... If writing emerged so late, it could not play a role in state formation. How then did the Mesopotamian city states function without record keeping?' Adams (1965: 40–1) concurs with his view that 'it is difficult to see the emergence of the towns as a consequence of any monopolistic control of the water supply of surrounding villages, and still more difficult to imagine the growth of their political institutions as a consequence of a need for a bureaucracy concerned with canal management.' In assessing this debate it is important to realize that the crude forms of writing would probably have been evolving well before the time of the first tablets that have survived to modern time.

[39] There is little evidence documenting the relative sizes of the private and temple economies. Most scholars agree that Sumer, after the introduction of writing, became a largely 'redistributive' economy, with most economic transactions being facilitated by religious authorities (see, for example, Schmandt-Besserat 1992). See Silver (1985) for a discussion of the private economy.

Policy Structure

Writing increased the scope for tax collection and management of large-scale public works. Agents could be effectively controlled and monitored, whether they were tax collectors or workers. Elaborate developments could be conceived and executed. The uniform application of taxes by officials who kept careful records allowed tax rates to be adjusted so as not to destroy the tax base, allowing a large volume of taxes to be raised from a group that extended well beyond kinship boundaries. The mechanism to accomplish these things was a permanent hierarchical organization whose employees were specialized in carrying out specific functions. Four classes of temple employees emerged: (*a*) the priests looked after religion and secular duties such as flood control; (*b*) the scribes kept records, collected taxes, managed stores of goods, established accounting prices for all their dealings, and supervised redistributive activities such as provision of goods to the needy; (*c*) skilled workers were employed mainly in textiles and metalworking; and (*d*) unskilled labourers built and maintained temples, canals, dykes, and worked the temple's lands. This temple-based bureaucracy became efficient at managing enterprises much more complex than could be handled by any previous oral-based organization.

Performance

The societies that evolved in Sumer were more complex and wealthier than previous societies. Sumerian agriculture produced a large surplus, providing living standards well above biological subsistence, sustaining an array of cities (some with populations in excess of 50,000). Crops were varied and game and fish were available in profusion. Canals originally built for irrigation provided an important means of transport (again illustrating the spillovers that so often accompany major innovations). Life was hard by modern standards, but it was vastly less harsh and frugal than what had been experienced by those who lived 1,000 years previously, let alone those who first made the transition from hunter-gatherers to settled farmers some 5,000 years before.[40]

Conclusion

The development of writing facilitated intensive and extensive economic growth as well as a host of other social and economic changes that accompanied the rise of cities. Most societies that failed to develop writing remained relatively simple economically and technologically. The only advanced society that did not have writing was probably the Inca civilization.[41] The general conclusion is that whatever

---

[40] See Mieroop (1997) for a detailed study of this life.

[41] The Incas are often quoted as an exception to the theory that writing is necessary for the continued existence of a complex civilization. We do not believe that the debate surrounding this issue is settled. Here is Dudley's explanation (1991: 40–1) of this exception. The Incas did have a means of recording both numerical and verbal information in the form of knotted cords that could be translated by those trained in the task. It was cruder and costlier to transmit and translate than Sumerian writing and hence led to a less complex and more centralized society than that of Sumer. However, the Incas had bronze with its military

the causal links in the early development of Sumerian society in the fourth century BC, in the absence of written records, the highly complex social organizations which characterized that society in the third century BC—to say nothing of those in the second century BC—would have been impossible.

Subsequent Developments

The subsequent history of writing in the Fertile Crescent illustrates a number of important themes that recur in the history of technology. First, the evolutionary paths of various languages depended to a great extent on *historical accidents* of the medium on which records were kept, and on the grammatical structure of the language being recorded. Sumerians wrote on clay tablets. This encouraged the abandonment of any curves and the resulting stylization of writing took its evolution rapidly away from pictorial representations towards phonetically based scripts. Egyptians wrote with ink on papyrus or chiselled symbols in stone. Both of these allowed curves and put little pressure for an evolution away from stylized pictorial representations. The grammar of Sumerian language also encouraged the development of symbols to stand for syllables but not for individual vowel sounds.

Second, whichever evolutionary path a particular language followed, its development was *path-dependent* and largely *irreversible*. Some languages, such as Chinese and Japanese, stayed with pictographs, which became highly stylized and turned into ideographs denoting various non-pictorial objects and concepts. Other languages developed phonetically. Faced with the choice between an ideograph-based language and a phonetically based one, and without an accumulation of past writings to preserve, it is hard to believe that any government would have chosen the former in, say, 1800. But by 1800 the written language that had been selected millennia ago was locked in by the very high cost of shifting from one to another (and by the potential loss of the accumulated literature).[42]

Third, established *vested interests* often block technological evolution even on lines that they had pioneered earlier. The grammar of Egyptian language encouraged the evolution of a separate symbol to represent the sound of each consonant. Indeed, by 2000 BC it was possible to write any Egyptian word using only twenty-four symbols. Yet hieroglyphics remained the predominant symbols well into the Christian era. This failure to make the shift to a truly phonetic and vastly simpler form of

---

scale economies and this led to a much larger empire in contrast to the pre-Bronze Age city states of Sumer that existed for nearly half a millennium after the invention of writing. Because it was highly centralized, Inca civilization could not withstand the shock of the Western invasion. After less than a century of existence, it fell in a very short time to a Spanish army of less than 200 men after Pizarro had killed its leader. From this evidence Dudley concludes that objective records are necessary but they do not need to be in the form of written words; where they were not, as in the case of the Incas, the degree of complexity of organization will typically be less than when written words are used, and the degree of centralization greater.

[42] In the 20th century two countries, Turkey and Korea, did make the switch, but for most the cost was just too high.

writing is an interesting lapse of technological development. A convincing case can be made that the problem lay with the scribes.

The real reason for not simplifying the system was vested interests. The scribes were the experts in writing; every scribe had undergone many years of training to make him proficient in all the intricacies of the scribal art; and the profession enjoyed considerable prestige.... It would have been against the interests of this influential group to substitute for their expertise a system of 24 signs which anyone could have mastered in a few months; the resistance of print unions to changing to a simpler technology offers a modern parallel to this attitude. (Saggs 1989: 74)

The same thing seems to have happened with the scribes in Sumer who resisted simplifying their language in ways that were developed elsewhere in the Fertile Crescent.

Fourth, *pluralism* often allows blocked lines of technological advance to be pursued in other jurisdictions. Neither the scribes of Sumer nor, later on, those of Egypt made the next crucial steps in simplifying language into a truly phonetic system. But others did so. In the latter half of the third millennium BC, Mesopotamian culture and its language spread into Syria. There, in the major trading city of Ebla, the scribes were not as well trained as those in Mesopotamia and they spoke neither Sumerian nor Akkadian, the two languages that were written in cuneiform. The challenges they faced led them to simplify cuneiform. Later, other people in Palestine, Syria, and Crete had scribes who had training neither in cuneiform nor in Egyptian. In their hands, many of the complexities and duplications of the older systems were stripped away. They ended up with a written language that used a little less than 100 characters, each of which combined one of the twenty consonants with one of the five vowels. The next critical step was to specify consonant sounds alone, using one symbol for each. This was only possible in languages where consonants can be specified on their own without ambiguity. The structure of Sumerian made this impossible while that of the Semitic languages was suited to this development. (Once again a lucky historical accident—at least for those speaking one of the Semitic tongues.) The Phoenicians developed a full alphabet of consonants sometime before 1000 BC. Some languages stayed at this point, leaving readers to fill in the vowels from the context as they read words spelt only in consonants. The Greeks, however, took the final step to a modern written language by developing symbols for the vowels.[43] This they had done by 750 BC.

Fifth, the importance of subsequent technological developments is illustrated by the decreasing disadvantage of ideographic languages during the late twentieth century. Computer keyboards, which were developed for phonetic languages, are now adapted to ideographic ones. Translation algorithms make it increasingly easy to move from one type of language to another. From an efficiency perspective, a hundred years from now it may not matter which type of language a society uses.

---

[43] There is debate on the lineage from Phoenician to Greek but we find persuasive the arguments of Saggs (1989: 85–7) that this is the line of descent.

V. BRONZE[44]

Unlike writing, the invention of bronze does not seem to have been a response to a specific challenge. Rather it was an important step in a long history of the incremental evolution of metals, which had been used for millennia alongside stone. (See Chapter 3 for a discussion of the intimate link between the earliest of hominids and their mainly stone tools.) Turning soft porous clay into hard, watertight pottery was the first discovery of the power of heat to change the nature of materials. This discovery of the transforming power of heat was a GPP that created many technological complementarities, particularly in metallurgy. The earliest substantiated use of copper is in the eighth century BC. The first use of smelting that can be substantiated—heating copper ore to around 700 °C—is in about 5500 BC in Anatolia. Here was a great discovery: metal could be extracted from ore by heating it. Repeated hammering could shape the smelted copper. However, this makes it brittle and impossible to work further. Another discovery was that, unlike stone, sufficient heat (just over 1000 °C) would melt copper, which could then be poured into a mould to harden into almost any shape. This required technological advances in furnaces, since open wood fires do not reach the required temperature. By the end of the fourth millennium BC, goods were routinely being produced by pouring melted copper into quite sophisticated moulds. It is unclear where bronze was first discovered but its first widespread exploitation in the West was in the rich societies of Sumer from which its use spread to all of Mesopotamia. Bronze rapidly replaced stone tools and weapons in many uses.

Effect on Structuralist Categories

Technology

Bronze is a copper alloy (small amounts of either arsenic or tin are added). It is easier to cast and stronger than hammered copper. However, due to the scarcity of tin, bronze was an expensive material.[45] Nonetheless, it came into widespread use in Sumer early in the third millennium BC.[46] Although Sumer had neither copper nor tin, it did have larger cities and more complex social and economic structures than elsewhere in the Fertile Crescent, and substantial purchasing power.

Bronze never completely displaced stone. It did so in weapons and high-quality civilian goods but it was too expensive to replace stone completely. Instead, stone merely retreated into more specialized niches until it was eliminated from all but a

---

[44] Although most authorities are in agreement about the sequence of events, Dudley (1991: ch. 27) seems to be one of the few to deal with the far-reaching military and civilian implications of the use of bronze. Our account of these is primarily based on his.

[45] The tin trade developed as one of the early examples of long-distance trade.

[46] Muhly (1980: 26) notes that the third millennium was a period of rapid innovation in metallurgy and contrasts this with the prevailing notion that this was a period of relative stagnation: 'this indicates an extraordinary development in metallurgical technology during the course of the 3rd millennium BC. The rate of technological change is quite astounding. The common belief is that before the 20th century ... technological development took place at a snail-like pace with long periods of utter stagnation.'

very few uses by iron. Bronze was employed in a wide range of civilian uses, as will be attested by a visit to any archaeological museum of the second and third millennia BC. Once bronze weapons came into widespread use, the technology of warfare developed by leaps and bounds to include siege weapons, defensive weapons, war chariots, and a plethora of other evidences of human ingenuity in destructive as well as constructive activities.

Bronze is the first technology whose most important effects were transmitted through military channels. So we must start with its military implications, considering the effects on our S-E categories in a different order than is usual.

Military Performance

Stone Age weapons had limited destructive power and warriors fought with light body protection. Bronze weapons and armour changed everything. McNeill (1982: 1) starts his classic book on military technology with the introduction of bronze weapons early in the third millennium BC: '[B]ronze metallurgy made specially skilled artisans indispensable for the manufacture of weapons and armor... [so that] warrior specialists emerged alongside metallurgical specialists, one class enjoying near monopoly of the other's product, at least to begin with.' Here we see the simultaneous emergence of specialists in warfare and in the working of bronze, as well as organized warfare.

Dudley (1991) argues that bronze weapons altered military technology dramatically. Because Stone Age battles tended to be man against man deploying weapons of limited destructive power, two fighting groups could expect the same number of causalities no matter what their relative sizes. This is what Dudley calls 'constant military returns to scale'. Under constant returns a large army will have an advantage over a small one, but even a very large army will be eliminated if it tries to conquer territories held by many smaller armies belonging to many separate towns and villages. The invading army's losses will be proportional to the total number of defenders no matter how they are split up into small groups. Thus, if faced with enough smaller groups, it will win several engagements but lose the campaign.

In contrast, bronze weapons gave an enormous advantage to the larger army. Using interlocking bronze shields, a larger army could advance in a phalanx and, by turning the flanks of the smaller army, surround and obliterate it while suffering disproportionately small losses. These circumstances are what Dudley calls 'military economies of scale'. When they are present, the invading army's losses over an entire campaign will be smaller the larger is the number of groups into which any given number of defenders are split. Under increasing returns, a well-equipped large army can conquer a vast territory defended by many smaller separate armies, even if the total number of defenders greatly exceeds that of the single conquering army. Thus, size became decisive in battles among equally well-trained and equipped soldiers.

Policy Structure

Some of largest changes caused by bronze were in the policy structure. First, the geographical boundary of the state, which Dudley calls the 'external margin', increased enormously as multicity empires emerged for the first time. This launched the age of imperial wars, which lasted into modern times. However, it took several centuries for the technology of bronze weapons and armour to be fully developed, for armies to be established and drilled in the disciplined behaviour required for an effective phalanx, and for appropriate military tactics to be worked out. During this period of about 2800–2500 BC, the cities of the Fertile Crescent fought many wars. Finally, the fully developed Bronze Age army evolved and scale effects came to dominate.[47] Sargon I, king of the Semitic city of Akkad, conquered the Sumerian cities between 2400 and 2350 BC.[48]

The second big effect of bronze was to shift the internal control of the state from the priesthood to lay rulers.[49] Armies began to be led into battle by city rulers, not by priests. Protection from aggression by adjacent cities and empires led to increasing importance of those who led the army in battle. More and more economic activities that used to be the province of the priests were taken over by the lay rulers.

Facilitating Structure

Defensive walls came to surround almost all Mesopotamian cities before the end of the first half of the third millennium BC. This was to a great extent a response to the outbreak of serious warfare between cities, involving the threat of lethal attack.[50]

Although the palace eventually supplanted the temple in civil administration, its officials could not control the economic affairs of a multicity empire as closely as could temple officials operating in one city. As a result, much decision-taking shifted to private individuals. Market behaviour became more widespread than in the cities of 3000 BC. Artisans and craftsmen traded their wares using newly introduced standardized weights of silver. The first contracts for the sale of land appear in the archaeological records at this time.

Many new economic innovations attest to the growing importance of internal market transactions. (Of course intercity and inter-area trade, which is at least

[47] Under increasing military returns to scale, what determined the size of empires? One possible explanation is that empires grew until the diseconomics of administering and controlling the areas at the boundaries balanced the scale economies in battle of the larger over the smaller unit. A second explanation is consistent with the argument we develop in Chapter 12: for any given state of technology, scale economies always reach a limit beyond which further increases in size begin to create cost-increasing diseconomies. In this case, the argument is that given the nature of bronze weapons, the topography of the region, and the difficulty of controlling ever larger armies in battle, there was an optimal size of army beyond which further increases in size reduced effectiveness. Once states became large enough to field armies of the optimal size, there were no further military pressures leading to further increase in size.

[48] The resulting Akkadian empire was not the end of Sumerian civilization but rather the beginning of the second of the three phases that historians use to divide its period of high importance.

[49] The archaeological evidence shows palaces beginning to appear around the middle of the third millennium BC, suggesting the emergence of a central authority other than the priesthood. The written record testifies to the declining importance of temple transactions.

[50] Walls are found around some earlier cities. Some of these were clearly for flood control while others seem to be defensive but these were probably to keep out marauders rather than armies. There is no evidence of walls that would protect against a determined onslaught of an organized force coming from another city or town before the third millennium BC.

10 millennia old, required individual transactions among private traders, but most intra-area exchanges did not do so until well into the third millennium BC.) Money made its appearance as a unit of account, although minted coins did not come until later. Rulers who could no longer determine economic activities by command promulgated laws governing these activities.[51]

Together the evidence of extensive private landholdings along with bustling foreign trade suggests a further shift in the line dividing private and public activity.... [In Sumer in 2800 BC], a wide range of activities had consisted of internal transactions among the dependants of the temple or palace. A complex system of equivalences or accounting prices had been developed by the officials of the royal or divine household to determine how goods would be distributed. These transactions were now increasingly relegated to the more impersonal mechanism of the market, at prices set by forces of supply and demand. (Dudley 1991: 70)

Performance

The beginning of the Bronze Age provides one of the most dramatic illustrations of the power of a GPT to alter the entire nature of society.[52]

- It altered the expression of aggression by initiating the age of imperial wars.
- With scale economies in military actions came multicity empires, whose growth was aided by the ability to tap large agricultural surpluses to produce public goods (as well as better satisfying the private consumption needs of rulers).
- The growing importance of warfare led both to the declining power of the priesthood, who became more and more confined to religious matters, and to the growing importance of lay rulers, who became full-fledged kings with much political power. This established a dualism between religion and state that had not existed in the earlier Mesopotamian societies, and that persisted in the West throughout most of the rest of its history.
- With multicity empires, the hold of the central authorities over economic matters weakened. What had been basically command and customary economies (at least for internal matters) evolved to a significant extent into market economies.

---

[51] The view taken here is contrary to the once accepted view of Polanyi (1957) that transactions mediated by private markets played little or no part in early civilizations. Although one could argue that Polanyi's political position predisposed him to take this view, we find compelling the objective evidence in such things as the growth in the size of the state beyond its capacity to regulate day-to-day transactions centrally, the increasing use of money, the rise in land sales, and the formulation of laws seeking to regulate much individual behaviour. See Snell (1997: 149–53) for discussion.

[52] When we say that bronze 'caused all these things' we are saying that, given the human propensity to exploit technological opportunities, the introduction of bronze was *sufficient* to have these effects. No one forced people to invent bronze weapons, but once a material with its properties became available, the possibilities were obvious and were quickly exploited. The palace might have triumphed over the temple in a struggle for power without bronze, but the military consequences of bronze were sufficient to end the theocracy and create a dual authority between the religious and the lay leaders. Again other forces that made the society more complex and extended the geographic boundaries of the state would have caused the command economy to be increasingly replaced by a market economy. But in this case the extension of the geographic boundaries that resulted from bronze technology was sufficient to cause this transfer.

- The technologies of societies with bronze as a material and writing as an organizational device were much more sophisticated and the output much larger than any society that existed before the beginning of the third millennium BC.

VI. IRON AND STEEL

Early steels were made by failing to remove enough carbon during the smelting of iron. They were the result of trial-and-error experimentation, and only worked with certain ores. Since steel remained difficult and costly to produce, it did not become widely used for multiple purposes until major production problems were solved in the nineteenth century. Thus most of our discussion of the early developments concern iron, which was only one material in a pyrotechnical revolution that included the invention and increasing use of early forms of glass, terracotta, lime plaster, and cement, all of which would eventually become important building and engineering materials. These all followed from the discovery of an important GPP, the transforming effects of fire. Our discussion of iron does not employ the standard breakdown between our S-E categories. This is partly because its development was spread over such a long period that it is difficult if not impossible to separate its effects on the facilitating structure from the effects of other changes going on at the same time, and partly because the earliest discovery and impacts of iron are not as well documented as other transforming GPTs.

Iron is one of the most versatile and pervasive natural materials in human society; 'at 1 billion metric tons output per year and requiring 5 percent of the world's energy, it is man's fundamental engineering material' (Wertime and Muhly 1980: 6). It is one of the most abundant metals. Because of its widespread distribution across the globe, it has been described as a 'democratic metal'. Iron's relative abundance and low price distinguishes it from its closest substitutes. Much like electricity, iron (mainly in the form of steel) is at the core of many of today's technologies, and is still being adapted to new uses.[53] Only with the advent of man-made synthetic materials has iron begun to lose its status as our most important materials technology.

In its meteoric form, iron was used sporadically as early as the neolithic agricultural revolution.[54] Its development as a practical materials technology progressed slowly and the use of its telluric form (terrestrial origins) became increasingly pronounced from about 3000 to 1200 BC. At this stage, iron was mined in short shafts or stripped from outcroppings. It took the form of poor-quality wrought iron. Furnace technology had not yet progressed to the point where cast iron or steel could be produced. The West's early Iron Age is commonly taken to begin in the eastern Mediterranean in about 1200 BC with the transition from using iron as an ornamental or precious material to using it in everyday practical ways. By this time, early

---

[53] It is interesting to note that it was iron that first induced people to speculate openly about the nature and causes of magnetism, which began the long search to understanding electricity.

[54] A handy summary of the development of iron's production, modification, and use can be found in Forbes (1967: 574–5, Tables 3 and 4).

furnace technologies had become sufficiently developed to permit the smelting of cast iron (early forms of steel were also produced, mostly by accident). Iron tools started to replace bronze, but the process was long and slow. What is called the late Iron Age begins at about 500–600 BC when the 'consolidation of new mechanistic and fire-oriented *weltanschauungen* toward the year 600 BC brought to an end a period of social disorganization in the Mediterranean [see below] and launched a new era of prosperity. The revolution picked up momentum as it was assimilated into a Greco-Roman society evermore oriented to fire-shaped material, rotary motion, mechanism, and growth' (Wertime and Wertime 1982: 22). Thus, the full development of iron, and the realization of its ultimate usefulness as a materials technology, took millennia.[55]

The Challenge

One challenge that may have contributed to the development of iron was the rising cost of bronze. In the second millennium BC the introduction of new agricultural implements such as scythes, sickles, hoes, shovels, and improved ploughs increased the demand for bronze while supplies shrank due to the disruption of trade that accompanied the political disturbances in the latter half of the second millennium BC. The result was an increase in the prices of everything made of bronze.[56] Wertime and Mulhy (1980: xviii) explain the replacement of bronze by iron as 'a combination of circumstances—the interruption of previous population growth; the disruption of trade in copper and tin; the accidental appearance of steel; the shift to new modes of fighting wars, cultivating crops, and carrying on household functions; the first impingements of wood shortages; and the growing influence of mass demands for metals'.

The Innovation

Although compared to bronze, iron was lighter, stronger, and cheaper, it did not displace bronze quickly because its widespread use required innovations in smelting technologies. Iron comes in three forms: wrought iron, which is soft and contaminated by slag; cast iron; and steel (each type contains a different amount of carbon and is smelted at different heats). To become widely used, naturally occurring iron

---

[55] As Wertime and Muhly (1980: xvii) note: 'The gap in every instance between the first appearance of iron, glass, or cement and its adaptation to a social milieu was a long and large one, anticipating the fate of nearly all major innovations in Western Civilization.'

[56] Wertime and Muhly (1980: 2) note: 'The appearance of such drastically new and disruptive technologies thus can be seen as the concomitant of a critical stage involving not just [correct amount of] the carbonization of iron to make steel but the shifting fortunes of agriculture and human populations in the eastern Mediterranean; the interruption of trade in copper and other metals; the movement of iron-carrying tribes from the Black Sea north, south, east and west; and possibly the first effects of a declining supply of charcoal and other fuels in the area.' Waldbaum (1982: 90) shares this view: 'Early experiments with smelted iron as a precious metal and the widespread availability of iron ores naturally led metalworkers to turn to iron when, as seems likely, decreased trade and shortages in supplies of tin drove the price of bronze too high.'

deposits must have their carbon reduced to produce steel, or increased to produce cast iron. Both operations require heat well in excess of what could be produced by early methods, such as fire pits and small, poorly ventilated furnaces.

The early development of steel occurred in the Armenian highlands (where some of the earliest developments in metallurgy took place—gold and copper ores were in use there as early as 5000 BC). Improving the usefulness of iron required removing impurities and, eventually, producing steel and cast iron. The Hittites started producing quality iron reliably for the first time around 1400 BC.

Draught was the key to a furnace's efficiency and the invention of bellows began a long trajectory of draught-producing innovations. First came single draught bellows, then alternating draughts produced by two or more bellows, ultimately ending up with continuous draught when water power was successfully harnessed. In the West, early blast furnaces, which used the gases produced during smelting as a reheating agent, appear in the fourteenth century (Forbes 1964: 190). Wertime and Wertime (1982: 6) see the invention and diffusion of the blast furnace as a crucial event in the ultimate success of iron as a pervasive modern engineering material.

Performance

The early evolution of iron is similar to that of virtually all other GPTs: slow development within a facilitating structure suited to the GPTs it would displace (bronze and stone). Only when it displaced its rival GPTs did iron start to generate major changes in the structure of the economy. The main contrast with most other GPTs is the duration of its stages. As the technology of producing iron slowly developed over the millennia prior to 1200, so did its uses (Snodgrass 1980: 336–7). Early in its development trajectory, iron served as a technically inferior but low-cost replacement for existing materials. As a cheap substitute for bronze, iron at most helped to accelerate the dynamics of the Bronze Age.

Millennia passed from its first use until its full developement as a GPT in the eastern Mediterranean around 1200 BC. Wertime and Wertime (1982: 22) note: 'Bronze did not "end" the Stone Age.... It is now clear that mass-produced iron, not elitist bronze, terminated the use of any remaining tools of stone, bone, and wood, about 1000 BC.' Iron slowly diffused to the rest of the West while its range of uses gradually expanded until it pervaded much of the economy. The transformative effects of iron on society are undeniable: 'Economically speaking iron smelting first made metal tools so cheap that they could be universally used for clearing forests and draining marshes and other heavy work. It is certain that the advent of iron changed the face of the world not only as a new material for arms but also by equipping man better in his struggle with nature' (Forbes 1964: 30).

The efficiency of iron production continued to develop over a further three millennia, until the twentieth century became the age of steel. Before that, iron enabled the development of the machine tool industry in the nineteenth century, which revolutionized methods of mass production; the development of the high-rise building, which transformed the urban landscape; and countless high-precision steel implements, including dental and medical instruments. Its production was a leading sector in the British Industrial Revolution and in the development of the US mass consumption economy. Iron and steel remain one of the most important and pervasive GPTs, even in the twenty-first century.

Surrounding Questions

Several pyrotechnical materials, including iron, were introduced in some unlikely places, and ignored in regions with other relatively well-developed technologies. The Inuit smelted iron soon after their arrival in North America. It was iron, not bronze, that was introduced into late Stone Age China.[57] On the other hand, most of the New World did not use iron (or glass, the wheel, writing, and cement).

Why, for example, did the Old Fertile Crescent and eastern Mediterranean so completely embrace iron, glass, cement, and terracottas as products of fire, while East Asia and the New World did less so or not at all. China...received glass as a diffused product across the silk routes of Asia. And China employed concrete only in the Ch'ing dynasty, at about the time of the coming of the Jesuits.... Meso-America and South America did use plasters, native metals, and some smelted metals with great skill.... But they stopped short of total integration of fire into their lifestyles. The Incan world...was gilded to look like the sun, but not mechanized to work like it. (Wertime and Wertime 1982: 22)

No one knows why. Wertime and Wertime's view (1982: 22) of the pyrotechnological path is similar to the concept of trajectories: that the sequence of innovations may be critical; missing crucial steps may prevent a society from realizing important modern innovations. Whatever the ultimate reason for the varied experiences of different societies, the question of why some societies made the transition and others did not is important in explaining the long-run development of different regions throughout the world.[58] Such diverse experiences with iron demonstrate clearly that inventions are not an inevitable consequence of opportunity and challenge—their occurrence is contingent on many factors.

Was the 'Dark Age' Due to the Military Consequences of Iron?

The end of the Bronze Age coincided with a 'dark age' for the civilizations of the eastern Mediterranean. Virtually every major city from Crete to the Egyptian border was sacked and burned. A dark age then settled on the area for several centuries in the last part of the second, and the first part of the first millennium BC. Historians have offered many explanations including fire and earthquake, but the phenomenon was too widespread not to have had some more fundamental cause. According to Wenke (1990), the most popular hypothesis is administrative breakdown. But that begs the question of why it happened at more or less the same time over such a widespread area.

---

[57] See Forbes (1964: 198–213) for a good introduction to early use of iron.
[58] Wertime and Wertime (1982: 22) note that the introduction of glass and cement 'mark a nearly irrevocable industrial and social commitment to a new fire-based matrix of life.'

We find Drews argument (1993) persuasive: his explanation lies in Iron Age military technology. The military scale economies created by bronze disappeared in early Iron Age warfare and did not reappear until tactics of using iron weapons in large armies were worked out over the next few centuries. Until then, ill-trained and ill-equipped (but no doubt brave) foot soldiers wielding cheap but effective iron weapons could defeat highly trained and highly organized armies equipped with bronze weapons and making extensive use of sophisticated war chariots. The result was the end of the ancient empires and a period of chaos. For a while, smaller, less organized groups of 'barbarians' held a military advantage, but this disappeared in favour of larger armies once the scale economies inherent in Iron Age warfare were developed in the form of new weapons and new tactics. This explanation puts iron alongside bronze as a material that had major social and economic impacts that originated from its effects on military technology. One interesting implication of this explanation is the existence of a feedback that is common in technological history. Iron weapons in the hands of the 'barbarians' allowed them to invade the ancient empires and bring about a period of upheaval. The resulting dislocation of long-distance trade raised the price of bronze and helped to hasten its replacement by cheaper, more locally available iron throughout the eastern Mediterranean.

VII. CLASSICAL TECHNOLOGIES

The first millennium BC saw the rise of the Persian Empire, the largest empire in the Middle East up to that time. Cyrus conquered Babylon in 539 BC and spread his empire to the shores of the Mediterranean. The civilizations of the Tigris–Euphrates valley then passed from being a centre of technological advance and political power. The Persians were well supplied with iron, by then the dominant metal. They had also mastered the horse, which became increasingly important as a military instrument over the last two millennia BC. Persian leaders were tolerant of the societies and religions of conquered races in a way that most previous empires had not been. This assisted them in welding many different peoples into one empire.

The first great opponents of the Persians were the Greeks and then the Romans. Their civilizations significantly advanced both science and applied technology. Living standards rose so high in these classical societies that what we think of as a modern phenomenon occurred: birth rates fell sufficiently to threaten a falling population. Slaves were an important part of their economies. Urban slaves probably achieved a higher living standard than the lower echelons of medieval cities (and it is not clear that rural slaves lived at a lower standard than the poorest dwellers of medieval villages).

Greek science is well known, including some of its practical inventions. For example, Greek geometry aided surveying and construction while the discovery of the principles of mechanical advantage laid the basis for a rational understanding of machinery. (Other societies had used these principles empirically but the Greeks reduced them to a science, an important GPP.) It is often argued, however, that the classical civilizations were not truly inventive technologically. What is clear is that neither the Greeks nor the Romans were responsible for innovating a GPT that would transform the classical world. We say innovated because the Romans certainly used and possibly independently invented the waterwheel. But they did not develop its widespread and varied uses, possibly because slave and animal power were cheap, while Mediterranean rivers were less reliable than those of northern Europe. What they did, however, was to improve, adapt, and apply to new uses the technologies that they inherited from previous civilizations, and to develop some significant technologies that fitted into the existing facilitating structures. The Romans were engineers par excellence, and their innovations did much to raise material living standards, even if none of them were transforming GPTs.

Here we merely list some of the key inventions and innovations of classical times, by way of illustrating that this was a vibrant period technologically. In the first millennium BC, kilns were developed in Greece that could reach over 1000 °C. Keys, lathes, bridges, square sails, steering paddles, and pulleys were all introduced during the same period. Even potters' wheels, which had been turntables spun by the potter, were altered to be run by a large flywheel turned by an assistant with a resulting increase in the quality and range of pottery. The list of technologies that first appeared, or were greatly improved, in classical times includes looms with warp weights and a stick spool, cement that would set under water, levers, screws, ratchets, pulleys, gears, cams, force pumps, compound pulleys, fore-and-aft rigging, chisels, punches, saws, water clocks, metal springs, lead pipes, surveyors transit, coin-operated vending machines, paved roads, sewers, garbage disposal, central heating, heated public baths, harvesting machines, and many scientific discoveries such as the corporality of air.

This is an impressive list. The common belief that the classical world was not technologically dynamic is probably best explained by the fact that no dramatic transforming GPTs were invented to catch the attention of casual observers and that most of the influential classical writers placed little value on technological advances.

Although quantitative measures of GDP are not available, there can be little doubt from qualitative information that living standards during the classical period were high relative to those achieved in most, if not all, previous Western civilizations. How they compared with Sumer in the mid third century BC is hard to estimate. However, the major technological advances in the intervening two and a half millennia, combined with a falling population towards the end of the period, probably indicated significantly higher classical living standards.

VIII.   THE MEDIEVAL AGRICULTURAL REVOLUTION

The second half of the first millennium AD witnessed a major agricultural revolution in Europe. Its technological foundations were the heavy plough, the three-field system, and the harnessing of horse power. Between the sixth and tenth centuries, northern Europe went from a marginal agricultural area into a highly productive one, particularly in relation to labour inputs.

Similar technologies would not be regarded as GPTs in a modern economy. They had a restricted variety of uses, and today agricultural technologies only impact a limited range of the entire economy. They were, however, general purpose with respect to virtually all agricultural commodities and, at the time, agriculture constituted the vast majority of contemporary productive activities (possibly over 90 per cent). So although they are a marginal case with respect to our definition, we treat the group as a GPT on the grounds that it started crudely, eventually came into widespread use across most of the economy, and, as we shall see, had many spillovers. Only their limited number of different uses makes them marginal as GPTs. In any case, GPTs or not, these were clearly transforming technologies with enormous impacts across the whole economic and social order of the medieval West. In so far as there was one, the basic GPT was probably the heavy plough, which created the pressures that led, on the one hand, to changes in the layout of fields and, on the other, to the development of efficient horse harnesses, horseshoes, and other new technologies related to powering the ploughs.

The Challenge

Both the urban markets and the supply of slave labour disappeared with the disruption that resulted from the barbarian conquests of the Western Roman Empire. As a result, the Roman latifundia—large farms producing for the urban market using slave labour—gave way to a new form of organization. Its eventual successor, after several centuries of evolution, was a system of large estates based on farm labourers who divided their efforts between their own smallholdings and the lord's land.

With the end of slave labour, the peasant family had to produce enough to feed and clothe itself, as well as to provide for the lord. So production became the key to survival. Peasants were motivated to improve productivity as long as some of that extra output remained in their hands.

Innovations

The heavy plough, often with wheels, dates back at least to the classical period where it was used in the eastern part of the Roman Empire. It was little used in the West until the sixth century when it slowly diffused over several centuries. Later, an angled mouldboard was added to turn over heavy sod.

The key organizational innovation was the replacement of the two-field system by the three-field system. It diffused slowly throughout most of Western Europe from the eighth to the twelfth century. Although, as is usual with technologies in this period, there is evidence of it having been used earlier elsewhere, it was still diffusing to some areas as late as the twelfth century.

A third important invention was the efficient horse collar. Throughout the classical civilizations, horses had been yoked with collars similar to those that worked well on oxen, which choked the horse as soon as it began to pull. This left the horse as a riding tool, important mainly in war and personal transport while the ox remained the main power for agricultural uses and for the movement of goods (plus the camel for some very long-distance transport). An efficient horse collar was introduced around the eighth century, apparently diffusing from Asia where it was developed by horse-dependent nomads.[59] The horse did not immediately replace the ox as a source of power. Instead, the ox retreated into niches in which it had special advantages, while the horse slowly became the dominant animal for commercial transport and most agricultural uses.

Effects on S-E Categories

Technologies

Many new subsidiary technologies were developed that helped to exploit these three major technologies. The list of tools that were invented or introduced during these first post-Roman centuries includes the harrow, the scythe, and the pitchfork. The harrow saved time and labour by eliminating cross-ploughing, while the other two instruments were important in the production of hay for horses.

Once the efficient harness made horses more useful, the nailed horseshoe was introduced to prevent early loss through broken or rotting hooves. Further important inventions included harnesses for agricultural instruments and wagons. These provided a great increase in the power that could be applied to any one item, something that was particularly important in clearing densely forested land and for ploughing the heavy soil of northern Europe.

Inputs

This set of innovations provides an interesting example of how GPTs sometimes alter the supply of inputs. By reducing the amount of land laying fallow, the three-field system raised the amount of cultivated land in each manor by 33.3 per cent at one stroke. It also allowed two plantings a year. Once the technical problems of harnessing had been solved, the new oat crop that was used for feed allowed the peasants to exploit horse power more efficiently.

The heavy plough and the horse allowed cultivation to spread from the light-soiled Mediterranean areas to the heavy-soiled (and forested) lands of northern Europe, which previously had not been available as inputs for European agriculture. Forest clearance, swamp drainage, and dykes to hold back sea and rivers were all developed in the push to convert the lands of northern Europe to agricultural production.

Facilitating Structure

Lynn White argued that the heavy plough precipitated a revolution in social organization—neither the first nor the last time that a new technology required major

---

[59] There is no reason why the collar and horseshoe could not have been invented in the West at any time over the previous 2,000 years but they were not. Nor is there much doubt that, if they had existed, they would have been used. This is an excellent example of how inventions and innovations that are feasible can remain unmade for long periods, as discussed in Chapter 3.

social restructuring before its potential could be realized. The new plough required a team of eight oxen in place of the two that could pull the scratch plough. To afford this amount of power, peasants had to pool their resources. Also, the difficulty of turning the heavy implement required that fields be laid out in long strips. Holdings could no longer be concentrated in single clearly marked square areas as in the two-field system. Scattered holdings in long strips, ploughed by communal teams of oxen, required joint decisions on all agricultural matters. This gave a social cohesion to the village and helped to establish a tradition of self-government.

Peasants were subjects of the local lord, who provided justice and protection in return for a share of their crops. However, they were largely self-governing in decisions regarding local matters. Although they could sometimes be oppressively demanding in what they took from the peasants, local lords in largely self-sufficient communities were typically much less oppressive in their demands than absentee landlords have been throughout history. After all, they were there to see the detrimental effects of excessive taxation on peasants' incentives.

Performance

The heavy plough, the three field system, and efficient horse harnesses greatly improved agricultural productivity. Peasants also enjoyed a more varied diet as one of the two fields was planted in the spring with a variety of new crops, including root crops and several types of nutritious beans. In the two- and three-field systems, one field was left fallow each year, with the result that at any one time half the land was cultivated under the two-field system and two-thirds under the three-field system. The planting of root crops that was made possible with three fields also allowed the soil to fix more nitrogen and maintain a higher level of productivity than was possible with the two-field system. Planting one field in autumn and one in spring also provided some insurance against crop failure. Horses proved more efficient than oxen in many uses, and the new harnesses allowed many previously impossible jobs to be accomplished with relative ease.

The heavy plough, open fields, the new integration of agriculture and herding, three-field rotation, modern horse harness, nailed horseshoes, and the whipple tree had combined into a total system of agrarian exploitation by the year 1100 to provide a zone of peasant prosperity stretching across Northern Europe from the Atlantic to the Dnieper. (White 1969: 17)

Related Issues

These events raise two issues. The first is a question: Why did a burst of agricultural innovations occur early in medieval Europe? The behaviour of peasants in adopting and adapting technologies that solved the problem of farming northern European land—problems that defied the Romans—is consistent with our view on the innovative capacities of humans where these are not suppressed by institutions hostile to change. The Roman system of latifundia provided little incentive for its labourers, mainly slaves, to improve the techniques of production and develop farming techniques suitable to conditions north of the Alps. Free peasants in the post-Roman era did solve these problems within what, by historical reckoning, is a relatively short time. The system that emerged could not have evolved incrementally out of the latifundia. It required a major structural reorganization that swept away the system of large slave-manned, market-oriented farms and replaced them with peasants working their own land, largely for their own benefit (with a village organization that coordinated their efforts).

The second is an observation. It is interesting that although there were some incremental improvements after 1100, the burst of agricultural innovations and productivity improvements in the first half of the medieval period was not matched by anything similar in the second half: 'During the next centuries [after 1100] there were no comparable improvements in agrarian technology, at least in the North' (White 1969: 17–18). This is consistent with our model of the logistic curve behaviour of GPT evolution (see Chapter 13). It seems probable that the best practice of the system of agriculture that evolved over the first half of the Middle Ages was reaching the limits of its potential to provide improvements in yields. It was increasingly difficult to secure further significant best practice improvements given the available technology, although productivity did vary greatly throughout Europe depending partly on proximity of good markets (Grantham 1999). A further burst of agricultural productivity required the introduction of a radically new organizational technology, one that would have been unlikely to evolve incrementally out of the old system. The incentive to try something new had to be provided and the power of entrenched vested interests to resist radical change had to be shaken. The Black Death seems to have provided both of these requirements by loosening the ties of the old system and providing strong incentives for the development of a new agricultural organization in northern Europe based on much more individualistic behaviour acting through markets.

IX.   WATERWHEEL

The medieval period saw the replacement of animate by inanimate power on a significant scale for the first time in the history of the West. Like many of the critical innovations that transformed medieval Europe, the waterwheel was invented elsewhere.[60] Once a society had wheels and axles for animal-powered transport, using water to push the same wheel seems a likely discovery. The best guess is that the waterwheel was invented independently in several places. But as observed earlier, societies without domesticated animals, and hence without wheels and axles for transport, seem rarely, if ever, to have invented the waterwheel.

---

[60] The first waterwheels known in the West were built by Romans. They were set horizontally in the water and turned a grindstone placed above it. The Romans later invented the vertical undershoot wheel, where the wheel was suspended in the stream that pushed its lower blades. It is unclear when water-driven mills spread into northern Europe but they were widely used by the 9th century. The Domesday Book, drawn up by William the Conquer just after 1066, recorded 5,624 mills in southern England alone.

The Challenge

Although used by the Romans, the waterwheel never became a significant source of power for grinding grain, possibly because of the abundant supply of slave labour. With the end of slave labour and the growth in agricultural productivity, grinding grain became a major problem and the waterwheel was the obvious solution. It spread through Europe as the source of milling power during the first centuries after the break-up of the Western Empire and by the end of the first millennium AD it was found in the vast majority of villages adjacent to rivers or streams of sufficient size.

Effects on S-E Categories

Technologies

Initially, the waterwheel was used exclusively to mill flour. The circular motion of the wheel drove the circular motion of the grinder. For most other uses, a method was needed to turn rotary motion into reciprocating motion. This can be done with either the cam or the crank.[61] The cam was known in classical times but was used only on small gadgets.

From about AD 1000 onwards, the waterwheel-driven cam was used to replace animate energy sources and to mechanize at least some of the production in a wide range of manufacturing processes. Early uses of waterwheels in Europe, together with the earliest established dates of thier use, include:

- making beer (987);
- treating hemp (1040);
- fulling cloth (1086);
- tanning leather (1138);
- sawing logs (1204);
- making paper (1238);
- grinding mustard (1251);
- drawing wire (1351);
- grinding pigments (1348); and
- cutting metal (1443).

There were many other uses. In particular, the iron industry was transformed by water power. Stamping mills broke up iron ore prior to smelting. Mills operated trip hammers for forging the blooms. Waterwheel-driven bellows allowed the heat of blast furnaces to reach crucial smelting temperatures, so that iron could be melted and cast in the way that bronze had been for millennia.[62] Cast iron became an important new product with many uses.

---

[61] The cam can take several forms. One is an eccentric wheel whose rim rises and falls against a lever that is thus made to take on a reciprocating motion. Another is a pin placed near the edge of the wheel, which raises a lever and then passes under it to let it fall. The crank is an axle with a kink in its middle that alternatively rises and falls as the axle rotates, carrying an attached rod forwards and backwards.

[62] The data are drawn largely from Gies and Gies (1994).

Inputs

Water in the form of fast-moving streams became a major new resource. This constituted an important shift in available energy as inanimate power was substituted for animate power.

Facilitating Structure

Virtually every village had its flour mill. The human capital invested in millers was significant and widespread—as is attested by the frequency of the surname 'Miller' in many European languages.

The locations of villages and other water-powered manufacturing activities were influenced by their need to be near running water to power their mills.

From the outset, water mills were capital-intensive. They were expensive to build and often required dams and weirs to create a sufficient head of water. As a result, techniques for pooling capital had to be innovated, particularly to finance mills for purposes other than grinding grain. They were often financed by the sale of shares. Owners sometimes formed what were, in effect, limited corporations to pool both the risks and the earnings of several mills in one locality.

Policy Structure

The growing use of water power for purposes other than grinding corn led to the construction of dams outside village boundaries. When such dams were built on heavily exploited rivers, one mill's dam often created a pool large enough to turn upstream owners' rapidly running rivers into lakes, thus destroying the value of upstream locations as sites for mills. This was a new problem raised by the new technology. Riparian property rights had to be established.[63] Eventually, upstream owners of river banks obtained the right to sue for damages against flooding caused by the builders of downstream dams. This was a clear case of property rights being worked out after, not before, the new technology. The absence of such rights did not impede the early development of the technology. But the technology did create a need to refine property rights.

Performance

The conflict-ridden adjustment that is so common with new technologies was seen with the mechanization of fulling, the beating of cloth to cleanse and thicken it, formerly done by the trampling feet of fullers. One group of hammers replaced many fullers. Riots occurred over job losses in several places, providing one of the first recorded cases of protests over technological unemployment. Carus-Wilson (1941: 39) described the mechanization of fulling as 'a revolution which brought poverty, unemployment and discontent to certain old centres of the industry, but wealth, opportunity and prosperity to the country as a whole, and which was destined to alter the face of medieval England'. This is a familiar technological

---

[63] See Gimpel (1993) for a full discussion.

story: loss of income for those with human capital invested in old techniques; general benefits to most others from reduced prices.

By AD 1000, European society was still underdeveloped by the standards of the great civilizations of the non-Western world. But this was a period when Europe began a trajectory of mechanization that eventually took its technology well beyond all others by the middle of the nineteenth century. Scholars still debate about how widespread the use of water power was for purposes other than milling, but its many uses are beyond doubt. Medieval Europeans seem to have developed a passion for mechanization. When presented with some new technology, their first idea seemed to be: 'How can we mechanize it?' For example, paper was first invented in the Orient and diffused through many countries before reaching Western Europe in the tenth century. Almost as soon as it arrived, the Europeans mechanized the process of beating waste material to create the required pulp. Yet another employment for the waterwheel had been found and put into widespread use.[64]

Both when it was mechanized and when it was not, European manufacturing expanded in scale and scope during the middle part of the Middle Ages. As Reynolds (1967: 185–6) puts it:

There was ... growing manufacture of textiles, pottery, leather goods, and many other things. The list of articles manufactured gets longer and longer, the products get better and better. Prices go up in terms of money but down in terms of man hours because of more efficient management, the application of mechanical power, improvement in tools and machinery, and better transport and distribution.

During this period, Europe's exports changed from basic products such as furs, grains, and minerals to more sophisticated manufactured products. Arms and armour exports reflected the high quality of Western military technology, just as bar iron and copper ingot exports reflected the high quality of European metallurgy, and utensil exports the quality of their manufacturing of some basic goods.

Postscript

In the twelfth century, windmills were introduced from the East, where they had been used to grind corn for centuries. Users in the West soon improved the

---

[64] Holt (1988, 1996, 1997) is one of the few dissenters who do not accept the importance of the medieval European's push to mechanize production. He argues that there is no doubt that 'throughout the period the production of raw material and finished goods remained labour-intensive and that virtually no process benefited from the application of water power' (Holt 1996: 110). We dissent and agree with the majority opinion to the contrary. For just one example, the transformation of the iron industry is beyond doubt and the ability to make cast iron through water-powered bellows on blast furnaces was a revolution in its own right. These bellows raised the temperature of blast furnaces to the high melting point of European iron ore. Also as Blaine (1976: 168) points out: 'We have two meticulous regional studies of the medieval fulling-mill: that by Bautier for France and by Carus-Wilson for England, both of which document its substantial importance by the thirteenth century.' Furthermore, the innovations in management and finance as well as the numerous lawsuits documented by Gimpel (1993: 18–20) would not have occurred if water mills and their accompanying dams were not in widespread use.

technology quite dramatically. Sails were turned from horizontal to vertical. More importantly, the 'post mill' was invented. This was a mill in which the whole structure containing the sails and the mill rotated on a large post so as to face the wind at all times. This transformed the indifferent power source provided by a fixed structure into a highly efficient machine for use on the northern plains where rivers ran slowly and froze in winter. By the thirteenth century, everything that water-driven mills were doing in hilly parts of Europe was being done by windmills in flat northern and eastern areas.

6

A Survey of GPTs in Western History (Part B): 1450–2010

We continue our tour through technological history, focusing on only the most important impacts of some key GPTs, again illustrating the kinds of things that can happen rather than exhausting the list of things that did happen. We also repeat our warning that although most of the technologies are presented around a motivating 'challenge', this should not be taken to imply an endorsement of a challenge-response model of innovation. Many GPTs arise with no obvious motivating challenge, and at other times clear challenges do not yield neat technological solutions. We use this organization merely to highlight the observation that very few innovations occur 'in a vacuum' and some do appear in response to perceived challenges, examples being the steam engine and the electronic computer. Also, as stated earlier, our identification of Western innovations is not meant to imply that many of these innovations were not also made elsewhere, sometimes earlier than in the West.

The knowledge of the effects of GPTs that we include here seems to us to be essential for understanding the role of GPTs both as drivers of technological history and as engines of long-term economic growth. This minimum of factual knowledge also serves to dispel some important myths about the effect of technological change on economies and societies.

I. THREE-MASTED SAILING SHIP[1]

Warriors returning from the Crusades in the twelfth and thirteenth centuries introduced Europe to many new luxury goods and the demand for them became a major cause of the growing Mediterranean trade. The need to move the rising volume of goods with more safety, speed, and efficiency induced many innovations in shipping in the thirteenth and fourteenth centuries. These included an efficient rudder fixed in the centre of the ship's stern, replacing the vulnerable and inefficient elongated oar suspended over the ship's side, charts for navigation, tide tables and compasses, which made navigation possible at night and under cloud cover. Italian

---

[1] It is debatable whether or not transportation technologies should be included as GPTs. Our reason for accepting them as such is given in the introductory remarks to Chapter 5. Whether or not they are regarded as GPTs, they certainly are transforming technologies.

cities used local levies to finance convoys, while marine insurance gave shippers a guaranteed payment for loss of goods and ship in return for a fee.[2]

The Challenge

By the fifteenth century, the Mediterranean economy was in decline. Increased incidents of piracy, obstruction of land-trading routes, and heavy taxation of spices by the Turks were contributing factors. The Portuguese responded by seeking a new route to the East, slowly and incrementally exploring down the coast of Africa. In the process, they found new Atlantic fishing grounds, and they began the European exploitation and expansion of the existing African slave trade (Solsten 1994: 23).

The Innovation

The major breakthrough in ship design that resulted in the Portuguese caravel, and several closely related designs, occurred in the fifteenth century. The generic design was a three-masted ship whose main propulsion was provided by two masts, each equipped with square sails, which are efficient in sailing downwind. Beating against the wind was nearly impossible with only a square sail, which was the standard rig in the cog that preceded it.[3] The three-master's ability to sail windward was provided by its special fore-and-aft rigging. Forward, a long bowsprit served to anchor triangular shaped foresails that gave the ship added stability and greatly added to its ability to beat into the wind. Aft, a third mast was equipped with a lateen sail—a sail hung from a single spar that is raised up the mast at a sharp angle by pulleys and held by guy ropes. This rigging allowed the sail to take on any angle facing to one side of the ship and so greatly enhanced the ship's ability to sail upwind.

A second set of innovations involved hull design. The old clinker design of overlapping planks gave way to planks that butted each other evenly and were sealed with caulking. This allowed interior reinforcing and load-bearing decks that eventually were able to carry an enormous weight of cannons and other equipment.

The Portuguese push down the coast of Africa was aided by a positive feedback loop, which, as we have noted with other GPTs, is common in technological change. The further they got, the more they needed better navigational aids and better ships; the better the navigational aids and ships that were available, the further they could go. When they began, they were using two types of small ships, the barcha and the barinel. Later, they shifted to the caravel, which they were building by the 1430s.[4]

In 1487, Bartholomew Dias sailed beyond the tip of Africa, proving that the Atlantic did in fact connect to the Indian Ocean. In 1498 Vasco da Gama reached India. In the mean time, the Genoese sailor, Christopher Columbus, set sail under

---

[2] See Unger (1980: 173) for more detail.

[3] A modern sailing vessel can sail to within 45° of the direction of the wind. So to make mileage in the exact direction from which the wind is coming, the ship must cover 2 miles of ocean for every mile made towards its destination. The best three-masted sailing vessels could beat to within only 60° of the wind's direction; cogs did much worse and so spent long periods in port waiting for favourable winds and much time at sea being blown in the wrong direction.

[4] See Diffie et al. (1977) and Hutchinson (1994) for more detailed discussions of these events.

the Spanish flag for India, and discovered America in 1492.[5] In 1500, Cabral discovered Brazil, launching Portugal into the New World alongside Spain. In 1519, Magellan set out with five ships. When the sole surviving ship returned, the world had been circumnavigated and the spices in the ship's hold were more than enough to pay for the expedition. In just over 100 years since the Portuguese began their expansion down the African coast, European navigators had discovered the outlines of the entire globe. As the sixteenth century wore on, ships improved in seaworthiness, navigation aids increased, and European knowledge of the world was filled in as more and more of it was mapped and charted. All of these developments gradually reduced the risks associated with long-distance travel by sea.

Effects on S-E Categories

Technologies

Like most great innovations, this type of ship had roots that stretched well back in history. Further, its burst of rapid development was followed by a long period—several centuries in this case—during which its basic form remained unchanged while it underwent many marginal improvements in its own, and related, technologies. These incremental improvements slowly but steadily increased its safety, efficiency, and range of applications both as a fighting machine and as a merchant vessel.

The most interesting spillovers to other technologies concerned magnetism and the compass. Europeans had long been aware of the problem of 'variation', that their compasses did not point to true north. When the Portuguese explored down the coast of Africa, the angle between magnetic and true north did not change drastically so they found no new problems with their compasses. But when Columbus crossed the Atlantic, his navigators found their compasses continually changing their angle with true north. From then on, compass variation became a serious navigational problem. It was an even more serious problem for the English than the Spanish and Portuguese because, cut off from the spice trade, the English were confined to northern waters where the angle of variation changed much more rapidly than in the tropics. In 1581, an Englishman, William Borough, published a book dealing solely with compass variation and its measurement. Robert Norman investigated inclination, finding that the compass always pointed below the horizon at an angle of 71.5°. These were problems that Aristotelian natural philosophy could not deal with, and those who were striving to understand magnetism began to become more confident in their opposition to the prevailing Aristotelian science.

Then in 1600, William Gilbert published *De Magneta* and thereby became the first early modern English scientist to gain international repute (Pumfrey 2002: 4). Gilbert systematized the observations of others and conducted a series of ingenious experiments with a model of the magnetic earth around which he 'sailed' making compass readings. With his daring hypothesis that the earth was a gigantic magnet, he turned magnetism from a body of empirical observations into a science. Locating

---

[5] The expedition included three ships of varying design but all equipped with three masts, two of which carried square sails, while the mizzenmast carried a lateen sail.

the magnetic north pole near, but not at, the true North Pole explained deviations; locating it below the earth's surface explained inclination. With this one book, English understanding of magnetism leapt ahead of the Chinese, whose piecemeal knowledge of magnetism had existed for centuries with no recorded attempt to make a science of it. Since magnetism is closely related to electricity, Gilbert also took one of the first steps, and it was an enormous step, towards the invention of the dynamo and practical electrical power. We say more about this remarkable work in Chapters 7 and 8, where we also further discuss the comparison with Chinese knowledge of magnetism. The development of the science of magnetism illustrates the often surprising complementarities between technologies—here the three-masted sailing ship on the one hand and magnetism and electricity on the other.

Inputs

As often happens, the new GPT altered the relative importance of many inputs. Wood for shipbuilding became an extremely important resource. Over the next few centuries much of England, Ireland, and many parts of the continent were deforested to provide wood for the ever-expanding number of ships at sea (as well as providing charcoal for the smelting of iron). Slaves taken from Africa became an important resource in the West for the first time since the dissolution of the Roman Empire. They were extensively traded and used in production in much of the Americas, both the islands and the mainland.

Facilitating Structure

An important aspect of the facilitating structure is location. With the three-masted ship, the central location of economic activity shifted to the Atlantic coast while the Mediterranean region 'subsided into relative backwardness, beginning shortly after 1500 and becoming sharply marked a century later' (Rowen 1960: 36). As the three-masted ship was developed and refined to a state where Atlantic coasting was relatively safe and regular, overland trade with Europe became a less important and more costly alternative. According to Braudel (1982: vol. II, 91–2), these developments sealed the fate of the Champagne fairs that depended on the overland routes.

The organization of firms and the mixture of their products changed greatly. The Italian system of trade had evolved over centuries to meet Mediterranean conditions. The development of the Portuguese sea route to the East undermined this established Venetian system, which slowly declined because its structure was not compatible with the style of market competition that was emerging in the Atlantic trade.

Supporting financial institutions also went through some major adjustments. As the Atlantic trade grew, many institutions were either born, or greatly enhanced, as a result of the need to invest large amounts of capital under very risky conditions. Joint stock companies and marine insurance were two of the most important examples. Italy's financial institutions arose around the large trading monopolies, and the institutions and financial instruments were designed to accommodate these large players (Braudel 1982: vol. I, 474 and vol. II, 433–55). Northern markets tapped new pools of capital by also catering to less wealthy investors.

Venetians had problems with labour and human capital. Because of the expansion of Atlantic trade, many sailors migrated from the Mediterranean to the north of Europe causing Italian seamen's wages to double over the sixteenth century. In the shipbuilding industry, skilled Italian craftsmen were trained in building galleys and their high wages allowed them to share in the monopoly profits from Eastern trade. But with the shift to the construction of round ships, the skills of the Italian shipbuilders lost value. But shipbuilders' wages had become entrenched in Venice and were not easily reduced. As a result, Amsterdam became a lower-cost builder than Venice (Braudel 1982: vol. II, 360, 365–6 and vol. III, 136, 190–2).

The systems of paying sailors had strong effects on the formation of human capital to meet the changing location of trade patterns. The English paid their sailors by the voyage while the Italians paid by the day. Although the Italian system was probably well suited to Mediterranean conditions, it caused problems when the Italians entered the Atlantic trade. English sailors would weather tough storms to complete a voyage quickly while Italian sailors would stay in harbour awaiting the most favourable winds. Thus the English sailors endured a process of learning by doing in facing the tougher weather than did the Italians.

Much new infrastructure was needed. Shipping along the Atlantic required its own structural adaptations. Port cities, some of them previously only fishing towns, became the centres of trade, banking, and shipbuilding. An elaborate apparatus was developed for production, distribution, and sale of basic materials going from the rest of the world to Europe, manufactured goods from Europe to Africa, and for slaves going from West Africa to the colonies. Large capital investments were required to provide the needed ships, port facilities, fortified bases, docks, storage warehouses, and a host of other facilities. Facilities were also established for the collection of slaves from West Africa (where they were mostly supplied by local black rulers), transporting them and distributing them to where they were to be employed.

There were many social changes. In particular, merchants became the class of the newly rich, their economic power eclipsing that of landowners in many countries, including England.

The different behaviour of the established agents in the Mediterranean countries and the usurpers in the Atlantic countries illustrates the value of the S-E approach and the evolutionary hand view of the market first discussed in Chapter 2. A maximizing model would have agents in both locations responding rationally to the new set of circumstances. As it was, agents in the Mediterranean countries were hampered by the inertias of established vested interests and long-established behavioural routines. Newly entering agents in the Atlantic countries were able to be more flexible. The evolutionary hand of the market showed that one set of policies was much better than the other by rewarding large profits to those on the Atlantic coast and inflicting losses on those in the Mediterranean. The former prospered and expanded while the latter languished and declined. The contrast in behaviour could not be explained without an arrow of time and a path-dependent view of the influence of past behavioural patterns on current decisions.

Policy and the Policy Structure

On a geopolitical scale, countries vied with each other in commerce and war for control of the vast new set of commercial possibilities. England and Holland vied for control of the Spice Islands and the Dutch finally won. England, Spain, and France vied for control of North America. Victory finally went to the American rebels from the English crown with a residual held by Spain for a while and England for longer.

The most successful governments, the English and Dutch, learned to cooperate with the new bourgeoisie rather than regard them merely as sources of tax revenue.

On the one hand, the government's ability to control commerce was weakened because it was much more difficult to police the seas than the land with the technologies of the time. On the other hand, cargoes landed at port were easily measured, and therefore taxed, which added to government revenues. For centuries tariffs were the largest single source of government revenues in many countries.

Performance

Soon after the Spanish and Portuguese reached India and the New World, great wealth poured into Europe in the form of precious metals, spices, and luxuries. Sugar, tropical fruits, and cotton followed. Colonies were established throughout the sixteenth century, and, at the beginning of the seventeenth century, temperate North America was successfully colonized. Settlements in Virginia and New England started a course of events that was to culminate less than two centuries later in the American Revolution, which established a country that was eventually to challenge and surpass Europe both economically and militarily.

The burst of 'Smithian growth' that ensued was based on globalized commerce rather than local manufacturing. The economy of Western Europe became a commercial one with foreign trade as the major generator of new wealth and power, the slave and spice trades founding many fortunes. The main economic (and political) power shifted from the Mediterranean, whose fluky winds and shallow harbours are not well suited to three-masted ships, to the nations on the Atlantic coast, where Mediterranean galleys rowed by slaves were inefficient in the rough Atlantic waves. Significant parts of the non-European world came under the influence of Spain, Portugal, Holland, England, and France, the five main countries with long coastlines on the Atlantic ocean. The colonizers encountered peoples who had not domesticated animals and thus had no immunity to the diseases that Europeans had been living with since the neolithic agricultural revolution. The majority of many affected local populations succumbed to these diseases, making it much easier for Europeans to establish and maintain such colonies.

Conclusion

Although these changes had many causes, including superior European weapons of all types, they could not have happened if Europeans had been unable to sail the entire high seas in reliable ships that were large enough to carry significant amounts of cargo and weapons. The introduction of three-masted sailing ships clearly changed the world dramatically—making it better for some and very much worse for others.

II. PRINTING

As we saw in Chapter 5, the existence of a written language is important to the development of a complex and technologically dynamic society. Because it so dramatically altered the cost structure of reproducing text, the printing press is an information and communication GPT of enormous importance.

The European mechanization of printing was the outgrowth of two earlier developments. The first was the introduction of paper, a Chinese invention that was made around AD 100 and that entered Europe from Islamic Spain in the twelfth century. Paper facilitated early growth in commercial activity by lowering the cost of storing information, and assisting 'the growth of credit in the use of documents for insurance and bills of exchange. With Arabic numerals it enormously enhanced the efficiency of commerce' (Innis 1972: 128). It also increased the relative importance of the vernacular over Latin, a trend that was accelerated by the printing press.

The second early development was printing with wooden cut blocks and engraved metal plates, the latter being used mainly to produce copies of objects such as playing cards. There had been printing in China utilizing negative surfaces cut into wood blocks since about the late sixth century. The blocks were costly to produce, which kept the unit cost of small print runs high. They also deteriorated rapidly with use, limiting the ability to lower unit cost by increasing print runs. This method of block printing was widely known in Gutenberg's time and survived in limited use until well after the introduction of the printing press.[6]

The Challenge

During the fifteenth century, a fall in the price of paper and the beginnings of the rise in literacy that greatly accelerated in the following century led to a search for a technology that could effectively replace the manuscript.[7] Numerous guilds and monopolies controlled the production of handwritten manuscripts, inflating their price and increasing the pay-offs to such a search.[8] This is one of the many historical cases where a transforming innovation was made in response to the demand arising

---

[6] Day (1996: 669) notes that 'the number of copies that could be printed from a block of wood was limited and, far more serious, when the print run was finished, the woodblocks had to be discarded and fresh blocks made for a different text.'

[7] Hirsch (1974: 10) notes four factors that contributed to an increased demand for printing services: (*a*) revival of learning in the 15th century; (*b*) improved transportation; (*c*) founding of new universities; and (*d*) lowering of the cost of paper.

[8] 'It was significant that these attempts were made in territory marginal to France, in which copyists' guilds held a strong monopoly, and that they were concerned with the production of an imitation of manuscripts such as Bibles, i.e. Latin Vulgate, which commanded very high prices, partly as a result of its size' (Innis 1972: 141).

from a perceived need (whereas in other cases the demand came after the innovation was made).

The Innovation

Gutenberg's revolution came with his use of metal rather than wood for the print blocks, with movable and reusable typeface, and with the press itself. In using metal for print blocks, Gutenberg was following the tradition of goldsmiths, who cut punches for trademarks, lettering, and inscriptions on cups, bells, and so on.[9] The press was an adoption of the winepress, introduced into Germany by the Romans 1,000 years previously. To be efficient, its mechanical motion had to be simple. Early improvements included making the turning action easier and allowing a shorter motion to depress the face.

Two mechanical challenges led to Gutenberg's most important innovations. First, the blocks used in the printing press had to produce precisely aligned text, regardless of the order in which they were used and despite their varying thickness. They also needed to be inexpensive and of consistent quality.[10] His solution was to invent the typecaster's mould, which was made of iron and copper and which held the blocks together. Second, an ink was needed that would adhere to the printing blocks, an ink with 'chemical properties very different from those of the ink with which impressions were taken from woodblocks' (Steinberg 1996: 8).[11] Here his solution was to develop an ink that 'was similar to that used by scribes, an aqueous solution of gum with either lamp-black or the more finely divided ferric gallate in suspension as the pigment' (Clapham 1957: 381).

Gutenberg's real genius lay in his ability to combine elements of various industries and specialities, bringing them together to produce a commercially viable technology. His invention of modern printing is an excellent example of an invention with many precursors; an invention that combined several existing technologies in novel ways, producing 'a revolution out of evolution'.[12]

After a slow start from 1450 to around 1500, the printing press diffused quickly thereafter. By the early sixteenth century there were 40,000 separate printed works in Europe, representing around 20 million individual books. As with the diffusion of any transforming GPT, many factors were at work, including the spirit of 'open-mindedness' after the Renaissance, an existing high level of demand for printing

---

[9] There is evidence that movable type was used in Korea and Turkey in the 13th century, but it does not appear that these early versions of the printing press influenced Gutenberg (Day 1996: 670).

[10] Gutenberg 'introduced to Europe, more than three centuries ahead of its general adoption by industry, the "theory of interchangeable parts" which is the basis of all modern mass-manufacturing technique' (Steinberg 1996: 8).

[11] This breakthrough was among the most important and may not even have been Gutenberg's. 'A major contribution to the art of printing was the invention of an improved ink consisting of a pigment . . . ground in a linseed-oil varnish: it remained the standard printers' ink for more than four centuries. The inventor is unknown' (Clapham 1957: 381).

[12] Although Mokyr lists printing with movable type as one of his macro inventions, it certainly was not a chance discovery appearing out of the blue without clear antecedents.

services, the general growth of European economies, and printing's freedom from guild restrictions.[13]

Effects on S-E Categories
Technology

Language systems display strong network externalities. For a communications network to grow, both senders and receivers must use the same language. Dudley (1991: 151) argues that early printing was caught in a low-level equilibrium: 'As long as most printed information was in Latin, a language that the great majority of people could not speak, there was little incentive to learn to read. However, since the majority of the literate public could read Latin, there was little incentive to publish in the vernacular.' Furthermore, the grammar, spelling, and word usage of the vernaculars typically differed from region to region. Printing could not reach the mass of people until the vernaculars were standardized. This required the development of national, or at least regional, languages and workable grammars. Both were developed by a combination of public and private efforts. In larger markets, especially France and Spain, where capturing even a small percentage of readers would offset the fixed costs of production, printers themselves reduced the variations in vernaculars. Religious and political authorities also played a role.

Over the course of the sixteenth century, the ratio of works published in Latin to all work published fell rapidly. These developments produced an enormously important derivative innovation complementary to the printing press: language went from being the domain of the elite, a fractured code that tended to divide, to a powerful unifying force. This change was instrumental in spreading the scientific method (Eisenstein 1983), changing the structure of the Church, assisting in the rise of the nation state, and effecting many cultural changes.

Facilitating Structure

Over the centuries, an infrastructure had grown up around the production of written works in monasteries, including facilities to train scribes, produce paper, and distribute manuscripts. Printing required an entirely new structure. Production shifted from monasteries to profit-seeking firms. These early printing firms tended to use only a few presses, with a single person doing the editing, typesetting, printing, publishing, and selling. Nearly 100 years passed before a finer division of labour began to emerge within the printing industry. By then, almost every major centre in Europe had an established printing press.

Although there was a range of capital requirements for the new printing firms, by and large, they all had high minimum efficient scales (MESs) of production, and in some cases the capital requirements were huge.[14] The sunk capital invested by early

---

[13] As Steinberg (1996: 8) notes: 'Letterpress printing was in the air, else Gutenberg's invention would not have spread with such lightning speed through the Rhine towns.'

[14] In Nunberg, Anton Koberger set up a printing shop that combined printing, publishing, and bookselling with 24 presses, served by over 100 workers (compositors, proofreaders, pressmen,

printers made them much more vulnerable to labour disturbances and downturns in business. It seems safe to infer from all this that the industrial concentration increased in the printing industry.

An important element of the facilitating structure is the distribution of human capital. The growth of printing threatened existing scribe-based labour, and in some cases they fought back.[15] However, such local efforts to block the diffusion of the printing press mainly failed. Printing created many new skill categories and changed the nature of others. For example, after the advent of printing, type founding became important as printers competed with different font types to win customers. The printing press brought many occupations under the same roof.

In the age of scribes, book-making had occurred under the diverse auspices represented by stationers and lay copyists in university towns; illuminators and miniaturists trained in special ateliers; goldsmiths and leather workers belonging to special guilds; monks and lay brothers gathered in scriptoria; royal clerks and papal secretaries working in chanceries and courts; preachers compiling books of sermons on their own; humanist poets serving as their own kind of scribes. The advent of printing led to the creation of a new kind of shop structure; to a regrouping which entailed closer contacts among diversely skilled workers and encouraged new forms of cross-cultural interchange. (Eisenstein 1983: 55)

There were many battles over property rights for the printing of specific texts: 'Competition over the right to publish a given text also introduced controversy over new issues involving monopoly and piracy. Printing forced a legal definition of what belonged in the public domain. . . . The terms plagiarism and copyright did not exist for the minstrel. It was only after printing that they began to hold significance for the author' (Eisenstein 1983: 121). Once again, we have an example of property rights issues following, not preceding, an important innovation.

Policy

From the start, the printing press weakened the Catholic Church's ability to enforce its 'policies'.[16] The Church saw the ability to transmit information with little alteration, and little control, as a threat. It tried to suppress the printing of Bibles and other important material: '[T]he shift in book production dealt a relatively swift

---

illuminators, and binders) (Steinberg 1996). Gutenberg received 1,600 guilders for his press (the chancellor of Mainz at the time made between 103 and 208 guilders per annum). Establishing the press at the monastery of St Ulrich cost 700 guilders; using contemporary prices this cost 19 tons of wheat (Hirsch 1974: 32). The total cost of establishing the press at St Ulrich was 55 tons of wheat.

[15] For example, one well-known story concerns Gutenberg's business partner, Fust, who took a print run of a dozen Bibles to sell in Paris. The local book-trade guild was '[a]larmed at the appearance of an outsider with such an unheard-of treasure of books; when he was found to be selling one Bible after another, they soon shouted for the police, giving their expert opinion that such a store of valuable books could be in one man's possession through the help of the devil himself and Fust had to run for his life' (Goldschmidt, quoted in Eisenstein 1983: 49).

[16] Printing lowered the costs of distributing decisions made by early 'policymakers'. Many identical copies of political edicts and Papal Bulls could now be produced in a fraction of the time and cost previously required. A major impact of printing was to shift the locus of political power away from traditional sources, as GPTs in the ICT area often do.

blow to the ecclesiastical influence, which had remained relatively strong despite the expansion of lay book production and the development of lay piety during the later Middle Ages' (Eisenstein 1983: 398).

In England, the character of the printing trade was fundamentally influenced by policy. Early attempts at attracting foreign printers to England were so successful that by the early sixteenth century, foreigners were dominating the industry. Several acts were then passed in an attempt to protect the English printing industry, restricting it in size and leading to greater government control.[17] These restrictions increased England's dependence on the Netherlands for printed materials and led to the rise of underground publications that avoided censorship.[18] Finally, towards the end of the seventeenth century, the policies were abandoned and the English printing trade expanded greatly. This experience illustrates the importance of European pluralism when items difficult to print in England were printed elsewhere.

The fall in the relative price of reproducing codes of law facilitated the increased separation of law from political power, building on earlier trends.[19] Printing created increased stability and uniformity in law. Secular leaders faced similar problems as did Church leaders in maintaining centralized control of the state. It was more difficult to alter codified policies and laws to suit a leader's changing goals than policies and laws based on tradition alone. The accumulation of laws and policies also increased the complexity of institutions, making it very difficult for a single person, or even a small group of individuals, to control them. Power increasingly devolved to the bureaucracy, which weakened the central authority.

Performance

Printing drastically reduced the number of man-hours required to produce a book. 'A man born in 1453, the year of the fall of Constantinople, could look back from his fiftieth year on a lifetime in which about 8 million books had been printed, more perhaps than all the scribes of Europe had produced since Constantine founded his city in AD 330' (Clapham 1957: 37). Even more important in the long run, that same man could purchase several hundred printed books for the cost of one scribal manuscript.

---

[17] Governmental decrees in 1586 and 1615 restricted the number of presses (London was allowed twenty-two) and a star chamber decree in 1637 further increased restrictions on the business of printing (Innis 1972: 150). Whereas through the 16th century every important town in North Western Europe had a press, '[i]n England the trade was artificially confined, more or less, to London by government restrictions' (Febvre and Martin 1997: 198).

[18] 'Abolition of the star chamber courts in 1641 was followed by intense activity in the publication of pamphlets and news books supporting parliament or royalty.... Success of parliament was followed by suppression, and the policy was continued after the Restoration' (Innis 1972: 150).

[19] The introduction and diffusion of the printing press had important impacts on the development of common law. The advent of the printing press allowed for the reproduction of important legal texts, which allowed the law faculty to teach law as a holistic body of knowledge. As Eisenstein (1983: 71) notes: 'The medieval teacher of the *Corpus Juris* was "not concerned to show how each component was related to the whole," partly because very few teachers on law faculties had a chance to see the *Corpus Juris* as a whole.' Printing also allowed for precedent, of critical importance for the common law, to be more easily recorded and diffused.

With the press came job printing. This important aspect of the printing revolution permitted made-to-order products. 'It lent itself to commercial advertising, official propaganda, seditious agitation, and bureaucratic red tape as no scribal procedure ever had' (Eisenstein 1983: 59). Job printing contained elements of mass production. Large runs of a single standard product, such as an advertisement, shared more with modern production techniques than with traditional craft production.

Not only were the total costs of producing a printed page lowered but the balance between fixed and variable costs of each item also changed dramatically. As well as having a high fixed cost of an individual printing establishment, the cost of producing each printed page was mainly the fixed cost of typesetting, while the marginal cost of producing an additional copy of that page was little more than the cost of paper. In contrast, the cost of producing additional hand copies of a given page were the cost of the scribe's time (plus the parchment or paper). By so altering the balance between fixed and variable costs, the mass production of books and pamphlets enabled communication strategies such as the Protestant appeal to the masses through pamphlets. Such a strategy would have been prohibitively expensive with scribe-copied manuscripts.[20] The Protestant Revolution could not have occurred, at least in the form that it took, without the printing press.

Dudley (1991) is one of the few economists to have considered the wider economic impacts of printing—using economic theory to link economic growth in Northern Europe to printing. He argues that the introduction of printing is one of the critical innovations that distinguish the early modern period, and the start of the dominance of North European states, from the previous era dominated by eastern traders and trade-based city states of southern Italy. (The three-masted sailing ship was another.) By allowing information to be cheaply and reliably reproduced, printing made centralized states less costly and threatened the Church's monopoly of knowledge.

The dual impact of this dynamic was felt most strongly in the Dutch Republic. Because the Netherlands maintained an open policy on publishing, many developments in printing originated there. For example, the Dutch publisher Plantin managed to integrate engravings into published works, revolutionizing scientific literature. Antwerp saw a rapid spread in printing services: 'A daily bourse at Antwerp required a permanent news service to provide information on the rating of business houses of different nationalities' (Innis 1972: 147). As Dudley (1991: 176) puts it: '[O]nce the highly educated Dutch created their own information network, the resulting efficiency gains were so great that they were able to bear a load of taxes that astonished their European contemporaries. Not only were the Dutch able to humiliate mighty Spain but they also succeeded in setting up an economic empire that stretched around the world.'

---

[20] Consider an example of a one-page pamphlet that took half an hour of a scribe's time to copy or two hours of printers' time to set and proof the type. If only one copy were required, the scribal method would be the lower-cost alternative. But if 1,000 copies were required, the scribal method, requiring 500 scribal hours of work, would be vastly more expensive than the printing method in which only 0.002 hours of typesetting were required per unit reproduced.

Among the already literate, printing increased the rate of learning and flow of standardized information. Some argue that learning by doing gave way to learning by reading, and the shift from learning from old men to children of both sexes led to fundamental changes in European culture and society (see, for example, Eisenstein 1983 and Steinberg 1996).

Printing 'standardized' the creation and diffusion of knowledge, in the sense that each copy was identical rather than being a transcribed and possibly 'edited' version of the original—edited by scribes who may either have wished to change the intent of the original text, or had simply made a mistake. 'The thoughts of philosophers, the discoveries of scientists, the writings of poets, and many other products of the human mind now swiftly became common property and were soon the precious heritage of all nations regardless of their national and personal origin' (Steinberg 1996: 54).

Printed texts provided a much broader knowledge base for individuals, thus increasing the 'productivity' of learning. Without an existing base of knowledge to build on, the same discovery can be made repeatedly, or made in isolation of other important discoveries, as happened so often in China. Recording the existing knowledge base, and allowing it to be distributed relatively cheaply, made learning less random. Learning could build on past advances and thus gained direction and purpose, leading to more consistent progress (Eisenstein 1983: pt. II).

Where disputation was the main route to new knowledge, as it was in the medieval universities, the limitations of manuscripts were not of great importance; when experiment became the main route to new knowledge, those limitations became important and printing helped to remove them.[21] Without access to well-kept reliable records, much of the scientific method is not feasible: 'It is not on his [the scientist's] command of technical literature—but also his capacity to put his findings in a form where they can be correlated with prior work—where they can be accepted or rejected by consensual validation—that helps to distinguish the scientist from the shrewd observer or from the speculative "crank" and the ingenious gadgeteer' (Eisenstein 1979: 477).

Day (1996: 670) argues that movable type is 'an invention that has exerted a more profound and widespread influence on mankind than any other'. It eventually came to impact almost every element of the facilitating structure. It helped to change the optimal size of the state, shift power from traditional monopolies of knowledge (e.g. the Church), bring on the Protestant revolution, and facilitate the development of the scientific revolution of the early modern period. It ultimately changed the way humans relate to the world.

In so far as it assisted the development of early modern science, and helped the Dutch to gain independence from Spain and then go on to develop a massive

---

[21] In Chapter 7, we argue that medieval universities provided the institution that preserved Western scientific knowledge allowing it to be passed on and added to systematically—which did not occur in China. Printing did the same thing in the early modern period just when many universities were becoming reactionary defenders of the old Aristotelian scientific paradigm. Furthermore, it made this knowledge much more widely accessible than when it reposed only in the universities.

commercial empire, printing contributed greatly to the economic growth of the early modern period, albeit indirectly.

Related Issues

Although we have focused on its early introduction, printing is also a vital part of any modern economy. In the nineteenth century, the locus of innovation in printing shifted from Germany to Britain. Britain's technicians who led the world in engineering knowledge produced the first printing presses made entirely from iron and driven by steam (Day 1996: 674–5).

In more modern times, printing technologies have migrated out of the printer's shop and onto every computer owners' desktop. The end result of Gutenberg's innovation, which democratized the *ownership* of knowledge, has been to democratize its *creation*. Printing technologies themselves are at the forefront of the modern ICT revolution in such forms as digital scanning and optical character recognition.

III. STEAM ENGINE

The European dependence on inanimate power began with the waterwheel and the windmill. Steam greatly increased that dependence by providing much more horsepower at a given site than could be provided either by water or wind and by breaking the need to generate power only at specific sites provided by nature. (Later in the century, electricity broke the other great limitation of all previous power sources by allowing power to be generated at one site and consumed at another.)

The mature First Industrial Revolution depended on the intersection of three separate technological trajectories: the automation of textile manufacturing; the development of the factory system; and the harnessing of steam power. In the first half of the nineteenth century, when steam engines entered factories in earnest, a dramatic and sustained rise in productivity began. By the last quarter of that century, steam power had penetrated virtually every corner of the economy, creating Britain's Victorian Age of steam.

Relative to all previous power sources, steam had a short lifespan as a prime mover. Having only a few specific uses in the early eighteenth century, and developing many more in the early nineteenth century with the development of high-pressure engines, steam was challenged by electricity and the internal combustion engine during the last half of the nineteenth century. By the middle of the twentieth century, it had been ousted from most of its uses by these two challengers and, by the end of the century, its main use was to drive steam turbines in plants generating electricity.

The Challenge

Rapid extensive growth in the eighteenth century increased the traditional sources of demand for coal.[22] Although inanimate power had been used for many purposes

---

[22] Much of this early growth was largely in the form of 'more of the same' without parallel increases in productivity. Nonetheless, as the scale of economic activity increased at an accelerating rate, this led to large increases in the demand for power.

throughout the Middle Ages (see the discussion of the waterwheel in Chapter 5), the power problems of the sixteenth and seventeenth centuries increasingly concerned the pumping of water from mines for which water power was of little use. As the British struggled to keep pace with a growing demand for energy, they mined ever deeper deposits of coal. These deep mines tended to flood, and various pumping systems had been used and refined throughout the Middle Ages but they were proving increasingly inadequate for the rising demands placed on them. Meeting the demand required a technology that could exploit a new, inanimate energy source. This source turned out to be coal-powered engines, which first employed the weight of the atmosphere as the driving force and then steam. The new engines were first used to pump water from mines but new applications were soon found, including pumping water to storage tanks on the tops of buildings and to the reservoirs above waterwheel-driven mills to ensure their continual running. Early in the history of these engines, traditional demands for coal dominated, but through the familiar positive feedback effect, this demand for coal led to the improvements of the engines, which increased the demand for coal.[23] During the eighteenth century 'serious attempts [were made] to improve the known sources of power—water, wind, and animal and the Newcomen steam engine (which, it must be remembered, would not drive rotary machinery)' (Lilley 1966: 101). All these sources underwent major developments. As often happens with new technologies, improvements in the existing competing technologies—water power and wind power in this case—helped to slow the diffusion of the new technology, steam power, in this case.[24] In the long run, however, sustained increases in energy output came mainly from steam.

The Innovation

The introduction and subsequent improvement of the steam engine was based on two developments that we discuss in detail in Chapter 7. The first was a series of scientific discoveries related to the nature of steam and the atmosphere. The second was the increasing sophistication of European engineering. These two trajectories came together with the growing British demand for new sources of energy in the seventeenth and eighteenth centuries.

[23] Pomeranz (2000) argues that growth in Britain may have stalled some time in the later 18th century had Britain not developed a technology capable of exploiting her large coal deposits. See Von Tunzelmann (1978), especially the introduction and conclusion, for a different view of Britain's 'energy crisis'.

[24] According to von Tunzelmann (1978: 125): 'It seems beyond question that the total power installed in 1800 was vastly higher in waterwheels than in steam engines, and additionally that it was still on the increase.' Throughout most of the nineteenth century, steam's closest technological substitute remained the waterwheel. Indeed, probably the most important advance of all in water power was made in that century with the introduction of the breastwheel. This used iron blades set at an angle of 45° to the water flow and received the water at its midway point. It greatly increased the amount of horsepower that could be generated by any given flow of water. A sliding hatch was also added, which improved the water pressure and allowed agents to use the waterwheel in periods of both high and low water. Other related developments included the introduction of the water pressure engine and the water turbine—quite new technologies that allowed for the exploitation of the water that had already passed through the waterwheel. These and other advances help to explain why, as von Tunzelmann (1978:140) notes, waterwheels were still an important source of power in 1850, while Chapman (1972) finds that water power effectively competed with steam through to 1870.

The first steam-powered pump used in production was developed in 1698 by the Englishman Thomas Savery. Thomas Newcomen produced a successful alternative to Savery's engine. The first Newcomen atmospheric engine, in which the weight of the atmosphere was the driving force, was put in place in 1712. While being improved by a host of small innovations, its basic principles remained unaltered over its lifetime, which extended into the twentieth century.

Newcomen's engine was used almost exclusively to pump water from mines. Watt's engine was the first engine in which steam was the driving force acting through a cylinder. It was typical of GPTs in that it began as a relatively inefficient machine with only a few uses[25] but increased over time in efficiency and range and number of applications.

When it entered cotton mills, it started with spinning, spreading to preparation, and finally to finishing.[26] Only later did it spread to woollens. In all of these textile uses, it turned the shafts that powered newly invented machines, and in some cases, it heated factories. Later, it spread to brewing and iron manufacturing, to water and rail transport, and, relatively late in the day, throughout the rest of the economy.

Steam's uses in transportation services had to await the development of efficient steam engines with a high ratio of power to weight (as discussed in Section V). By 1850, the steam engine had arrived at more or less its final form and was used widely in land-borne transport, and was diffusing to marine uses.[27] Steam spread slowly to water transport partly because, in a now familiar pattern, sail increased in efficiency in competition with steam. River steamers and harbour tugs came first since sail was poorly adapted to both uses. Steam then powered passenger travel over short distances at sea, such as crossing the English Channel, where delays caused by unfavourable winds created highly unpredictable changes in crossing times. Then came long-distance passenger traffic and high-value freight. Finally, well into the twentieth century, sail gave way to steam on bulk goods, such as wheat and coal with low ratios of value to weight. This is typical of the slow penetration of most GPTs to one part of the economy after another, rather than being adopted everywhere more or less simultaneously.

---

[25] At one time or another, the textile industry employed all types of steam engine. Savery engines were used to power mules in Manchester by drawing water over a waterwheel. These were eventually replaced by Newcomen atmospheric engines (due to larger markets and the falling costs of the Newcomen engine) in almost all aspects of textile production by 1770. In the 19th century true steam engines entered the factories providing increased power, speed, and reliability.

[26] The diffusion of steam was uneven in textiles as elsewhere. Producers of woollens were much slower than producers of cotton to adopt the steam engine. Landes (1969: 104) points out that in 1850 woollen producers received one-third of their power from water whereas cotton producers received one-eighth. Firm size, unique technical challenges, and other factors impacted the spread of steam from sector to sector.

[27] Rosenberg and Trajtenberg (2004) provide an interesting analysis of how one important version, the Corliss engine, greatly assisted the spread of steam power to US factories.

Effects on S-E Categories

Technology

As textile producers began to appreciate the advantages of steam power, its complementarities grew. Newly invented processing, spinning, and finishing technologies were re-engineered to exploit steam power. When it entered textile factories, it greatly increased the speed of operation, which in turn required stronger threads and tougher spindles. These, and a host of other similar 'minor' innovations, allowed the full potential of steam to be realized in textile factories. Ultimately, it helped to create large increases in productivity that were not matched in water-powered textile mills.

Steam went on to enable many other technologies, including the GPTs of railways and iron steamships, both of which were transforming technologies in their own right. It also enabled a host of other lesser but nonetheless important technologies. For example, the steam tractor challenged horse power on many farms, providing not only power to pull ploughs and harrows but a stationary source of power through its flywheel, which could power many machines such as threshers and saws.

Facilitating Structure

Because early steam engines were largely used to perform tasks that were already done with existing technologies, such as pumping water out of mines, the embodiment of these earliest engines entailed relatively small adjustments to the facilitating structure. However, as the steam engine evolved to take on new uses, increasing structural adjustments were required.

Under the putting-out system, the majority of a producer's investment was in inventories of raw materials that were circulated through a chain of private producers. Small-scale production was the norm and barriers to entry were low. Water-powered factories entailed significant increases in the cost of fixed capital and in the MES of production. There were even larger increases when steam replaced water. Engines had to be embodied in relatively expensive capital goods—the engine itself, sheds to house it, solid foundations, and linkages to the factory. The higher fixed costs and MESs led to an increase in vertical integration in impacted sectors and an increasing concern with the costs of capital.[28]

The industrial geography of Britain was transformed in numerous ways. Industries based on water power needed to concentrate along fast-flowing streams. Steam-powered factories tended to cluster near sources of coal, giving rise to the great industrial towns of the English Midlands.

The production, installation, operation, and maintenance of the steam engine required significant changes in the structure of the labour force. There was an increase in the demand for mechanical skill, a demand that was mostly absent in agricultural economies. The revolutionary transition from craft production to early

---

[28] Von Tunzelmann (1994: 298–9) argues that this led to a focus on 'cost savings in natural resources or in time—savings in labour and capital costs were frequently the objectives, although all interacted'.

forms of mass production required a number of micro inventions, including the development of standardized parts and a skilled workforce of engineers. Watt himself used engineers to mass produce steam engines no longer specifically built for each individual customer. (See Chapter 7 for more on Britain's engineering capabilities.) Steam contributed to deskilling in the textile industry for handicraft workers, but demanded a skill premium from some other textile workers, including those who ran and maintained the machines. Workers lost much of the self-determination they enjoyed under the putting-out system. The poor working conditions of the early factory eventually spawned a new labour movement, political parties, and even a literary movement.

Policy

The First Industrial Revolution proceeded largely without any systematic intervention from government. Parliament did not help to build a modern financial sector, fund transportation infrastructure in a widespread and coordinated way, provide additional incentives to adopt new technologies, manage fiscal or monetary policy with growth in mind, nor help to train a new labour force with appropriate skills for a new industrial nation.[29] Nonetheless, Britain industrialized relatively quickly.

Still, the use of the steam engine, and the rise of urban factories, created pressing policy issues. Many of these were local and specific to single uses of the engine rather than generic to steam power itself. Some were so large as to require broader policy changes. These broad policy issues are so numerous and diverse that we only illustrate them here with two cases. When it entered factories, the steam engine gave employment to men, women, and children, bringing them and their low wages to the attention of middle-class reformers who had been largely unaware of the rural poverty that had existed for millennia. Laws were passed to govern child labour and working conditions. Britain also saw the rise of powerful unions and the many laws governing them.

Steam helped to create an economy that could support an army and navy trained in the newest technologies (many themselves based on steam power) that made Britain the superpower of the day. It played a role in maintaining the British empire. For example, the creation of railroads in India assisted Britain's continued dominance there up until the Second World War. Steam transformed naval warfare and made it much easier to police the seas. Ships could sail from harbour without waiting for favourable winds and could sail the world without fear of weather-related disasters as had happened, for example, when a significant portion of the British fleet was lost on the Goodwin Sands during the great hurricane of 1703.

---

[29] As Mokyr (1999: 46–7) notes: 'During the heydey of the Industrial Revolution, even social-overhead projects that in most other societies were considered to warrant direct intervention of the state were in Britain left to private enterprise. Turnpikes, canals, and railroads were built in Britain without direct state support; schools and universities were private.'

Performance

The steam engine ushered in the Victorian Age of steam. Within a relatively short period, historically speaking, driven by the factory system and steam, Britain went from being a primarily rural society—both for agriculture and manufacturing—whose social structure was based on tradition, to an urban, factory-based society. Being a gentleman came to be relatively less and less important as the nineteenth century became the age of the entrepreneur.[30] The landscape came to be dotted with large steam-driven factories, the burning of coal in those factories turning the green countryside grey with soot. But with the environmental challenges came much new wealth. The new factories produced an ever-widening array of products, and for a fraction of their previous price. The well-being of the populace was finally no longer dependent on the harvest, with the great majority of Britain's inhabitants enjoying food security, and better and cheaper manufactured necessities than ever before—not to mention their slowly growing consumption of non-necessities. Large railways cut across the landscape, connecting markets and moving people. They moved cargo to local ports, where water-based transport that was becoming increasingly steam-driven, hauled it all over the world. A cluster of innovations—the telegraph (an information and communications technology), railroads and steamships (transportation GPTs), and the steam engine (a power GPT)—helped to create a globalized market in which steam played a central role.[31]

Steam in the form of engines installed in the iron ships transformed the world's transportation system. In combination with the steam railway and refrigeration, it opened up large portions of the world to produce foodstuffs and raw materials for European consumption.[32]

We have already noted that steam engines and mechanical technologies were typical of GPTs in having their initial impacts on a narrow sector and in taking a long time to diffuse over a wide range.[33] The slow diffusion of best-practice steam

---

[30] Note that this was only a change in the *relative* importance of the determinants of social status, and one that did not persist. By the early 20th century, being a gentleman (a well-defined class that required certain attributes, including the right parents, the right accent, and the right eduction at an acceptable public school) was still crucial for social acceptance. It was said in mid-20th-century Britain that it took three generations to make a gentleman: the first made the money in the industry; the second were educated at a public school but were ashamed of their parents; and the third really made it into the gentleman class. As Darendorf (1982) has argued, an important sociological difference between Britain and the USA was that the British never truly accepted the monied class. The British rich left their productive activities behind as soon as they made money; in the USA, the Rockefellers and Carnegies *became* the upper class. The change in England from the 18th century, in which a science-intoxicated public rushed to learn more about Newton's laws and a 19th-century entrepreneurial economy dominated by innovators, to the 20th century, in which engineers were regarded as of low social status, and education of the elite was centred on the Classics and required years of hard work to master both classical Greek and Latin, is an amazing phenomenon that has attracted too little attention from economists and sociologists. But if one is to explain the relative 19th- and 20th-century performances of Britain on the one hand and those of Europe and the USA on the other, this must be an important issue to investigate.

[31] See Williamson (1996) for more on the extent of the global economy and some of its effects.

[32] See Rosenberg (1982: especially ch. 3) for more on this.

[33] As Crafts (1985: 7) notes: 'Even in 1870 use of steam power was to a considerable extent concentrated in textiles, with 580,000 out of 1,980,000 HP.' There are few estimates of how fast 'steam-based h.p.'

engines reduced the early impact of steam power on the growth of productivity and output. But by late in the First Industrial Revolution the steam engine had enabled a spectacular increase in Britain's total output as well as significant changes to the income distribution and standards of living.[34] Crafts (1985)—who has carefully documented the gradual nature of productivity and output growth in Britain from the eighteenth through the twentieth century—stipulates that steam power induced an 'industrial revolution'. He is careful to note that it took longer than early researchers thought.

Attempts to measure spillovers from GPTs, such as the steam engine, have typically come up with relatively small numbers. This is true to a great extent because most measures look for contemporaneous 'free lunch' effects. As we argued in Chapter 4 and its Appendix and illustrated many times in Chapters 5 and 6, many important spillovers are neither contemporaneous nor of the 'free lunch' variety. Technological complementarities spread over many decades, sometimes centuries. For example, the steam engine enabled the mature factory system located in the new industrial towns with machines working at speeds and stresses that water power could not accomplish. It also enabled the railroad, the iron steamship, and a host of lesser products and processes that were developed over the century following the introduction of the high-pressure engine early in the nineteenth century. Also, the new technological opportunities that are created by GPTs, including the steam engine, do not necessarily have to increase measured TFP. Even if investments in these new lines only return their opportunity cost, measured by what can be earned by investing in existing technologies, they contribute to growth by preventing the marginal productivity of capital from declining, as would eventually happen if no new technologies were invented. (See Appendix to Chapter 4; Carlaw and Lipsey 2002; Lipsey and Carlaw 2004 for details.)

The harnessing of steam was a key technological development. It dramatically accelerated the shift in sources of power from the animate to the inanimate that had begun with water and wind power. Steam remains important today; in many places the steam created from superhot nuclear material is used to drive steam turbines and is an important source of power.

diffused. Best estimates indicate that the diffusion slowed around 1860: '[I]t has been suggested that there were no more than one thousand engines in use in 1800; guessing at an average size of 10 h.p., ... one arrives at an aggregate capacity of perhaps 10,000 h.p. Fifteen years later, according to the French observer Baron Dupin, this total had risen, for Great Britain alone, to 210,000 h.p.; and by the middle of the century it had further increased more than sixfold. For the United Kingdom in 1850, Mulhall estimates 500,000 h.p. of stationary engines, [and] 790,000 h.p. of mobile engines, mostly in the form of railway locomotives' (Landes 1969: 104). While its importance grew throughout the 19th century, its rate of growth had already slowed by 1860.

[34] According to current research, it appears that living standards did not improve much at all for the great mass of the working poor before 1820—after that date most stipulate that almost all aspects of British society enjoyed a positive impact on their quality of life (see Feinstein 1998).

IV MECHANIZATION[35]

The concept of mechanization—using machines to do what was formally done by human hands and human brains—is an example of what we defined in Chapter 4 as a GPP. It is an idea or concept that has many of the characteristics of a GPT, with the major exception that it is not a single generic technology characterized by a set of instructions describing a product, process, or organizational form. Instead, it is a principle that is employed in many different technologies.

The processes that are mechanized and the various machines that do the job cannot be classified as a single technology. But the concept of mechanization fits the characteristics of a GPT in many other respects: the first applications were crude compared to modern ones; the concept has slowly spread over most of the economy's production processes and many of its products; and each new application brings many Hicksian and technological complementarities. Of course, the new applications that confer the complementarities are typically themselves genuine technologies and sometimes GPTs. We pointed out in our earlier discussion that, unlike technologies, GPPs cannot be typically classed as either product, or process, or organizational. In the case of mechanization, it can be seen in processes, as with the early textile machinery and the modern highly automated factory, and in products, as with ships and cars that are guided by automatic pilots.

Although some mechanization had been practised for millennia, its sustained trajectory began in the early modern period with textile machinery. Towards the end of the sixteenth century, Leonardo da Vinci enunciated the programme to mechanize textile machinery and eliminate most tasks currently done by hand. The subsequent evolution is discussed in detail in Chapter 7. Here we only note that it took about 200 years, and many ancillary innovations, for the programme to be far enough advanced for it to pay to move textile machinery from the cottages into the newly evolving factories. In the early factories, the machines were powered by hand or water. Then, early in the nineteenth century, steam moved into the factories

---

[35] Economic historians and students of technology do not always distinguish between mechanization and automation, speaking, for example, of the textile machines of the First Industrial Revolution as automated machines. This is not surprising since *The New Oxford Dictionary of English* (1999) draws no clear distinction between the two. Here are four relevant definitions:

- *Automation*: the use or introduction of automatic equipment in a manufacturing or other process or facility (114)
- *Automatic*: (of a device or process) works by itself with little or no direct human control (114)
- *Mechanize*: introduce machines or automatic devices into (a process, activity, or place) (1149)
- *Machine*: an apparatus using or applying mechanical power and having several parts, each with a definite function and together performing a particular task (1108)

We extend the concept of a machine to things whose parts relate to each other electronically rather than mechanically and would distinguish between an ordinary machine that does some job under human control and an automated machine that responds to changing stimuli *as if* it were controlled by a human brain. In this sense, a device that allows a worker to spray-paint a car as it passes down the assembly line is a machine, while one that recognizes the car and the parts to be painted, and then does the job without human intervention as the car passes down the line is an automated machine. Fortunately, nothing that we do subsequently depends on a clear distinction between mechanization and automation, so we say nothing further about it.

and further innovations were needed to allow the textile machinery to meet the higher speeds and stresses demanded by steam power. By then, this machinery had become one of the prime driving forces in the First Industrial Revolution.

The concept of mechanization spread to other types of manufacturing and, by the end of the nineteenth century, factories with some degree of mechanization were visible throughout much of the manufacturing sector. In the twentieth century, assembly lines led to more advanced forms of mechanization. Then, more radically, computers and robots entered the factory, leading to the automation of many machines and the clean modern, manufacturing plant in which the number of operatives per unit of output is vastly less than it was in earlier centuries. When electronic switches replaced many of the mechanical moving parts in modern machinery, computer-controlled automation spread over much of the non-manu-facturing sector. For example, the machinery that flies an airplane and pilots a ship is largely automated thorough computer control, as are the machines that record music and handle finances. (Note that our concept of machines includes not only devices whose parts relate to each other mechanically but also electronically.)

V. RAILWAYS

Early railways exhibited two characteristics typical of new GPTs: their original employment was single use, transporting coal from the pithead to ports on canals, rivers, and sea coasts; and they were use-radical but not technology-radical. They were use-radical because they could not have evolved through incremental improve-ments to the technology that they challenged—canal and road transport. They were not technology-radical because they had a long evolutionary history. The first railways were carts operating on wooden rail beds that were used to haul heavy coal out of mines as early as the start of the seventeenth century (at first they were moved by hand, then by horse). Later, they were extended to surface transport to move that coal over short distances from the pithead to harbours and rivers (see Ransom 1996: 555). They were often constructed on a grade that allowed gravity to do much of the work of moving loaded carriages downhill.

The history of rail technology provides an excellent example of the complex complementarities that evolve among GPTs. First, the development of rail would have been radically different in the absence of another significant GPT, the steam engine (and later the internal combustion engine and electricity). Rail initially was complementary with canals and the horse-drawn vehicles, but when it eventually joined with steam, it grew into a general purpose giant that dominated these alternatives. In its turn, it was challenged by the motor vehicle and, later still, by air transport. Both of these were themselves powered by another GPT: the internal combustion engine. But even this strong competition did not eliminate rail, but only narrowed its range of uses. Even today, railways remain an efficient method for transporting goods with low ratios of value to weight over long distances and for transporting people over the middle distances, which account for much of the world's travelling needs.

The Challenge

The inland transportation needs in the era of Smithian growth that followed the introduction of the three-masted sailing ship were mainly served by an extensive network of canals.[36] As trade expanded before and during the First Industrial Revolution, pressure grew for the development of more efficient methods of transporting goods. Canals were efficient for bulk trade goods, but they were susceptible to seasonal changes in weather (dry summers lowered water levels; wet winters raised them), and were becoming increasingly busy.[37] Canals also required large amounts of water, which put them into competition with water-powered factories. Further, as canals became longer and grades increased, the system of locks grew in scope and complexity. At some point the water pressure on the lock gates constrained further expansion (see Evans 1997).

Rail was not a major competitor to the canal system. Instead, short hauls over road and rail largely served to complement canals. The advent of steam-powered railways greatly increased the speed at which cargo travelled, and canals could not fight back effectively against this new competition since as the speed of a barge increased, the friction generated by the bow wave rose exponentially: 'at horse speeds, a canal could compete with the railways; at steam speeds it could not' (Evans 1997: 216). Canals were on the defensive from about 1820 onwards, and in a familiar story, the pressures to improve the system increasingly came from reacting to developments in rail: '[Until 1825], the canals' technical aspirations were largely directed toward solving internal problems having to do with locks and water supplies. After this, their problems were set externally and they tried to emulate the railways' (Evans 1997: 217).

As with the steam engine, coal played a key part in the development of rail. Early coal mines were located close to relatively cheap water transport network. As the reserves of the best mines were depleted, new mines had to be developed further from such convenient locations. Horse-drawn and, later, steam-powered rail networks helped to alleviate the resulting transportation bottlenecks. There was also a mutual causation loop between coal mining and rail. Steam's success depended on access to relatively cheap coal, while coal's success depended on the development of efficient railways, and the railways' ultimate success depended on steam, which was generated by coal.

The Innovation

There were several distinct innovations in the development of rail transport. Prior to the introduction of the steam engine, the main innovation was the introduction of

---

[36] Canals had been used in almost every corner of the globe for centuries prior to the introduction of the railroad. In the years running up to the invention of rail transport, the density of the canal network was increasing almost everywhere, especially in Europe and China. In the latter country a tremendous engineering accomplishment managed to connect several crucial waterways and the coast.

[37] Although roads were another possible substitute, throughout the early part of the 19th century, the poorly developed technology of road building made them inefficient methods for transporting bulk cargo relative to rail and water (see Evans 1997).

iron rails that dramatically reduced friction relative to that of a wooden track or a dirt road.[38] The second main innovation came when rail transport was combined with steam. The technology required to make this feasible was a steam engine that could generate the necessary high ratio of horsepower to weight. Trevithick's improvement on Watt's steam engine, employing high pressures and eliminating Watt's separate condenser, allowed a large increase in the steam engine's ratio of horsepower to weight, resulting in a parallel decrease in the cost per horsepower of rail transport (Ransom 1996: 558–9).

The problem of how to develop enough steam in the boiler was eventually solved by using tubes in the firebox. Another problem—generating sufficient draft to pull the exhaust from the smokestack quickly enough—was solved by Booth's invention of a jet that helped to expel exhaust and draw fire. At about the same time, George Stevenson came to understand the importance of a properly graded roadbed and curves appropriately designed to minimize resistance. Together, all these insights went into the success of the Stevenson Rocket, which helped to introduce the age of steam transportation. Once efficient steam locomotives were coupled with a workable understanding of railroad design, the number and total mileage of rail lines increased dramatically. By 1850 there were around 6,800 miles of track carrying steam-powered locomotives in England alone.

Effects on S-E Categories

Technology

The issue of competing standards often found with new technologies occurred early in railway history in the form of different gauges of track.[39] Each gauge had its strengths and weaknesses. For example, broad gauge accommodated more powerful locomotives while narrow gauge was cheaper to lay. Both persisted well into the twentieth century. Where two gauges were used in the same system, however, costs and delivery times were increased by the switch of rolling stock that was needed to move between the gauges.

The development of railroads powered by mature steam locomotives, and later by diesels, resulted in a cascade of induced innovations. It also set in motion a number of smaller innovations that increased the efficiency of rail. 'The technological sources of productivity growth included a series of important inventions specific to the railroads—air brakes and automatic couplers—the substitution of steel for iron rails, and the gradual improvement in the design of locomotives and rolling stock' (Rosenberg 1982: 69).

More recently, standardized shipping containers have increased the efficiency of rail acting as a part of an interlocking transportation network. These allow cargoes to

---

[38] 'The obvious step forward of making the rails entirely of cast iron seems to have occurred in South Wales, where ironworks were using iron edge rails, deeper than they were wide, in the early 1790s' (Ransom 1996: 556).

[39] Railways of less than 2 feet width are generally termed narrow gauge; broad-gauge rail tends to be much wider, ranging from 3 to 5 feet.

go from their first shipper to their ultimate destination without the loading and unloading costs that were formerly required when changing from one transportation medium to another.

A stream of innovations in high-speed passenger trains, including electromagnetic systems, tunnelling technology, methods for dealing with grades, and bridging technology, continue to improve efficiency. High-speed rail spans many parts of Europe and most of Japan. Rail now links Britain to continental Europe through the Channel Tunnel.

Facilitating Structure

Rail transport changed the locational decisions of firms, the effective geographical distribution of resources, and the concentrations of human populations probably more than any previous transportation technology. Cities did not need to be located on a river or ocean, and producers did not need to locate near to their customers.

Prior to the widespread introduction of rail in the USA, time often varied capriciously among adjacent locations. Since the shipment of goods and people by rail had to be carefully coordinated over large regions, these variations created serious safety issues. Early on, the introduction of rail induced an effort to standardize time zones and time zones.

Rail also altered the nature of regional competition and concentration among firms by greatly lowering the unit cost of land transportation and increasing the division of labour in many sectors. This helped to erode the market power of local monopolists who had been isolated from competitors by high transport costs. It also led to the development of the modern multi-unit firm.

As Chandler (1977) argues and Rosenberg (1982) concurs, rail was the key innovation at the core of a system of interrelated technologies that led to a new form of production and consumption. The railroad allowed reliable delivery of large shipments of inputs and outputs, a precondition for modern manufacturing techniques, just as in the next century the ICT revolution allowed international coordination, thus contributing to the globalization of manufacturing.

The managing of this time-sensitive, large-scale movement of products and inputs required a level of coordination whose precision was hitherto unknown. This was particularly so in the USA because of its huge land mass:

Of the new forms of transportation the railroads were the most numerous, their activities the most complex, and their influence the most persuasive. They were the pioneers in the management of modern business enterprise. . . . By the early twentieth century modern business enterprise, with its large staff of salaried managers and its clear separation of ownership and control, completely dominated the American transportation and communications networks—networks that were so necessary for the coming of mass production and mass distribution and for the rise of modern business enterprise in other sectors of the economy. (Chandler 1977: 80)

Telegraphic communications were a critical complementary technology that permitted faster speeds for trains and in turn required more complex forms of organization within the railway companies. In an excellent example of technological complementarities, these new forms of organization later spread to other industries.

Eventually, with the advent of refrigeration, improved communications, and new efficient trucking technologies, the railroad became a component of one of the most important technology systems of the modern US economy. Railways turned a number of regional US markets into one national market for many manufactured goods, creating scale economies that were unavailable to European producers. In combination with steamships, they became the foundation of a growing tourist industry. Rail, steamship, and refrigeration allowed new areas in the Americas and the Antipodes to produce foodstuffs for consumption in Europe. This significantly lowered the price of food in Europe and contributed to the growth of overseas economies.

Policy

Railroads are a notoriously 'lumpy' investment, often requiring massive sums. This often put government financing efforts at the centre of railroad construction. In Canada, for example, rail was financed both directly through government expenditures and indirectly through government land grants.[40]

Dudley (1991: ch. 6) argues that the combination of rail and telegraph significantly impacted the evolution of European states by increasing the optimal size of the state. Dudley's argument is (as it was with bronze, discussed in Chapter 5) that an important determinant of the size of states is the degree of military economies of scale. Prior to rail, the marshalling of large armies was a slow process and could often be defeated in detail by splitting the enemy forces into small units before engaging them. Rail and telegraph created significant military economies of scale allowing a large state to deliver troops quickly to an area, effect a victory with disproportionately lower losses, and leave those troops in place to be supplied by the rail network—compared with what could be done by a smaller state. These technologies also created the need for complex mobilization plans, which once set in motion, were hard to reverse, a characteristic that some historians have argued was a significant cause of Europe's drift into war in the summer of 1914. As the size of the state increased, the marginal tax rate fell while total government revenue rose. This dynamic, according to Dudley assisted growth and helped to promote the modern welfare state:

Even after these changes in territorial boundaries and tax levels, however, Germany still had resources to burn. For nearly three-quarters of a century, German political leaders had at their disposal a great surplus of resources beyond what was necessary to control their territory militarily. This surplus made it possible to introduce the world's first program of social insurance in the 1880s. (Dudley 1991: 216)

---

[40] Undoubtedly, some of this track was the result of a railroad bubble. For example, in Canada government subsidies led to overinvestment in rail (Lewis and MacKinnon 1987). What is clear is that thousands of miles of track would survive as productive investments, confirming the importance of rail to the economies of the 19th and 20th centuries.

Regardless of whether Dudley's thesis is correct in detail, the impact of railroads as a nation-building device is beyond dispute. In the USA, railroads helped to forge a sense of nationhood. Canada was so worried about the security of its Western territories that the transcontinental railroad was seen partly as a defence against US expansionism. Russia built the Trans-Siberian railroad for similar purposes. The British used an extensive railroad network in their colonies to effect control of a globe-spanning empire. These observations touch on a host of policy implications that are presented here only in the broadest of brush strokes.

Performance

One of the big surprises with early railroads concerned the demand for passenger traffic. In a dramatic illustration of the uncertainties that accompany a new GPT, virtually everyone associated with the early railroads had expected them to be predominantly a means of transporting freight. Yet this new technology tapped a latent demand for travel that had been quite unsuspected by those who stumbled into serving it. Both the time and money cost of travel fell. Trips that had previously taken days now took hours and trips that had taken weeks took days. A society in which many people had never travelled more than a few miles from where they were born was transformed in many ways by the new travel patterns. For example, there was an increase in the genetic diversity of humans as the pool of potential marriage partners was expanded by travel, particularly in Britain and Europe.

Railroads had important long-run effects on most modern economies. They facilitated the industrialization of Britain and other European nations, as well as the USA. Chandler has powerfully argued in the context of the US economy that the cluster of innovations that included the railroad and the telegraph was crucial in helping to create in the USA the world's first mass production–mass consumption economy.

Fogel (1964) challenged this view of rail's central importance to industrialization by asking what it would cost to 'remove' rail from the nineteenth century US economy. His answer was that the 'social savings' due to the introduction of rail was a mere 0.6 per cent of GDP in 1890.[41] The basic argument is simple: there are no indispensable technologies since everything has close substitutes. In the case of rail, there were canals, cart and horse, and, eventually, automobiles. Thus removing rails would only entail a marginal increase in the price of transportation.

Fogel's work has had many criticisms and rebuttals. These range from the technical through the empirical to the historical. We here focus on one criticism that we find persuasive. Notionally removing one technology from a technology cluster does not allow us to measure anything like the total impact of that technology, particularly if it is a GPT with a large number of technological complementarities whose effects are widespread over space and time. As Rosenberg (1982: 58–9) argues: 'The growing productivity of industrial economies is the complex outcome of large

---

[41] Hawke (1970) came to a different conclusion for Britain. He estimated that removing the railroad from the British economy would have reduced GDP by 4.1 per cent in 1900.

numbers of interlocking, mutually reinforcing technologies, the individual components of which are of very limited economic consequence by themselves.' Railways encouraged intracontinental communications through the telegraph; they led to new forms of business organization that spread to the rest of the economy; they allowed a single US market to emerge, encouraging the development of the US system of manufactures, which in the final analysis allowed the USA to overhaul their European competitors, including Britain, in the race for industrial ascendancy. (See discussion of technological complementarities in Chapter 4, where we used railroads as one of our key examples.) These are massive technological complementarities that are missed completely by statistical studies of the type conducted by Fogel—and they matter.[42]

VI. ELECTRICITY

Until the mid nineteenth century, the world had seen only two generic energy systems: animate and mechanical. The next 100 years added two more, electronic and atomic, with quantum energy as a future prospect.[43] Electricity delivers energy as a flow of electrons, which gives it a much higher degree of flexibility than any mechanical source of power. We live today in an electronic age where much of what we do economically, socially, and politically is dependent on electricity. For example, it is *the* power source behind the ICT revolution that started with the telegraph, and developed through the radio, television, computer, satellite communication, laser, and the Internet. 'Of the great construction projects of the last century, none has been more impressive in its technical, economic, and scientific aspects, none has been more influential in its social effects, and none has engaged more thoroughly our constructive instincts and capabilities than the electric power system' (Hughes 1983: 1).

The Challenge

When the dynamo was invented in 1867, steam was still evolving along many productive trajectories, not yet having fully supplanted water power on land or sail at sea. Thus the technology to generate electricity did not arise to meet any obvious energy crisis in the technologies it displaced. Over the seventeenth and eighteenth centuries, electricity appears to have been studied mainly because scientists wanted to understand its nature. With the invention of the voltaic cell in 1800, electricity in the form of a direct current became useful in a limited range of applications. The most important of these was the telegraph, which, for the first time in history, provided a publicly available means of communicating information faster than humans or

---

[42] See Freeman and Louçã (2001: 194–8) for a similar criticism.

[43] Atomic energy has only been used directly in destructive, military applications. For constructive applications it has almost exclusively been used to generate heat to make electricity. So to date it is correctly seen as a form of electricity-generating technology and not as a generic category in itself.

animals could carry it.[44] Throughout the nineteenth century, electricity was touted by many as a new marvel with tremendous economic potential, although until the dynamo was invented most of that potential remained unrealized.

The Innovation[45]

In Chapter 8, we discuss the long trajectory of developing scientific knowledge that culminated in the invention of the dynamo.[46] Here we merely note that, like steam, the history of electricity reveals a mixture of discoveries and inventions, each complementing the other. The nature of electricity had to be discovered and methods of generating it had to be invented.

Early adopters of electricity faced a choice between two types of current to carry electricity from source to use. Direct current (DC), which was championed by Thomas Edison, among others, had many advantages over alternating current (AC). The speed of a DC motor could be regulated more efficiently then an AC motor, the risk of electrocution was less, and there were a few key applications that could only be done with DC, including electrolysis and electroplating. The crucial disadvantage was that the power could only be efficiently transported over short distances. In a clear case of learning by using groping into an uncertain future in a profit-oriented but not profit maximizing fashion—the relative advantages and disadvantages of AC and DC had to be learned by experience. In 1893, the decision was made to use AC for generating and distributing the power from the Niagara project in the USA.[47] Thereafter, the technology for generation and transmission evolved into something close to its modern form: the universal electricity supply utility, a system based upon the generation of alternating current in massive central power stations for distribution via a transmission network extended across a wide geographic area to residential and business customers.[48]

Effects on S-E Categories

Electricity had profound effects wherever it was introduced. Since we cannot pretend to be exhaustive, we concentrate in this case mainly on effects in the USA.

Technology

It took nearly fifty years after the invention of the dynamo for electricity to move from a crude and narrowly applied technology to a fully established transforming

---

[44] Semaphore systems, in which flags transmitted information visually from one tower to another, were the first practical means of moving detailed information faster than it could be carried by humans or animals, but this was never a practical means of moving masses of information over long distances and its use was mainly confined to the military.

[45] Much of this section is based on Nye (1990).

[46] See Bowers (1996) for a good presentation of the history of electricity.

[47] Bowers (1996: 372) notes: 'All public electricity supply systems are now entirely AC, although the last DC supply in Britain—to a Fleet Street newspaper—remained in use until 1985.'

[48] This evolution is itself an interesting story. See Bowers (1996), Hughes (1983), Nye (1990), and Schurr (1990) for more details.

GPT that impacted the entire economy. Electricity's first uses were limited mainly to street lighting and street railways. Thomas Edison's Menlo Park laboratory was one of the first commercial research establishments where R&D was institutionalized and directed at commercial ends. Slowly, as technical problems were solved, the number of uses expanded, the techniques and locations of production were trans-formed, and a range of new products and industries arose. For example, an assort-ment of electrically driven household machines including washing machines, dish washers, vacuum cleaners, irons, refrigerators, deep freezers, and electric stoves transformed household work and eliminated much of household drudgery.

As a power delivery system, electricity required many complementary innov-ations. As it became more widely used, increasing demands were placed on the original methods of generation, and new methods were actively sought out. One of the most important innovations in power generation was the construction of large hydroelectric dams in which fast-flowing water was used to turn turbines—a modern application of the age-old principle of the waterwheel.

Delivery technologies also had to be developed. The modern electrical grid is a complex technological system producing power through a dynamo (itself powered by various methods such as smashing atoms, burning coal, or running water through turbines), sometimes storing that power (through various types of batter-ies), transporting it in the form of electron flows to the place of its final use, and then transforming that electron flow into useful energy at its destination. No one element is of much use without all the others.

Facilitating Structure

Electrification required large investments in the many capital goods that produce, distribute, and use it. Both the managerial and the physical organizations of the firm were fundamentally altered by electricity. When water was the motive power, the scale of the factory was largely determined by the available supply of water power, which imposed both a fairly rigid minimum and maximum efficient size. The use of water and steam required most production machinery to be directly connected to their source of power. A factory was powered by a large shaft from which the power was distributed via a set of pulleys and belts. Because of heavy friction loss in belt transmission, the machines that required the most power were placed closest to the drive shaft, and factories were built with two storeys to get more machines close to the shaft situated near the ceiling of the lower floor. The entire system had to run if any part of the factory was in use while if any part was down for repair, the entire factory had to be shut down.

Electric motors were originally used in a facilitating structure that was adapted to steam engines. Using electricity to power a plant designed for steam was typically more costly than using steam power, but gains in flexibility more or less made up for this. Later, a separate motor was attached to each machine (the unit drive). After a prolonged learning period, the layout of the factory was changed dramatically. Machines were arranged according to their position in the production process, rather than their power needs. Only when this alteration in the facilitating structure was completed, was the full potential of electric power in factories realized (David 1991*b*). There were other gains as well. Once overhead transmission mechanisms were eliminated, improvements were possible in illumination, ventilation, and cleanliness. The unit drive eliminated belt slippage, which had reduced the quantity and quality of output (we touch on similar issues in the *Performance* section). The whole factory structure was redesigned: a single-storey structure was cheaper to build (no need to reinforce the first floor to support the weight of the machinery on the second floor). Refitting and repair no longer required shutting down all those machines driven by one main shaft. The continuous process assembly line would have been impossible without electricity.

The size of a plant that used unit drive machines was no longer determined by the efficient size of a central power delivery system. In assembly plants, electricity increased scale economies; in parts manufacture, small-scale production became efficient because an electric motor could be attached to each machine tool. The result was a system of relatively small decentralized parts producers supplying large centralized assembly plants—a method of production that is still used today.

Electrification eliminated many jobs outright and drastically altered those that remained. It lowered the basic skill level required for many previously skilled jobs. Workers no longer needed to be 'mechanics', as they were no longer in charge of keeping their piece of machinery running. Machine tools had once required the operator to perform a wide range of tasks, but the electrification of the workplace transferred the 'skill' to the machine itself, because after electrification, workers did little more then feed blanks into a machine. Highly skilled glass blowers were replaced with bottle-making machines. In mines, the skilled mule drivers and their assistants were driven out of work by electric locomotives. A highly skilled worker was needed to maintain proper heat levels in furnaces run on coal, gas, oil, and wood, whereas an electric oven could be set to the proper level with the push of a button. All these are counter-examples to the assumption commonly made in growth models that technological change always increases the demand for human capital among the workforce. Rather it changes the demand for certain types of human capital, making the type appropriate to the new technology relatively more valuable and other types appropriate for displaced technologies less valuable.

Policy

The spread of electricity altered scale economies not only for its users but also for its producers. Early electrical plants produced direct current, which could not be distributed efficiently over long distances, so they were small and localized. With the introduction of alternating current, power could be transmitted over long distances, allowing producers to consolidate their generating stations to take advantages of economies of scale. Electrical generating plants became natural monopolies. While considerable effort was focused on bringing the large electric utility companies under government control in the USA, owners fought vigorously to resist or reverse the process. Their efforts, along with a public mistrust of government plus large-scale economies, restrained public regulation of large US monopolies in most states.

An issue facing urban policymakers was the impact new electric trolleys would have on the city. This created a multitude of political issues. 'As the streetcar became a significant fixed cost of everyday life, it also became the focus of political controversies about safety, fares, transfers, length of franchises, and ownership' (Nye 1990: 97).

Another issue surrounding the provision of electricity concerned the servicing of markets with low demand densities. In the USA, these were areas largely devoted to agriculture, the last sector of the economy to be electrified. The lack of modern sources of power for the rural parts of the USA was seen as a major policy challenge, especially because the monopolization of the electricity market was already becoming a policy issue. This was in direct contrast to the European experience, where '[m]ore than two-thirds of German, French, Dutch, and Scandinavian farmers enjoyed not only electricity but reasonable service rates by the end of the 1920s' (Nye 1990: 287). In 1933, the new Roosevelt administration created the Tennessee Valley Authority (TVA). In 1936 the Rural Electrification Act made low-cost loans available to firms, families, and other branches of government in order to facilitate the expansion of the nation's power grid. The effort was eventually successful in giving rural Americans reliable access to electric power.

Performance

As with most GPTs, many of the microeconomic benefits of electricity were not anticipated but discovered only through use. Electric lights illustrate this learning. Compared with gas lighting, they did not give off the acidic fumes that harmed fabrics, making them particularly useful in textile factories; they did not give off large amounts of moisture, making them particularly useful in the many lines of manufacturing and retailing where humidity control was important; they did not leak gas, making them particularly useful in industries where fire and explosion were constant dangers; they could be placed anywhere that light was needed providing an even light that neither flickered nor produced deep shadows. They did not increase the temperature of the factory. More generally, a steam-powered factory was a dangerous place in which to work, and although an electrically powered factory had its own dangers, it was typically safer, quieter, and cleaner. These sorts of unanticipated gains illustrate why the assumption of perfect foresight found in many GPT models is problematic, and why the assumption of profit-orientated groping towards an uncertain future is closer to reality.

In the early twentieth century, electric supply systems exhibited endogenous efficiency gains from such sources as technical scale economies, economies in training the workforce, network scale economies through load balancing, and a range of learning effects, which were enhanced as generation and transmission equipment became more standardized. Although some of this was foreseen by a few farsighted persons, the details had to be worked out in learning by doing and learning by using. For example, it was not until the 1920s that the potential advantages of the unit drive system were fully understood and exploited. Although electrification in the USA rose by about 25 per cent from 1909 to 1919 and again from 1920 to 1929, only in the latter decade did unit drives begin to be widespread enough to cause significant increases in aggregate productivity growth. Although few steam-driven factories were built in the USA after 1900, it was not until the end of the 1930s that the electrification of US industry was substantially completed. The long lags were due to many forces, not the least of which was the durability of established steam plants whose marginal costs of operation tended to be less than the full costs of new electric power plants.[49]

At the macro level, there were four identifiable long-term trends related to the use of electricity: a large increase in electricity's share of total energy produced and consumed; a growth of productivity; a persistent decline in energy required per unit of output; and a drastic increase in per capita power consumption. These trends have contributed greatly to the increase in modern living standards, much of which comes in the form of unmeasured improvements to many important service flows (e.g. quality of lighting, air conditioning, heating, etc.).

By the early 1940s, the facilitating and policy structures of the US economy had been altered drastically to fit the needs of electricity, mass production, and the automobile. There followed a long secular boom from 1945 to the early 1970s in which technological change took place more incrementally, and within a stable facilitating structure that was reasonably well adapted to the underlying technolo gies. We are living in the age of electricity Many of the most fundamental tech-nologies of today, and tomorrow, would be technically impossible in its absence. Electricity has transformed the structure of the economy in ways that few, if any, other GPTs in history have ever done in the 10,000 years since the neolithic agricultural revolution.

Related Issues

Not Just a Reduction in the Price of Power

As we have frequently argued, GPT-induced transformations, such as occurred with electricity, cannot be analysed as if they were mere reductions in the price of existing energy sources. Electricity enabled production techniques and a host of new products that were technically impossible with any mechanical form of energy.

Electrification ... was not merely a cheaper form of energy but one fundamentally different from either steam or water power. Electric light, drive, and heat greatly increased the flexibility of factory location, design, and size. Electrical technology changed the working methods of a wide range of industries, including coal mines, oil wells, machine shops, chemical plants, textile mills, aluminium plants, printing houses, steel mills, food processors, automotive manufactures, and companies adopting Ford's form of mass production.... These new modes of manufacturing overturned the old industrial system. (Nye 1990: 232–3)

As an illustration of what we argued in Chapter 4 about how to model the effects of new GPTs, none of these changes would have resulted from a fall in the prices of steam power, even to zero.

---

[49] The data in this paragraph are from David (1991*b*).

Not Identifiable as a GPT by Observing the Generating Industry Alone
We discussed in Chapter 4 why our criteria do not allow a GPT to be identified solely by what happens in the industry that produces the GPT itself (see page 108). Instead, our definition tells us that for a technology to be a GPT, it needs to have (*a*) much initial scope for improvement; (*b*) multiple uses; (*c*) uses across much of the economy; and (*d*) many technological complementarities. This is why in our earlier discussion we rejected the argument of Moser and Nichols (2004) that they could establish that electricity was not a GPT by studying patents for the improvement of electricity generation. To emphasize this important point, we apply our criteria to the question of whether or not electricity is a GPT.

First, we have already discussed a few highlights in the evolution of the electricity-generating industry following the invention of the dynamo in 1867—from small stations generating direct current to early small ones generating alternating current to the slow rise of large-scale hydroelectric plants with massive dynamos and the development of an accompanying distribution system with high-tension wires, transformers, and the like. Those who believe that electricity does not fulfil this first criterion of having much initial scope for improvement need to refute the mass of historical evidence as laid out in books such as Bowers (1996), David (1991*b*), Hughes (1983), Nye (1990), and Schurr (1990).

Second and third, although being widely used and having many uses are separate criteria, it is convenient to discuss them together. The evidence that these two criteria are fulfilled is so much around us that an appeal to common observation is sufficient to establish its truth. We have listed above some of the myriad different uses of electricity in the modern world and the ubiquity of some of these, such as electric lights and computers. For a simple self-conducted test, observe what happens in any modern city when the electricity supply fails—and also note that much of what is still working relies on emergency back-up generators.

Fourth, as for having many technological complementarities, we have argued that much of the impact of electricity was transmitted throughout the rest of the economy through changes in engineering relationships rather than changes in prices. We have also noted many of these, such as the complete reorganization of the factory enabled by the adoption of the unit drive on machines. Another of electricity's major technological complementarities was the creation of a whole range of new products that were not technically feasible with previous power sources, and the rise of industries to produce them—radios, televisions, lasers, vacuum cleaners, and computers, which in turn enabled email and the Internet.

The evidence on these last three points could fill books and much of it is alluded to in our section on electricity. This is the evidence. As we observed in Chapter 4, the fact that we do not need a host of researchers to gather it, or regression techniques to analyse it, does not make it any the less cogent evidence.[50]

---

[50] In the case of older GPTs that are not part of our common, everyday experience, a more systematic gathering of evidence may be required to show that these four conditions were fulfilled. Even then, our discussions in Chapters 5 and 6 show that the necessary evidence is often easy to come by and requires little more than gathering available material and focusing it onto the four necessary criteria.

VII. THREE ORGANIZATIONAL GPTS

In this section, we look at three important organizational GPTs: the factory system; mass production; and lean production. Because each was an outgrowth of the previous system, we treat them together. The factory system is the fundamental organizational GPT that has enabled mass and lean productions, and it is a matter of judgement whether we regard these as three separate GPTs or as major adoptions of a single GPT.

For most of human history, production took place in the home and artisans' shops.[51] The sector on which the Industrial Revolution made its first impact, textiles, was organized on a putting-out system, in which raw materials were provided to small-scale craft producers. Some of these survived the Industrial Revolution; most did not. One of the central aspects of that revolution was the substitution of the centralized large-scale production of homogenous goods for decentralized small-scale production of crafts goods.

When production was first moved from the cottages, it went to what Mokyr calls 'manufactories'. These were small, crude installations that offered very few efficiency gains over putting-out. They were merely a 'concentration of former artisans and domestic workers under one roof, in which workers continued what they were doing before, only away from home' (Mokyr 2002: 120). Manufactories centralized some aspects of production, and could be quite large, but they were not factories.

The modern factory system developed when the new textile machinery entered the early manufactories. Human power was replaced first by water power, then by steam power, and finally by electricity. As one power source replaced another, the MES of many manufacturing operations increased so that throughout the nineteenth century factories became larger and more organized.

MASS PRODUCTION

Aspects of mass production exist whenever interchangeable parts are used in production.[52] While British industry pioneered mass production in heavy industry (Musson 1980), the US system of manufactures[53] was a precursor of mass production in light industries. Using standardized parts, US firms produced standardized consumer goods with lower quality and price compared to the goods produced by Europe's craft techniques, which focused on quality rather than price.

---

[51] Mokyr argues that the important change in organization during the Industrial Revolution was not in the separation of ownership from production, mechanization, or even an increased division of labour. To some extent all these developments pre-dated the Industrial Revolution. Instead Mokyr (2002: 125) argues that 'the Industrial Revolution marked the beginning of the process in which the household would eventually lose its position as the prevalent locus of production'.

[52] Venetians used pre-built, interchangeable parts and a form of mass production to make galleys on a canal assembly line in preparation of the battle of Lepanto in 1571 (Beeching 1982: ch. 9).

[53] As described by Rosenberg (1994: ch. 6).

Mass production techniques based on specialized machine tools and interchangeable component parts first appeared [in the USA] in armories and gun factories in the 1830s; spread to related industries, such as watch and sewing machine manufacture after mid-century; and became characteristic of locomotive, steam engine, and other heavy machinery manufacture late in the nineteenth century. (Nelson 1980: 6)

The Challenge

Some of the most important stimulants to the development of fully fledged mass production in the early twentieth century were the limitations of early factories producing complex consumer goods, such as the automobile. Unlike textile production, for which the organization of early factories was well suited, the technology of early twentieth-century factories required something very close to craft production for modern assembly activities (Freeman and Perez 1988).[54]

The machine tools that were in use up to the early 1900s could only work soft metals, so these were machined in their soft state and then hardened. Since the parts warped during hardening, each part was unique, making mass production impossible. Instead, each part had to be individually machined and then worked into its place in the overall assembly.

The Innovation

Early in the twentieth century, machine tools were developed that could cut prehardened steel, thus making it possible to produce a part of sufficiently common standard dimensions and quality so that specific parts became interchangeable in their assembly. When Ford could not persuade his parts manufacturers to produce parts that were sufficiently standardized, he manufactured them in-house. He then reorganized his factory along lines of the principles of scientific management enunciated by Taylor (1903) early in the century.[55] Standardized parts were assembled by workers who were less skilled than craftsmen and who did relatively few, well-defined tasks. While craftsmen used to move from job to job and were responsible for locating their own parts, Ford had the parts delivered to the assemblers. These developments, the complete and consistent interchangeability of parts, the simplicity of attaching them to each other, and specialized, relatively unskilled, and stationary workers are the essence of mass production. The last step, not the first,

---

[54] Craft producers are highly skilled workers using simple but flexible tools to make exactly what the consumer asks for—one item at a time. Mass producers are unskilled workers using expensive single-purpose machines to churn out standardized products in high volume. Lean producers combine the advantages of craft and mass production, while avoiding the high cost of the former and the rigidity of the latter (Womack, Jones, and Roos, 1990).

[55] Ford's use of Taylorist principles well illustrates Freeman and Louçã's contention (2001: 246): 'The real significance of "Taylorism" was not that it introduced "scientific management" but that...it provided a rationale for a whole set of organizational innovations. These displaced the old model and substituted a management-intensive style based on the professionalization and specialization of the various functions of management.'

was the assembly line, which was Ford's own innovation. The line moved the partially assembled car from one worker to the next, setting an inexorable pace to the whole process in which each worker did one simple job.

Later, when parts manufacturers became proficient in the use of the new technologies, it turned out that centralizing all parts production within the assembly firm was inefficient and Ford, who refused to learn this lesson, lost out to General Motors. In the end, the production of automobile and many other manufactured products became a two-level system, in which large assemblers used parts mainly produced by many decentralized parts manufacturers, some of whom were extremely small. This is another clear case of learning by doing. Because Ford's suppliers did not see the potential of the new machine tools, Ford had to produce the parts himself. But once he had proved his point, his system turned out to be less efficient than the separation of parts producers from assemblers. The evolutionary hand punished Ford with reduced profits until the company learned this lesson in a way that other automobile firms already had. A static view would hold that Ford made a mistake in adopting an inefficient mode of production in the first place and eventually paid for it in lost profits. A dynamic view is that, given the lack of foresight in his parts producers, Ford's best policy was to produce everything himself but his mistake was, as is so often the case with the dominant firm, in not realizing that, as learning progressed and the technology developed, the best form of organization had changed.

Mass production eventually came to dominate almost all aspects of manufacturing, first in the USA and later in Europe. It also spread to more and more sectors of the economy, often in surprising ways. One of the last sectors to be fully impacted by mass production techniques has been services. In the 1950s, for example, McDonald's pioneered the application of the lessons of mass production to the restaurant industry—and was soon followed by many others.

Effects on S-E Categories

Facilitating Structure

To list all the changes brought about by mass production would take a book, so here we touch on a few of the major structural changes that illustrate some aspects of organizational GPTs and their channels of impact.

Mature mass production techniques required major changes in the design of factories. Bringing the product to the workers instead of leaving it stationary while workers moved between stations required two major changes. Large amounts of standardized parts had to be delivered to each worker's station and the factory had to be laid out to facilitate the passing of the product through successive stations until it was completed.

Mass production increased the MES of operations of assembly plants, making oligopoly the norm. In contrast, the lower efficient scale of parts manufacturing left them operating in a more competitive market structure.

The large fixed costs of assembly made unfettered price competition among assemblers a destructive strategy.[56] Competition was largely in advertising and product differentiation while prices were mainly set as a mark-up on full costs.

The development of mass markets and '[t]he new speed and volume of distribution brought a revolution in marketing' (Chandler 1977: 485). This was just one aspect of organizational innovations that impacted almost all sequences in both the supply chain of large firms and their distribution systems.

With the rise of large industrial concerns, methods of finance had to change. The firm as a 'legal fiction' was developed along with holding companies, trusts, and other methods of circumventing competitive pressures. Also, financing the capital expenditures to compete in a national (or world) market required surrendering much decision-making power to one's creditors.

Mass production led to dramatic alterations in the geography of production. In the USA, cities such as Chicago, St Louis, Detroit, and Pittsburgh, which had grown slowly for decades, expanded rapidly. The continual search for new markets by mass production firms was a strong force behind the continuing globalization of finance and trade.

The nature of the Fordist labour force has been the topic of much research. Here we touch on two illustrative issues: deskilling and management. Mass production led to a general deskilling of the manufacturing labour force. Assembly line workers performed narrow repetitive tasks that allowed little room for creativity or self-expression. These negatives were overcome with higher pay. Scholars such as Freeman, Perez, and Boyer have pointed out that such a linking between pay and productivity was crucial in facilitating the joint development of a mass production–mass consumption economy.

The mass production, multi-unit conglomerate was not compatible with the traditional family-run firm that preceded it. Professional managers were required. Over time, the personal involvement of owners in the running of industry was effectively eliminated.[57] Because they sat at the nexus of a large labour force in need of supervision—the owners of the firm, and often large numbers of shareholders—these managers came to play a key role in the new mass production economy. Chandler (1977: 491) argues that economists 'have paid almost no notice at all to the managers who, because they carried out a basic new economic function, continued to play a far more central role in the operations of the American economy than did the robber barons, industrial statesmen, or financiers'.[58] He concludes that

[56] With high fixed and low marginal costs, price competition can lead to a Bertrand equilibrium, in which price equals marginal cost so that fixed costs cannot be covered. The strategies in the text can be seen as establishing routines that were designed to prevent this outcome.

[57] 'A study of the 200 largest nonfinancial companies in 1963 indicates that in none of these firms did an individual, family, or group hold over 80 percent of the stock. None were still privately owned. In only 5 of the 200 did a family or group have a majority control by owning as much as 50 percent of the stock. . . . In 1963 . . . 84.5 percent of the 200 largest nonfinancial companies were management controlled' (Chandler 1977: 492–3).

[58] But many institutional economists in the tradition of Thorston Veblen did pay attention to this development (see, for example, Burnham 1942).

'by the 1950s the managerial firm had become the standard form of modern business enterprise in major sectors of the American economy' (Chandler 1977: 493). With these changes came a host of others. For example, wealth became less a matter of owning productive assets than managing them, which led to an increase in social mobility. For another, an agency problem developed between the managers' interest in their own incomes and the owners' interests in the firm's profits—a conflict that is evident in the behaviour of many of today's managers.

Performance

Mass production had many effects observable at the micro level. For example, it allowed factory owners to save on all inputs—something that we earlier observed to be a common feature of many, perhaps most, new technologies. The assembly line obviously saved on labour costs by using only unskilled labour, and fewer of them than the craftsmen of earlier production processes. It also allowed for savings in capital as the value of inventories fell more dramatically than fixed capital formation increased.

Within cities, the widespread ownership of automobiles—something that would have been impossible without the cost savings of mass production—allowed people to move from the core to the peripheries and allowed the large supermarkets to dominate retail sales, driving out most of the 'mom and pop' grocery stores. In response to the mobility conferred by the automobile, gas stations, hotels, and other units suggesting a mobile population dotted the landscape.

At the macro level, we argue that the boom that followed the Second World War and stretched until the mid-1970s was a manifestation of the stage in a GPT's life when one or more transforming GPTs has permeated the economy and the facilitating structure has adapted to it. (The stages in the life of a GPT are outlined in more detail in Chapter 12.) Their full set of applications can then be developed within a structure that accommodates rather than inhibits it. The electrification of factories, the mass production system, the internal combustion engine and the petroleum industry that it required, as well as the alteration in consumption patterns that it enabled, were the major technologies that underlay the post–Second World War boom.[59] In many consumer durables sectors that were of fundamental importance to improving living standards over most of the twentieth century, mass production led to dramatic increases in output and corresponding decreases in prices. Industries producing automobiles, refrigerators, airplanes, stoves, washing machines, and even services such as fast food were all similarly affected.

---

[59] Many scholars, such as those in the Regulation School (Marxists and post-Keynesians who argue that technology requires an articulating system), also argue that the spread of mass production was a key contributor to the post-war boom. Others, however, contest this claim either explicitly or implicitly. For example, modern growth theorists do not typically mention mass production as a factor in US growth. Students of national systems of innovation acknowledge it, but many do not stress it. In contrast, many political economists put mass production at centre of study. Economic historians are divided on its importance: Piore and Sabel (1984) dispute the centrality of mass production while Chandler gives it a key place in all of his work.

LEAN PRODUCTION

Lean production is one of the few transforming GPTs that evolved out of the one it challenged and largely replaced. It kept the concept of mass-producing low-priced goods on an assembly line but it changed radically the degree of specialization of labour and capital with consequences that were dramatic.

The Challenge

Toyota Motor Company had entered the automobile industry at the urging of the Japanese government shortly before the Second World War. After the war, Japanese automobile firms wanted to get into full-scale production in competition with the Europeans and Americans. Foreign producers were also anxious to start up in Japan.

Early on, the Japanese planning body, the Ministry of International Trade and Industry (MITI), made two key policy interventions: it prohibited foreign firms from investing in the Japanese motor industry and it established high tariffs on imported cars. Without these prohibitions, the Japanese industry would probably have become a branch plant industry using US technology, as did the Canadian industry. Instead, there was an influx of small, new local firms into the protected Japanese automobile industry.

In response to this influx, MITI attempted a third policy intervention: to rationalize the industry by turning the twelve existing Japanese firms into three big firms, each specialized in one branch of cars and trucks with little competition among them. MITI's plan was based on the classic infant industry argument for tariffs, which is to allow the local infants to *move downwards along* a static falling long-run total cost curve and finally become as good as everyone else. Given the size of the Japanese market, this policy required that there be only a few firms, hence MITI's attempt to 'rationalize' the industry. The theoretical basis for this policy was static neoclassical theory. The experience of government-supported national flag carriers elsewhere suggests, however, that if MITI had had its way, the Japanese firms, who would have lacked the necessary scale economies and the incentive to engage in the uncertain activity of major technological innovations, would have collected the rents available from a protected home market, never becoming major players internationally.

The Japanese automobile firms resisted MITI's attempt to prevent 'excessive' competition and engaged in strong rivalrous behaviour against each other. The challenge facing them was that the Japanese market was not large enough to enable the firms to reach their MESs using US mass production technology. What actually happened then is an illustration of S-E theory. The firms' endogenous innovative response in the 'very long run' was to invent the wholly new production technique of lean production, which *shifted* their long-run cost curves to levels below those of the North American producers and lowered their MESs. This contrast between the neoclassical and the S-E theories of infant industry protection is further discussed in Chapter 16.

The Innovations

Toyota took two decades to develop lean production before the Japanese firms were able seriously to challenge North American and European producers. The new technology has many aspects and we only mention a few by way of illustration.[60] Our comparisons refer to the two industries as they were in the late 1980s. (Since then North America–based firms have adopted many of the aspects of lean production.)

US automobile producers used large stamping presses that would stamp the same part for months. After a long production run, a day or more was required to change the dies to stamp a different part. This method of production led to significant scale economies, which worked against the Japanese producers. One of Toyota's innovations was to develop a method of changing dies in a matter of minutes, permitting the efficient production of variety on a small scale.

In the process, the Japanese discovered, quite unexpectedly, that it actually cost less per unit to make small batches of each part rather than the large batches made in the USA. Two sources of this cost saving were important. First, small batches eliminated the carrying costs of huge inventories. Storage and coordination costs were minimized by receiving parts only as they were needed. Second, since the parts were used almost as soon as they arrived at the plant, defective parts were discovered before many were received. The latter discovery greatly cut the costs caused by defects and led to a more reliable final product. In contrast, US mass production techniques allowed many defective units to pass down the line to be repaired after assembly. Despite devoting considerable resources to fixing errors, many defects were missed in the final stages of production and were passed on to consumers.

Making the Japanese system work required a highly skilled and motivated workforce. Toyota ceased assigning one repetitive task to each worker, and instead used the workers as parts of a team with rotating leaders, giving them a sense of the entire production process. Each team was assigned a number of related jobs and production goals. Often the team was given some discretion to determine how best to meet these goals. Workers were even rotated between divisions—a worker from production might spend time in engineering. Workers were also put in charge of stopping the assembly line, something that only foremen could do in US plants. Stops were encouraged to deal with defects before assembly was completed. After an initial chaotic period of learning by doing, this led to a dramatic decline in the number of defects in Japanese automobiles. The result was a reputation for reliability that continues to this day.

Lean production also differed in all other aspects of the firm's activities, including the design of new models, where Japanese methods allowed new designs to be developed and put into production in about half the time needed by US and European firms.

---

[60] A full description can be found in Womack, Jones, and Roos (1990).

Facilitating Structure

Lean production required large changes in the organization of production in affected industries. But unlike mass production, it did not have large repercussions on the facilitating structure outside of industry. It also has led to large changes in the organization of labour within the firm. Introducing it into North American firms was another example of the conflict-ridden process that typically occurs when well-established procedures have to be changed to accommodate new technologies. Unions were reluctant to give up forms of organizing labour, such as strong job demarcations, that had evolved over decades to fit mass production techniques.

Results

Lean production proved so efficient that Japanese firms gained rapid increases in market share when they seriously challenged the North American and European markets in the 1980s. But for a series of restrictive trade arrangements, including voluntary export restrictions (VERs), the Japanese share would have been much larger than it became. Also more than one US and European automobile manufacturer would almost surely have been driven out of business (either through insolvency or take over) by the remarkable success of this public policy–induced, private sector–created innovation of a new organizational GPT.

Further Considerations

The experience with lean production illustrates a number of interesting generalizations that have been put forward in earlier chapters:

1. Organizational GPTs can be as important in raising productivity as those involving products and processes.
2. Governments sometimes can pick winners, as when MITI singled out the postwar automobile industry for encouragement.
3. Governments can err in trying to control the development of evolving firms, as MITI did when it tried to create three national champions who would not have been in competition with each other. (These and other related policy issues are taken up in more detail in Chapters 16 and 17.)
4. Domestic competition is an important incentive, especially when innovation is required for continued success.
5. Even when innovation is planned by firms, it usually has many unexpected results, as when lean production methods turned out to reduce the costs associated with defective parts and increase the reliability of the final product.
6. New technologies often use less of all inputs for any given amount of output.

VIII.   SOME FUTURE TRANSFORMING GPTS

We conclude this chapter with some thoughts about possible future transforming GPTs. (Note that the computer-led ICT revolution was discussed as a case study towards the end of Chapter 4.) This section is more speculative than that of the other GPTs. Since the full development and realization of these technologies is still in the future, and since no one can predict their ultimate effects with any surety, we do not use our usual S-E categories to organize this discussion.

One theme common to many of the most important technologies of the near future is that they result from the 'science of the small'. As science continually pushes against the limits of size, it is increasingly possible to control the fundamental building blocks of nature. Here we look at two such developments: biotechnology and nanotechnology.

Biotechnology

Although biological engineering through selective breeding is as old as the neolithic agricultural revolution, modern biotechnology begins with the 1953 discovery of the structure of DNA as the carrier of the genetic code. Understanding the double helix structure of DNA was a key GPP. It launched a new era of research that took the world '[f]rom discovery of DNA's molecular structure to Federal Express overnight delivery of custom-made, designer DNA molecules—and all in the space of forty years' (Regis 1995: 17).[61] The GPP of understanding DNA was turned into a GPT by several inventions that made it a practical technology. First was the discovery of a family of enzymes called restriction endonucleases, which can recognize a particular sequence in DNA and cut it at the required point. Then came the technique that allowed the various fragments of DNA to be separated into homogeneous groups. After that was recombinant DNA in which fragments of DNA are joined by use of a 'sealing enzyme' called ligase. Cancer cells, which have the property of unstoppable growth, can then be used to reproduce the recombinant DNA at will. With these inventions, biotechnology became a true process GPT, which like any other, could be used in the manufacturing (or creating) of many different products.

Like all GPTs, it was not clear just what applications would emerge before each technique was perfected and applied—although in a general way it was obvious to most observers that the possibilities were enormous (as was the case with the discoveries surrounding electricity). As always, the discovery of new knowledge was well ahead of its practical applications, although these are beginning to multiply exponentially—a typical feature of transforming GPTs. We mention a few examples.

The field of biotechnology is undergoing a 'revolution' as the application of advanced computing power, as well as complementary advances in other fields—e.g.

---

[61] Although, the time between successive GPTs has narrowed over the centuries, the gestation period of individual GPTs does not seem to have shortened much since the industrial revolution. Impressionistically speaking, in 2003, fifty years after the double helix revolution, biotechnology is not obviously further ahead or behind in its development trajectory compared with where electricity was in 1917, fifty years after the invention of the dynamo, and the computer in the early 1990s, fifty years after the development of the first electronic computers.

physics, chemistry, nanotechnology—rapidly accelerate its rate of innovation. Custom-made strands of DNA indicate the overlap between nanotechnology and modern biotechnology in the science of the small: each strand may be built from the
bottom up, from the base constituents of DNA itself.

Even at this relatively early stage in its development, at the start of the twenty-first
century, it is clear to many that the innovations resulting from research into
biotechnology will have important transforming effects on many aspects of the
economy. Here we briefly touch on some of the sectors where biotechnology is
already having important impacts.

Applications

Since biotechnology concerns the building blocks of life, one of its largest impacts is
on the field of health care. One important goal is to use the patient's own genetic
material to manufacture biological 'parts', from skin to organ tissue, which can
replace defective material without fear of rejection by the patient's immune system.
Gene therapy allows problem cells to be 'corrected' by introducing cells into the bone
marrow of a patient, creating a powerful method for combating very serious diseases
in relatively advanced stages of their development. Only slightly further away is the
ability to construct therapeutic molecules from scratch, using computer models to
discover the best fit for the surface of a protein. This development will help to realize
the search for therapies based on theoretical developments rather than trial-and-
error experimentation.

The impact of biotechnology on food production has already been remarkable.
The Green Revolution was an early development in bioengineering. Genetic engineering of grains is being used to modify many crops with the hope of ultimately
engineering 'optimal plants for every growing condition and market niche' (Grace
1997: 102). Plants can now be made resistant to fungal diseases by exposing them to
a genetically engineered weak version of the disease to activate their immune
system—a procedure analogous to inoculation in humans. Genetic engineering is
being used to improve the freezing tolerance of grains and grapes with big potential
effects on extending the area of cultivation of some key crops. In a practice called
'genetic farming' genetic engineers are also using plants and animals as factories to
manufacture drugs, industrial chemicals, fuels, plastics, and medical products. Here
we see the familiar GPT development as the procedure branches out to affect more
and more industries that initially were unrelated to biotechnology. Genetic engineering also has promise for environmental clean-up as pollution-eating bugs are
developed.

The application of biotechnology to agriculture presents some of the thorniest
issues confronting policymakers today. The implementation of biotechnology has
been full of uncertainties about harmful side effects and, so far, the results have not
met the optimism of some early researchers. Regardless of how the agricultural
applications of biotechnology turn out, one can be sure that public resistance to
genetically engineered foodstuffs will slow their development and diffusion. But
since the optimal level of the technology's implementation cannot even be guessed

at, some observers fear it has not been slowed sufficiently while others argue it has been slowed too much.

Bioprospecting is steadily locating new medicines and other useful materials in forests and seas. For example, animals that cohabitate with poisonous species often produce antitoxins of great potency—materials that, once understood, can be manufactured in laboratories. Other possibilities just on the horizon include salt-resistant, protein-digesting enzymes that may be useful in cleaning industrial machinery; compounds made by algae and sponges that help plants to germinate and grow; and marine enzymes that combine readily with other chemicals and are then useful in processing medicines, food products, and cosmetics (Grace 1997: 170). Bioengineering is also being extended into the forest industry. Of the many new techniques, one of the most promising is micro propagation, which clones trees. Its advantages include cheap, fast, mechanized production of trees for reforestation, and the ability to genetically engineer and clone stocks of transgenic trees.

Impacts on the Facilitating and Policy Structures

Biotechnology will cause many deep and widespread changes in structure. Since much research concerns probing heretofore unexplored areas of biology, it is creating tremendous pressure on the existing policy structure. In particular, many successful efforts to change intellectual property rights to cover plants and other organisms were made by large pharmaceutical companies. This has created conflict at the international level, with developing countries (especially those in South America, and some parts of Asia) trying to protect what they see as their natural endowment of environmental diversity.

Biotechnology will transform many industries. Some will become more productive versions of their current selves (e.g. forestry and mining); others may be transformed beyond recognition (e.g. health care and agriculture). Although the details are still hard to predict, we can be sure that major adjustments will occur throughout the facilitating structure.

Perhaps most important of all are the medical implications of biotechnology, which no doubt will ultimately be profound. On the policy side, new methods of genetic testing may render much more information on a patient's current and future states of health, which has tremendous implications for the provision of service and health insurance. This poses all kinds of policy questions about what knowledge should be kept in the public domain and what should be allowed to become private property. Increasing average lifespans from 70 to say 110 years over the course of half a century would require enormous adjustments in all aspects of the facilitating and policy structures (e.g. labour laws, social security, health benefits, housing, product mix).

Although successes and failures cannot be predicted in detail, it is clear that there will be an impressive range of successful medical applications transforming medical practice in myriad ways.

Within 50 years, we expect comprehensive genomics-based health care to be the norm in the U.S. We will understand the molecular foundation of diseases, be able to prevent them in many cases, and design accurate, individual therapies for illness. In the next decade, genetic tests will routinely predict individual susceptibility to disease. (Collins and Jegalian 2000: 17)

We interpret this to be a statement about scientific *possibility*, not economic *likelihood*. As usual, predictions about the actual social implementation of such technological advances range from utopian to dystopian. As Bailey (2000: 61) notes: 'The biomedical revolution of the next century promises to alter our culture, our politics, and our lives.'

Conclusion

Biotechnology seems to be evolving as did past GPTs. It is sufficiently developed to ensure that it has many potential uses, but not developed enough to allow much beyond informed guesses at some of the revolutionary uses on the horizon. Commercial risks are great because the industry is operating under conditions of genuine uncertainty. Pay-offs are sometimes a decade or more into the future and failed research efforts are plentiful.[62]

One of the unfortunate uncertainties around biotechnology is the large degree of social risk. Risks of unfortunate, even disastrous, side effects are a major concern, especially since uncertainty is everywhere—there is no way we can rule out the possibility of producing a product that does serious harm before we learn how to control it. Public resistance illustrates the conflicts that typically arise with new technologies. The opposition may hold up the introduction of many products and processes that will eventually win acceptance years from now, just as they may also hold up the introduction of products and process that eventually will prove harmful. The conflicts surrounding biotechnology amply illustrate two points we have made repeatedly: first, the development and diffusion of a new GPT is often a conflict-ridden process; and second, technology develops much faster when the criterion of acceptance is success in the marketplace than when it is political approval (see our discussion on pages 42 and 417). There is little doubt that public protests, working through political and extra-legal channels, have slowed—*for better or for worse*—the evolution of the biotechnological GPT.

Nanotechnology

Compared with the other GPTs that we have considered, the promises of nanotechnology are more distant. Conceptually, however, this fundamental alteration of *all* materials production promises the greatest revolution in production since flaking chips off flints produced the first stone tool. This is because the very materials we use will be designed by humans and not simply found. Again, as is typical with GPTs, this move to designed materials has a rather long history (dating back to the various metallurgical developments of early history). It gathered momentum in the first half of

---

[62] Under these circumstances public assistance can be important in influencing the pace and direction of new developments. Although current research is heavily financed by private sector companies, many of the technologies would have been much slower to develop if early research had not been supported by the public sector.

the twentieth century with the introduction of synthetic plastics. Today we are on the verge of rendering the distinction between natural and synthetic materials obsolete.[63]

Basics

Nanotechnology refers to the technologies that operate on materials one-billionth of a metre or less in size—about the thickness of a drop of water spread over one square metre. It comes in two basic forms: 'top-down', which pulverizes larger lumps of material until they are of nano-size; and 'bottom-up', which works with individual atoms and molecules. Most of the really dramatic applications come from the bottom-up approach and we confine ourselves to that branch from here on.

Current technology removes the unwanted parts of a material to be left with what is wanted or needed. Nanotechnology handles individual atoms and molecules, building them precisely into desired aggregates, which may be no more than two or three molecules, or may be an object observable to the naked eye. The power to rearrange atoms at will, not long ago thought forever out of reach, is a genuine process GPT, which like all process technologies can be used to make many different products. It will have staggering implications for the production of economic output.

Nanotechnology has a number of key characteristics. The first and most important is the ability to place an atom or molecule into a precise location. The second is the ability to produce goods for little more than the cost of the raw materials. These two combined may ultimately allow us to produce a shape or structure (obeying the basic laws of physics) of any material from any material. The third, and least well understood in terms of its ultimate impact, is the ability to produce self-replicating machines. This last aspect of nanotechnology causes the most concern amongst critics considering the possible negative effects.[64]

Nanotechnology is being used to produce medical machines the size of a few hundred atoms to practice nanomedicine, which includes non intrusive surgery. At the intersection of the biotechnology and nanotechnology revolutions is the research into nanobots that regulate the bloodstream, the construction of microfluids for use in the body, and using nanotechnology to insert drugs into specific cells or even to construct an artificial immune system.

Nanotechnology will be used to reduce the size and cost of computers. Enormously powerful quantum computers may not even use electronics. Nanoproducts may simplify housekeeping with dirt-digesting machines that will make possible a whole range of products, such as self-cleaning dishes and carpets, while keeping household air permanently fresh.

The largest and most important implications of nanotechnology will probably be in materials technology. Manipulating matter at the molecular level, especially the

---

[63] For example, there is no way in which iron synthesized by nanotechnology would be in any sense different from naturally occurring iron.

[64] As Drexler (1986: 172) puts it: 'Tough, omnivorous "bacteria" could outcompete real bacteria: they could spread like blowing pollen, replicate swiftly, and reduce the biosphere to dust in a matter of days. Dangerous replicators could easily be too tough, small, and rapidly spreading to stop.'

ability to self-replicate, allows it to be treated much like 'data'. We can transform it, manipulate it, reproduce it, and transmit it with precision.

[N]anotechnology could have more effect on our material existence than those last two great inventions in that domain—the replacement of sticks and stones by metals and cements and the harnessing of electricity. Similarly, we can compare the possible effects of artificial intelligence on how we think—and on how we might come to think about ourselves—with only two earlier inventions: those of language and of writing. (Minski 1986: vii)

Nanotechnology does not yet have all the characteristics of a GPT. It has yet to enter the economy in an important way, and many of its applications are either still only on the drawing board or in designers' imaginations. Yet if nanotechnology realizes even a fraction of its potential, it will become one of the most important GPTs of the twenty-first century.

Structural Impacts

Guessing at the adjustments in the facilitating structure that would be brought about by a major shift to nanotechnology is still in the realm of science fiction. But if fully realized, nanotechnology promises dramatic changes to all aspects of the facilitating structure. If one were to accept an optimistic outlook with regard to its possible impacts, the list would be endless: raw materials would no longer need to be transported to the factory, the factory itself would become mobile, waste products would be reduced, the distribution of geographic wealth would be dramatically impacted (e.g. deposits of iron or coal would cease to be meaningful), the nature of work would need to be completely reconsidered (many researchers speculate on an entertainment society replacing our information society). The list goes on. This leads Drexler (1986: 20) to conclude:

To have any hope of understanding our future, we must understand the consequences of assemblers, disassemblers, and nanocomputers. They promise to bring changes as profound as the Industrial Revolution, antibiotics, and nuclear weapons all rolled up in one massive breakthrough. To understand a future of such profound change, it makes sense to seek principles of change that have survived the greatest upheavals of the past. They will prove a useful guide.

Since the development of nanotechnology is truly uncertain, it is easy to exaggerate the opportunities for technological dynamism offered by this radical new technology. However, since the technology displays so many of the characteristics of past transforming GPTs, we are confident that at some point society will have to address the challenges and opportunities offered by nanotechnology. In so doing, much of our present economic, political, and social structures will be transformed almost beyond recognition.

IX. OMITTED GPTS

Of the list of twenty-four GPTs that we gave at the beginning of Chapter 5, we have discussed nineteen in detail. The others were omitted solely in the interests of space, not because of any judgement of ours about their relative importance. In this section, we devote a short paragraph to each of the omitted GPTs.

The *iron steamship* increased speed, safety, and punctuality in sea travel. It made luxury international travel a reality at least for the rich. Combined with refrigeration and the telegraph and fed by the railroad, it globalized the market for agricultural products, both animal and vegetable. Argentinian beef, Australian mutton, and bread made from Canadian wheat became staples on European tables. Mounted with guns and suitably armoured, it evolved into the twentieth-century dreadnought, which revolutionized naval warfare.

The *internal-combustion engine* started as a stationary engine powered by coal gas and evolved into a mobile engine powered by petroleum. Its high power to weight ratio enabled the development of lighter-than-air craft and also the automobile, at least in its present form.[65] It gave rise to the oil industry that altered the wealth of many nations and changed the course of foreign policy in so many ways. Installed in tanks and trucks, it ushered in an age of mobile warfare that made the Second World War so different from the First. It also contributed greatly to global pollution.

The *motor vehicle* altered social and economic relations in myriad ways. Its production became a major source of employment and wealth creation, particularly in the USA. It was the origin of the assembly line and many other of the twentieth century's productivity-improving innovations in the technique of mass production. It contributed to the development of sprawling suburbs that had begun with trams and commuter passenger rail services. It enabled the suburban shopping centre and the domestic long-distance tourist industry, ringing the death knell on the pattern of holidays and vacations taken within short distances of people's residences.

The *airplane* shrunk the world dramatically. When it evolved into the large jet-powered commercial aircraft, it ushered in the affordable two-week holiday taken anywhere in the world, international conferences, and commercial sports leagues that spread over wide distances—the whole nation in the USA and most of the continent in Europe. For example, US professional baseball and hockey were confined to the area that could be reached by an overnight bus journey until the advent of the jet aircraft, after which the leagues quickly spread nationwide. As military aircraft, it transformed land warfare. Flown from aircraft carriers, it did the same on sea, ending the centuries-long era of the battleship as queen of the seas.

The *Internet*, a part of the twentieth-century ICT revolution, is the offshoot of the computer and fast communications networks. It is a good example of a technology whose use was not even guessed at by those responsible for its original development. It has transformed long-distance communication. Through email it has virtually eliminated the sending of letters by surface mail. It has allowed NGOs to gather groups of protesters quickly, ending the age of routine behind-the-scenes diplomacy.

---

[65] If the gasoline engine had not existed, steam would have powered an ever-growing number of forms of surface transports. How close the steam-driven non-rail surface evolution would have come to the gasoline-driven evolution that was actually experienced is a matter of conjecture.

It has led to an explosion of information available to ordinary citizens who learn, shop, organize diverse efforts, play games, meet temporary partners and permanent mates, all through the medium of the 'net'.

X. CONCLUDING THOUGHTS

This survey of transforming GPTs illustrates why we argue that one cannot explain the long-run growth record of the West, or the world, without understanding technology. Further, one cannot properly understand technology when it is formulated merely as a scalar in a production function. Instead, one must comprehend each technology's characteristics and channels of structural impacts. Along with the masses of incremental changes in technology that are important sources of economic growth from year to year, every once in a while comes a new GPT that causes major structural adjustments and changes in our way of life, as well as rejuvenating the growth process by presenting a whole new research programme for finding improvements in, and applications for, the new GPT.

We have also documented the empirical basis for many of the stylized facts laid out in earlier chapters. GPTs do typically start very crudely, they do start with a narrow range of uses and a restricted number of applications. As they develop, however, they do spread to have multiple uses and to impact entire economies in many, many dimensions.

In Part III, we reorganize those effects in a more theoretical manner, in order to set the stage for formally modelling the GPT-driven growth process in a way that is constrained by some of the key facts that we have outlined here. But first, in Part II, we turn our attention to the dramatic appearance in the nineteenth century of sustained growth in the West, both of the extensive and the intensive variety.

Part II

The Transition to Sustained Economic Growth in the West

In this part, we deal with the West's achievement of sustained extensive and intensive growth, both of which occurred during the nineteenth century. To the question: 'Why did it occur at all?' we answer in Chapter 7 that the transition to sustained extensive growth was the result of the First Industrial Revolution, which occurred in Britain in the late eighteenth and early nineteenth centuries, and the subsequent institutionalization of R&D, together with the close linking of technological and scientific development, both of which occurred during the Second Industrial Revolution in the latter part of the century. We trace the roots of the Industrial Revolution back as far as the Middle Ages, following their growth up through the evolution of early modern science and technology, which we argue were more closely related than is often accepted.

To the question: 'Why did this revolution occur in eighteenth- and nineteenth-century Britain and then spread fairly quickly to the European continent?' we answer in Chapter 8 that a highly contingent and country-specific explanation is required. In Chapter 1 we followed Geoffrey Hodgson in calling our approach one of 'historical specificity' as opposed to 'theoretical generality'. Since current formal models of growth are general ones, predicting the emergence of sustained growth anywhere in the world as soon as certain broad macro conditions are met, we argue that they cannot formalize the explanation of why, where, and when it happened. Instead, our explanation is couched in terms of appreciative historical theorizing about specific events in specific places. To the question: 'Why did this revolution not occur anywhere outside of the West, in spite of the high degree of technological development of some other societies?' we answer in Chapter 8 that no other country had Western science, which was a necessary condition for the two Industrial Revolutions.

In Chapter 9 we deal with the relation between income and population growth that determines how much of extensive growth gets translated into intensive growth. Here we do find that the assumed relations are simple enough to allow us to model some of them and learn from such formal theorizing. We find that when we embed non-Malthusian household behaviour into a Solow growth model, a powerful externality produces macro behaviour that is very close to, but not identical with, Malthusian predictions. But when we add additional sectors to the model and alter the production function in the direction of increasing empirical relevance, these Malthusian results largely disappear.

In Chapter 10 we ask: 'Why did population dynamics change sufficiently to turn the West's sustained extensive growth into sustained intensive growth some time in the latter part of the nineteenth century?' Here again we argue that appreciative, historically based theorizing is necessary to deal with the complex set of issues involved in any potentially satisfactory explanation.

Although we have not said the last word on the issues of why, where, and when sustained growth emerged, we hope we have given strong support to the need to approach such questions mainly through appreciative historical theorizing rather than exclusively through formal model building. Some day, someone may succeed in building a model which predicts that the Industrial Revolution would occur in late eighteenth and early nineteenth-century Britain and not elsewhere in the world—a model that has other testable implications so that it is more than just an *ex post* rationalization—but it will have to be a model that contains vastly more country-specific and historically specific variables than any of today's formal growth and population models.

7

The Emergence of Sustained Extensive Growth in the West

I. INTRODUCTION

There have been long periods of growth in the past, as well as shorter bursts—what Goldstone (2002) calls efflorescences. But the growth that started some time in the nineteenth century is much more rapid than anything that has been seen previously. It also shows signs of being self-sustaining in ways that past growth was not.[1] In this chapter, we consider the emergence of sustained extensive growth that occurred during or shortly after the First Industrial Revolution.[2] The bulk of the chapter is devoted to events leading up to the First Industrial Revolution. Only towards the end do we deal with the issue of why those events led to a period of sustained growth rather than just another short-lived burst.

Two Approaches

Two main approaches to explaining the emergence of sustained growth are discernible in the literature. One is to construct a formal model that will 'explain' the transition. None of the existing growth models that are based on a neoclassical macro production function are country-specific. Nor are the popular two-stage, endogenous-population models designed to explain the transition from sporadic slow growth (or even zero growth) to sustained high growth. In all these models, growth occurs whenever an economy fulfils some small set of necessary conditions, usually concerned with saving and investment in the growth models, and with investment in human capital for children and/or urbanization in the population models. Indeed, practically all these models make modern sustained growth inevitable sooner or later for all economies. Thus, they are not designed to explain how sustained growth started in one country and not in another *or* why it sometimes comes to halt in countries as widely separated as Nigeria and Argentina.

---

[1] As we point out in more detail at the beginning of Chapter 9, this must be a tentative judgement because there appear to have been at least three periods of sustained growth in the West that lasted many centuries more than the current period beginning with the First Industrial Revolution—two of them followed by disastrous declines.

[2] The details of the timing depend partly on how growth is measured, for example, in terms of technological change or productivity.

In stark contrast, most economic historians and students of technological change are agreed that the Industrial Revolution was not about to occur in any other part of the world, and was a contingent event even in Britain—it might not have happened but for a host of conditions, some of which we investigate in this chapter. We accept this latter view and argue that to explain the Industrial Revolution there is no alternative to a historical treatment that stresses the unique aspects of Europe's centuries-long trajectory of science and technology and of Britain's initial push to industrialization. This requires a combination of historical analysis and appreciative theorizing.

Three Questions

Three questions need to be addressed about Britain's Industrial Revolution that initiated sustained extensive growth in the West: *Why* was there an Industrial Revolution? Why did it occur *where* it did? Why did it occur *when* it did? In short: Why? When? Where? This chapter is devoted to developing our answer to these questions. We start by summarizing some key points.

Why?

To consider the conditions that led to the Industrial Revolution, we argue that the focus must be on the generation of technological knowledge.[3] Specifically, we argue that the answer to the 'why' of the Industrial Revolution is that it stemmed from a view of the universe as an ordered machine governed by natural laws that goes back at least to the medieval scholastic philosophers and to research programmes that were initiated in the early modern period to mechanize all aspects of textile production, to discover alternative sources of power, and to understand magnetism. Fulfilling these programmes required what we regard today as both technology and science—areas of study united under the single rubric of natural philosophy in the medieval and early modern periods. We argue that early modern science provided a necessary condition for the Industrial Revolution, a critical condition that was absent in other civilizations, which might otherwise have developed their own such revolutions.[4]

---

[3] A view shared by Mokyr (2002: 29): 'The central conclusion from the analysis is that economic historians should re-examine the epistemic roots of the Industrial Revolution, in addition to the more standard economic explanations that focus on institutions, markets, geography, and so on.'

[4] Importantly, we do not consider the generation of a mechanical science as sufficient to explain the Industrial Revolution. Any number of contingent events can prevent a scientifically sophisticated society from generating its own industrial revolution. We argue instead that the commonly cited causes form a bundle that contains *more than* sufficient conditions. In other words, the Industrial Revolution as a historical event is strongly overdetermined—not a surprise since many specific events in history are overdetermined. Any number of subsets of those purported causes could have done the job, which implies that eliminating any one of them would not have stopped the emergence of sustained growth. This is why we regard mechanistic science as different from the other 'causes'. It is, we argue, a necessary condition. Eliminating science from any bundle of conditions explaining the Industrial Revolution would have prevented it from occurring. This is a strong thesis as regards the role of knowledge.

An important implication of our view is that the mechanical technologies of industrialization did not develop contemporaneously with industrialization, but long before. We trace the attitudes that produced them back to fundamental questions posed by medieval science. Then we trace their actual development to the trajectories of the four key technologies of the Industrial Revolution—textiles, factory system, steam, and electricity—and to the early modern science that assisted them.[5]

Where?

To the question of 'where' we answer that it could only have happened in north-western Europe, because only there were people developing a scientific approach to understanding and controlling the physical world. More specifically, we argue that within north-western Europe, it could only have happened when it did, in Britain. Britain was the only country in which the new Newtonian mechanics was widely taught, understood, and practised throughout the eighteenth century. This lead in mechanics ensured that, if the Industrial Revolution was to start in the eighteenth century, it could only start in Britain. If Britain had been prevented from developing the revolution, say for political reasons, it might well have happened elsewhere in Europe. Even so, it would have been much delayed, as is illustrated by the actual difficulties in diffusing the early nineteenth-century British technologies to the Continent.

The science of mechanics developed over a long trajectory, and had its roots in developments in medieval and early modern science. In fact, in so far as industry and science were 'revolutionized', those revolutions were made possible by a string of linked technological and scientific advances that stretched back for centuries. Importantly, the trajectory of these developments was strongly affected by the European desire to mechanize almost all aspects of production. 'The later Middle Ages, that is roughly from A.D. 1000 to the close of the fifteenth century, is the period of decisive development in the history of the effort to use the forces of nature mechanically for human purposes' (White 1962: 79).

Science's channels of effect were subtle. Scientific theories were not developed in the lab or the classroom to be tested and commercialized on the shop floor. Nor did they always guide and inform basic research in a linear fashion. Instead, science provided a host of questions and a direction to research that facilitated the development of mechanics as *the* way to understand the natural world. It led to the

---

[5] In doing so, we argue for a return to the views of earlier writers on the Industrial Revolution such as Musson, Robinson, and Schofield (see Musson 1972; Musson and Robinson 1989; Schofield 1963). They held that science was much more important in determining the when, where, and how of the Industrial Revolution than is accepted today. We go one step further by arguing that the development of science was a *necessary* precondition for the Industrial Revolution. Mokyr (2002: 29) makes a similar argument: 'I submit that the Industrial Revolution's timing was determined by intellectual developments and that the true key to the timing of the Industrial Revolution has to be sought in the scientific revolution of the seventeenth century and the enlightenment movement of the eighteenth century. The key to the Industrial Revolution was technology, and technology is knowledge.'

development of a cultural context in which craftsmen could talk to natural philosophers, and vice versa. In the absence of mechanistic science, the feedback from knowledge to technology would have been much dampened and the development of crucial technologies much delayed.[6]

In Chapter 8, we apply this view of European exceptionalism to investigate the question of why there was no Industrial Revolution in two other seemingly promising regions: the Islamic countries and China. We argue that the Islamic countries missed out on several of the key developments that contributed to the European Industrial Revolution. In contrast, China had at the beginning of the eighteenth century many characteristics that matched those found in Europe. But what it lacked was the necessary condition for such a revolution: early modern science.

When?

As to the question of 'When', our thesis yields no specific date for the Industrial Revolution. By the late eighteenth century, however, the trajectory of textile mechanization reached a state where it became profitable to move production out of cottages into 'proto-factories'. Then, as textile machinery, water power, and steam power evolved over the next few decades, production became established in what modern observers would recognize as full-blown factories. By that time the Industrial Revolution would have been hard to stop.

The factory system was the critical organizational GPT that made the Industrial Revolution something more than just another stage in the mechanization of production, which had been proceeding since the medieval period. This GPT might have been accelerated or decelerated a bit by countless contingent events that would have affected the trajectory of research into textile mechanization. But the evolution of that research programme had to follow its own logic of cumulative knowledge. It is hard to imagine the factory system of production becoming efficient much earlier. Similarly, steam power evolved over 200 years of cumulative incremental research into the science and technology of atmospheric pressure and steam power. When the engine was finally developed sufficiently to be introduced into factories, the full development of factory system and its extension to most of the economy's manufacturing sectors began.

Three Answers

Although these questions are distinct and we have already given a few of the elements of our answers, it is not possible to separate our full answers into distinct narratives. For this reason, we present the relevant material throughout most of this chapter and then, near its end, we provide our answers, most of the substance of which will require little more than back references to what has already been said.

---

[6] The modern view among historians of science—that the roots of the scientific revolution lay in the medieval period (see, for example, Grant 1996; Lindberg 1992; Shapin 1996; Huff 1993)—complements our position that the technologies of the two Industrial Revolutions had been evolving since the medieval period in a continual positive feedback process between what we now distinguish as science and technology.

II. EARLY ROOTS

To understand the emergence of the sustained growth that occurred with the Industrial Revolution, we need to look at some early developments that profoundly influenced the science and technology that lay behind it. Nothing that we say in this and the next chapter is meant to imply any judgement about the *superiority* of one religion over another. Our argument is that Christianity and Islam developed along *different* paths, to a significant extent because of historical accidents, but that these paths profoundly affected more than just the differences in the religious dogmas that evolved in the two civilizations; they affected the trajectories of science and technology.

The Christian West Before 1000

We take classical learning as given and begin with the rise of Christianity (although a full explanation would start with classical natural philosophy). Early Christians were a minority population who were forced to persuade converts rather than relying on force or numbers. Starting in Judea, Christianity spread westward, first under threat of persecution and then, after the Edict of Milan in 313, as a religion with rights similar to others. During that time, it was competing for attention in the culturally sophisticated societies of the Roman Empire.

Two things followed from this history. First, the church fathers had to come to terms with prevailing traditions. Thinkers such as Saint Augustine accepted into Christianity many Greek ideas, particularly from Plato. Christianity also had to accept major aspects of Judaism and it was no easy task to reconcile Old Testament Jewish teachings with those of Christ and his disciples. Philosophical and religious arguments persisted for centuries and the need to deal with them required the church fathers to be philosophers.[7] 'It was the slow percolation of Christianity that enabled it to adjust to the ... world around it and thus prepare itself for a role that could not have been envisioned by its early members' (Grant 1996: 2).

Second, because Christianity had to accept the lay authority that it sought to persuade to its beliefs, a pluralistic tradition of lay and religious authority was established from the outset. No other stance was possible until AD 391 when Christianity became the officially recognized religion of Rome. Given the power of the emperors, it is hard to see how a theocracy could have been created even then, although the clerics might have attempted to infiltrate the lay government with the aim of eventually usurping political power and proclaiming a theocracy. The church fathers did not take this course, probably for the very good reason that a much safer path lay in accepting lay authority as long as the church was given sway over religious matters.

---

[7] Grant (1996) stresses the specific problems created by the doctrine of the Trinity, which was accepted by the Western Church but rejected by the Eastern, Greek orthodox, branch. This subtle doctrine leads to many philosophical quandaries in reconciling the belief in one God with a trinity of Gods: the Father, the Son, and the Holy Ghost.

The early Greek fathers of the Christian Church diverged in their opinions on how their revealed religious knowledge related to Greek scientific knowledge. Some rejected all Greek science, relying solely on revealed truth. Others argued that Christianity could profit from incorporating most of Greek science and philosophy. This gave rise to the 'handmaiden' view, which eventually prevailed with the powerful support of Saint Augustine, among others. Greek science was then seen as inherently neither good nor bad, its value depending on how it was used by Christian thinkers. Thus, Christianity reconciled itself with Greek learning rather than rejecting it as an alien and evil force as it might well have done.

Medieval Institutional Innovations

The eleventh century ushered in a period of stability and expansion in the West. Stronger monarchies appeared. They extended both the internal and external margins of the state with law and order and more secure borders.[8] Economic activity expanded. Industry was partially mechanized by the increasing use of the waterwheel and agricultural innovations greatly increased the food supply (see Chapter 5). Population grew everywhere, particularly in the reviving cities. The new urban prosperity led to an emerging demand for education.[9]

Urban schools grew in number and size to become a substantial educational force. The first round of expansion was in the church schools located in the major urban centres. In later periods, relatively more centres of lay learning developed, but the Church's role in the provision of European education remained important into the twentieth century. Teachers and scholars were attracted to the new centres of learning. The teaching curriculum expanded well beyond that of the monastic schools to include subjects such as logic, law, and medicine. The new schools were in the forefront of attempts to rationalize many activities. According to them, reason and logic—rather than faith in revealed doctrine—should be applied to everything that was studied, from commercial practices to theology. This rationalism pervaded religious as well as lay thinking. Church dogma right up to, and including, the existence of God was subject to rational argument. For example, in the eleventh century a major church thinker, Saint Anselm, invented the ontological proof of God. In this and other works, he applied a secular philosophical method to church doctrine in order to make it more persuasive to non-believers.[10]

---

[8] Dudley (1991) defines the internal margin of the state as the proportion of GDP that can be successfully raised as taxes and the external margin as its geographical boundaries. See our discussion in Chapters 5 and 6.

[9] There is an interesting modelling issue here. Urban areas were the main source of educational demand at least until the 18th century. What caused the difference between the rural and the urban demand for education? We suggest two forces. First, the returns to education seem small in rural settings where farming ability is all that matters, but higher in urban settings where many alternative employment opportunities are available. Second, incomes are typically lower in rural settings than in the urban middle class, who created the new demand for education. The higher urban incomes could be in the range where there is a high-income elasticity of demand for education for its own sake.

[10] But as Lindberg (1992: 195) observes: '[T]he risks were serious: if reason can prove theological claims, presumably it can also disprove them. This is not a problem as long as reason arrives at the "right"

The new eleventh-century learning first used known Latin sources. Most of these were popularizations of Greek classics translated into Latin during the time of the Empire and intended for those who could not read Greek. Scholars soon realized that they were well behind the advanced scholarship of ancient Greece and modern Islam. In the later part of the eleventh century, an increasing number of translations were made from both Greek and Islamic sources. The latter became increasingly accessible because of the Christian reconquest of Sicily and parts of Spain.[11] Particularly important were the translations made by the collaboration of a Christian and an Islamic scholar from the great library of Toledo, which had avoided the widespread destruction that accompanied the Christian reconquest of that city in the eleventh century. Together, over the latter half of the twelfth century, they translated nearly 100 books on such subjects as astronomy, mathematics, medicine, philosophy, and logic.[12] It was only after translations such as these that Aristotle's writing became widely known. This, as we shall see, was an influential historical accident.

Four key developments took place contemporaneously with the new learning and were closely related to it: the rise of a pluralistic and evolutionary concept of law; the development of the concept of the corporation; pluralism in government; and the birth of universities. Although these were interrelated, we must perforce discuss them separately.

The Legal Revolution[13]

Once the Germanic tribes settled down after the various waves of migration, they left their imprint on the Western portion of the Roman Empire, which they had taken over piecemeal. In their society, everyone and everything had its price. Wrongs were settled by customary recompense. If these customary recompenses were not paid, the groups engaged in blood feuds. As time passed, these customs were increasingly codified. But literacy was so sparse that the writings were mainly for reference by future scribes.

[I]n this Germanic world lie the origins of a jurisprudence.... The first institution to open the way to this was the acceptance of kingly or collective power to declare what was to be recorded. All the Germanic kingdoms moved towards the writing down and codification of their law. (Roberts 1993: 240)

---

answer; but what shall we do if, having committed ourselves to reason as the arbiter of truth, we find reason and faith in opposition?'

[11] This rise of European learning in the 11th and the 12th centuries was only bringing Europe closer to Islam where advanced scholarship had flourished for several centuries.

[12] See Fletcher (2003) for a full account of this remarkable collaboration.

[13] Our treatment in this section is based mainly on Huff (1993: ch. 4). Although Huff, and others writing on this issue, take a comparative approach, we are concerned here with what happened in the West. In Chapter 8, we ask why sustained growth did not emerge elsewhere and, although there are differences between the West on the one hand and China and Islam on the other in almost every point we make here, we concentrate only on why science did not develop in those other areas. If science were a necessary condition for the emergence of sustained growth, its absence is sufficient to explain the failure to do so elsewhere.

But the most important legal changes came in the twelfth and thirteenth centuries, which saw the creation of 'a variety of new forms and powers of association that were in fact unique to the West, since they were wholly absent in Islamic as well as Chinese law' (Huff 1993: 120). In the West, the king had often asserted his claim to be the source of all law. That power was broken in the investiture controversy (1050–1122) over who had the right to appoint bishops. The controversy was largely won by the Church, which withdrew the spiritual authority that kings had formerly claimed, and created a body of cannon law that was the West's first modern system of law designed to be universal in scope. That law was largely the work of the Italian monk Gratian.

Gratian began with the concept of natural law, which lies between divine law and human law. Natural law 'is found in both divine revelation and in human reason and conscience' (Berman 1983: 145). Because natural law is also God's will, neither the king's nor the Church's law is superior to it.

This was a major achievement in that reason and conscience were held to be at least as important as custom and revelation. Gratian worked out tests, such as duration, universality, uniformity of application, and reasonableness, to ascertain if customary behaviour should prevail. These tests had the effect of making legal rules relative rather than absolute:

What took place in the eleventh, twelfth, and early thirteenth centuries in Western Europe was a radical transformation that created, among other things, the very concept of a legal system with its many levels of autonomy and jurisdiction and its cadres of legal experts.... [This] was not only an intellectual revolution, but a social, political, and economic revolution whereby new legal concepts, entities, procedures, powers, and agencies came into being and transformed social life. (Huff 1993: 124–5)

The result was that Western law came to be seen as evolving in adaptation to changing circumstances. In contrast, thinkers of many other religions, including Islam, held that laws had been laid down once and for all by prophets and could only be changed when they had been misinterpreted or misunderstood. Furthermore, the split between civil and ecclesiastical law and the power of corporations, such as guilds and universities, gave rise to the concept of degrees of jurisdiction absent from Islam.

Corporation

A key institutional development during this period was the concept of treating a body of people as a corporation, which is separate from the state and distinct from the individuals who compose it. It can be argued that the Christian Church was the first corporation in Western society. Although the Christian leaders often sought to dominate lay authority after their Church became the official religion of Rome, they always recognized the separate authority of lay governments. Pluralism between religious and lay authority was thus a part of the West's tradition from the outset of the Church's supremacy over other religions.

Guilds were the first lay corporate institution. They gave substantial power and protection to those practising one particular trade. Later came the universities, and after them several cities. The plethora of corporations, each with its own range of authority, was a key development in the West's growing pluralism.

[E]ach collectivity that achieved corporate status...enacted laws to govern its members and thereby whole new systems of law—for example, urban law, merchant law, royal law— developed that served to counterbalance jurisdictions and prevent the monopoly of power and authority over the whole realm. Thus guilds, associations of merchants, and various assortments of workers and tradesmen became law-making bodies. They enacted ordinances to regulate their membership, to fix prices, control trade, and standardize business transactions. (Huff 1993: 137)

This independent power of corporations created a split between civil and ecclesiastical law on the one hand and the power of corporations on the other. Importantly, it produced the concept of *degrees of jurisdiction*. Thus, in the centuries after the decline of the Western Roman Empire, guilds were progressive institutions that protected groups of economic producers from the excessive and arbitrary power of the state and Church. They played a key part in the development of pluralism.[14]

Universities

As the urban schools that were established in the eleventh century grew in size, the best schools attracted the most outstanding scholars and students. 'Most masters and students were foreigners in the cities in which they taught and studied and, consequently, had no rights and privileges. Operating individually, they were no match for the municipal, state, and church authorities with whom they had to negotiate teaching conditions' (Grant 1996: 35). In self-defence, they developed what amounted to a guild of local scholars. Over time, they became a self-governing corporate group composed of teachers and their students, enjoying a considerable degree of autonomy from local and national interference. During the first half of the thirteenth century, a number of these schools evolved into universities.

An important university produced fame and revenue for its city, which gave the university authorities substantial power. They could threaten to move to another city if local officials asked for unacceptable conditions. They also became adept at gaining patronage from a local personage, such as a baron or prince. Thus 'for the most part the universities managed the rare and remarkable feat of securing patronage and protection without interference' (Lindberg 1992: 208).

Initially, when scholars taught as individuals, they were the arbitrators of their own success. But once they became members of a guild, collective behaviour evolved. The corporation set and enforced standards and granted licences to become teachers.

---

[14] Epstein (1998) plays down the political power of guilds, and their ability to shield members from market forces. He also argues that they were a source of innovation and diffusion in the medieval economy. Although it may be, as is commonly argued, that craft guilds eventually became entrenched roadblocks to the adoption of new technologies, Epstein disagrees, arguing that guilds never became inefficient at generating innovation and diffusing skills, but that they were abolished by state fiat.

Within broad limits set by the need to conform (or at least appear to conform) with church dogma, members of a university were free to pursue virtually any intellectual avenue and to enjoy many privileges, not the least of which was that they, and their students, were granted clerical status. The universities also came to teach a more or less common agenda across most of Europe. Aristotelian logic was important, as were traditional arts subjects, as well as moral philosophy, natural philosophy, and metaphysics. Medicine, law, and theology were taught in graduate faculties. Aristotelian natural philosophy became increasingly important, covering metaphysics, physics, meteorology, psychology, and natural history. 'For the first time in history, there was an educational effort of international scope, undertaken by scholars conscious of their intellectual and professional unity, offering standardized higher education to an entire generation of students' (Lindberg 1992: 212).

Makdisi (1981, 1990) has argued that the concept of a university, as a place where scholars and their pupils gather to study the full range of known scholarship, is an Islamic invention, which spread to the Christian world through contact with the West, bequeathing to it a number of concepts that survive to this day. But what never happened in the Islamic world, and what was crucial in the West, was the development of the university as a corporation. Thus, as with so many other innovations, the West was not the original inventor; instead it critically improved on technologies and institutions that it had copied from elsewhere.

In the twelfth and thirteenth centuries, the universities made the study of Greek and Islamic science a major part of the curriculum and developed a system of examinations. Through these, and other similar measures, 'the West took a decisive (and probably irreversible) step toward the inculcation of a scientific world view that extolled the powers of reason and painted the universe—human, animal, inanimate—as a rationally ordered system' (Huff 1993: 189).[15]

Government Institutions

Unlike the universities and the legal system, the growing pluralism of Europe's political institutions was an unconscious evolutionary development, not a conscious creation. In fact, it was mostly resisted when recognized by those in power.

At one extreme of sovereignty, the ruler owns everything. Vassals and their tenants had only a lifelong interest in the land, which led to struggles as the tenant's death approached. To some extent, all societies share aspects of this system—Islam, China, India, Europe, and most of the ancient empires including the Persian. In Europe during the early medieval period, however, the rights of non-government agents grew as age-old de facto property rights became harder to alter unilaterally. For example, the rights of peasants to alienate or gift their land became increasingly recognized by local courts. Rosenberg and Birdzell (1986: 61) argue that from the

---

[15] By the early modern period, as is the case with most institutions that gain political power, universities tried to suppress elements of the newly emerging science. As we document in Chapter 6, their attempts were made much more difficult by the existence of the printing press and the production of standardized texts.

relatively centralized perspective of most other societies, European feudalism looked like anarchy.[16] The king parcelled out land to lords, who in turn parcelled some out to their vassals, creating mutual, two-way obligations—some of which were affirmed by the Magna Carta. The interest was hereditary, precluding costly and wasteful power struggles at death. In contrast to centralized forms of government, the feudal arrangements assisted the rise of the market economy because they strengthened an existing trend towards pluralistic arrangements with mutual obligations and personal ownership. Rosenberg and Birdzell argue that these interlocking obligations, and the lack of political unity in Europe, were important in limiting the government's power to inhibit innovation in science, religion, and technology in the early modern period.

Competition among the political leaders of the newly emerging nation-states, each anxious to retain the revenues and credits available from a merchant class and each aware of the political danger of allowing neighboring states to increase their capacity to finance military power, was an important factor in overcoming the inherited distaste of the rural military aristocracy for the new merchant class. Had the merchants been dealing with a political monopoly [as in China], they might not have been able to purchase the required freedom of action at a price compatible with the development of trade. (Rosenberg and Birdzell 1986: 136–7)

The size of the contribution made by political diversity in the West's growth is an open question, but it was positive.[17] Important though it may have been, it certainly was not a necessary condition for some kinds of growth as is shown by the continued development of China documented by Pomeranz (2000). Indeed, the established trading relations in India, China, and the rest of Asia were so profitable that Europeans strove to get even a small share of them after they had entered those areas. Where pluralism was probably more important was in science. It helped Western science to avoid the attacks of the established religion—attacks to which Islamic science finally succumbed—and it created the autonomous spheres of activity that were so lacking in China.

Another source of political pluralism was the independence that many of the large trading cities achieved during the urban revival in the latter half of the Middle Ages. Many cities declared themselves independent communes, free from feudal obligations. Although they owed allegiance to the king and paid taxes to the royal treasury, they were largely self-governing in local affairs and were free to establish their own civic laws, rules, and regulations. Such an arrangement is unthinkable in a unitary

---

[16] Japan also had a feudal system, which may or may not have had something to do with its willingness to be more open to Western ideas than was China (prior to its opening up following the Japanese–US trade treaty of 1854). Be that as it may, what Japan did not have was Western science, and when it did enter into a period of sustained growth, this was based for many decades on the diffusion of Western science and technology and only later on endogenous science and technology.

[17] There is an obvious trade-off involved. If warfare is too constant, it becomes overly disruptive to trade. But an overly secure state can become overbearing. Nonetheless, it appears that many scholars are now willing to locate important precursors of industrialization in feudal Europe although others dissent. (See especially the comparative analysis of feudalism by Pomeranz 2000.)

state and would have been unsustainable if the legal reforms discussed earlier had not recognized separate, sometimes overlapping, spheres of legal jurisdiction.

The Role of the Medieval Church in Scholarship

When lay learning more or less disappeared in the centuries following the dissolution of the Western Roman Empire, learning was maintained and cultivated by the monasteries.[18] It is not surprising, therefore, that when the new lay interest in education arose in the eleventh century, clerics were in close touch with it and were prominent in helping it to develop. Indeed, the distinction between religious and lay centres of instruction that characterizes the modern Western world did not then exist.

Many of the works that became available in the West for the first time—such as geometry (from the Greeks) and algebra and astronomy (from Arab regions)— presented no challenges to existing religious thought. The obviously useful content of these 'exact sciences' did not impinge on matters of Christian dogma. In contrast, potential conflicts between the two were suggested by broader works on 'natural philosophy', which included much of what we today call science. However, the Christian thinkers sought to Christianize this branch of classical learning rather than rejecting it. 'In broad terms this meant bringing together in a single whole views based upon the amalgam of Jewish history and poetry called the Bible (in the Greek translation known as the Septuagint, which dated *c.* 200–100 BC) with the philosophy and science of the advanced urban civilisation of Greece—a formidable task' (Kearney 1971: 13).

Reconciling classical learning with religious doctrine became one of the most important research programmes of the twelfth and thirteenth centuries. Scholars such as Thierry of Chartres, who lived in the first half of the twelfth century, argued that divine intervention was restricted to the initial moment of creation and all subsequent events followed natural laws. To discover these natural laws was to discover God's purpose.

We have already noted that the early revival of learning was confined to Latin texts, which included many literary works and Plato's dialogues, but not the works of Aristotle. Plato's mysticism sat reasonably well with medieval church doctrine, which in any case, had absorbed a large dose of Platonism in its formative years.

Coping with Aristotle

As the translation movement gained momentum in the second half of the twelfth and into the first half of the thirteenth century, the works of Aristotle came into circulation in new Latin translations, as also the commentaries on him by Greek, Roman, and Islamic writers. Although Aristotle offered a vastly more useful body of

---

[18] During the upset following the barbarian invasions, the Church evolved two important new institutions, monasticism and the papacy. Monasticism began in the East in the latter part of the 3rd century AD and spread to the West. In the 5th century, a crumbling society gave strength to the idea of withdrawal to lead a life of study, contemplation, and worship. This attracted many people of intelligence and high status.

knowledge than did Plato, his teachings were more difficult to reconcile with Christianity than Plato's had been. By the mid thirteenth century, when Aristotle had fully entered the curriculum, questions that were hotly debate inside and outside the universities included

the constitution, nature, and conditions of the transformation of nature; whether the world is singular or plural; whether the earth turns on its axis or is stationary; 'whether every effecting thing is the cause of that which is effecting'; whether things can happen by chance; whether a vacuum is possible; whether the natural state of an object is stationary or in motion; whether luminous celestial bodies are hot.... It is hard to imagine a more concentrated diet of scientific questions pertaining to the nature, composition, mechanisms, and patterns of the natural world. Perhaps even more difficult to imagine today is the mandatory discussion of all these questions by the whole student body in the arts curriculum. (Huff 1993: 192–3)

Three points of major conflict between Christian and Aristotelian teachings soon became important: (*a*) Aristotle's doctrine that the universe had always existed and would always exist seemed to contradict the biblical story of Genesis; (*b*) his view of 'the prime mover' left no room for miraculous divine intervention subsequent to the act of creation; and (*c*) according to him, the soul died with the death of the body. University teachers and graduates who were in positions of power and authority conducted scholarly debates on these issues.

Works by Robert Grosseteste, Roger Bacon, Albert the Great, all churchmen and scholars, culminated in the writings of Saint Thomas Aquinas (*c*. 1225–74). He argued that Aristotelian and Christian philosophy were different roads to truth. They could sometimes lead to different truths but never to truths that contradicted each other. Apparent contradictions were the result of errors in translation or interpretation.

Conservative Counter-Attack

Early conservative critics of Aristotle, and of Aquinas's interpretations, were concentrated in the University of Paris, and in 1210, they banned the reading of Aristotle's works on natural philosophy and related commentaries. In 1231, Pope Gregory IX modified and repeated the ban and appointed a commission to purge Aristotle's treatises of error. The commission never reported and, by 1255, the ban was regularly ignored in Paris.

Although the initial intellectual battles were confined to Paris, the conservatives reacted more strongly and more generally in the second half of the century. They were especially provoked by some radicals who went beyond Aquinas's position, seeking to provide complete explanations of everything with no reference to church doctrine. After some preliminary skirmishes, the edict of 1270 condemned 129 points, some of them due to Aquinas. Teaching them were grounds for excommunication, the ultimate penalty in an age when eternal damnation was a very real possibility in the minds of all Christians. Although the condemnations did succeed in purging some post-Aristotelian teachings from the curriculum for a time, they were never fully effective. Less than fifty years later, and while some of his teachings were still on the proscribed list, the Church made Thomas Aquinas a saint.

There were at least two important reasons for the eventual failure of the condemnations. First, the Church never sought to suppress Greek learning but only to reconcile it with Christian teaching. Prohibition of certain doctrines was a drastic last resort, not a first reaction to apparent conflict. Second, the university was a corporate body with substantial independence. It could set its standards and provide protection to its scholars to teach and think what they wished within only very loose requirements to conform with church doctrines. The new learning was relatively safe from enemies from outside the universities but not, of course, from those within. In any case, many scholars learned to circumvent the prohibitions either by treating Aristotle's problems 'hypothetically' or by repeating his arguments so that they could ostensibly be refuted while really elaborating on them.

One of the most important issues that was studied during that time is variously called contingency, particularism, or occasionalism. According to occasionalist doctrine, if God is free to do anything at any time, then the state of the world at any one moment in time is contingent on the particular will of God at that time. As a result, similar causes need not produce similar effects because the will of God may change between two occurrences of the same cause. In contrast, according to the religious version of the doctrine of naturalism, God created the world according to natural laws and then endowed humans with free will to determine their own affairs.

After centuries of debate, Christian thinkers rejected occasionalism and accepted naturalism. They argued that, although God could have created any world, he chose to create this world with its causes, effects, and natural laws. Thus, immutable natural laws explain what we see in the world of our experience, except in the case of rare divine interventions in the form of miracles. To discover the laws of nature is, therefore, to discover the work of God. Science is reverent, not blasphemous.

This naturalism is one of the most salient features of twelfth-century natural philosophy. [The philosophers] . . . shared a new conception of nature as an autonomous, rational entity, which proceeds without interference according to its own principles. There was a growing awareness of natural order or natural law and a determination to see how far natural principles of causation would go in providing a satisfactory explanation of the world. (Lindberg 1992: 198–200)

Faced with debate over the same issue, Islamic scholars eventually settled on occasionalism, in which the world *is* recreated according to God's will each day. This view resulted in the orthodox Islamic position that it is blasphemous to seek to discover scientific regularities that will allow prediction of the effects that follow from given causes.[19] As an important consequence of these contrasting positions, science during the medieval period was pursued with the active encouragement of the church in the West and in spite of religious hostility in Islam.

---

[19] '[T]he Ash'arite view of man and nature, based on Islamic atomism (known as occasionalism), was very much opposed to the well-ordered, even mechanistic and physically determined conception of the natural order that evolved in the writing of the Christian theologians of the twelfth and thirteenth centuries, (Huff 1993: 105).

Triumph of Free Scholarship

Importantly, by the time Aristotle entered the curriculum, the corporate status of the university was firmly established and the Church was already committed to reconciling Christian doctrine with the newly rediscovered Greek science. One can only speculate as to what might have happened if the revival of learning had unearthed Aristotle first, as it did in Islam. Certainly, Aristotle's teachings were fully embraced by the Christian Church while major parts of it were rejected by the Islamic clerics. The historical accidents of the different timing of the discovery contributed to each of these outcomes. Although we can never know what would have happened had the West discovered Aristotle early in its revival of learning, we can be sure that those who opposed the reconciliation of Christian dogma with Greek learning would have had a much better chance of halting that programme. If they had succeeded, the whole subsequent history of science and religion would probably have been altered. Two important lessons of this story are, first, that historical accidents have large potential consequences and, second, that the path that turned out to lead to the Industrial Revolution was not predetermined, but was instead laid down step by step as events transpired, and, if some key events had been different, the path could well have gone off in a very different direction.

Once the conservative counter attacks had been thwarted, the medieval universities reaffirmed the place of Aristotle's naturalistic doctrines at the centre of the arts curriculum. His ideas were important in developing the religious–intellectual mind-set of the medieval period. 'Anyone who reads these works [of Aristotle] or compares them with the philosophical writings of China cannot fail to see the uniqueness of the Aristotelian emphasis on explaining the natural world in terms of fundamental elements, causal processes, and rational inquiry' (Huff 1993: 335). When this had been done, 'a powerful, methodologically sophisticated, intellectual framework for the study of nature had been institutionalized' (Huff 1993: 337). By the fourteenth century, most academics and church thinkers regarded the world as subject to natural laws, which had been promulgated by God and were meant to be discovered by his human subjects.

III. THE EARLY MODERN PERIOD

The Rise of Western Science

The new science, which became a uniquely Western science, developed in the fifteenth, sixteenth, and seventeenth centuries. It slowly replaced the Aristotelian–Christian world view with a new mechanical view of the universe. In it there was no clear distinction between pure and applied science or science and engineering; all were covered in the twin concepts of the 'exact sciences' and 'natural philosophy'. In astronomy, Copernicus reinterpreted existing observations into a startling new heliocentric model. Galileo provided observations that substantiated it. Kepler used old and new observations (mainly from Tycho Brahe) to develop his three laws of motion, which applied solely to heavenly bodies. Newton unified these by deducing them from a single theory of motion that applied to all things terrestrial and celestial. His were the first truly modern scientific laws.

   Although the mechanistic world view was developed in the early modern period, non-mechanical views remained influential well into the eighteenth century. For example, William Gilbert (1544–1603), whose *De Magnete* turned magnetism from a body of empirical observations into a science and was thoroughly modern in its use of data, thought that the heavenly bodies were imbued with spirit. This was not unique to this period, intellectual transitions often find important thinkers with one foot in the old system and one in the new. They contribute substantially to changes whose revolutionary implications they only dimly perceive, and do not always approve.[20] This was true even of Newton. Only with Newton's popularizers was the mysticism stripped away from his theories—presenting an uncompromisingly mechanical view of the universe.

Continuity in Subject Matter

The science of the medieval period provided a vital legacy to the early modern era. It posed many questions that became part of the agenda of early modern scientists. While these scientists gave novel answers, they were responding to issues first posed by medieval thinkers. They were, in effect, continuing a medieval research agenda. Out of this developing research agenda came new directions in physics, biology, meteorology, psychology, and geology, all of which had once been a part of natural philosophy. Medieval science led researchers and writers to develop an interest in scientific methodology. They tried to understand, in a systematic way, what we can know about the world and how one might go about gaining that knowledge. Medieval science produced rationalistic assumptions about the nature of the world and passed that world view on to early modern scientists. As Grant (1996: 170) points out: '[A] scientific revolution could not have occurred in Western Europe in the seventeenth century if the level of science and natural philosophy had remained what it was in the first half of the twelfth century.'

Discontinuity in Method

Medieval natural philosophers were not opposed to observation and relied heavily on the works of Aristotle, who was an astute observer of nature. Although they engaged in sophisticated discussions of many important scientific issues, a priori reasoning was held to be the major road to new knowledge. The early modern scientific revolution was based on a change in method: accepting experiment as *the* way to settle debates about empirical issues. As a result, much of pre-Newtonian science developed through myriad piecemeal empirical discoveries concerning issues that had been debated by scholastic philosophers for centuries.

---

[20] See Kearney (1971: 22–48) for a detailed discussion of the various medieval views of many who contributed to the development of early modern science.

Religion and the New Science

By the beginning of the early modern period, the flexibility of the scholastic philosophers in creating a system of thought that reconciled Christianity with Greek science had given way to rigidity now that their system had been fully developed. 'All this vast scheme had been so riveted into the Ptolemaic view by the use of biblical texts and theological reasoning that the resultant system of the universe was considered impregnable and final. To attack it was blasphemy' (White 1896: 120).

This view was strongly held by the highly influential Jesuit order whose members were steeped in Aristotelian science. Thus many considered it blasphemous when Galileo insisted that Copernicus's heliocentric system described reality rather than just being a useful predictive hypothesis. The Roman Church responded by declaring the new view to be heretical early in the seventeenth century and confining Galileo to house arrest. This put the Catholic Church on the side of those who opposed the new world view. Furthermore, it helped to bring 'the new science out of the domain of the universities and the learned disputations of the natural philosophers. Science made its way onto the intellectual agenda of all educated Europeans' (Jacob 1997: 25). As Aristotelian science fell further into disrepute, the Catholic Church became less and less involved with modern science. Its strong opposition managed to crush much scientific enquiry in southern Europe within one generation after Galileo's condemnation: 'In those countries where the clergy embraced the new science, or were at least neutral toward it, science flourished. Where science remained suspect or was persecuted, as occurred in parts of Catholic Europe dominated by the Inquisition, relative intellectual stagnation in science was the price to be paid' (Jacob 1997: 19). As a result of the Catholic Church's hostility, the centres of the new science migrated north, particularly to Protestant countries, although France initially tolerated the new science.

As Catholics were largely opposed to the new learning, to support it was anti-papist and, therefore, a desirable stand for at least some Protestants. Some Continental leaders of Protestantism, such as Calvin and Luther, rejected heliocentricism. In England, however, the new science was largely accepted by 1670. Later, Quakers and then liberal Anglicans began to preach elements of Newton's laws and mechanics as the works of God (Jacob 1997: 60).

The new printing press helped enormously to free science from state and religious control. A printing press could be set up anywhere for a relatively low cost while monasteries with learned scribes were less easy to duplicate and much easier to control. Thus, when authorities were hostile in one area, a book could easily be printed in another area, often where presses had been newly established. For example, many of Galileo's later works were published in Holland rather than Italy. At first, the Catholic Church opposed the printing press because of the freedom of expression that it would obviously confer, as did the authorities in China and Islam. The Chinese and Islamic authorities were successful in their efforts, but the pluralism in Europe rendered ineffective any attempt at outright suppression or rigid censorship of the printed word.

'In the 1690s when Anglican clergy in London were preaching Newton's science complete with atomism, Italian followers of the new science were under trial in Naples' (Jacob 1997: 28). Because of free universities and the ability to publish at least somewhere in Europe, religious opposition, whether Catholic or Protestant, only delayed but did not eliminate scientific advance: 'The triumph of the Copernican revolution was thus a vindication of the efficacy of the institutional structures that had been put in place to encourage, protect, and preserve spheres of neutral space within which offensive, revolutionary, and even heretical ideas could be openly debated' (Huff 1993: 356).

These structures were one of the most important legacies of the medieval thinkers. They were a part of European pluralism in which universities were to some extent free from state and religious control. Another contributor to the victory of science over religious repression was the pluralism of political control. When Catholic countries turned against the new science, some Protestant countries welcomed it, particularly the Netherlands and England. One of the great advantages of pluralism is that when repressive forces gain control in some places, there is usually somewhere else to run to.

IV.   FOUR PHASES OF INDUSTRIAL MECHANIZATION

Although both the view of the universe as a rational machine subject to scientific laws and the institutions of learning and pluralism were rooted in the medieval period, the explicitly technological roots of the Industrial Revolution only became continuously visible in the early modern period. To consider what happened from that time on, it is useful to divide the whole period of industrialization into four phases (which of course overlapped and shaded into one another):

1.   Early modern mechanization (1450~1770): Cottage-based putting out; slow emergence of early 'manufactories'—sheds and cottages containing hand-powered textile machines—and some water-powered facilities containing textile machinery start to appear.[21]
2.   Early factory phase (1770~1820): proto-factories become more important, larger in scale; some were designed to exploit early forms of steam power but most were powered by waterwheels.
3.   Steam-driven factory phase (1820~80): steam is used in textile production and then other products, extending into transport through railways and ships.

---

[21] Such organizations existed outside textiles as well, but it was with textiles that they found the widest diffusion. Similar developments were occurring in many other places, including India and China, which makes it all the clearer that the technological break with the non-Western world came in the later two stages: first, when automated textile machines were placed in genuine factories and second, when the factories became powered by steam engines.

4. Science-led industrial phase (1880~1975): characterized by such products as steel, chemicals, internal combustion engines, and electric motors, whose development often required a clear understanding of scientific laws.[22]

The first of these phases, which we consider in this section, pre-dated the Industrial Revolution; the second and third are usually referred to as the First Industrial Revolution; and the fourth as beginning with the Second Industrial Revolution.

Early Modern Mechanization

Although the period 1450–1770 can be distinguished as a separate period in the history of mechanization, it really represents an acceleration of the medieval drive to mechanize as many manufacturing processes as possible. Early on, this took the form of applying water power to a range of new tasks as discussed in Chapter 5. During 1450–1770, the desire to mechanize production benefited from the newly emerging mechanistic science, and the scientific method of experimentation. Early modern science was applied to questions that needed to be answered before some key trajectories of technological advance could be established.

Science and Technology in the Early Modern Period

Today we think of science as a system of theoretical laws formulated to predict outcomes not observed when the laws were developed. It is based on clear divisions between pure science and applied science, between natural and social sciences, and between different disciplines within each of these. Today when people talk of science, they usually mean 'pure natural science', thinking in terms of universal laws such as Einstein's field equations.

Things were different in classical, medieval, and early modern times. All science was then contained in one discipline, natural philosophy. The distinctions between pure science, applied science, and engineering did not emerge until the latter half of the nineteenth century: 'We separate science from religion, science from technology, theories from practices. They did not' (Jacob 1997: 104).

The commonly heard argument that science was irrelevant to the Industrial Revolution typically denies a link between the modern concept of science and the Industrial Revolution. To be sure, scientific laws were not used to deduce technological applications as a modern view of a feedback from science to technology might have it. Indeed, there were no general scientific laws as we understand them today. Science as it was then understood was engaged in a piecemeal application of the new empirical methodology to settling many issues that had been debated for centuries by the scholastic philosophers and that originally stemmed from Aristotle. All the advances that occurred between 1450 and 1650 are found in any standard history of science, although none were formulated as universal laws. The accumulating evidence slowly refuted much of Aristotle's writings, and this in turn required

---

[22] We terminate this phase in 1975, which can be thought of as the beginning of the 'post-industrial era'.

the development of a new overarching framework that could explain the emerging conflicts. Newton's *Principia* (1687) provided just that. Musson and Robinson (1989: 11) note the confusion over the role of science may be 'the result of a false system of categories, which distorts the fact that when the scholar and the instrument-maker cooperated in the sixteenth and seventeenth centuries, as they often did, they were both acting in the character of proto-scientists'.[23]

The discoveries that took Western Europe to the threshold of the Industrial Revolution, and took Britain over it, reveal a significant two-way relationship between these piecemeal scientific discoveries and technological applications. The new world view of a mechanical universe that was generated by the scientific discoveries of the early modern period fostered an interest in mechanizing human activities wherever possible.[24] The new mechanics

was used not merely to calculate the movement of heavenly bodies, but also in practical arts such as navigation, cartography, ballistics, mining, and surveying, and these gave rise to the craft of instrument-making: the manufacture of telescopes, microscopes, barometers, chronometers, micrometers, dividing and gear-cutting engines, etc. (Musson and Robinson 1989: 23)

The Influence of Newton

Isaac Newton (1642–1727) was the single most important figure in the new science. Although his towering place in science is well known, less attention has been paid to his place in the popular culture of the century that followed the publication of *Principia* in 1687.[25] This book was the great synthesizing work for the new science. Its laws of motion presented a mechanical interpretation of the behaviour of all things in the universe, large and small, near and far.

With the invention of calculus—the mathematical language of Newton's general laws—science took a decisive step that had eluded the Greeks.[26] It provided the

---

[23] We reference here the reprint of Musson and Robinson's classic text, originally published in 1969. On 19th century science and it's connection to the mechanical arts, Uglow (2002: xx) notes: 'At the time, "science" meant knowledge; interest in the material world was "natural philosophy." And when people spoke of the "arts," they did not mean only the fine arts but also the "mechanic arts," the skills and techniques in agriculture, say, or printing. So the relationship of philosophy to the arts could mean the usefulness of natural knowledge to industry—almost the opposite of what we mean today.'

[24] Mokyr (1999) argues that many of the things scientists were investigating in the early modern period had no direct relevance for current technological problems. This is as it had always been right up to the 20th century, and still is in many fields today. What matters is that *some* of the things they were investigating *did* have relevance to current technological problems.

[25] Our discussion of this aspect of Newton's work is based on the pathbreaking research of Jacob (1997). She has meticulously documented the degree to which Newtonian science and mechanics permeated British society, as well as being accepted by the clergy. See also Stewart (1992) on the spread of Newtonian science. Christianson (1984) is a fine biography that puts Newton into the context of his times.

[26] The Greeks got very close to calculus but were unable to resolve the apparent paradoxes that arose when considering rates of change at a point in time or space, as stated by Zeno. Indeed, even after calculus became a working tool, its apparent paradoxes persisted well into the 20th century, to be resolved finally when the interpretation of a derivative as a ratio of little bits (see Thompson 1910) was replaced by its interpretation as the end result of a limiting process (see Courant 1934).

mathematics of instantaneous motion and rates of change at a point in time and space. Its impact was indeed revolutionary, both in its mechanical world view that influenced most of science over the next 200 years, and in its obvious practical applications that influenced several generations of innovators who followed, particularly in England and Scotland and later throughout all of Europe. 'In the eighteenth century, thanks primarily to Newton's work, mechanics became an organized body of readily accessible knowledge' (Jacob 1997: 8). Indeed, it does not seem an overstatement to say that Newtonian mechanics provided the intellectual basis for the First Industrial Revolution, which in its two stages, was almost wholly mechanical.

Brought together by a shared technical vocabulary of Newtonian origin, engineers, and entrepreneurs—like Boulton and Watt—negotiated, in some instances battled their way through the mechanization of workshops or the improvement of canals, mines, and harbours.... [B]y 1750 British engineers and entrepreneurs could talk the same mechanical talk. They could objectify the physical world, see its operations mechanically and factor their common interests and values into their partnerships. What they said and did changed the Western world forever. (Jacob 1997: 115)

Increasingly, those engaged in manufacturing in the eighteenth century required at least a passing familiarity with Newtonian mechanics, or at least to be able to hire and converse with those who did. Obviously this required a level of mathematical competence. In Britain mathematics was already quite widely taught by the 1720s. The growing interest in mathematics is indicated by a doubling of the number of mathematical textbooks in the first half of the century (Jacob 1997: 110). Newton's work was further popularized by those who wrote textbooks and gave public instruction. In a historically unprecedented turn, the once exclusive domain of scholars became the science of the educated layperson. Enthusiastic audiences, containing cross sections of persons who could hardly be imagined attending any twentieth-century lecture on modern science, were seen across Britain. Popular journals, including one addressed mainly to women, helped to spread the new knowledge. While all Catholic and most Protestant clerics on the Continent were still opposing Galileo's theories, many Anglicans were preaching Newton's ideas from the pulpit. As Stewart (1992) puts it:

Newtonianism was soon represented in the public world as holding the keys to the solution to a wide range of obstacles in mechanics, mining, hydraulics, and various technical enterprises. (xxxi–xxxii)

[T]he world of the public lecturer and experimenter was prescient with meaning for the acceptance of natural philosophy and, through its practitioners, of the legitimacy of the domination and manipulation of nature upon which a materialist society came to rest. The industrialization of eighteenth-century Britain was as much a function of this attitude as a response to economic or technical factors. (xxxiv)

By the beginning of the eighteenth century, the Royal Society of London for the Promotion of Natural Knowledge, founded in 1662, had become a prestigious society whose membership included both scientists and interested laypersons.

Unlike its French counterpart, the Royal Society was a private institution and admitted not just scientists but also men of property and influence who were interested in using the new science productively, and who became a conduit for diffusing it throughout the society. The Royal Society was an institutional innovation; nothing quite like it had come before. Its eclectic membership studied the latest scientific facts and theories and eagerly took up what they had learnt in conversations, on the job site, in further reading, and in public lectures and demonstrations. The Royal Society provided an important institutional framework to promote and shape the evolution of scientific thought and the acceptance of science among the general public.

The degree to which Newton's new mechanical science permeated British society and was used by innovators and entrepreneurs, such as the Watts and the Boultons, separated England from all other European countries—only the Netherlands came close.[27] This knowledge entered into the public domain in a world in which science was 'all the rage'. It was in the air and practical engineers and inventors breathed it every day. By 1750 the scientific revolution had created in Britain 'a new person, generally but not exclusively a male entrepreneur, who approached the productive process mechanically, literally by seeing it as something to be mastered by machines, or on a more abstract level to be conceptualised in terms of weight, motion, and the principles of force and inertia' (Jacob 1997: 6–7).

Smeaton is a case in point; his 'work was outstanding as an example of experimental method in science, and how it could be used to shed light on engineering problems' (Pacey 1975: 208). Smeaton actively employed Newton's 'laws of reasoning by induction' to study the properties of the waterwheel. His work demonstrated the superiority of the overshot wheel to the undershot, and the superiority of the breast-wheel to both the under- and overshot wheels. Many of Smeaton's results were published by the Royal Society, ultimately proving to be widely influential.[28] According to Pacey (1975: 209) Smeaton 'clearly saw that the comparison of his maxims with experimental measurements involved the same methodological problem as Newton's comparison of theory and observation in astronomy'.

The influence of mechanistic science was felt not just in the development of machinery but also in canals,[29] harbours, mines, and a host of other applications.

---

[27] While some French academics desired a science that could be applied to the problems of industry and production, the actual application of science in France was much different from Britain. Jacob (1997: 169–70) notes: 'Their oftentimes theoretical approach brought to industry a social and cultural style best described as aristocratic and hierarchical. It was comparatively less egalitarian than the trial-and-error, even competitive, exchanges around scientific or technical knowledge that occurred between entrepreneurs and civil engineers within scientific societies and academies in Britain and more rarely, the Low Countries.' Jacob also places importance on the hierarchical nature of French society at this time and the barriers this posed to the efficient diffusion and employment of scientific knowledge.

[28] As Pacey (1975: 211) puts it: 'It is perhaps significant that many of the large water-powered factories erected during the Industrial Revolution were equipped with breast-wheels, although this type had rarely been used previously.'

[29] Jacob notes that the accelerated construction of canals in the late 18th century brought many industrialists in close contact with engineers, both to provide expert knowledge to improve the efficiency

The role of science in all of this was not that of general laws leading to the development of specific applications. Instead, it permeated the thoughts and attitudes of ordinary people, providing them with the theoretical mechanics and the practical mathematics that facilitated technological change. This illustrates the fusion of theoretical and applied science, as well as engineering, which characterized the scientific world well into the nineteenth century.[30]

Mechanization of Textile Production[31]

The early part of the Industrial Revolution was *not* produced by a technology-radical innovation, a sudden discontinuity in process technology. Instead, it was the end result of technological trajectories that stretched over several centuries.

The early modern passion for mechanization was nowhere more obvious than in textile production. In the late fifteenth century, Leonardo da Vinci (1452–1519), the greatest scientific visionary of the early modern period, conceived a programme to mechanize most of the operations in the textile industry. His projects 'mark the opening up of invention as a conscious reaching forward to distant objectives in which the immediate possibilities are forgotten and the attention is concentrated on the complete realization of the abstract principle' (Usher 1988: 271). His drawings predicted much of what happened over the next 200 years. Although he made important inventions in textile machinery, many of his ideas languished because mechanical technology was not yet up to delivering what he was able to conceive through the application of the mechanistic scientific–philosophical doctrine. Technology had to catch up with scientific imagination, not the reverse. His vision was slowly realized over the next 300 years by piecemeal discoveries and innovations of which the following is but a small sample.

The draw loom was developed in the fifteenth century and the stocking frame later in the sixteenth century. As well as making hose, it was the basic invention that 'underlies the whole family of knitting and lace-making machines developed in the eighteenth and nineteenth centuries' (Usher 1988: 281). A flyer was developed for the Saxon wheel in 1530. One technical issue facing early attempts to mechanize was shuttle rebound; solutions were suggested in 1678 and 1745. The solutions did not work for materials wider than ribbons, but were important for ribbon production. A shearing engine, using the principle of scissor blades, was conceptualized in da Vinci's time. Work progressed on the technology until 1792 when a mechanism similar to a lawnmower solved the problem. According to Usher, 'the early

---

of canals and to provide testimony to Parliament to secure approval of various projects. In these efforts, '[t]hey had come to accept the professionalization of scientific knowledge of a mechanical sort, to rely solely on engineers, preferably famous ones—if they were to be found. The promoters sat through parliamentary cross-examinations of experts, following in detail their estimates of the weight of water lost through the diversion of river water into a canal' (Jacob 1997: 203).

[30] Even then, the clear distinction between these branches of science was slow to develop. For example, Lord Kelvin, one of the most important theorists in science at the end of the 19th century, and president of the Royal Society in 1890, made many applied technological discoveries.

[31] This section fills out the brief discussion of mechanized textile machinery given in Chapter 6.

application of mechanization to most aspects of silk manufacture strongly suggests that mechanical problems were the main detriment to applying mechanization to the spinning of wool, flax, and cotton. Silk doubling and twisting were successfully mechanized soon after da Vinci pointed the way. The basic form of the ribbon loom was invented in the sixteenth century but important improvements continued to be made over the next 200 years. Finally, Kay (1745) controlled the pedals by tappets whose motion could be coordinated with other motions of the machine. Thus as early as 1760, the ribbon loom embodied all the essential mechanical principles of mechanized weaving. 1730 saw a patent for the preparation of twine, while a patent for a machine for opening and dressing wool was issued in 1733. That year also saw the momentous invention of the flying shuttle. Later in the century, came the well-known spinning jenny and the mule.

Although the flying shuttle was a key invention, it created a series of mechanical problems, whose solution required many decades of effort. The problems arose when the attempt was made to substitute mechanical means for the hand of the weaver on the picking stick of the flying shuttle. Key developments occurred in 1803–5, 1813, 1821, and 1822.

While pure science played a role in some of the developments in the mechanization of textile manufacturing (e.g. the development of the Jacquard loom was influenced by new ways of organizing information), most developments were influenced by what we could now call engineering expertise—advances in spinning preceded those in weaving because the mechanical problems were less. But that engineering expertise was evolving as part of the whole mechanization programme that was both encouraged and facilitated by the early modern scientific–mechanistic world view, and then more dramatically by Newtonian mechanics and mathematics.

This long history of incremental mechanization illustrates a general problem found with the development of each major type of textile machine. Typically, it was long after basic theoretical principles had been solved that engineers could implement them. This process required many incremental and often complex inventions, each one designed to eliminate a human task. According to Usher (1988: 288), the history of the mechanization of draw loom weaving 'has long been obscured by writers who were unwilling to recognize the essential cumulative character for mechanical achievements'.[32]

Did Science Really Matter?

For decades, historians have debated whether or not early modern science was an important determinant of the Industrial Revolution.[33] Early in the debate, Schofield,

---

[32] The story goes back to the 15th century when a loom was invented that worked for narrow fabrics. A series of improvements occurred over the centuries. For example, spinning by rollers was developed in 1733 and the mounting of spindles on a moveable carriage to duplicate the operation of pulling out the yarn came soon after. The process was completed by Jacquard early in the 19th century.

[33] See Jacob (1997), Kearny (1971), Landes (1969), Mokyr (1990, 2002), Musson and Robinson (1989), Schofield (1963), and Stewart (1992) among others.

Musson, and Robinson argued that pure science played a key role in facilitating Britain's industrialization and that there were many direct links between a newly emerging body of scientific knowledge and Britain's 'wave of gadgets'. Musson and Robinson were aware they had not yet established such a link, but to them it was inevitable that it would be established by future research.[34] The link is not yet accepted. Instead, in his groundbreaking work, *Prometheus Unbound*, Landes made an argument that became widely accepted. He argued that the technological developments of the Industrial Revolution were the product of educated craftsmen, themselves guided in their efforts largely by trial and error and tinkering. Many technologies, Landes argues reasonably, were also developed fortuitously.[35] Many modern economic historians hold a similar view, that the scientific revolution and the Industrial Revolution were not significantly causally connected.

Our position is a return to the views of earlier writers such as Musson and Robinson. We argue that mechanistic science of the West was crucial in determining the when, where, and how of the Industrial Revolution.[36] More specifically, we argue that early modern science, mechanistic science, was a *necessary* condition for the Industrial Revolution. Science as it existed in nineteenth-century Britain was necessary for the full development of the key GPTs of the Industrial Revolution, and that science could never have developed in the absence of the scientific revolution of the early modern period.

Most inventors in the eighteenth century were educated persons in touch, directly or indirectly, with developments in science. They were of course not scientists in white lab coats, but neither were they untutored tinkerers. Even Landes (1969: 63), having argued elsewhere that science had little to do with technological developments, observes:

Even more striking is the theoretical knowledge of these men. They were not, on the whole, the unlettered tinkerers of historical mythology. Even the ordinary millwright as Fairbairn notes, was usually 'a fair arithmetician, knew something of geometry, levelling and mensuration, and in some cases possessed a very competent knowledge of practical mathematics. He could calculate velocities, strength and power of machines; could draw in plan and section....' Whatever the reasons for British precocity in this domain, the results are clear.[37]

This reveals a lot: at no previous time, and at no place in the West outside of Britain in the eighteenth century, could one say such things about ordinary millwrights

[34] See Musson and Robinson (1989).

[35] White (1978) argues a similar position. A careful perusal of Landes (1998) shows no change in his position on this issue.

[36] Lipsey first made this argument in a paper presented in 1997 to the Economic Growth and Policy Program of the Canadian Institute for Advanced Research and then in a paper prepared jointly with Clifford Bekar and Kenneth Carlaw to a conference 'On the Origins of the Modern World: Comparative Perspectives from the Edge of the Millennium' UC Davis, 15–17 October 1999. See the more extended discussion in the Preface to this book.

[37] For the quote within the quote, Landes' reference is: Fairbairn, Willam (1864), *Treatise on Mills and Millwork*, 2nd edn., 2 vols. (London), I, vi.

(or their analogues in other times or places).[38] These millwrights had access to, and accessed, a pool of mechanical theory and applied knowledge. This knowledge underlay the great mechanical inventions of the Industrial Revolution, including the steam engine and the great engineering work that preceded it in the eighteenth century. There is no mystery in what Landes observes if one accepts the importance of pre-nineteenth-century science and the unique penetration of Newtonian mechanics into British society.

Early Factory Phase

The latter few decades of the eighteenth century witnessed a radical innovation that we first discussed in Chapter 6. This was the introduction of a new organizational GPT, the factory system, and along with it, significant changes in the facilitating structure such as the location, organization, and concentration of industrial production. The factory system was both a use- and a technology-radical innovation in the sense defined in Chapter 4.

In contrast, the solutions for automating textile production that were embodied in the factories of the early Industrial Revolution were, as we have seen, neither use- nor technology-radical innovations, beginning the culmination of an evolutionary process that had begun several centuries earlier. It is only the already noted tendency to credit the last step with the whole solution that makes the developments in textile machinery in the later part of the eighteenth century seem to be a discontinuous result of something that happened only in that century. As Usher (1988: 293) puts it in his classic book:

It is the rule rather than the exception that the final achievement should be credited with the total accomplishment.... Each step in the process is equally essential and though they do not encounter absolutely equal resistance, it is nonetheless true that significant difficulties are not at an end even when the principles are fully worked out.

What happened was that the long incremental evolution of automated textile machinery reached a stage where it became efficient to take production out of the cottages into sheds filled with human-powered machinery and smallish water-powered mills.[39] These relatively sudden changes in the economy's organizational GPT and its facilitating structure have often been mistakenly construed as sudden changes in process technology.[40]

---

[38] We confine these observations to the West because we cannot demonstrate the absence of these abilities at all other times in all other places. We suspect, however, that the qualification is not necessary since many of the capabilities depended on knowledge of what were then exclusively the domain of early modern Western science and engineering.

[39] We do not enter into the debate as to the proximate cause of the move out of cottage production into manufactories. All we need to note here is that while factories slowly asserted their efficiency over putting-out, the competition was close since non-factory production lasted through *all* of the 19th century, diminishing in importance slowly rather than suddenly disappearing in the face of an obviously greatly superior form of production.

[40] We focus here on the evolution of the factory as a GPT as well as the two main complementary technologies, steam and textile machinery. We spend little time on the transition from cottage production

As Crafts (1985) has shown, national productivity and real wages[41] did not rise greatly during this early phase of industrialization. As a result, some economists who equate changes in TFP with technological change have argued that there was no significant technological breakthrough at the time. This is why we have earlier stressed the need to use our S-E decomposition to break the relation between technological change and TFP, or any other measure of productivity. The early factory stage was typical of most new GPTs. When it began, agents were not sure what form of organization would prove to be efficient. Many experiments were made and there was significant overinvestment in various factory experiments. Eventually, the evolutionary hand sorted out those who made good decisions, or were lucky, from those who made bad decisions, or were unlucky. After decades of experimentation, the factory evolved mainly into a largely water-powered structure in which automated textile machinery produced a much larger volume of output than the earlier manufactories and proto-factories, which as we observed in Chapter 6, were often just sheds housing workers who themselves provided the power to textile machinery.

As with many GPTs, while the technology was being worked out, and the facilitating structure was being altered to accommodate it, there was little 'productivity bonus'. Also, with many GPTs even when productivity rises in the sectors where the technology is first introduced, it typically takes decades before its use spreads through enough of the economy to have a major impact on national data. So it was with the textile factories in this early part of the First Industrial Revolution. Nonetheless, the manufacturing part of the economy was being restructured on a factory basis in a move that was pregnant with the potential for sustained growth. But the growth had to wait until the next phase when automatic textile machinery was combined with steam power and the factory system spread to sectors beyond textiles.

Science played a key role in these early phases of the Industrial Revolution as well. Early factories were a continuation of the evolutionary trajectory of textile manufacturing. The discontinuity came only in the organizational GPT, and only in the elements of the facilitating structure needed to give effect to the new factory system. The required engineering expertise was evolving as part of the whole mechanization programme, which was both encouraged and facilitated by the early modern scientific–mechanistic world view. Accumulating knowledge allowed those we would now call engineers to do things in 1650 and then in 1750 that they could not have done 100 years earlier. If these technological developments came from 'tinkering', it was a 'tinkering' that was enabled by 200 years of accumulated 'scientific' knowledge based

---

to factories. See Szostak (1991) for an explanation of this evolution that is broadly consistent with our view. Szostak argues that the driving force behind the emergence of the factory system was organizational rather than, in his terminology, technological, and that these organizational changes, which we would call changes in organizational technology, were ultimately driven by changes in transportation technologies.

[41] See Feinstein (1998) for real wages.

on the evolving research programme to mechanize all aspects of textile production.[42] If what was invented in the eighteenth century seem mere 'gadgets' to modern eyes, they were engineering triumphs to contemporaries.[43]

Steam-Driven Factory Phase[44]

By the early nineteenth century, developments in steam engines made it efficient to replace water and human powers with steam power. Production moved from sheds and water-powered mills to steam-powered factories. Though there had been some huge water-powered factories containing water frames and mules, there is little doubt that the average size of factories increased significantly when production moved to the new industrial cities and changed over to steam power. New machines and new factories had to be designed and built. Metal replaced wood in most machines and a whole new machine tool industry was developed. Industry became more concentrated as the scale economies of steam-powered factories called for much larger productive units than did water power. (We discuss this phenomenon in detail in Chapter 12.) The appeal of their cheap mass-produced goods to ordinary people provided the necessary market. Major adjustments to the whole structure of the economy were required as masses of people moved to the new industrial towns, urbanizing the society to an extent not seen since classical times. Fuel, raw materials, and finished goods needed to be transported. This required an extensive network of canals and railroads. The new modes of transport introduced by the railway and later by the iron steamships altered many economic relations. The changes also initiated rising wages as steam power served to raise productivity. Steam complemented developments already occurring in textiles, where many incremental innovations in textile machinery had slowly been raising productivity (e.g. number of spindles employed, strength of yarn spun). This was the age of steam that was discussed in Chapter 6. Here we concentrate on the development of the steam engine as an important part of our story of the close relation between early modern scientific understanding and applied technology.

Once again, there was no revolution in the process technology. By the third decade of the nineteenth century, both the steam engine and the factory had evolved to the extent that steam was able to power the new textile machines. The change was use-radical as defined in Chapter 3, since there was a discrete shift in the power source whenever establishments changed from human and water powers to steam power. However, the change was not technology-radical since the steam engine that entered the factories had been evolving over approximately 200 years, and the important

---

[42] Education may have also played a role in these developments. In a review of the contribution of human capital to economic growth in the Industrial Revolution, Mitch (1999: 270–1) finds that while formal education contributed little directly to economic growth, it may have facilitated and guided innovation.

[43] See Mokyr (1990) and Ashton (1955) for the use of the terms 'tinkering' and 'gadget' respectively.

[44] See Von Tunzelmann (1978) for the classic study of the development of the steam engine. See also Von Tunzelmann (1994).

changes made in textile machinery to accommodate the superior speed and increased stresses that arose with steam power were incremental not radical.

This shift induced a radical change in the facilitating structure as production moved to the new industrial towns that we associate with the First Industrial Revolution. As so often happens, however, a use-radical change, this time in a power source, and a discontinuity in the evolution of key elements of the facilitating structure, have often been misconstrued as a discontinuity in the evolution of the technology—a 'technology-radical' shift.

Development of the Steam Engine

Steam was the first major new source of power for the West since windmills. Its development started with early modern science and its development trajectory is a prime example of a positive feedback running between what we now call science and technology. Although no one can prove that the steam engine could not have developed purely through empirical trial and error, three things are clear: first, it did not develop in a purely empirical fashion historically; second, a purely empirical approach would have taken far longer if it could have happened at all; and third, in the absence of mechanistic science, the efficiency of the steam engine would have been greatly reduced.

Although inanimate power in the form of water and wind was used for many purposes throughout the Middle Ages, the English power problems of the sixteenth and seventeenth centuries mainly concerned the pumping of water from ever-deepening mines and supplying municipal water systems, jobs for which wind and water power were ill-suited. The principles underlying the suction pump were not understood because little progress had been made in understanding one of the great scholastic research issues, the nature of a vacuum. Galileo considered the suction pump but to no avail. Torricelli studied the pump's failure and made the first correct analysis of air pressure. Pascal elegantly repeated Torricelli's experiments and published works that put the theory of atmospheric pressure on a firm basis. Independently, Otto von Guericke experimented with air pressure and produced the first workable airtight cylinder and piston driven by atmospheric pressure. As well as adding to knowledge about vacuums, his cylinder provided a technological advance that was necessary for the subsequent development of the steam-driven piston. 'The discovery of the atmosphere thus profoundly affected the development of science... [and] it was no less important in its impact on technology' (Cardwell 1971: 11). While none of these early discoveries resulted in sweeping scientific laws, they were all scientific advances, as science was then understood.

Once the science behind the suction pump was understood, the pump was extensively redesigned (showing the feedback from scientific understanding to technological improvements). In 1675 Samuel Moreland obtained a patent for a plunger pump. The new pump displayed many innovations that were crucial for further increases in efficiency and power. One change saw the plunger work through a gland and stuffing box. This basic principle was later important in the development of the piston engine and it was eventually used in a wide variety of machines.

Another important scientific problem concerned understanding the nature of steam. Investigations of steam began in the sixteenth century, but work was hampered by the mistaken theory that steam was just a form of air. Early work by Cardan and Porta provided a better understanding of the relation between the two. De Caus (1576–1630) took the decisive step when he ascertained that steam was a form of water. Importantly, he understood that steam would return to its liquid state on cooling. These 'were scientific discoveries of the utmost importance. They were the principles upon which the work of Worcester, Savery, and Papin was largely based' (Usher 1988: 343).

Understanding that air and steam were different allowed contemporary observers to realize that steam had greater energy potential than did air pressure. This conclusion did not pass unnoticed by practical observers, who were on the lookout for new power sources. The potential of steam was understood long before it could be practically harnessed: 'Men could see the possibilities clearly enough but they had no means of bringing them within the realm of the practicable' (Cardwell 1971: 12).

The first true steam engine was a hybrid. The 'water-commanding engine' was developed by Edward Somerset, the second Marquis of Worcester, who made use of the studies of Caus and Porta on mechanics (Thurston 1878: 16). His engine used both atmospheric and steam pressure. While there is no record of its commercial use, its principles were sound and Thomas Savery used them in his first commercial steam pump, the 'fountain engine'. The vacuum created by the condensation of steam in Savery's pump raised water from its source into a container at pump level, then the injection of steam forced the water out of the container and up to the desired destination. To get sufficient energy for the second stage of the lift, the pressure had to be higher than current metallurgy safely permitted. The engine's boiler was therefore liable to explode. The Savery engine had limited use, mostly in mines. It was also used to pump water to reservoirs above waterwheels and to supply water tanks located on top of large structures.

But the fountain engine did not lead to a 'modern' steam engine, an engine that used pressure to drive a cylinder. Many considered the possibility of using atmospheric pressure to drive a piston. For example, Christiaan Huygens and Abbe Hautefeuille planned to explode gunpowder in a cylinder to create a vacuum below the piston. Papin, a mathematician, argued that steam could be used to push a cylinder upwards, and if the cylinder were then cooled, the resulting vacuum would allow the atmospheric pressure to push the cylinder downwards.[45] Thomas Newcomen developed the first working steam engine. Newcomen was country-bred, but kept abreast of scientific developments in his correspondence with Robert Hooke of the Royal Society. His use of a cylinder to drive a piston connected to a driving mechanism represented an important breakthrough. The downstroke of the Newcomen engine, the power stroke, was driven by atmospheric pressure when a partial vacuum was created in the cylinder through cooling the steam that had been

---

[45] Papin was a mathematician who, after escaping from the persecution of Protestants in France, worked in the laboratory of Robert Boyle, the founder of the Royal Society.

drawn into it during the upstroke. The upstroke was powered by the action of a counterweighted beam that was linked to the top of the cylinder. Since it did not drive a column of water upwards, as Savery's engine did, the boiler and cylinder operated at safe levels of pressure. The engine marked 'the effective beginning of the utilization of the new sources of power with which scientists and inventors had been struggling actively for about a century' (Usher 1988: 350).

It was James Watt who turned Newcomen's atmospheric engine into a true steam engine. Originally 'he was an instrument-maker and a scientist, not an engineer. He had no experience of Newcomen engines nor it seems of any other large-scale machines, and his knowledge was derived from readings of Desaguliers and Belidor' (Cardwell 1971: 42). In 1765, Watt conceived of the separate condensing chamber, which meant one could avoid having to cool and reheat the cylinder in Newcomen's engine on every sequence of strokes. This improved the engine's efficiency by cutting down on heat loss. More importantly it allowed the engine's motive power to become steam rather than atmospheric pressure. Watt took out patents in 1781–2 embodying his solution to the problem of rotary motion, creating a double-acting engine in which steam pushed the cylinder in each direction (The complex parts for Watt's engine were beyond the capacity of contemporary ironworkers, and technical advances were needed in metal working before the new principles could be fully exploited.)

Converting Newcomen's atmospheric engine into a steam engine required all Watt's talents as an instrument-maker and draftsman. It also required a mathematical exactness that Watt had developed over the course of his studies—his letters and diaries demonstrate that he understood basic scientific principles required to work on his steam engine (Jacob 1997: 119–20). Watt exploited the available science (although the second law of thermodynamics, important to the ultimate development of later engines, came later). Aspects of the required science were developed by Joseph Black, 'one of the founders of the scientific study of heat' (Cardwell 1995: 157). Black had many accomplishments: he developed the first truly quantitative measures of heat, the concepts of specific heat capacity, and the idea of latent heat. While it will never be clear how much Watt was influenced by Black—direct links between the two have not been conclusively established—it is difficult to believe that Watt did not know of, and use, Black's work (especially in a world in which all those associated with the Royal Society were aware of each other's work).[46]

---

[46] Cardwell, for example, does not accept the common view that Black had no influence on Watt. He (1995: 157–9) writes that Watt learned the fundamental concept of heat capacity from Black and used Black's work on heat conductivity to develop his replacement for the metal cylinders then in common use—a wooden cylinder, treated with linseed oil and baked. Uglow (2002: 101) also details a close relationship between the two, noting that after Black explained his theory of latent heat to Watt, 'Watt now saw that the great drawback with the Newcomen engine was the loss of this extra heat through the alternate heating and cooling of the cylinder. Although Black's theory, he said, did not *suggest* his improvements to the engine, his knowledge and method...helped his work immeasurably.' Herman (2001: 320) goes further, describing Black as Watt's 'friend and teacher'.

To fully exploit the energy potential of Watt's engine required a much higher steam pressure than Watt was comfortable with. However, when Watt's key patents expired in 1800, he lost his control over the development of the engine. This, coupled with improvements in iron making, which produced boilers and cylinders that could withstand increasingly higher pressures, allowed Trevithick to develop a working high-pressure engine in 1801.[47]

Did Science Matter for the Steam Engine?

Landes (1969: 61, n.1) argued that science contributed little to the development of the stream engine, 'which is often put forward as the prime example of science-spawned innovation'. However, he (1969: 104)[48] later states that there is 'some truth' to the observation that early on Newcomen's engine owed something to recent scientific discoveries. He also notes that Watt derived ideas and technical competence from his association with contemporary scientists. Landes then goes on to argue: 'One thing is clear, however, once the principle of the separate condenser was established, subsequent advances owed little or nothing to theory.' This is a little like saying that the orbit of a rocket owes little to chemical fuels; after all, once they reach orbit, rockets no longer use chemical fuels as propellants. But just as rockets require chemical fuels to ever achieve orbit, the trajectory leading to steam power required science for 200 years. Even if we accept for the sake of argument that once steam was fully developed as a power source, its further incremental refinement owed little to science, that does nothing to diminish the fact that science contributed greatly to the trajectory that led to the engine.[49]

In his early work, Thurston (1878) notes that the developers of the steam engine's principles were mathematicians, physicists, and/or practical engineers: Cardan and Porta were mathematicians; Porta and Huygens knew chemistry and physics; Savery was familiar with mechanics and mathematics. It is hard to conceive that these same people could achieve what they did using only trial-and-error empiricism.

The development of the steam engine relies on an interrelationship of new piecemeal scientific knowledge and practical engineering. Engineers frequently made use of scientific principles only recently understood. As Thurston (1878: 37) puts it:

At the beginning of the eighteenth century every element of the modern type of steam engine had been separately invented and practically applied. . . . It now only remained for the engineer

---

[47] These were all stationary applications of steam power. The development of an effective locomotive required the solution to two further problems that we have already described in Chapter 6 (see page 192).

[48] In this paragraph, all subsequent quotes from Landes are from page 61.

[49] It is, of course, not true that the incremental improvement of steam did not benefit from science. The mid 19th century development of the Corliss steam engine, which was responsible for the transition of much US manufacturing from water to steam power, relied heavily on state-of-the-art engineering knowledge. This was systematic knowledge that we include in science, not empirical knowledge developed by trial and error. It could not have been arrived at without the underpinning of early modern science in general and Newtonian mechanics in particular and could not, therefore, have been achieved outside of the West. On the development and significance of the Corliss engine see Rosenberg and Trajtenberg (2004).

to combine known forms of mechanism in a practical machine which should be capable of economically and conveniently utilizing the power of steam through the application of now well-understood principles, and by the intelligent combination of physical phenomena already familiar to scientific investigators.

This idea is also shared by Musson (1963: xvii), who argued:

[A] great deal of experimentation of that time [sixteenth and seventeenth centuries] had utilitarian applications, and there is no doubt that the underlying principles of the steam engine—the creation of a vacuum by condensation of steam in a closed vessel and the utilization of atmospheric and steam pressure—were originally discovered by natural philosophers, or scientists as we would now call them, in the seventeenth century.

Finally, from Cardwell (1971: 54):

In the first place, no 'common-sense' appreciation of the heat losses involved in the operation of the Newcomen engine would have justified Watt's inventions. What was needed was the measurement of the actual amounts involved. This Watt was able to provide, for he belonged to one of the most active scientific groups in the world; a group which was, moreover, pioneering the scientific study of heat.

Clearly, science played an important role in the development of the steam engine.

Subsequent Developments in this Period

What sustained technological change and economic growth during the later stages of the steam-driven phase? The general answer is that this period was typical of the diverse developments that occur once a new GPT has been established and it is being refined and extended to more and more productive activities. Once the factory system had been developed in textiles, it slowly spread to other types of manufacturing. New products and new processes were developed as that extension occurred. Wood was abandoned as the prime material for machines. Although wooden machines could stand up to the pressures of hand or water power, they were inadequate to withstand the pressures involved with steam power. As a result of the need for machines made of metal, an entire new industry, the machine tool industry, came into being. Massive amounts of investment were required for the new factories and the industrial towns that served them and their workers. So also was heavy investment required in the transportation network that facilitated the growing economic activity. The amazing results of all this creative activity occurred within what Freeman and Louçã would call the new technoeconomic paradigm, and what we think of as the working out of the later stages of the development of a new GPT, the factory, when its potential had been vastly extended by the addition of a second GPT, the steam engine. These activities sustained technological change and economic growth at a positive although uneven rate until the middle of the century when its impressive achievements were put on view in the Great Exhibition of 1851. By then the early stages of the science-led phase can be discerned with the benefit of hindsight even if they were not obvious to many contemporary observers.

Science-Led Industrial Phase

During the early factory and the steam-driven phases, the innovations in the leading sectors were virtually all mechanical. Many of the non-mechanical innovations in other sectors were based on empirical trial and error without a strong scientific underpinning. This was true, for example, in metallurgy. Importantly, these advances did not lead mechanical advances but, instead, were made largely in response to pressures coming from the mechanical sector to develop such things as better steam engines and to replace wooden machines with metal ones. So those sectors that could use Newtonian mechanical science were leaders and those that were based purely on trial and error were followers.

During the science-led-phase—the so-called Second Industrial Revolution—industrial development was led by many non-mechanical sectors. It is generally agreed that the Second Industrial Revolution was heavily science-based. Chemicals and steel were two of its key products while electricity and the internal-combustion engine were its new energy sources (see Chapter 6). Advances in chemistry, especially as it was applied to textile production, were particularly important. New dyes that were first developed in Britain but most fully exploited in Germany, led to the development of the new discipline of chemical engineering. By 1900, both theoretical and empirical advances were supporting continuing innovations in dyes, bleaches, and detergents. All these required applications of fairly advanced Western science.

The key point in the above discussion is that in all three phases of the Industrial Revolution the leading sectors were the ones most influenced by science while those that were evolving purely by trial-and-error groping were lagging behind, and being pulled along by the leading sectors. Science did matter.

Electricity, which we discussed in Chapter 6, is one of the most pervasive GPTs of all time. It played a key part in this phase of industrialization. As with textiles and steam, its development followed a long evolutionary course. It took nearly 300 years of cumulative research into all of its aspects to complete the West's research agenda of understanding electricity and magnetism, of which the following are just some highlights. In 1600, Gilbert published *De Magnete*, which turned isolated empirical knowledge about the behaviour of compasses, some of which was known to the Chinese and some of which had been known by the Greeks, into a scientific theory in which the central hypothesis was that the earth itself was a gigantic magnet. Its attraction of the compass needle explained all of the needle's behaviour, both when it was obviously systematic and when it was apparently erratic. In an excellent example of the complementarities between apparently unrelated technologies, it was the three-masted sailing ship that took Europeans far enough away from home shores to be seriously bothered by the compass's erratic behaviour, and it took the new scientific approach to document this behaviour systematically and then explain it in an embracing hypothesis. (See Section I in Chapter 6 and Section II in Chapter 8 for further discussion.) In 1670, Otto von Guericke invented a machine to produce an electric charge. At the start of the eighteenth century, Du Fay showed the difference between positive and negative electric charges. The earliest form of condenser, the

Leyden jar, was invented in 1745. In 1752, Benjamin Franklin showed that atmospheric electricity was identical in form to the charge produced by a Leyden jar. In 1766, Priestly proved that the force between electric charges varies inversely with the distance between the charges. De Coulomb subsequently invented an instrument to measure electric charges accurately. In 1800, Volta produced the first electric battery. In 1819, Oersted demonstrated that a magnetic field existed around an electric current. In 1831, Faraday demonstrated that a current flowing through a coil of wire could induce a current in a nearby coil; he also developed the theory of electric lines of force. In 1840, Joule and von Helmholtz demonstrated that electricity was a form of energy and that it obeyed the law of conservation of energy. Joule also showed that the magneto converts mechanical energy into electrical energy. In 1845, Wheatston and Cooke patented an electromagnet to replace a permanent magnet in telegraphs. In 1866, Wilde described a machine that used an electromagnet to turn unlimited amounts of mechanical energy into electrical energy. In 1867, Wheatstone and Siemens invented a practical dynamo and the electric engine had arrived. In 1873, Maxwell published his *Treatise on Electricity and Magnetism*, which mathematized Faraday's theory of electrical magnetic forces.

The arrival of practical electric power in the late nineteenth century was thus the fruit of a long evolutionary collaboration between science and technology. By no stretch of the imagination could it have occurred without both early modern and nineteenth-century Western science.

V.   GROWTH BECOMES SUSTAINED

In Chapter 1, we discussed the concept of sustained growth, observing that although it is a well-defined concept in theoretical models, it is not well defined in empirical applications. We then suggested that the empirical criteria for sustained growth were, first, that it is obviously not a short burst of growth that comes to an end in a matter of a few years or at the most a few decades and, second, that there are reasons to believe that the growth is self-sustaining.

Two centuries of growth in the West at a significantly positive, although varying, rate is sufficient to meet the first criteria. But what about the second criteria, that growth be self-sustaining? We see at least three main reasons for believing that this criteria is also met today, at least in the West (and in some other areas as well): scientific research has been institutionalized; applied R&D has also been institutionalized; the trajectories of science and technology have become much more intertwined than they were in the past. We look at these in turn.

Institutionalization of Scientific Advance

Starting in the late nineteenth century, Western science has been institutionalized, primarily in universities. At the same time, there has been a vast increase in the amount of resources, human and physical, allocated to scientific investigation. As a result, the evolution of modern science along its own natural trajectory, observable at least as far back as the beginnings of early modern science, had been greatly accelerated—and there are as many trajectories as there are branches of science. One discovery in science and mathematics has led to another in a cascade of newly discovered and interrelated knowledge. This process is cumulative and self-reinforcing in the sense that the solution to one problem typically gives rise to other problems.

Institutionalization of R&D

Also in the late nineteenth century, firms, universities, and governments began to set up research labs, which engaged in everything from pure to highly applied research. The 'invention factory' established by Thomas Edison at Menlo Park in 1876 'is usually credited with pioneering the organization of invention in the field of communications and electricity' (Rosenberg and Birdzell 1986: 249). Many other companies followed, although not immediately. By the turn of the century, the involvement of industry in organized R&D was significant and growing.

By the early years of the twentieth century, industrial research had clearly turned toward the development of new products and processes. If the knowledge required for innovation lay on (or even a little beyond) the frontiers of science, the industrial laboratories worked the frontiers. (Rosenberg and Birdzel 1986: 251)

Today, R&D is a major activity encouraged by significant tax incentives in most Western countries. Large oligopolistic firms in many branches of manufacturing and service industries engage in organized research as a major weapon in the competition with their rivals. These efforts are conspicuous in drugs, medical supplies, aeronautics, transports equipment, lumber products, and biotechnology, to name but a few of the most obvious examples.

Science and Technology Intertwined

Science and technology have become much more interrelated than they ever were in the past. Prior to the eighteenth century, new GPTs were empirically based, being discovered and developed experimentally, mainly by practical craftspersons. Such GPTs arrived episodically since there was no natural trajectory leading from one to the next. Up until the mid nineteenth century, Newtonian mechanics explained most of what was observed and provided the intellectual underpinnings of the technologies of the First Industrial Revolution, as well as large engineering works such as bridges and canals, and the shafts, pulleys, and crankshafts of the new factories. Although scientific knowledge did assist technological developments in the nineteenth century, it was still possible for experienced craftspersons to invent significant new technologies on a strictly trial-and-error basis. It was also possible for ordinary skilled workers to have a knowledge of the relevant Newtonian science.

All this changed when most technologies, including GPTs, began to have a basis in pure science. The first two were the steam engine and the railroad, where the interactions between what we now think of as science and technology were clear. By the time the West developed the technologies of the Second Industrial Revolution, such as electricity, steel, and chemicals, the connections between science and technology had became strong and direct.

At about the same time, universities began to develop departments of applied science, which had direct links to the commercial world, training scientists and engineers for employment in the private sector and doing research that was directly relevant to technological development. The USA and Germany have been particularly successful in such endeavours and, as a result, have maintained a lead in many industrial products that have a strong base in applied science. In Chapter 4, we discussed Rosenberg's analysis of the modern links that make even pure science endogenous to economic incentives, responding to the incentives produced by the market economy, which in turn are generated by the needs of developing technologies.

When, by the end of the nineteenth century, problems with the Newtonian view became increasingly apparent, the new science began to go 'underground'. Early in the twentieth century, Poincaré and Einstein laid the foundations of a new quantum science of the behaviour of subatomic particles. Later, non-linear systems became important, bringing with them the understanding of chaotic behaviour, butterfly effects, and other seemingly exotic types of behaviour. These and other new understandings completed the overthrow, begun with Heisenberg's uncertainty principle, of the world view of mechanical determinism that had stemmed from Newtonian physics. Long before then, science had gone where ordinary craftspersons, skilled labourers, or even the typical university graduate could not follow. Some minor inventions that are incremental improvements to existing technologies can still be made by those ignorant of modern science, but for virtually all contributions to the majority of technological trajectories in products and processes, to say nothing about developing new GPTs, are the sole province of scientifically educated persons. The major exception is organizational technologies, where new radical forms of organization, such as lean production, often require no more than common sense, intuition, and a good grounding in mechanics.

Thus, fast-evolving scientific trajectories that directly link to the introduction of new technologies, especially GPTs, have created self-reinforcing and interlocking technological trajectories. One only has to think of the dynamo enabling the practical generation of electricity, which enabled the radio, television, and electronic computer, which in turn enabled the whole ICT revolution, followed by the Internet; combined with another trajectory in biological science it produced biotechnology, and then, in conjunction with some of the new physics, enabled nanotechnology. Still just on the horizon is the quantum computer with computing power, which dwarfs anything that can be produced by electronic computers.

Further Growth Not Inevitable

Just because there are reasons why modern growth in the West tends to be self-sustaining, it does not follow that such growth will be sustained indefinitely. Given a few macro levers, any economist worth his or her salt could end growth in any Western country. He or she could use some of the well-known macro levers such as initiating a hyperinflation through excessive monetary expansion and introducing confiscatory personal and corporate income tax rates. These are crude but effective means of stopping growth, but some more subtle measures such as were discussed in Chapter 3 would also do the job over a decade or so: measures that suppressed invention and innovation, driving entrepreneurs abroad, discouraging foreign investment, and adopting educational policies that did not equip the younger generation to take part in the evolving globalized economy.

The moral is that there is no assurance that just because growth has been sustained for a couple of centuries it will continue indefinitely. After all, it was probably sustained for up to a millennium in a couple of previous Western historical experiences in areas that are now relatively economically undynamic—the Middle East and the eastern Mediterranean.

VI.   THE THREE QUESTIONS ANSWERED

We now return to the three questions that we posed at the outset of this chapter. *Why* was there an Industrial Revolution that set the West off on a path of sustained growth that was extremely rapid by historical standards? Why did it occur *where* it did—in the West in general and in Britain in particular? Why did it begin *when* it did—in the last half of the eighteenth century and not, say, 150 years earlier or later? To answer these questions, we merely need to gather together points established in the chapter.

Why the Industrial Revolution?

Long Evolution

The Industrial Revolution was not a sudden event that came more or less from out of the blue. Instead, it was the contingent culmination of evolutionary paths that had been in place for centuries. The medieval period saw the development of a pluralistic society, which ultimately freed natural philosophers to pursue a uniquely powerful form of science that explained the world in terms of mechanical laws. In society, a division developed between lay and religious areas of jurisdiction. In government, many competing nation states arose, as well as many powerful independent cities. In the private sector, the self-governing corporation grew up to insulate first the Church, and then universities, professions, and crafts from the full power of the state. In law, a division developed between king's law and religious law, and within the king's law among natural, civil, and criminal law. In philosophy, the view developed that nature was governed by God-given natural laws. To discover these laws was to discover God's works and hence the pursuit was pious and not blasphemous. The search for these laws in a pluralistic society allowed a multitude of views to be expressed and debated according to strict rules of logical enquiry. This put the Christian Church, which by a lucky historical accident had avoided the theocracy that caused difficulties in many other societies, on the side of those who sought to explain the world in terms of mechanical laws of nature. Then, as the

Catholic Church started to turn against early modern science, the Reformation created a new branch of the Christian religion that welcomed it, at least in some Protestant areas—probably to some extent because welcoming it was anti-Catholic.

In the early modern period, three research programmes were begun: to mechanize textile production; to harness atmospheric pressure (and eventually steam power); and to understand magnetism. These evolved slowly through incremental changes as knowledge accumulated in a path-dependent way. They reached fruition in the eighteenth and nineteenth centuries when they became key drivers of the Industrial Revolutions. These research programmes relied on what we now regard both as technology and science.

The First Industrial Revolution from the mid eighteenth to the early nineteenth centuries made extensive use of the new Newtonian science and the mechanistic world view that it promoted. Some of the mechanical inventions might have been made without knowledge of science but others, particularly the steam engine, needed it. The really major improvements in productivity in the early nineteenth century that resulted from combining the steam engine with the new automated textile machinery—machinery that until then had been hand- or water-driven—could, therefore, not have occurred. A non-Western Industrial Revolution devoid of Western science would have stalled early in the nineteenth century—even in the doubtful event that it could have got that far.

Even if the fully automated European textile machinery *c.*1800, and the steam engine, were by some near miracle developed in a society without Western science, the Second Industrial Revolution of the latter part of the nineteenth century could never have happened anywhere but in Europe. That revolution was firmly science-based and could not have happened in a country that did not have access to Western science.[50]

---

[50] Mokyr (2002: 29) distinguishes between the total useful knowledge in a society, which he calls Ω, and techniques, which are 'essentially sets of instructions or recipes on how to manipulate nature', which he calls λ. He defines a subset of λ as singleton techniques. These have a narrow base in Ω which, in the limit, is so narrow that all that is known is that the technique works. He then argues that 'much technological progress before 1800 was of that nature. Although new techniques appeared before the Industrial Revolution, they had narrow epistemic bases and thus rarely if ever led to continued and sustained improvements' (2002: 19). During the Industrial Revolution, according to Mokyr, technological knowledge became less and less of the singleton type and the complementarity of λ and Ω became stronger until, late in that century, it was so strong that technological and scientific knowledge became self-sustaining in a positive feedback system. In contrast, we trace the shift from λ knowledge to Ω knowledge much further back in time than does Mokyr, highlighting the continuous nature of science's long-run development. While in many fields it was well into the 19th century before Ω and λ became sufficiently complementary to create a positive feedback loop, in other fields, the development started in the early modern period. We illustrate with three key cases: (*a*) the trajectory that began with Leonardo da Vinci and led to the breakthroughs in textile manufacturing; (*b*) the kind of mechanics that underlay the First Industrial Revolution in many fields, such as the building of harbours and canals as well as textiles and the steam engine, were turned into Ω knowledge and unified by Newton's laws of motion and his calculus; and (*c*) the trajectory of discoveries that led to the use of electricity stretched cumulatively over 200 years. These technological trajectories that were central to the Industrial Revolution cannot be regarded as a succession of isolated pieces of singleton knowledge. So although we agree with Mokyr's argument of why

Institutional Memory

Many cultures, particularly those of Islam and China, produced breakthroughs in science and technology that were equal to, or significantly better than, those of medieval and early modern Europe. However, Europe alone generated the incremental, cumulative advances in science that were necessary to produce modern mechanistic science, the science of the First Industrial Revolution. Such cumulative advances require a form of 'memory'. Technology and science require different forms of memory. Artefacts provide a memory for the non-tacit aspects of technological knowledge. Tools, machines, new crops, and so on all provide a method for passing aspects of technological knowledge through time.[51] Artefacts have a physical existence and technological improvements are embodied in better artefacts; they are there for all to use and to improve on in their turn.[52] So, for most of history, artefacts have provided an unplanned, and largely unmanaged, technological memory.

Science requires a different form of memory, an institutional memory. There is no automatic memory provided for scientific knowledge. Creating an institutional memory for science was an important contribution of the medieval European university: libraries recorded knowledge, classrooms were used to teach it, and scholars contributed to its evolution. Just as Greek academies did in classical times, universities helped to provide continuity in the evolution of medieval scientific knowledge.

These significant roles of physical and institutional 'memory' are important in answering an objection to our thesis: Why is it that other regions in the world, especially those with important historical achievements in science and technology, failed to produce modern mechanistic science and sustained innovation? An important part of the answer is that they lacked the independent institutions that provided an effective memory needed for cumulative scientific advances. (This point is further discussed in Chapter 8.)

Why in Britain?

The conditions we have summarized that led to the Industrial Revolution were only found in the West. This leads us to ask if the Industrial Revolution could have

---

sustained growth took off in the late 18th and early 19th centuries, we argue that from 1450 to 1750 several lines of cumulative scientific and technological advance were very far from providing only singleton knowledge in several areas that were most important for the Industrial Revolution. In sum, we argue that the conditions Mokyr correctly identifies as essential to the Industrial Revolution are rooted much further back in history than he contends.

[51] Technologies are occasionally lost. For one reason, at times of great upheaval they may fall into disuse to be forgotten, as was the case with several Roman technologies. For another reason, the technology may be used by only a few persons whose successors may lose interest, as was the case with the great Chinese water clocks that were used for astrological purposes by some emperors, then ignored by later ones.

[52] It may help to record technological knowledge in written form and to pass it on through formal instruction, but this was seldom necessary before the 19th century.

happened at about the time it did but in another Western country, such as France or Germany?

Many Contributing Causes

In considering this question, we recall our belief that many historical events are 'overdetermined' in the sense that at any one time there often exist multiple sets of causes that are sufficient for a particular occurrence. We can identify some of these, but it makes no sense to argue about which of several existing sufficient causes (or groups of causes) actually was *the* cause. For example, many forces contributed to Britain's technological success and indeed there were probably more than enough sufficient causes for that success. As Landes (1969: 71) put it:

[W]hat sets Britain off is a question of degree. Nowhere else . . . was the countryside so infused with manufacture; nowhere else, the pressure and incentives to change greater, the force of tradition weaker. It was all of a piece: improving landlords, enclosures, commercial farming, village shops, putting-out, mines and forges, the active mortgage market—all combined to break the shackles of place and habit, assimilate country and city, and promote a far wider recruitment of talent than would have otherwise occurred.

To this list we would add: more security of real and financial property, strong restraints on arbitrary behaviour of the monarchy, better intellectual property protection, ample supplies of raw materials and markets provided by colonies, and a host of other factors that helped rather than hindered Britain's industrial and commercial success.[53] Various combinations of these 'causes' might have been sufficient for the Industrial Revolution to occur in Britain. Books have been written on each of them.

One influential work by North and Thomas (1973) stresses the role of property rights. We accept the importance of property rights in any explanation of long-run growth. Their absence can completely stifle innovation and investment. However, we maintain, first, that they are only one element in a bundle of causes that contributed to the Industrial Revolution and, second, that the historical evidence does not support a linear relationship from property rights to innovation. Technologies often create new demands on property rights regimes, which then are changed to serve in ways that facilitate yet more innovation. This seems true in cases ranging over time from the spread of water-powered machinery in the Middle Ages to the modern biotechnology revolution and digitally recorded music, all of which raised their own property rights problems. These are typically resolved after, rather than before, the technologies are beyond their initial development stages. So it seems to us that the causal relations run more often from technology to property rights than vice versa. This is not to say that property rights have been unimportant because, if the

---

[53] Pomeranz (2000) has argued that the two important conditions for the British Industrial Revolution were the existence of easy-to-reach coal and colonies. That they were important, we do not doubt. But were they necessary? We doubt it. Even so, there is no problem in having more than one necessary condition. Even if colonies and/or coal were necessary (which we doubt), that does not preclude the necessity of science; the explanations are potential complements.

problems that are raised by new technologies are not satisfactorily resolved, the development and diffusion of these technologies will be slowed, or in extreme cases, halted.

Science as a Necessary Condition

Our answer to the question 'why in Britain?' is that while there were many contributing causes as we have listed, Newtonian mechanical science was a necessary condition for the First Industrial Revolution. While other countries as widely separated as France and China had many of the other conditions, only Britain had a mechanical science that permeated the whole society with both a mechanistic world view and the techniques to handle what were at the time complex problems in mechanics. Jacob's research, which we have quoted liberally, has revealed just how deeply Newtonian science entered the thinking of British industrialists, engineers, entrepreneurs, and ordinary people in the eighteenth and early nineteenth centuries.

Many aspects of British industrialization that puzzled Landes are explicable when seen in the light of Britain's scientific development. After pointing to the 'higher level of technical skill and greater interest in machines' in England compared with other European countries, Landes (1969: 61) argues: 'This should not be confused with scientific knowledge.' In contrast, we argue that these British abilities and interests were influenced by scientific knowledge. Britain's technological developments were stimulated and assisted by such knowledge, particularly Newtonian mechanics.

Landes (1969: 61) goes on to say that his view 'makes the question of British mechanical skill the more mysterious'. Indeed it would be mysterious if that skill had nothing to do with science, as Landes suggests. Instead, when one takes Britain's unique development of a Newtonian mechanistic research programme into account, there is no mystery. The British comparative advantage was based on a mixture of practical and scientific knowledge (as science was then understood).

Why Not Elsewhere in Europe?

Britain's success was based on more than just an ability to 'tinker', in which Mokyr locates Britain's distinct advantage. He (1990: 242) argues that 'Britain did not have a significant scientific advantage that would explain its technological leadership'. Later Mokyr (2002) reiterated the point, arguing that while Europe's scientific culture distinguished it from other areas of the world, and should be part of any explanation of why the Industrial Revolution happened first in Europe, different levels of science do not explain the different patterns of industrialization within Europe—'compared to China or classical antiquity, the gap anywhere in Europe appears to have been shallow' (Mokyr 2002: 64). Indeed, according to his argument, the countries that were scientific leaders need not have been the economic leaders:

Nor did the national differences matter all that much: as long as knowledge could move readily across boundaries, both scientific and technological 'leads' would be temporary. Even if all the theorists had lived in France and all practical entrepreneurs had lived in Britain, abstract knowledge should have moved from France to Britain, been turned into technology there, and eventually returned to the Continent in the form of machines and the men who knew how to operate them. *This is roughly what happened between 1760 and 1850.* (emphasis added)

However, scientific and technological knowledge does not, as Mokyr seems to be saying in the above quote, move quickly and costlessly across the borders that divide firms, let alone across international boundaries. Even at the level of entrepreneurial firms, the profits that motivate growth-creating technological change are the rents that individual innovators earn before other competitors learn to copy them. The British nation had a lead in the requisite mechanistic science and this was parlayed into several decades of industrial leadership.

We argue that the differences between British and French science and engineering were significant. Jacob (1997: 46) puts it this way: 'The combined legacy of Cartesian and scholastic teaching may account for the fact that by the 1790s French colleges were noticeably deficient in teaching devices needed for mechanical applications.' The result was that 'educated Frenchmen of the generation prior to the 1750s missed any formal education in practical Newtonian mechanics as well as in the entire Newtonian philosophical outlook' (Jacob 1997: 50). Because French teaching lacked the mechanical applications that were commonplace in England, they lacked the Newtonian applied science that was the underpinning of the First Industrial Revolution.[54] Mokyr (1990: 242) quotes Kuhn as saying that the views of the English were predominantly experimental and mechanical while the French were predominantly mathematical and deductive 'seems to have stood the test of time'. The French made many inventions but the English excelled in commercial applications because they understood the mechanics that were needed to make ideas work.

The length of time it took for what some consider quite basic technological developments to diffuse to the Continent is consistent with the idea that Britain was ahead of those countries in the understanding of Newtonian mechanics. Ultimately, the full diffusion of the technologies of the First Industrial Revolution to the Continent took a generation. Often the technology was diffused by British technicians who took the technology to the Continent and made it work. Furthermore, when it did come, one of the countries where it took root earliest was Belgium, which was the Continental country where knowledge of Newtonian mechanics was most widespread. If, as some have argued, the Continental countries were on the verge of an Industrial Revolution, and had the scientific prerequisites for it, diffusion would have been much faster and easier than it actually was.

The argument that Britain was ahead of the Continent in those developments that led to the First Industrial Revolution does not imply that if Britain had failed to produce that revolution, it would not have happened elsewhere in Europe. Everything that we have said puts Europe (at least northern Europe) well ahead of any

---

[54] We are not arguing that the French lacked inventiveness. After all, Papin invented an early form of steam engine, others invented the hot-air balloon, and developed an efficient signalling technology to transmit complex messages using semaphore towers faster than ever before. What they did not excel at, at least compared with the British, were inventions requiring a high degree of mechanical expertise.

other region in the push to mechanize. If for some reason, possibly political, Britain had ceased its technological development some time in the early eighteenth century, there is no reason to believe that the Industrial Revolution would not have happened on the Continent. Its development would have been postponed, but not terminated.

When In Britain?

We have argued that the Industrial Revolution could only have happened in Europe because only Europe had the necessary condition of early modern science, and that it happened first in Britain because that country was ahead in the Newtonian mechanical science that underlay the First Industrial Revolution. The 'when?' of that revolution is implicit in our argument about the trajectories of what we today would distinguish as early modern science and technology (and what was then regarded as just natural philosophy). As we have observed, the project to mechanize all textile manufacturing was initiated by da Vinci and stretched over 200 years as more and more complicated technological problems were solved. Their solution required, among other things, improved technological abilities, better designs, and better materials.

The pace of these interrelated, path-dependent developments might have been accelerated or decelerated a bit for many reasons, but it proceeded with easier problems being solved first and more difficult ones later on, until the machines were developed enough that it paid to take them out of cottages into what became factories. The second part of the revolution came when the trajectory that led to the steam engine reached the type of high-pressure engine that fitted well into the textile factories. So the Industrial Revolution was really the combination of two evolutionary paths in technology that had been going on continuously for centuries and an organizational GPT, when work moved out of the cottages into early factories and later into the new industrials towns.

Although many events might have unfolded differently enough to alter the timing somewhat, it is inconceivable that they could have advanced things by more than a few decades. Too much cumulative knowledge and too many changes in attitude were needed to compress these events by much. Other events might have slowed the industrial development. For example, many things would have been different if the Stuarts had won the civil war or if the Glorious Revolution of 1688 had not occurred. But unless scientific enquiry had been seriously suppressed, it seems unlikely that the key trajectories would have been lengthened by more that a few decades.

A Postscript on Timing

There has been substantial debate about the exact timing of the emergence of sustained growth in the West. Resolution of this debate can be assisted by making two distinctions that we have repeatedly emphasized. First, changes in productivity are not the same thing as changes in technology. For example, sustained growth driven by a succession of GPTs is consistent with zero change in TFP.[55] Although this is not what we would think of as the normal case, the point is that changes in TFP, or

---

[55] See Appendix to Chapter 4 and the discussion of TFP in Chapter 15 for more details on this.

in any other measure of productivity, do not measure technological change. The GPT that drove much of the Industrial Revolution was the factory system, which was experimented with starting in the eighteenth century. Like all major GPTs, it was not obvious what form would be best and many different ones were tried, running at one extreme from sheds with a few individuals providing human power to the new machines to large water-powered factories with hundreds of employees at the other extreme. Also, like many GPTs, the margin of efficiency of the new form of production over the old was small at first. The slow decline of cottage industry and the slow depression of the wages of hand loom weavers over the nineteenth century are good indications of the way in which the new system gradually asserted its superiority over the old as it was improved and extended to cover more and more types of production.[56] (Note that this is a typical story of new GPTs as explained in Chapters 4 and 13 and illustrated in Chapters 5 and 6.) So it is not surprising that at the time when entrepreneurs were slowly feeling their way towards improving the new GPT and learning how to use it efficiently, total production and measured productivity only changed slowly.[57]

Second, we need to distinguish between extensive and intensive growth. The emergence of sustained extensive growth occurred some time in the early nineteenth century. Its seeds were sown with the early factories whose efficiency was not notably greater than cottage industry until steam entered the factories from the 1820s onward. But it is clear from the trajectories of factories, steam, electricity, internal-combustion engines, chemistry, and metallurgy that sustained extensive growth had been assured technologically by the mid nineteenth century, if not before. Sustained intensive growth awaited the fall in the birth rate that came in different Western countries at different times in the nineteenth and early twentieth centuries. These are distinct events. We can imagine one without the other, at least for quite a long time. Today, when population is brought under control in some very poor countries (often as a result of female education), there is a transition to intensive growth without any acceleration in technological change or extensive growth. Similarly, it is possible to have extensive growth matched by population growth with no intensive growth for very long periods of time. So, what we have discussed in this chapter is the transition to sustained extensive growth, while intensive growth will be discussed in Chapters 9 and 10.

To the question 'When did sustained extensive growth actually emerge?' we answer: 'Some time in the early nineteenth century.' But to the question 'When were the seeds of this emergence first sown?' we answer: 'Some time at the beginning of the early modern period, while the construction of the seeds themselves began in the medieval period.'

---

[56] The proportion of textile workers employed outside of the factory system was still 30 per cent in 1841, falling to 12 per cent in 1871, and reaching 2 per cent by 1901. In metal trades, the figure was 65 per cent in 1841 and 25 per cent by 1871. By 1901, less than 10 per cent of the entire industrial labour force was working outside of the factory system (Usher 1920).

[57] The annual rate of increase in British output was 0.26 between 1760 and 1830 according to Clark (2001); it was 0.17 per cent from 1760 to 1800 and 0.52 per cent from 1800 to 1830 according to Crafts and Harley (1992).

8

Why Not Elsewhere?

In the eleventh century, at the beginning of its revival of learning, Europe was uncivilized and technologically backward by the standards of both China and the Islamic empire. By the beginning of the sixteenth century, Europe was well ahead of the Islamic countries in science and technology and was rapidly accumulating new knowledge in both these areas. At the same time, Islam had entered a period of scientific and technological stagnation. China was the equal of Europe in many areas until some time in the eighteenth century.[1] Yet by the end of the nineteenth century, a large gulf had opened up between the West and China in terms of technology and rates of economic growth.

In Chapter 7, we argued that a set of specific characteristics and events explain why sustained extensive growth emerged in Western Europe, why it happened late in the second millennium, and why it was originally located specifically in Britain, then spreading to the rest of the Continent. In this chapter, we ask a related question: Why did sustained growth not emerge elsewhere? Why did some other countries not generate their own industrial revolutions and the self-sustaining growth of science and technology that accompanied it? We concentrate on China and Islam as the most likely candidates for such a development, since no other non-Western country came close to Islam's science and technology in the thirteenth century and to China's technology in the eighteenth century. Our proximate answer for China and Islam is that, despite being early technological leaders, they did not generate industrial revolutions because, among other things, they failed to develop mechanistic science. This of course raises the question of why this happened. We offer some explanations based on comparisons and contrasts with conditions that favoured the development of European science.

I. WHY NOT IN ISLAM?

The areas of the eastern Mediterranean and the Fertile Crescent did not suffer the same disruptions from the barbarian invasions that beset the Western Roman Empire. Then, in the seventh century AD, the Islamic religion was born and within

---

[1] For the 18th century, Pomeranz (2000) argues that in terms of life expectancy, birth rates, death rates, caloric intake, and possibly even literacy, China was comparable to Britain. Since comparable estimates of GDP are not available for the period, Pomeranz generally employs indirect measures to compare China and Britain.

less than 200 years, its followers had created an extensive empire whose regions were economically rich and intellectually sophisticated. The Islamic military conquests were different from the earlier barbarian invasions in that local institutions were left free to continue functioning more or less as they always had. Greek learning was never lost in the conquered countries and science and technology continued to flourish in them. Many innovations came to the West via Islam, either having been created there or having diffused from China, where they had originated. When they went east in the First Crusade (1096–9), European Christians encountered a civilization that was superior to theirs in philosophy and science, and at least their equal in technology. Why did such an advanced society, which was heir to the same Greek learning that formed the basis of medieval scholastic philosophy, fail to generate its own sustained growth? We began our investigation in Chapter 7 of why the West achieved sustained growth with the origins of Christianity. Similarly, we start our investigation into why the Islamic countries failed to do so with the rise of Islam.

Early Development of Christianity and Islam[2]

The early followers of both Christ and Muhammad were relatively unsophisticated people who spread their religions within relatively sophisticated societies. However, the development of the Islamic religion was markedly different from that of Christianity in ways that mattered for the subsequent history of science and technology.

First, in contrast with the Christian need to convert by persuasion, Islam was spread by the sword. Within twenty years of Muhammad's death in 632, armies of the first four caliphs had conquered Palestine, Syria, Egypt, Iraq, and most of Persia. Subsequently, during the period 661–750, the armies of the Umayyads pushed Islam's borders to the Indus River in the east and through North Africa to Spain in the west. In 732, exactly 100 years after the prophet's death, Charles Martel claimed defeat of the Islamic armies near Poitiers in France. Although the causes are not clear, Islam's Western expansion ended there.[3]

Second, during and after the expansion of the Islamic empire, little attempt was made to convert the conquered infidels. Indeed, the empire was remarkably tolerant of diverse cultures and religions. Nonetheless, the incentives for locals to convert were substantial.[4] Little is actually known about the process of conversion, but during the first hundred years, Islamic converts made up probably no more than 10 per cent of the conquered people. By the end of 300 years of Muslim rule, however, the greater part of the conquered population had converted to Islam in their own self-interest with no need for intellectual persuasion (Hourani 1991: 46–7).

---

[2] We keep a narrow focus on the issue of why technological and scientific advance stagnated in the Islamic countries, a development on which scholars are more or less agreed—although, of course, there is room for disagreement about the causes.

[3] Roberts (1993: 262) suggests that there were no obvious military reasons for stopping and that 'possibly it was just because the Arabs were not much interested in European conquest, once away from the warm lands of the Mediterranean littoral'.

[4] Non-Muslims were forbidden to marry Muslim women, to give evidence against Muslims in the law courts, and were denied entry into many positions of power.

Third, the Islamic religious leaders lacked the strong incentives that were present in Christianity to become natural philosophers. The religion itself had a relatively simple dogma that avoided some of the complexities of Christianity, such as the doctrine of the Trinity. No attempt was made to reconcile the religion's dogma with Greek science, about which the religious leaders remained largely ignorant for the first centuries of their ascendancy. Also, since no attempt was made to persuade a sophisticated public to convert, the religion's leaders did not need to engage them in intellectual debate on their own terms. Thus, although many of the conquered areas contained highly sophisticated societies with many scholars who were well versed in all branches of philosophy, including natural philosophy, the religious leaders themselves did not develop a serious knowledge of philosophy. All of this mattered because, as in the West, the religious leaders had the power to challenge and often suppress unacceptable ideas and, unlike in the West, there was no sharp distinction between religious and secular leaders.

In summary, since Christianity spread by persuasion, its religious leaders were forced to become knowledgeable in all branches of current thinking, including philosophy. Since the Islamic empire was created by conquest and was adopted voluntarily over a couple of centuries by many of the conquered people, the religious leaders were under no pressure to become educated in the learning of the societies they conquered—and they remained largely ignorant of it.

Islamic Science and Technology

The Arabs who built the great Islamic empire were largely desert peoples. Although their empire inherited much of the science and technology of the Eastern Roman empire, that knowledge remained in the hands of non-Arabs for some time after the great conquests. Thus, the development of the Islamic tradition in learning took several centuries and followed a path that was very different from that of Christianity. The initial generations of Muslim rule saw no widespread translation movement as 'it was not necessary to translate from Greek or Syriac into Arabic, since most of those who carried on the tradition [of learning] were still Christians, Jews or Zoroastrians, and even those who had been converted would still have retained their knowledge of [Syriac and/or Greek], the languages of thought' (Hourani 1991: 75–6).

In the 820s, after a new capital city had been created at Baghdad, a centre of learning was established, and intellectual contact between speakers of Arabic and Greek was sought:

By the late eighth century, Islamic scholars, speaking and writing in Arabic, became aware of a vast body of Greek scientific literature. Recognizing that the absence of scientific literature in the Arabic language was a serious cultural and intellectual deficiency, they set out to translate Greek science and natural philosophy into Arabic. (Grant 1996: 206)

For the next 200 years, the whole of Greek learning was translated from Syriac into Arabic, and in the process, the Arabic language was expanded to 'make it an adequate medium for the whole intellectual life of the age' (Hourani 1991: 76). Over the following several centuries, residents of Islamic countries, many of whom were Christians or Jews, mastered Greek science and added to it significantly. '[C]ultured Muslims were willing to invest in Greek science because they believed (rightly or wrongly) that it had value' (Lindberg 1992: 171). The early Islamic philosophers were free thinkers in developing theories of knowledge that built directly on Greek philosophy. They believed that philosophical knowledge was the highest form of knowledge and that revealed religion was little more than superstition.[5]

Science Versus Religion

As we saw in Chapter 7, the doctrines of occasionalism and naturalism came into conflict early in Christian history, with naturalism winning the day.[6] This facilitated the reconciliation of religion with science, which must accept some variant of 'naturalism'. When scientists search for scientific laws they must hold that, whatever God decided when he created the world, and whatever miracles he occasionally performs, virtually all worldly events are the result of natural regularities—the laws of nature.

A similar conflict arose early in the history of Islam and a fundamental split developed between the philosophers and the religious scholars. After much debate, Islamic religious scholars accepted occasionalism and rejected naturalism. They held that God's will determines all day-to-day events that we observe. To attempt to discover natural laws is thus to predict God's behaviour, which is a blasphemous activity.

As a result of this split, Islamic orthodoxy came to recognize two kinds of science: (*a*) Islamic science based on the Koran, which consisted largely of interpretations of the holy writings; and (*b*) foreign science, which was mainly Greek—as translated into Arabic and elaborated by Islamic natural philosophers. Subjects such as arithmetic, geometry, and astronomy were accepted because these were useful religiously. For example, arithmetic was used to divide inheritances, and to establish the times of prayer. The cultural elite of the Arabic-Islamic civilization made a strong commitment to such forms of learning. There were many libraries scattered through Islam, some containing thousands of manuscripts.[7]

In contrast, natural philosophy was never accepted by Islamic religious thinkers as a legitimate study. Unlike Western clerics the great majority of Islamic clerics knew little of the science that their fellow citizens were pursuing, and, therefore, many regarded it with suspicion (Lindberg 1992: 173). Scientific studies were thus conducted in private between tutors and individual pupils.[8] Since there was no central

---

[5] See (Huff 1993: 67ff.) for a full discussion.

[6] De facto occasionalism is, however, alive and well in the minds of many ordinary Christians today, as shown when God is thanked by the football player for his touchdown, the crash survivor for his deliverance, or the observers of countless natural disasters who ask 'How could God have permitted *that*?'

[7] Rosenberg and Birdzell (1986) observe that a well-stocked European library in the medieval period might have contained a mere eighty manuscripts.

[8] 'The distinction between the intellectual elite and the masses was to become a commonplace of Islamic thought. Philosophy continued to exist, but was carried on as a private activity, largely by medical men, pursued with discretion and often met with suspicion' (Hourani 1991: 78).

authority in Islam strong enough to suppress it totally, the study of natural philosophy did continue and scholars maintained some independence to develop ideas that were in apparent conflict with religious beliefs. They were, however, never given the institutionalized support of belonging to a powerful corporate body. Thus, they did not develop the institutions that were needed to provide a collective memory and to pass on their knowledge in a systematic and evolving way to students operating within the mainstream. '[T]hose who pursued the religious sciences had the upper hand and periodically denounced those who pursued the foreign and ancient sciences' (Huff 1993: 69).

As Makdisi (1981: 271) observes: 'Islamic education like Islamic law is basically individualistic, personalist.' Education in medieval Islam was centred around masters who tutored students according to their own wisdom. The students collected personalized permissions from individual scholars, not a certificate of mastery in a particular subject matter. In natural science, all instruction occurred outside of colleges and the student had to travel from scholar to scholar.[9]

Under this system, scholars who held contrary views, or attempted to advance new systems of thought, found little institutional support, so that they were often vulnerable to criticism from secular and religious authorities. Huff (1993: 77) notes that another problem was that there were no 'mechanisms whereby received wisdom ... could be separated from the false and disproven'.

Nonetheless, by the beginning of the thirteenth century, Islamic countries had the world's most advanced 'exact sciences', especially in optics, astronomy, geometry, trigonometry, and medicine. Many important scientific developments had occurred in the Islamic countries, although significantly, as Huff (1993: 321) observes, 'these scientific activities were often scattered geographically, isolated in their influence, and conducted in semi-secrecy'. In spite of many difficulties of communication and religious interference, 'the work went forward and, over the course of time, indispensable elements of scientific practice accumulated and became a unique heritage of human endeavour' (Huff 1993: 321).

This work is a monument to human inventiveness and curiosity. Given the lack of institutional support, the wonder is not that Islamic scholarship failed in the end but that it produced so much and flourished for so long. What it had going for it was a highly educated, set of curious intellectuals, the written word, libraries to provide continuity, and hospitals and observatories to give institutional support to some investigators. What it lacked, as well as those things mentioned earlier, was a set of institutions that provided an autonomous sphere of activities sufficiently strong to repel a religious counter-attack similar to the one that was repulsed in Europe when conservatives resisted the attempts of Aquinas and his contemporaries to reconcile the Old Testament with Aristotelian science.

---

[9] As Huff (1993: 81) puts it: 'Because Islamic law did not recognize corporate groups and entities, it prevented the evolution of autonomous status groups—professional as well as residential groups—within which legal privileges and universalistic norms, for example, the norms of science, objectivity, and impersonal justice, could be established and applied irrespective of personal, religious, or political considerations.'

Decline of Islamic Science

Even as the West was translating and learning from Islamic scholarship, the seeds of the differences that were to separate Islam from European intellectual development were beginning to bear fruit. Dates differ, but most authorities agree that some time in the fourteenth century Islamic science had entered a period of decline that took it from its heights of the twelfth century to a backward and stagnant position by the fifteenth century. Lindberg (1992: 182) expresses this judgement on the decline of Islamic science:

In assessing this collapse, we must remember that at an advanced level the foreign sciences had never found a stable institutional home in Islam, that they continued to be viewed with suspicion in conservative religious quarters, and that their utility (especially as advanced disciplines) may not have seemed overpowering. Fortunately before the products of Islamic science could be lost, contact was made with Christendom, and the process of cultural transmission began anew.

Two significant changes occurred around the thirteenth century. First, the Islamic world was transformed from 'a commercial monetary economy to one which, despite an extensive and important foreign and transit trade, was internally...based on subsistence agriculture' (Lewis 1970: 114). Second, Arabic-speaking peoples lost their independence to the Turks. The Persians and the Turks developed their own Muslim culture and assumed both political and cultural leadership over Islam (Lewis 1970: 114–15). After the thirteenth century, conservative religious forces gained increasing power. According to Lewis (1970: 115–16):

The development of a static society and the predominance of a static formalist theology led to a decline in independent speculation and research.... Literature was restrictive and lacked vitality.... The most striking feature of the time is the increased stress on form for artists, on memory for scholars.

By 1517 the Mamluk Empire had been conquered by Ottoman Turks. Arabic-speaking people were marginalized; only a few regions retained any real independence under Ottoman rule. Over the next 400 years the Ottomans created and ruled over an empire that was powerful both militarily and commercially and that challenged Europe. There continued to be astronomers, observatories, hospitals, and universities, but all slowly came under the influence of religious conformism. Many of the great libraries and astronomical observatories were destroyed by religious zealots. In short, under Ottoman rule, both science and technology first stagnated and then regressed.[10]

---

[10] 'During the centuries of the Ottoman rule there had been no advance in technology and a decline in the level of scientific knowledge and understanding.... [T]here was little knowledge of the languages of Western Europe or of the scientific and technical advances being made there. The astronomical theories associated with the name of Copernicus were mentioned for the first time, and even then only briefly, in Turkish at the end of the seventeenth century, and the advances in European medicine were only slowly coming to be known in the eighteenth' (Hourani 1991: 259).

Towards an Explanation

What were the reasons for the decline of Islamic science? Why did it not give birth to modern science and the technologies that were related to it? It is often argued that the peace, prosperity, and patronage under which earlier Islamic science had prospered disappeared as pressure mounted both from Christian counter-attacks in Spain and Mongol pressure from the East. The Christian counter-attack, which began in the middle of the eleventh century, had regained the bulk of Spain by the early thirteenth century. The Mughals sacked Baghdad in 1258. Huff argues cogently, however, that these external reasons are unconvincing. He counters that Spain was a geographical fringe province whose loss did not affect the behaviour of the core Islamic regions in the eastern Mediterranean. He also points out that Arab learning flourished under Mughal rule. For example, Islamic astronomy reached its highest peaks under the Mongols after the construction of the Maragha observatory around 1260.[11] We accept that the decline had more to do with a combination of institutions and scientific world views than with externally dictated events.

Corporate Bodies and Institutions

As already observed, Islamic culture did not develop the concept of a corporate body independent of the collection of its members.[12] This had profound effects on Islamic universities, which remained only the sum of the individuals who gave instruction, each of whom issued their own certificates of competence to his or her 'graduating' students. Thus the collective, generalized, and impersonal standards for evaluating scholarship that were developed in the West were absent from Islam. Nor did Islamic scientists develop institutions and attitudes that would provide autonomy for scientific enquiry safe from the restrictions on thought imposed by religious and social dogma. Furthermore, because they had no corporate identity that could be altered, Islamic colleges had to carry on as intended by their founders, making it difficult for them to respond to growth and change.

The failures of two institutions that might have nurtured modern scientific activities are instructive. The first is hospitals. To some extent the Islamic hospitals were able to avoid the prohibition on the teaching of foreign ideas. By the thirteenth century, some medical doctors had discovered important facts, such as the nature of the heart and the circulatory system, not known in the West until the eighteenth century. Yet this work did not blossom into modern learning and, as Browne (1962)

---

[11] Once they had conquered an area and slaughtered those who had resisted them, the Mongols were remarkably tolerant of various religions and forms of learning (see, for example, Weatherford 2004).

[12] We suspect that the rise in the West of the concept of the corporation, one of history's fundamental organizational GPTs, can be explained in terms of historical accidents. The Christian Church arose beneath a strong state and to develop its influence it had to develop a corporate status separate from the state and, once that was done, other corporate structures followed naturally. In Islam, because the century of conquest was built on a unified version of church and state, separate institutions were not needed and did not develop. But whatever the reasons, the absence of a corporate structure had important consequences for the development of science, and this is what matters for our argument.

observed, the Iranian physicians whom he met in Teheran in 1887 had no knowledge of modern medicine.[13]

Four reasons seem important in accounting for this different trajectory of Islamic hospitals:

1. Medical education was largely confined to the hospitals and not taught in schools of higher education as it was in the West.
2. The dissection of human bodies was strictly forbidden by religious law.
3. The idea was widespread that illness was God's punishment for wrongdoing so that there was no such thing as natural causes of illness.
4. Since physicians could not join together in an autonomous self-regulating guild or corporation, their scientific standards had no way of becoming firmly established in the institutional structure of Islamic civilization. They remained under the supervision of a religious officer.

The second key institution that failed was the observatory. Many were built but later destroyed by religious zealots. The basic tenants of astronomy and astrology were antithetic to Islamic doctrine of occasionalism, which held that to attempt to predict the future was blasphemous. Nonetheless, many astronomical observations were made and many advances occurred within the framework of Ptolemaic astronomy. Significantly, as we have observed, the greatest of the Islamic observatories, the Maragha observatory, was built under Mongol rulers. It was advanced in its equipment and was home for a massive library. The observations and calculations of its astronomers went beyond the Ptolemaic system, comparing favourably with those of Tycho Brahe on which Kepler built his laws of planetary motion. Yet within fifty years of its foundation, it had been destroyed and religious conformity replaced the enquiring spirit that it cultivated. As Huff (1993: 212–13) puts it:

It hinged on the problem of institution building. If in the long run scientific thought and intellectual creativity in general are to keep themselves alive and advance into new domains of conquest and creativity, multiple spheres of freedom—what we may call *neutral zones*—must exist within which large groups of people can pursue their genius free from the censure of political and religious authorities. In addition, certain metaphysical and philosophical assumptions must accompany this freedom. Insofar as science is concerned, individuals must be conceived to be endowed with reason, the world must be thought to be a rational and consistent whole, and various levels of universal representation, participation, and discourse must be available. It is precisely here that one finds the great weaknesses of Arabic-Islamic civilizations as an incubator of modern science.

World view

We have seen that natural philosophy, out of which came first the rationalist world view of the medieval scholastics and then the mechanistic world view of early

---

[13] Browne (1962: 93) as quoted in Huff (1993: 178).

modern scientists, was never systematically pursued in Islam with institutional backing. The conflicts that inevitably arose between religious dogma and Aristotelian teachings were resolved very differently in Islam and in the West. When the conflicts became fully understood by Islamic religious leaders who had slowly became more and more powerful, the teachings of Greek philosophy and science were banned from institutions of higher learning. The result was that while Europeans accepted Aristotle into established institutions, the Islamic authorities rejected him, and with him, much of Greek science and, even more importantly, the Greek scientific attitude.

Islamic culture contained a strong bias against allowing the masses open access to knowledge since they were judged to be incapable of comprehending such matters and, therefore, were not to be addressed in such writings. One practical result of this distrust was the rejection of the modern printing press after it arrived from Europe in the fifteenth century. The Islamic authorities resisted the use of printing because they saw it as encouraging ordinary people to interpret the holy writings for themselves rather than as dictated by the clergy, a fear shared by the Catholic Church. European Protestants, on the other hand, embraced printing for the very same reason. Right through the nineteenth century, Islamic (and Chinese) teaching consisted of committing large tracts to rote memory. As well as keeping learning from the masses, the suppression of the printing press denied thinkers a means of spreading their ideas quickly and submitting them to peer review.

Law

There was no concept of an evolving body of Islamic law since the holy writings were accepted as the complete record of God's commands. The law had been laid down by the prophet. In theory, it could be interpreted but not changed, and was the same no matter what the level of authority at which it was administered. As a result, the Islamic method of disputation was designed to find fault with the reasoning of those who went before, not to evolve towards a new understanding. In practice, new interpretations did effect some changes. But Islamic legal and religious thought remained integrated and unitary, not separated and pluralistic, as it was in the West.

Thus Islam lacked the West's pluralism of overlapping jurisdictions involving church, government, guilds and institutions of learning, as well as different types of law—criminal, civil, ecclesiastical, corporate, and natural. Furthermore, the concept of the single holy law ruled out corporate autonomy, whether for guilds, cities, universities, scientific societies, or businesses. The autonomous educational institutions that evolved in Europe in the twelfth and thirteenth centuries had no counterpart in Islam.[14]

---

[14] An explanation that goes one step beyond where we are stopping would probably link these two reasons by explaining the rise of unitarianism in Islam and pluralism in the West.

Decline of Islamic Technology

The same attitudes that encouraged science in Islam for centuries encouraged technological dynamism. Many early technological innovations that were adopted in Europe originated either in Islam or China (diffusing through Islam to Europe). By the same token, the attitudes that eventually suppressed science in Islam also suppressed technological advance. After the decline of Islamic science, virtually no civilian technological innovations originated in Islam and diffused to Europe.

As time passed, values such as disinterested inquiry and organized scepticism, which encourage doing something new both in science and in technology, were increasingly found only in small circles of physicians and philosophers outside the centres of learning in Arabic-Islamic civilization. Importantly, they received no support from Islamic institutions, nor validation by the Islamic elite. Conservative religious views also gained increasing influence so that the very idea of innovation often came to imply impiety, possibly even heresy. According to Huff (1993: 234): 'One tradition of the Prophet in wide use [in the latter period] claims that the "worst things are those that are novelties, every novelty is an innovation, every innovation is an error and every error leads to Hell-fire" '. In this context, Huff (1993: 234) also quotes Lewis (1953) as saying: 'In its extreme form, this principle has meant the rejection of every idea and amenity not known in Western Arabia in the time of Muhammad and his companions, and it has been used by successive generations of ultra-conservatives to oppose tables, sieves, coffee and tobacco, printing-presses and artillery, telephones, wireless, and votes for women.' These attitudes were always present among the orthodox, but as time went on, religious orthodoxy gained supremacy.

Conclusion

So the decline of Islamic science can be traced to a number of developments that were different from those in the West, many of them due to historical accidents: a theocracy with no concept of degrees of jurisdiction or of a developing code of laws; religious hostility to established science and free enquiry; no major institutional innovations such as the corporation—in the form of guilds, universities, independent cities, and business organizations. In short, while the West was developing a pluralistic society, Islam was solidifying a monolithic, relatively rigid, theocratic society.

The parallel decline of Islamic technological dynamism is evidence for the thesis we argued in Chapter 7 concerning the close relation between science and technology in the medieval and early modern periods. We have argued a direct link between Newtonian mechanical science and several of the key technologies of the First Industrial Revolution. But this is not all that matters. Much of the common ground for scientific and technological advance is provided by nebulous, but nonetheless important, general habits of thought and attitudes of free enquiry—a belief in the ordered and rational world, a mechanical view of the universe, a desire to 'get to the bottom of things', belief that life can be made better, a willingness to depart from traditional ways of doing things, and a belief that knowledge, attitudes, and institutions can and should evolve. When science is in the air, technology flourishes on the ground.[15] The decline of Islamic learning and science, which is understandable, was accompanied by a decline in technological dynamism. We explain the latter by linking it with the former.

II. WHY NOT IN CHINA?

As mentioned earlier, Pomeranz (2000) has demonstrated that from the early modern period through to the late eighteenth century, Chinese living standards compared favourably with those in Europe. He also argued more contentiously that Chinese literacy was probably on par with that of Western Europe in the eighteenth century. On Chinese technology, Needham's works (1954) documented a technologically dynamic China, which had invented many of the technologies subsequently important in Europe. The thrust of Needham's scholarship on technology has never been seriously challenged.

These observations present what seems like a 'paradox'. Why is it that the Chinese—if they were more or less equal to early eighteenth-century Britain in living standards, literacy, and technology—did not generate their own industrial revolution? If Britain had not been the first industrial nation, would China have taken its place? How long might that process have taken?

We argue that China lacked the science necessary for a fully fledged industrial revolution. We cannot survey the whole complex history of Chinese science. Instead, we confine ourselves to noting a few general aspects, focusing on two examples important to industrialization: mechanics and electricity. We then go on to suggest reasons why Chinese science never developed into a cumulative, evolving body of knowledge in spite of the existence of many fine individual scientists.[16] Finally, we note that the absence of institutionalized science precluded the Chinese from making the jump from the many empirically based technologies that they had developed and preserved to the many technologies that underlay the British Industrial Revolution and that allowed the West to make its breakthrough to sustained growth.

Chinese Science[17]

As well as documenting the enormous advances in Chinese technology over the millennia, Needham argued that Chinese science was superior to that of the West during the Middle Ages, and at least its equal throughout the seventeenth and

---

[15] Of course, not everyone need have these enquiring attitudes. Conservative, even reactionary, forces are found everywhere. But where conservative attitudes flourish among thinkers, they will also be found among enough ordinary people to slow the course of technological change.

[16] One of the early works dealing with this question was written by the Chinese scholar Yu-lan (1922). It focuses much more than we do on China's unique world view to explain its lack of science. While Chinese philosophies may well have hampered the development of their science, it is arguable that if there had been scope for cumulative scientific development, the advances they did make could well have led them to a mechanistic science despite their world view.

[17] We take our material on the state of Chinese science mainly from Qian (1985), a Chinese-born physicist, trained first in Chinese and then in American science.

possibly the eighteenth centuries. He also argued that the Chinese philosophical approach might have proved to be the basis of the 'new' science utilizing fields rather than mechanical (what he called 'billiard ball') concepts. His views on science have been accepted by some but have been challenged by others. (See in particular Bodde 1981; Huff 1993; Qian 1985; Sivin 1980.)[18]

While we accept Needham's powerful evidence with respect to technology, we argue that on science his critics have made an overwhelming case. Indeed, the facts seem to be that China did not have even the beginnings of systematic cumulative modern science. There were many great scientific thinkers in China, but too often their ideas flourished briefly, only to be lost.[19]

General Problems

Chinese mathematical thought operated under a serious constraint in that it lacked a system of rigorous proof. Outside of mathematics, Chinese scientists faced the same constraint in lacking a standard of logical proof provided by Aristotelian logic. They also had no system of deductive geometry (Mokyr 1990), and lacked trigonometry, an essential tool for mathematical astronomy. As a result, the Chinese were forced to employ Arabic astronomers from the thirteenth century onwards.

Chinese thinkers seldom moved from practical discoveries to general principles. When they did, they often failed to preserve the results for future generations. For example, the Chinese did prove the Pythagorean theorem in the form: $3^2 + 4^2 = 5^2$. However, there is no record that they ever tried to prove the general formulation (i.e. $a^2 + b^2 = c^2$) in a sustained way and, if they did, the general result was not passed on to future generations. Interestingly, however, the truth of the theorem was taken for granted and often put to practical use. In the sixteenth century, the Chinese scholar, Zhu, did great work on musicology, resonance, and tonal scales. However, he never mathematized his findings. One of the reasons for success in the West was the ability to generalize over a wide range of studies. In contrast, Zhu was historically 'too unique a talent, and his scholarship produced too limited a masterpiece' (Qian 1985: 78).

In disagreeing with Needham's view that Chinese science was close to Western science until the seventeenth century, Qian (1985: 48–9) states: 'With regard to ... exact science, not only would traditional China give nothing, but it was for centuries not even in a position to receive: from the thirteenth century to the end of the

---

[18] It has been argued to us that these authors are unreliable, because they are strongly biased towards making China look inferior, which they accomplish by viewing Chinese science through Eurocentric eyes. Be that as it may, we have not seen any convincing evidence conflicting with their conclusion that, whatever its accomplishments, China lacked the base of modern science that was a necessary condition for the science-led phase, very probably for the steam-driven phase, and in our opinion also for the early factory phase of the Industrial Revolution.

[19] The impressive list of Chinese scientific discoveries, many of which provided what Mokyr would classify as singleton knowledge, and many of which were subsequently forgotten, is too long to include here. A partial list would include advances in mathematics, understanding fossil evidence, and advances in optics. But as we argue later in our section *No Institutional Memory for Science*, none of these discoveries were pursued in ways that established sustained cumulative trajectories.

nineteenth century, time and again China declined to import and digest the best of Hellenic science.' For example, when they employed Arabic astronomers in the thirteenth century, they took the results they wanted without attempting to learn how to produce them for themselves. Either they were not interested in learning the Arab's techniques or they were unable to do so because of the lack of complementary scientific knowledge.

Mechanics

We have observed in Chapter 7 that Newtonian mechanics provided a critical input into the innovations that created the First Industrial Revolution and the great engineering feats that preceded it. This mechanics had evolved through Greek science, particularly concerning buoyancy and the lever; Galileo's and Kepler's work on mechanical phenomena; and Newton's laws that synthesized previous discoveries.

With respect to buoyancy, Needham had argued that the Chinese knew Archimedes' principles. Aside from his substantive consideration of Needham's specific arguments, Qian (1985: 54) observes that if Needham were correct, there should be many references in Chinese literature to the important concept of specific gravity.[20] But there are few, and those that do exist are obscure and debatable— hardly, as Qian (1985: 56) observes, the stuff of ordinary usage:

[I]f Chinese hydrostatic development were to contribute to the 'mechanical revolution'—that is to say, to catch up with Western development up to the eve of the Newtonian culmination— it required: (1) a general formulation about a floating body; (2) a general formulation about an immersed body; and (3) an explanation that unifies these and other hydrostatic facts (in particular those summarised in the Pascal principle). It is now clear that even with the most favourable interpretation of the practice of Han technicians, the actual Chinese situation in this respect can only be described as empiricist and underdeveloped, and remained so for a long time.

The second piece of Greek mechanical science that was important for later developments was the principle of the lever. According to Qian, the operation of the lever was understood in China, but was stated more generally by a writer during the Han dynasty than by a subsequent writer 300 years later.

As Qian (1985: 67) observes of Western mechanics: '[It] was "modernised" in three steps: Archimedes' theorems of the lever and buoyancy; Galileo's and Kepler's theorems on a variety of mechanical phenomena; and Newton's synthesis....

---

[20] Qian's refutation of Needham's arguments about buoyancy is based on three points: (*a*) Needham argues without further evidence that the character 'zhun' means weighing in water—Qian find this dubious; (*b*) to get the composition of an alloy by weighing the water it displaces requires knowing that an alloy contains only two components, which there is no evidence that the Chinese knew; and (*c*) one text to which Needham refers speaks of floating of lotus seeds to determine specific gravity of a brine—Qian feels this is partly right and partly nonsense (floating them upright or sideways, which the author feels matters, makes no difference). 'There is definitely no science here, and if it is viewed as a technology, it is false technology' (Qian 1985: 55).

Chinese mechanics, as we have discussed before, had fulfilled the first half step, but never moved beyond that independently.' Thus the mechanical science that contributed so much to the British Industrial Revolution was almost totally absent from China.

Electricity

One of the best known of Needham's arguments is his contention that the Chinese knowledge of magnetism put China close to the West in early knowledge of electricity. Knowledge of magnetism is divided into six parts: (1) attraction; (2) direction; (3) declination (a compass needle does not always point to true north); (4) local variation (the direction in which the needle points varies due to local disturbing forces); (5) inclination (the needle does not always point in a horizontal plane); and (6) the earth is a giant lodestone that attracts the compasses needle. The Chinese and the Greeks discovered the first two at more or less the same time. The Chinese discovered the third 400 years before Western sailors discovered it in the fifteenth century. It seems that the fourth was also known to the Chinese. The fifth and the sixth, however, were unknown to them. Yet the sixth is what turns magnetism from a wholly empirical body of knowledge into a theoretical science, where the 'earth is a lodestone' hypothesis explains the other observations, given only the assumption of (1). This is what Gilbert (1544–1603) did for the West in his famous treatise *De Magnete*. According to Pumfrey (2002) this great book 'created a whole new "field" of magnetic science' (136) and 'has, with some justification, been called the first thoroughly experimental treatise' (6).[21] So when European scholars made the study of magnetism into a science in the later part of the sixteenth century, the Chinese study of magnetism 'did not surpass a qualitative description of magnetic declination. The richness and trail-blazing role of *De magnete* provide a foil that accentuates contemporaneous Chinese negligence of, or insensitivity to, physics' (Qian 1985: 80).

In Chapter 7, we briefly touched on some of the highlights in the long trajectory of cumulative scientific discoveries that led from Gilbert in the sixteenth century to the development of the dynamo in the latter half of the nineteenth century. Since the Chinese had not even advanced their knowledge as far as the full contents of *De Magnete*, it is no exaggeration to say that they were centuries of research away from the development of the practical generation of electricity.

A Great Leap Forward?

Finally, we come to Needham's conjecture that the new quantum mechanics implies a different view of causality that is more akin to Chinese thought, and that Chinese science could have taken the lead in developing this new approach. According to this argument, if Western science had not existed, China might have made the jump from Aristotelian to modern post-Newtonian science. It is hard to take this view

---

[21] See Chapter 7 on electricity and Chapter 5 on the three-masted sailing ship for further discussion.

seriously. Science builds on itself, and it usually does this by progressing from the more to the less obvious. For this reason, Euclidean geometry preceded modern geometry. Euclid is the stuff of everyday experience and it is useful for everyday tasks. Non-Euclidean geometry was first an intellectual exercise prompted by the interest in what would happen if Euclid's assumption that parallel lines stay parallel when extended indefinitely was wrong. Two specific theoretical issues arose out of these thought experiments about parallel lines (the issues concerned whether such lines would meet or would diverge) which led eventually to the two branches of non-Euclidean geometry. Later this new work proved useful in analysing the universe made possible by Einstein's physics. Similarly, Greek and early modern mechanics is grounded in everyday experience and is useful. It is simply not credible that people who had not gone through the astronomy of Copernicus and Kepler, and the mechanics of Galileo and Newton, as well as the calculus and the behaviour of linear dynamic systems could have jumped to modern mathematics and the 'new physics' of quantum electrodynamics.

Towards an Explanation

Why, in spite of so many individual achievements, did Chinese science fail to achieve the cumulative growth that took Western science to its commanding position in the nineteenth century? To begin to answer the question we illustrate two themes that permeate the literature on Chinese science and why it eventually came to stagnate. The first comes from Huff (1993: 320): 'The pursuit of sciences in China was relegated to the periphery of intellectual endeavor. For that reason ... it is not puzzling that Chinese culture and civilization ... did not give birth to modern science.' The second comes from Qian (1985: 103–4)[22]:

In traditional China, a territorially unified autocratic rule was effectively aided by and symbiotically combined with an equally unified system of ideological control. Its philosophical spirit was introspective, its academic scope was officially limited and exclusively politico-ethical, and its basic attitude discouraged innovative practices and rationalistic inquiries. This politico-ideological situation contrasted sharply with European pluralism, which was fully embodied in its feudal separatism, national rivalries, and religious disputes.

Many dramatic contrasts between China and the West are suggested by these quotations and we elaborate on some of them in the next section.

No Institutional Memory for Science

Chinese ingenuity and scholarship has many examples of individual achievements that equalled and often preceded those in the West. But few if any of these were systematically built on over the centuries and many were lost, sometimes to be rediscovered by later generations. '[We] ... encounter repeated instances where some topic was picked up by an interested scholar but then was subsequently

[22] A form of this argument is also made by Jones (1981, 1988), who focuses on China as a unified state and the negative implications of this for innovation and the development of science.

disregarded' (Qian 1985: 60). Here are but three of the many examples. First, there was a flowering of mathematical work under the relatively tolerant Sung dynasty. But the use of mathematics rapidly declined under the neo-Confucian revival at the end of the Sung dynasty. Qian (1985: 64) argues that the reason was that Chinese mathematics was an official enterprise: 'There were not enough autonomous roots of mathematical scholarship among learned circles. Once official encouragement declined, mathematics declined rapidly.'[23] Second, there were brilliant experiments in optics in the eleventh century by a person unaware of previous experiments made several centuries earlier. Third, Needham argued that Zhu Xi was the first to have 'appreciated the true nature of fossils, 400 years before Leonardo da Vinci'. He was, however, an exception in advocating the dispassionate study of nature. Later generations ignored his approach. His insights were not built on by subsequent followers and largely disappeared (Qian 1985: 117).

What was lacking? First and foremost were institutions of scientific learning with a corporate structure similar to the universities that emerged in Europe in the Middle Ages. In their absence, there was nothing to provide a collective memory for scientific discoveries that would preserve them and allow them to be built on cumulatively. Although the Chinese developed institutions that preserved knowledge and art in many spheres including history, scientific libraries that gathered together and preserved important works about the natural world were largely absent: 'In fact, the Chinese repeatedly lost significant portions of their literary heritage' (Huff 1993: 319).

A second consequence of the lack of independent universities was the absence of institutions to protect individual scholars who might be advancing knowledge in ways that threatened established authorities. This lack of institutional support implied that scholars had to rely on official sanction. But sustained sanction was lacking as was even sustained toleration of independent scholarship directed at discovering the nature of the world. When the court was interested, various studies were tolerated, supported, and often flourished. When the court lost interest or became hostile, support was withdrawn and the effort languished. What had been established was then often lost.

Centralization

One of the most important aspects of pre-twentieth-century Chinese society was its high degree of centralization. Of course, the actual control exercised by the central government varied with its administrative ability, and in the centuries just before the abdication of the last emperor in 1912, state power progressively weakened. But throughout Chinese history, formal arrangements were lacking for separate corporate spheres of jurisdiction and control, for subnational governmental units sharing

---

[23] Mokyr (1990: 237) makes a similar point with respect to technology: 'Because most entrenched bureaucracies tend to develop a strong aversion to changing the status quo, state-run technological progress is not likely to be sustained over long periods. The Chinese miracle is indeed that it lasted so long. It ended when the state lost interest in promoting technological change.'

power with the central government, and for legal divisions such as civil and criminal law.

Because of the dominance of the imperial authority, towns and cities never gained the official semi-independence and corporate status that they achieved in the West. Everything that was done at any lower level of administration was done in the name of the emperor. Such European procedures as edicts and taxes that were created and enforced by city bureaucracies and courts were unknown. The Chinese bureaucracy was also secretive about such science that it did encourage, particularly mathematics and astronomy. This secrecy worked against the accumulation of a publicly available body of knowledge on which successive generations could build. As Huff (1993: 309) observes: 'Needham's account of the study of astronomy in China is littered with references to the security-minded manner and the semi-secrecy in which these disciplines were kept.'

Attitudes

In the West, history was seen as an unfolding of either the laws of nature as in Christian philosophy or of God's will as in Islamic theology. In contrast, Chinese thinkers searched for ethical virtues and ways of harmonizing with nature, rather than for natural laws and ways of understanding nature. Confucianism was purely 'politico-ethical' and discouraged interest in God's design of the universe in contrast with Christianity (Qian 1985: 114).[24] Balazs (1964: 22) notes:

Lacking systematic hypotheses expressed in mathematical terms and verified experimentally, Chinese science never got beyond the protoscientific stage, despite the fact that this initial stage was full of promise and that there was plenty of scientific aptitude.... Most probably the main inhibiting cause was the intellectual climate of Confucianist orthodoxy, not at all favourable for any form of trial or experiment.

Law

Questions of law and legal authority are important because they help to define spheres of jurisdiction that determine the degree of pluralism within a region or country. Not stemming from a deistic religion, Chinese law does not contain the idea of the commandments, either of God or any authority superior to, or even parallel with, the emperor. Not surprisingly, therefore, the Chinese did not develop the concept of natural law embedded in nature and separate from human law. No distinction was made between legal and ethical behaviour, which were regarded as

---

[24] Western thinkers saw the world in Greek atomistic terms. In sharp contrast, Chinese thinkers saw the world organically. It was to be understood in terms of harmonies and the primary forces of such opposites as ying and yang. These are not thought of as antagonistic but as following natural complementarities that are not governed by laws of nature. This approach has value in many lines of activity such as Chinese holistic medicine as opposed to Western specialized medicine. But it was not conducive to the kind of reductivist Western science that underlay the great scientific and technological advances of the First and Second Industrial Revolutions.

synonymous. Thus the rule of law was never a Chinese concept. Virtually all Chinese legal rules had many exceptions applying to particular groups.

The magistrate was an official of the emperor and could not be challenged. He was required to settle cases by impartial investigation, not by hearing advocacy from each side. Thus a profession of lawyers who were advocates for the defence and the prosecution never developed in China. Furthermore, the magistrates had—except under the Sung dynasty when separate legal exams were held—no legal training. They were appointed to the civil service as a result of passing the common examination based exclusively on literary works.

Chinese law did not recognize separate spheres of jurisdiction such as criminal and civil law or corporate and private law. Thus 'zones of autonomy' were not well established for subgroups in the society such as professionals. Instead, Chinese officials tended to be hostile to the emergence of any semi-autonomous social group, including merchants.[25]

The law was only secondarily interested in defending the rights—especially the economic rights—of one individual or group, and not at all in defending such rights against the state. What really concerned it ... were acts of moral or ritual impropriety or of criminal violence which seemed to Chinese eyes to be violations or disruptions of the social order. (Bodde 1963: 171)

All these developments had important consequences because, as Huff (1993: 273) puts it:

[W]ithout some spheres of autonomy, no groups can emerge as professionals, that is, legitimate specialists who represent the highest levels of thought and action in a particular sphere of human endeavor. Historically speaking, the first nonecclesiastical professionals to emerge [in the West] are probably judges and lawyers.

Examination System and Educational Curriculum

The examination system began under the Han dynasty about 2,000 years ago, went through a period of change and expansion of curriculum in the relatively liberal Sung period about 1,000 years ago, and was narrowed and solidified by the Ming in the mid fourteenth century, hardly to change again until it was abolished in the twentieth century. Anyone could attempt the annual exams, and if successful, would gain entrance into the imperial bureaucracy. On the one hand, this system had the great advantage of being open to all and thus recruiting ambitious and successful scholars from all ranks of Chinese society. On the other hand, its content was non-scientific and non-analytical. It stressed Confucian classics, poetry, and official histories, which had to be memorized and reproduced in the exams.

---

[25] Balazs (1964: 17) argues that merchants came under quite extensive control: 'The state in China was a managerial, an interventionist state.... Nothing escaped official regimentation. Trade, mining, building, ritual, music, schools, in fact the whole of public life and a great deal of private life as well, were subjected to it.' Pomeranz (2000: 248–51) has a more mixed review. He (2000: 70) argues: 'Overall China was closer to market-driven agriculture than was most of Europe including most of *western* Europe.' He goes on to argue the same for land but stipulates that the Chinese state did involve itself with relatively more aspects of the land market.

Furthermore, the imperial academies differed from Western universities, being merely 'bureaucratic subdivisions of the administrative structure that could be expanded, reorganized, or abolished at a moment's notice, as they often were' (Huff 1993: 306). They were largely staffed by active or retired civil servants, and they took the content of these examinations as their curriculum. With the invention of woodblock printing, the state printed textbooks, which it distributed to all schools. With an unchanging curriculum, the rigidity of woodblock as opposed to movable type printing was no disadvantage. In short, the Confucian-based system of education and training for those in charge of most aspects of life inhibited 'the creation of a suitable methodology for studying the phenomena of nature' (Bodde 1963: 307).

The contrast with Western universities of the medieval period is striking. There we find fiercely independent corporate structures, whose members taught a curriculum based heavily on science, stressing disputation in search of new understanding always following the strict rules of logic. Law and medicine flourished under the protection of the universities as independent studies leading to independent, largely self-governing professions interested in abstract principles that underlay particulars.

A Commercial Example

The sojourn abroad organized by the Chinese court in the early fifteenth century provides an excellent example of several themes: the power of the state, the restrictions placed on merchants, and opportunities created and then lost. The effort began when government shipyards constructed over 2,100 sea-going vessels. During the first thirty years of that century, massive Chinese fleets, containing hundreds of vessels carrying thousands of men, travelled to various ports in Asia. These fleets dwarfed in size and number of vessels anything that Europeans sent out later in that century for their early trade with the East. However, the main purpose of the expeditions was to spread knowledge of Chinese culture, and to spread the fame of the emperor among 'barbarians'. Goods were carried but more for gifts than trade. Once the move had been made, some more conventional, commercially oriented voyages also occurred. But like so many other endeavours in which the Chinese were well ahead of the Europeans, these efforts came to naught. A new emperor came to the throne and those around him scorned commerce and opposed contact with the barbarian world. So, after a period of debate and indecision, all further expeditions were halted: 'By 1500, anyone who built a ship of more than two masts was liable to the death penalty, and in 1525 coastal authorities were enjoined to destroy all ocean-going ships and to arrest their owners. Finally in 1551, it became a crime to go to sea on a multimasted ship, even for trade' (Landes 1998: 96).

This experience illustrates much of Chinese success and failure. The fleet that was put to sea in 1405 was beyond anything that European technology could have produced at the time, or for the next 200 years. Its purpose, however, was state glorification, not commerce. Its grandiose nature made a heavy drain on state finances, a drain that was one of the reasons for abandoning the enterprise. Centralized state control implied that when the state turned against outside adventures, the whole country did.

In contrast, the West was at that time just beginning its sea-going explorations of the outside world. Although the early developments had some state assistance, they were clearly in the cause of commercial gain. Had one European state turned against exploration and foreign commerce, seeking to stop it in the way that the Chinese authorities had done, the immensely profitable opportunities would have led its own private citizens to continue their efforts—as they would have done in China if the unitary state had not been so efficient in imposing its will. Had one European state actually succeeded in stopping exploration and trade, other states would have been eager to exploit the profitable opportunities.

Consequences for Technology

As already observed, the Chinese invented many of the technologies that diffused to the West. Many, such as the waterwheel, were used extensively in China; others, such as gunpowder, were not. We argued in Chapter 7 that an institutional memory is not usually needed for technology since the artefacts themselves and their continued use by the public provide all the memory that is needed. It is interesting to note, therefore, that some Chinese technologies that were used mainly, or even exclusively, by the emperors' court were lost sight of. The most spectacular case is the great Chinese water clock whose complex technology dazzled visitors in the tenth century.[26] In the twelfth century, the clock was dismantled and most of it parts were carried away by invaders from the North. Knowledge of its technology was soon lost. Granted, the immediate cause of the loss was an act of war, but in the pluralist West such useful knowledge would rarely have been so centralized that it was lost when one embodiment of it was destroyed. After all, the great library of Alexandria was destroyed without the loss of the bulk of classical science and literature—although many individual items were lost forever. The decentralization of knowledge and scholarship in the West ensured that even so catastrophic a loss as that of the Alexandrian library did not lead to the loss of a large amount of accumulated knowledge. Shortly after the loss of the Chinese water clock, Europeans invented their own clocks using mechanical escapement techniques rather than water power. These clocks had important subsequent effects on social and economic relations and the development of science and technology. (See Landes 1983 for a detailed analysis.)

There were other lost technological opportunities in China. Printing never progressed from the woodblock techniques, which suited the imperial court well but which would have been inadequate to serve needs if printing had been spread among the general public as it quickly did after the invention of moveable type in the West. Gunpowder remained a toy in China while in Europe it became a lethal technology of war and later an important industrial tool. Indeed, the cannon and gun were one of the key technologies that conferred military superiority on Europeans when they ventured beyond European borders in their new three-masted sailing ships.

---

[26] See Landes (1983: ch. 1) for a full discussion.

What is more important than lost or unexploited technologies is that the absence of Western science precluded the Chinese from making the transition from the technologies found in Europe and China in 1700 to those common in Europe in 1900, but totally absent from China. Needham argued that Chinese science simply took a different form from European science, and that it could have led to the same sorts of breakthrough. As we argued in Chapter 7, the technologies of the First Industrial Revolution were largely mechanical and their scientific bases were Newton's laws of motion and the calculus, while the Second Industrial Revolution was based on Western scientific techniques in such subjects as chemistry, electronics, and metallurgy. Distinctly different bodies of scientific knowledge and methods of enquiry could not have given rise to the technologies of either of these industrial revolutions.

The ignorance of Newtonian mechanics put the Chinese at a major disadvantage compared to those like Smeaton and Telford who created the many advances in eighteenth-century Britain. It also made it difficult if not impossible to develop the kind of textile machinery that was used in Britain by the beginning of the nineteenth century and that underlay the early factory part of the Industrial Revolution, as outlined in Chapter 7. The absence of easily codified scientific knowledge of the nature of the atmosphere, steam, and heat would have made it extremely difficult— probably impossible—to develop the high-pressure steam engine that was the basis of the steam-driven stage in the First Industrial Revolution, both in the factories and in transportation. Finally, the absence of any knowledge of chemistry or electricity made the Second Industrial Revolution quite unthinkable in China. So, although a purely trial-and-error approach might have got Chinese industries to where the British were in 1790, it could not by any stretch of the imagination have got them to where they were at the time of the Great Exhibition in 1851, to say nothing of 1890 when the science-driven phase of the Second Industrial Revolution was in full spate.

Many of the key technologies that contributed to the emergence of sustained growth in the West just could not have developed independently in China. These include the fully developed factory system with high-pressure steam engines combined with advanced automated textile machines, the transition to a self-sustaining growth of systematic knowledge, the creation of applied sciences, the applications of chemistry and electricity, and the development of the research laboratories, which were a key part of the West's invention of how to invent.

III. CONCLUSION

In this and the previous chapter, we have offered our explanation of why sustained extensive growth emerged in Europe in general and in Britain in particular. We have also suggested why it did not occur elsewhere. While we do not expect to have said the last word on these much-debated subjects, we do hope to have argued fairly conclusively that this key event in long-term economic growth cannot be adequately dealt with in the context of any current, or foreseeable, formal model of economic growth (with or without endogenous population).

We consider some of these models in Chapters 9 and 10 and in Part III, but our position is that, given the state of the art of model building, understanding the complexities of the forces acting to produce modern sustained growth requires historical analysis and appreciative theorizing.

The emergence of sustained extensive growth required the development of the science that became unique to the West. Newtonian mechanical science assisted many of the developments in eighteenth-century England, greatly helped the development of automated textile machinery, and, even more so, the high-pressure steam engine. It was without any doubt essential for the key technologies of the Second Industrial Revolution that were based on electricity, metallurgy, and chemistry.

The development of the necessary mechanistic science can be traced back at least to the revival of learning and the rise of scholastic philosophy in eleventh- and twelfth-century Western Europe. The unanswered questions with which those philosophers struggled sowed the seeds of early modern science, which allowed investigators to use new empirical tools to settle old questions. Out of this piecemeal empirical testing of many Aristotelian hypotheses came much new scientific knowledge. This knowledge was finally synthesized by Newton into a new mechanical world view that replaced the Aristotelian teleological world view.

There were some key conditions that encouraged the growth of modern science in the West and discouraged it elsewhere. These include: the Christian Church's acceptance of Aristotelian science and the need to reconcile it with Christian theology, which gave a measure of protection to scholars that was lacking in both Islam and China; the provision of an institutionalized memory for scientific advances in the form of the autonomous universities and their libraries—developments that were not found in Islam and China; pluralism, in the form of the corporation, distinct areas of different legal authority and bodies of law, and levels of political jurisdiction. The latter gave rise to protected spheres of action where individuals could get on with investigations that often threatened the established secular and religious authorities. All of these were to a significant extent lacking in the theocracy of the Islamic empire and its successors as well as in imperial China.

The technologies that created the First Industrial Revolution can be traced back to a European concern with mechanization, already manifest in medieval times by such things as the application of the waterwheel to myriad tasks and the development of the mechanical clock. They were given a great boost by the mechanical world view that grew up around early modern science, particularly through the development of an understanding of the heliocentric solar system, which was not discovered elsewhere. Leonardo da Vinci was the great prophet of mechanization who laid down a research programme of mechanization of textile production that took over 200 years to fulfil completely.

At the same time as textile production was being partially mechanized, early scientists were beginning investigations along two other key lines: (*a*) air pressure, vacuum, and steam, which led to the initial development of a working atmospheric engine and then of Watt's steam engine; and (*b*) magnetism and electricity, which led, after 250 years of scientific discoveries, to the invention of the dynamo.

Thus the technologies of the Industrial Revolution did not spring from entirely new developments in the eighteenth century but were instead the culmination of the trajectories that were established at the beginning of the early modern period—and whose roots stretched further back in time. Countries outside of the West had not even begun to establish equivalent trajectories and, thus, were centuries away from endogenously developing their own industrial revolutions.

9

Population Dynamics: Relation Between Extensive and Intensive Growth

Up to this point, we have been mainly concerned with extensive growth. In Chapters 9 and 10 and their appendices, we direct our attention to intensive growth—growth measured in per capita figures rather than in totals. Chapter 9 deals with the relation between the two types of growth in somewhat general terms but concentrating on the period from the dissolution of the Western Roman Empire to the First Industrial Revolution, from about AD 500 to 1750. Appendix 9A summarizes the evidence that family size has been a choice variable throughout most of Western history. Appendix 9B presents the equations of our formal models of population dynamics. Chapter 10 considers the West's transition to intensive growth that occurred during the nineteenth century.

This chapter first gives a brief survey of both extensive and intensive growth over the millennia. From this we derive a number of generalizations, or stylized facts, that we seek to explain. We then introduce three broad types of theories that offer explanations of the relation between extensive and intensive growth: the Malthusian; the neo-Malthusian; and the non-Malthusian. Next, we describe our own three models of how these two types of growth are related. Finally, we draw a number of conclusions of which the following are a few key illustrations:

- The commonly used models that make the macro behaviour of the economy depend solely on the behaviour of individual families miss a number of potentially important relations that operate at a level beyond the control of individual families. The most important of these is a 'family formation externality', which acts to generate higher than optimal population growth.
- Most theories that obtain Malthusian results assume that individual families behave in a Malthusian manner. We show that Malthusian-type behaviour is possible in macro growth models in which individual families act in a wholly non-Malthusian manner.
- If the almost universally accepted assumptions about the nature of the production function are altered to come closer to empirical reality, the results of the amended models change dramatically, producing wholly non-Malthusian explanations of the West's demographic behaviour and hence of the relation between extensive and intensive growth.

I. GROWTH OVER THE MILLENNIA

To develop what we require Chapters 9 and 10, we need to discuss briefly both the extensive and intensive growth that have occurred through the millennia. This will provide us with some empirical generalizations that require explanation.

Long-Term Extensive Growth

Total output has grown significantly since the neolithic agricultural revolution. The primary evidence, as we observed in Chapter 1, is the growth in the world's population. Between the neolithic agricultural revolution and the Industrial Revolution population grew from an estimated 10 million to 1 billion, a growth rate of about 0.046 per cent per annum. By assuming zero intensive growth, this figure provides a minimum estimate for extensive growth.

The history of technological change in the West suggests that there have been long periods of sustained extensive growth, followed by periods of constant or even falling GDP. Initially, the neolithic agricultural revolution brought with it a large increase in population, which was estimated by Hassan (1981) to go from 10 million to 50 million in the course of a couple of millennia, representing a rate of increase possibly ten times what it had been in previous millennia. So there was a major acceleration in the rate of extensive growth over that time.

It is also clear that there were very large increases in output in Sumer and later in the whole of Mesopotamia after writing was invented and disseminated in the latter part of the fourth millennium BC. This period saw the rise of the great hydraulic societies in which large cities developed for the first time in the West's experience. This was followed by the introduction of bronze and its many derivative technologies, the associated rise of multicity empires, and the continued growth of a highly urbanized society. Most of the technologies that are seen in this period had probably already been developed before the end of the third millennium BC, although institutions continued to evolve over the next 1,000 years. For example, the laws known as the Code of Hammurabi date from the eighteenth century BC.

It is not clear what happened to growth in Mesopotamia from 2000 to 500 BC during which time the fortunes of the area were subject to many fluctuations. The Hittites sacked Babylon in 1595 BC, ending the Babylonian dynasty that had been established by Hammurabi some centuries earlier. The beginning of the Iron Age around 1200 BC was accompanied by incursions of 'barbarians' who sacked most of the cities along the Mediterranean rim, leading no doubt to a period of negative growth. Around 900 BC, the Assyrians began to build an empire centred in northern Mesopotamia. They in turn were defeated by the Babylonians in 612 BC, setting up the last great Babylonian empire. Finally in 539 BC, that empire was conquered by the Persians, by which time the centre of Western technological advance had already shifted decisively from Mesopotamia to the countries bordering on the Mediterranean.

The first millennium BC saw a recovery from the 'dark ages' that had accompanied the beginning of the Iron Age. The Greeks and Etruscans produced advanced societies that had significant amounts of urbanization supported by independent farmers. Later in the millennium, both were absorbed into the Roman empire, with its large commercial farms, the latifundia, based on slave labour. The great adversary of the West, the Persian empire, also arose in that millennium. Between them, Greece and Rome produced many hundreds of years of growth in population and total output.

Another great setback came to western Europe with the 'barbarian' invasions that accompanied the dissolution of the Western Roman Empire. Although there was no equivalent setback for the Eastern Empire, there is little evidence of further intensive growth there either. During the period of the dissolution of the Western Empire, output no doubt fell dramatically in Western Europe as the highly developed Roman economy gave way to a more or less subsistence-agrarian economy, with a very low degree of urbanization. Then, slowly, Europe recovered. Agricultural developments and land clearing led to increases in population, a more varied diet, and, after AD 1000, to substantial urbanization. Total output no doubt increased through much of that period. There was very probably another burst of sustained (Smithian) growth caused by the great expansion of trade that followed the European explorations enabled by the three-masted sailing ship. The rate of extensive growth then accelerated during the nineteenth century to take output to levels never before seen.

There is debate about whether the growth between 500 and 1800 is best regarded as a period of sustained or of episodic growth, which Goldstone (2002) calls 'efflorescences'. In the medieval and early modern periods, major technological innovations were widely separated in time and, therefore, we take the view that 'episodic bursts of growth' better describe the growth of that period than 'sustained growth'. But in the absence of more detailed data than are now available, this issue cannot be settled definitively.

Long-Term Intensive Growth

The persistence of extensive growth on average is clear; what is not so clear is the course of intensive growth. A major qualitative historical investigation would be needed to advance understanding significantly on the issue of the course of intensive growth over the last 10,000 years of the West's experience. In the absence of such a study, we must content ourselves with a few observations suggesting that, contrary to much folklore, living standards were not static throughout the entire period from the neolithic agricultural revolution to the First Industrial Revolution.

Bursts of population growth appear to have accompanied most of the major GPTs that enabled periods of extensive growth. This was true after the neolithic agricultural revolution and in Sumer when writing assisted the growth of new, highly productive forms of agriculture. It was also the case in the medieval period when a steady increase in population followed the development of the three-field system, the heavy plough, and the efficient horse collar, which in turn led to a large increase in the amount of land under cultivation and in agricultural efficiency. Thus it appears that much extensive growth was translated into population growth rather than into intensive growth. But how much remained to raise living standards, rather than feeding more mouths, is much debated.

There is a substantial and growing body of evidence showing that many farmers worked harder, were more prone to famines, and were less healthy than hunter-gatherers who lived well before the neolithic agricultural revolution. Western living standards may well have been lower in 7500 BC than in 16,000 BC. However, this decline, if it did occur, cannot be blamed on the technologies of the agricultural revolution, since the hunter-gatherer societies had come under severe pressure from which agriculture allowed them to escape. The pressure was due partly to the extinction of many of the large animals on which the earlier humans had relied for food and partly to climate change that caused many of the surviving game animals to move north in pursuit of cooler temperatures. This is a familiar story of problems caused by unsustainable growth due to the successes of earlier technologies (in this case, hunting technologies) being alleviated by further technological developments (in this case, the domestication of crops and animals).[1]

Coming ahead in time, it is difficult to argue that the major improvements in the technologies of food, clothing, shelter, carrying and storage, metallurgy, agriculture, and non-human power that occurred from, say, 8000 to 3500 BC did not raise material living standards to some extent. (These technologies were reviewed briefly at the beginning of Chapter 5.) Clearly, the life of a farmer in 3400 BC was much more influenced by sophisticated technology than that of a farmer in 9000 BC. Also, the increased production of such 'non-essentials' as jewellery and decorated utensils, as well as increased urbanization, suggests a growing agricultural surplus that supported work that was not needed to maintain life at a bare subsistence standard. (How this might happen is stylized in our two-sector model presented later in this chapter.)

Still later, the area of the Tigris–Euphrates valley was transformed by writing, irrigation, and bronze, plus their many derivative technologies. Early written records in these areas in about 2800 BC, along with evidence about small family sizes cited in Appendix 9.1, suggest a major increase in living standards over the 400–500 years that followed the first use of writing. Also, from 2800 BC, with the invention of bronze, to about 2000 BC, there was a major increase in the sophistication of society and economic affairs, with the first extensive use of money (but not coinage), laws governing commercial relations, property rights, and other modern sounding institutions. Urbanization grew to an extent never seen before. Highly decorated utensils, elaborate tools, funereal arrangements, jewellery, and many other artefacts found by anthropologists and displayed in well-known museums all attest to a large amount of productive effort begin devoted to non-food production and therefore creating living standards well above subsistence. Other evidence for this period is the growing volume of public goods produced in such forms as temples, palaces, parks, gardens, and other such edifices, all of which absorbed substantial amounts of resources. Judging by the extent of warfare and increasing use of costly weapons, many of which were made of expensive bronze, the total and per capita resources devoted to

---

[1] In Chapter 5, we briefly discussed the much-debated issue of why humans became settled agriculturalists during the neolithic agricultural revolution.

organized warfare had grown steadily from almost nothing at the end of the fourth millennium BC to a very large amount towards the end of the third millennium BC. Although military activities may not have contributed to living standards, they are a part of GDP and should be counted as part of intensive growth. Possibly they also had some of the many technological spillovers from military to civilian uses that we associate with modern defence spending, particularly in the USA.

It is not clear what happened to living standards in Mesopotamia during 2000–500 BC. However, living standards no doubt fell in the latter half of the second millennium BC when 'barbarians' sacked and destroyed most of the major cities from Crete to the Egyptian border. This ushered in a 'dark age' that lasted for several centuries. Greco-Roman civilization, which arose in the first millennia BC, was probably the richest yet seen in the West. The increase in average lifespan and the reductions in death and birth rates, and the resulting declining population, is indirect evidence of a high living standard during the height of these civilisations. (See Appendix 9.1 for a summary of the methods of controlling family size that have been used in the West for many millennia.) Citizens were substituting leisure activities for time spent producing and raising children. Also the list of new consumer goods and services and other technologies summarized in Section VII of Chapter 5 suggests that living standards for urban-dwelling citizens were substantially higher than those 1000–2000 years earlier. Although it is hard to judge, it is not clear that Roman slaves toiling in agricultural areas lived at a lower material standard than those at the bottom of the social scale in Europe in AD 700, while the many who worked in urban areas very probably lived better.

During and immediately after the dissolution of the Western Roman Empire, living standards no doubt fell drastically as a subsistence-agrarian economy replaced the highly urbanized, technologically sophisticated Roman economy. But soon after that, independent villages, populated mainly by free peasants, solved the problem of making the heavy soils of northern Europe productive, something the Romans had never done. As a result, the supply of agricultural land rose dramatically as did the efficiency of land use. Diet became much more varied and, until the full development of the feudal system in the second half of the medieval period, peasants were probably able to consume the great majority of their own outputs. Again, evidence of control over family size is consistent with some of the rising productivity being used to support increased per capita consumption rather than larger families (see Appendix 9.1).

Then, from about AD 1000 until the First Industrial Revolution, urbanization, public works, and military expenditure again grew, indicating a gradual agricultural surplus able to feed an increasing number of non-food producers, both local lords and their retainers and urban dwellers. The evidence is spotty with respect to living standards in rural areas where the vast majority of the population lived. Historians point to a growing food shortage in the thirteenth century caused by population increases. If food was becoming scarcer from the eleventh to the thirteenth centuries, living standards must have been above subsistence during the earlier part of that period and must have varied over the centuries. Also, evidence from times of poor crops and famine suggests that most of the suffering was experienced by the poorest 20–30 per cent of the rural population. Since the evidence also suggests significant dispersions of wealth and income in medieval villages, even if this lower echelon lived close to subsistence, the others must have been spread out above it, and some well above it. Furthermore, detailed studies of family budgets show that peasants were gaining increases in income from non-agricultural sources at precisely this time[2]. (See Dyer 1989, especially Chapters 5 and 6.) If so, this suggests that total income of the typical peasant family was not at subsistence; nor was it constant. Later, when the putting-out system spread through Europe in the late Middle Ages, the new organizational technology provided peasants with a secure secondary source of income that mainly required the free time of female peasants.[3]

Further, Allen (2001) has shown that in the late medieval period, real wages behaved differently in various European countries in the 200 years following the Black Death. Even if the labourers in the country with the lowest real wages were at Malthusian subsistence, those in countries with higher real wages (England in particular) must have been above it and had living standards that varied over time. Major setbacks occurred with such general events as the Black Death and more regionally with such destructive wars as the Mughal invasions in the east of Europe, the Hundred Years War between England and France in the west of Europe, and the Thirty Years War that devastated much of what is now Germany. However, if we take the nineteenth-century living standards of Russian serfs and pre-potato-famine peasants living in the west of Ireland as close to the biological subsistence level, it is clear that for most of the medieval and early modern periods the majority of Europeans lived well above that standard.[4]

Finally, with the First Industrial Revolution, Western Europe moved into a regime of rapid and sustained growth. Around the time when the West was making the transition from episodic to sustained extensive growth in the nineteenth century, there was a 'great divide' in the behaviour of population causing a dramatic shift in the West's relation between extensive and intensive growth. There was a fall in crude death rates, followed later in the century by a fall in crude birth rates. These developments were initially accompanied by an upward surge in the rate of population growth and then by an even more dramatic fall. By some time in the twentieth century, most countries in the West had achieved birth and death rates that were not far from those that would hold population constant—and falling below them in an increasing number of countries. Early in the twenty-first century, many industrialized countries are avoiding declining populations largely through immigration from the less developed countries.

---

[2] Even if we arbitrarily assume that their food consumption were at subsistence, the secondary income must have raised living standards above it.

[3] Although peasant agriculture has always required much heavy work, that work is localized at various times of the year such as planting and harvesting. In between, there are extended periods when heavy labour is not required, particularly in the winter.

[4] See Dyer (1989) for medieval standards.

Thus there were two separate inflection points in the West's trend growth rates over the last 200 years. First, there was an emergence of sustained and rapid (by historical standards) extensive growth, and then there was the emergence of sustained and rapid (by historical standards) intensive growth. The two are conceptually distinct, although they may have been related in the West's case, about which we say more in Chapter 10.

Generalizations

Several important empirical generalizations concerning growth in the West can be made from the previous discussion:

1. On average, since the neolithic agricultural revolution, there has been an enormous amount of extensive growth, albeit at a rate that seems slow by modern standards.
2. There have been major setbacks when there was very probably negative extensive growth extending over several centuries, one being the period around the end of the Bronze Age and another around the dissolution of the Western Roman Empire.
3. Most of the extensive growth has gone to support a rising population, with periods of rapid extensive growth caused by the introduction of major new technologies being followed by bursts of population growth, while a much smaller part has supported rising living standards.
4. There seems to have been bouts of intensive growth that were sustained over quite long periods of time, particularly those that followed the introduction of writing and bronze in the civilizations of Mesopotamia and that covered the rise of classical civilization, first in Greece and then in Rome. These two periods were without doubt much longer in duration than the 200 plus years of growth that have followed on the First Industrial Revolution in the West. Modern growth is probably unique in the rate at which it has been sustained over the last 200 years, but it is not unique in the duration of a strong positive trend to the growth rate.[5]
5. In the absence of detailed historical work far beyond the scope of this book, it is impossible to say how much of the growth, both extensive and intensive, was in the form of episodic bursts following the introduction of key new technologies and how much was sustained over a period of more than 100–200 years, but both the periods mentioned in point 4 would seem to have been sustained over several centuries, possibly a millennium. We suspect that much of the rest of the growth, both extensive and intensive, would be better described as episodic rather than sustained, although that is only a guess and a contrary argument can be derived from any history of technological development such as Mokyr (1990) or Landes (1998).

---

[5] We say 'probably' because no quantitative comparison exists between modern growth and some of the great periods of growth in the distant past.

II. RELATED EXTENSIVE AND INTENSIVE GROWTH

Section I provides us with a set of broad generalizations that require explanation. They also suggest, more specifically, that there is some relation between the growth rates of total income and of the population. This relation, if it exists, helps to determine how extensive and intensive growth are related to each other. To investigate these relations, we need to study the dynamics of population growth.

Conflicting Views

We distinguish three basic views—Malthusian, neo-Malthusian, and non-Malthusian—on how the behaviour of population influences the relation between extensive growth, which is driven primarily by technological change, and intensive growth, which is a major determinant of living standards.

Malthusian

A simple statement of the Malthusian view runs as follows. The birth rate is biologically determined at or near the biological maximum.[6] Humans reproduce so quickly that population growth tends to outstrip productivity growth.[7] This holds living standards at the biological subsistence level, where the positive checks of high infant mortality, periodic pestilence, and plagues stop population from growing further. If productivity growth raises living standards above subsistence, the positive checks are weakened and rapid population growth quickly pushes living standards back to subsistence, where they are again held constant by the positive checks. As a result, living standards have remained throughout most of human experience at, or close to, the subsistence level—at least until the nineteenth century when Malthus wrote his famous book, *An Essay on the Principle of Population*.[8] We take the main assumption of any Malthusian-type theory to be that the birth rate is not a choice variable. We take the main conclusion to be that all extensive growth is translated over the long run into population growth, with any effect on intensive growth being reversed over the time it takes for population to respond fully to increases in total output. Notice that real per capita income is held at the 'subsistence level' because the death rate is negatively related to real per capita income. A positive check to population caused by anything on the output side, such as a change in climate or the exhaustion of key resources, is not a Malthusian explanation.

---

[6] Since throughout all of history, some women did not pair with males, some were barren although paired with males (through either their own or their mate's reproductive problems), and many died in childbirth, the average number of live births per adult woman was always significantly less than the maximum number of children borne by a woman who experienced none of these.

[7] Malthus (1872: 12) assumed that people lacked sufficient foresight to see the consequences of increasing the size of their families: 'But, man cannot look around him, and see the distresses which frequently press on those who have large families.'

[8] Followers of Malthus would later add that only the rapid growth produced by the First and Second Industrial Revolutions allowed output to get decisively ahead of population growth, ushering in history's first period of sustained intensive growth.

Many economic historians have followed Malthus in seeing the world as caught in a Malthusian trap. The following quotation is typical:

In ages past, better living standards had *always* been followed by a rise in population that eventually consumed the gains. Now [during the First Industrial Revolution], for the first time in history, both the economy and knowledge were growing fast enough to generate a continuing flow of improvements. Gone, Malthus's positive checks and the stagnationist predictions of the 'dismal science'; instead, one had an age of promise and great expectations. (Landes 1998: 187, emphasis added)

Cohen (1995), North (1981), and MacFarlane (1997) have all expressed similar views.

It is worth noting that to assume that population expands whenever income exceeds subsistence is to adopt the methodologically dubious practice of imposing behavioural assumptions on a derived relation instead of on the behavioural relations that determine it—in this case the birth and death rates. Whenever separate assumptions are made about these two rates, it is no longer necessary that the two will be equal (a necessary condition for a stable population) at the biological subsistence level (or any other exogenously given level).[9]

Neo-Malthusian

Recently, several economic theorists have taken a neo-Malthusian position. Their models are mainly directed to explaining the West's transition from extensive to intensive growth that occurred some time in the nineteenth century.[10] We consider this issue in Chapter 10 and here we are interested only in the implications of these theories for the period prior to the First Industrial Revolution. They typically adopt the non-Malthusian assumption that the birth rate is a family choice variable. To this is added the assumption that parents would like to have larger families than they do have but that family size is constrained because they are living at a 'subsistence level of income'. If incomes rise, parents elect to have larger families so that the family remains on the subsistence level. This models the European economy as being

---

[9] We illustrate this point with the simplest possible example. Let the behaviour of the birth rate and the death rate be linearly related to real per capita income:

$$B = a + cR$$

and

$$D = e + fR$$

where B is births, D is deaths, and R is real per capita income; $f < 0 < (a, c, e)$ and $a < e$. A necessary condition for population to be stable is that $B = D$, which solves for

$$R = (e - a)/(c - f)$$

This equilibrium income may be at or above the subsistence level. It will not change as technology changes but will change if the relation between deaths or births and income changes.

[10] See, for example, the symposium on 'Population and Economic Growth', *American Economic Review*, Papers and Proceedings, May 1999.

trapped in a low-income equilibrium where increases in income led to increases in the birth rate that held real per capita incomes constant. The economy then broke out to a sustained growth path some time just before, or at the beginning of, the Industrial Revolution. Usually the period considered by such theorists extends only as far back as Europe from the dissolution of the Western Roman Empire, but if the theories are valid, they should apply to the entire human experience (unless conditions are specified that make them non-applicable to the 8,000 or so years between the neolithic agricultural revolution and the dissolution of the Western Roman Empire).

In this chapter, we concentrate on the same period, AD 500–1750, but leave on the table the issue of the relation between the two types of growth in earlier periods. In Chapter 10, we consider the transition to sustained intensive growth that occurred some time during the nineteenth century. We take Galor and Weil's model (2000) as the most fully developed of these neo-Malthusian models and use it for the main comparisons of neo-Malthusian theories with ours. We outline the parts of their model that are relevant to the present discussion in Box 9.1—we only summarize those assumptions and implications that are relevant to a comparison with our model and do not cover the wealth of sophisticated formal analysis that they use to develop their model.

A slightly different version of the neo-Malthusian theory is due to Easterlin (1998). He assumes that over most of the period under consideration, birth and

---

Box 9.1. The Galor and Weil Model

The following are the assumptions and implications of the G&W model that are important for comparisons with our model.

1. Each person lives two periods: one as a child and one as a working adult who is head of a one-person family.
2. Children do not consume.
3. The single parent (whom we refer to as 'it') divides its time between raising children and producing 'food' for its own consumption.
4. The time spent raising children is divided between the time cost of raising each child and the time cost of conferring units of education on each child.
5. The parent's utility is a function of the amount it consumes and the future income of its children, measured as the number of children it raises multiplied by the wage per efficiency unit of labour in the next generation and the amount of human capital with which it endows each child.
6. There is a Malthusian subsistence constraint below which the parent's income cannot fall.
7. When the Malthusian subsistence constraint binds, the parent cannot devote as much time to child-raising as it would wish. The subsistence value of consumption is produced and the remaining available time is allocated to child-raising activities; so any increase in productivity causes more time to be devoted to raising more children with the parent's food consumption unchanged.
8. When the subsistence constraint is not binding, the parent devotes a constant fraction of its available time to producing for its own consumption and a constant

Box 9.1. (continued)

amount to raising children, although the proportions of time devoted to the two child-raising activities of raising more children or educating existing children vary over time.

9. The amount of each adult worker's human capital is a function of the amount of education it receives as a child and the depreciation of that capital before it reaches working age. That depreciation is an increasing function of the rate of technical progress and a decreasing function of the amount of human capital.

10. The amount of human capital that parents elect to confer on their children is a non-decreasing function of the rate of technical progress.

11. The rate of technical progress is an increasing function of the size of the population and the amount of human capital with which each worker is endowed.

12. It does not pay to devote time to conferring human capital on children until the rate of technical change is sufficiently high and, until then, all time that is freed up by increasing productivity in food production is devoted to increasing the size of family.

The behaviour of the model is divided into three regimes: (*a*) the Malthusian Regime, in which the subsistence constraint is binding and a slow rate of technical progress leads to an increase in family size with no change in adult consumption and no change in human capital; (*b*) the Post-Malthusian Regime, which can support several different equilibria but, in the absence of stochastic shocks, will be in equilibrium with zero education for children, a binding subsistence constraint, and a modest rate of growth of productivity (see Galor and Weil 2000: 819, fig. 4); and (*c*) the Modern Growth Regime in which the increasing rate of population growth accelerates the rate of technical progress until it pays parents to reallocate the amount of time spent raising children so as to have fewer children, each endowed with an increasing amount of human capital.

death rates were such that parents could not raise as many children as they desired and could support. As a result, rational parents made no attempt to control family size, even where they were aware of birth control methods.

In both these versions, parents can choose the size of their families but elect to remain at subsistence income because they would like larger families than they have, in one case because it would push them below subsistence and in the other case because they are prevented from raising more children by a high death rate. Since it is clear from the evidence stated above that European peasants did not typically live at a biological subsistence living standard, neo-Malthusian theories that refer to a subsistence level trap must refer to a level well above biological subsistence. Any viable neo-Malthusian theory should explain how, and at what level, that constant standard was determined and why, if ever, it changed. We take this matter up again towards the end of Chapter 10.

Non-Malthusian

To non-Malthusians, the causes of early medieval growth are found in many profound technological changes such as the introduction of the three-field system, the heavy plough, and the growing use of waterwheels—as well as a host of other less dramatic technological advances chronicled in books such as Rosenberg and Birdzell (1986), Mokyr (1990), and Landes (1998). The non-Malthusians argue that the rises in total income were taken out partly in increased population and partly in higher living standards, the balance between the two varying from time to time and from place to place. Typically, however, they argue that this is what the evidence shows although they do not model how it might have been the outcome of rational individual behaviour.

For example, Jones (1988) argues that the belief that sustained growth is a strictly modern phenomenon is based on the incorrect belief that the Industrial Revolution was a unique phenomenon in human history—not just in its specific technologies, which were of course unique, but in the length of its period of technological change and productivity growth. For Jones, other periods of history have seen similar phenomena that probably differed quantitatively, but not qualitatively. In addition, he correctly points out that to judge living standards one must consider the production of all goods and services, not just foodstuffs. These include both 'non-essential' goods and services produced by the private sector and public goods. Jones argues that the production of public goods was one way in which agricultural surpluses were translated into goods for general consumption. We formalize his argument later in this chapter.

Modelling the Relation

To investigate these issues, we construct a number of models of endogenous population growth. These models have several purposes. First, their behaviour sheds light on the implications of various assumptions about how fertility and mortality, and hence population growth respond to economic stimuli. Second, we want to be able to explain fertility rates, family sizes, and per capita incomes that rise and fall over the centuries. Third, we want to be able to explain periods in which family size and population move in opposite directions as a result of variations in the number of families. Fourth, we wish to they investigate how populations and living standards are affected by a number of shocks, such as changes in technology, productivity of children relative to adults, death rates, savings, obsolescence rates, and willingness to marry. Finally, our models are intended to help us to understand the observed behaviour of actual populations and of the relation between extensive and intensive growth. Here, as already explained, our focus is mainly on two periods: Europe between the dissolution of the Western Roman Empire and the First Industrial Revolution in this chapter and in Chapter 10, nineteenth-century Europe, which saw the two great transitions in growth rates, first to sustained extensive growth and then to sustained intensive growth.

A Key Assumption: Family Size as a Choice Variable

When constructing our own models of population dynamics, the assumption about how family size is determined is critical. Appendix 9.1 presents a brief summary of the evidence that persuades us that people in the West had means of regulating family size by many methods that were in the public domain and subject to public discussion from the earliest times right up to the first part of the early modern period, and available through word of mouth at least into the eighteenth century.

The methods used have varied somewhat over the millennia, but they typically included varying the age of marriage, sexual practices that do not result in conception, an array of birth control techniques, abortion, and infanticide (by which we mean bringing about the death of a newborn child either directly by killing it or indirectly by means such as exposure). Evidence of the use of these methods suggests that not only was it possible to exert some control over family size but also that such control was indeed exercised, at least until somewhere around the late eighteenth or early nineteenth centuries. Taken together, the evidence seems conclusively to rule out any strict Malthusian theory where the birth rate is at some high biologically determined figure so that real incomes are pushed near to the biological subsistence level. So from here until the concluding part of the chapter we confine ourselves to the neo-Malthusian and non-Malthusian schools of thought and we assume that family size (at least in the West) has almost always been a choice variable.

The Next Steps

We now introduce three models of population dynamics: an individual household; a one-sector economy, producing only food; and a three-sector economy, producing food, a manufactured good, and a public good. The models are discussed and evaluated in general terms in this chapter and laid out formally in Appendix 9.2. One of our main objectives is to discover the implications of three key assumptions concerning what influences the fertility decisions of parents: that they value per capita consumption, that they value children as productive assets, and that they value children for their own sakes. With this information in hand, we can evaluate some of the positions taken by the schools of thought discussed above and investigate possibilities with respect to the behaviour of the West's living standards. We consider the three models separately rather than just going straight to the three-sector model because we wish to compare our results with the majority of other treatments of endogenous population that deal, either explicitly or implicitly, with only one sector, agriculture.

III.   MODEL 1: INDIVIDUAL HOUSEHOLD

In this model, we investigate the choices of the household with respect to consumption and fertility when it is presented with an exogenous increase in its ability to produce income. We discuss the model in the text, lay out its equations in Box 9.2, develop it fully in Appendix 9.2, and, where relevant, we make parenthetical comparisons with the model of Galor and Weil—hereafter G&W.

Assumptions

We make three critical assumptions about family behaviour.

Assumption 1: Parents value their family's per capita consumption, not its total consumption. Some models have used the more theoretically tractable assumption that total and not per capita consumption enters the family's utility function. Since we see no basis in historical evidence, or in the theory of rational behaviour, to

Box 9.2. Equations for the Individual Household (Model 1)

The family's utility is increasing in per capita family consumption and the number of children up to some maximum determined by the second argument in the function:

$$u = \left(\frac{f}{p+h}\right)^{\alpha} (p+h) - q(p+h)^{\gamma}, \ \alpha \in (0, 1), \ \gamma \in [1, \infty), \ q \in [0, \infty) \qquad (9.1)$$

where f is the household's total production of food, p is parents (always equal to two), h is the number of children in the household, and q, α, and γ are parameters. Simple manipulation produces:

$$u = f^{\alpha}(p+h)^{1-\alpha} - q(p+h)^{\gamma} \qquad (9.2)$$

The household's production function is:

$$f = A(p + zh)^{\beta}, \quad z \in (0, 1) \quad \beta \in (0, 1) \qquad (9.3)$$

where A gives the combined effect of the fixed inputs of land and capital and productivity, z converts children into adult equivalents, and β is a parameter. Substituting (9.3) into (9.2) yields the utility function in the form that we use it:

$$u = A^{\alpha}(p + zh)^{\beta\alpha}(p+h)^{1-\alpha} - q(p+h)^{\gamma} \qquad (9.4)$$

justify that assumption, we accept the analytical problems that our assumption entails. (In G&W there is no distinction between total and per capita family consumption because there is only one parent and children consume nothing.)

Assumption 2: One of the two reasons why parents value their children is that they contribute to agricultural production. This conforms to much evidence that children were productive assets in farming communities, at least until modern times.[11] Children are, however, less productive than adults and the family's labour force is measured in adult equivalents by multiplying the number of children by a parameter of $0 \leq z \leq 1$. (In G&W children do not contribute to agricultural production.)

Assumption 3: In addition to valuing their productive contribution, parents derive direct utility from their children so that, *ceteris paribus*, they prefer more to fewer children up to some large number, after which further children begin to confer a disutility. (The utility function 9.1 contains a term that represents the direct positive utility of children and a term that acts as a counterbalance so that there is a maximum number that parents desire.) The positive utility of children may arise for many reasons such as parents deriving direct pleasure from their young or expecting to be supported

[11] Indeed the evidence that the firstborn of many village parents occurred less than nine months after marriage is consistent with the hypothesis that children were so useful on farms that engaged couples had sexual relations to prove that the woman (who was typically blamed for infertility) was not barren, conception being followed quickly by marriage, and failure to conceive by breaking off the engagement (see Appendix 9.1).

later in life by their grown children. (G&W assume that children are only valued for the direct utility they give to their parents, which is derived from their ability to earn income when they become adults. They attribute this to either altruism on the part of parents or parental desire be supported by their children in old age.)

It follows from assumptions 2 and 3 that, for a given family income, an additional child adds to the family's output, and directly to parents' utility (up to some maximum number of children) but simultaneously reduces utility by reducing the family's per capita consumption whenever marginal product of the last child is below the family's average product (which is always the case with the production functions that we use in our first three models).

Our model is completed with the following additional assumptions.

Assumption 4: A family comprises two adults, each denoted by p, who choose the number of their children, h. For convenience we often work with the size of a family as $j = 2p + h$. (In G&W there is only one parent, which avoids many of the analytical complications that we encounter with our models.)

Assumption 5: Each adult and child is endowed with an exogenously determined amount of time to allocate to food production, which stands for all necessities such as food, clothing, and shelter.

Assumption 6: Food is produced with the Cobb–Douglas production function $f = A(p + zh)^\beta$, displayed in equation 9.3 of Box 9.2. In this function, A stands for productivity and the contribution of fixed factors, which in the first model are land and capital; and the labour input is the parents, p, plus their children, h, multiplied by the child productivity parameter, z.

Assumption 7: To avoid cumbersome expressions that add nothing to the analysis, our birth rate includes only those who are born alive and whose lives are not ended quickly through infanticide.[12]

Assumption 8: Children are raised at no direct time cost, which we believe mirrors the evidence that given the large extended families in most medieval villages, the amount of time mothers spent working the fields was not competitive with the amount of time they spent raising children. (In G&W the cost of rearing children and endowing them with human capital is the parents' time cost.)

Assumption 9: Parents care only about their own utility and that of their children while they are at home. This assumption is further discussed later.[13] (In G&W the parent cares about its own consumption and the income stream that will accrue to its children when they become adults.)

Our assumptions that children contribute to family food production at an efficiency less than adults but lower per capita food consumption introduces a heterogeneity

---

[12] Thus we treat infanticide as a method of birth control. All that matters, however, is that infanticide is one effective method of controlling family size. (An increase in infanticide can equally well be analysed as a decrease in the birth rate or as an increase in the death rate of children.)

[13] Implicit in our assumption is that parents do not have dynastic preferences such that they maximize their own and all of their descendant's utility over the infinite horizon.

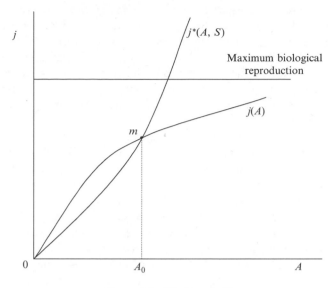

Figure 9.1. *The household*

between parents and children that, when combined with the non-linearity of the model, precludes solving it analytically. For the moment, therefore, we assume that children are as productive as adults ($z = 1$ in equation 9.3). This allows analytical solutions to be derived. Later we allow z to be less than unity.

Manipulation and Results

The model is manipulated by maximizing the utility function with respect to the number of children, checking its second-order conditions to ensure that the result is a maximum, then manipulating the first-order conditions to obtain a demand for family size that can be substituted into the production function to obtain a demand for food and dividing that by the size of family to obtain per capita family food consumption—all of which is laid out in detail in Appendix 9.2.

The behaviour of the model is shown in Figure 9.1, which plots size of family, j, against the productivity parameter, A. The curve labelled $j(A)$ shows how desired family size varies as productivity is varied parametrically, assuming no minimum subsistence requirement. As would be expected from the family utility function, desired family size increases with income but at a diminishing rate.[14] The second curve, labelled $j^*(A, S)$, is the family size that holds the household on the biological subsistence constraint, defined as the minimum amount of food children need on average to survive till marriageable age (i.e. the maximum size of family that can be

---

[14] This is a plot of the demand for family size given in equation 9A.2.6 on page 342. Given the constraints on the parameter values, this relation has a positive first derivative and a negative second derivative, as shown in the figure. It is clear from the algebra that j increases without limit as A increases,

supported at the biological subsistence level for any given productivity level).[15] As shown algebraically in the footnote, this curve rises at an increasing rate as A increases. The intuition is that a proportionate increase in the parameter A and in the size of family would leave per capita income unchanged if children did not add to production. To the extent that they are productive, such an increase leads to a rise in per capita income, which can only be reduced to its original level by further increases in family size. Because of decreasing returns, increasing family size raises total output but lowers per capita output.

Each of these curves gives the locus of equilibrium points as A is varied parametrically, one for the Malthusian model, $j^*(A, S)$, and the other for our model, assuming that achieving minimum substance is not a requirement, $j(A)$. The horizontal line shows the biological maximum number of children that a family can have, which is an obvious constraint on family size.[16]

Where family income cannot be less than subsistence income, the locus of equilibrium family size as A varies will be the lesser of the js determined by each curve. Thus, over the range from zero to the intersection point of the constraint with the demand for children function, m, family size increases along the subsistence constraint as A increases, and the whole family remains by choice at the biological subsistence level. For As to the right of the intersection point, the subsistence constraint is no longer binding and family size increases with A at a sufficiently low rate to allow the family's per capita income to rise. In other words, to the right of point m, the household has a positive income elasticity of demand for both children and per capita consumption.

This model can be used to establish a number of interesting results (which are obvious from the Figure 9.1). First, with homogeneous households, changes in productivity have the following effects:

1. As productivity rises up to some critical value, the family remains at biological subsistence and the choice is made to consume additional income by having larger families at an unchanged per capita income.

---

and hence j must eventually exceed the biologically maximum birth rate. We regard this extreme result as unrealistic and confine ourselves to the range over which j is less than that maximum possible rate. This restriction affects none of our analysis since our concern is to investigate the consequences of a positive income elasticity of demand for per capita consumption and family size. Our results holds for all As when j is less than the maximum biological birth constraint.

[15] The curve is derived as follows: Letting the family's total income that will just provide subsistence for each of its members be f^*, we can write: $S = f^*/j$. Substituting for the definition of the production function, we get a relation between j and A that describes the household size that puts it at the subsistence level of food income:

$$j^* = (A/S)^{(1/1-\beta)}$$

[16] To put Easterlin's assumption into our language, he assumes that the typical family is to the right of the intersection point between $j(A)$ and the maximum biological reproduction constraint. The latter then determines family size.

2. Above the critical level of productivity, increases in income from increased productivity are consumed partly in larger families and partly in higher per capita consumption.

Since the evidence quoted earlier in this chapter makes it clear that the typical European peasant did not live at the biological subsistence level, result 1 is of no further interest. From here on, we assume that the typical peasant family lived above biological subsistence, that is, to the right of point *m* in Figure 9.1. (The behaviour in point 1 is similar to the G&W model except that we assume that the subsistence constraint never binds on the typical household, while they use the constraint to explain behaviour during the whole of what they call the Malthusian Regime, which must be a large proportion of the whole period under consideration. When the constraint no longer binds, G&W's parents do not want larger families as income rises while ours do.)

Second, consider heterogeneous households. Although the authors of all other formal models do not consider the issue of heterogeneous households, the historical evidence is that a significant group of people, possibly 20–30 per cent, lived close to the subsistence level while the rest had incomes significantly above it.[17] Adding this heterogeneity produces further results.

3. Periods of unexpectedly low productivity may cause hardship or even starvation among families who have chosen to live at the subsistence level. This is not because they are having the biologically maximum possible size of family (indeed their families will be smaller than those who are above subsistence), but because their tastes dictate that they live at the subsistence level. Hardship and starvation occur not because the parents have more children than they expect to be able to support but because of unexpected declines in income.[18]

4. Increases in living standards can occur as everyone's productivity rises, allowing more people to choose to move off the subsistence constraint. This occurs even though substantial numbers remain on that constraint and are still subject to hardship and starvation in the face of unexpected declines in income. This point provides a warning for those who infer from the persistence of periodic famines that Malthusian pressures and subsistence living standards were the norm. Periodic bouts of famine affecting a significant section of the population are consistent, as this model shows, with rising real income for the entire population, rising average food consumption, and a growing proportion of the population consuming above the subsistence level—subject only to the requirement that a significant number of the society's heterogeneous households remain at or very near, the biological subsistence level.

---

[17] This number of course changed from year to year and place to place. But a reasonable estimate is that in any given year (between 750 and 1750) a rural peasant living in northern Europe had at least a 70 per cent chance of living above subsistence (see Geremek 1997; Dyer 1989).

[18] This last point comes closest to the Malthusian model since it is the death rate that causes the population level to move back to subsistence. However, it is not 'blind breeding' but unexpected negative productivity shocks that cause the increase in the death rate.

These results have a decidedly non-Malthusian ring. When productivity rises enough to make the *biological* subsistence constraint non-binding on a particular household (which we take to be most households most of the time), the household takes out only part of any increase in income in increased family size and part in higher per capita consumption. Over this range of income, the actions of individual households, responding to any given family income, do not depress living standards to biological subsistence. It follows that if there is a Malthusian trap under the assumed conditions, it must be due to some force exogenous to the family choice variables. In Section IV, we investigate this possibility by embedding our model of the individual household in a standard Solow growth model of the whole economy.

IV. MODEL 2: SOLOW GROWTH WITH ENDOGENOUS POPULATION

When we combine Model 1 with a Solow-style aggregate growth model, we find what we call a 'family formation externality'. It produces Malthusian-like results in spite of the non-Malthusian behaviour of the typical family. Let us see how this comes about.

Assumptions and Manipulation

The equations of this model are laid out in Box 9.3 and their formal manipulation is explained in detail in Appendix 9.2. On production, we assume a Cobb–Douglas aggregate production function with labour and capital as variable inputs, which have combined coefficients that sum to less than unity (because of the contribution of fixed land). Each family's income is its proportionate share of total production.[19] Married couples and their children undertake all food production. Children are less productive than adults and the adult equivalent of the child labour stock is the number of children multiplied by a parameter z ($0 < z < 1$). Total production is a function of the labour force measured in adult equivalents and capital, with land held constant. Dividing total output by the number of families then determines income for the family. As far as shifts in the production function are concerned, we treat technological change and its resulting changes in productivity as exogenous, while treating population as endogenous. This allows us to study the effects of specific technological shocks that give once-for-all increases in productivity. Treating

---

[19] This procedure is implicit in all growth models based on a single aggregate production function. It implies that when increased population lowers the marginal product of labour, each and every family's marginal product is lowered. In practice, the marginal products of different families were differentially affected by increases in population. Those who hung on to their own land undivided suffered no loss. Those who had to farm land subdivided between various heirs, or who tilled newly cleared, inferior land, suffered the effects of diminishing returns. If we sought to allow for differential effects of increasing population, we would need separate production functions for each class of family, which is ruled out of our aggregate model. We discuss the significance of this simplification later.

Box 9.3. Equations for the One-Sector Model (Model 2)

Total production is a function of the labour force measured in adult equivalents $(p + zh_t)$ and capital, K_t:

$$F_t = A(N_t(p + zh_t))^\beta (K_t)^\eta, \quad \beta \in [0, 1], \ \eta \in [0, 1], \text{ and } \beta + \eta < 1 \tag{9.5}$$

where N is the number of families. The aggregate capital stock is $K_t = N_t k_t$, where k_t evolves according to:

$$k_t = \frac{N_t s f_t + (1 - \delta) N_{t-1} K_{t-1}}{N_t}$$

where $s \in (0, 1)$ and $\delta \in (0, 1)$ are the savings and depreciation rate. Food per family, f_t, is:

$$f_t = \frac{F_t}{N_t} = A N_t{}^{\beta + \eta - 1} (p + zh_t)^\beta k_t^\eta \tag{9.6}$$

The utility function is the same as (9.1) except for the deduction from consumption of the fraction of income that is saved:

$$u_t = \left(\frac{(1 - s)f_t}{(p + h_t)} \right)^\alpha (p + h_t) - q(p + h_t)^\gamma \tag{9.7}$$

The survival rate is an increasing function of per capita income:

$$\Pr(survival) = \lambda_t = 1 - e^{-d\left(\frac{f_t}{(p + h_t)}\right)} \tag{9.8}$$

d is a calibration parameter set to produce a probability of survival of approximately 50 per cent and its value is given in Box 9A.2.1 on page 344.
Number of families formed is:

$$N_t = \frac{(\lambda_{t-1} N_{t-1} h_{t-1})}{\theta_t} \tag{9.9}$$

(If everyone marries (and the sexes are equal) $\theta = 2$; otherwise it is some larger number.)
We make θ_t a function of per capita income:

$$\theta_t = \frac{2}{x} \tag{9.10}$$

where

$$x = 1 - e^{-m\left(\frac{f_t}{(p + h_t)}\right)}$$

where

$$S_A = \lambda_{t-1} N_{t-1}[p + h_{t-1}] e^{-m \frac{f_t}{(p + h_t)}}$$

is the number of last period's children who survive to adulthood multiplied by the proportion who remain single. m is a calibration parameter set to ensure that θ_t is greater than 2 and its value is given in Box 9A.2.1. The number of children $N_t h_t$ multiplied by the survival rate and divided by θ_t then determines the number of families in period $t + 1$ and so on.
In the steady state, $h_t = h_{t-1}$, $f_t = f_{t-1}$, and $N_t = N_{t-1}$.

technological change as occasional, exogenous shocks is also in keeping with the view that technological change was not self-sustaining in pre-Industrial Revolution Europe but came in sporadic bouts that were often the results of accretions of what Mokyr terms singleton knowledge. New GPTs can be treated as particularly large and long-lasting increases in the productivity parameter, A.

On the household side, we use a model of overlapping generations. Each agent lives two periods: one as a child and one as an adult. We assume that a fraction of children die before becoming adults; only adults can marry; and only a fraction of these actually do marry. To be consistent with the historical evidence, the survival rate of children is assumed to be an increasing function of per capita income. To be consistent with the findings of Wrigley et al. (1997)—that couples had to accumulate a significant amount of capital before marrying and that this was easier when the economic conditions were better—we make the propensity to marry an increasing function of per capita income. People who remain single are assumed to produce a subsistence living for themselves, so they have no effect on the food production of households with children.[20]

Families save a constant fraction of their production and add it to their personal capital stock, which depreciates at a constant rate. In many overlapping generation models, savings behaviour is derived from the maximizing behaviour of the household. We model savings behaviour parametrically for two reasons: (*a*) for consistency with the Solow growth model; and (*b*) doing so simplifies the maximization problem so that we can focus on the choice variable of interest (family size) in the household maximization problem.

In line with the evidence quoted earlier in this chapter, we assume that the biological subsistence constraint is never binding on our typical household over the entire period in question. Thus, the representative household is operating to the right of the intersection point *m* in Figure 9.1.

Finally, to apply our simulation to real data we need to know how many years elapse per generation. The length of the average generation is measured by the age at which a woman has her median child. So, for example, if a woman has her fourth child out of seven at age thirty-three and that child does the same, there is a period of thirty-three years between generations. Although age of marriage varied over more than the 1,500 years since the end of the Western Roman Empire, Europeans typically married later than many other peoples who often married shortly after (or even before) puberty. Our reading of this and other evidence suggests three generations per century and we assume this figure, although the number might be as high as four during some subperiods.

---

[20] This assumption is consistent with the historical observations that single people generally were employed as household servants or as labourers in manufacturing or agriculture, earning subsistence wages. Unmarried individuals are counted in the population but per capita output is measured as the output of families divided by the number of people in families. Treating unmarried persons as one-person households who enter production of the subsistence good greatly increases the complexity of the model but, as some experimentation shows, changes none of its qualitative properties.

As already mentioned, the non-linearity in the model makes it extremely difficult to sign analytically any of the relations between variables and parameter values under general conditions. Since we do not want to continue with the restrictive assumption that children are as productive as adults ($z = 1$), we accept the analytical intractability and proceed as follows. We calibrate our parameters with historically reasonable values, which we call the *base case values*, and numerically solve for the endogenous variables. (All such details are presented in Appendix 9.2. See Box 9A.2.1 on page 344 for the definition and base case values for all the parameters.) Given any set of reasonable initial conditions on the capital stock, the initial population, and the initial productivity, and given the chosen parameter values, the utility maximizing choice of parents in each generation causes the model to evolve as follows. The total population in period t is the number of persons in families plus the number who remain single. Each married adult couple in the current period makes a single utility maximizing decision as to how many children to have, which determines both the size of their family and their family's food consumption. The number of children multiplied by the survival rate and the propensity to marry then determines the number of families in period $t + 1$ and so on. In the steady state, the number of children per family, the number of families, and per capita food consumption are all constant from period to period.

When the model is allowed to settle down in its steady state values for the base case parameter settings. Population is not, except by accident, at the optimal size that a social planner would choose. We then generated a set of comparative static results by comparing the steady state equilibrium of the calibrated model with the steady states that occur after an alteration in the base case values of each of the parameters taken one at a time. Box 9.4 gives all the qualitative results while the most important are discussed below. In contrast to Model 1, this macro model produces something that looks very much like a Malthusian trap but at a level of income that is determined endogenously. Let us look first at the 'trap'.

Malthusian Pressures in Response to Income Changes

In Model 1, a rise in productivity causes a rise in family size and a rise in per capita real income. This is not the case when the household is embedded in a Solow-type macro model.

A Once-for-All Shift in Productivity

A once-for-all shift in the productivity parameter A causes an initial increase in real income and leads households to consume some of this increase in per capita income and allocate some to sustain more children, which is the same as the behaviour predicted by Model 1. However, the rise in family size increases population in this generation and family formation in the next. Because of diminishing returns in agriculture, the rising population reduces per capita income. Population goes on growing until, in the new steady state, family size and per capita income return to their initial values. The only variables that change are the number of families, total

Box 9.4. Results for the One-Sector Model

Induced changes in endogenous variables (+ = up, − = down, 0 = no change)

Direct effect of parameter change	Family size $(p + h)$	Number of families (n)	Population (P)	Income per family member	Capital stock (K)	Capital per family (k)	Probability of surviving childhood	Percentage adults who marry
Productivity rises $\Delta A > 0$	0	+	+	0	+	0	0	0
Utility value of consumption rises $\Delta\alpha > 0$ β 'small'	−	+	+	+	+	+	+	+
Utility value of consumption rises $\Delta\alpha > 0$ β 'large'	+	+	+	−	+	−	−	−
Utility value of children falls $\Delta q > 0$	−	−	−	+	−	+	+	+
Children become less productive $\Delta z < 0$	−	−	−	+	−	+	+	+
Probability of surviving childhood rises $\Delta d > 0$	−	+	+	−	+	−	+	−
Desire to marry falls $\Delta m < 0$	+	−	−	+	−	+	+	−
Saving rate rises $\Delta s > 0$	−	+	+	+	+	+	+	+
Depreciation rate on capital rises $\Delta\delta > 0$	0	−	−	0	−	−	0	0

population, and total capital stock, all of which increase in equal proportion. Thus, the effects of once-for-all increases in productivity (or in the exogenous supply of land) are completely eaten up by new families. This is the result that we earlier called the family formation externality: although individual households choose to have more real income and slightly larger families when a productivity rise increases their incomes, larger families increase the population, generation by generation, until real family incomes are depressed to their original level and family size reverts to the number that just holds population constant. We have assumed that parents are unaware of this family formation externality. There is, however, nothing any individual family could do about it even if it were aware of the externality, since it is collective and not individual action that creates the externality.[21]

Easterlin (1998: 87) objects to such a result arguing that 'if consumption were so threatened, would human beings be oblivious to the impact on their well-being of the growth in dependency [family size]. If a rise in dependency creates a threat either to maintaining existing consumption levels or future improvements therein, will individuals passively accept this consequence?' But the whole point of an externality is that it is beyond the power of any individual agent to alter its effect.[22]

This is where the results of our model agree with Malthusian theory. If the family's choice of the number of children depends on its real income and if there is a unique equilibrium, a once-for-all increase in productivity will, at least in this one-sector model, cause per capita income and family size to increase in the transition phase (which may last several centuries). Eventually, however, population will grow until per capita income is returned to its original level—always assuming, of course, that no further disturbances occur. These dynamic adjustments are spread over a substantial period of time. For example, with a shock that doubles productivity, it takes nine periods, or 300 years on our assumption that a generation is thirty-three years, for 99.5 per cent of the adjustment to take place.

It is important to notice that although this result is similar to that obtained by many other endogenous population models, the behaviour that drives it is different. In most other models, including G&W's, family income is held at a constant level because as real income rises, households elect to take out all the extra income in having more children. The result is a reflection of individual decisions, and rather unlikely ones at that. We see no evidence that over the whole pre-industrial period, the typical household was electing to live at the subsistence level of income, and that as productivity rose over the centuries (as it surely did), the average size of family increased. In contrast, households in our model always elect to take out part of their income in additional per capita consumption and only part in additional children. This, however, causes the rate of family formation to increase, thus setting the externality in motion. Household income is then driven back to its original level,

---

[21] We must consider if this externality depends on the selfish nature of the parents in not taking into account the welfare of their children when they become adults and subsequent descendants. At the other extreme, if parents in each generation took into account the well-being of their descendants in *all* subsequent generations, the negative family formation externality might disappear. Continuous growth in productivity could then lead to continuous growth in income per person. Some experimentation leads us to conjecture, however, that an infinite planning horizon is needed to eliminate the externality. Under more reasonable assumptions that the household considers the effect of its behaviour on only a finite number of future generations, we believe the externality always persists, as it does in those numerical examples that we have worked out.

[22] Indeed, we first built our population models to prove something similar to Easterlin's contention. We argued that because parents would wish to take out part of their rising income in more consumption, we should see across the whole economy that an improvement in technology was associated with a rise in both family size and a rise in per capita consumption. This is what happened in our Model 1, which relates only to a single family. But when we embed this behaviour into a model of the whole economy in Model 2, the family formation externality eliminated the increases in per capita consumption that individuals had initially elected to enjoy.

but not by the direct choice of individual households, and the average size of family remains constant over the centuries.

A Constant Rate of Growth of Productivity

Although once-for-all increases in productivity eventually get consumed in support-ing more population at an unchanged level of per capita income, a constant rate of productivity *growth* leads to a higher *level* of per capita income. To show this, we let the model stabilize at the base case values and then imposed various rates of growth on the productivity parameter. In each case, per capita real income grew slowly over the centuries, but finally stabilized at an increase over the base case just less than the rate of growth of productivity. For example, given the numerical values chosen to calibrate our parameters, a 5 per cent growth rate in productivity per generation eventually raised the level of per capita income by 4 per cent. When family size stabilized at this slightly increased value, all further increases in productivity were taken out in a continually rising number of families and a rising population.

Determinants of the Equilibrium ('Subsistence') Level of Income

Now let us turn to the determinants of the floor level to which income is returned after any once-for-all increase in productivity. In most other descriptions and models of a Malthusian trap, including G&W's, the floor level of income is either at biological subsistence or some unexplained 'customary' level. Since historical evidence suggests that incomes were seldom at biological subsistence in the West, this leaves the level of 'subsistence income' in most neo-Malthusian theories as an arbitrary assumption. In contrast, our equilibrium level of per capita income is a function of several of the model's parameters. The influence of each of these parameters can be seen by considering what change in each is required to raise the floor level of income.

Children Become Less Desirable

Children can become less desirable for either of two reasons: first, tastes can change to lower the direct utility generated by any size of family (modelled by an increase in the parameter q in the utility function 9.7 in Box 9.3); second, children can become less productive (modelled by a reduction in the parameter z in the production function 9.5). The latter change can result from any of several forces such as a change in the production regime,[23] a change in the ability to employ children due to restrictive child labour laws, an increase in the direct costs of rearing children induced by the need to hire supervisory help from outside the family, or a rise in the opportunity cost of mothers' time spent at home.

A fall in the desirability of children or a fall in their productivity causes parents to have fewer children in the present period. This lowers family formation in the next

---

[23] By the production regime, we mean the nature of the final products and the production functions used to produce them.

period. Population falls as a result and real per capita income rises, as does per family capital stock and the survival and marriage rates. The aggregate capital stock falls as a result of fewer families and a lower population.

Digression on the Costs of Growth

The last result illustrates the contrast between the short-term costs and long-term benefits that often arise in the context of economic growth. The first generation loses unambiguously whenever their children become less productive, either as a result of reductions in their productivity that lower the demand for their services or of child labour laws that prevent them from supplying these services. If there were no family formation externality, as in Model 1, and as in models where Malthusian results follow directly from the Malthusian behaviour of individual families, there would be an unambiguous loss for all families in all generations. But the action of the family formation externality in Model 2 turns the short-term loss into a long-term gain by restricting population growth. As long as adult productivity does not change, population will fall as family size is reduced. The result is a once-for-all increase in per capita living standards—an increase that will be stretched over several generations and thus last 100–200 years, depending on the speed of adjustment.

Increase in the Utility of Per Capita Consumption

An increase in the utility of consumption, such as might happen with the introduction of new commodities, increases the weight given to per capita consumption relative to the direct utility value of children. Households can seek to increase their per capita consumption either by having more children to increase production, which we call the production effect, or by having fewer children to lower the number of persons among whom a given output is to be shared, which we call a substitution effect. Which alternative is chosen depends on the marginal product of labour. In either case, the results are rather surprising and illustrate the important interaction between family fertility choices and such macro relations as survival rates. The results cannot be predicted solely from a knowledge of the decisions of individual families regarding consumption and family size.

If the marginal product of children is below some critical value, the substitution effect dominates and the increase in the utility of consumption has the initial effect of reducing family size in order to increase consumption. Net family formation initially decreases but as family incomes rise, the survival rate of children and the marriage rate of adults both increase in subsequent generations causing population to start to increase. In the new equilibrium, the size of family is smaller and population and number of families are both slightly larger, as are per capita income, probability of survival, marriage rate, and capital stock (in the aggregate and per family). So the increased population (14.2 per cent in the example we used) is made up of slightly more families (5.9 per cent more in our example) of smaller size (18.3 per cent smaller in our example). Since adults are more productive than children, this shift raises per capita income. The higher equilibrium income (39.4 per cent in our example) leads to an increase in the child survival rate and a fall in the proportion of persons remaining single.

If the marginal product of labour is above its critical value, some but not all of these results are reversed. The production effect now dominates and family size is initially increased in order to produce more. Initially, per capita consumption rises as production is increased. However, net family formation increases in subsequent generations causing population to rise. In the new equilibrium, population, number of families, family size, and aggregate capital stock are all increased, while per capita income and per capita capital stock fall below their initial values. So the attempt to produce more output by having more children ends up, through the operation of the family formation externality, reducing per capita income below its initial level. The child survival rate also falls while the proportion of adults remaining single rises.

Reduction in the Probability of Surviving or of Marrying

The initial effect of an exogenous reduction in the probability of children surviving to adulthood or in the propensity of those who do survive to marry is a fall in family formation that causes population to fall. The final result is fewer, larger-sized families with a dramatic fall in population, higher real income, and more capital per head.

The reason for these results is that the initial changes reduce the force of the family formation externality. For given family decisions on size and real consumption, fewer children survive and/or fewer of those do form new families. The result is a significant fall in population that, *ceteris paribus*, increases real incomes substantially. The size of family increases as parents elect to take out some of their additional income in more children but the decline in net family formation more than offsets this, so there is a smaller population made up of many fewer families, each of somewhat larger size.

Rise in the Savings Rate

The initial effect of a rise in the savings rate is to increase the size of the capital stock. This causes income to rise and family size increases in response. This increases family formation in the next generation. The number of families rises greatly while their size falls slightly, causing the population to rise considerably. The aggregate capital stock increases greatly, while the stock per household increases somewhat. In equilibrium, there are more families of smaller size, each with more capital, resulting in an increase in population. Real family income increases slightly as do the probability of survival and the marriage rate.[24]

---

[24] This is a case in which the signs of the changes shown in Box 9.4 are not as revealing as the magnitudes. To illustrate, we calculated an example in which the savings rate rose from 0.1 to 0.2. The ratios of the new to the original values of the endogenous variables were as follows: number of families 1.76, size of families 0.94, population 1.6, aggregate capital stock 3.64, capital per household 2.07, income per head 1.09, survival probability and marriage rate 1.06 and 1.03.

Thus the family formation externality causes most of the effects of increased capital stock to be taken out in an increased population. The reason is that the approximate doubling of the capital stock per head raises the marginal product of labour, but this is almost completely offset by the doubling of the labour force.

This is a case in which our symmetric application of the family formation externality to all peasants is a severe limitation. If some peasants hold on to their own initial plot of land and do not subdivide it, they do not suffer the effects of the externality. In contrast, peasants who work on subdivided or newly cleared marginal land suffer its full impact. The net effect of a rise in the savings rate will then be to increase inequalities between the incomes of 'have' and 'have not' peasants.

It is worth noting that a fall in the depreciation rate does not have an identical effect. Instead it leads to an increase in population that wholly offsets the initial effect of rising income through a rise in the capital stock.[25]

The results on both the savings and depreciation rates are striking. In the Solow growth model, these rates influence the level of income but not its rate of growth. In Model 2, the depreciation rate has no influence on the level of per capita income. All it does is help to determine the size of the population and its decomposition into the number of families and their size. The savings rate has a major effect on the capital stock, but it also has a small effect on per capita income. For example, a doubling of the savings rate in the base case increases per capita income by 9 per cent. Thus a free gift from nature in the form of a lower depreciation rate yields no permanent increase in per capita income, while the pay-off to increased frugality in the form of a higher savings rate is positive but extremely small.[26]

Summary: Sources of Once-for-All Increases in Living Standards

The above discussion on the determinants of the equilibrium level of income provides the following predictions concerning changes that will lead to a once-for-all increase in per capita income:

---

[25] The initial effect of a rise in the depreciation rate is a fall in the capital stock. This lowers income and family size. The resulting fall in population continues until real income is restored to its original level, as is family size. The variables that change in equilibrium are the number of families, the population, and capital per head, all of which fall in the same proportion, and the capital stock, whose percentage decrease is twice that of the other variables that change. The reason for these surprising results is that family income and family size must return to their original values. This can only happen if income per head is unchanged. Given a constant propensity to save, the higher depreciation rate would then impose a lowered capital stock and, *ceteris paribus*, a lower real income. A smaller population compensates for this tendency, so that the higher marginal product of labour offsets the effects of the family's reduced amount of capital.

[26] At first glance, one might have thought that a rise in the savings rate and a fall in the depreciation rate would have identical effects. This is not so because a rise in the savings rate affects per capita consumption and hence is weighted by α in the utility function. Thus, the change in the saving parameter must work its way through the utility function in a non-linear fashion, while changes in δ have a direct, linear effect on the model.

1. a sustained increase in the rate of productivity growth: for example, a rise in the annual rate of productivity growth from 0 to 0.5 per cent per year, which is about 10 per cent per generation, will lead in Model 2 to a once-for-all increase in real per capita incomes of about 8.1 per cent, spread over 200–300 years, which will be perceived as a sustained rate of growth of about 1 per cent per generation over this period;
2. a fall in the direct utility value of children;
3. a fall in the productivity of children due to a change in the production regime of the sort often associated with urbanization;
4. child labour laws that restrict the ability to use child labour (points 3 and 4 are modelled by a fall in z in equation 9.5);
5. a rise in the direct costs of rearing children, such as occurs when the family support that exists in villages is exchanged for the relative anonymity of cities or when the price of hired help rises;
6. a rise in the market value of the mother's time (points 5 and 6 can also be modelled by a fall in z if we assume that the parameter measures the relative productivity of children net of any cost of rearing them);
7. a rise in the utility of consumption if the marginal product of labour is below some critical value. Although we do not model it, new products are an obvious possibility for increasing the utility of consumption;
8. a fall in the utility value of consumption if the marginal productivity of labour is above some critical value;
9. a rise in the death rate of children;
10. a rise in the desire for adults to remain single;
11. a rise in the savings rate.

Thus, unlike most of the neo-Malthusian models, our model does not imply an arbitrary level of subsistence income that is constant over more than the 1,000 years between the dissolution of the Western Roman Empire and the onset of the First Industrial Revolution. Instead the level of per capita income that tends to be maintained is a function of many parameters, some of which are observed to change over the centuries.

Sustained Growth

The only way in which increases in productivity can produce sustained intensive growth in this model is if there is an *accelerating rate* of productivity growth. Once we make the assumptions in a one-sector economy model that the desired size of family is an increasing function of per capita consumption and that preferences are not infinite horizon dynastic, per capita consumption is bolted down by the need to hold births equal to deaths in equilibrium. The externality is totally binding and nothing that causes a once-for-all change in productivity can cause per capita income to rise permanently, whether the cause is an increase in the amount of land available for cultivation, as in the early Middle Ages, or technological progress, as with the heavy plough, or anything else that shows up as a change in the productivity parameter A.

The more productivity shocks there are, the larger is the population, but there is no change in equilibrium per capita consumption. A series of favourable shocks such as were recorded in the 1,200 or so years under consideration can do no more to the *equilibrium* level of per capita income than can a single shock. However, the higher the *growth rate* of any of these influences that shift the productivity parameter A, the higher is the *level* of per capita income. So in this model, technologically dynamic societies will have higher levels of real incomes than technologically stagnant ones, but no matter how high the rate of extensive growth, there is no sustained intensive growth.

This powerful result does not come from assuming Malthusian behaviour among individual families. It occurs even though there is a positive income elasticity of demand for consumption because all that it requires is a positive income elasticity of demand for children, no matter how small that elasticity may be. The lower the elasticity, the longer time it will take for the externality to reduce real income to its original level after a favourable productivity shock, but any positive elasticity will do the job sooner or later.[27]

Key Questions

The results of this section are based on a very simple aggregate production function such as is typically found in macro-growth models with either exogenous or endogenous technical change. This is also the implicit approach of many of the economic historians who have espoused the Malthusian position. These observations suggest three important questions:

1. Is the prediction of zero-intensive growth due to the family formation externality robust with respect to the addition of more sectors?
2. Is the critical assumption that families have a positive income elasticity of demand for children at all levels of income correct empirically and will alternative assumptions alter the key conclusions of the model?
3. Is the Cobb–Douglas production function determining the results or are the results robust with respect to the substitution of different production functions in the one-sector growth model?

V. A MULTI-SECTOR MODEL

In this and the next two sections we address the above questions in turn.

---

[27] To be precise, what is required is that there be a positive income elasticity of demand for children when the birth rate is such that population is constant. This critical birth rate in turn depends on many other factors such as the rates of child mortality and adult marriage. But as long as children have a positive utility when population is constant, any income shock will cause the birth rate to rise and set the family formation externality into play. (It does not matter that for some large size of family the marginal utility of children reaches zero as long as this size is above the equilibrium size that holds population constant.)

Limitations of a one-sector model

The assumption that only a single product is produced is suspect for biasing the results since, in reality, rising real income may be taken out only partly in more agricultural goods, partly in public goods, and partly in non-agricultural goods and services.

Public goods have played an important role in consumption throughout history. For example, the state has been an important source of public structures financed from taxation. Particularly in warmer climates, such as those experienced in the Mediterranean area, much activity takes place out of doors, and public goods such as parks, avenues for paseos, arenas, and public buildings are important parts of the consumption bundle of ordinary individuals. The state also provides law and order, justice, and punishment. Military protection has been an important public good since the dawn of organized warfare that followed the introduction of bronze early in the third century BC (see Chapter 5). Defence provides value for everyone. Although, as we have already observed wars of expansion may not benefit peasants, the associated expenditures are a part of GDP, and if we are interested in the growth of GDP, we must take such expenditures into account.

The other great public institution, the Church, levied taxes (only to some extent voluntary) on its believers, who, until modern times, were the vast majority of the West's population. With these funds, it provided public goods such as cathedrals, monasteries, and services such as administration of the sacraments and help to the poor. To individuals who used churches as centres for social as well as religious activities, and who thought that contributing to the good works of the Church was a payment towards a ticket to paradise, this was a major source of private utility. Some of the public goods on the above list were services that were consumed when they were produced; others were long-lasting capital goods—so long-lasting that many of them are still with us.

A second important limitation of the one-sector model is its neglect of private goods other than food, which we defined as a composite good covering the necessities of life. Indeed, most of those who have espoused Malthusian theory have concentrated on actual food production more or less to the exclusion of other types of output. In practice, however, rising real incomes could be, and typically were, consumed only partly in more food and partly in increased consumption of other goods and services. Throughout the period in which we are interested, many of these goods were produced within the village, either by the efforts of the peasants themselves or of specialized artisans such as blacksmiths. In the later part of the period, however, the putting-out system came to play an important role in shaping the economic life of medieval Europe. It provided peasants with a source of income not tied to the land. Although piece rates were low, the income they earned allowed peasant families to enjoy modest increases in living standards that could not have been generated by their village's own agricultural sector. In so far as these goods were produced during what would otherwise have been leisure time, the entire earnings from putting-out represented a net increase in material living standards. People often wonder about peasants living at or near the subsistence level having leisure time. But agriculture is a seasonal activity, particularly in northern climates, so during off seasons, farmers have substantial leisure time. (The inability to model such an activity is another limitation of the aggregate, constant elasticity production function in which all available inputs are used all the time.)

Model 3: Food, a Manufactured Good, a Public Good

We repeat our point made with respect to Model 2: we treat technological change as exogenous because the population dynamics in which we are interested are independent of the causes of technological change. So it is easiest to study the relation between technological change on the one hand and population and living standards on the other hand by changing technology parametrically, even though, as the rest of this book attests, we believe that episodic technological changes were generated by endogenous innovative activity.

Model 3 is Model 2 with the addition of two new goods: a manufactured good and a public good. Its equations are given in Box 9.5 and their manipulation is discussed in detail in Appendix 9.2. Here we concentrate on the basic outlines of the model and its results. As before, one private good, *food*, stands for the necessities of life. The other private good, *manufacturing* output, is produced by the adult peasants according to a standard diminishing returns function. This good is produced with the labour of the parents, but not their children, and with a given amount of capital and material inputs that are supplied by the owner of the production. So adults must divide their time between the production of food and the manufactured good while children are only useful in food production. These assumptions are meant to model the putting-out system of pre-Industrial Revolution Europe.

The *public good* is a durable commodity that is produced by the state and paid for by taxes levied on peasant's food production. It is entirely non-rivalrous.[28] The stock of the public good is added to each period by its current production, which is obtained by applying the tax rate to the output of food and multiplying it by a parameter that turns the tax revenue expressed in food into the public good and depreciating it at a fixed rate δ.

The utility function of each family (equation 9.11) contains the per capita family food consumption, which is obtained by multiplying food production by one minus the tax rate to yield food consumption. The manufactured good enters as an amount per family, since it is assumed to be a public good within the family on the grounds that much of it is available to all family members, but rivalrous between families. The public good enters as a total, since its entire stock is assumed to

---

[28] We can allow for a portion of public goods to be services by adjusting the depreciation rate on the stock of public goods. If for example 20 per cent of all public goods are services and 80 per cent are durables with a 5 per cent annual depreciation rate, we can depreciate the whole stock of public goods at the rate of 24 per cent.

Box 9.5. Equations for the Three-Sector Model (Model 3)

The household's utility function is:

$$u_t = \left[\frac{(1 - s - T)f_t}{(p + h_t)}\right]^{\alpha} (p + h_t) - q(p + h_t)^{\gamma} + (G_t)^{\kappa} + (j(m_t))^{\chi} \qquad (9.11)$$

where T is the tax rate, G_t is the total quantity of the public good, and m_t is the per family quantity of the manufactured good, j is a calibration parameter, $\alpha, \kappa, \chi \in [0, 1]$ and $\gamma > 1$.

The aggregate and household productions of food is given by the following:

$$F_t = A(N_t(p_{f,t} + zh_t))^{\beta}(K_t)^{\eta}, \quad \beta + \eta < 1 \qquad (9.12)$$

$$f_t = \frac{F_t}{N_t} = AN_t^{\beta + \eta - 1}(p_{f,t} + zh_t)^{\beta} k_t^{\eta} \qquad (9.13)$$

which are equations (9.5) and (9.6) in Box 9.3, except that $p_{f,t}$ is the parental contribution to the household's food production. Household capital is the same as in Model 2 (unnumbered equation in Box 9.3):

$$k_t = \frac{N_t s f_t + (1 - \delta)N_{t-1} K_{t-1}}{N_t} \qquad (9.14)$$

The stock of the public good is:

$$G_t = nT(N_t f_t) + (1 - \varphi)G_{t-1} = nTF_t + (1 - \varphi)G_{t-1} \qquad (9.15)$$

where φ is the depreciation rate on public goods and n is productivity parameter that turns the private good into a public good.

The total production, and household production of the manufactured good are given by the following:

$$M_t = B(N_t)^{\nu}(p_{m,t})^{1-\nu} \qquad (9.16)$$

$$m_t = \frac{M_t}{N_t} = BN_t^{\nu-1}(p_{m,t})^{1-\nu} \qquad (9.17)$$

In addition, we have the following parental time constraint:

$$p = 2 = p_{f,t} + p_{m,t} \qquad (9.18)$$

Real per capita income is:

$$y_t = f_t/(2 + h_t) + w_1 G_t + w_2(m_t) \qquad (9.19)$$

where w_1 converts the public good into units of f_t and the price of m_t relative to f_t is w_2, which is equal to the ratio of the marginal product of labour in food to the marginal product of labour in manufacturing.

contribut equally to each family's utility. Real per capita income is thus defined as family food consumption divided by the number of people in the family, plus the production of the manufactured good per family multiplied by the relative price of that good plus the total stock of the public good multiplied by an implicit price that turns it into food equivalents.

Manipulation and Results

As pointed out earlier, analytical solutions are extremely cumbersome to generate when z is not unity. So, as in Model 2, we simulate the model using the base case values for the parameters shown in Box 9A.2.1, on page 344, to generate numerical values for the variables. Sensitivity analysis shows that our qualitative results are not significantly changed by altering the parameter values over a wide range (as long as the parameter restrictions are met). Having computationally solved the model for the base case parameter values, we then introduce various changes in parameters and compare the new steady state values with those of the base case state. The qualitative results of these comparative dynamic exercises are summarized in Box 9.6 and discussed below.

For comparative purposes, we do one experiment with the manufacturing sector removed so that the peasants produce only food while the public good is paid for by taxes. Consider in this case an increase in the productivity parameter for food production. When this happens, peasants get a rise in income and choose to have more children, which sets the family formation externality in operation. When the new equilibrium is reached after many generations, the net effect is a rise in the number of families with the same per capita food production. However, more families implies a larger tax base, which causes an increase in tax revenue and hence an increase in the stock of the public good. This continues until the larger additions due to the larger current tax revenues just balance the increased depreciation from the larger stock. Thus, unlike the one-sector model, peasants do gain from a once-for-all increase in productivity, but only because the rise in population causes a rise in aggregate tax revenue and hence an increase in the equilibrium stock of the public good. Similarly, when general equilibrium effects are taken into account, a rise in the tax rate that lowers the disposable income of the present generation ends up making future generations better off because they return to the initial level of per capita food consumption but with access to a larger stock of public goods.

When the productivity parameter grows at a constant positive rate, there is a once-for-all increase in per capita food consumption. Because there is also a continual rise in population, there is a continual rise in aggregate tax revenue and hence a positive rate of accumulation of the public good. Now, in spite of the family formation externality, peasants experience a continual increase in living standards because of the continual growth in the amount of the public good.

Box 9.6. Results for the Three-Sector Model

	Family size	Number of families	Population	Food per person	Manufacturing output per household	Stock of public good	Household income without public good	National income	Total household utility	Utility without public good
Increase productivity in manufacturing $\Delta B > 0$	–	–	–	+	+	–	+	+	+	+
Increase productivity in agriculture $\Delta A > 0$	+	+	+	–	–	+	–	+	+	–
Decrease productivity of children $\Delta z > 0$	–	–	–	+	+	–	+	–	+	+
Tax rate rises $\Delta T > 0$	–	–	–	+	+	+	–	–	+	–

Increase in Agricultural Productivity

We now replace the manufacturing sector and again consider a once-for-all increase in the productivity of agriculture in this three-sector model. The results may seem surprising.[29] Initially, as in the one- and two-sector models, agents want more children because they have more income, but this sets the family formation externality in motion. The family is also induced to allocate more resources to the now more productive agricultural sector by taking adult resources out of manufacturing. Population continues to grow until, in the new steady state, family per capita food production is *less than it was initially*, as are the survival rate of children and the marriage rate of adults. Family production of manufactured goods is also reduced. The only variable positively contributing to family utility is the public good, which has increased in size because of the increase in the tax base following the increase in population.

What is the source of the difference between the results of this model and the two-sector version with no manufacturing? In all the models, equilibrium requires that the birth rate be such that population is constant. Unless there is change in the survival or marriage rates, this requires that the birth rate return to its original, pre-shock, level. In the one-sector model and in this model with no manufacturing, the only effect of an exogenous increase in agricultural productivity is to increase parents' desire for children. When food consumption returns to its original level in both cases, a new steady state is established in which all micro variables are unchanged except that there are more families and hence a larger population. There is, however, an additional effect to consider in the full Model 3. The increase in agricultural productivity shifts labour out of manufacturing into agriculture, something that was impossible when there was only one sector in which the family could work. So when per capita food income is driven down to its original pre-shock level, the family wishes to allocate more labour to agriculture, thus having a higher per capita food income, and more children than in the original equilibrium. The only way, therefore, that the birth rate can be returned to its required level is for per capita income to be driven below its initial level.[30] So, an increase in agricultural productivity has two effects: (*a*) it lowers real family income measured by the consumption of food and manufactured goods; and (*b*) it increases utility through an increased stock of the public good.

Increase in Manufacturing Productivity

For our next experiment, we increase productivity in manufacturing relative to the base case. The results are the opposite of those following from increased agricultural productivity. Initially, peasants reallocate adult labour out of agriculture into manu-

---

[29] When we first developed this three-sector model, we conjectured that it would unequivocally allow technological progress to raise welfare as long as the operation of the family formation externality was confined to agricultural production while both food and manufactured goods had positive income elasticities of demand.

[30] If the survival and marriage rates did not alter, the birth rate would have to return to exactly its pre-shock level. However, as income falls below its pre-shock level the survival and marriage rates both fall so the equilibrium birth rate is re-established by a combination of smaller families, lower survival, and lower marriage rates.

facturing and this lowers per capita food production and desired family size. The family formation externality now operates in reverse. The population falls until, in the new steady state, family size, number of families, and population all decrease. The per capita consumption of food and the per family consumption of the manufactured good both increase.

Decrease in Children's Productivity

For a third experiment, we impose a decrease in the productivity of children in food production. Parents now want fewer children and this fall in family size puts the family formation externality into reverse. In the new steady state, family size, number of families, and population are all decreased, while the consumption of food per person and manufactured goods per family are both increased, and the stock of the public good falls due to the decline in the tax base.

Increase in the Tax Rate

For a fourth experiment, we increase the tax rate, but constrain it to be less than the level that maximizes total tax revenues. Another seemingly perverse result emerges. A tax increase that hurts the present generation turns out to be advantageous to future generations. The additional tax causes parents to reduce family size, and now family formation falls. Since there is a reduction in the productivity of labour in agriculture (net of the tax on agricultural production), parents allocate less effort to food production and more to manufactured goods. So after population has adjusted, per capita income measured in the consumption of both food and manufactured goods is increased but consumption of the public good falls—probably a welfare increasing trade-off for most peasants most of the time. The end result is fewer families of smaller size, a smaller population, more food per person, more manufactured goods per family, and a smaller stock of the public good.

Taxation to provide public goods raises welfare without increasing the size of family and hence provides a means of raising real income while avoiding the family formation externality. It also allows a steady increase in productivity to be taken out at least partly in a steady increase in living standards (even if not in per capita food consumption), which does not happen in the case of the one-sector model.[31] This is an interesting conclusion, because as we have already observed, public goods have been important throughout history.[32] This result provides another excellent example of how misleading the results of partial equilibrium analysis can be. When population is held constant, the present generation of peasants lose from any increase in the tax rate because their disposable income falls. But when population adjusts, the

---

[31] This is a point also made forcibly by Jones (1988).

[32] Of course, some fraction of the public goods expenditure may serve to lower death rates and raise birth rates. All we require, however, is that some fraction does not. In any case, we suspect that such connections are much stronger today, due to the importance of spending on health and environment, than they were in earlier times.

disposable income of future generations is restored (while their consumption of the public good rises).

A related source of continually rising real income is productivity improvements in turning units of food into units of the public good. If the productivity of this process improves continually, the stock of public goods, and hence the collective utility that it provides, will grow continually for any given level of taxation.[33]

VI. OTHER POSSIBLE DETERMINANTS OF FERTILITY

We now turn to the second issue raised earlier in this chapter: the importance of our assumption that families have a positive income elasticity of demand for children at all levels of income. So far, we have constructed all our models on the assumption that desired family size is a function of parents' per capita income and that the birth rate can be varied to give effect to this desire. It is possible that the first of these basic assumptions is wide of the mark empirically.

One possibility is that the size of family reacted to influences that varied with the size of the population, either directly or through some chain of related intermediate variables. To illustrate the consequences of this assumption, we use the simplest possible direct effect. This is obtained by adding to the utility function a term that makes desired family size a decreasing function of population, *ceteris paribus.*[34] When the models are solved with this one alteration, a rise in agricultural productivity causes an immediate rise in both per capita food consumption and the number of children. Family formation rises over the generations but this now sets up two forces that cause family size to fall back to what is needed to hold population constant: (*a*) per capita income starts to fall; and (*b*) population starts to rise. In the new steady state, family size is lower than it was originally because of the increased population density. Per capita food consumption is increased as is the family's consumption of manufacturing goods. The survival rate of children and the marriage rate of adults are both higher but these are more than offset by the smaller family size. Thus, increases in productivity now lead to an increase both in population and in per capita family income.

Could such a force be found in reality at any time over the last 1,500 years? In the early part of the Middle Ages, new land was being cleared so that increases in population did not imply increased density of habitation. Later, when most available land was under cultivation, increased population did require increased density of cultivation with less land per person and more pressure on public goods such as the

---

[33] In so far as tax revenue is spent on welfare, as much of the church's revenue was spent, we will not get these results. Tax-financed welfare payments take the ability to purchase food from some families and give it to others. So total purchases of food are unchanged and there is no overall effect on living standards. Our results depend on the amount of the tax revenue that is spent on a public good (or in Model 3, the revenue could also be spent on the manufacturing good).

[34] The term that gives a diminishing marginal utility of children, $-q(p + h_i)^\gamma$ in equation (9.11), is made to shift towards less utility as population grows by replacing the parameter, q, by a term that is a decreasing function of the total population, $q_t = \psi(P_{t-1})^\zeta$. See Appendix 9.2 for the complete description of this change in the model.

village mill and blacksmith facilities. Then it is possible that the congestion associated with rising population density did act to restrain births. A similar result occurs if the death rate rises as the population density rises. This could be the result of externalities in public health caused by factors such as pressure on limited water and sanitation resources or public health facilities.

Another way in which increasing density of population might lead to a decline in the birth rate is if the reduced opportunities associated with increased population density reduced the marriage rate. In this case, the birth rate of married couples need not change but there are fewer married couples for any given size of population. Now a rise in agricultural productivity has similar effects to those outlined above, except that the effect of increased population density works to reduce the birth rate indirectly through a reduction of the marriage rate with the same effect on population dynamics.

There is yet another possibility that depends on the rate of emigration. Increased density of population, with the congestion and decline of opportunities for new entrants to the labour force that it implies, could lead to increased emigration— either to cities earlier in the period[35] or to the colonies later in the period. Once overseas colonies had been established by the European nations, emigration provided an important safety valve to relieve the effects of overpopulation. The story of the effect of an increase in agricultural productivity is then just as seen above, except that the increased population density works through the emigration rate rather than the birth or marriage rates.

In all these cases, an increase in agricultural productivity leads to both a rise in population and a rise in living standards. The Malthusian spectre is seen partly in the unintended reduction in living standards over what each family originally intended because of the operation of the family formation externality. But it is not a complete reversal since some increase in living standards is sustained, the amount depending on how much the rates of birth, death, marriage, or emigration respond, either directly or indirectly, to the increased density of population.

So an important topic for further research is to locate any forces that limited the desired size of family and were directly or indirectly related to population density. In the mean time, we can do no more than list this as one of the possibilities of how extensive growth could result in some intensive growth—a possibility that should at the very least refute the common presumption that neo-Malthusian theories are the only game in town.

VII. THE IMPORTANCE OF USING A CES PRODUCTION FUNCTION

We economists are so used to employing constant elasticity of substitution (CES) production functions because of their analytical tractability that we often forget

---

[35] In so far as peasants were bound to the land, this would require escape, which became increasingly common as time went by.

some of their very unrealistic properties. In many applications, these can be ignored without serious implications, but this is not so in the present case. Indeed, the assumption of a Cobb–Douglas aggregate production function (or indeed any constant elasticity function) biases the results in at least two unrealistic ways.

First, the marginal products of all variable inputs always remain positive in any CES production function, never reaching zero for any finite ratio of the variable inputs. One result is that all land is used no matter how small the labour force. In a world in which land is extended over real space and movement through that space is costly in time and money, there will be a finite maximum amount of land that is economical for each peasant family to use, even if land were free. Indeed, we know that after the Black Death reduced the overall European population dramatically, large tracts of land were transferred to pasture or allowed to revert to their natural state.

Second, the marginal product of any factor declines from the outset in all CES functions, including Cobb–Douglas. This is a highly unrealistic assumption. In practice, there are substantial indivisibilities in the inputs of agricultural labour. People come in indivisible units and the land they work on is extended over space. Both these characteristics create fixed costs of moving from one job to another and hence increase marginal returns to labour over some range of labour input (as is assumed in any introductory textbook).

Now consider the effects on choice of family size with each type of production function, assuming a one-sector economy for simplicity of analysis. When faced with a CES production function, parents whose only concern was their per capita consumption would elect to have no children, even if children were as productive as adults (i.e. even if $z = 1$ in Models 2 and 3). Thus the only way to create a positive demand for children is to give them some direct utility value, as we did in all our models.

In contrast, when the production function has the range of increasing marginal returns to labour, as we would always expect it to have in agricultural settings, parents who were only concerned with per capita consumption and derived no direct utility from their children would want a family size that maximizes average income. This explanation of how parents would choose the size of their family is different from the one in our models—and in all other models of endogenous population where parents are assumed to value children for the direct utility that they confer. It makes family size depend on the production function alone. If we assume for illustrative purposes (as we did in Model 1) that children are as productive as adults, the desired size of family occurs where the marginal productivity of children is falling and that of the last child equals the average product of the whole family.[36] This is shown in Figure 9.2, where L_1 is the desired family size, while Box 9.7 shows a worked example.

---

[36] The condition for the maximizing number of children is a little more complex when children are less productive than their parents.

Box 9.7. Equations for a Range of Increasing Returns to Labour

Let the production function for each peasant family be:

$$f = A(bL^2 + cL^3)$$

where f is food, L is labour, A is a productivity parameter, and $c < 0 < b$.
The marginal and average products are:

$$MP = A(2bL + 3cL^2)$$

and

$$AP = A(bL + cL^2)$$

Average product is a maximum where:

$$\frac{dAP}{dL} = A(b + 2cL) = 0$$

or

$$L = \frac{-b}{2c}$$

which is independent of A.

Note that both marginal and average products eventually became zero, which is what we would expect when each peasant has a finite amount of land to cultivate.

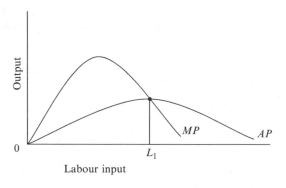

Figure 9.2. *A range of increasing returns to labour*

Now consider how a model with this type of production function would behave. First, a rise in productivity could have any possible effect on desired family size, depending on how it shifted the production function. For example, if every point on the marginal and average productivity curves shown in Figure 9.2 shifts up proportionately, the labour input that maximizes per capita income, and thus the desired size of family, remains unchanged. This is the case for any production function where productivity is shown by a constant multiple applying to the whole function, $Af(L)$. Increases in productivity then lead to increases in real income with the average size of family unchanged. If the intersection point shifts left, the desired family size decreases; if it shifts right, desired size increases.

Second, consider what happens if the desired family size that maximizes family per capita consumption is such that population is increasing. The consequences cannot now be handled by a model that employs a single aggregate production function. Each family unit has its own production function and newly formed families must find new land to work, or else existing land must be subdivided. In the former case, population can go on growing at constant per capita incomes as long as new land is available, as it was for much of the early part of the period in question. Indeed, if the new land that is made available because of the invention of such things as the heavy plough is more productive than existing land, per capita income can rise. In the latter case in which new land is no longer available, existing land must be subdivided among more and more families. The optimal size of family will then shrink as the land available to be cultivated by each family shrinks. In this case, the population will reach an equilibrium when the size of holding is such that the size of family that is optimal for each holding is just sufficient to hold population constant. If the production functions of each family obey constant returns to scale, a proportionate reduction in land and labour inputs will lead to no change in average output per unit of labour, thus leaving living standards unchanged. If there are scale effects due to indivisibilities over the relevant range of inputs, per capita output may fall.

These are dramatic results. If we assume a production function in closer agreement with the facts than any CES function, and also assume that children are valued only for their contribution to family production, we find that increases in productivity lead to increases in living standards even in a one-sector model.

What such a theory leaves unexplained is the gradual increase in the population of Europe over the period in question, which went from about 27 million in 700 to about 140 million in 1750, a rate of increase of about 0.16 per cent per annum or about 0.5 per cent per generation.[37] Given our base case values of a children's survival rate and the propensity of adults to marry, about 40 per cent of all children born alive will marry in the next generation. This requires that families have on average about five live births to produce two who will marry in the next generation, hence holding population constant. An average of about 5.025 children will lead to an increase in population of 0.5 per cent per generation. If we allow for two major outbreaks of the Black Death that decimated the population, an overall growth rate of 0.766 per cent will produce the observed population increase between the two end points. A slightly larger family size is then required to produce the observed rate of population increase over the whole period. This is not far off from the sketchy evidence on family size. If we add two equilibrating forces that operate when the rate

---

[37] Estimates vary considerably but for our overall purpose the variations are not overly important. These two figures are from M.K. Bennett in *The World's Food* as quoted in Slicher (1963: 78).

of growth of population outstrips the rate of growth of productivity, we can get even closer to an explanation. Land may be subdivided, which lowers the optimum size of family and slows the population growth rate, and there may be increased emigration to the cities, which slows the rate of rural family formation. These back-of-the-envelope calculations are not meant to be conclusive but they do cast doubt on the belief that the observed data for European population growth require a Malthusian explanation.

VIII.   WHAT HAVE WE LEARNT?

- It is important to distinguish the behaviour of individual families from the behaviour of the whole economy. Theories that require that all observed macro relations mirror the choices of individual families miss many of the mechanisms that can influence the relation between extensive and intensive growth.

- There can be Malthusian macro results without any Malthusian micro behaviour. For example, the family formation externality requires only that parents have a positive income elasticity of demand for children. Then as long as any increase in income, induced by an increase in productivity or anything else, leads to any increase in desired family size—and there are no other equilibrating forces that work alongside the externality—the formation of new families over the generations will lead to an increase in population, which will eventually eat up any increase in food production.

- Family size and real income can move in the opposite direction from population. Thus it is possible to have larger families living at a higher real income but with a smaller population because there are fewer families.

- Given the uneven distribution of landholdings, the existence of some famine in times of poor crops is consistent both with a large proportion of the rural population living above the subsistence level and with that proportion increasing over time as increasing productivity raises average incomes.

- Because of the family formation externality, it is possible to explain a floor level of income that is not at the subsistence level. In our model, this depends on the following factors: the infant survival rate, the propensity for adults to marry, the utility of consumption relative to the direct utility of children in combination with the productivity of children relative to adults, and the savings rate.

- Because of the operation of the family formation externality, changes that lower real income in the short run can act to raise it in the long run. Examples are: increased taxation, which is used to create public goods that are of genuine value to ordinary families; a fall in agriculture productivity, which shifts productive effort towards manufactured goods; a fall in the productivity of children; and child labour laws, which restrict the use of children in production.

- In any situation in which children are valued for their contribution to output and the marginal productivity of labour declines from the outset (e.g. in any CES production function or its truncated short-run version, $Y = L^\alpha$), per capita family income is maximized when the number of children is zero. Thus there must be a desire for children separate from their contribution to production to explain why parents have any positive number of children. The obvious assumption to make in the above case is that children are valued for their own sake, or as we put it, they confer a direct utility to their parents.

- Another assumption is then required to prevent the size of family increasing until the marginal utility of children is zero. The obvious assumption here is that children also imply some cost that tends to limit family size. If this 'cost' limitation is that children reduce per capita consumption, *ceteris paribus*, then the family formation externality always exists. Whenever there is an increase in income, there is an increase in desired family size and the externality operates in subsequent generations.

- The strongest Malthusian-type results come from one-sector models. Public goods and any good that does not affect the family's decisions on family size can cause real income to rise without Malthusian pressures being exerted. In our model, this works because the operative limitation on family size is the effect on per capita food consumption. The ability to consume more manufactured or public goods does not lead to an increase in family size.

- If there are checks on the decision to increase family size other than the negative effect of additional children on family per capita consumption, the effect of the family formation externality is weakened. For example, increasing population density may lead, either directly or indirectly through some chain of intermediate variables, to a reduction in the number of adults who marry (either because fewer children are born, more die during childhood, fewer adults decide to marry, or more emigrate from the rural setting). If so, an increase in income due to a rise in agricultural productivity will leave per capita income above its original level but below the level initially achieved after the productivity increase.

- The commonly used CES production function has two counterfactual properties that strongly influence the results of any model that uses it. First, the marginal product of each input only approaches zero asymptotically so that no matter how small are the supplies of labour and capital, all land will always be cultivated. Thus the function cannot handle situations such as followed the Black Death when the drastic reduction in the rural population caused much land to go uncultivated, being used for pasture or reverting to its natural state. Second, the marginal product of each input falls for any positive value of that input. Indivisibilities of any sort such as those connected with the indivisibility of humans, the physical extension of land combined with positive cost of movement, imply a range of increasing returns.

- If there is a range of increasing returns to labour before diminishing returns set in, as argued in any first-year economics textbook, and if the point of maximum average returns is at more than two units of labour, a positive number of children is required to maximize real per capita income. In this case, the assumption that children confer a direct utility to their parents is not necessary to explain the decision to have children. (The same is also true if children do confer direct utility but the direct marginal utility of an extra child, measured in units of agricultural output, is less than the marginal contribution of an added child to per capita output.) In either case, the desired number of children may not increase when productivity increases. There are then no Malthusian forces to weaken the income-enhancing effects of increases in productivity.

APPENDIX 9.1. HISTORICAL RECORD ON THE CONTROL OF FAMILY SIZE

In this Appendix we present a very brief summary of the historical record on the widespread knowledge and practice of methods of controlling family size that appears to have existed in the West at least since the earliest civilizations.

The Ancient World

Nomadic societies have much lower birth rates than settled societies. Births are spread much further apart. Breastfeeding, which tends to inhibit ovulation, is typically sustained for several years. This long period of energy loss, plus constant movement, tends to keep nursing mothers below the critical level of body fat typically needed for conception. The result is births spread three to four years apart even without any other form of birth control. Thus, societies in the hunter-gatherer stage seldom needed to fear Malthusian positive population checks, unless sudden shifts in environment dramatically lowered their food supplies, which is a non-Malthusian event.

There is substantial evidence of birth control and infanticide in Mesopotamian and Egyptian societies. One of the earliest dated documents mentioning specific birth control techniques comes from the Kuhn gynaecological papyrus of about 1850 BC.[38] Some of the many contraceptive pessaries described therein include acacia gum. As Riddle, Estes, and Russel (1994: 31) observe: 'Modern researchers have found acacia to be spermatocidal. When compounded, it produces the lactic acid anhydride, which is used in modern contraceptive jellies.' The document also mentions three different methods of birth control: an application of a gummy substance to cover the 'mouth of the womb', a substance made of honey and sodium carbonate that was applied to the inside of the vagina, and a pessary made from crocodile dung. Prolonged lactation of up to three years was also used as an Egyptian birth control device. There is scanty evidence about family size but it seems to have been too small in the nuclear families of Mesopotamia to suggest an absence of all attempts to control birth. For example, families recorded on the 'census list' in Harran, the upper Euphrates River, had an average of 1.43 children (Snell 1997: 81).

The Classical World

At the height of their civilization, the Greeks managed quite small families through a combination of birth control, abortion, and infanticide. Greek historian Polybius (*c.*200–118 BC) indicates that couples limited themselves to one or two children.

---

[38] Although this is long after the invention of Egyptian writing, it is not long after its use for non-economic matters. It took many centuries after writing was developed to record economic transactions, before it spread to record other matters. So the date of this document does not tell us the earliest times at which birth control knowledge was propounded. It only tells us that one of the earliest non-economic uses of writing was to record birth control information.

The contraception properties of certain plants were known in Greece as far back as the seventh century BC (Riddle, Estes, and Russel 1994: 30). The contraceptive effects of a plant named siliphion were documented by the Greek botanist, Theophrastus (*c*.370–288 BC). This plant was so well known for its contraceptive and abortifacient properties that prices were significantly increased due to demand and, by the first century AD, it was worth 'more than its weight in silver' (Riddle, Estes, and Russel 1994: 30). Unfortunately, siliphion only grew in a strip of land about 125 miles long and 35 miles wide near the coastal city of Cyrene (located in modern-day Libya) and did not respond to attempts to cultivate it in various areas throughout Greece. The demand for siliphion was so great that it became extinct some time during the third or second century BC.

Although siliphion was harvested to extinction, other plants also proved to have contraceptive and abortifacient properties. A close relative of siliphion, but not quite as effective, was the asafoetida plant. Many ancient writers on the subject of gynaecology, including Hippocrates, declare the effectiveness of these plants and several other 'potions' used for both contraceptive and abortifacient practices. Other plants that were commonly used were the seeds of Queen Anne's lace, willow, date palm, pomegranate, pennyroyal, artemisia, myrrh, and rue. Some of these plants were toxic but ancients knew the proportions that could be safely consumed (Riddle, Estes, and Russel 1994: 30–1). Modern studies have proved that many of these plants are indeed effective contraceptives. For example, evidence suggests that Queen Anne's lace seeds are an effective post-coital anti-fertility agent. It is still used today as a contraceptive by women in India and in the Appalachian Mountains of North Carolina.

Sexual practices that did not result in conception, such as oral, anal, and homo-sexual intercourse, were also common throughout the ancient world. They were not condemned until the medieval Church accepted the doctrine that procreation was the God-ordained function of sexual intercourse (Riddle 1992: 5).

Roman experience was similar to that of the Greeks and, of course, much influenced by them. Contraception, abortion, and infanticide were commonly practised in ancient Rome. Too many children could fragment the family property as each child inherited equal portions of the family's estate. (Female shares were in the form of a dowry.)

The Roman Empire was a time of high prosperity by all historical standards. According to Riddle, Estes, and Russel (1994: 34) the anthropologist J. Lawrence Angel found evidence that 'people were living longer during the pre-Christian centuries from the second millennium until about the first century AD'. At the same time the population within the bounds of the Roman Empire began a decline that lasted until the dissolution of the Western Empire. The population of Europe is estimated to have declined from 32.8 million to 27.5 million during the first five centuries of the first millennium AD. (Riddle, Estes, and Russel 1994: 34).

Further evidence is provided by Angel's study of the average number of births per woman, showing its fall from 5.0 in 2000 BC to 4.7 in 1500 BC, 4.1 in 1150 BC, 3.6 in 330 BC, and 3.3 in AD 120.

Again according to Riddle, Estes, and Russel (1994: 34), Angel and Bisel's data show 'that birth rates in Roman times had fallen below what was necessary to maintain the population'. It appears that adult lifespans rose over the period while the number of births fell. The decline in births appears to track the fall in the death rate that occurred as living conditions improved through the centuries of Greek and Roman civilizations. This is evidence that births were being adjusted by the family in response to what was for them an exogenous fall in the death rate, with the object of controlling family size.

The killing of unwanted children has been a method of population control as far back as one can discern—although discussion of the method was sometimes suppressed. In Rome, newborn children could be sold, killed, exposed to the elements, and, in the case of deformed children, drowned. In a letter written in 1 BC, a husband instructs his pregnant wife, 'if it is a boy keep it, if a girl discard it,' and the Roman poet Juvenal mentions children 'abandoned beside cesspools' (Rose 1997). In AD 374, exposure became illegal although still often practised (Adkins and Adkins 1997: 340).

In the face of the evidence briefly sketched here, we must agree with Riddle, Estes, and Russel (1994: 34) that historical demographic studies show that peoples of the ancient and classical West regulated family size quite effectively.

The Middle Ages

Quantitative evidence on infanticide is provided for England by Russell, who uses burial site excavations to argue that infant mortality, particularly among females, was related to economic variables.[39] During the four subperiods that Russell studies (1–350, 351–540, 541–750, and 751–1000) the number of males per 100 females was 129, 113, 122, and 132. Assuming the number at birth was close to 100, this suggests a loss of females in each period of 18.7, 7.1, 13.8, and 25.9 per cent. 'It is quite possible that the 7.1 percent of girls born in the plague period might have died naturally amid plague conditions. It is very unlikely that the higher rates of the other three periods occurred without human interference with the lives of children'[40] (Russell 1985: 158).

Although the Christian Church opposed infanticide as a method of controlling family size, 'if the excuse of poverty was given, the penance was not very heavy' (Russell 1985: 158). Russell (1985: 159) argues that the choice of infanticide was conditioned on economics: 'Medieval folk, knowing their environment, also knew of their chances for a good life. Unlike today, the "right to life" was not as important as the right to a good life'. The archaeological evidence gathered from grave site excavations for the first millennium AD shows that surviving children were neither

---

[39] Parkin (1992) argues that these data from burial sites are unreliable because it is difficult if not impossible to tell male from female using pre-pubescent skeletons. However, other material evidence and writings confirm the widespread use of infanticide and exposure over the millennia.

[40] There was a widespread plague in Europe during the period 540–750, although the precise nature of the disease is unknown.

malnourished nor disease-ridden and Russell argues that, while the practice was brutish, infanticide allowed surviving children 'good conditions for growth'.[41] Further evidence that control of family size extended to all sectors of society is that wealthy households tended to have more children than poorer families during medieval and renaissance times (Riddle 1992: 3; Roberts 1993: 437–8).

The Early Modern Period

There is well-documented evidence that family size was a choice variable in England in the early modern period. It relates to two sets of evidence: on marriage and on the production of live children.

According to Wrigley et al. (1997), a newly married couple in Western Europe was expected to establish a new household. Big fixed costs were associated with household formation. Males needed substantial human and some financial capital. Apprenticeship or service in husbandry were means of obtaining these. Females had to be able to run the domestic household. This required that they learn the necessary skills of food preparation, garment making, and all other aspects of household management in a long apprenticeship with the older females in their household.

To establish a new household involved substantial initial expense and a relatively high level of continuing cost. In most cases it meant the purchase, or acquisition in other ways, of such things as pots, pans, fire irons, mugs, platters, cutlery, chairs, tables, chests, beds, and bed linen as well as the ability to meet rent payments or their equivalent. (Wrigley et al. 1997: 123)

In many other societies 'a couple on marriage joined an existing household and the husband might wait many years before becoming the head' (Wrigley et al. 1997: 123). These sociological differences produced several important contrasts between the West and other societies.[42] First, Western marriage tended to come later in life, after the requisites had been provided—much later than other societies where marriage tended to come soon after physical maturity.[43] Second, a significant portion of the population, males and females, never married. This contrasts sharply with other societies in which few people remained single after reaching sexual maturity. Third, the age of marriage tended to vary with overall economic circumstances that influenced the speed with which an individual could become economically independent.[44] Although the data in Wrigley et al. refers to the early modern period, the practices to which they refer were also common in the medieval period.

---

[41] Of course, infanticide might also have been motivated by subsistence living. Our point is only that people had the knowledge of how to control family size and acted on that knowledge.

[42] As always we may wonder if there is some hidden economic reason why these sociological differences evolved. But whatever their origins, they provide a proximate explanation of the differences in nuptiality.

[43] According to Wrigley et al. (1997: 122): 'Hollingsworth has shown that in late Tutor and Stuart times the daughters of noble families married young, with a preponderance of teenage brides, though by the mid eighteenth century elite practice had ceased to diverge so markedly from the national norm [of much later marriage].' This fits the explanation of late marriages of ordinary people since the daughters of nobles would not have the same economic constraints as ordinary people, nor would their suitors.

[44] Macfarlane (1997) provides evidence that the practices of controlling age of marriage, birth control, and infanticide were also deeply ingrained in Japanese culture.

The net effect of these institutional differences seems to have been not only later marriages but fewer children per married couple. Macfarlane's evidence supports this view. Fertility rates were lower on average in England than in the rest of the world. The average in England was around 30 per 1,000, while 'a normal pre-industrial society' averaged 45 per 1,000. Wrigley and Schofield (1981) provide evidence that in much of Europe during the seventeenth and eighteenth centuries, women were on average marrying for the first time at the age of twenty-six or older. The overall effect was to lower the average birth rate and to make it sensitive to economic conditions. Our interpretation of Wrigley and Schofield's evidence is that there is both a short-term and long-term relationship between marriage and births.

Evidence from the parish registers shows a fairly constant rate of first births from one to ten months after marriage. At this point, the rate of firstborns drops quickly. We explain this data as follows. In rural society, children are an important input into the family production function. When couples strike out on their own in an agricultural world, marriages must produce a sufficient number of children. A simple insurance policy guaranteeing fertility for couples entering into marriage is to get pregnant prior to marriage. So courting couples had sexual intercourse and, if the female got pregnant, the couple could safely marry. If not, each party could look elsewhere for a fertile partner.[45] The data that Wrigley and Schofield present is consistent with this type of information problem. Thus we argue that their data reveals a short-term relationship between fertility and marriage. Couples seeking to enter marriage sought to get pregnant as a precondition of the marriage.[46]

The long-term relationship that Wrigley and Schofield argue is readily borne out by their data that the later a couple married, the fewer children they had.

A sharp rise in marriage age or in the proportion never marrying therefore implied a matching fall in fertility as the proportion of the fertile period that the average woman spent in marriage fell. ... [A] rise in nuptiality in the eighteenth century was sufficient to increase fertility by about fifty percent from its low point in the middle of the seventeenth century. (Wrigley and Schofield 1981: 175–6)

Birth Control Goes Underground

In the late medieval period, medicine came increasingly into the hands of university-trained doctors, while the preparation of drugs passed into the hands of the guild of apothecaries. Neither doctors nor apothecaries were trained in birth control techniques. At the same time, treatises on birth control were no longer commonly written. As a result, birth control knowledge was transferred from the literary traditions in the public domain to oral traditions passed on by midwives and ordinary women, both of whom were usually illiterate. Nonetheless, as Wrigley

[45] It is worth noting that this practice implies a much higher rate of infertility among unmarried women compared with the entire population.

[46] Wrigley and Schofield look for a spike in births 9–10 months after marriage and do not find one. This would be evidence of the absence of a short-term relationship only if marriage typically preceded the attempt to become pregnant.

and Schofield's data strongly suggests, birth control continued to be practised in many circles, although the knowledge ceased to be publicly available and hence was no doubt denied to some.

The enclosures and the Industrial Revolution caused a major shift in population away from the villages whose tight social support system of relatives and neighbours helped to keep birth control knowledge alive. In the social upheaval of the migration to the cities, most of the existing social support systems were destroyed and it took time before new ones evolved.[47] Before this could happen, it is quite likely that some of the birth control knowledge was lost to many midwives and working-class mothers. Certainly there was a perceived need in the later part of the nineteenth century to bring birth control knowledge to working-class wives.

Our survey leads us to conclude that the balance of evidence favours the assumption that family size (at least in the West) has almost always been a choice variable. It has been controlled by methods that have varied somewhat over the millennia, but which typically include varying the age of marriage, sexual practices that do not result in conception, an array of birth control techniques, abortion, and infanticide (by which we mean bringing about the death of a newborn child either directly by killing it or indirectly by such means as exposure).[48]

We have concentrated on the prevalence of methods to control family size. However, where direct evidence on family size is available, it suggests that throughout the last 2,000 years in the West, the average number of children per family was less than would be expected if no attempt had been made to control it.[49] For example, Livi-Bacci (1997: 13) estimates the maximum total fertility per woman at sixteen. Yet, according to him, the only society that came close to producing such a large number of children per couple was the Hutterites of the Canadian Prairies in the nineteenth century. The fertility rates found there were around ten children per female. All this evidence conflicts with the following hypotheses:

---

[47] In the tight societies of villages, people supported extended families and close friends by providing food in time of need, care in times of sickness, 'babysitting' when needed, and much sharing of the wisdom of experience, particularly from older to younger persons. These support systems were destroyed when people left the villages but were eventually reconstructed in the slums of the great industrial towns, as shown, for example, in Young, Dunlop, and Willmott (1957).

[48] Parkin (1992) argues that many investigators confuse direct killing, which he calls infanticide, and indirect methods, which include exposure. For our purposes, all methods of ending a newborn infant's life by conscious decision can be grouped under the single heading, which for convenience we call 'infanticide'.

[49] Note that lags in learning allow rational choice of family size to be compatible with people continuing to choose a birth rate that pushes population towards subsistence after some exogenous event alters the environment. To illustrate, let there be some rapid change in circumstances, such as medical advances, that cause the death rate to fall rapidly. It may take a substantial time for attitudes and behaviour patterns that were appropriate to the old regime to be discarded and for those appropriate to the new regime to be understood and then adopted. In the mean time, population may rise dramatically. The most obvious example is the introduction of modern medicine to the less developed world where high birth rates had been needed to produce sufficient children to work the farm and sufficient adult offspring to provide for the parents' old age.

1. Because of high death rates people were able to raise fewer children than desired (Easterlin 1998).
2. Out of ignorance or design parents made no attempt to control family size (Malthusians).
3. Desired family size exceeded what could be supported at a subsistence level so that its size was controlled at that level and, as a consequence, it rose along a trend line as increases in productivity increased the number of children who would be supported at subsistence over the medieval and early modern period (Galor and Weil 2000; other neo-Malthusians).

APPENDIX 9.2. FORMAL MODELS OF POPULATION DYNAMICS

In this appendix we lay out the formal construction of our models with a minimum of interpretative discussion. In order to make it self-contained, there is some duplication between it and the chapter's main text and boxes.

A.I. MODEL 1: INDIVIDUAL HOUSEHOLD

Our first model concerns the behaviour of a single family. We make the following assumptions:

- It takes two adults to make a family, which is endowed with an exogenously determined amount of time and an endogenously accumulated amount of capital to allocate to food production.
- Children are raised at no direct time cost.
- Parents care only about their own utility and that of their children while they are at home. Parents' utility varies directly with the family's per capita consumption and the number of children in the family, the direct marginal utility of which, diminishes steadily and eventually becomes negative. Both per capita income and number of children are determined by the parents' choice of family size.
- As well as adding directly to parents' utility, children are productive inputs in the family's production function but are less productive than adults. (In some of our models, we relax the assumption of heterogeneous productivity between parents and adults so that we can derive analytical solutions.)
- Thus, for a given family income, an additional child adds directly to the family's utility (up to some maximum number of children) and to the family's output, but simultaneously reduces utility by reducing the family's per capita consumption.
- The household produces and consumes a single product, food, f, under conditions of diminishing marginal returns to the variable input labour.

Our assumptions require the household's utility to be an increasing function of its size (up to some maximum number of people) and of its per capita consumption (without limit). The following is such a function:

$$u = \left(\frac{f}{p+h}\right)^{\alpha} (p+h) - q(p+h)^{\gamma}$$

$$\alpha \in (0, 1), \; \gamma \in (1, \infty), \; q \in (0, \infty) \tag{9A.2.1}$$

where f is the family's total production of food, p is parents (always equal to two), and h is the number of children in the family. The first argument shows per capita consumption and family size both contributing positively to utility. The second argument causes the marginal utility of children eventually to become negative, implying that the family will always have a finite desired size.

Simple manipulation produces the form in which we use the function:

$$u = f^{\alpha}(p+h)^{1-\alpha} - q(p+h)^{\gamma} \tag{9A.2.2}$$

The second reason for wanting children is that they contribute to family income:

$$f = A(p + zh)^{\beta} \quad \beta \in (0, 1), \; z \in (0, 1) \tag{9A.2.3}$$

A gives the combined effect of the fixed inputs of land and capital and productivity while z converts children into adult equivalents. Substituting (9A.2.3) into (9A.2.2) yields:

$$u = A^{\alpha}(p+zh)^{\beta\alpha}(p+h)^{1-\alpha} - q(p+h)^{\gamma} \tag{9A.2.4}$$

Maximizing with respect to h:

$$\frac{du}{dh} = A^{\alpha}(p+zh)^{\beta\alpha}(p+h)^{1-\alpha}\left[\frac{\beta\alpha z}{(p+zh)} + \frac{(1-\alpha)}{(p+h)}\right] - \gamma q(p+h)^{\gamma-1}$$

$$= 0 \tag{9A.2.5}$$

The first-order condition is non-linear and, therefore, neither the demand function for family size nor that for income can be explicitly derived.[50] However, for given numerical values of the parameters and initial starting values, the number of children that satisfies (9A.2.5) can be found.[51]

Analytic solutions are also possible under the assumption that $z = 1$ (i.e. children are equivalent to adults in production). Making this assumption allows for useful and explicit illustrations of some comparative static results. (Similar results are generated numerically in Section A.II where the simulated aggregate model in which z is not constrained to unity.) With $z = 1$ and $j = p + h$, we derive the demand function for family size as:

$$j = \left[\frac{A^{\alpha}(\beta\alpha + (1-\alpha))}{\gamma q}\right]^{\frac{1}{\gamma - \beta\alpha - (1-\alpha)}} \tag{9A.2.6}$$

---

[50] The problem of non-linearity is common in many models of endogenous fertility and population growth (see Rosenzweig and Stark 1997: 1141–60).

[51] A check of the second-order condition confirms that this is indeed a maximum.

Substituting j into the production function $f = Aj^\beta$, yields the demand for income:

$$f = A^{\frac{\gamma-(1-\alpha)}{\gamma-\beta\alpha-(1-\alpha)}} \left[\frac{\beta\alpha + (1-\alpha)}{\gamma q} \right]^{\frac{\beta}{\gamma-\beta\alpha-(1-\alpha)}} \qquad (9A.2.7)$$

Per capita family income is

$$\frac{f}{j} = A^{\frac{\gamma-1}{\gamma-\beta\alpha-(1-\alpha)}} \left[\frac{\beta\alpha + (1-\alpha)}{\gamma q} \right]^{\frac{\beta-1}{\gamma-\beta\alpha-(1-\alpha)}} \qquad (9A.2.8)$$

Both equations (9A.2.7) and (9A.2.8) are increasing in A. The partial derivative of f/j with respect to A is positive as long as $\gamma > 1$, which is the restriction initially imposed. This restriction implies that, as family productivity rises, or the opportunity cost of children falls, the demand for children rises but less rapidly than the demand for food, so that per capita family income also rises. In other words, there is a positive income elasticity of demand for both per capita consumption and children. The behaviour of this model is shown in Figure 9.1 and analysed on pages 305–308 of Chapter 9.

A.II. MODEL 2: A SOLOW GROWTH MODEL WITH ENDOGENOUS POPULATION

To embed the household in a model of the whole economy, we use a Solow growth model with the added assumption that the population is endogenously determined by parental choice of family size.

Assumptions

We use a model of overlapping generations and define all the model's variables in Box 9A.2.1.

- A fraction of children die before becoming adults.
- Only adults can marry; and only a fraction of these actually do marry.
- Those who do marry determine the size of their families so as to maximize their own welfare, which is a function of the number of their children and their family's per capita income, the latter being negatively related to the size of their family.
- Married couples and their children undertake all food production.
- The biological subsistence constraint is never binding on our typical household over the entire period in question. Thus, our typical household is operating to the right of the intersection point m in Figure 9.1.
- Since a child can do fraction z of the work an adult can do, the total number of adult equivalents in the agricultural labour force is the number of families in the current period, N_t, multiplied by $(p + zh_t)$.

- Families save a constant fraction, s, of their production and add it to their personal capital stock, k_t, which depreciates at a constant rate, $\delta \in (0, 1)$.

Box 9A.2.1. Parameters with Base Case Values in Parentheses

A = the constant on the production function **(500)**
β = the coefficient on labour in the production function **(0.33)**
η = the coefficient on capital in the production function **(0.33)**
α = the coefficient on per capita consumption in the utility function **(0.6)**
γ = the coefficient on children in the negative term in the utility function **(1.45)**
p = the parents of a household having children **(2)**
q = the constant on the negative term for children in the utility function **(0.5)**
d = the coefficient on the survival function **(0.07)**
m = the coefficient on the function determining the proportion of people who marry **(0.2)**
s = the savings rate **(0.1)**
δ = the depreciation rate on capital **(0.6)**
z = the constant that converts child labour into adult equivalents in the production function **(0.5)**

Total production, F_t, is a function of the labour force measured in adult equivalents and capital, with land held constant:

$$F_t = A(N_t(p + zh_t))^\beta (K_t)^\eta, \quad \beta \in (0, 1), \ \eta \in (0, 1) \tag{9A.2.9}$$

The aggregate capital stock is $K_t = N_t k_t$, where k_t evolves according to

$$k_t = \frac{N_t s f_t + (1 - \delta) N_{t-1} K_{t-1}}{N_t}$$

Food per family per period, f_t, is:

$$f_t = \frac{F_t}{N_t} = A N_t^{\beta + \eta - 1} (p + zh_t)^\beta k_t^\eta \tag{9A.2.10}$$

The utility function is the same as (9A.2.1) except for the deduction from consumption of the fraction of income that is saved and invested in the family's physical capital stock:

$$u_t = \left(\frac{(1 - s)f_t}{(p + h_t)}\right)^\alpha (p + h_t) - q(p + h_t)^\gamma \tag{9A.2.11}$$

Substituting the production function into the utility function yields:

$$u_t = [(1 - s) A N_t^{\beta + \eta - 1}(p + zh_t)^\beta (k_t)^\eta]^\alpha (p + h_t)^{(1 - \alpha)} - q(p + h_t)^\gamma \tag{9A.2.12}$$

The first-order condition for maximizing u_t with respect to h_t yields:

$$\left[(1-s)AN_t^{\beta+\eta-1}k_t^{\eta} \right]^{\alpha} (p+zh_t)^{\beta\alpha}(p+h_t)^{(1-\alpha)} \left[\frac{\beta\alpha z}{(p+zh_t)} + \frac{(1-\alpha)}{(p+h_t)} \right]$$

$$- q\gamma(p+h_t)^{\gamma-1} = 0 \tag{9A.2.13}$$

The demands for family size and food are functions of time because both are functions of N_t, which depend on the number of people born in the previous period. When $z \in (0,1)$ the non-linear nature of the model makes it difficult to derive analytically the demands for children per household and per capita food consumption. Either we can continue with the assumption of Model 1 where $z = 1$ and look for analytical solutions or we can accept the non-linearity and solve for our variables numerically for given parameter values. We choose the latter approach because we wish to allow the costs and benefits of children to vary independently of the productivity of adults.

Given any set of initial conditions, the model evolves as follows. The number of children in period $t-1$ is equal to the number of families multiplied by the number of children per family, $N_{t-1}h_{t-1}$. In any generation only a proportion, λ, of children survive to marriageable age. To be consistent with the historical experience, this survival rate is made an increasing function of per capita income:

$$\Pr(survival) = \lambda_t = 1 - e^{-d\left(\frac{f_t}{(p+h_t)}\right)} \tag{9A.2.14}$$

d is a calibration parameter chosen to produce a probability of survival of approximately 50 per cent and its value is given in Box 9A.2.1. The population in period t is related to the population in period $t-1$ as follows. Take the number of children borne in $t-1$, $N_{t-1}h_{t-1}$, and multiply it by the survival rate to get the number who survive to become adults eligible to form families in period t. To obtain the number of families actually formed, divide the eligible population by θ_t, which is the number of children who must survive to become adults in order for one family to be formed:

$$N_t = \frac{(\lambda_{t-1}N_{t-1}h_{t-1})}{\theta_t} \tag{9A.2.15}$$

If everyone marries (and the sexes are equal), $\theta_t = 2$; otherwise it is some larger number. (The value of θ_t is 2 divided by the proportion of the population who marry.) To be consistent with the findings of Wrigley et al. (1997), we make θ_t a function of per capita income:

$$\theta_t = \frac{2}{x} \tag{9A.2.16}$$

where

$$x = 1 - e^{-m\left(\frac{f_t}{(p+h_t)}\right)}$$

m is a calibration parameter set to ensure that θ_t is greater than 2 (approximately 2.3) and its value is given in Box 9A.2.1. Each adult pair now makes a single utility maximizing decision that determines the size of its family and its family's food consumption. This decision determines F_t, f_t, h_t, and $f_t/(p + h_t)$.

The total population in period t is the number of persons in families plus the number who remain single:

$$P_t = N_t(p + h_t) + S_{At} \qquad (9A.2.17)$$

where

$$S_A = \lambda_{t-1} N_{t-1} [p + h_{t-1}] e^{-m \frac{f_t}{(p + h_t)}}$$

is the number of the last period's children who survive to adulthood multiplied by the proportion who remain single. People who remain single are assumed to produce a subsistence living for themselves. They have no effect on the food production of households with children. The number of children $N_t h_t$ multiplied by the survival rate and divided by θ_t then determines the number of families in period $t + 1$ and so on.

In the steady state, $h_t = h_{t-1}, f_t = f_{t-1}$, and $N_t = N_{t-1}$.

The non-linearity in the model makes it impossible to sign any relations between variables and parameter values under general conditions. Instead, we calibrate our parameters with historically reasonable base case values. We then generate a set of comparative static results by comparing the steady state equilibrium of the calibrated model with the steady states that occur after some alteration in each of the base case values taken one at a time.

Calibration

Our base case is defined by the parameter values given in bold after the definitions in Box 9A.2.1. We calibrated the model in two ways. First, the values of those parameters that have a direct interpretation were chosen to be not inconsistent with values seen in the historical record for a starting period early in the medieval era. Land, labour, and capital were given equal weights in the production function, hence $\beta = \eta = 0.33$. The weight on capital is consistent with contemporary income shares calculated from aggregate income accounts. For much of the period in question, the capital stock comprised seed, which was a significant share of food income for the agricultural household and which had a fairly high depreciation rate, plus agricultural equipment, which had a long lifespan. The share of labour in production is chosen as a residual so that the contribution of land in production is equivalent to that of capital. We assume that parents put more utility weight on real income than on children by setting $\alpha = 0.6$. The savings rate is set at 10 per cent and the depreciation rate at 60 per cent per generation of thirty-three years (see below) or 1.43 per cent per year, $\delta = 0.60$.

Second, we chose the other parameter values, A, d, m, γ, and q, so as to give historically reasonable initial values to those endogenous variables whose absolute values had behavioural interpretations: average number of children, h, is 7.17, giving a family size of just over 9, the survival rate of children, λ, is 46 per cent, of which 83 per cent marry ($\theta = 2.4$). The other numbers for income, population, and number of families have no absolute significance as the units in which they are measured are arbitrary.

Comparative Analysis

The model was allowed to settle down in its steady state values for the base case parameter settings. We then altered the model's parameters one at time. Box 9.4 on page 312 gives the results of these experiments, which are discussed in detail in the text of Chapter 9.

A.III. MODEL 3: A THREE-SECTOR MODEL

We now add two more sectors to our Solow model. The first is a public good produced by the state and financed by taxes levied on the peasant's production of food. It is a true public good as its total stock enters into the utility functions of each peasant family. The second new commodity is a manufactured good that is produced by adult peasants who must then divide their time between two types of productive activity: food and the manufactured good. Children are only productive in agriculture. The family's total production of the manufactured good enters its utility function (in contrast with food, which is entered as a per capita figure) on the assumption that the manufactured good is non-rivalrous within the family but rivalrous as among families. The new model's parameters and their base case values are also laid out in Box 9A.2.1. (The two-sector model with agriculture and a public good is obtained by setting all of the m terms to zero.)

The household's utility function is:

$$u_t = \left[\frac{(1 - T)f_t}{(p + h_t)}\right]^\alpha (p + h_t) - q(p + h_t)^\gamma + (G_t)^\kappa + (j(m_t))^\chi \qquad (9A.2.18)$$

where T is the tax rate, G_t is the total quantity of the public good, and m_t is the quantity of the manufactured good, j is a calibration parameter, $\alpha, \kappa, \chi \in (0, 1)$ and $\gamma \in (1, \infty)$.

The aggregate and household production of food is given by (13.2) and (13.3):

$$F_t = A(N_t(p_{f,t} + zh_t))^\beta (K_t)^\eta, \quad \beta \in (0, 1), \ \eta \in (0, 1) \qquad (9A.2.19)$$

$$f_t = \frac{F_t}{N_t} = AN_t^{\beta + \eta - 1}(p_{f,t} + zh_t)^\beta k_t^\eta \qquad (9A.2.20)$$

which are equations (9A.2.9) and (9A.2.10), except that $p_{f,t}$ is the parental contribution to the household's food production. Household capital is the same as in Model 2:

$$k_t = \frac{N_t s f_t + (1 - \delta) N_{t-1} K_{t-1}}{N_t} \qquad (9A.2.21)$$

The stock of the public good is

$$G_t = nT(N_t f_t) + (1 - \varphi) G_{t-1} = nTF_t + (1 - \varphi) G_{t-1} \qquad (9A.2.22)$$

where $\varphi \in (0, 1)$ is the depreciation rate on public goods, $n > 0$ is a productivity parameter that turns the private good into a public good.

The total production, and household production of the manufactured good are given by the following:

$$M_t = B(N_t)^{\nu} (p_{m,t})^{1-\nu}, \quad \nu \in (0, 1) \qquad (9A.2.23)$$

$$m_t = \frac{M_t}{N_t} = BN_t^{\nu-1} (p_{m,t})^{1-\nu} \qquad (9A.2.24)$$

In addition, we have the following constraint:

$$p = 2 = p_{f,t} + p_{m,t} \qquad (9A.2.25)$$

Real per capita income is:

$$y_t = f_t / (2 + h_t) + w_1 G_t + w_2 (m_t) \qquad (9A.2.26)$$

where w_1 converts the public good into units of f_t and the price of m_t relative to f_t is w_2, which is equal to the ratio of the marginal product of labour in food to the marginal product of labour in manufacturing.

The three-sector model is then manipulated in the following way. Substituting (9A.2.20), (9A.2.21), and (9A.2.22) into (9A.2.18) yields:

$$u_t = \left[(1 - s - T) A N_t^{\beta + \eta - 1} (p - p_{m,t} + z h_t)^{\beta} k_t^{\eta} \right]^{\alpha} (p + h_t)^{(1-\alpha)}$$
$$- q(p + h_t)^{\gamma} + G_t^{\kappa} + \left(jBN_t^{\nu-1} \right)^{\chi} (jp_{m,t})^{\nu\chi} \qquad (9A.2.27)$$

We maximize equation (9A.2.27) by differentiating with respect to h and p_m to obtain two first-order conditions. But first we simplify (9A.2.27) by letting

$$H_t = (1 - s - T)^{\alpha} A^{\alpha} N_t^{\alpha(\beta + \eta - 1)} k_t^{\alpha\eta}$$

So that:

$$u_t = H_t (p - p_{m,t} + z h_t)^{\beta\alpha} (p + h_t)^{(1-\alpha)} - q(p + h_t)^{\gamma} + G_t^{\kappa}$$
$$+ \left(jBN_t^{\nu-1} \right)^{\chi} (jp_{m,t})^{\nu\chi} \qquad (9A.2.27)$$

The first-order conditions are:

$$\frac{\partial u_t}{\partial h_t} = \alpha\beta H_t z(p - p_{m,t} + zh_t)^{\alpha\beta - 1}(p + h_t)^{1 - \alpha}$$

$$+ (1 - \alpha)H_t(p - p_{m,t} + zh_t)^{\alpha\beta}(p + h_t)^{-\alpha} - \gamma q(p + h_t)^{\gamma - 1} = 0 \tag{9A.2.28a}$$

$$\frac{\partial u_t}{\partial p_{m,t}} = -\alpha\beta H_t(p - p_{m,t} + zh_t)^{\alpha\beta - 1}(p + h_t)^{1 - \alpha}$$

$$+ \nu\chi(BN_t^{\nu - 1})^{\chi}(jp_{m,t})^{\nu\chi - 1} = 0 \tag{9A.2.28b}$$

Now to generate a reduced form that is sufficiently tractable to allow us to simulate the optimal solution numerically, let:

$$\alpha\beta = \nu\chi \tag{9A.2.29}$$

This allows us to solve (9A.2.28b) for p_m. Substituting the solution for p_m into (9A.2.28a) and with some algebraic manipulation we get the following reduced form expression that encapsulates the two first-order conditions for the family's utility maximization:

$$\alpha\beta H_t z \left[(p + zh_t) - \frac{(p + zh_t)}{1 + j\left[\frac{j(jBN_t^{\nu - 1})^{\chi}}{H_t}\right]^{\frac{1}{\alpha\beta - 1}}} \right]^{\alpha\beta} (p + h_t)^{1 - \alpha}$$

$$+ (1 - \alpha)H_t \left[(p + zj) - \frac{(p + zh_t)}{1 + (p + h_t)^{1 - \alpha}\frac{B\chi}{H_t}} \right]^{\alpha\beta} (p + h_t)^{-\alpha} - \gamma q(p + h_t)^{\gamma - 1} = 0 \tag{9A.2.30}$$

This reduced form, first-order, optimizing condition can now be calibrated using the parameter values chosen. The numerical values of h_t that satisfy the condition are then solved computationally. These values can then be used to back out the numerical solution for $p_{m,t}$ and thus determine numerical values for the rest of the endogenous variables in the system.

We now turn to the importance of our assumption that families have a positive income elasticity of demand for children. We have constructed all our models on the assumption that desired family size is a function of parents' per capita income and that the birth rate can be varied to give effect to this desire. One possibility is that the size of family reacts to influences that vary with the size of the population. This is obtained by adding to the utility function a term that makes desired family size a decreasing function of population, *ceteris paribus*. (In the text of Chapter 9 we discuss some reasons why such a relation might hold in the real world.)

This adds a second disincentive to increasing family size. In addition to the effects of additional children lowering per capita consumption for any given income, we let the direct utility of children be negatively related to population density. Since land is fixed, this disincentive varies directly with total population, *P*. When the models are solved with this one alteration, a rise in agricultural productivity causes an immediate rise in both per capita food consumption and the number of children as usual. But in contrast to the earlier models, family size returns in equilibrium to its initial level but with a higher per capita food production compared to the initial situation.

Thus we replace q in equation (9A.2.18) by $(\psi P_{t-1})^\zeta$, where ψ and ζ are positive parameters to obtain:

$$u_t = \left[\frac{(1-s-T)f_t}{(p+h_t)}\right]^\alpha (p+h_t) - (\psi P_{t-1})^\zeta (p+h_t)^\gamma + (nG_t)^\kappa + (j(m_t))^\chi \quad (9A.2.18')$$

It is obvious from (9A.2.18) that $\dfrac{\partial u_t}{\partial P_{t-1}} < 0$

10

The Emergence of Sustained Intensive Growth in the West

In Chapter 9, we observed that the West underwent two distinct transitions in growth performance: first, the emergence of *sustained* extensive growth some time in the late eighteenth or early nineteenth century; and second, the emergence of *sustained* intensive growth later in the same century. We have argued in Chapters 7 and 8 that the West's transition to sustained extensive growth was a contingent historical event that, for very good reasons, took place first in Britain. We have further argued that it could not have happened elsewhere in Europe within, say, half a century or more, since the requisite scientific knowledge and technological expertise in mechanics that was needed took some time to be diffused from Britain. Nor could it have occurred endogenously elsewhere in the world within centuries, since none of the other civilizations were near to achieving the necessary scientific knowledge that without doubt underlay the Second Industrial Revolution and, we argue, also the First. So we did not try to model the transition to sustained intensive growth, as we know of no formal models, nor can we conceive of any, that would encompass the sort of considerations that explain why Europe made the transition while China and the Islamic countries did not. Such a model would have to predict sustained growth to occur first in Britain, then in the rest of the West, particularly Western Europe and the USA, but not elsewhere. The first non-western country to industrialize was Japan, and interesting issues are raised as to why that country of all others managed successfully to adopt and adapt the techniques of the West's Industrial Revolution. Whatever were the important contributing local conditions, its growth was dependent on the diffusion of technology imported from outside rather than on indigenous Japanese science and technology—a development that was to come much later in the twentieth century.

The second transition was to sustained intensive growth. It came later in the nineteenth century and was driven by two phenomena that occurred after the First Industrial Revolution. Both are justly called revolutions. The first concerned morbidity and the second, fertility. These two fundamentally changed the relation between extensive and intensive growth that had existed for centuries—even allowing for some intensive growth between 500 and 1750, there is little doubt that the major proportion of all extensive growth was translated into increased population rather than increased living standards.

I. EXPLANATIONS

We argue that this second transition was also a contingent historical process that cannot be captured in any of the formal models of which we are aware.

Mortality

The mortality revolution took place mainly in the mid to late nineteenth century as death rates plummeted, first in the West, then elsewhere. As a result, population started to rise rapidly during that century. There has been debate as to whether the cause was economic growth per se or specific technological changes in the under-standing and control of infections and diseases, as well as new public health measures such as better sanitation, sewers, and hospitals. We largely accept, with some caveats laid out below, Easterlin's arguments (1998: ch. 7) that it was due to the development of specific technologies, not to growth in general.

Arguing that it was merely due to a generalized growth in incomes would seem to require that people knew how to do it all along but did not have sufficient income. The evidence is otherwise. It was specific advancements in knowledge on the causes and control of diseases and public health initiatives that accounted for the change. For example, until the nineteenth century no one knew that germs caused disease and no one knew that dirty conditions caused infections—the fight to establish conditions of cleanliness among doctors and nurses in hospitals was a long and bitter one. The importance of specific technologies seems clear for the West and it seems even clearer if one looks at the less developed world. There the availability of Western medicine and public health measures led to declines in mortality without any major accelerations in rates of extensive growth and, in many cases, at levels of real income below those in the West at the onset of the Industrial Revolution.

While accepting this explanation, we also note that it still leaves room for a relation between the Industrial Revolution's extensive growth and the mortality revolution. The need for public health was greatly magnified when Britain became urbanized as a result of the steam-driven phase of the Industrial Revolution. Rural squalor was not evident to reformers in the way that urban squalor was (a point emphasized by Rosenberg and Birdzell 1986: 171–3), while the congestion of the cities no doubt accentuated the problems of public health. Also, rising total incomes made it easier to provide the tax revenues needed to finance the improvements mentioned above, virtually all of which were public goods, developed in the private sector but installed by governments.[1] So the increase in scientific and technological knowledge, together with the urbanization caused by the second part of the First

---

[1] Easterlin (1998: 76) argues, however, that this was not an important factor because 'the measures necessary to implement advances in health technology do not seem to have required, on average, anything like the capital expenditure necessary for modern economic growth'. This is not an altogether compelling argument since 19th-century public sector revenue sources were small relative to those available for financing private capital expenditures today. A somewhat stronger argument is that the imposition of these same measures in less developed countries in the 20th century required only a small fraction of their total health expenditures.

Industrial Revolution, brought about the mortality revolution, with a subsidiary role being played by the general increases in living standards (which were still quite modest at that time).

Fertility

From about 1880 to 1914, there was a fertility revolution that dramatically lowered birth rates in the West. In the high-income countries, birth rates began to fall to levels that first approached, then often went below, what was required to sustain the population. Thus, in many of the richest countries, population increases slowed dramatically and later in the twentieth century, populations began to fall, except where they were held up by immigration from the poorer countries. This revolution spread slowly to the rest of the world and has not yet reached some of the world's poorest regions. What caused this fall in fertility? We first give what seems to be the most common explanation among economists, then we offer our own.

Human Capital

Nothing that we say below is intended to cast doubt on the consensus that human capital was becoming increasingly important as the nineteenth century progressed. The increase in knowledge embedded in the human capital of decision-makers was responsible for the changes in public health and urban cleanliness that contributed greatly to the mortality revolution. As the nineteenth century progressed, human capital became increasingly important for many jobs. Large manufacturing and financial businesses required elaborate record-keeping, which in turn required an army of clerks who were both literate and numerate. Neither are we disputing the strong evidence that increasing education and income in developing countries are correlated with a declining birth rate.

What we wish to question is a very specific theory about the direction of causation. Many economists, including Galor and Weil (2000), have argued that the main cause of the fertility revolution was the increase in the return on human capital, an increase that did undoubtedly occur. This they argue led parents to substitute number of children for the human capital with which each could be endowed. Thus, in these theories, the desire to endow each child with more human capital (given limited resources) caused parents to reduce family size.

While not disputing that this may be one of the many causes of the fertility revolution, there are two sets of reasons, relating to timing and cost, that cast doubt on its being the major cause. First, with respect to timing, the evidence is that the return to human capital did not rise significantly in Britain until the twentieth century. Crafts (1985: 141) notes that until late in the Industrial Revolution, Britain's 'trading base was built on coal and unskilled labour rather than large accumulations of human capital'. His research is echoed by others studying the role of the Industrial Revolution in Britain: the accumulation of human capital does not explain a significant portion of the intensive growth in this period. So the general British decline in fertility seems to have preceded not succeeded the increase in the demand for human capital among unskilled and semi-skilled workers, who were the majority of the working population. Also, fertility fell first in France and in the USA long before it fell in Britain and before the First Industrial Revolution diffused to those countries. This timing is inconsistent with the theory that the decline in fertility was driven by reactions to the human capital needs of the Industrial Revolution, in which case it should have happened first in Britain, not in France and the USA. The Second Industrial Revolution that took place late in the nineteenth century clearly raised the need for human capital but that revolution was centred in Germany, which, by the beginning of the twentieth century, was clearly overtaking Britain as Europe's industrial leader—a trend that probably would have been increasingly dominant if it had not been interrupted by the devastation of the First World War and its aftermath. Yet the birth rates declined earlier in France and Britain than in Germany, this timing also being inconsistent with the theory that the main cause of the fertility revolution was the need to educate children with increasing amounts of human capital made necessary by the Second Industrial Revolution.

Second, with respect to cost, when compulsory education was introduced, it was provided by the state, although a few with higher incomes opted out and paid for their children's private education. So most ordinary persons faced no trade-off between the number of children and the human capital their offspring could acquire.[2] Although they did pay for their children's education out of their taxes, the marginal cost of educating an additional child was zero as long as education was financed from public funds. It was well into the twentieth century before education beyond the compulsory age became common enough to produce a significant trade-off for the majority of parents between the number of children and the human capital with which each could be endowed. Even after the Second World War, when the West's fertility revolution was largely completed, relatively few European youths went onto those branches of higher education where parents were burdened with fees and support costs. Most left school at, or soon after, they reached the age at which their compulsory schooling ended. For the others, there was often significant state support. In Britain, for example, an incomes-tested grant system ensured that the parents of those who secured university entrance did not have to make significant contributions to fees or support of their children unless they were in the higher-income brackets.

Our Explanation

We argue that there were several mutually reinforcing reasons for the fall in fertility. These reasons have been advanced by many others and we make no claim to originality. We advance them here only as an alternative to the single cause explanation of the need to endow one's children with increasing amounts of human capital. First, there were two changes in the production regime (changes that make us doubt

---

[2] There is also the question of time as well as money cost. Undoubtedly, there is a time cost involved in raising children but there is no evidence that working-class parents devoted sufficient time to home education to create a trade-off between limited amount of time available and per capita human capital with which they could endow their offspring.

that a single aggregate production function can describe the entire period). There was a transfer of production out of the cottages and into the factories that is associated with the First Industrial Revolution. This implied that parents were no longer faced with the decision of how much labour to apply to a fixed amount of land. Instead, they were faced with given wage rates for men, for women, and for children. The textile machinery of the First Industrial Revolution created many jobs for children, some of which they could do more or less as well as adults, and others where their small nimble fingers were superior to those of adults. Since wages were low, there was an incentive for whole families to work in order to gain a living income. These considerations created an incentive to keep family size large, while influences that worked in the opposite direction were the time and money costs of raising children, which tend to be higher in urban than in rural settings (where the social support system of the extended family and neighbours help to reduce the costs of child raising). Later in the century, there was a shift of the cutting-edge technologies from the predominantly mechanical to predominantly science-based, such as chemical and electrical, that accompanied the transition from the First to the Second Industrial Revolutions. This tended to lower the value of children in many lines of production.

The second set of causes concerns public policy. During the second half of the nineteenth century, child labour laws and compulsory schooling tended to lower further the contribution that children could make to family incomes and so decreased their economic value to parents. Also social security and pension schemes that were slowly developed over the late nineteenth and early twentieth centuries reduced the importance of children as a cushion against their parents' old age when work might become impossible.

Third, as the twentieth century progressed, gradual increases in the opportunities and wages available to women raised the opportunity cost of the time taken to raise a family.

Fourth, the increased need for human capital very probably did make some contribution. Parents who opted out of the public education system, or who supported their children in post-secondary education, did make significant financial sacrifices. But this is not sufficient on its own to explain the decline in fertility in the late nineteenth and early twentieth centuries among the bulk of the families whose children were educated in the public system.

Finally, we note a set of forces driven by the tastes of adults with respect to their own consumption rather than their concern over their children. Urban life not only raises the cost of raising children, it also presents forms of consumption that are alternatives to those associated with the family-centred lifestyle. These alternatives increased over time as new forms of entertainment, such as those associated with improved public transport and the bicycle, presented new alternatives for the allocation of parents' income.[3] In today's high-income and car-centred world, it is

---

[3] In the USA, the private automobile no doubt played an important part in presenting the parents with many alternative ways of using their funds. However, this was not important in Europe where automobiles remained luxury commodities until well after the end of the Second World War.

hard to appreciate the enormous increase in personal mobility that went with the introduction of bicycles at prices that ordinary people could afford. What ensued was not just a simple case of a high-income elasticity of demand for entertainment that led to fewer children. That explanation would require that children were an inferior good. Instead, the case is more complex than a simple argument based solely on income elasticity would suggest. As the choice set of new commodities expanded and the cost of the items fell, they came within reach of more and more households. Consuming these new goods and services took not only money but scarce time. Thus the opportunity cost of raising children was increasingly measured in time not available to consume leisure goods and services as well as in income forgone.[4]

In this vein, the long-term upward trend in real incomes may imply that, in Easterlin's words (1998: 110): '[E]ach generation is raised in a progressively more abundant material environment. Consequently, each generation develops a new and higher socially defined "subsistence level" that must be met before it can afford to have children.' This implies holding the birth rate to a level well below the rate of growth of aggregate real income. Recall that in the models of Chapter 9 an increase in the utility value of consumption, combined with a falling productivity of children in production, lowers desired family size.

The fertility revolution seems to provide an illustration of what we have several times observed in earlier chapters: specific historical events are often overdetermined in the sense that there exist more than enough sufficient reasons to produce the event being studied, in contrast to what is usually required in economic models that typically employ unique causality. In such cases, debates about which of the sufficient causes *really* caused the event tend to be counterproductive. We suspect that all the forces listed above contributed to the West's precipitous decline in fertility. To go further requires not more elaborate models but more careful study of detailed demographic data for the various countries of the West. Explanations can then be tested against much more detailed data on birth and death rates; family size; demand for human capital; male, female, and children's wage rates; cost, availability, and use of home help; and a number of other relevant statistics for each country in the West over the time span of the demographic revolution. Since most sweeping theories that explain what happened by invoking only one or two forces, such as an increased demand for human capital, are not consistent with the full body of existing facts, the data can provide the awkward facts that are needed to constrain new, more elaborate theories.[5]

---

[4] For a while, the cost of servants was low enough so that even those on quite modest incomes could afford some home help. This reduced the time and income loss of child raising, mitigating the trade-off between consuming the new products and living the old lifestyle. But as women's wages rose, the cost of home help of all kinds rose, until by the end of the Second World War live-in home help all but disappeared, except for those in quite high-income brackets. By then, consumption of many of the new leisure-time goods and services was clearly an alternative to raising a large family.

[5] One of the hallmarks of the natural sciences is their respect for awkward facts. As one of us has put it elsewhere: '[A]n "externally driven research programme" (EDRP), ... is one that is driven by, and constrained by, observed facts. A classic example from astronomy is the search over two millennia for an explanation of the observed behaviour of the planets in which "awkward facts", such as small perturbations in the orbit of Mercury, defeated many beautiful theories until the truth was finally brought to light' (Lipsey 2001: 198). Had Kepler dismissed these small factual deviations from his theory as unimportant variations

In the mean time, we merely show in Box 10.1 how the fertility revolution can be accommodated in our one-sector model, providing a competing explanation to the ones offered by the other models of the emergence of sustained growth, so that evidence is needed to judge between them.

Box 10.1. The Model Altered to Reflect the Fertility Revolution

We repeat below the family utility function first given in equation (9.1):

$$u = \left(\frac{f}{p+h}\right)^{\alpha}(p+h) - q(p+h)^{\gamma} \quad 0 < \alpha < 1 < \gamma \tag{10.1}$$

We now make two changes. First, when people move to the city, f becomes $w_m + tw_f + hzw_c$, where the terms are the wage rate of males; the wage rate of females multiplied by the proportion of time spent in the workforce, t; the wage rate of children, w_c, multiplied by the number of children, h, multiplied by the fraction of the adult working year that the child can work, z. Second, we interpret q as being the opportunity cost of having children:

$$q = q(r, w_f, p_s, S, p_f, p_m)$$

where r is the proportion of the mother's time that must be lost from work in order to have and raise children; w_f, the female wage rate; p_s, the wage of home help; S is the amount of home help; p_f, the price of necessities bought by the household; and p_m, the price of luxuries. The partial derivatives of q are positive with respect to the first four terms and negative with respect to the last two. The precise form of the function can await specification when numerical simulations are made.

Now consider the developments that we have been discussing in the text. The loss of the village support system should raise the amount of time a mother needs to spend in raising children, r, and/or the amount of hired help used in child raising, S. A rise in female wages should raise both w and p_s. Technical progress should lower p_f and p_m, the real price of necessities and luxuries. All of these have the effect of raising q, the opportunity cost of raising children, and, as we saw in Chapter 9, a rise in q lowers the equilibrium size of family. Also, new child labour laws and the technologies of the Second Industrial Revolution should have the effect of lowering z in the equation (9.3), which as we also saw in Chapter 9 lowers the equilibrium family size.

These changes can be incorporated in our model as exogenous shifts. We do not seek to make them endogenous because, as we have argued at length, we know of no formal theory that can incorporate enough contingent, context-specific events to explain why these changes occurred first in one country after another in the West, and not elsewhere until well into the twentieth century, and then only in a few other countries.

Since all of the changes in the nineteenth century worked to raise q in the second expression above, it is clear that with appropriate parameterization, the demand for children could be reduced to the level between two and three, which would just hold population constant without the need for any Malthusian or real income checks on births and deaths.

---

from the broad 'truth' of his earlier hypotheses, he would never have made his pathbreaking discovery that the age-old idea that heavenly bodies must move in circles was shatteringly wrong.

In our modelling exercises, we had to embed the family's choice in a model of the whole economy to see its implications for population. In the present case, however, we do not need to worry that the family formation externality may upset this result. As long as the number of births is at or below what is required to hold population constant, there will be no externality that increases population in ways that individuals would not choose. Of course, real incomes rise over time (which will be shown in the expression in Box 10.1 as increases in the wages of males and females), and, *ceteris paribus*, this leads to an increased demand for children. However, as long as the opportunity cost of children rises fast enough to offset the effect of the increased real wages, family size can be kept at or below four. Eventually the opportunity cost can become so high that the birth rate falls below two per family whatever the level of family real income.

So, as yet, there is no certainty as to the relative importance of the suggested causes of the fertility revolution. It may well have been the result of a combination of all the causes mentioned above. Be that as it may, the revolution did occur in most of the developed countries at more or less the same time. *From that time on, a theory of the West's extensive growth also became a theory of its intensive growth, at least to a fairly good approximation.* So after this event, we do not need to model endogenous population to model both extensive and intensive growth in the West as we do in Part III.

II.   THE THREE GENERIC THEORIES ONCE AGAIN

Towards the beginning of Chapter 9, we outlined three generic theories of population dynamics: the Malthusian, the neo-Malthusian, and the non-Malthusian. We can now summarize our conclusions with respect to each.

Malthusian Theories

Malthusian-type theories are accepted by so many that it is worthwhile summarizing all the reasons we have developed for rejecting it. First, the evidence given in Appendix 9.1 shows that methods of controlling family size were widely known and practised during much of the West's history. Second, it is clear that throughout the post-Roman period, living standards were not at subsistence and we cannot be certain that living standards were static over the period. Third, since the neolithic agricultural revolution, it is clear that there were periods of growth in both total and per capita income that were sustained over centuries, particularly the 1,000-year periods in Sumer following the invention of writing and in the Mediterranean following the disruptions that accompanied the end of the Bronze Age.

There is one other possibility that needs to be considered with respect to the Malthusian assumption that family size was not a choice variable. Easterlin (1998: 96) quotes Titmus (1966: 91) to the effect that the typical English working-class mother in the 1880s married in her teens and experienced ten pregnancies. This does not suggest widespread use of birth control. Easterlin expresses agreement with Titmus, and goes on to assert that family size was not a choice variable until modern times. What he does not point out, however, is that the behaviour reported by Titmus was a big change from that of earlier periods. In early modern periods, English women typically married in their mid twenties and had many fewer pregnancies. (See the detailed evidence presented in Wrigley et al. 1997 and briefly reviewed in Appendix 9.1.)[6]

The evidence shows that the knowledge of birth control techniques was in the public domain until some time in the late Middle Ages. Then medicine slowly came to be practised by university-trained doctors and the preparation of medicines passed to the guild of apothecaries. Neither of these groups were trained in birth control techniques. Birth control knowledge was passed on after that mainly by midwives and ordinary women, both of whom were usually illiterate. It is likely that much of this oral knowledge was lost in the transition from village to city that accompanied the Industrial Revolution. (See a fuller discussion in Appendix 9.1.) So Titmus's observation about nineteenth-century working-class mothers is consistent with our earlier non-Malthusian evidence if there was a significant loss of oral traditional knowledge in the late eighteenth and early nineteenth centuries—knowledge that had to be regained in the late nineteenth and early twentieth centuries when, among other things, there were public movements to teach methods of birth control to working-class wives.

Neo-Malthusian Theories

General Criticisms

Neo-Malthusian theories all assume that the increases in food production associated with improved productivity induced increases in population that held income at some floor level, usually called 'subsistence'. Given that this cannot be biological subsistence, the level of the floor is typically left unexplained.

Some economic historians have argued that the subsistence level is customary and occasionally ratcheted upwards. To be operative, this theory requires an explanation of the disturbances that move the level upwards. Our study of technological history suggests that new products are a possible influence to point to here. Each upward

---

[6] Easterlin (1998: 100–1) goes on to observe that '[t]he most important evidence comes from sample surveys of Third World populations conducted in the 1960s and 1970s, when fertility was still quite high'. Among other things, he argues that people in the Third World do not typically realize the causal links between births and various factors that we know would influence them. For example, peasants on the Indian subcontinent often believe that postponing marriage increases the number of children (Easterlin 1998: 101). Yet, at least according to Malthus and much folklore, the Irish long understood this link and used late marriages to control family size. It is also clear that family size was held low, sometimes well below four in classical times where leaders worried about declining populations. Thus Easterlin's evidence that family size is not a choice variable in some places does *not* necessarily apply to the West over the last two millennia. In particular it is not clear that the 20th-century experience of the Third World countries with respect to the absence of conscious choices of family size is relevant evidence for Europeans in the period 500–1780. They knew different things and had different customs.

ratcheting should, however, be accompanied by a reduction in desired family size and we see no evidence of this through the period under consideration, at least until the nineteenth century. So although this as a possible explanation of the population dynamics of the nineteenth century, it seems to have little to offer by way of explanation for the entire earlier period.

Most versions of neo-Malthusian theory assume that parents had control over family size. They thus assume that an increase in population followed an increase in income because parents elected to remain on the subsistence level of income, preferring larger families to more food for each member. We have no direct evidence on such preferences but it seems highly unlikely to us that parents chose to stay on the subsistence level of income because they put such a high value on more children throughout the whole period under consideration.

Easterlin

In Easterlin's theory, population is the result of three forces: (*a*) the demand for children, defined as the number of children parents typically desire to raise to adulthood; (*b*) the supply of children, defined as the number of children that parents would raise to adulthood (given the conditions of the society) if they made no effort to control family size; and (*c*) the cost of fertility regulation, which depends on social as well as economic variables. According to Easterlin:

1. demand exceeded supply over most of the period under consideration so that rational parents made no attempt to control family size, even where they did know about birth control methods;
2. when the mortality revolution occurred, supply gradually expanded to exceed demand;
3. as a result, population first rose dramatically, and parents then began to control births in an attempt to lower supply to the level of demand, 'the single most important factor causing the fertility decline is itself the Mortality Revolution and particularly the great reduction in infant and child mortality that accompanied the Mortality Revolution' (Easterlin 1998: 95).

In point 1, he seems to argue in some places that birth control knowledge was absent in the West until modern times and at other places that, although it was known, it was not practised because the supply of children fell short of the demand. We have rejected the first interpretation in the previous section. The second interpretation, that parents knew how to control family size but chose not to do so, avoids the implication of most neo-Malthusian theories that the size of family increased as a secular trend over the whole period. However, this theory still requires the awkward assumption that parents preferred to live at the subsistence level because they valued extra children so highly that they would not restrict the size of their families in order to raise their per capita consumption above subsistence from AD 500 to 1800. His theory also requires the assumption, which does not seem to conform with the weight of the evidence surveyed in Appendix 9.1, that family size was at the maximum biologically possible throughout the period.

On point 2, we have already argued that the large increase in fertility during the late eighteenth and early nineteenth centuries was associated with the loss of birth control knowledge among the working class during the move from village to city and the new technologies that lowered the death rate in the nineteenth century. Before the working class could respond by lowering the birth rate, birth control knowledge had to be recovered, which happened slowly during the late nineteenth and early twentieth centuries.

In point 3, he states that the main reason for the nineteenth-century fertility revolution was not merely that the survival rate had risen so much that the supply of children was rising well above demand. That would indeed account for some control of births, but it does not account for the fall that occurred in family size because parents were choosing to raise far fewer children to maturity than had been done since classical times. If the main reason for the fall in fertility was the fall in mortality, family fertility would fall only until family size was stabilized at the level that existed before the fall in mortality. What is needed for an explanation of the transition to sustained intensive growth is an explanation of why the birth rate declined *much more than* the death rate. Instead, we agree with Easterlin's later discussion where he provides reasons why there was a fall not just in the desired birth rate but in the desired size of family as well. Since his list is close to ours, we do not give it here.

Galor and Weil

We selected Galor and Weil as providing the most sophisticated of the formal theories of the two transitions, first to sustained extensive, then to sustained intensive growth. Some aspects of their theory are clearly not meant to mirror reality but only to make the model tractable. But if a theory is to be taken seriously, all of its empirical implications must be considered as open to testing.

Our major criticism of all the formal models of the transitions from episodic to sustained extensive and intensive growth, including G&W's, is their 'historical generality'. They predict that if a few macro conditions are met, any society will make the two transitions in question. We argue instead that both these transitions were contingent processes that could have been otherwise but for some context-specific events that are not included in any of the general models. To meet even the most basic facts, theorists need to explain why the transition to sustained extensive growth happened endogenously only in Britain and then diffused to the rest of Europe, and why it did not happen endogenously anywhere outside of the West. This is an example of the need for what Hodgson calls historical specificity. (See the discussion of historical specificity in Chapter 1.)

Consider the two transitions in G&W's theory. Strictly, G&W's theory shows no transition from episodic to sustained extensive growth since their rate of growth of productivity is assumed to be a function of the size of the population, whose growth is slowly accelerating over the whole period. (There are two abrupt transitions from each of their first two regimes to the next, but these are in the formal structure of the model, not from episodic to sustained extensive growth.) Aside from making accelerating extensive growth inevitable, these characteristics do not seem to fit the facts of European history very well. The rate of growth of population and the rate of technical change show no signs of continually accelerating over most of the time between the fall of the Western Roman Empire and the beginning of the First Industrial Revolution. Indeed, it seems clear that the big changes in agricultural productivity occurred in the first 500 or so years following the dissolution of the Western Roman Empire and that there was much less technological change in agriculture during the later part of the medieval period than in the first part. (See our discussion of medieval agricultural technologies on pages 160–164 of Chapter 5.) Furthermore, large countries did not grow faster than small countries. Two of the fastest growing countries in the early modern period were Holland and Britain. An implication of G&W's model is that Germany and France should have had a faster rate of economic growth than Britain and should, therefore, have experienced the First Industrial Revolution sooner than Britain.[7]

The transition to intensive growth is a little less mechanical than their mere acceleration of extensive growth, which is sustained throughout the entire period. It comes when the rate of growth is high enough that parents decide to have fewer and fewer children in order to endow those they do have with increasing amounts of human capital.[8] So any society will eventually grow at an accelerating rate and such growth will inevitably become fast enough to induce the transition from sustained extensive to sustained intensive growth as a result of the parents' decision to have fewer, better educated children. Apart from its non-contingent nature, our disagreements with the theory of this transition is that the evidence does not support the view that an increased need for human capital among the working class was the major cause of the West's revolution in fertility rates in the nineteenth century. Nor do we see why the demand for human capital should depend mainly on the rate of change of technological knowledge rather than its level. It is hard to accept, for example, that

---

[7] If it is world and not national population that is relevant, there is nothing to explain different growth experiences in various countries and areas, only a prediction of accelerating growth everywhere.

[8] G&W's parents are making a two-period maximization with the incomes their children will earn as adults as one of the arguments in their utility function. Once the Malthusian constraint is no longer binding, an increase in parental income, *ceteris paribus*, leaves the number of children and their education unaltered (Galor and Weil 2000: 815 proposition 1 (c)). What does affect the division between child numbers and child quality is the rate of technical progress (Galor and Weil 2000: 814). Parents are interested in the amount of human capital a child acquires and carries over to adulthood, which is an increasing function of the amount of education given to the child and a decreasing function of the rate of technical progress between childhood and adulthood. The negative effect of technological progress is diminished the more the education that a child receives (Galor and Weil 2000: 813). So as the rate of technical progress accelerates, the return to educating an existing child eventually exceeds the return from adding one more child to the family. Parents begin to substitute quality for quantity, thus slowing the rate of growth of the population. From that time on as technical progress accelerates further, parents elect to have fewer children who are better educated. In the final stable equilibrium of the Modern Growth Regime, population may be constant, growing, or declining. In the case of constant population, the level of education and rate of technical progress are constant. If population is growing, both the amount of education and the rate of technical progress will be rising as well. If population is falling, the level of education and the rate of technical progress will fall as well. In all cases the rate of increase of per capita income is positive and constant over time.

the demand for human capital would be less in today's knowledge-intensive economy than in the 1945–75 period when growth rates were higher than they are today. Neither do we see any cross section evidence that in countries experiencing modern sustained growth, the rate of technological progress and the level of education are positively correlated with the rate of population growth.[9]

Non-Malthusian Theories

Nothing in non-Malthusian theories denies the strong positive relation between extensive growth and population increases. The issue is whether or not there was anything left over for increases in living standards over the centuries. We have developed theories that allow for modest increases in living standards during the period 500–1750. First, even if the family formation externality holds per capita food consumption near some floor level, modest increases in real incomes are possible through the increased consumption of the manufactured and public goods. Second, there are many possible checks other than a reduction of living standards due to diminishing returns that can work to slow the rate of population growth whenever it tends to exceed the rate of growth of productive capacity. There may be emigration to the cities or to other countries, birth and marriage rates may fall as population density rises, particularly given the need in European countries to amass significant amounts of capital before marrying and the observed fact that, in contrast to any other societies, substantial portions of the European populations never married. (See the discussion of these points in Appendix 9.1.) When those other checks also exist, the effects of an increase in productivity will be divided between a population increase, as brought about by the family formation externality, and an increase in living standards that occurs because population is checked by other forces than falling living standards. Third, in so far as peasants desired to maximize real per capita family food consumption in a setting in which the marginal and average products of labour rose over an initial range and then fell, increases in productivity would be translated into increased per capita consumption with no accompanying burst of population growth. These circumstances may then be combined with the possibility that, given death and marriage rates, the choice of optimum family size

---

[9] Galor and Weil argue that other evidence supports their theory.

1. Maddison reports zero GDP growth from 500 to 1500. But this is close to a guestimate with little of the impressive evidence he brings to support his conclusions about growth in the later periods.
2. Real wages are estimated to be about the same in 1800 as in 1300. But real wages in the city are irrelevant and agricultural real wages reflect what the landless could earn. As the number of landless was growing over the period, this observation is consistent with rising income for the majority who had land.
3. Mokyr, Pritchet, and Lucas all argue that sustained growth is a modern phenomenon. But the absence of sustained growth does not preclude episodic growth (extensive and intensive), which is all that has been alleged about the pre-industrial period (and in any case G&W have sustained extensive growth throughout all their periods).
4. The evidence they quote on population is all accommodated within our model of population dynamics and none of it is inconsistent with episodic extensive and intensive growth.

just happened to be what produced something quite close to the observed population growth rate—a rate that was modified only slightly by any of the possible equilibrating forces that we have analysed above. Since this would have required something around five or six live births per family, this is a possibility that cannot be lightly dismissed.

III.   CONCLUSION AND SUMMARY

In Part II, we have moved towards an explanation of some key aspects of the West's economic growth. We first asked why the transition to sustained economic growth occurred in the West late in the second millennium AD. We argued that, given the present state of modelling techniques in the social sciences, the explanation of why it happened when and where it did can only be dealt with by historical analysis. The revolution had its historical roots in the European revival of learning in the latter half of the medieval period. The Christian Church played an enormously important part during that time in fostering learning, and providing and staffing educational institutions. Then, with the dawn of the early modern period, the scientific revolution swept away the old Aristotelian system and replaced it piecemeal over the next 200 years with new empirical knowledge that culminated in a new world view propounded in Newton's *Principia*. This masterpiece not only systematized the new knowledge of how things behaved but it also provided the mechanistic science, and the mathematics, that assisted the great engineering works that preceded the Industrial Revolution and many of the mechanical inventions that made it possible, particularly the high-pressure steam engine.

During the same period, the research programme to mechanize all aspects of the textile industry that was promulgated by Leonardo da Vinci went forward, with technically easier problems being solved first and harder ones later. During the latter half of the eighteenth century, these two trajectories culminated in a series of classic inventions, which set the Industrial Revolution in full swing. Western science played an important part in these lines of development: first mechanistic science, then other branches such as chemistry, metallurgy, and physics in the Second Revolution of the last part of the nineteenth century. Without Western science, the Second Industrial Revolution would have been impossible. We argue that science and technological trajectories that were entwined with it also played a key part in the First Industrial Revolution, explaining both its timing in the eighteenth century and its location in Britain.

We then asked why this transition did not occur elsewhere. Many reasons contributed to the explanation of why China and the Islamic countries did not create their own indigenous industrial revolutions. But one key necessary condition that was missing in both civilizations was anything close to the mechanistic science that Newton synthesized and those non-mechanical branches that underlay the Second Industrial Revolution.

Next, we considered the relation between extensive and intensive growth. We started with the hypothesis that if families had positive income elasticities of demand for both children and per capita consumption, the productivity growth that occurred from 700 to 1750 in Europe would have led to increases both in population and in living standards (both extensive and intensive growth). We found, however, that in the Solow growth model, a powerful family formation externality caused population to rise sufficiently to hold living standards at a floor level determined from within our model (although not at biological subsistence). Living standards could still rise because of an accumulation of public goods and an increased consumption of manufactured goods. They could also rise if there were a change in any of the things that influence the family formation externality, such as a rise in the utility value of consumption (which might come about by the introduction of new products for consumption) or a fall in the usefulness of children in production.

Also, we found that if there is a range of increasing returns to labour, as is no doubt true in real farming situations, there will be an optimum number of children even if children confer no direct utility on their parents. This gives rise to a totally non-Malthusian explanation of Europe's experience. We present it here as a potentially testable hypothesis.

Hypothesis

The optimum family size was about five to six children and given the ratio of marriages in generation $t + 1$ to births in generation t of around 0.4 (the rest either die in childhood or do not marry), net family formation was just large enough to produce the observed rate of population growth of about 0.766 per cent per generation. Because the marriage rate varied positively and the death rate negatively with real incomes, there were episodic bursts of population associated with episodic technological advances, and these partly reduced real incomes below what would have happened if population had not changed. But the working of checks other than those associated with falling living standards prevented the increase of population from reducing real consumption of agricultural commodities back to their pre-change levels. Furthermore, increases in village production of manufactured goods and an increased supply of more elaborate public goods and services raised real incomes independently of what was happening to food consumption.

None of this is to deny that real incomes were very low by modern standards and that they did not rise either rapidly or in a sustained way. To some extent our externality that produces Malthusian-seeming results very probably acted to turn much extensive growth into population growth. But accepting this is a long way from maintaining that real incomes were static from 500 to 1500, let alone until 1750—a position that, along with many economic historians, we do not accept.

Explaining the transition from sustained extensive growth brought about by the Industrial Revolutions to sustained intensive growth requires only that we explain the West's fertility revolution. There are several possible causes that were no doubt in operation and that probably contributed to this decline. We cast doubt on the explanation offered by many economists that the *prime cause* was a desire on the part of parents to equip their children with much more human capital than in previous times, leading to smaller, better educated families. Detailed studies that use all the available facts as controls may get closer to ordering the importance of the various causal forces. However, once the birth rate fell in advanced industrialized countries for whatever reasons, their sustained extensive growth became sustained intensive growth. From then on, models of GPT-driven sustained extensive growth also became models of GPT-driven intensive growth.

In Part III, we model the West's sustained GPT-driven, long-term growth in total output. If we can explain extensive growth in any period after the demographic revolution, we have pretty well explained intensive growth, so we do not need to consider population dynamics further.

Part III

Modelling Sustained GPT-Driven Growth

In Part II, we offered an explanation of the emergence of sustained extensive and intensive growth in the West, which happened mainly in the nineteenth century. In Part III, we develop models of GPT-driven, sustained growth—models that we argue are appropriate tools of analysis once sustained growth has been established. It would be natural to expect the material in Parts I and II to lead us directly to an evolutionary modelling of innovation and technological change at the microeconomic level. Instead, we have chosen a different strategy, that of first building a macro model of GPT-driven growth and then amending it incrementally to incorporate an increasing number of S-E characteristics. Ours is an attempt at incremental rather than radical innovation in modelling evolutionary growth.

We chose this course for several reasons. First, many other economists are currently investigating micro-evolutionary models and we felt that our comparative advantage did not lie in adding to this literature. Second, as far as we can see, the development of micro-evolutionary models has not yet produced theories capable of dealing routinely with what is observed about aggregate, economy-wide, technologically driven, economic growth. Third, the first generation of aggregate GPT models does not seem to have given rise to a burst of model building analogous to what followed the early interest in micro-evolutionary approaches, particularly after the publication of Nelson and Winter's pathbreaking *Theory of Economic Change*. We think this is because the equilibrium concept used in the first generation of aggregate GPT models did not easily lend itself to an extension to the many complications needed to go beyond the crude assumptions that were necessary to make these models work. Fourth, an earlier simulation model developed by two of us (Carlaw and Lipsey 2001,

2006), which was designed to make some modest advances in GPT modelling at the aggregate level, turned out to be versatile enough to handle more realistic complexities that take the model closer to S-E characteristics. Finally, no one knows the potential of a particular line of theoretical enquiry until that line has been investigated—a theme that recurs throughout Part I with respect to technological innovations. Thus, when something new is being attempted, there is value in having many different attacks on the same problem, which in this case is explaining long-term growth and technological change as an evolutionary process. We see our approach as complementary to, not competitive with, models that deal more explicitly with evolutionary processes at the microeconomic level.

Chapter 11 surveys the literature on GPTs and other similar concepts, such as Freeman and Perez's technoeconomic paradigms (1988), and Mokyr's macro inventions (1990). This provides us with points of contrast when we develop our own formal theories later in this part.

Chapter 12 studies the concept of returns to scale, which is important in empirical and theoretical studies of sustained growth. We argue that the standard theoretical treatment of scale effects is scholastic in attempting to deduce conditions under which scale effects will exist from highly abstract formulations that have little or no empirical content. We then go on to explain why scale effects are so important in technological history but are so hard to observe. Finally, we consider the place of scale effects in macro growth models.

Chapter 13 begins a series of abstractions, each taking us further away from the rich details in Parts I and II, but closer to a tractable macro model of sustained GPT-driven growth. Our first level of abstraction looks for commonalities among the GPTs that we have discussed in Part I. Our second level divides the evolution of the 'typical' GPT into five phases. Our third level divides this evolution into two categories, the efficiency with which a GPT delivers its services and the range of its applications, both of which evolve over time according to a logistic formulation.

Chapters 14 and 15 complete our series of abstractions by building and applying a model of GPT-driven growth in which the logistic formulation of Chapter 13 plays a key part. This gives us a baseline model to act as a standard of comparison when considering the various complications that we introduce sequentially. These are intended to make the model evolve in the direction of an S-E approach, incorporating an increasing number of things that empirical evidence suggests to be important characteristics of GPTs and the growth that they sustain. A full evolution in this direction, which would include many structuralist and evolutionary characteristics at lower levels of aggregation, is a major research programme that we can only begin in this book. We hope, however, that Chapters 14 and 15 indicate the outlines of, and take the first steps in developing, such a potentially fruitful programme. In the mean time, we are able to model many of the complexities that empirical evidence shows to be important for GPT-driven growth, but that make the standard first-generation models intractable—uncertainty, a succession of non-identical GPTs, spillovers between the sectors, the facilitating structure, and more than one GPT in existence at the same time. We are also able to use the model to show (*a*) why TFP does not measure technological change; (*b*) the circumstances in which full information, rational expectations, and adaptive expectations formed under conditions of uncertainty produce similar or widely divergent outcomes; and (*c*) how sustained economic growth can be achieved even when all accumulating factors are produced and producing under conditions of diminishing returns.

11

GPTs and Related Concepts
in the Literature

Relatively few papers and books have been written on the subject of what we have called transforming GPTs. Important related concepts developed by writers using historical and appreciative theoretical approaches are Mokyr's macro inventions (1990), technoeconomic paradigms by Perez (1983, 1985) and Freeman and Perez (1988), Freeman and Louçä's technological revolutions (2001), and Lipsey and Bekar's enabling technologies (1995). Nelson and Winter's technological regimes (1982: 258–60) have some similarities but are closer to the more limited concept of a technological trajectory that we discussed in Chapters 2 and 4 than to a GPT. So we only note the similarity in passing. Models that provide a formal analysis of GPTs using endogenous growth theory are Bresnahan and Trajtenberg (1992), Helpman and Trajtenberg (1998a, 1998b), and Aghion and Howitt (1998). Carlaw and Lipsey (2001, 2006) build from this first generation of GPT models to allow for an examination of the economic impact of the arrival of more than one GPT spaced out over long intervals of time.

In addition, several authors have studied specific technologies as examples of GPTs. Harris (1998) examines the Internet as a case study of a GPT, Rosenberg (1998) examines chemical engineering as a GPT, and Rosenberg and Trajtenberg (2004) consider the Corliss engine as a specific manifestation of the GPT that is the steam engine.

This chapter is divided into two sections: first, we present a brief critical survey of the historical–appreciative literature to provide a complement to our own analysis in earlier parts of this book, where we discuss many aspects of GPTs; and second, we survey the first-generation GPT models as a background to our own second-generation models, which we present in Chapters 14 and 15, and that go well beyond the original ones in several dimensions.

I. HISTORICAL AND APPRECIATIVE THEORIES OF GPTS

Several authors use historical and/or appreciative theories to develop concepts close to GPTs. In this section, we briefly review how these concepts relate to GPTs.

Technoeconomic Paradigms

The concept of a 'technoeconomic paradigm' (TEP), which we briefly discussed in Chapter 3, covers a collection of related technologies *and* their associated economic structure.[1] It is defined as a systemic relationship among products, processes, organizations, and the institutions that coordinate economic activity. A typical paradigm is based on a few key technologies and commodities that are mutually reinforcing, a few key materials whose costs are falling over time, a typical way of organizing economic activity, and a typical pattern of geographical location. Although all the elements of a TEP are assumed to be systemically related, the force that usually changes a TEP is what we would call a new transforming GPT that fundamentally alters the relationship among technologies and between technology and the facilitating structure of the economy. Freeman and Perez are not specific on this last point but it seems to be implicit in their whole analysis.

The TEP is similar but not identical to the combination of our concepts of a GPT *and* the associated facilitating structure. The main similarities are that both approaches cover major technologies that drive long-term economic growth and that both cover much more than just technology, including much of the economic, social, and political structures that give economic effect to technologies. Generally, however, a TEP is a much more inclusive concept and it differs from our GPT-facilitating structure framework in a number of ways.

First, consider technology. A TEP includes the whole set of technologies that characterize a technological era, some major and some minor, some closely related and some not so. A typical TEP era is likely to include several dominant GPTs, possibly one in each of our main classes: ICTs, materials, power, transportation, and organization. They fit together in a systemic whole, ordered by an emergent coordinating process that is not fully specified.

In contrast, a GPT is a major technology but all of the derivative technologies that it enables are treated as separate entities. In our version, these GPTs need not fit together as a *unique* systemic whole. At present, for example, the prevailing technology system includes ICTs, artificial materials, biotechnology, and the beginnings of nanotechnology. At any one time, these will be coordinated (more or less well) into a working whole, as any system is. But it is quite possible to conceive of something like the current system, with electricity and modern ICTs, but without one or more of the other modern technologies, including such GPTs as artificial materials, biotechnology, or nanotechnology. We allow for the possibility of a variety of more or less integrated technology systems by permitting various possible combinations of GPTs, which do not have to fit together in a unique bundle, which may or may not have a facilitating structure that is well adapted to them, and any one of which can arrive at times when the current GPTs are not in a crisis caused by an exhaustion of the new investment possibilities that depend on them.

---

[1] The concept was introduced by Perez (1983, 1985). Other examples are Freeman, Clark, and Soete (1982), Freeman and Soete (1987), and Freeman and Perez (1988).

If each of these individual technologies in a TEP required all the others in order to function, the concept of the whole integrated paradigm would be more than just a description of what it is. But since, as we just obsereved, the current ICTs could have existed with or without the materials revolution, with or without biotechnology, and with or without nanotechnology, the concept of the current TEP that integrates whichever of these happen to be in existence seems to be just a description of the existing set of technologies. This is not to say that technologies are completely independent of each other so that *any* combination is possible. Instead, there is a hierarchy of technologies. For example, virtually none of today's GPTs would be possible without electricity and few of them without computers.

Now consider the non-technology part of the TEP. This includes those elements of our facilitating structure that are fully adapted to the prevailing technologies, as well as other non-economic variables discussed below. Because the concept of a TEP is that of a fully adapted paradigm, it can only include the *adapted* part of our facilitating structure. In contrast, our facilitating structure is the *existing* and continually evolving structure. Many of the pressures that drive change stem from the lack of adaptation of significant parts of the existing structure to newly arriving technologies. This can happen on any scale, not just what Freeman and Louçã call structural crises of adjustment as one TEP gives way to another.

TEPs are used, among other things, to develop two important points about the process of technological change. First, the dynamics of economic growth are intimately linked to the development of new technologies and the evolution of their relationships to the economic, political, and social structures. Second, the introduction of a major new technology system tends to have pervasive structural effects throughout the economy—a 'structural crisis of adjustment'. Our model, in which new GPTs drive economic growth and typically require major changes in the facilitating structure before their full effects can be felt, covers both these points but in a more piecemeal fashion.

Perhaps the best way to illustrate Freeman and Perez's concept is to quote from their description of two of the TEPs that they identify. In their view, Fordist-style mass production is the TEP that dominated the post–Second World War era up until the mid-1970s.

The technological paradigm which predominated in the post-war boom [1945–70] was one based on low-cost oil and energy-intensive materials (especially petrochemicals and synthetics), and was led by giant oil, chemical, automobile and other mass durable goods producers. Its 'ideal' type of productive organisation at the plant level was the continuous-flow assembly-line, turning out massive quantities of identical units. The 'ideal' type of firm was the 'corporation' with a separate and complex hierarchical managerial and administrative structure, including in-house R&D and operating in oligopolistic markets in which advertising and marketing activities played a major role. It required large numbers of middle-range skills in both the blue- and white-collar areas, leading to a characteristic pattern of occupations and income distribution . . . . The paradigm required a vast infrastructural network of motorways, service stations, airports, oil and petrol distribution systems, which was promoted by public investment on a large scale already in the 1930s, but more massively in the post-war period. (Freeman and Perez 1988: 60)

Freeman and Perez identify a new TEP that emerged in the late 1970s and incorporated the then new technologies of computers, lean- or just-in-time organizations, and new materials. They also note that the transition to this new TEP was characterized by uncertainty on the part of many adopting agents and resulted in many structural frictions within the adopting economies.

The 'ideal' information-intensive productive organisation now increasingly links design, management, production and marketing into one integrated system—a process which may be described as 'systemation' and which goes far beyond the earlier concepts of mechanisation and automation. ... [Its manifestation in production is the new technology of lean production or flexible manufacturing.] The skill profile associated with the new technoeconomic paradigm appears to change from the concentration on middle-range craft and supervisory skills to increasingly high- and low-range qualifications, and from narrow specialisation to broader, multi-purpose basic skills for information handling. Diversity and flexibility at all levels substitute for homogeneity and dedicated systems. The transformation of the profile of capital equipment is no less radical.... The deep structural problems involved in this change of paradigm are now evident in all parts of the world. Among the manifestations are the acute and persistent shortage of the high-level skills associated with the new paradigm, even in countries with high levels of general unemployment, and the persistent surplus capacity in the older 'smokestack', energy-intensive industries such as steel, oil and petrochemicals. (Freeman and Perez 1988: 60–1)

As is clear from the above quotations, the TEP concept is holistic; it integrates technology, the facilitating structure, policy, and the policy structure that we separate in our S-E framework developed in Chapter 3. This concept is, however, close to ours in the sense that it stresses the interaction among the elements of technology and structure.

Technological Revolutions

Overview

Freeman and Louçã (2001) develop a view of the West's economic history from the time of the First Industrial Revolution as a series of TEPs, well-integrated systemic sets of social and economic orders, each following the other with an intervening period of 'structural crisis of adjustment' as the whole order is adjusted to each new TEP. (It is not clear to us, however, that their driving force, which creates a structural crisis and the transition from one TEP to another, is always assumed to be a major new technology.) In contrast, our S-E view sees technologies arriving more or less continually, some fitting well into the prevailing facilitating structure, some requiring adjustments of more or less breadth and magnitude, while the occasional one transforms just about everything. This is a more piecemeal view of the evolutionary process than the systemic one of the TEP.

But the differences are probably less than the similarities. No doubt TEP theorists would agree that technologies are developed continually and that some require more adjustments to the existing order than others. We certainly agree that occasionally a new GPT, such as electricity or the computer, comes to pervade more or less everything, requiring massive adjustments to the facilitating structure. When these adjustments are made, they and the major new technologies come to characterize a whole era. Nonetheless, we find it more useful to identify each specific new arriving technology and its impact on the specific elements of structure and to analyse it individually, only later studying the system as a more or less well-integrated whole in terms of its performance effects.[2]

It seems to us that the two theories are somewhat different ways of formulating the historical evolution of growth-induced transformations—ways that have as many similarities as differences. They can, therefore, be regarded as complementary in the sense that the different ways of looking at the same growth experiences may give rise to somewhat different insights.

Details

Freeman and Louçã argue that their succession of TEPs forms the basis of five identifiable long waves of economic and social history for the past 300 years in the West. The foreword to their book by Richard Nelson provides a succinct summary:

> The analysis of economic growth developed in this book is organized around the concept of 'long waves'. The long-wave theory espoused by the authors does not argue for any tight regularity of timing and duration. Rather, the central argument is that economic growth as we have experienced it needs to be understood in terms of a sequence of eras. Each era is marked by a cluster of technologies, whose progressive development drives experienced economic growth. The argument is not one of technological determinism. In the long-wave theory espoused by the authors, the effective development and implementation of the particular technologies that are central in an era require an appropriate and supportive structure of institutions, a point of view that goes back at least as far as Marx, and was early developed in its present form by Carlota Perez.... The succession of different economic eras generates 'long waves', the authors argue, because progress based on the core technologies of one era operating under their suited institutions sooner or later runs into diminishing returns, and economic progress based on those technologies inevitably slows down. The resumption of rapid economic growth then requires the emergence of a new set of driving core technologies, and the reformation of institutional structures to suit the new needs. As the authors stress, the change from one era to another very often has been associated with a change in the locus of economic leadership. (Freeman and Louçã 2001: vii)

Freeman and Louçã build their theory of technological revolutions on five subsystems of society—science, technology, economy, politics, and culture. Each subsystem evolves along its own wavelike trajectory, but interactions among them imply that they also respond to movements in the others with lags and feedbacks. In their view (Freeman and Louçã 2001: 121), the TEP approach has three innovative features:

---

[2] We owe a considerable debt to TEP authors because their concept first started us thinking about the structural links that are associated with GPTs. Our reasons for not just adopting the TEP viewpoint in full are spelt out in Lipsey and Bekar (1995: 63–71).

1. it is an appreciative theory based on the overlapping subsystems;
2. it analyses crisis and transition in terms of 'sychronicity and maladjustment' among the subsystems, which also determines the timing of fluctuations; and
3. social conflicts are generated by the coordination process, which they see as being 'power in all of its forms, from the production of legitimacy to strict coercion'.

We accept and have no further comment on their first point. However, the second raises some interesting issues. The variable most relevant to understanding historical dynamics is this coordination process. In their theory, it is not carried out by a specific mechanism or institution in a society. Instead it emerges as the result, at one level, of actions—actions that integrate conflicts, actions based on convention, and actions carried out through institutions—and power, strategy, and domination at another level. In Chapter 2, we outlined Dosi and Orsenigo's analysis (1988) of how heterogeneous agents are coordinated through learning, selection, and institutional structures. This is the model that Freeman and Louçã may have in mind for their coordinating mechanism, although they do not state it explicitly.

The result of coordination, according to Freeman and Louçã, is some degree of congruence among the five major subsystems of the economy. Unfortunately, their theoretical sections do not outline this critical mechanism in any detail, although some examples of it do occur in widely scattered places in their history chapters. For example, in their first wave, the British Industrial Revolution, they identify a broad social consensus exemplified by Smith's *Wealth of Nations* combined with the Renaissance, the Scientific Revolution, and the Reformation as the coordinating mechanisms that lead to the '*congruence* of favourable developments in all the main subsystems of British society' (Freeman and Louçã 2001: 177–8). Their second wave has the coordinating mechanisms of changes to (*a*) organizations, in terms of growing size of firms with growing market power; (*b*) management, in terms of a hierarchy of professionally qualified managers; and (*c*) institutions, in terms of a transition first to laissez-faire and then to more socialist political structures. Nowhere, however, is their mechanism clearly explicated in more general terms that are separated from specific examples. This is a pity since it is such a key and potentially valuable part of their theory. The lack of a more general statement gives rise, however, to the worry that it is an *ex post* rationalization of whatever happens, and has no predictive ability in the sense that common characteristics of the coordinating process could be listed and predicted to arise in the next transition from one TEP to another.

This is what we have done with GPTs in Part I and do more of in Chapter 13, leading to predictions about the broad course of any new GPT. Examples are:

1. the logistic nature of the time paths of improvements in the GPT's own efficiency and in the diffusion of its applications (which we discuss in more detail in the Chapter 13);
2. the general impact of GPTs on the facilitating structure, such as new GPTs almost always needing to be embodied in new capital, while altering the

structure of the demand for human capital, the optimal location of many productive activities, and the concentration of industry; and

3. the channels through which different GPTs exert their influence (as studied in Chapter 13).

On their third point, we differ from Freeman and Louçã in that we see social conflicts arising, not out of a particular coordination process but out of the specific dislocations between technology and the facilitating structure caused by the arrival and adoption of transforming GPTs, which may or may not be at the junction between two of Freeman and Louçã's TEPs. In our scheme, the arrival of such technologies transform the power and coercion mechanisms, change property rights and social norms, and require massive divestments and investments in capital of all forms to accommodate and exploit the new GPT. This may be what Freeman and Louçã are referring to in their third point but, in the absence of a specification of what the coordination mechanism is and how it might evolve, we cannot be sure.

Mokyr's Macro Inventions

Mokyr distinguishes what he calls micro and macro inventions. He (1990: 13) defines the former as 'small, incremental steps that improve, adapt, and streamline existing techniques already in use, reducing costs, improving form and function, increasing durability, and reducing energy and raw material requirements'. According to him, they result from an intentional search for improvements (Mokyr 1990: 295) and they occur far more frequently and produce more gains than macro inventions.[3] Macro inventions are defined as 'inventions in which a radical new idea, without clear precedent emerges more or less *ab nihilo*'. These are dependent only on the genius or luck of its inventor (Mokyr 1990: 13). A macro invention must be technically and economically feasible, and occur in a socially sympathetic environment (Mokyr 1990: 291). This concept seems in some ways close to a GPT since many macro inventions rejuvenate the long-run growth process and have a large number of complementarities with new and existing technologies. However, while the list of what Mokyr calls macro inventions contains some that clearly are GPTs, such as the steam engine and the dynamo, others clearly are not, such as the bicycle and the screw propeller.[4]

---

[3] 'In terms of sheer numbers, micro inventions are far more frequent and account for most gains in productivity' (Mokyr 1990: 13). We agree with the former statement but in light of our discussion of technological externalities in Chapter 4, we believe that the latter is not a verifiable assertion.

[4] The following list of inventions that Mokyr (1990) calls, or alludes to as, macro inventions suggests to us that it is not altogether clear what distinguishes his two types of inventions; nor does it seem to us that the twofold classification is exhaustive: the three-field system (33, 295), the heavy plough (32, 295), the windmill (44–5, 294), spectacles (54, 294), the weight-driven mechanical clock (49, 294), blast furnaces and the casting of iron (48), the printing press with moveable type (49), coke as a power source, (62, 294), the stocking frame (68), the steam engine (85 ff), the breast wheel (90), the hot-air balloon (110), chlorine bleaching (99, 294), gaslighting (109), the power loom (97–8), the bicycle (130), the Jacquard loom (100, 292, 294), chemical fertilizers and pesticides (296–7), the gas engine (131), screw propellers (128), the

We disagree with Mokyr on the following points. First, we do not think it illuminating in terms of any economic effects to divide all inventions into two classes one of which is intentional and the other, accidental; nor do we think Mokyr is consistent in confining macro inventions to those that emerge without clear precedent as shown in footnote 3. Second, we do not think that the big inventions are less important than the small ones. While accepting that small inventions contribute much to economic growth, we hold that the really big inventions, GPTs in our terminology, rejuvenate the growth process and, without them, growth would sooner or later slow down and possibly come close to a halt (see Chapters 13 and 14). Third, we do not accept that all, or even most, of the really big inventions, either his macro inventions or our GPTs, appear more or less out of the blue, presumably as isolated acts of inspired creativity. In Chapter 4, we have argued that few inventions are what we defined as 'technology-radical', emerging without clear technological antecedents. Most GPTs have clear antecedents stretching well back before the time at which they emerged as GPTs, as do many of Mokyr's macro inventions. We do argue that many technologies are 'use-radical', since they could not have evolved incrementally out of the technology that they replace. But all sorts of technologies, from major to minor ones, are use-radical, including many that are not on Mokyr's list of macro inventions. So we do not find his distinction useful because whether or not they were intentional or technology-radical has no effect on outcomes in which we are interested, and looking at his list, we find no way to tell if a specific invention is or is not macro.

Lipsey and Bekar's Enabling Technologies

Lipsey and Bekar (1995) studied 'enabling technologies', which are distinguished by their extensive range of use and their complementarities. These authors utilize a broad sweep of history to identify and then define these technologies. The identification comes from observing periods of history where such technologies have revolutionized life in terms of changing the structure of economies and the way in which production is organized. The definition comes from the effect of these technologies on the economic system. Lipsey and Bekar define deep structural adjustments (DSAs) as major changes in the entire structure of the economy and go on to say that these are caused by many, but not all, new enabling technologies. From the cases studied and the description of DSAs, two things are clear: first, their concept of an enabling technology is an early and less clearly defined version of the concept of GPTs as defined by Lipsey, Bekar, and Carlaw (1998a); and second, DSAs refer to what they later call large changes in the facilitating structure that are induced by new transforming GPTs.

---

pneumatic tyre (130, 133), Bessemer-type steel (291), aniline purple dye (119), the dynamo (291), pasteurization (291), and indigo dye (120). Some of the items on the list were accidental discoveries, such as aniline purple, while others had a long history, sometimes stretching back for centuries, such as the invention of the dynamo.

II.   GROWTH WITHIN A SINGLE GPT

A number of formal models of the growth that is driven by the arrival of a single GPT are presented in Helpman (1998). These are mainly inspired by the seminal work of Bresnahan and Trajtenberg (1992). They introduced the term 'general purpose technology' and sketched a formal framework for examining the phenomenon that concentrated mainly on the impact of a single GPT. In addition to these papers, we review a paper by Aghion and Howitt (1992) that models the process of creative destruction brought about by the endogenous choices of agents to innovate. While Aghion and Howitt do not explicitly deal with GPTs, they do model a number of the characteristics of technology and technological change that apply to GPTs.

Bresnahan and Trajtenberg

In their seminal article on GPTs, Bresnahan and Trajtenberg (1992) argue that technologies have a treelike structure, with a few prime movers at the top, which set a research agenda for subordinate and complementary technologies. They define GPTs as having three characteristics: pervasiveness, technological dynamism, and innovational complementarities. Pervasiveness, for Bresnahan and Trajtenberg, means that a GPT is used as a component input in many downstream sectors because it provides a generic function, such as rotary motion. Technological dynamism results from the GPT's ability to support continuous innovation and learning in a research programme related to the GPT. Innovational complementarities exist because of mutually reinforcing productivity gains generated by the GPT for its downstream applications and vice versa.

The consequences of improving the GPT are reduced costs in the applications sector, improvement of downstream products, and adoption of the GPT in an increasing range of downstream production activities. The decisions to improve the GPT induce more innovational effort in the applications sector, which feeds back via the complementarities to induce more improvements in the GPT. This relationship implies that there is a non-convexity in the production feasibility set for R&D. Thus, there is potential for a coordination problem between applied R&D and the GPT sector. Depending on ownership, there could exist a variety of information asymmetries and coordination failures related to such things as the intertemporal sequencing of innovational effort.

Bresnahan and Trajtenberg also define a horizontal complementarity among downstream sectors, whereby each application sector benefits by the marginal addition of another application sector because of the positive effect this has on the quality of the GPT. This horizontal externality creates further coordination problems, which lead Bresnahan and Trajtenberg to conclude that a close examination of the feedbacks and trade-offs involved with particular intellectual property protection policies is desirable before they are implemented. In their view, policies such as the strong protection of the intellectual property of a GPT might exacerbate this horizontal externality and thus limit the valuable development of complementary downstream technologies.

Their model has only one GPT. It is never replaced and is owned by a monopolist who optimally chooses how fast to improve it, based in part on how fast improvements are occurring in the applications sectors. The users of the GPT also make profit-maximizing choices on how fast to improve their specific applications, based in part on how fast improvements are occurring in the GPT. The dynamics come from an application of Maskin and Tirole's Markov Perfect Equilibrium (1987) in which the upstream monopolist and downstream application sectors make sequential choices. The model converges to a stationary equilibrium that depends only on the last two moves made in the sequence. Bresnahan and Trajtenberg define a continuum of equilibria running from the myopic, non-cooperative equilibrium, with a low rate of innovation, to a perfectly coordinated equilibrium, in which all complementary relations are recognized and the rate of innovation is highest. This second equilibrium produces the socially optimal rate of innovation, because it fully internalizes the strategic complementarities. They are able to obtain this optimality result because, along with all the other GPT theorists considered in this section, they explicitly assume the absence of any uncertainty—an assumption we regard as being at variance with all known facts about technological change. (Also, the maximum possible rate of innovation so achieved is optimal only if all costs associated with changing technologies are ignored.)

Helpman and Trajtenberg

Helpman and Trajtenberg (1998a) extend the Bresnahan and Trajtenberg paper by modelling a version of the Bresnahan and Trajtenberg 'technology tree' using a general equilibrium framework that allows them to track the effects of a new GPT in macro aggregates, and model the diffusion process of a new GPT.

At any one time, there is a single GPT in use. It is employed only by the sector producing final goods and neither by the sector producing R&D nor by the sector producing the GPT's supporting components (a limitation that we avoid in our models in Chapters 14 and 15). The productivity of the GPT depends on the number of supporting components that are created by the R&D sector and produced in a given quantity for use alongside the GPT in the final output sector. A new GPT is not put to use until enough units of the complementary component have been developed to make it more productive than the incumbent GPT. The components are specific to one GPT and are used in a refinement of the production function found in Grossman and Helpman (1991), which in turn is based on the Dixit–Stiglitz utility function developed for their model of monopolistic competition. This function has the property that as new complementary components are added, total output increases while productivity per component falls. Thus, there is a finite limit to the GPT's technological development trajectory.

The model contains a vertical complementarity between the GPT and its supporting components and a type of horizontal substitutability between the supporting components themselves. This last relationship replaces Bresnahan and Trajtenberg's innovational complementarities that refer to strategic complementarities between owners of GPTs and the application sectors using the GPTs. However, the components developed for a particular GPT are all substitutes for each other. We note that this might be true for some technologies, such as competing versions of monitors for computers or competing versions of automobiles in the same market segment, but the assumption is certainly not true for many of the subtechnologies of a given GPT, such as the Internet and the computer, which are complementary to each other and to the GPT of electricity. Thus, Helpman and Trajtenberg have reversed the Bresnahan and Trajtenberg horizontal complementarity. Furthermore, it is usually the case (as noted by Bresnahan and Trajtenberg) that GPTs are themselves components of their application technologies. For example, steel is a complementary component in the steam engine, internal combustion engines, buildings, and all other technologies that use it, not the other way around as the Dixit–Stiglitz formulation leads them to suggest. So the GPT evolves by becoming components of a widening range and variety of applications, not by using more components that are developed as inputs for it.[5]

For theoretical convenience, GPTs arrive exogenously and 'unexpectedly'. They are immediately recognized and one of two things happen, depending on the state of production under the old GPT. First, if the R&D activity surrounding the old GPT had already produced all of the economically viable components, then at the time the new GPT arrives all the resources in the economy are devoted to production. Thus, new R&D activity will divert resources out of production, where they produce monopolistically competitive rents, into R&D, where they produce no rents. This causes a temporary slowdown of measured output. Second, if the new GPT arrives while components are still being developed for the old, R&D related to the old technology stops immediately and resources are diverted from both the R&D for the incumbent GPT and the production sector to R&D for the new GPT. This also causes an output slowdown. In either case, enough components are eventually developed so that the productivity of the new GPT exceeds that of the old GPT and productive activity switches from using the old GPT into using the new one.

Helpman and Trajtenberg (1998b) model the process of a new GPT's diffusion. The GPT may be potentially adopted by many sectors with different productivities in using it. (If each sector had the same productivity in the GPT, there would be instantaneous diffusion across all sectors as soon as the number of components created in the R&D sector was sufficient to induce anyone to use it.) Each sector develops components for the GPT in sequence by diverting resources from produc- tion to R&D, starting with the one that has most to gain from the new GPT. This is known in advance (which illustrates the lack of uncertainty in the model). Having done its initial R&D, each sector except the final one to adopt the GPT waits until the next to last phase of the economy's R&D is completed, and then they all rejoin the R&D process to complete the final phase.[6] Thus Helpman and Trajtenberg's model is

---

[5] Some empirical applications that we have heard presented in seminars accept this substitutability of supporting components without apparently noticing its counterfactual status and how much the assump- tion biases their further results.

[6] This artificial-sounding process is imposed to deal with some technically difficult modelling problems.

really one of diffusion in terms of when R&D is performed, not in terms of when the GPT is implemented. The R&D diffusion process drags out the dynamic pattern in the transition from one GPT to another.

Since they build from the (1998*a*) model, Helpman and Trajtenberg (1998*b*) maintain the counterfactual assumptions that all components are substitutes for each other and that components from the applications sector are used as inputs to the GPT rather than the GPT being used as an input component to applications developed in the downstream sectors.

Aghion and Howitt (1992)

Aghion and Howitt (1992) develop a model of technological change and creative destruction that is not a model of GPTs. We consider it here because it is a model of endogenous technological change that deals with the relevant modelling issue of the arrival rate of technology. It also employs modelling techniques for dealing with endogenous technological change upon which future GPT models might draw. In their model, the rate and impact of innovation is determined by a combination of endogenous and random factors. The model has a stationary equilibrium in which the rate of innovation is determined by the expected value of a Poisson arrival process. This arrival rate is determined by the equilibrium labour effort devoted to discovering new technologies and a parameter of the Poisson distribution. Innovations arrive at a continuous rate determined by the stationary equilibrium. The size of the productivity gain associated with an innovation increases with effort to create larger innovations (not explicitly defined) and is balanced on the margin against expected cost. These costs are the opportunity costs of obtaining smaller monopoly rents sooner for a smaller innovation, and since Aghion and Howitt assume that larger innovations happen with a lower probability, the opportunity cost increases with the size of the innovation. This characterization of productivity impacts is unlike the reality we observe where different technologies have different and often unforeseen impacts. However, their objective was not to model the hierarchical structure of technology but rather to develop a model of economic growth that takes account of the creative destruction, which occurs as a result of the endogenous decisions.

Aghion and Howitt (1998)

Aghion and Howitt (1998) set out to deal with two of the problems of empirical relevance in Helpman and Trajtenberg (1998*a*). First, the timing of slowdowns occurs immediately on the arrival of the new GPT, something that Aghion and Howitt say is inconsistent with David's observation (1991*b*) that it may take several decades for a major new technology to have significant impact on macroeconomic activity. Second, they argue that reallocations of labour into R&D when the GPT arrives cannot be large enough to cause a productivity slowdown of the sort that is observed in reality. They interpret David to mean that there should be an initial period in which the macro data are unaffected by the arrival of the GPT.

To consider the first empirical problem concerning the timing of the slowdown, Aghion and Howitt build a model in which there are three distinct phases. Their main innovation is the introduction of the first phase in which the GPT has arrived but output remains constant. They offer three reasons for this constancy: measurement error, complementarities, and their new concept 'social learning'. They focus on the third reason for the explanation.

Their model is similar to Helpman and Trajtenberg's modelling of complementarities in that each sector that produces final output engages in R&D to produce sector-specific components for the GPT before it can be used in that sector. However, unlike Helpman and Trajtenberg, they require that each sector must first acquire a template to go with the GPT before the sector can begin the process of developing components. Firms can acquire the template through independent discovery using their own R&D or from imitation of other firms that they observe. Their R&D is conducted by sector-specific labour that has no other use. Nothing changes in measured aggregates during the phase of template discovery because no resources are being reallocated, so there is no change in output. The initial probability that any firm in any sector will independently discover its template is low. But the probability of acquiring a template increases as discoveries are made because firms can imitate by observing the successes of other firms. So the more templates that have been discovered, the higher is the probability of success for those firms that have not yet made the discovery, and so the rate of template discovery accelerates over some range. Once each firm discovers its template, it enters the second phase. This phase is the same as the first phase in Helpman and Trajtenberg (1998a). Once the template is discovered, firms move resources out of output production into R&D to produce the components that are defined by the template and that are required for implementation of the GPT. This diversion of labour resources causes an output reduction. The rate at which firms discover an implementation from their R&D efforts is an increasing function of the number of firms in the second phase and a random Poisson arrival process. Upon successful discovery of an implementation, each firm moves into the third phase, which is where output growth occurs.

Generalized labour (not counting the sector-specific labour that remains unemployed once a template is discovered in the first phase) is the resource constraint, each unit of which can produce either one unit of the component or output according to the production function. Of course, the second phase contains assumptions that are not based on empirically believable behaviour but that are explicitly designed to obtain results which avoid the property they criticize in Helpman and Trajtenberg. Also as with Helpman and Trajtenberg (1998a), Aghion and Howitt use the Dixit–Stiglitz production function and assume that components are created for the GPT, rather than the GPT being a component in a wide set of applications. Thus, they encounter the same problems as Helpman and Trajtenberg (1998a) in that all components are substitutes rather than some being complements, so that the intuition of how a GPT operates when it enters a production system is reversed from what is observed.

Aghion and Howitt argue that the second problem is relatively easy to deal with because a 'massive and fundamental' change in technology would cause adjustment and coordination problems. They state that these show up as changes in sunk capital, increased rate of job turnover due to higher rates of innovation, and an accelerated rate of obsolescence. They do not model this sunk cost problem.

III. CONCLUSIONS

The literature on historical and appreciative theories of GPTs and other similar concepts concerns broad sweeping views of major technological changes that drive socio-economic and structural change. This literature does not provide formal models but is rich in the complex detail of how technologies in general and GPTs in particular can have revolutionary effects on whole economies. A common theme is that the evolutionary, path-dependent process that generates GPTs and then integrates them into the economic system is complex and filled with uncertainty. Individual agents are not capable of foreseeing the full implications of any GPT because its effects stretch over many decades and cut across many lines of decision-making, and impact on many social and economic institutions.

The existing formal models of GPTs are technically complex but, nonetheless, capture very few of the complexities of actual GPTs as revealed by the students of history and technology. These models are open to three sets of objections:

1. Some awkward assumptions, which are inconsistent with the stylized facts presented in Chapter 4, are used in order to create models that are solvable, for example, GPTs arriving exogenously, a specific pool of labour being used only for making GPT templates, GPTs requiring components rather than being components in their downstream applications, and components associated with GPTs all being substitutes for each other.
2. Many of the complexities of the character, evolutionary path, and technological complementarities with other technologies including other GPTs are ignored in order to create models simple enough to be handled by standard maximizing techniques.
3. All of the models assume that the entire economy is composed of a single GPT and its related technologies. Thus none of the issues related to how the behaviour of different GPTs affect the macro behaviour of the whole economy can be investigated.

All these three are features of an emerging research agenda and so these comments should be understood as markers for further research rather than arguments for ignoring these first pioneering attempts at modelling the impact of GPTs.

What these comments do show is a need to develop a different modelling methodology in order to avoid some of the awkward and unrealistic assumptions needed to make these first-generation models work, as well as incorporating more of the stylized facts. In particular, an explicit modelling of uncertainty and the use of a non-stationary equilibrium concept is called for. This is the modelling task that we take on in Chapters 14 and 15 building from our earlier work.

12

Scale Economies in Economic Growth

Part III is devoted mainly to the development of formal theories of sustained economic growth. Before doing so, however, we need to consider the place of scale economies at the microeconomic level, in technological history, and in aggregate models of economic growth. We are mainly concerned here with those scale effects that are associated with physical production technologies. Arthur (1994) in his pathbreaking work on increasing returns to scale was concerned with any effect that lowered unit costs as output increased. He also devoted much attention to the issue of product selection when several versions of a new product, either a capital or a consumer good, competed with each other for acceptance. Here, we are mainly concerned with the long-term effects of scale economies that are associated with the technologies of production, as these are the ones that are of most interest in the models of long-term sustained growth that we develop in subsequent chapters.

The history of technological change is replete with cases of new technologies that are associated with scale effects. Many innovations have permitted the exploitation of pre-existing large-scale economies; others have drastically shrunk the efficient scale of operations. Understanding what is at issue here poses some problems of interpretation since the normal theoretical explanation of scale effects concerns changing the scale of activities with a given state of technology, while we are concerned mainly with scale effects that arise as technologies change.

We start with a brief survey of the treatment of scale effects in microeconomic theory, relating the existing abstract theory to some empirical observations concerning technology. We argue that the typical theoretical treatment found in the literature is scholastic (with all the strengths and weaknesses of the scholastic philosophers discussed in Chapter 7) in that it attempts to deduce real-world behaviour from highly abstract arguments that have little or no empirical content. For example, none of the entries in *The New Palgrave: A Dictionary of Economics* that are relevant to scale economies offer any significant help on the empirical sources of scale effects. There is only one mention of an empirical technological relation in all of the articles. Eatwell (Eatwell and Newman 1987: vol. 4, 166) states: 'There are some examples in which outputs are an increasing function of inputs for purely technical reasons.' He goes on to cite the relation between the capacity of a pipeline and the material used in its construction as the diameter of the pipe is increased. One would hardly guess from Eatwell's article, let alone the other relevant *Palgrave* entries by Baumol, Becattini, Oi, Silvestre, and Vassilakis, in which not one technological relation is mentioned, that technological relations lie at the heart of so many observed cases of scale economies. For example, in Silvestre's article 'Economies and Diseconomies of Scale' he (1987: 80–3) mentions only indivisible inputs, set-up costs, and Adam Smith's division of labour as sources of scale economies.

I.   ISSUES OF SCALE IN MICROECONOMIC THEORY

If the scale of operations is to be increased, the capital goods that deliver capital services can be increased in two distinct ways: they may be *replicated*, which means creating units identical to those already in use; or differently designed goods may be used to operate at a larger scale of output. In this second case, we speak of *reconfiguration* of the capital goods to distinguish this activity from *replication* of identical capital goods. Reconfiguration does not necessarily mean the invention of a wholly new design. Where the different goods use only known technological knowledge, this is a *long-run reconfiguration* occurring in the context of constant technology. When the different goods embody newly developed technologies, we speak of *very long-run reconfiguration*.

The standard theory of production uses a single-stage production function showing output of the *i*th product as a function of the service flows of *n* inputs:

$$X_i = \psi_i(s_1, s_2, \dots, s_n) \tag{12.1}$$

In micro-theory textbooks, equation (12.1) is usually assumed to be a linear homogeneous function so that multiplying all inputs by the scalar, λ, multiplies the output by λ. Most of these books argue that, in the absence of indivisibilities, constant returns to scale obtain in the long-run. Decreasing returns to scale are ruled out in the absence of a hidden fixed factor because if all else fails, production facilities can be replicated. Sometimes the existence of constant returns is simply assumed because of its tractable algebraic characteristics; sometimes, however, it is argued. The argument typically starts with some version of the proportionality postulate. This was stated by Koopmans (1957: 76), one of the founders of the formal approach to production theory, as follows:

[I]f an activity $a = (a_1, a_2, \dots, a_n)$ is possible, then every activity $\lambda a = (\lambda a_1, \lambda a_2, \dots, \lambda a_n)$ of which the net outputs are proportional to those of *a*, with a non-negative proportionality factor, λ, is also possible.[1]

According to Koopmans, the proportionality postulate implies that increasing returns to scale are impossible unless there is an *indivisibility* or lumpiness in one or more of the inputs. If there were no such indivisibility of inputs, the technique that proves superior at the higher scale could, in his words, always be 'subdivided proportionately' to produce efficiently at the lower scale.[2] It seems clear, in this

---

[1] In this activity analysis treatment, a_1 can be thought of for our purposes as the output, and $(a_2, \dots, a_n)$ as inputs.

[2] Koopmans goes on to make clear that he regards such indivisibilities as common in the real world and so does not believe that constant returns are typical of many real-world production functions.

context, that Koopmans means by 'indivisibility' the impossibility of reducing all the inputs $a_1, \ldots, a_n$ by the same proportion $0 < \lambda < 1$.[3]

Notice that this deduction—scale effects can only result from indivisibilities in capital goods—is made from a highly abstracted formulation that contains no empirical content concerning the activity in question. No empirical constraints are used in the formulation of the concept of an activity. Nor are capital goods explicitly modelled. The correct deduction is not that scale effects can only result from a lumpiness of inputs but that this abstract formulation has removed all possible sources of scale effects other than those that are associated with some characteristic of the input flows, of which lumpiness is the obvious candidate. This kind of reasoning is close to that used by the scholastic philosophers whom we considered in Chapter 7. They were interested in real-world phenomena but thought that truth about them could be discovered by abstract a priori reasoning alone.

Of the many problems with formal arguments based on this principle, the most basic is its high level of abstraction. The reader is never invited to consider what 'subdividing an activity proportionately' might mean in particular empirical technological circumstances. So let us take the unusual step of asking what the postulate implies in the case of some specific real-world production activity.

Assume that activity a is the manufacture of a steam engine that will deliver 100 horsepower per period. The inputs are a specified set of materials, power, services of various machine tools, and services of various types of labour. Assume that we now wish to produce a steam engine that will deliver 50 horsepower per period. 'Subdividing the activity proportionately' might mean reducing all the dimensions of the steam engine in equal proportion. Or it might mean altering all of the inputs— materials, machine tool hours, power, labour, etc.—in equal proportion. Notice that these are *alternative rather than identical ways* of 'subdividing the activity', an observation that must immediately suggest some ambiguity in the concept of subdividing.

First, consider altering the inputs. Some inputs are three dimensional solids (e.g. the base on which the engine is mounted), others are two-dimensional surfaces (e.g. the walls of the boiler), and yet others are effectively one-dimensional (e.g. the various wire cables). So building a working engine that uses exactly λ as much of each input is likely to be physically impossible and certainly would result in a technically inefficient engine, as pointed out by implication in the basic engineering literature.

Next, consider shrinking all the dimensions of the engine in the same proportion. Because of the different dimensionality of the parts, this will alter the material contents of the engine in different proportions. Also scaling all of the engine's dimensions by some fraction λ and providing it with λ as much fuel will *not* alter its output of power in the proportion λ. For one reason, the ratio of heat loss through the engine's cylinders to the power delivered by those cylinders rises as the

---

[3] Vasillakis (1987: 761) invokes indivisibilities in his explanation of how increasing returns may be related to the division of labour.

size of the cylinder falls. (Since the time of Isaac Newton, practical engineers have known that a small body loses heat faster than a large body. See for example, Cardwell 1995: 158.)

In summary, one can build a steam engine that will produce 50 rather than 100 horsepower per period, but this cannot be done either by scaling all the dimensions of the 100 horsepower engine by 50 per cent or (what is *not* the same thing) by reducing all the inputs that go to make up the engine by 50 per cent. This discussion suggests that we look to real-world relations to find sources of scale economies and not to some abstract a priori argument that rules them out by definition.

Scale Effects Arising from the Technology of Producing Capital Goods

Early Austrian capital theorists (e.g. Böhm-Bawerk 1889; Wicksell 1893) asked: Why is roundabout production chosen when it requires waiting? They answered, without wholly convincing arguments, that the explanation lay in the superior productive power of indirect (capital-using) over direct (non-capital-using) means of production. Eaton and Lipsey (1997) have sought to make this proposition more secure by deducing scale effects in the technology of producing capital goods on the basis of a very small, but critical, input of empirical knowledge. What follows is a short intuitive version of the main points in their formal proof by contradiction.

Assumptions. (1) There is a positive cost of waiting (i.e. the interest rate is positive). (2) Capital goods are needed to yield given flows of services over time and a decision must be made on the amount of durability to build into these goods. (3) The technology of building capital goods displays constant returns in the sense that the long-run reconfiguration of a capital good to embody λ more or less capital services implies that the cost of producing that capital good changes in the proportion, λ.

Implication. Interest costs are minimized by minimizing the capital good's durability.

Empirical observation. Virtually all real capital goods could be made to be less durable than they now are. So if the amount of services embodied in a capital good is a measure of its 'lumpiness', and if embodied services vary directly with durability, *endogenous lumpiness* must be created when capital goods are produced (i.e. the decision is made to embody more services in a capital good than are physically necessary).

Contradiction. The empirical observation of endogenous lumpiness is inconsistent with the implication drawn from the three basic assumptions: unit costs of delivering a capital good's services are minimized by minimizing durability.

Conclusion. Since assumption (1) is known to be true and assumption (2) may be taken to be to verified by observation of the great majority of capital goods (we know of no exceptions), the conclusion is that assumption (3) must be false. This assumption is then altered as follows: *There is a universal scale effect in embodying services in capital goods: as durability of the capital good is increased, there is some range starting from zero over which the services that it embodies rise faster than the cost of adding to the good's durability.*

This scale effect appears to be rooted in the physical nature of durable goods, which yield their services over time, and it seems likely to us that this is the scale effect that the Austrians were looking for when they tried to explain the efficiency of roundabout production. Examples are given in the next three subsections.[4]

Scale Effects Arising from Geometrical Relations

We live in a three-dimensional world that entails many scale effects, both increasing and diminishing. These effects typically require neither input indivisibilities nor violation of the neoclassical assumption that the production function for final output displays constant returns to scale, since the causes of the scale effects are found in the long-run *reconfiguration* of the capital goods that deliver services to producers of non-capital goods.

The geometrical relation governing any container typically makes the amount of material used, and hence its cost (given constant prices of the materials with which it is made), proportional to *one dimension less than* the service output, giving increasing returns to scale with respect to the inputs of materials over the whole range of output.[5] For example, the capacity of a closed cubic container of sides s is s^3. The amount of material required for construction is $6s^2$. So material required per unit of capacity is $6/s$. This relation holds for more than just storage containers. Blast furnaces, ships, and gasoline engines are a few examples of the myriad technologies that show such geometrical scale effects.

Also, costs of construction (other than materials) often increase less than in proportion to the increase in the capacity of any container. For example, the amount of welding required to seal the sides of the container referred to above is proportional to the total length of the seams, which is $12s$ or $12/s^2$ per unit of capacity. So not only are both the amount of material and the cost of welding per unit of capacity falling as the capital good's capacity is increased, they also fall at different rates.

Scale Effects Arising from Physical Laws

In the case of most long-run changes, a different design of capital goods is required if a different capacity rate of service flow is to be delivered efficiently. The physical nature of the world in which we live typically implies non-constant returns to outlay: the cost of producing a unit of the capital service varies as the output capacity of the capital good is varied. If these effects are to be allowed for in the neoclassical production function given above, they will show up as a change in the price of a unit of capital services produced from the reconfigured capital goods. Here are a few of the many possible examples.

The geometrical reasoning given in the previous subsection cannot produce a final conclusion about scale effects related to containers; one needs to know some physics as well. It is imaginable, for example, that as the capacity of a container is increased, the

---

[4] No claim is made that these categories exhaust all possible sources of scale effects.

[5] For example, if the output is a two-dimensional pasture, the input is a one-dimensional fence; if the output is a three-dimensional storage room, the input is two-dimensional walls.

walls would need to be thickened proportionally, making the volume of material increase linearly with the container's capacity. Physical relations dictate that in most cases this is not so. Although some thickening is often required, in many (probably most) cases, the thickening is less than in proportion to the increase in the surface area. In such cases, the volume of material increases less than in proportion to the increase in capacity (although more than in proportion to the increase in surface area).

To make a light bulb last longer, what is required is to alter the strength of the filament without a proportionate change in most of the other materials that make it. To make a light bulb deliver a larger wattage of light, what is needed is to change the resistance of the filament with no change in the glass or the socket of the light bulb. This gives increasing returns to reconfigurations designed to alter either the duration or rate of flow of the services of the light bulb over a wide range of duration and wattage.

There are many scale effects associated with ships. First, the maximum speed that a displacement hull can be driven through the water is proportional to the square root of the length of the hull on the waterline (planing hulls obey different laws). No amount of a priori reasoning could reveal this rather mysterious relation (Hiscock 1965: 138). Second, while a ship's carrying capacity is roughly proportional to the cube of its length on the waterline, geometrical relations plus the physics governing structural strength of a hollow body dictate that the ship's cost is related approximately linearly to its waterline length (Rosenberg and Birdzell 1986: 83). Third, altering the ship's size also alters its handling and safety characteristics in complex ways. Fourth, as the size and other characteristics of a ship are changed, there is an alteration in the materials best used for its construction. Thus, building larger ships alters carrying capacity, construction costs, operating costs, speed, and other handling characteristics, each in a different proportion.

If all the dimensions of a bridge are altered in the proportion λ, its structural strength is altered by $1/\lambda$ and its weight by λ^3 (under the simplifying assumption that it is optimal to use the same types of materials in bridges of all sizes) (Adams 1991: 81). In other words, bridges and other similar structures, exhibit diminishing returns in the sense that as their size and the amount of materials used in their construction are increased, their strength increases less than in proportion. This structural relation is one of the most important sources of diminishing returns to reconfiguration that limits the extent to which other sources of increasing returns can be exploited by building larger versions of some generic capital good.

According to the physics of heat, the heat loss from blast furnaces is proportional to the area of its surface, while the amount of metal that can be smelted is proportional to the cube of the surface sides. This is a source of increasing returns in the relation between fuel used and output capacity of such furnaces.

As with blast furnaces, the heat loss from a steam engine's cylinder is proportional to the cylinder's surface area while the power it generates is proportional to the volume of the cylinder. This is one of the several reasons why the thermal efficiency of a steam engine is an increasing function of its size over a wide range starting from zero. This in turn is why steam-powered factories were built much larger than the water-powered factories that they displaced. There are no similar effects with electric motors, which is one reason why small-scale parts manufacturers (feeding into large-scale assemblers) became efficient when electricity replaced steam as the major power source of industry.

These examples illustrate that when the rate of output is altered in the long run, and capital is altered by reconfiguration rather than replication, the nature of the world in which we live will almost always produce a complex set of scale reactions, some tending to reduce the unit cost of output, some tending to increase it. Other reactions will alter the capital good's performance characteristics in ways that are only indirectly reflected in the relevant service flow. With long-run reconfiguration, the typical theoretical thought experiment of multiplying all inputs by the same constant λ is irrelevant. Engineers are never given a bundle of inputs and told to design a piece of capital. Instead they are given the output specifications and told to design the most efficient capital good to produce it.

Scale Effects Arising from Complementarity and Risk of Breakdown

As observed in Chapter 3, a capital good usually comprises several components that are technological complements to each other. Each component of a capital good is typically subject to a number of stresses and strains over the lifetime of the entire good. Bridges, buildings, and other structures must withstand various shocks generated by weather. An internal combustion engine must withstand strains each time it starts. Electronic communication networks must withstand power surges. Airlines must withstand the closures of airport nodes due to weather. Technological complementarities plus uncertainty about how long each component will last, or how resilient each will be to shocks over their lifetimes, create a problem for builders of capital goods.

Carlaw (2000, 2004) shows that scale effects result from the complementarities among components that make up capital goods and the risk associated with how long each component will last. This risk is modelled as the ability to withstand stresses that either arrive in each period with some probability or that arrive with some uncertain magnitude in any given period. The intuition of how scale effects arise in his model can be illustrated with a simple example.

First, suppose a given capital good has only one component. Assume that the probability that the component will be hit by a destructive stress in any given period is 0.5 and the builder of the capital good wants it to yield services for three periods at a rate of one unit of service per period. When a stress arrives, it does so at the beginning of the period, and the component delivers its services in that period only if the number of stresses it has been designed to withstand has not then been exceeded. Assuming a zero rate of time discount, the expected total value of services over three periods increases linearly as the component is built to withstand more stresses.[6] Second, suppose a capital good comprises two components, each with the

---

[6] If the component is built to withstand no stresses, the probability of surviving three periods is 0.125 and the expected total services is $3(0.125) = 0.375$. With the ability to withstand one stress, the probability

same but independent probability (0.5) of a destructive stress occurring at the beginning of each period, and the loss of one component renders the good useless. In this case (again assuming a zero rate of time discount), the expected value of total services increases at an increasing rate over some range as the number of stresses each component can withstand is increased.[7] Within each component the inputs that create its durability are assumed to be divisible. (Although we have an integer problem, it is an artefact of the model's construction where we assume discrete stresses in each period.) So the cost-minimizing agent will create durability to exploit the scale effects inherent in the nature of multiple component systems and environmental uncertainty. Furthermore, even if the system were to comprise a very large number of small complementary parts, each would still be made durable (able to withstand more than one shock) to exploit the latent increasing returns to scale that exist due to the technological complementarities and probabilities of failure among the components of capital goods.

Interestingly, this analysis reverses Koopman's argument that scale effects exist because of indivisibilities. In this case, scale effects exist because of the uncertain nature of the world in which we live and the technological complementarities among components of capital. Indivisibilities are then an endogenous phenomenon that are created because of scale effects, just as Eaton and Lipsey (1997) argued they were.

Scale Effects and the Neoclassical Constant Returns Production Function

To see the compatibility of scale effects and a neoclassical constant returns function, we adopt the terminology of the Austrian economists rather than of the national income accountants: capital goods are 'intermediate goods' and consumer goods (and services) are 'final goods'. Let the production function for a final good, G, be linear homogenous in inputs $j_1, \ldots, j_n$:

$$G = f(j_1, \ldots, j_i, \ldots, j_n) \tag{12.2}$$

where j_i is some service provided by an intermediate good, for example, power measured in horsepower provided by a steam engine just large enough to deliver the required flow efficiently. Then let all the physical input flows be doubled and, by definition, the output flow will also be doubled. But now a larger steam engine can

---

of surviving three periods is 0.5 and the expected total services is $3(0.5) = 1.5$. With the ability to withstand two stresses, the probability of surviving three periods is 0.875 and the expected total services is $3(0.875) = 2.625$. With the ability to withstand three stresses, the probability of surviving three periods is 1 and the expected total services is 3.

[7] If each component is built to withstand no stresses, the probability of surviving three periods is 0.0156; with the ability of each to withstand one stress, it is 0.25; with the ability to withstand two stresses, it is 0.766; and with the ability to withstand three stresses, the probability of surviving three periods is again obviously 1. Expected total services in each case are calculated as in n. 6. We see in this case that there is a range of increasing returns from zero to two hits. But building the components so that each can withstand a third hit yields diminishing returns for this last unit of durability. In other words, the average cost curve is U-shaped.

be built to provide the flow of $2j_i$. Given the normal economies of steam engine construction and operation, this larger flow will be delivered at a lower unit cost. So the assumption of linear homogeneity of the production function for final goods is maintained and the scale effects that are going on behind the scene in the production of the service flow show up as a pecuniary economy for the final goods producer. As long as the intermediate stages of production in which the capital services are produced are not modelled, the fiction of overall constant returns can be maintained. Box 12.1 gives a simple example of this relation, which is chosen because its transparency allows the issues to be easily identified.

Box 12.1. An Example of Increasing Returns to Scale

Let there be a firm that is in the business of pasturing other people's horses. One square unit of fenced space is required to accommodate one horse. Assume that the sides must be linear, in which case cost minimization requires that the field be square. The grass is free and the only production cost is the fence, which is continuously variable. When the firm wishes to pasture more horses, it increases the size of its fenced field.

Write the firm's production function in terms of the input of capital services, P, measured in square acres of pasture, and the output, H, measured in the number of horses pastured:

$$H = P \qquad (12B.1)$$

This is the neoclassical constant returns production function relating inputs of factor services to the flow of output. It is, however, the second stage in a two-stage production process.

Now write the production function for the capital service, pasture. The input, F, measured as the total number of feet of fence, produces a capital good, P, measured in square feet of pasture:

$$P = (F/4)^2 \qquad (12B.2)$$

This production function is the first stage in the two-stage production process.[8] It displays increasing returns since

$$dP/dF = F/8 \qquad (12B.3)$$

is increasing in F. So, as the length of the fence is varied by the multiple λ, output of pasture acres varies by λ^2.

In this two-stage process, the inputs that go into the first-stage production of the capital good can be called the primary inputs—the fence in this case—and the outputs of the capital good, which are the inputs that go into the second-stage production of the final good, can be called the intermediate inputs—in this case the service of fenced pasture.

---

[8] The first stage also consists of two separate operations: first, a capital good is produced; and second, it is used to provide service flows, which are used in the production of the final good. These two operations are combined by defining the capital good in terms of its service output. Thus equation (12B.3) is simultaneously the production function for the capital good, fenced pasture, and for the flow of capital services of fenced pasture per unit of time.

Box 12.1. (continued)

Next, substitute the capital service production function of (12B.2) into the output production function of (12B.1) to get:

$$H = (F/4)^2 \qquad (12B.4)$$

This is the production function for final outputs in terms of primary inputs, the fence that makes the capital good, which provides the capital service of protected pasture. It displays increasing returns since

$$dH/dF = F/8$$

is increasing in *F*.

Finally, letting a foot of fence cost one unit of money, the total cost of fencing the pasture is *F*, and the cost per pastured horse (unit cost of output) is:

$$C = F/H$$

$$= 16/F \qquad (12B.5)$$

which is monotonically decreasing in *F*, giving increasing returns to outlay.

All this is obvious and no doubt tedious, but the demonstration is important for that reason. There are *no indivisibilities* in this example. The physical nature of the capital good is unchanged and the area of the pasture is a continuous variable. The neoclassical production function, defined in terms of inputs of service flows, displays constant returns to scale. Yet there are scale economies rooted in the geometry of our three-dimensional world. These economies will, however, never be seen, as long as production functions are modelled only in terms of the second stage of production, so that no account is taken of real physical relations that govern the production of capital services by the capital good.[9]

Scale Effects Arising from Indivisibilities

Standard theory has always recognized indivisibilities, or *exogenous* 'lumpiness' as a source of scale effects and modern industrial organization theory has identified a large number of such indivisibilities associated with imperfect competition. There are many once-for-all costs that create indivisibilities, such as the cost of developing a new product or a revised version of an old one, the cost of establishing a brand name, the cost of entering a new market, and so on. With many of today's consumer goods, production runs last no more than a few years, sometimes only a few months, and the cost of developing new products is a significant part of the total costs of

---

[9] Some readers have objected that (12B.4) is no more than a function of a function, which can be assumed to be the production function of the integrated firm with which neoclassical theory is concerned. Our response is: Of course it is just a function of a function, as are all production functions for integrated firms when the production functions for intermediate goods are substituted for the service flow that they provide. The point of the present argument is that we have no justification in assuming constant returns, or any other relation for that matter, until we model the circumstances under which the intermediate service flows are themselves produced. It is the 'redesign' of capital goods that is the source of non-linearities in the production function either for final goods or for the integrated firms.

producing that product. In these circumstances, firms face declining unit costs in terms of quantities and values of inputs as the output of each product line is increased over that product line's lifetime.

An interesting historical case is in the reproduction of the written word that we discussed in Chapter 6. Until the introduction of the printing press, virtually all the costs of reproducing a book were the variable cost of the scribe's time. After the printing press was introduced, the bulk of the costs were the fixed cost of typesetting, and the marginal cost of another copy of a book or pamphlet was quite small. The early Protestants' appeal to the masses though the printed word would have been quite impossible without this cost structure (Dudley 1991: ch. 5).

This printing example illustrates the misleading nature of the commonly heard statement: 'Since all costs are variable in the long run, the long run must be characterized by constant returns to scale.' The ability to replicate establishments implied that the printing industry could expand at constant costs of producing establishments but each and every establishment produced each and every book at a falling cost per copy.

Technological Limits to the Size of Production Units?

In this section we, consider the technological forces that influence the size of individual production units. Such units may be plants for manufacturing, individual ships or airplanes for transport, individual offices for advertising firms, etc. For simplicity, we refer to all these as production units—of which a firm may own one or many.

It is a characteristic of most of the above examples that scale effects are embedded in the physical nature of the world in which we live. Many of these specific sources cause scale effects that are unbounded: the larger the fence, the lower the cost per unit of pasture enclosed; the larger the ship, the faster its hull can be propelled through the water; the larger the blast furnace, the lower are both the construction costs and the heat requirements per unit of ore smelted. If there were the only influences in operation, the size of each production unit would tend to expand until only one unit existed, resulting in a universal monopoly in each product line, mitigated only by the cost of transporting goods to geographically extended markets. In practice, however, there are many other offsetting influences that limit the size of production units.

In some cases, physical relations limit size. It has already been noted that the structural strength of any three-dimensional body diminishes as its dimensions are increased, *ceteris paribus*. For example, a small airplane can tolerate a hard landing that, scaled up proportionately, would destroy a 747. In many cases, turbulence arising from the motion of a body through a gas or a liquid increases more than in proportion to the increase in the dimensions of the body. In other cases, complementary technologies cannot support a larger size of the main technology.[10]

---

[10] As emphasized in Chapter 3, most complex technologies have a fractal-like structure in that they are made up of many cooperating technologies, each one of which is in turn made up of cooperating technologies, and so on, through layer after layer of complexity. Scale effects in any one of these layers will cause scale effects in the main technology.

The smallest workable size of production is seldom the most efficient. As size increases, many characteristics encounter favourable scale effects while others, either in the main technology or in complementary subtechnologies, encounter decreasing returns that eventually dominate. Further increases in the production unit's capacity then result in rising costs per unit of capacity delivered. The optimal size of productive unit is thus the one at which the economies of scale in some aspects of the technology just balance the diseconomies in other aspects.

Now consider the long-run average cost curve for a single production unit under conditions of reconfiguration. This is Viner's long-run cost curve drawn tangent to a series of short-run cost curves, each one for a different reconfiguration of the production unit. As one moves along it from left to right, the capital good is being redesigned to deliver increasing amounts of the services per unit of time. The precise shape of the curve depends on technical relations, which cannot be discovered without a detailed knowledge of the engineering characteristics of the specific technology in question. A priori reasoning cannot tell us about the existence and range of such scale economies and diseconomies.

We have, however, argued that all capital goods display a range of scale economies but that there are limits to the ability to exploit those economies at any given state of technological knowledge. This leads to the prediction that the long-run cost curve has a negatively sloped portion at the left and a positively sloped portion at the right. Note that this is true even in the case in which probability theory shows the cost of protecting against adverse hits on the components of a technology. In other words, there is a range of increasing returns followed by a range of decreasing returns to scale under conditions of long-run reconfiguration of capital.[11] If the curve has a single minimum point, there is a unique scale of operations that minimizes costs of production in the long run. It is possible that the curve may have a flat portion in the middle, with constant returns to reconfiguration, which leads to the use of the term 'minimum efficient scale' to indicate the lowest output at which costs reach a minimum.

It is important to recall that here we are speaking of single production units. Things are different for a firm. It can expand by reconfiguring its capital as long as there are long-run increasing returns to reconfiguration. Once decreasing returns to reconfiguration are encountered, a firm that has the possibility of replicating identical production units need not encounter a rising portion of its long-run cost curve. While output is below the level of a single production unit's MES, the cost curve of the firm that owns it is falling. Then as more identical production units are added, the familiar scalloped average cost curve is encountered, which approaches a horizontal line as the number of plants increases without limit. For example, an airline may use a small commuter jet to service a route with a low passenger density. If demand increases, it may replace its jets with larger jets that operate at lower cost per

---

[11] Carlaw (2004) shows that the diminishing returns portion of the U-shaped average cost curve can also be due to the costs of deferring consumption in order to build capital goods.

passenger mile (long-run reconfiguration). Eventually, if demand continues to increase, it will be using the largest jets available and further increases will be met with more and more of these jets (replication) at constant operating costs.

II. 'SCALE' EFFECTS IN TECHNOLOGICAL HISTORY

In economic history, falling unit costs of output are often observed to accompany many technological changes. These effects are associated with the very long-run reconfiguration of capital that accompanies technological change and so are not the scale effects that economists typically define under conditions of constant technology. Nonetheless, they produce important changes in unit costs when new technologies allow efficient alterations in the scale of operations, and they are directly related to the causes just outlined.

Technological Change: When Bigger Is Better

'Historical increasing returns' arise because the scale effects are permanently embedded in the geometry and physical nature of the world in which we live, but our ability to exploit them is dependent on the existing state of technology. An excellent example of this effect can be seen in the history of blast furnaces. Originally, hand- and animal-driven bellows could only deliver an effective flow of air to quite small blast furnaces. In the medieval period, waterwheel-driven bellows allowed air to be injected with more force so that furnaces could be increased in size, reaping the benefits of lower construction costs and lower heat requirements per unit of output. In the nineteenth century, steam pumps again increased the feasible size of the furnaces, reaping further scale effects. Later, the technique of preheating the air before injecting it allowed an even larger area of molten metal to be effectively bathed in oxygen, further increasing the efficient size of blast furnaces. In each of these cases, the scale economies in materials used and heat loss were balanced by diminishing efficiency of the air delivery system as the size of furnaces increased beyond some critical size. Successive innovations in the air delivery system allowed further exploitation of the scale effects in construction and heat utilization, but each time only up to some critical point.

The exploitation of virtually every cause of a scale effect that we listed in the sections on geometry and physical relations is limited by the current state of technology. New technology is, therefore, required to allow further exploitation of these effects. Here are some important further examples. Every time agents learn to build and operate larger ships, airplanes, or buildings, they reap the unit cost reductions implicit in the relations laid out above. New materials associated with the twentieth-century materials revolution have allowed many processes to be carried on at a larger scale, so reaping more of the favourable scale effects inherent in the basic processes.

Chandler (1990) points out that the combination of the newly developed railway and the telegraph in nineteenth-century USA vastly increased the size of the market.

Unit costs of production fell in many industries that had technologically determined scale economies, which could not be fully exploited in small local markets. Cigarettes, light machinery, electrical equipment, metal manufacturing, oil refining, rubber, paper, glass, aluminium, and steel are just some of the many industries that grew in the latter half of the nineteenth century to become technologically driven oligopolies, serving the US national market. This growth in size and in production efficiency were impossible until the technological innovation of efficient railroads expanded market size and allowed the potential scale effects that had always existed to become realized in practice.

The steady high volume, or throughput, needed to achieve and maintain potential economies of scale and scope could rarely be attained as long as the flow of goods depended on [local markets]....The railroad provided the technology not only to move an unprecedented volume of goods at unprecedented speed, but to do so on a precise schedule, that is, a schedule stated not in terms of weeks or months but of days and even hours...and the telegraph became a critical instrument in assuring safe, rapid, and efficient movement of trains. (Chandler 1990: 53–4)

Notice that to evaluate all these cases, one needs empirical knowledge of technical relations that exist in the real world. No attempt is made to deduce anything about historical scale effects from the mere definition of some relation such as a production function or some a priori, untested postulate such as the proportionality principle.

Technological Change: When Smaller Is Better

Technological change often makes it efficient to reduce the scale of individual operations. For example, the technology of the internal combustion engine, both gasoline- and diesel-powered, gave it a much lower MES than the steam engine. Those engines displaced the steam engine as a supplier of energy at the lower output levels at which the steam engine could be used, but only at high unit cost, and entered small-power-requirement niches from which the steam engine was fully precluded, such as hedge clippers and lawnmowers.

The electric motor disintegrated the steam-powered factory. Assembly moved to large-scale, electrically powered plants while parts were produced in many small-scale operations each using a few unit-drive, electrically powered machine tools. The production functions for many manufacturing goods thus went from a single function for the integrated steam plant to a two-stage production arrangement with one set of functions having small MESs for parts producers and another set with large MESs for assemblers.

Even more radical shifts may come with hydrogen fuel cells. Their technology is still being developed but it is possible that they will be a truly constant return to scale technology with small-scale production units being just as efficient as large-sized units. In this case, every power user may generate its own power supply. The transition to such a radically new technology would require enormous adjustments in the facilitating structure. The production function of virtually all producers would alter drastically with power requirements making no contribution to the determination of their MESs.

Replication and Scale Effects

As noted in Box 12.2 the possibility of replicating identical units, which are required to ensure that firms never encounter decreasing returns to scale, is an empirical question that cannot be settled by a priori theorizing. For the rest of this section, however, we confine our discussion to the frequently encountered cases where replication is possible.

Box 12.2. Replication and Decreasing Returns for Firms

It is clear from what has been said in the text that we expect to find eventually decreasing returns to long-run reconfiguration of single production units. They typically have an optimal, cost-minimizing size beyond which there are diseconomies of larger-scale production.

But what about the firm? In the theoretical literature on scale effects, it is common to argue that, because of the possibility of replication, one should never expect to see diminishing returns to scale at the firm level. This argument is another example of the common attempt in capital theory to deduce empirical behaviour from a priori arguments. The correct prediction is 'where replication is possible, one should never expect to see diminishing returns to scale'. This raises the empirical question: 'Under what circumstances is replication possible?' In *The New Palgrave*, Eatwell (Eatwell and Newman 1987: 166) answers this question without recourse to empirical knowledge: 'barring indivisibilities, there can be no barrier to replication. ... In other words, there can be no such things as decreasing returns *to scale*.' In a similar vein, Silvestre (1987: 81) states:

[A]n exact clone of a production process that exhaustively lists all factors of production should give exactly the same output. The failure to double the output suggests the presence of an extra input, not listed among the arguments in the production function, that cannot be duplicated.

This common style of scholastic argument against decreasing returns to scale implicitly assumes that replication is always possible in any real-world production process, as long as there are no input indivisibilities. But this is an issue that cannot be settled by a priori reasoning based on an abstract model of the production process—a model that omits many of the conditions that affect output other than factor inputs as usually understood.[12] To go further requires an appeal to empirical evidence. Here we can only illustrate the possibilities. On the one hand, to produce more razor blades, a new plant identical to existing ones can be set up in a greenfield site and managed independently. This should yield constant returns to scale and to outlay. On the other hand, if more output is required at a point in space, replication may not be possible.

---

[12] If the list of possible missing inputs is defined as *anything* that might cause the neoclassical production function to display decreasing returns, such as climate, or spatial conditions, the proposition becomes tautological. For it to be non-empty empirically, it must be possible to conceive of observations that would conflict with it. This is not possible if, when the cause of each apparently conflicting example is identified, that cause is then defined as an unstated fixed input.

Box 12.2 (continued)

Here is one spatial example that was important in economic history. As British coal mines went deeper and deeper in the eighteenth century, they went below the level of the water table and flooding became a problem. At first, horses were used—both to turn the capstans that drove pumps and to haul the water, bucket by bucket. This, along with some other techniques, sufficed for a while. But as more and more water had to be removed from the ever-deepening shafts, the number of horses used at a specific pithead increased. Although there is no practical limit to the amount of energy that can be obtained from horses if there is room for them to operate, there were physical limits to the number that could be applied to any one pithead. Long before that absolute limit was reached, costs per unit of horsepower increased due to such problems as non-linear increases in difficulties of coordinating the operation of horses, both when at work and when changing shifts. There was no input indivisibility, only spatial problems in applying inputs to a point in space and coordination problems in dealing with larger quantities of inputs—problems that no amount of abstract theorizing about production functions could reveal. There was no point replicating by building another pit; more power was needed at each pithead as mines went deeper. (The steam engine solved the problem by delivering far more power at a single point than horses could.)

This example is only an illustration of the general proposition that one cannot deduce anything about scale effects if one knows nothing about the physical conditions under which production is occurring. For example, replication is possible in some circumstances, where no worse than constant returns is predicted, and not in others, where the possibility of decreasing returns arises whenever the physical conditions dictate decreasing returns to reconfiguration.

Industries that have potential scale economies rooted in such things as the geometry and physics of the real world, and where replication is possible, will typically operate under long-run constant cost and very long-run 'historical' increasing returns. Consider the example of the smelting of ore already discussed. At any moment of time in the past, the industry operated under long-run constant returns. For any given state of technology, there was an optimum size of smelter that minimized average costs. Each smelter could be expected to operate more or less at capacity. Expansions of output then took place mainly by replication of smelters and hence at constant costs of production. Thus the industry had a horizontal long-run cost curve. In the very long run, however, the industry operated under historical increasing returns to scale. Technological advances, reviewed earlier in this chapter, periodically raised the efficient scale of operations of each individual smelter and caused costs to be reduced as the new technology enabled larger smelters. While the new smelters were replacing the old over a long period due to the long life of smelters, observed costs were falling. But once all smelters had come to embody the new technology, further expansion of output took place by replication at constant costs.

This observation has implications for empirical measurements. Empirically measured long-run cost curves will be negatively sloped only if firms have market power and each operates one unit of the required capital equipment at less than its MES. In most cases, even firms with market power have many units of each type of capital, for example, many blast furnaces, many airplanes, or many drill presses. So one will see constant costs of production due to replication even though each machine tool embodies large-scale economies (economies that will have been exhausted by building each at its optimum capacity). Empirically, the phenomenon of very long-term scale effects due to new technologies can only be observed when a new technology is in the act of replacing an older one.

Analytically, the effects of historically falling costs associated with new technologies that lower the unit cost of production by altering the efficient scale of production units are most likely to be observed as a shift in the aggregate production function than by any of the more conventional methods of measuring scale effects. Such a shift will typically be interpreted as the results of technological change. For sure, it is enabled by such change but its magnitude depends on the amount of scale economies that the new technology allows producers to reap. Later in this chapter we discuss modelling problems associated with such shifts.

III. SCALE ECONOMIES IN MACRO GROWTH MODELS

We have argued several times in this book that the aggregate production function is a theoretical artefact that has no micro underpinnings in the real processes that drive long-term economic growth. Given the present state of economics, the function can be aggregated from a set of perfectly competitive industries but not from the complex set of industries—competitive, large and small group monopolistically competitive, oligopolistic and monopoly—that inhabit the world of our actual experience. Thus, to attempt to model and understand the real forces that drive growth in terms of a single aggregate function is to attempt the impossible and risk being misled. To elaborate on this argument in the present context, we first look at how growth theorists have used the aggregate production function and then show why such a function cannot incorporate many of the forces that we argue have driven long-term growth.

Macro Production Functions in Conventional Growth Theory

Solow, and virtually all those who followed him in the burst of growth theorizing, which lasted until about 1970, mostly assumed constant returns to scale and exogenous technological change. Micro studies of technology had argued that technological change was endogenous from at least the 1970s—with earlier precursors going back to John Rae in the nineteenth century and Joseph Schumpeter early in the twentieth century. Endogenous technological change finally became mainstream in aggregate growth models in the 1980s with seminal papers by Romer (1986) and Lucas (1988). (An earlier endogenous growth model by Kaldor and Mirrlees (1962) was seminal in influencing applied research in Europe but was largely ignored by theorists.)

The standard macroeconomic treatment following Solow (1957) defined the aggregate production function in terms of traditional inputs. Taking the Cobb–Douglas case:

$$Y = F(K, L) = AL^{\alpha}K^{\beta}, \quad \alpha + \beta = 1 \tag{12.3}$$

Constant returns to scale are assumed on the empirical grounds that at the firm level, replication of identical productive facilities with technology held constant should allow output to grow in proportion to inputs. (But note the point made in the Appendix to Chapter 4 that there are unspecified inputs in terms of such things as raw materials and the carrying capacity of the environment that need to grow in proportion to the standard inputs.) Knowledge is *not* assumed to be an input in that function. Instead, changes in technology brought about by new knowledge produced by R&D are assumed to alter the firm's production function, usually by increasing the value of the parameter A. Potentially the parameters α and β can also be altered by technological change and no doubt are at the firm and industry level. They are, however, generally taken as constant in empirical work, with the relatively stable factor shares of labour and capital in the US national accounts, at least since 1950, pointed to as justification for this assumption.

Models that treat knowledge as an input, as in (12.4), are in striking contrast.[13] In Cobb–Douglas form, the aggregate production function becomes:

$$Y = F(K, L, Z) = AL^{\alpha}K^{\beta}Z^{\gamma} \quad \alpha + \beta + \gamma = 1 \tag{12.4}$$

where Z is the stock of knowledge.[14]

Since this formulation is assumed to be capable of being aggregated from micro relations, it implies that when each firm increases its output by replicating existing plants with constant embodied technology, each must add to its stock of knowledge in the same proportion as its other inputs. One firm could add to its proportion of the stock of an unchanged national stock of knowledge by taking knowledge from others (assuming it is rivalrous), but what one firm can do, all cannot. If the stock of knowledge is to be increased in total, this must be new knowledge. Given that technology is assumed to be constant, this is a logical contradiction and, therefore, an undesirable implication. Furthermore, there is no known behaviour similar to that of replication that would predict constant returns to all traditional inputs *plus* new knowledge for each and every firm. Constant returns in (12.4) must then be assumed to be a fortuitous accident. Another consequence of the formulation in (12.4) is that, as in the Solow model, sustained intensive growth at a constant rate is only possible if there are exogenous changes in A. Thus, the agents' choices, including what they devote to R&D to change knowledge, do not influence the long-run growth rate.

Endogenous growth theory uses an alternative formulation of the aggregate production function allowing for increasing returns to scale. For example, using the formulation in (12.4) it assumes $\alpha + \beta + \gamma > 1$. This use of scale effects

---

[13] Mankiw, Romer, and Wiel (1992) provide a similar type of model where instead of the knowledge stock, Z in the aggregate production function in (12.4), they use human capital H.

[14] There is a problem here in distinguishing Z and A. Since changes in technological knowledge shift A, the parameter Z must be human capital excluding such knowledge. If Z is assumed to include all knowledge and A is not a function of Z, then the assumption is being made that growth cannot be sustained at a constant rate by equal rates of growth of physical capital and knowledge with labour held constant.

generates sustained positive growth over the long run. To illustrate, we use the production function defined in Romer (1986).

$$c_i = F(k_i, K, x_i) \tag{12.5}$$

where

$$F(\psi k_i, \psi K, \psi x_i) > F(\psi k_i, K, \psi x_i) = \psi F(k_i, K, x_i)$$

c_i is the output produced by firm i. k_i is the knowledge state of firm i in which it consciously invests and x_i is a vector of additional inputs, which are in fixed supply in the economy, such as physical capital, labour, and other factors used by the firm. K is the state of knowledge obtained from aggregating across the $k_i s$ of all firms and represents a positive social spillover from the private accumulation of knowledge. ψ is a scalar. As shown in the second line in (12.5), Romer (1986) assumed increasing returns to all factors of production and constant returns to those factors that the firm had control over. To generate sustained growth, he assumed at least constant or increasing returns to investment in the generic knowledge input k_i and the aggregate state of knowledge, K, in each firm's production function. Romer (1990) justified this assumption because knowledge is non-rivalrous in use.

Lucas (1988) assumed at least constant returns to the accumulating factors of physical and human capital. In one version of his model, he then added a spillover modelled as a positive aggregate externality in the accumulation of human capital that gave increasing returns to accumulated factors.

Barro (1990) simply modelled the aggregate production function as having the form $Y = AK$ where Y is total output and K is the accumulated stock of generic capital (human and physical).

As Romer (2001) points out, a common characteristic of these models of endogenous knowledge-driven (i.e. technology-driven) growth is at least constant returns to accumulating factors, whether they are labelled generic knowledge, technological knowledge, physical capital, or human capital.

In these models, endogenous choice variables, including investment in physical capital, resources devoted to R&D, resources devoted to human capital accumulation, and population, can influence an economy's rate of growth. However, a number of empirical studies on post–Second World War data show that the predictions of the model do not seem to be supported (see, for example, Jones 1995; Backus, Kehoe, and Kehoe 1992). Contrary to the predictions of the models, population, savings rates, resources devoted to human capital, and resources devoted to R&D have all risen in the countries included in these studies, with no discernible effect on their long-run average growth rates. Some, such as Jones (1995), have interpreted these empirical results as implying that there are decreasing returns to produced factors. Others, such as Howitt (1999), argue that there are constant or increasing returns to the accumulating factors but assume that it is the amount of R&D activity per sector that determines the growth rate and that the number of sectors within the economies studied is growing so that the average amount of factors per sector is constant. In such models, growth is steady in the face of population growth, while increasing amounts of resources being devoted to total R&D activity will cause growth to increase. Jones (1995) argues that such models still have predictions not borne out by the evidence since resources devoted to R&D and human capital accumulation have been increasing without increases in average growth rates.

Production Functions in S-E-Driven Growth

In contrast to the previous discussion, we argue that the economics of technical change cannot be caught in a single aggregate production function having an unchanged form. To see what is involved, we need to consider the effects of innovation on both scale effects as discussed earlier in this chapter and technological externalities as defined in Chapter 4.

Innovation shifts the long-run micro cost curves for individual producing units downwards, but they are still U-shaped in the sense that for a given state of technology there are scales of operation for individual production units that are sometimes too small and sometimes too large to be efficient. We say that the new technology introduces historical increasing returns to scale when the long-run cost curve of production units using the new technology is negatively sloped at the MES for production units operating with the old technology. In contrast, the new technology introduces historical decreasing returns to scale when that cost curve is positively sloped at the MES for production units operating with the old technology. Both these changes are cost-reducing and hence growth-inducing.

When the cost curves shift, production units will be altered in size until their new MESs are reached—assuming there is sufficient demand to purchase the resulting output. After that, wherever replication is possible, firms encounter constant returns under replication for a given technology. Later, when there is another technological breakthrough, adjustment under increasing or decreasing returns will again take place until the efficient new sizes of establishments are installed.

Figure 12.1 shows a stylized version of the shifts in plant production functions brought about by the shifts first from water to steam and then from steam to electricity. Steam caused the typical size of manufacturing plants to be increased under conditions of increasing returns. But once the new MESs were reached, further growth came from replication under constant returns. Electricity introduced increasing returns to scale for assemblers and diminishing returns to scale for parts manufacturers, both judged from the MES of the typical steam plant. Parts producers shrunk in size while assemblers grew, both encountering historical falling costs until their new MESs were discovered and reached. After that, growth of output was once again by replication.

This is a picture of firms getting and exploiting scale effects in fits and starts. With some new technologies, historical increasing returns to scale lead to growth spurts associated with increases in the size of production units. With other new technologies, decreasing returns to scale lead to growth spurts associated with decreases in the size of production units. Sometimes, both changes were associated with a single new technology as was the case with electricity.

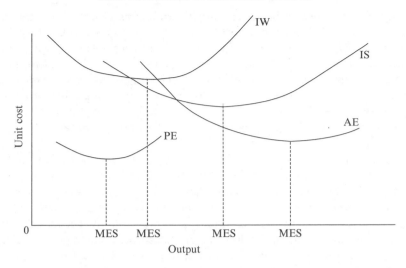

Figure 12.1. *Some stylized long-run average total cost curves for various types of manufacturing plants*
(IW, integrated water-powered factory; IS, integrated steam-powered factory; PE, typical parts producer using unit-drive, electrically powered machine; AE, typical electricity-powered assembly plant.)

An aggregate production function relating measured inputs to GDP could be fitted to the data covering these periods if the data were available, just as it can always be fitted to any data for the relevant inputs and outputs of any micro or macro production set. But its macro structure would not capture what was happening to the MESs or any other aspect of the changes in the micro structure of the typical production facility in the industries that were driving growth. This is because a single aggregate production function displays either constant, increasing, or diminishing returns overall. If there are increasing returns, growth explodes; only if there are constant returns to the accumulating factors, is steady-state growth possible. The kinds of fits and starts of scale economies that emerge through technological change and are exploited once and for all in each production unit, after which further increases occur at constant returns because of replication, cannot be modelled in a single aggregate function. Such a function can be made more or less to fit the data for total inputs and outputs but it cannot model what is generating that data whenever growth occurs because of the alterations in the efficient scale of operations as shown by the examples above.

So much for transitory scale effects typical of technological change, but what also matters for aggregate growth is the technological complementarities introduced by new technologies. As we have so often observed, each new GPT brings with it a set of research opportunities to be exploited. This exploitation does not, however, occur smoothly since it frequently encounters bottlenecks and salients. Also, growth is always in danger of slowing over time as the potential of existing GPTs becomes more fully exploited. New GPTs then rejuvenate the process by presenting a new research programme based on new technological complementarities. It is sometimes helpful to characterize GPTs as massive salients for which many existing and many not-yet-invented technologies become bottlenecks when the GPT arrives. It is the salient nature of GPTs and the process of resolving the bottlenecks they create that generate long-term growth patterns. This engine works at the micro level in fits and starts that are muted at the macro level, and, as we argue in Chapter 13, it may typically follow a logistic time path. These complex forms of behaviour cannot be modelled by one aggregate production function whose form remains constant over long time periods.

Instead, the models we develop in the following chapters use several sectors, each with its own differently evolving production function. This allows us to focus attention on the complementarities and to model knowledge that grows irregularly. Our models' growth processes are largely conditioned by these characteristics of each new GPT, much as we observe in our micro observations. The models display diminishing returns to accumulation that are interrupted by temporary bursts of historical increasing returns with the arrival of a new GPT. But these increasing returns to scale are only a temporary phenomenon. In all cases, there are limits to the scale effects of each new GPT.

13

Appreciative Theories of GPTs

In Chapters 5 and 6, we examined the rich historical experience concerning GPTs and in Chapter 11 we described the existing theories about them. In Chapter 12, we described the treatment of scale effects in the literature and examined such effects in the context of technological change. In this chapter, we go through three levels of formal abstraction as we move from our historical analysis to formal theories of GPTs. Although the first section is long and may appear tedious at first reading, it is an important step in going from the historical descriptions of Chapters 5 and 6 to the full-scale modelling of Chapters 14 and 15.

I. FIRST LEVEL OF ABSTRACTION: ADJUSTMENTS OF THE S-E CATEGORIES

We first provide a detailed treatment that extracts the common experiences we have found in Chapters 5 and 6, placing them into our S-E classification system of technology, facilitating structure, policy, policy structure, and performance. The last classification, performance, takes us into some substantial digressions on such topics as sustainability and accelerating change. Although the experiences we categorize here are important in understanding the role that innovation plays in the growth process, most of them have no counterparts in existing models of GPTs. These have invariably assumed that the short- and long-run effects of GPTs are determined by the technology itself and its predetermined need for supporting technologies. While this may be a reasonable place to begin formal theorizing, we argue that many of the most important effects are determined not by the GPT's own characteristics taken in isolation but by how the new GPT interacts with other existing technologies, the facilitating structure, and public policy.

To start, and for analytical purposes only, we take technological shocks as exogenous. Further, we focus mainly on GPTs. To analyse how the system responds to various shocks, we adopt the heuristic of assuming that all elements of the S-E decomposition are initially fully adjusted to an existing static technology. Thus, none of the agents who control the various elements of technology, structure, or policy have any incentive to alter what is under their control. We then introduce a single exogenous change in technology and enquire into all of the induced changes. This comparative static style of equilibrium analysis is used solely for purposes of understanding how the various elements fit together. In practice, we expect the entire system to be evolving continuously, never reaching anything remotely resembling either a static equilibrium or a balanced growth path. With this caveat in mind, we consider a given change in technological knowledge. This will cause induced changes in other parts of technological knowledge, the facilitating structure, public policy, the policy structure, and performance.

The statements that follow are meant as statements of historical facts generalized from the detailed observations of many technologies, including those summarized in Chapters 5 and 6. In each case, we give one or two illustrative examples but readers of the earlier chapters will be able to add many more. At the outset, we note that the effects studied below are not necessarily exclusive to GPTs. Major changes in our S-E categories are often induced by changes in product and process technologies that are not themselves GPTs. For example, large structural changes followed the introduction of the telegraph. Financial information, production, and transportation could all be much more efficiently coordinated both nationally and internationally once information was transmitted in seconds rather than weeks. However, the transforming GPTs on which we concentrate tend to have a wider range and deeper magnitude of effects than other technologies.

Price and Technology Effects

As a first step, we must consider the channels by which the effects of any initial technological shock are transmitted to the rest of the economy. Neoclassical analysis concentrates mainly on prices and price changes. So the effects of new technologies are often seen as a fall in the price of the service provided by the old technology. Thus, for example, Jorgenson (2001:8) writes that 'the impact of the relentless decline in semiconductor prices is transmitted through falling IT prices'.

But we know that this is only a part of the story. Another major impact of semiconductors is that they enable the production of entirely new things as well as the improvement of old things in ways that have little to do with prices. Instead, the changes occur because the technological relations that govern and limit what we do are dramatically altered by a new GPT. Thus, many impacts of a new GPT are based on relationships that do not act primarily through price changes. (Seeing some of the major effects as occurring through changes in technological relations that cannot be modelled as price changes is an example of what in Chapter 2 we called 'structural contrasts'.) For example, one of the most profound effects of the replacement of waterwheels by steam engines in early nineteenth-century British factories was that factories were freed to locate wherever economic advantages were greatest. As a result, industrial production moved from the countryside, where fast-moving water was abundant, to the new industrial cities to which the latent power was transported in the form of coal. No decrease in the price of water power could have brought about this change, since water power must be consumed where it is generated and the possible sites for its generation are given by technical conditions. Currently, computers and the Internet are enabling a vast array of new products, processes, and organizational forms that were not technically feasible in the pre-computer age.

Effects on Technologies

Next we consider the many effects of a new GPT on technological characteristics. Although the details differ across classes of GPTs, there are certain typical inter-actions that are shared by all GPTs. Some of these are a direct consequence only of the technological characteristics of individual GPTs. Others depend on how specific GPTs interact with each other.

Effects that Depend Only on the Characteristics of the New GPT

Most new GPTs start as relatively crude technologies with a limited number of uses (often one), and only slowly develop the whole range of characteristics that we associate with a GPT. This initial evolutionary path is related to how agents learn about new technological ideas under conditions of uncertainty—learning by doing, by using, and by conscious experimentation. Writing started as a numerical method of recording transactions and took centuries to develop into a full-blown tool for recording all information. Steam power started as a crude technology for removing water from English coal mines, and over 100 years passed from the first working steam engine until it was perfected and used throughout much of the economy. The electronic computer started as a single-purpose technology designed to solve a limited number of military problems. It took twenty to thirty years for it to be improved sufficiently for its use to begin to spread beyond specialized niches, and then another twenty to thirty years for its penetration of virtually the entire economy.

As it develops in efficiency and sophistication, a new GPT enables many other new technologies that could not have existed in its absence, giving rise to new products, new processes, and new industries. All such developments will be spread over a long period of time both because some must await the achievement of a certain level of efficiency in the main GPT and because the cumulative nature of new learning implies that new developments come in a sequence with later ones depending on earlier ones. The list of products and processes that would not be possible without human-made materials, electricity, or the computer stretches over pages, and these were developed over decades, sometimes even centuries.

Effects that Depend on Interactions with Other Technologies

Effects following from the interactions between a new GPT and existing technologies depend on many things such as whether the new GPT is in competition with, or complementary to, each existing technology. Where the incumbent and the challenger are in competition, the relative productivities of the two matter and these will evolve over time. These effects depend on the characteristics of both the new GPT and the existing technologies, some of which will be other GPTs. Each set of relations between new GPTs and established technologies will generate its own transitional and long-lasting effects. Some of the more important ones are discussed below.

A new GPT will typically come into competition with a range of existing technologies that are doing some of the things also done by the new technology. In some cases, the new technology will quickly become superior to the older competing technology. For example, when unit-drive electric motors challenged steam in factories, they quickly established their supremacy as a power delivery system and few new steam-driven factories were built thereafter. In other cases, the initial margin of advantage is small and the transition correspondingly slower. This was the case when early factories competed with the putting-out system and when power looms competed with hand loom weavers.

As the new GPT develops, it will eventually come into competition with other technologies that were initially unaffected by it or were even complementary to it. Steam had only stationary applications to begin with, and then with the development of the high-pressure engine and the solution of several other technical problems, it spread to land transport to compete with horse-drawn vehicles on land and later with wind on the sea. As harbour tugs, steam first cooperated with sail and then, as the efficiency of the iron steamship improved, it competed with sail in a series of niches that it successively occupied: short-haul passenger services, long-haul passenger services, specialized and high-value freight, and finally freight of a low value per ton. Motor vehicles were first complementary with rail in moving material to the railhead but later, as the efficiency of their engines improved along with such complementary inputs as the road system, they provided strong competition to rail. When the new technology becomes dominant, it sometimes internalizes, or cooperates with, a revised version of the old technology. For example, the steam turbine, a combination of waterwheel and steam technologies, remains in use today as an electricity-generating device.

Sooner or later, a new GPT may begin to compete with technologies that are not themselves near the end of their development trajectory. Many of these older technologies are eventually overcome by the new technology, but only after a period of intense competition in which both technologies become more productive. The efficiency of water power was significantly advanced after it came into direct competition with steam for powering factories. The sailing ship was greatly improved after steam began to compete with it. When the new technology finally demonstrates its clear superiority over the old, R&D money shifts away from the old technology so that its productivity stagnates. This shift of R&D is not, however, a cause of the introduction of the new technology but a consequence.

In some cases, there may be little or no competition with the established technologies because the new technology fills a new niche. Regular, long-distance, trans-oceanic trade was created by the three-masted sailing ship, which had no established marine technology with which to compete over long distances. The internal combustion engine provided services that existing steam technologies could not—fast-starting engines that were efficient at small horsepower ratings and had relatively low ratios of weight to power. Only when it was combined with electricity did the hybrid diesel–electric engine seriously challenge steam in such uses as ships and railways.

Sometimes a new GPT is complementary with a different type of existing technology, in which case these new uses will create incentives for the improvement of the older technology's efficiency. This was true, for example, of power and materials during the

Industrial Revolution. Stronger materials were required before high-pressure steam engines could be perfected. It is also true of electricity and ICTs today. In many cases, a new technology will cooperate with existing technologies with no competition between them, as when the computer used electricity and the Internet used the computer. In other cases, technologies may work together in cooperative arrangements as main technologies in a technology system, as when the railway, the iron steamship, refrigeration, and the telegraph created a global market for many farm products in the latter half of the nineteenth century.

In every case that we have considered, the full effect of a new GPT (on productivity among other things) depends on the difference between the range of applications and the productivity of the new GPT on the one hand and the technologies it competes with and/or complements on the other hand. Since both technologies evolve, the effect is time-dependent and cannot be predicted solely from knowledge of the new GPT's own initial (or final) characteristics. This illustrates one of our main themes that a major shortcoming of all existing formal theories of GPTs is that the technology is often modelled as operating in isolation, not in various relations of competitiveness and complementarity with existing technologies, some of which will be other GPTs. Until this is done, there is a risk that existing models will be seriously misleading in suggesting that the key effects of new GPTs depend only on a set of characteristics common to all of them.

Effects on the Facilitating Structure

Technological knowledge is clearly linked to the facilitating structure, since to create economic value, most knowledge must be embodied. This gives rise to a number of characteristic links running from new GPTs to the facilitating structure. We first mention two very general effects. We then consider the channels by which these effects are transmitted. Finally, we consider in more detail the transitory effects as well as the long-lasting effects.

General Effects

When a new technology is introduced, various elements of the facilitating structure will be changed adaptively. For example, the technological knowledge for the mass-produced automobile had to be embodied in factories and cars. Large investments in infrastructures, such as roads and petroleum production and distribution, were required to give them value. New ICT-driven organizational technologies had to be embodied in new flatter, rather than the older hierarchical command structures in firms and in non-paper-based methods of organizing activity within offices. New technologies often require new skills and education facilities to produce them, as well as new production facilities of different size and location from existing ones. Office work created by the Industrial Revolution demanded levels of literacy and numeracy never before required from any but a small number of people. The newer technologies used to produce iron and steel required much larger scales of operation in 1900 than the older ones used in 1800.

412 Modelling Sustained GPT-Driven Growth

Since much time is required to effect these changes, the evolution of the facilitating structure is likely to lag behind the evolution of technology, particularly when technology is changing in ways that require large adjustments in that structure. When railways were first introduced, it took much time for the structures needed to manage and organize their efficient operation to be worked out and installed. Altering the educational system to deal with the demands of the new knowledge society in which the typical person cannot expect to remain in the same job for a working lifetime has been a long and ongoing process, full of uncertainties as to what alterations are desirable.

Channels of Effect

Although all GPTs end up inducing changes in the economy's facilitating structure, GPTs in different classes typically make their effects felt through different channels.

Power delivery systems. New power delivery technologies often have direct impacts across the entire economy. Products and processes that are powered by them are typically radically redesigned and sometimes wholly new ones are enabled by the new power sources. Steamships were a radical redesign of sailing ships as were cars from horse carriages. Airplanes were made possible by, among other things, the internal-combustion engine. Electricity caused a major redesign of the factory and enabled its reorganization in ways that greatly increased its efficiency. It also enabled the redesign of many older products, as when the electric tram replaced the horse-drawn vehicle, and the creation of many new products, such as refrigerators, electric lights, and radios. The efficient size of firms altered in many different industries and public policy responded to the resulting changes in market power.

ICTs. Whereas new power technologies usually have their first impact through new capital goods, ICTs usually have their initial impacts on institutions, and methods of organization. (Of course there must be new capital investment to embody the new technologies.) Later, the institutional and organizational changes will induce changes in product and process technologies, the latter being typically embodied in new capital goods. The introduction of writing in Sumer and of printing in the Netherlands allowed for a large increase in government tax revenues. These in turn had big effects on such things as irrigation, agricultural techniques, and architectural technologies in Sumer and on new financial and commercial technologies in the Netherlands. The modern computer-based ICT revolution caused an ongoing major reorganization of production and administration, both within firms and within geographical regions, as organizations became flatter and production more dispersed. These new methods of coordination led to many new technologies for production, distribution, and design.

Transportation. Changes in transportation technologies can often be employed without major alterations in the ways other existing technologies are currently embodied in capital goods, or the ways machines are laid out on the shop floor. What changes almost immediately is the optimum location and concentration of industry. The three-masted sailing ship transferred the location of the predominant economic activity from the Mediterranean to the Atlantic coast. In some cases, a new transportation technology may create entirely new industries or new ways of doing business. For example, as we saw in Chapter 6, Chandler (1990) outlines the huge, multifaceted effects created in the USA by railroad technologies in the late nineteenth and early twentienth centuries.

Materials. Changes in materials typically cause many product and process technologies to be redesigned, either out of necessity or because they enable changes that increase efficiency and exploit the latent scale effects discussed in Chapter 12. Later, effects are felt in changing institutions and methods of organization. The invention of bronze had its initial effects on product technologies, but eventually led to a major extension of the boundaries of the state, to a greatly increased importance of markets, and to a restructuring of the government (with power passing from the priesthood to lay rulers). The introduction of iron as a generally available material led to alterations in many tools and instruments of warfare. As a result, the organization of production and of military tactics and procedures underwent many changes.

Organizational technologies. These typically have their first impacts as changes in the division of labour internal to the firm, the physical layout of production facilities and the policy structure. The First Industrial Revolution was an organizational GPT that saw production move out of cottages and into early factories. New methods of managing and financing production were required. Later, the new forms of organization enabled many new innovations in products and processes. The factory allowed human and water power to be replaced by steam power, which required a large scale of production to be efficient. This in turn led to many improvements in textile machinery as the pace of production and the stress on the materials increased. After organizational GPTs are introduced, they typically induce a number of technological innovations in other categories, since the new organizational technology highlights new opportunities to adapt the facilitating structure. For example, lean production spread from the automobile industry, where it was first developed, to many other lines of manufacturing, and led to important incremental improvements in information technology, particularly for controlling the production and delivery of parts.

Transitional Impacts on the Facilitating Structure

New investment is needed to bring new GPTs into use. As with just about any new innovation, GPTs require investment to create the capital goods, new organizational forms, and new infrastructures that are needed to give them effect. The only difference from other new technologies is that the slow evolution and diffusion, but eventually widespread applicability, of new GPTs will typically encourage a higher volume of investment spread over longer periods of time and across more agents than most lesser innovations. These are capable of giving rise to investment booms such as accompanied the railroads, the automobile, and the radio (one part of the ICT revolution). Even well-justified investment booms may give way to bandwagon effects of overinvestment and to subsequent busts, which, if the GPT is large enough, could contribute to a serious recession. We do not wish to stress these contentious possibilities but need to mention them because of their potential importance.

The transition from old to new structures often cause many problems that, although transitory, can stretch over decades and sometimes be a source of strife. Periods in which one or more new GPTs are beginning to transform much of the facilitating structure and causing revisions in public policy are typically periods of great uncertainty. Existing arrangements that worked well in the previous technological regime begin to work less well and sometimes become dysfunctional. No one is certain of what adjustments, large and small, are needed to the structure and to public policy. So debate tends to rage with rational persons taking different positions on what is needed.

Agents know that adjustments in the elements of the structure that they control are needed but are uncertain about what these adjustments should be. Thus many investments in structural changes may turn out to be unprofitable.

Business leaders, government, and organized labour may all view the required adjustments in a hostile manner since they are being asked to make changes in institutions and procedures that worked well in past decades (because they were adapted to the previous technological regime).

For example, people may be uncertain as to what changes are needed in the educational system. What is happening to the required skill mix and what kind of new skills are needed and what type of old skills will become redundant? Such debates raged towards the end of the nineteenth century with Britain and Germany taking very different decisions. The Germans decided to establish trade schools where those who did not go on to formal higher education received an excellent training in some trade. The British concentrated their resources on higher education for a small elite and devoted fewer resources for training the working class in the skills needed in the new factories. This gave Germany a comparative advantage in the production of state-of-the-art but standard consumer durables—an advantage that persisted for over 100 years.

Currently the new technologies are providing freely available digitally recorded music, enabled by the computer and the Internet. Existing copyright laws appear ineffective in protecting composers, performers, and publishers and there is much uncertainty concerning how public policy should react.

Since no one can know the future course of the evolution of any new GPT, there is much uncertainty concerning the best accommodating adjustment to make to the facilitating structure. New GPTs require firms and public bodies to rethink their policies with respect to many things such as R&D, investment in new and old technologies, location and size of production facilities, organization of production, management, and finance. Since all agents are making adjustments simultaneously, the appropriateness of one agent's action will depend partly on how other agents decide to act. Rational agents in both the private and public sectors may disagree about appropriate responses, both because they have different sets of incomplete information about relevant events and plans, and because different agents can make different judgements about how best to act under uncertainty (even in the unlikely event that all agents possess the same information). A study of the debates over the last few decades concerning the reorganization of firms, labour practices, education, and government policies reveal both genuine disagreement based on uncertainty and resistance motivated by the desire to protect special interests.

The durability of many of the elements of the facilitating structure delays adjustment even when there is agreement as to what changes are needed. Existing capital will not be replaced by new capital embodying some superior technology as long as its variable costs of operation can be covered. This was one of the main reasons for the long delay in electrifying the whole manufacturing sector in North America and Europe, where it was decades before steam plants depreciated sufficiently to have their operating costs rise above the full costs of a new electrically powered plant. The new pattern of industrial location and firm concentration will not be finalized until all the firms and plants are adjusted to the new technology. The optimal design of plant and management practices may not be obvious after the introduction of a new technology, as was the case with the computer. The understanding of what is needed by way of new infrastructure may take time, as will its design and construction—consider for example, the long discussion about the new 'information superhighway'. Similar adjustment lags apply to human capital where the full adjustment may have to wait until existing workers are replaced by a new generation trained in the requirements of the new technologies.

Firms, industries, and whole countries that do not make the necessary adjustments quickly enough often lose out to other firms, industries, or countries. As emphasized in Chapter 2, this is one of the main sources through which the evolutionary hand works to accomplish adjustments to change. For example, the Venetians did not recognize the need to alter their methods of transport and their trading organizations fast enough after the three-masted sailing ship had drastically altered trading routes and arrangements. This hastened the decline that was being brought about by their unfavourable location with respect to the new routes.

Some elements of the facilitating structure do not respond to economic incentives because they are determined by non-economic forces such as religion and public policy. The effects of a new technology on performance may be influenced by these unresponsive elements of the structure. Public policies, even when they are not trying to protect some existing rents, are often slow to react with needed alterations in the infrastructure and the educational system. Governments in some less developed countries were typically slow to accept that changing technology made investment in telephones and other ICTs much more important than investment in such old technologies as heavy manufacturing.

Long-Term Changes in the Facilitating Structure

New process GPTs often require a reorganization of many existing production processes before their full potential can be realized. The heavy plough altered the way in which agricultural production was organized in early medieval villages. Automobiles were initially produced in similar conditions to those used for carriage production, but within a decade or two, the production process evolved to a scale and form of organization unknown to carriage-makers.

New GPTs typically require new skills on the part of the labour force. The textile machines of the First Industrial Revolution required much less skill than did the hand-operated machinery used in the putting-out system—so much less that children could do many of the jobs. As the factory system matured, its steam-driven machinery required much maintenance and repair from its operatives. Later, when the more reliable unit-drive electric motors came to power factory machines, repair and maintenance could be devolved to a few specialists so that operatives required no significant skill. Operating motor cars and aircraft required different skills from those needed by carriage drivers and mule handlers. Early computers required a great deal of skill to operate and program. However, successive generations of more user-friendly machines required less and less skill and less and less ad hoc programming from users.

New management structures are often required to make new process GPTs work efficiently. The capital-intensive forms of hydraulic agriculture that were enabled by writing required centralized decision-making with respect to investment. The factories of the First Industrial Revolution required an entirely different management and control structure than did the putting-out system. Electronic computers added little to productivity when they were first installed in a structure designed for paper records and verbal communications. Over time, the organization of management and production were drastically altered to take advantage of the power of computers. Electronic data archiving, retrieval, and manipulation slowly took the place of paper systems for filing and transmitting information. Firms became flatter and less hierarchical in organization.

New GPTs often alter the efficient locations of economic activity. The efficient geographical location of production facilities changed radically when steam replaced water, and when electricity replaced steam. The advent of low-cost transport and reliable worldwide communication systems made possible the worldwide decentralization of parts production that occurred in the later years of the twentieth century.

New GPTs have different technologically determined scale economies. These effects have already been discussed at length in Chapter 12. As a further example, we note that the restructuring of firms that was driven by the ICT revolution has led to the devolution to independent producers of many activities that were formerly undertaken by integrated firms. Everything from office cleaning to product design is less often done in-house. The result has been a more competitive structure for the economy in many lines of activity.

New GPTs cause many permanent changes in the facilitating structure that destroy existing sources of rents and create new ones. The permanent alterations in potential rents caused by a new GPT are accomplished with substantial strife as agents defend the threatened sources of existing rents. At the beginning of the nineteenth century, the Luddites who were skilled craftspeople resisted the integration and mechanization of production that accompanied the British Industrial Revolution. In the 1950s and 1960s British printing unions effectively resisted the introduction of automatic methods of printing books and newspapers. More recently, many unions bitterly resisted the reorganization of work induced by the lean production methods of

Toyotaism. Faxes and email destroyed the rents available to postal services, which were previously, along with courier services, the only medium for the transmission of hard copies. (Much of this rental income was used to cross subsidize unprofitable postal operations.) Rosenberg and Birdzell (1986: 309) provide the following list of institutional innovations that were all bitterly resisted in their time because each hurt some groups with political power: the joint-stock company, the department store, the mail-order house, the chain store, the supermarket, the trust, the integrated-process enterprise, the branch bank, the conglomerate, and the multinational corporation. When those with vested interests in old sources of economic rent have substantial political power, a long period of conflict often occurs. Also, owners of firms in industries threatened by superior new technologies, either domestically or internationally, have often sought government assistance to protect them from competition coming from more efficient units. Subsidies, tariffs, and regulation of technological advances are some of the tools typically used.

GPTs typically require new infrastructure. The internal combustion engine enabled cars, trucks, and airplanes, all of which required a massive infrastructure in such things as roads, airports, guidance and control systems, as well as everything that was needed for the discovery, manufacturing, and distribution of petroleum products. Electricity required very large investments in production and distribution systems as did the widespread use of petroleum, which needed to be discovered as well as produced and distributed.

Effects Emanating from the Facilitating Structure

So far we have looked at changes in the facilitating structure that are induced by changes in technology. The reverse causation is also present: exogenous changes in the *facilitating structure* can induce changes in each of the other S-E categories.

Technology. The internal organization of firms and the type of competition among them affects the R&D that they do, and hence the rate and type of new technological knowledge that is generated.

Inputs. Where firms locate, and which of the available production processes they use, will affect the value of resources, and their rates of use and replacement.

Public policy. Changes in the concentration of industry, urbanization, and deurbanization are among the many changes in the facilitating structure that often cause reactive changes in public policy.

Policy structure. The induced changes in policy just mentioned will often require changes in the policy structure to give them effect.

Economic results. Economic results can be affected in obvious ways by changes in virtually any of the elements of the facilitating structure, the amount and type of new capital equipment, the organization, location, and concentration of firms and industries, the education and financial systems; and the infrastructure.

Effects on Public Policy and the Policy Structure

Changes in GPTs typically induce reactive changes in policy and the policy structure. All of the changes that we list below are associated with modern GPTs but some were not associated with GPTs in the past, when public policies were often, but not always, much less important than they are today.

Induced Changes in Policy and Policy Structure

Technology often determines which public policies are feasible. Policing the seas with sail was much more difficult than with steamships. Today traffic can be controlled and everything that a driver does can be monitored with GPS and recording devices on cars in ways that were impossible fifty years ago. Access to doctors and prescriptions can be monitored through smart cards and hence controlled in new ways. International organizations can monitor and control the production of nuclear armaments due to advanced means of surveillance. The last two examples are the result of the ICT revolution as are many other policies made feasible by new ICTs.

New GPTs typically present many challenges to governments looking for optimal reactions. Old policies become irrelevant or even harmful and new policies are needed. Over the last thirty years of the nineteenth century, both Germany and the USA set up educational institutions to train personnel in the new sciences and engineering skills that were required by the Second Industrial Revolution. Britain failed to follow suit and relied on its traditional methods of part-time education and training on the job. These methods were probably suitable to the mechanical thrust of the First Industrial Revolution but were increasingly inadequate to meet the requirements of the Second. This was an important cause of the decline of British industry relative to industries in the USA and Germany. At the end of the twentieth century, biotechnology presented difficult policy issues concerning what should be patentable. Ethical considerations concern such contentious issues as choice of a child's sex (legal in the USA and illegal in Canada), cloning and brain stem research (mainly illegal in the USA and legal in the EU). These lead to debates and legislation that controls and in some cases slows development. Similar problems will no doubt arise with 'nanotechnologies'.

New policies are typically needed to assist a technology to become a fully fledged GPT. The issues involved here are discussed in Chapters 16 and 17. Few if any modern GPTs have been developed without substantial public sector assistance in early stages of their development. The list includes commercial aircraft, computers, biotechnology, and nanotechnology. Publicly funded research bodies, including universities and research laboratories, are active in most countries. In many countries, some of the assistance comes directly from the government. In the USA it often comes through the procurement activities of the Department of Defense.

New technologies that change the degree of concentration in many industries often require a policy reaction. Government regulations in those industries that become less concentrated may become outdated while policy may be slow to recognize the rise of concentration in other industries, new or old. ICT-driven globalization has also increased the amount of international competition so that a high degree of domestic concentration may no longer be a serious threat because the firms are competing internationally. A host of modern forms of cooperation for the development and diffusion of technologies, such as alliances, licensing agreements, and cooperative ventures, are no longer sufficient to prove intent to monopolize. Often they are ways of responding to international competitive situations. Domestic competition policies need to be deeply and quickly adjusted to keep abreast of the technologically driven changes in the conditions of international competition.

New policies instituted in response to new technologies often require changes in the policy structure. New organizational structures are needed to create and enforce international cooperation caused by globalization and to apply a host of new policing techniques, such as genetic identification and television camera surveillance. As governments face new problems created by the new technologies, the old hierarchical departmental structures are becoming as obsolete as they earlier became in private sector firms. Increasingly, civil servants deal with issues that cut across traditional department boundaries. A newer flatter structure seems called for but is not easy to create in the face of an entrenched public sector bureaucracy, which is not subject to bottom-line constraints.

Adjustments in public policy and the policy structure tend to occur with long lags. As we have earlier observed in another context, uncertainty can make unclear what reactions are needed. Even after what is needed has becomes clear, the process of adaptation can be slowed by inertias in political decision-making, plus the resistance of those who are hurt either by the new technologies or by the accommodating changes in public policy.

Exogenous Changes in Public Policy and the Policy Structure

So far we have seen how public policies, and the policy structure needed to give them effect, can be changed in response to changes in technology and the changes in facilitating structure that they induce. Policy and the policy structure may also be changed proactively in an attempt to influence technological change. This may be done directly through such policies as R&D subsidies and tax credits. It may also be done indirectly by acting on other S-E categories. Monopolies may be broken up with the intention of inducing more interfirm competition in prices and innovation. Tax, educational, and research systems may be altered with the intention of encouraging more entrepreneurial activities. Technological change may also be affected inadvertently when, for example, policies designed to protect the environment lead to a burst of innovative activities, or when controls designed to support the exchange rate inhibit the importation of new technologies embodied in foreign-produced capital goods. Policies with respect to inputs may also have indirect effects on technology—usually inadvertent. For example, prohibition on clear-cut logging and certain mining practices have led to innovations to improve the efficiency of the production methods that are still permitted.

Effects on Economic Performance

We have discussed the effects of GPTs on the facilitating structure, policy, and the policy structure. We come now to their effects on economic performance. Such effects will mainly occur only after the new technologies have been embodied in the various elements of the facilitating structure.

The Long-Term Effects of a Succession of GPTs

As we have repeatedly argued, technological change in general, and the introduction of new GPTs in particular, are at the root of long-term sustained intensive growth. We have already reviewed the evidence for the existence of very long-term extensive and intensive growth at the beginning of Chapter 9 and we say nothing more about this important topic here.

The Effects of Individual GPTs

As we have argued earlier, the impact of a new GPT on its own sector, let alone on the whole economy, depends on how it relates to the technologies currently in place. To know how a GPT will affect the growth rate, we need to know such things as (*a*) its current and projected productivity relative to that of the technology it is replacing; (*b*) whether the new GPT is a substitute for, or a complement to, existing technologies in other categories; (*c*) how the new GPT relates to the existing facilitating structure of the economy; and (*d*) the properties of the GPT itself.

The major effects of a typical GPT are felt only slowly at first when it is in a relatively crude form; then as the GPT is improved and applied more extensively, effects are felt at an accelerating rate for a long time, and finally they slow again, as its potential for enabling new inventions and innovations becomes exhausted. This produces something like the logistic curve discussed in more detail later. David (1991*b*) has shown the initial slow rise of this curve with respect to electricity. Very long lags exist because it takes much time for (*a*) the range of a GPT's use and applications to evolve; (*b*) ancillary technologies to be developed; and (*c*) changes to be made in all the elements of the facilitating and policy structures that support it. Typically, several decades are required for a GPT to make a major impact, and that impact may then stretch over more than a century—and sometimes millennia as with iron—as new technologies that are enabled by the GPT are developed.

GPTs and Productivity Slowdowns

It is commonly held that new GPTs will be accompanied by a slowdown in the rate of growth of productivity and that the ICT revolution accounted for the slowdown that occurred from about 1975 to 1995. In Chapter 4, we considered and rejected this general hypothesis. (See discussion under the subheading 'The Myth of the Productivity Paradox' in Section IV of Chapter 4.) Here we merely note that the existing formal theories of GPTs that predict slowdowns do not even model the forces that we argue are important, particularly the relation between a new GPT and those that it challenges and those with which it cooperates. In contrast, most existing theories assume that only one GPT is in use at any one point in time, and that its isolated evolution determines the economy's macro behaviour. They are not therefore designed to explain two sets of observed facts: first, that some new GPTs are accompanied by slowdowns while others are not; and second, that where slowdowns do occur they vary in duration and intensity from one GPT to another.

Product Versus Process Technologies

Process technologies typically lower costs, and prices usually follow them downwards. The employment effects will then depend on the demand elasticities for the products in question. For example, for many decades in the first part of the twentieth century agricultural products had low price and income elasticities, while manufactured goods had high elasticities. Thus, the effect of new price-reducing process technologies in these two sectors differed, with employment in agriculture falling while employment in manufacturing rose. Later, prices and income elasticities of demand for manufactured goods fell while those for services rose and new process technologies lowered employment in manufacturing and raised it in services. More generally, where process technologies are improving rapidly, demand sometimes expands sufficiently to cause employment to rise, making adjustment relatively easy as labour can be drawn from anywhere in the rest of the economy. In other cases, demand expands more slowly and employment falls in spite of increases in output, making adjustment more difficult because unemployment is concentrated in the dynamic sectors and redundant labour must find jobs elsewhere.

The experience with product technologies is usually different since a major new product is successful only if there is sufficient demand to buy it at a rising volume.

The effects on measured productivity also will typically be different. Measuring the productivity-enhancing effects of process technologies has few conceptual difficulties relative to measuring the effects of new product technologies. It is much easier to say what is happening to productivity when the cost of producing existing products is changing than when the main effect of technological change is the introduction of new products.

A GPT will generally affect both product and process technologies, and often organizational technologies as well. Because technological advances in these two types of technologies can have different effects on the performance of the economy, the balance of any GPT between innovations in product and process technologies may matter. A GPT that is biased towards process innovation will encourage productivity growth but raises the issue of how much the demand for the existing range of goods will respond. A GPT that is biased towards product innovation is less conducive to measured increases in productivity and raises issues of how the consumption of existing goods and services will respond to free up the purchasing power needed to buy the new commodities.[1]

Factor Markets and Income Distribution

For purposes of modelling the long-term effects of individual GPTs, we have made the common assumption of full employment of all productive resources. This is a defensible assumption for the very long term but over shorter periods new GPTs can have major effects on employment and unemployment. The theory of long waves

---

[1] We are indebted to Rick Szostak for raising the important issue of the different effects of product- and process-biased GPTs.

associated with new constellations of GPTs and related technologies championed by
Freeman and Louçã predicts recessions and major bouts of unemployment during
the crises associated with the transition from one major technological regime to
another. Without going as far as accepting long-wave cycles, it is possible to accept
that this transition will sometimes be associated with significant amounts of structural unemployment until the labour force reacts to the new pattern of demand by
altering such characteristics as their occupations, skills, and geographic location.

For example, Freeman and Louçã (2001: 184–7) review the large amounts of
unemployment and 'pauperism' that accompanied the mature phase of the First
Industrial Revolution in Britain:

The spectacle of mass unemployment (estimated by Carlyle apparently at nearly 15 percent of
that total labour force) in what was then the wealthiest and most prosperous country in the
world clearly struck him as an extraordinary paradox, and it is difficult not to feel that this was
a period of turbulent transition rather than one of steady prosperous growth, conveyed by
some of the adherents of smoothed trends in reconstructed estimates of GDP growth.
(Freeman and Louçã 2001: 186.)

A new GPT typically requires a different mix of skills and usually some quite new
ones. If at the old prices there is a shift in the pattern of demand, there will be changes
in relative prices of different sorts of labour and the transitional effects depend on the
relative speeds of the demand shifts and the supply responses. In the industries in
which demand is rising rapidly, those already in the occupations gain more the slower
the supply adjusts. Where demands are shrinking, those remaining in the occupations
lose more the slower the supply adjusts. As a result of these lagged supply adjustments
in the face of relatively rapid shifts in the pattern of demand, the distribution of
income may become more unequal. Once the pattern of demand has stabilized in
conformity with the needs of the new GPTs, the supply adjustments will catch up to
some extent and the inequalities in the distribution of income will narrow.

What happens in the long run depends among other things on the demands for
human capital generated by the new GPT relative to the older one that it replaces.
Because the new technologies of the ICT revolution led to an increased demand for
low-skilled and high-skilled jobs, while the older GPT required more medium-skill
jobs and few low- and high-skill ones, the inequalities in the (pre-tax transfer)
distribution of income widened in many countries. Although the increased inequalities were the manifestation of induced increases in the inequality of the distribution
of human capital, the overall results were, nonetheless, more inequality in the (pre-
tax transfer) distribution of income. Furthermore, by globalizing the market for
products of low-skilled labour, globalization has tended to drive down the wages of
such labour in developed nations.

The results have been dramatic. For each of the first seven decades in the twentieth
century, average incomes rose and the distribution of income narrowed. Every income
group became better off but the poor did relatively better than the rich. Then, some
time in the seventh decade, this trend was reversed and since 1980, inequalities in the
distribution of income have widened dramatically. There is still debate about

the causes but we believe that the new technologies have been one of the major driving forces. Part-time work has risen and these, and many other low-wage jobs, do not come with the benefits that accompanied old time manufacturing jobs, such as health insurance and pension funds. Median male wages have fallen and household incomes have risen only slightly (buoyed up by rising female incomes). Bankruptcies among low-income families have soared. For low-income families, labour force participation of both adults is a necessary condition for holding incomes at or near the poverty line. In many countries, the tax expenditure system softens these growing inequalities significantly. In the USA it does very little to change the distribution of income that the market produces. This national growth of haves and have-nots, particularly in the USA, may be one of the most important social issues of the next few decades. It may contribute to a growing divide, economically, politically, and socially, between the two growing extremes of the income distribution. (See, for example, Baumol, Blinder, and Wolff 2003; Head 2003; Shulman 2003; and Warren and Tyagi 2003 for further details.)

What happens to the distribution of income will also depend on what the new technology does to the extent of the market. The three-masted sailing ship, the railroads, and the ICT revolution greatly extended the size of markets. But the first only did so for output and resource inputs. Railroads extended the market for goods in the USA to cover the whole country. As well as extending the market for parts of manufactured goods by allowing production to be coordinated worldwide, the ICTs also greatly extended the market for services. For example, radio, recordings, movies, television, and the Internet have all extended the market for entertainers, creating what is now a truly global market for their services. The same thing is happening in many other fields. For example, computerized surgery will soon allow surgeons in a major hospital to compete with surgeons elsewhere for operating on those who are rich enough to afford their services. This globalization of markets for labour services tends to increase inequalities in the distribution of incomes[2] (see, for example, Frank and Cook 1995).

The above discussion suggests that we should be cautious in accepting theories that build the same specific labour market effects into all new GPTs (as do most existing formal theories of GPTs that deal with the labour market). What happens in the transition, and in the longer term, depends on how the pattern of labour demand that is associated with the new GPT relates to the pattern associated with the technologies it challenges or displaces. There is no reason why this relation should

---

[2] Here is an example. There are two geographical areas each with a population of 100 persons whose incomes are equally distributed from 100 to 200. The markets are initially separated and each is served by two professionals of one variety (such as lawyers) who each serve half of the customers. The better of the two professionals in each market serves those with the higher incomes. So the average incomes of the customers of the two will be 125 and 175. Now let the two markets be unified by some technological change. The best of the four professionals now serves the top quarter of the income distribution in the combined market with a customer average income of 187.5; the other three have customers with average incomes of 162.5, 137.5, and 112.5 respectively. The enlarged market allows more stratification of skills and larger differences in incomes than when smaller markets were each served by fewer professionals. (The standard deviation of the four professionals' clients rises in this example from 50 to 56.)

be the same, GPT by GPT. In other words, transitional and permanent labour market effects are more likely to be determined by the interrelations between the characteristics of each new GPT and the characteristics of technologies that it challenges and those with which it cooperates than by some given set of characteristics common to all GPTs when each is operating in isolation.[3]

Observed and Unobserved Discontinuities

GPT-driven growth has major discontinuities in the sense that the R&D programme associated with each new GPT could not have evolved incrementally from the GPT that preceded it. Major technological advances cause discontinuities in the opportunities for new investment in particular sectors and radically alter the relation between inputs and outputs at the microeconomic level. For example, the economy-wide R&D programme for applying electricity was very different from that for applying the steam engine. Thus technological change that actually occurs at the micro level is neither smooth nor balanced. There are, however, many reasons why such discontinuities are seldom observed at the aggregate level. First, at any one time, there typically exist several GPTs, each at different stages of its evolution. Second, GPTs start in isolated sectors and only slowly assert their dominance over the old technologies that they challenge and eventually largely replace. Third, when some major new technology spreads slowly from firm to firm, discontinuities will only be observed at the firm level. Even there, radically new technologies often perform little better than those they replace for quite long gestation periods, during which learning by doing and learning by using occurs. In such cases, each firm's productivity will change continuously. This discussion illustrates that observing realized changes in productivity at the aggregate level, or even the micro level, is a poor way to gauge the extent to which technological changes are actually occurring.

Accelerating Change

One aspect of performance that has been debated over the last few decades is whether or not technological change is accelerating. At the beginning of Chapter 5, we gave two pieces of evidence for acceleration: over the last 10,000 years, the time between GPTs has fallen from millennia to centuries to decades, while the gestation period between the initial invention and becoming a fully fledged GPT has also fallen.

One important reason for this acceleration lies in the West's invention of how to invent, which we discussed towards the end of Chapter 7. In earlier times, people tackled technological problems piecemeal. Late in the nineteenth century, however,

---

[3] Because we are making general points with respect to all GPTs, we have not discussed the literature concerning the extent to which the growing inequality in income during the last quarter of the 20th century was driven by technological change. Although the evidence was not altogether clear, we believe much of it is consistent with the hypothesis that technological change was one of the major causes of this rising inequality. Whatever the final judgement may be on this particular case, it will not affect our general discussion of how new GPTs can impact on the distribution of income.

practical innovators set up R&D laboratories, and these, together with new university departments of applied sciences, created an institutional structure whose *raison d'être* was technological change. To a significant extent, change was no longer on the outside, pushing in against the established forces of stability; instead, the conservative forces that were hurt by change were now resisting the established institutionalized forces of change. Resist they did, sometimes with significant results, although such successful resistances are now more often reduced to rearguard actions of limited scope and duration.

Throughout history, new GPTs have arrived episodically, causing in their turn episodic bouts of structural adjustment. Once the facilitating structure had become more or less fully adapted to the new technology, a period of secular boom followed. During this latter period, a stream of further product and process innovations slowly exploited the full potential of the new GPT within a facilitating structure well adapted to it.

This suggests a worry. If change accelerates in the sense that one GPT follows another before the facilitating structure and public policies have had time to become well adapted to the first, a new set of problems may arise. There will not be a settled period in which any new GPT has time to be more or less fully exploited in the context of a facilitating structure and set of public policies that are well adapted to it. Instead, new changes will be required by the new GPT before the set of changes required by its predecessor have been well advanced. As yet, we see no evidence of this, but the reduction in the amount of time between GPTs must make this a serious possibility. In Chapter 15, we make a start at modelling this possibility.

Two Insights

The earlier discussion of productivity effects is one aspect of an important insight that follows from the S-E approach: there are no necessary relations among the magnitudes of change in technology, in the facilitating and policy structures, and in performance. We say no more about this here because it has already been discussed in Section IV of Chapter 4 under the subheading 'The Myth of the Productivity Paradox'.

A second important insight that follows from S-E theory is that there is no necessary relation between the magnitude of the change in technology and the changes it induces in the facilitating structure. Some important new GPTs, such as the laser, fit well into the existing facilitating structure and require few structural changes. Others that we have called transforming technologies require massive changes in the facilitating and policy structures, changes that may radically alter our ways of life. What we see most obviously are the changes in the facilitating structure and these are then often confused with changes in technology.

An example of the above two points is provided by the First Industrial Revolution in Britain. During the first half of this revolution, from 1780 to 1820, production was moved out of the home and into the newly evolving factories, creating the beginnings of the factory system, which was the basis of so much that followed and that continued to evolve over the entire century. The new factories (often no more than rented sheds) housed automated textile machines that were driven by power supplied sometimes by humans and sometimes by waterwheels. This profound technological change, this time in an organizational GPT, was accompanied neither by significant increases in overall productivity nor in real wages. (An early-day growth accountant might have been telling the people in 1815 that the 'New Economy' was an illusion.) Then, mainly after 1820, steam power was introduced into factories. This union of two *already well-established technologies*, automated textile machines and the high-pressure steam engine, brought major changes in the facilitating structure as much of the population moved to the new industrial towns, while significant gains occurred in productivity and real wages. So a period when technological change was less fundamental than it had been from 1780 to 1820 was accompanied by larger increases in productivity and larger changes in the facilitating structure than occurred from 1780 to 1820.

Confusion is all too likely when technology, structure, and performance are changing in different ways and the events are interpreted by a theory, such as one involving the neoclassical aggregate production function, that does not distinguish among these.

Is Growth Sustainable?

One of the most important questions concerning long-term performance is one that we first raised Chapter 1: Can growth be sustained into the indefinite future? We first briefly address the general worry that since the world's resources are finite, growth must be unsustainable in the very long term. If all resources were non-renewable, all economic activity, whether growing or static in magnitude, might eventually become unsustainable. But even this is not quite certain since a finite stock of non-renewable resources can last infinitely if the usage declines asymptotically over time—a not impossible achievement in a technologically dynamic society with a constant population. Fortunately, many resources are not of the non-renewable type. Furthermore, the law of conservation of mass energy shows that one does not destroy mass energy but merely transforms it into other forms. Also, the world is not a closed system, receiving a continuous flow of new energy from the sun. So there seems little substance in the general worry that over many centuries all forms of growth are unsustainable because of ultimate resource limitations.

Next we break the large question about the sustainability of growth into three smaller ones and discuss each in turn. Can sustained growth be produced by (*a*) capital accumulation on its own? (*b*) the accumulation of all factors? (*c*) technological advance?

Only capital accumulation. Diminishing returns create a limit to growth based on pure capital accumulation with a constant technology and population. This limit is predicted by standard constant returns to scale (CRS) growth models in which only capital accumulates. (See the discussion in Chapter 12 on scale effects in macro growth models.) In any CRS version, extensive growth approaches zero as the capital stock increases without limit.

The accumulation of all factors. The standard macro model based on a constant returns aggregate production function in which the inputs are labour, physical capital, and human capital predicts that if all these grow at a constant rate (Hicks neutral), extensive growth will also be sustained at that rate. To consider this kind of growth with truly constant technology, we need the thought experiment we have used several times before. Hold all technologies constant at what was known at some base period, say 1900. Then accumulate at some given rate more physical capital that embodies those base period technologies, more human capital in the form of more education in what was known in the base period, and more population. Here are a few illustrative examples of what the constant-technology experiment would reveal if conducted between a base period of 1900 and today.

- Feeding 6 billion people with the agricultural technologies of 1900 would have been impossible.
- Exhaustion of specific resources would have become a serious problem. Since most new technologies are absolutely saving in resources, producing the real value of today's manufacturing and service output with 1900 technologies would have required vastly more resource inputs than are currently being used. Furthermore, with no changes in technological knowledge, the scope for economizing on scarce resources and replacing them by plentiful ones would have been greatly restricted.
- The marginal utility of income would have diminished rapidly as people accumulated larger and larger stocks of the 1900-design durable goods, and consumed increasing amounts of 1900-style services and perishables.

While this is, of course, speculation, the main point is that continued growth of labour and physical and human capital with truly constant technology would have produced enormous problems—so many that it seems safe to conclude that sustained growth with truly constant technology and a constant rate of accumulation of all the factors included in the usual growth models is impossible.

To reconcile the above view with the prediction of constant growth from the theoretical model, we need to recognize that the capital that would need to grow would include such resource inputs as acres of agricultural land, suitable land for new cities, quantities of mineral and timber resources, available 'waste-disposal' ecosystems, supplies of fresh water, and a host of other things that are ignored by the standard theoretical growth models and most applied measurements of capital. (Since technology is assumed to be constant in the above exercise, this growth cannot be the result of increased efficiency in the use of natural resources due to new techniques.)

Thus if technology were really held constant, growth of the accumulating factors could not be sustained indefinitely because of pressure on non-accumulating factors, particularly broadly defined natural resources. These pressures would arise from a variety of causes. One is the exhaustion of such non-renewable resources as specific minerals and petroleum and the lack of available substitutes (since technology is being held constant). Another source is too rapid exploitation of renewable resources, such as overfishing and cutting forests faster than they can regenerate. Yet another source is overtaxing the environment's ability to handle the by-products of rising production. Heat must be dissipated and pollution removed. All animate activity produces waste and the environment handles it naturally up to some carrying capacity. After that, problems arise. Rivers become polluted; air becomes contaminated; the ozone layer becomes depleted; and so on. With technology constant at 1900 levels and GDP rising towards today's level, these environmental problems would have become disastrous well before 2000.

Technological advance. As we argued in Chapter 1, there is no necessary limit to growth based on advancing technological knowledge. Now that we have studied GPTs in more detail, we need to reconsider that argument. At the outset, we stress that there can be no certainty in any argument concerning the future. However, since we humans must plan ahead, we must look to the future. Arguments about what we might expect to experience are useful in assessing possibilities. That is all we can do. With these caveats in mind, we argue that if there are limits to future growth, they are far less likely to come from limits to innovative activity than from other sources, such as failures of human will, human institutions, or human inaction.

When we allow for continuing technological change, this provides an alleviation of the pressure put on natural resources when labour, physical capital, and human capital are all accumulating. Some of these pressures are more worrying than others. Although the exhaustion of particular resources can cause local crises, new technologies have always produced alternatives in the past. When charcoal became scarce, techniques for smelting iron with coal were developed. When high-grade iron ore was in short supply, methods of using very low-grade ore were developed. When the price of petroleum rose drastically in the 1970s, research into alternative fuels soared and only fell off when the price of petroleum dropped (in an impressive example of the endogeneity of technological change). There is no doubt that alternatives to petroleum will be developed long before the reserves are completely exhausted, because as supplies get scarcer, prices rise, creating an incentive to invent and perfect alternatives. Although it is hard to predict the results of the biotechnology revolution, which is still in its early days, there is little doubt that it will develop new resources to supplement or supplant existing ones. Thus there is always a danger that conserving some existing resources due to a worry about exhaustion may carry them over from the present, when they have a high value, into the future, when they will be effectively worthless.

Another alleviating factor comes from the cost-saving effects of technological advance. The evidence is that advances in technological knowledge typically lead to decreases in the amount of all resources used per unit of output—a process that Grübler (1998) calls 'dematerialization'. Problems associated with resource use have been caused not because each unit of output requires more units of resource inputs but because more outputs have been produced for two reasons: (*a*) to support an expanding population and (*b*) to allow much of that population to raise their material living standards by increasing per capita consumption. The world's rate of population increase is slowing and total world population is predicted to peak at somewhere around 8–10 billion people some time around the mid twenty-first century.[4] This will remove one of the causes of pressure on resources. From then on, the problems associated with increasing resource use will arise only when the rate at which output is rising exceeds the rate at which inputs per unit of output are falling.

Too rapid a rate of exploitation of renewable resources is something that can also be controlled by public policy. It takes effort to make the necessary regulations and it takes public will to enforce them, but it is not beyond human wit to exert much effective control over resource exploitation. We may fail to protect some of these resources but, if so, it will not be because we lack, or cannot develop, the technology to do so. Similarly, overtaxing the recuperative powers of the natural world is preventable. Areas of overtaxing have to be identified and methods of dealing with the pollution developed—often through the discovery of new technologies—and then instituted.

One problem is disagreement over the seriousness of some particular concern and, therefore, how many scarce resources it is worth devoting to deal with it. A prime example is global warming. The prevailing opinion is that global temperatures have risen significantly since the Industrial Revolution. While almost all experts agree that the increases are significant, there is disagreement as to how much of the rise in temperatures is due to human intervention. Furthermore, while almost everyone agrees that the problem is large, there is some disagreement as to how much harm will be done by any given change in temperatures and, therefore, how many resources it is worth employing now to alleviate the warming. These disagreements matter because they create political room for those who wish not to burden industry with more regulations. But if the world came to accept that the consequences of leaving the current warming trend unchecked would be serious, technology is available, or could be developed, to eliminate most of these causes within decades rather than centuries—although the short-run problems could still be formidable. The problem is not therefore, with technology but with human assessment of the costs and benefits of doing nothing versus adopting various costly prevention programmes now.

Nothing said above is meant to imply that global warming and other environmental issues are not serious. It is conceivable that we will so mismanage these as to destroy growth for a long time to come and even reduce living standards by large amounts. But if we do so, it will probably not be because the problems cannot be solved technologically once they are appreciated. Humans are technological animals and there are no practical limits to new technological knowledge. If we do create environmental disasters, it will more likely be because we are unwilling to face up to our problems, or to create the institutions necessary to deal with them, or any number of other social, political, or psychological reasons—but not because solving them is technically impossible. (Note that a 'solution' might include abandoning the use of a particular technology because its harmful side effects cannot be eliminated.)

---

[4] Over the last decade or so, projections for the population peak have been revised downwards several times.

One major caveat to this argument is that no one can rule out the possibility that our productive activities will produce some catastrophic effect with a sufficient lag between cause and effect so that, by the time the effect is understood, it is too late to remove the cause, or a sudden phase state shift will produce disastrous results faster than any reaction is possible even with the most enlightened policymakers. An example, would be a sudden ending of the Gulf Stream with catastrophic effects on northern Europe. So the probability of such future events cannot be reduced to zero by foreseeable technological means. They are part of the uncertainties involved in technological change. But so far they have not been large enough to stop growth.

Finally, we come to a major alleged limitation to sustained growth with technological change: the existence of diminishing returns to new knowledge.[5] We study this possibility first to see what light our analysis of GPTs can shed on it and then in more general terms concerning the very nature of knowledge.

It is helpful to distinguish between the effects of the development of a single GPT and the replacement of one by another. As we argue in detail later in this chapter, any one GPT's trajectory of applications, which includes enabling many individual derivative technologies, will typically follow a logistic curve, eventually having an ever-slowing rate of new applications and productivity growth. Thus, if no further GPTs were invented, growth would sooner or later slow, and possibly peter out.

Now consider a succession of GPTs. In this case, we are placing no artificial limitations on the generation of new ideas. As we have said before, and as we model in Chapter 14, new GPTs present agents with a new research programme to develop new process, product, and organizational technologies. As long as transforming GPTs continue to be invented, there is no obvious reason why growth cannot proceed into the indefinite future. Scientific and technological history gives no reason to suspect that the flow of new GPTs will dry up. Indeed, several new potential GPTs can be seen emerging at present, in particular biotechnology, hydrogen fuel cells, and nanotechnology, all three of which give promise of transforming products, processes, and organizations across a wide spectrum of the whole economy—*if* they become economically viable over their whole range of potential applications.

Let us now look at knowledge generation in more general terms. Ever since the science of economics began, the landscape of economic models has been dominated by diminishing returns to the accumulation of capital when labour and technology are constant. Knowledge, however, is not like goods and resource inputs. Goods and resources are rivalrous; if one person uses them, others cannot. In contrast, knowledge is non-rivalrous; when one person uses an idea, this does not prevent another person from using the same idea simultaneously.[6] Thus, the accumulation of

---

[5] Diminishing returns is only necessary but not sufficient. Diminishing returns would only slow growth, not stop it. To stop growth, the net returns to further knowledge would have to reach zero. No one can say what will or will not happen over some number of millennia, but over time spans that are relevant, this seems so unlikely as to have a vanishingly small probability.

[6] Some economists seek to equate ideas and human capital. However, as Paul Romer has frequently pointed out, the two are significantly different in that human capital is rivalrous—if I visit a firm and use

knowledge, with labour and capital constant, is not subject to decreasing returns in the same way as is the accumulation of capital, with ideas (technological knowledge) constant. This is due largely to the characteristic of knowledge that it can be combined and recombined with other pieces of existing or yet-to-be created pieces of knowledge to form new technologies, which in turn create even more opportunities. The implication is that investment need not be subject to decreasing returns, as long as it embodies new technological knowledge. Thus, when ideas are the key factor in growth, incomes can go on growing indefinitely without fear of being checked by the law of diminishing returns.

One common argument for diminishing returns to knowledge is that people use the best ideas first and then go on to less productive ones. But this does not apply to technological change. As we have seen, a case can be made for diminishing returns to new ideas within the later stages of the evolution of one GPT, such as the steam engine or the printing press. But there is no reason to expect diminishing returns in the shift from one GPT to another, because there is no reason to believe that the increment to total output coming from a succession of totally new ways of doing things will decrease over time. For example, going from water to steam was going from one mechanical source of energy to another. This move created many possibilities for new technologies based on steam. But these paled by comparison to the opportunities opened up when society went from steam to electricity, from a mechanical to an electronic form of power. In the realm of fundamental new ideas, neither theory nor evidence supports the view of the diminishing economic returns to the accumulation of knowledge over the long term.

Economic analysis will no doubt be used in the future to analyse many dismal economic events [and there will be many]. But the days when the underlying basis of the subject justified the title 'dismal science' are over. The modern title should become 'the optimistic science'— not because economics predicts inevitable growth or the arrival of universal bliss, but because its underlying structure, altered to incorporate the economics of knowledge, implies no limit to real-income creating, sustainable growth, operating in a basically market-organised society. If we cannot achieve sustained and sustainable economic growth, the fault dear Brutus must lie with ourselves not with some iron-clad economic law that dictates failure before we start. (Lipsey 1994: 351)

Technological change continues on average to produce, as it always has, more output for less of all inputs, to find substitutes for non-renewable resources, and to find solutions to the problems caused by the externalities of growth. There is no reason to believe that it will not be able to go on doing so into the indefinite future. We may fail to solve some of the problems created by growth but the reasons are unlikely to lie in any inherent limitations of the power of new technological knowledge to cope with these problems.

---

my skills to help it today, I cannot simultaneously visit some other firm and use my skills to help it—while ideas are not—once an idea is developed, everyone can use it simultaneously.

II. SECOND LEVEL OF ABSTRACTION: A STYLIZED EVOLUTION OF A GPT

In this section, we move to our second level of abstraction by stylizing the evolution of GPTs into five distinct phases, which we use in our formal modelling of a succession of GPTs in Chapter 14.[7] Although we have emphasized that no two GPTs are the same in all respects, they do have similarities that make analytical categorization possible. These phases relate to a new transforming GPT and the GPT that it challenges. Complementary GPTs have different evolutionary paths as they tend to reinforce each other's evolution towards increased efficiency and increased ranges of application.

Phase 1. A new GPT is introduced into the facilitating and policy structures that were designed for a pre-existing set of GPTs. In this phase, the amount of investment and output attributable to the new GPT is small.

Phase 2. The facilitating structure, public policies, and the policy structure are redesigned to fit the new GPT—this stage is often long-drawn-out, full of uncertainty, and prone to conflict since the adjustments create many winners and losers. There is often a burst of investment in such things as R&D and new capital (both physical and human), without a correspondingly large increase in output.

Phase 3. The principles of the new GPT are applied to produce many new products, processes, and organizational forms *within a newly evolved facilitating and policy structure, which is by now fairly well adapted to it*. This phase is the time when the new technology tends to yield the largest pay-offs in terms of productivity, real wage increases, and investment booms.

Phase 4. The opportunities for application of the GPT's principles to new product, process and organizational technologies diminish and, if new GPTs are not introduced, the growth process will slow—at least in so far as it is related to the GPT in question.

Phase 5. The GPT is challenged by a new competing technology. The established GPT may either be displaced fairly quickly or may undergo a burst of productivity gains because intense competition develops with the challenging GPT. Sooner or later, however, the new GPT displaces the old one. The replacement may be total or partial.

Each of these phases varies greatly from GPT to GPT depending on the productivity potential of each, and when and how challengers arise. A stylized version of these phases is shown in Figure 13.1, whose axis labels are explained in Section III.[8]

---

[7] Freeman and Louçã (2001: 146) develop a six-stage classification for the evolution of whole technology systems, which are a set of related technologies with accompanying structure. Although not identical, their phases are close to ours.

[8] Many GPTs persist in Phase 3 for a very long time (e.g. printing, electricity, iron, and steel) and as such might be perceived as exceptions to these phase sequences since there does not as yet seem to be any slowing in the number of new technologies that they enable. The question remains open. We think it likely (as with most GPTs we have studied) that either the limit of each of these GPTs as enabling technologies will be reached or a rival will arrive to displace it.

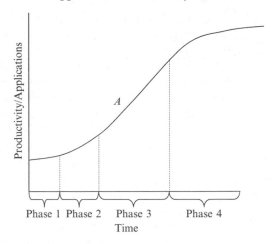

Figure 13.1. *Productivity/Applications curves for a GPT*
Curve *A* stands for two quite distinct curves with different scales on the *y*-axis. It can be regarded as *either* a productivity curve *or* an applications curve.

Phases 1–4 follow in chronological order. But since a new GPT may arrive at any time, and challenge an existing GPT at any stage of the incumbent's evolution, Phase 5 does not necessarily follow Phase 4. The new competing GPT may arrive in Phase 4, when the possibilities of the established GPT have mainly been exploited, or it may come in Phase 3, when the existing GPT still has plenty of unexploited potential. In this latter case, Phase 4 may be skipped altogether. All that can be said is that the longer the arrival of the new GPT is delayed, the stronger is the incentive to invent a new one because the existing GPT will be getting further and further into Phase 4 of its development with falling rates of both productivity growth and new applica-tions.[9] When it does come, the new GPT rejuvenates the growth process—in the sense that whatever the phase of the existing GPT when it arrives, it will ultimately cause more growth than would have occurred in its absence.

One important way in which growth is sustained is when one GPT enables another GPT and then another, as when electricity enabled the electronic computer, which enabled the Internet. Such cases present some conceptual problems. In one sense, the potential of the original GPT is not diminishing but in another sense it has passed on to a mature stage in which it is merely a component of the newer GPTs, which are the ones that are presenting the new research programmes. The resulting new burst of growth would not have occurred without the new GPTs. For example, the original potential to utilize electric motors on products and processes to replace other power sources was eventually exhausted. Electricity was, however, also a necessary input for the computer and the Internet. But without these new GPTs, the applications of electricity and the improvements in the efficiency of its production and distribution

---

[9] Note that these are micro predictions with respect to the GPT in question. Whether or not they are observable at the macro level depends on the importance of the particular GPT to the whole economy.

might have entered Phase 4. Instead, by enabling the computer and the Internet, which entered in their early phases, the growth process that would have been much weaker without them was sustained.

If we go through our list of GPTs from Chapters 5 and 6, we find a few GPTs that behave like electricity. Instead, most retreat fairly quickly into specialized niches when challenged by a new GPT in their own class, thus entering our Phase 4 if they were not already there. Stone and bronze retreated into very specialized niches. Sail gave way almost completely to the steamship and later diesel- and diesel–electric-powered ones. The windmill and the waterwheel virtually disappeared, although the waterwheel stayed on in the form of the turbine for generating hydroelectricity and the windmill is making a modest comeback as a power generator. On land, steam was almost completely supplanted by electricity and the internal-combustion engine, although it stays on as a generator of electric power. In contrast, iron and steel lasted in major uses for millennia and electricity has lasted for 150 years, going on to enable a massive number of modern technologies including several GPTs. But electricity and oil may well be supplanted as the world's major power sources over the course of the next hundred years or so when major alternatives such as hydrogen fuel cells, solar, geothermal, and revamped atomic plants come online in major ways.

III.   THIRD LEVEL OF ABSTRACTION: A LOGISTIC CURVE MODEL OF THE EVOLUTION OF A GPT

We now move to our third level of abstraction by grouping the performance characteristics of a GPT into two logistic curves: one for the GPT's evolving efficiency and one for the set of derivative technologies and applications that spring from it. This gives us two generic types of performance indicators that measure (*a*) the cost of producing the GPT's own services and (*b*) the results that it accomplishes directly or enables indirectly—which in Chapter 4 we called its technological complementarities and spillovers.

The Efficiency Curve

For our appreciative theory of the GPT's efficiency, we need to abstract from several important characteristics of actual GPTs. First, the full description of the performance of a single GPT requires several attributes. For example, a machine may deliver its services at a certain cost, a certain speed, and a certain degree of safety for its operatives, while a consumer durable is typically characterized by a number of attributes such as capacity, durability, reliability, and so on.

Second, a GPT has many different product and process applications and its efficiency may evolve differently in each. Early on, a GPT will typically be more efficient than the GPT it is challenging in a few applications but less efficient in others, as early cars were less efficient than horses for most uses and early electrically powered plants were less efficient than most steam-powered plants until associated design and organizational problems had been solved. Then, as its overall efficiency improves, it will become more efficient and gradually replace the old GPT in more and more uses. For example, the computer was first used by the military for specialized tasks; then in major research projects with large computational problems of a fixed nature; then in a few offices; then, equipped with transistors and a central processor, as an adjunct in large offices; then, as the personal computer revolution progressed, as a stand-alone piece of equipment on office desks; and, finally, as something commonly found in homes. Over the same period, its range of uses widened from mere computation, to handling manuscripts, to assisting the design of products, to the control of inventories, to guiding moving vehicles, to being the 'brains' of robots in factories, and to a major communication device when it was married to the Internet, to mention just a few of its evolving uses.

Third, a GPT may reach more than one limit to its efficiency as it evolves and technological developments may allow it to breech some of these. Thus, one logistic curve may not be enough to describe the full experience of any one GPT. For a given basic design, such a curve would exist. There was, for example, only so far that one could go with hard-wired computers using vacuum tubes as switches—although if the transistor had not been invented, we could have expected many improvements in vacuum tubes. But software and transistors each gave a discrete upward shift in the technology's productivity. Today, there is a limit to how many circuits can be carved on a silicon wafer, a limit that will be reached before long. A discrete jump in computing efficiency can then be expected when quantum computers are perfected. In line with the definitions we gave in Chapter 4, we regard electronic computers as one generic GPT and quantum computers as another.[10] Sooner or later some upper limit on efficiency seems to apply to all GPTs. Consider ships for another example. There was just so much that could be done to improve the efficiency of a sailing ship. Most of that had been accomplished by 1900 when the clipper ships still travelled many of the oceans. But, by then, a new technology that had been invented for other purposes had transformed the typical passenger-carrying sailing ship into the iron steamship with a great jump in efficiency (and comfort). Similarly, propeller aircraft were reaching limits dictated by existing technologies and by nature[11] when jets caused a discrete jump in efficiency and then evolved over their own logistic curve. Supersonic travel required considerable induced technological innovations in many aspects, such as metals and controls.

To build the first simplest version of our theory of GPTs, we abstract from these complications. We avoid the first and second by assuming that the performance of any process technology is fully described by the unit cost of the services it produces and that these are the same in all of its uses. This requires valuing many kinds of attributes such as durability (through a depreciation cost) and safety (by the cost of

[10] Quantum computers use totally different physical principles and, although quantum computers will do many things the electronic computer does only faster, they will also do many things that electronic computers cannot do.

[11] For example, the maximum speed of the tips of the propeller is just below that of sound, which was a natural limit that would have required a technological breakthrough to transcend—a breakthrough that was never made.

insuring against the risk).[12] Similarly, we assume that the same holds for product technologies so that we can describe them by the unit cost of their services per unit of time. For a refrigerator, it may be a cubic foot of space cooled to x degrees, for a computer it may be the number of operations per second. We call all of these 'outputs', whether they are produced by capital or by consumer goods. We then let a technology's efficiency (or productivity) be measured by the output of its services per unit of cost per unit of time (e.g. x kilowatt hours per dollar of cost). In later versions of our formal models presented in Chapter 15, we relax this simplifying assumption allowing, for example, for different uses of the GPT with different efficiencies in each use. We avoid the third complication by assuming that the GPT improves in efficiency smoothly without reaching any intermediate ceilings from which it escapes when there is some further technological breakthrough. We formalize this discussion by assuming that the evolving efficiency of a typical GPT can be described by a logistic curve with time on the x-axis and efficiency on the y-axis.

The Applications Curve

As we have seen in earlier chapters, the evolution of a GPT and its derivative technologies creates a set of technological complementarities and other spillovers. This enables many subsequent technological changes in new product, process, and organizational technologies as well as improvements in existing ones. Because these occur slowly at first, then accelerate, and finally slow down as the potential of the GPT is more fully exploited, the cumulative applications of each GPT tend to follow a logistic curve. We call this the 'applications curve'. If we were going to use this curve in our modelling, as we do use the efficiency curve, we would need a metric with which to measure applications. Developing this would be no easy task. Fortunately, when we come to model applications, we define a number of discrete sectors, and increasing applications merely means that the GPT is used in more of these existing sectors, or in totally new sectors. In an n sector model, the logistic applications curve would determine the number of sectors in which the GPT was newly used in each period. In this chapter, however, where we are doing appreciative theory, we merely need an intuitive idea of an applications curve to distinguish between the evolution of a GPT's efficiency and its range of applications. We regard this curve as measuring the cumulative value of all the GPT's applications made so far, both direct and indirect.

A Single GPT

Figure 13.1 shows a logistic curve describing the efficiency of a single GPT from Phases 1 through 4.[13] Figure 13.2 shows two arbitrary types of jumps (of the many

---

[12] The fact that many performance effects can be reduced to a single price does not vitiate our previous arguments that many of the enabling effects of GPTs cannot be expressed as price reductions.

[13] We ignore for the time being the possibility of a temporary increase in the rate of efficiency growth as the old GPT competes with the new one in Phase 5.

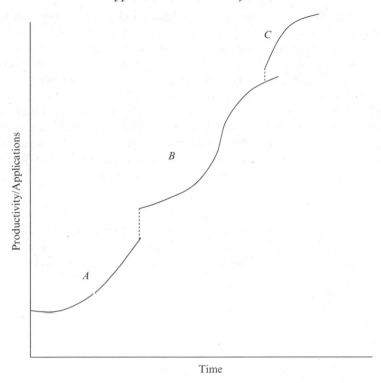

Figure 13.2. *Productivity/Applications curves for a succession of GPTs*
The curves show the transition from *A*, which is still in Phase 3, to *B* and then from *B*, which has already reached Phase 4, to *C*.

possible) to illustrate what we have assumed away. In the first case, technology *A* is improved by a discontinuous breakthrough that creates path *B*, such as the invention of computer software. This takes some time to perfect so that the new path follows a logistic curve with slow development at first and acceleration later. In the second case, another breakthrough shifts the development path upwards but this does not require a long gestation period, instead it fits into the earlier development, merely removing a constraint. The path then follows that from *B* to *C* with no slow initial period.

Figures 13.1 and 13.2 can also serve as illustrations of the notional applications curve. (Since both applications and efficiency are logistic, we can use one generic version for both curves.) While the efficiency curve usually takes a discrete jump when a breakthrough occurs in the evolution of one GPT, this may or may not happen with applications. It is quite possible that the applications grow continuously while productivity jumps discretely when the breakthrough occurs. For example, the breakthroughs that dramatically increase efficiency often occur at the early stages of a GPT's evolution, when it has only a few applications and these are not yet creating large amounts of value, as happened, for example, when computers switched from being hard-wired for specific problems to being directed by software. In such cases, the change in the value of applications will be small. Also, if the demand for the technology's services is inelastic in the application where the breakthrough occurs, efficiency may rise while value of applications (in that one use) falls, or both may jump discretely. For example, when a GPT is widely used, a rapid rise in its productivity in all or most of its uses may be accomplished by a correspondingly rapid rise in the value of its applications. So, to be consistent with historical evidence, we argue that jumps in efficiency need not be associated with jumps in applications—that is, Figure 13.2 may or may not apply as an applications curve when a discrete breakthrough occurs in the evolution of the GPT. We emphasize that many different paths are possible.

Sequential GPTs

Assume for the moment that there is only one type of GPT—say energy, materials, or communications. It is now reasonable to think of GPTs as arriving in a linear sequence. Of course there is uncertainty as to when the GPT will arrive. Sometimes

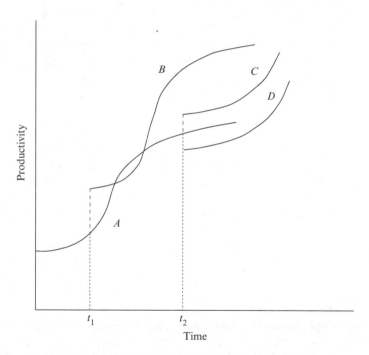

Figure 13.3. *Productivity curves for different patterns of two successive GPTs*
The incumbent *A* is replaced by several alternatives (*B, C, D*) that pass the various selection criteria described in Chapter 14.

the new GPT will come early in the trajectory of the old GPT, sometimes late. But as one GPT begins to traverse the flattening part of its logistic trajectory, the pressure for the invention of a replacement builds up. Whenever the new GPT does arrive, and a new developmental trajectory is established, there is no guarantee of a jump in efficiency. If the new GPT is relatively more efficient from the outset, and therefore quickly replaces the existing one, the trajectory of the new GPT will lie everywhere above the old. This is illustrated in Figure 13.3 where the initial technology is producing path *A* and the new one that arrives at time t_2 produces path *C*. Often, however, the new and the old exist side by side. This will typically be the case when the average efficiency of the new lies below the old one for some time. This is shown in Figure 13.3 by a technology that arrives at time t_1 and produces path *B*. It is also possible that a new GPT will initially perform less well in practice than it seemed to do on the drawing board and in prototype models. In this case, there may be an initial decline in efficiency, although sooner or later the new GPT's efficiency will exceed that of the one that it challenges. Such a case is illustrated in Figure 13.3 by the shift from path *A* to path *D*. Handling all such problems as these is difficult, both conceptually and in the construction of formal models. We postpone further consideration until Chapters 14 and 15.

14

Formal Models of GPT-Driven Sustained Growth: The Baseline Model[1]

We now move to our final stage of abstraction by developing a formal model of GPT-driven growth. In this chapter, we present what we call our baseline model and some results that follow from it. This is mainly a tool-forging chapter. In Chapter 15, we elaborate the model to incorporate progressively more characteristics that our S-E theory suggests are important.[2] Along the way, we are able to obtain some interesting results, including some surprising comparisons between rational and adaptive expectations, and a demonstration of how inadequate total factor productivity is as a measure of technological change.

The model in this chapter builds on the model that we presented in Carlaw and Lipsey (2001), later published as Carlaw and Lipsey (2006, forthcoming). Our main text describes the model verbally and outlines its results. The boxes provide stand-alone formal representations of the models. We make this division so that the discussion of the intuition of the model is not interrupted by the algebra in the main text and so that readers with a preference for formal modelling can first study the stripped-down mathematics of the models that are presented in the boxes.

I. OUTLINE OF OUR BASELINE MODEL

The assumptions of our baseline model are intended to capture some of the key stylized facts concerning GPTs that were presented in previous chapters but are omitted from all the GPT models that we reviewed in Chapter 11. We use a series of footnotes to compare our assumptions with those made in the other models.

---

[1] The simulation models discussed in chapters 14 and 15 are available as MatLab code at www.econ.canterbury.ac.nz/people/carlaw.shtml and www.sfu.ca/~rlipsey

[2] Lipsey (2001) defines an internally driven research programme (IDRP) as one whose models develop in reaction to problems created by the programme's previous models, with little or no control exercised by empirical data. In contrast, he defines an externally driven research programme (EDRP) as one whose models develop in response to empirical tests or applications of the programme's earlier models. Ours is an EDRP because the assumptions we make in our baseline model, and the variations that we make in later models, are all designed to make them come closer to what has been learned from economic historians and students of technology about the characteristics and behaviour of GPTs as well as the economic growth that they drive.

The baseline model has three sectors: (*a*) a single consumption good, which we refer to as 'the consumption sector'; (*b*) R&D that produces applied knowledge, which is used to develop applications of each GPT to specific purposes, called 'the applied-R&D sector'; and (*c*) fundamental research that produces pure knowledge, which leads to new GPTs, called 'the pure research sector'. All sectors employ the same generic resource and are therefore related to each other by their resource opportunity costs, as measured by foregone current consumption.[3] Each sector has a production function that displays diminishing returns to the resources that are used. In the absence of any new GPT, each of the three production functions shows constant or diminishing returns to the knowledge stock that it uses.[4]

The stock of accumulated applied R&D knowledge, A_t, is the stock of existing applied technology, while the stock of useful pure knowledge, G_t, is the current state of technology with respect to GPTs. Thus, technology is 'flat' within each sector, while its structure is modelled by the hierachy of the interrelated sectors, each using distinct technologies.

When a new GPT does arrive, there is often, but not always, a temporary burst of historical increasing returns of the sort we discussed in Chapter 12. These increasing returns are only a temporary phenomenon because in reality there are technological limits to the scale effects that can be exploited by each new GPT.[5] So we do not have the kind of permanent increasing returns to accumulation that are found in some of the endogenous macro growth models that we discussed in Chapter 12.

These assumptions allow us to focus attention on technological complementarities and to model knowledge that grows irregularly. The growth process in our baseline model is conditioned by the characteristics of each new GPT and the criteria agents use in deciding whether or not to adopt it.

We know from the studies reported in Chapters 5 and 6 that new GPTs create technological complementarities that rejuvenate the growth process.[6] They enable new product, process, and organizational technologies, the developments of which sustain the productivity of both fundamental and applied research as a long-term trend, if not from year to year. In our baseline model, we confine these complementarities to process technologies. When a new GPT is developed, it has a direct complementarity with pre-existing knowledge and current resources in the applied R&D sector, making these more productive. Output from the applied R&D sector

---

[3] Aghion and Howitt (1998) employ three sectors in their model, Helpman and Trajtenberg (1998*b*) employ *m* identical sectors in their diffusion model, and all other first-generation GPT models use two sectors.

[4] See equation 14.2 in Box 14.1 for returns to new applied knowledge, A_t, in the consumption sector; see equation 14.5 in Box 14.3 for returns to that knowledge in the pure research sector; and see equation 14.3 in Box 14.1 for returns to new knowledge of how to use the existing GPT, G_t.

[5] These increasing returns can be measured easily enough at the level of the production unit. For example, the savings in inputs (both in physical and monetary units) that accompanied the various innovations in the smelting of ore that were referred to in Chapter 12 were relatively easy to measure.

[6] These complementarities were defined in Chapter 4 and distinguished from the narrower class of technological externalities.

enables the GPT to have an indirect complementarity with the consumption and pure knowledge sectors because applied R&D knowledge is useful in those sectors, making resources and prior knowledge in each more productive.[7,8]

We use separate logistic curves to represent the evolution of each GPT's impact on the marginal productivity of applied R&D, and hence on the consumption sector. This is our efficiency curve from Chapter 13. It models the observation that GPTs start crudely and only slowly increase the efficiency with which they deliver their services. (Since at this stage the GPT is only used directly in the applied R&D sector, our other curve in Chapter 13, the applications curve, is not relevant.[9])

In common with all other models of GPTs, technology is assumed to have a hierarchical structure, meaning that some technologies are necessary antecedents for others.[10] This is in contrast to standard aggregate growth models where technology is typically modelled as featureless.

Technological change is modelled as a succession of GPTs that establish the path-dependent research agenda for further applied R&D.[11]

We introduce uncertainty in pure knowledge production in three ways:

1. the productivity of resources devoted to pure research in every period is subject to random fluctuations;
2. the time period between the arrival of successive GPTs is of uncertain duration (but typically long); and

---

[7] Bresnahan and Trajtenberg's vertical and horizontal complementarities (1992) are similar to our technological complementarities. Other GPT models have a complementarity only between the GPT and its supporting components, which are created by the R&D sector for use alongside the GPT in the final output sector. The components themselves are substitutes for each other, which does not mirror what we see with many complementary components that comprise technology systems such as those described in Chapter 4.

[8] In Helpman and Trajtenberg (1998*a*), the effect of GPTs is registered through the rate of component development, which is linear. In Helpman and Trajtenberg (1998*b*) the effect of the GPT is registered through the combined effect of component development and the diffusion process, which holds back the impact of the GPT until all sectors that can use it have developed a threshold number of complementary components. Thereafter, the GPTs impact linearly on the economy. Aghion and Howitt (1998) assume an epidemic effect where the development of the GPT actually causes a transitory reduction in output after a period of constant output. An increase in output finally occurs as a result of an epidemic diffusion process in their model.

[9] This is the first major departure from Carlaw and Lipsey's earlier model (2001, 2006). They allowed the full productive impact of a GPT to enter the system upon the GPT's discovery. It is also in contrast to Helpman and Trajtenberg (1998*a*, 1998*b*) and Aghion and Howitt (1998) where once the GPT arrives in a given sector, its efficiency depends linearly on the development of components. Helpman and Trajtenberg (1998*b*) and Aghion and Howitt (1998) develop detailed theoretical mechanisms for what we define as the applications curve in Chapter 13. In each of these cases, the pattern of output is determined by the diffusion process across firms and sectors where the efficiency of the GPT in each sector increases with the development of components up to some maximum.

[10] For example, as we have noted elsewhere, the electronic computer cannot exist without the power technology of electricity.

[11] All the GPT models that we surveyed in Chapter 11, except ours, verbally describe this succession of GPTs but concentrate on the formal dynamics of a single GPT from the time that it is exogenously introduced until it reaches full maturity.

3.　the effect of a newly arrived GPT on productivity in the applied R&D sector is partly determined endogenously by the amount of resources devoted to the pure research sector since the last GPT was invented, and partly by two random variables defined in Box 14.3: ϖ, which shifts the whole logistic efficiency curve upwards or downwards, and ϑ, which changes its maximum height and hence alters the duration of each of the GPTs phases and its full productivity-raising potential.[12]

These latter two variables model the fact that a technology that looks good on the drawing board, or in prototype models, often performs differently, either better or worse, when put into full use.

For any given period, we assume that agents allocate resources among the three sectors according to their expected current marginal product in each. Under certain assumptions, this is equivalent to perfect competition.[13] Whatever the specific rule agents use for making these allocations, we require only that they respond to relative intersectoral differences in perceived rates of returns.[14]

In our model, agents do not know the precise future consumption pay-off to resources allocated to pure and applied research because they do not know the probability distributions that are generating the disturbances on the outcomes, nor can they infer them from the behaviour of previous GPTs. So they form expectations of the pay-offs to investments based on their perceptions of the current period's marginal productivities. Given these expectations, they allocate resources so as to maximize the value of current consumption.[15] This is meant to model agents behaving as we discussed in Chapter 2: groping into an uncertain future in a profit-oriented way. In Chapter 15, we examine the implications of allowing them to have other types of foresight.

---

[12] In contrast, the arrival dates of new GPTs and their impacts are exogenous in all other models except those of Aghion and Howitt (1992, 1998). The arrival rate of these authors' technologies is subject to a Poisson arrival process but nonetheless, in the steady-state equilibrium the rate is constant.

[13] Within the framework developed here, we could model the consumption sector and/or the applied R&D sector as being characterized by monopolistic competition. The sector in question would comprise several products differentiated by a parameter. Because adding the complication of monopolistic competition does not change the qualitative results, we retain the simpler assumption of perfect competition.

[14] None of the GPT models by other authors reviewed in Chapter 11 have endogenously generated GPTs. Therefore, there is no allocation of resources to a sector that generates new GPTs, such as our pure knowledge sector. Aghion and Howitt (1992) have endogenously generated technological change where the allocation of labour to producing technological change is derived from a perfectly foresighted maximization based on a stationary Poisson distribution. In all of the GPT models, the allocation of resources to the sectors developing components and templates for the newly arrived GPT is based on forward-looking expectations with stationary distributions.

[15] As an alternative to our simple assumption, we could have assumed that agents are forward-looking but do not foresee changes in the marginal products in all lines of production, which implies that they perform the dynamic programming problem in each period taking the perceived marginal products in all lines of activities as being constant at their current period values. In the subsequent period, they repeat the procedure with the new marginal products encountered in that period. Since in our model this assumption and the one in the text amount to the same thing qualitatively, we adopt the one in the text because it is vastly simpler.

In all other treatments, agents are modelled as having perfect foresight about the future evolution of new GPTs. Our assumption of no foresight seems closer to what we observe than the assumption that agents are sufficiently foresighted to maximize over the whole of a GPT's lifetime—a lifetime that can easily extend over more than 100 years. Nonetheless, one might wonder if agents could learn over successive GPTs and thus eventually be able to anticipate the course of each new one. We reject this possibility because GPTs are technologically distinct from each other so that the histories of past GPTs provide little precise quantitative evidence about how new ones will behave (although, as we observed in Chapter 13, there are some broad qualitative similarities among GPTs). For example, knowing how the steam engine affected the economy over the several hundred years of its evolution would tell agents virtually nothing about the empirical details of the evolutionary paths to be expected over the next couple of hundred years for all the economic impacts of electricity at the time when the dynamo was invented in 1867.

The model generates a non-stationary equilibrium, such that neither the levels nor the rates of change of the endogenous variables converge to constants. There is a transitional competitive equilibrium in every time period, given the expected marginal productivities of inputs in each sector. But because of technological advance, the nature of the spillovers, and the absence of perfect foresight, the marginal products change from one period to the next in ways that are not anticipated. Although growth never stops, a very productive new GPT can accelerate the average growth rate over its lifetime, while a less productive one can slow it. This last characteristic allows us to focus on the historical, path-dependent, and variable pattern of growth. In contrast, other models typically use a steady state equilibrium concept.[16] One advantage of our treatment is that it does not require increasing returns to the accumulating factors in order to obtain sustained growth. Another advantage is that our model does not predict that devoting more resources to R&D necessarily increases the growth rate—a prediction made by most other endogenous growth models that does not seem to conform with the observed facts.

The assumption of stationarity is often justified on the grounds that it is necessary for models to conform with the stylized facts of growth (see, for example, Jones 1988). Although our equilibrium concept is non-stationary, the model's results conform with many of these accepted facts concerning economic growth.[17] When our model is

---

[16] Because agents are assumed to be able to foresee and to maximize over the lifetime of the GPT in all other GPT models, a stationary equilibrium is derived from the infinite horizon utility maximization. Even in Aghion and Howitt (1992), where there is randomness in the arrival rate of new technologies, the rate of innovation is constant in equilibrium. This is because their innovation arrival rate is derived from the expected value of the Poisson distribution with a parameter determined by the equilibrium flow of labour services into research.

[17] It is sometimes argued that non-stationary models are to be avoided because any shock has permanent effects and commonly leads to 'butterfly effects'. While our model is non-stationary, it sometimes behaves in ways that are almost indistinguishable from standard models built on stationary equilibrium concepts. (See the first model in Chapter 15.) Also, even when we introduce some strong positive feedbacks, the model does not explode, generating instead variable growth rates that have no long-term tendency to accelerate over time.

extended to cover more than one country, different growth patterns are generated, consistent with the observations that aggregate incomes and growth rates vary across countries and that some countries grow faster than others, changing their relative income standing over time. Each country will also have a non-constant growth rate over time. In spite of these variable growth rates, the ratio of our accumulating factor (generally treated as capital in standard models) to output is constant through time, which is consistent with the empirical record of the USA over the last century. To the best of our knowledge no other growth models mange to reconcile the twin observations of varying growth rates over the long term and constant input/output ratios.[18]

To summarize, our model has the following key characteristics that incorporate some of the stylized facts presented in previous chapters. GPTs arrive at randomly determined times with an impact on the productivity of applied R&D that is determined by the amount of pure research knowledge which has been endogenously generated since the last GPT and elements of randomness. The three sources of randomness outlined above imply that in the short term, outcomes are influenced by the particular realizations of the random variables, allowing the average growth rate of output over the lifetime of each successive GPT to differ from that of its predecessor. The average growth rate over long periods of time, in which several GPTs succeed each other, is determined endogenously by the accumulation of knowledge (i.e. technology). This is partly endogenous, determined by the allocation of resources to pure research, and partly exogenous, determined by random factors affecting the productivity, timing, and size of those resource allocations. Furthermore, while some GPT-driven research programmes are richer than others, there is *no* reason in our model to expect that successive GPTs will always either accelerate or decelerate growth on average over their lifetimes. This formalizes our argument in Chapter 4 that there is no expectation that each new GPT will produce a 'productivity bonus' in the form of an acceleration to the rate of productivity growth, either temporarily or permanently.

II. TWO-SECTOR ILLUSTRATION OF GROWTH REJUVENATION

In this section, we treat the pure knowledge sector of our baseline model as exogenous in order to illustrate the rejuvenating effects of GPTs on the growth process, and in Section III, we endogenize the arrival of GPTs.

---

[18] Since we have yet to set up a multination version of our model, we have nothing to say about the possibilities of the international convergence of growth rates, although we are pretty sure that whether growth rates will converge or diverge in our model will depend on the particular values given to the various parameters. This is consistent with our belief that there is no general tendency in the world for one result or the other to hold under all circumstances. Instead, the tendency towards divergence or convergence will be context-specific. What useful theories can then do is to predict the conditions under which each outcome is likely.

The Model

The equations of the model are shown in Box 14.1. The fixed total of resources is allocated between the two sectors (equation 14.1). The first sector produces the

---

Box 14.1. A Two-Sector Model that Illustrates the Growth Rejuvenation Process

A generic resource input, R_t, is allocated between the consumption sector, $r_{c,\,t}$, and the applied R&D sector, $r_{a,t}$:

$$R_t = r_{c,t} + r_{a,t} \qquad (14.1)$$

Consumption output, c_t, depends on the resources devoted to it and the stock of applied knowledge, A_t, which is the productivity parameter for the consumption sector:

$$c_t = (\mu A_{t-1})^{\alpha_1} r_{c,t}^{\alpha_2} \text{ with } \alpha_i \in (0, 1], \, i = (1, 2), \text{ and } \alpha_2 < 1 \qquad (14.2)$$

The parameter $\mu \in (0,1]$ is set to one here but is used in the three-sector model.

The flow of applied R&D knowledge, a_t, in equation (14.3) is a function of $r_{a,t}$ and the productivity coefficient, G_{t-1}. The current stock of applied knowledge, A_t, is the accumulated flow of produced knowledge, a_t, plus the previous period's stock, A_{t-1}, which is reduced by an obsolescence factor, ε:

$$\begin{aligned} a_t &= \nu(G_{t-1})^{\beta_1} r_{a,t}^{\beta_2} \\ A_t &= a_t + (1 - \varepsilon)A_{t-1} \end{aligned} \quad \text{with } \beta_i \in (0, 1], \, i = (1, 2), \text{ and } \beta_2 < 1 \qquad (14.3)$$

The parameter ν, which is a calibration parameter for subsequent simulations, is set to unity for this model. The restrictions on the parameters α_i and β_i ensure diminishing returns to resources in consumption and applied R&D and either constant or diminishing returns to pure knowledge in both sectors. We use the constant returns assumption on pure knowledge for the simulation of our baseline model. G is the stock of useful knowledge produced by the pure research sector and embodied in the current GPT. In this two-sector case, the productivity parameter for applied research, $\nu(G_{t-1})^{\beta_1}$, is treated as a collection of parameters, whereas in subsequent models G is an endogenous variable.

The maximization problem with intertemporal substitution can now be expressed in the following Bellman equation:

$$V(A_t, \, t) = \max_{\{r_{c,t}, \, r_{a,t}\}} c_t + \rho E[V(A_{t+1}, \, t + 1)]$$

$$s.t.(14.1)-(14.3)$$

where ρ is the discount factor and E is the expectations operator. For an easier expression of the problem that does not affect any of the qualitative results, we simplify by allowing the stock of applied knowledge to have immediate impact in the production of consumption goods as follows:

$$c_t = (\mu A_t)^{\alpha_1} r_{c,t}^{\alpha_2} \text{ with } \alpha_i \in (0, 1], \, i = (1, 2), \text{ and } \alpha_2 < 1 \qquad (14.2')$$

The period-by-period optimization problem is:

$$\max_{r_{c,\,t},\,r_{a,\,t}} c_t = (\mu A_t)^{\alpha_1}(r_{c,\,t})^{\alpha_2}$$

s.t.

$$a_t = \nu G_t^{\beta_1}(r_{a,t})^{\beta_2} \tag{14.4}$$

$$A_t = a_t + (1-\varepsilon)A_{t-1}$$

$$R_t = r_{c,t} + r_{a,t}$$

There is an implicit assumption here that the underlying utility function is monotonically increasing in consumption.

consumption good under conditions of diminishing returns to the resources allocated to it. Its production (shown in equation 14.2) is a function of the resource input, $r_{c,t}$, and a productivity variable, A_t (the μ in equation 14.2 is set to unity as it is only used in the three-sector model). This productivity parameter is determined by the stock of applied knowledge that is produced by the applied research sector (equation 14.3). The current flow of output of the knowledge produced by this second sector depends on two things: the amount of resources it employs, $r_{a,t}$, and a productivity parameter, G. This parameter is the stock of useful pure knowledge that is embodied in the currently used GPT. It is exogenous in this two-sector version of the model. The applied research sector produces a flow of applied knowledge, a_t, under conditions of diminishing returns to the resources used. The stock of applied technological knowledge, A_t, is augmented by the current output of that knowledge and becomes obsolete at a rate determined by the parameter ε. This stock of knowledge enters into the productivity coefficient of the consumption good sector so that, as the stock accumulates, productivity rises in that sector.

Because the results of applied research in the current period immediately affect the productivity of consumption in the same period, there is no intertemporal substitution in the model [19] Thus the maximizing trade off is between the output of resources devoted to consumption production with a given production function and the output of resources that go into applied research to improve productivity in the consumption sector. A marginal reallocation of resources from the consumption sector to applied research directly reduces the production of consumption goods, while indirectly increasing their production by raising the productivity of those resources that remain in the consumption sector. Maximization of consumption output in one period requires that these two marginal amounts be equated.

Simulation of the Model

In order to simulate the model, we must give values to its parameters. The specific numbers, which are shown in Box 14.2, were chosen for various reasons. First, several different parameterizations were tested to check the robustness of the qualitative results and these were found to be robust to wide ranges of values

---

[19] The models in Boxes 14.1 and 14.3 initially incorporate intertemporal substitution, but the model is simplified by eliminating this substitution without affecting the qualitative results.

Box 14.2. Numerical Simulation of the Two-Sector Model

The following are the parameter values used for the simulations whose results are shown in Figures 14.1–14.4:

$\alpha_1 = 1$	$\alpha_2 = 0.3$	$\beta_1 = 1$	$\beta_2 = 0.3$
$\nu = 1$	$\mu = 1$	$A_0 = 1$	
$R = r_{c,t} + r_{a,t} = 1,000$	$\varepsilon = 0$		

G is 1 initially and then changes exogenously to 10 in period 51.

---

satisfying our basic assumptions. Second, nothing in our subsequent analysis turns on these particular values. Third, in line with the argument in Chapter 13 (see the discussion in Section I under the subheading *Is Growth Sustainable?*), we chose some parameter values to ensure that knowledge has constant returns. Fourth, we chose other parameter values to ensure diminishing returns to resources in both lines of production. The initial value of the stock of applied knowledge does not matter since we allow the simulation to run for a sufficient number of periods that initial values have no influence. We assume no depreciation of that stock. The resource constraint is set to an arbitrary positive real number.

Resources are allocated in a recursive manner. In each period, agents take as given the productivity coefficients that determine the marginal products of resources in each sector. On this basis, they allocate resources between the two. Because the new applied knowledge generated in each period raises the marginal product of resources in the consumption sector, some resources must migrate out of applied R&D so as to establish competitive equilibrium in each successive period. Thus, we have a Solow-style model. In the absence of exogenous changes in either the endowment of resources or the productivity of the applied R&D sector, the economy asymptotically approaches a steady state. In it, the stock of applied knowledge stops growing because resources have become so productive in consumption relative to applied R&D that it does not pay to forgo any current consumption to generate increases in future consumption. All the resources are then allocated to the consumption sector, whose productivity remains constant.[20]

Figure 14.1 shows the time series for the outputs of the consumer goods and for the stock of accumulated applied knowledge. Figure 14.2 shows the time series for the allocations of resources in the two sectors. As productivity grows in the consumption sector, resources move out of R&D into the consumption sector. We simulate the arrival of a new GPT in period 51 by exogenously increasing the productivity parameter of the production function for applied knowledge. This increases the marginal productivity of resources devoted to R&D, causing a diver-

---

[20] Obviously, we can solve directly for the steady state equilibrium in this framework by optimizing over the infinite horizon. However, we adopt this recursive approach in this simple two-sector model because it is the appropriate mechanism for allocating resources in the more complex three-sector models characterized by uncertainty.

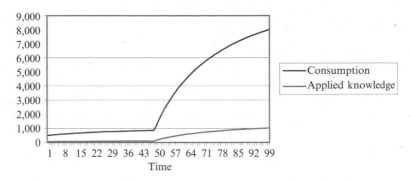

Figure 14.1. *Two-sector simulation: consumption output and knowledge stock*

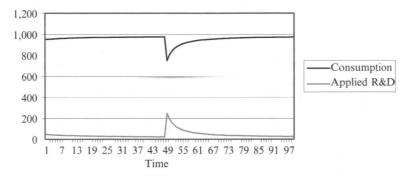

Figure 14.2. *Two-sector simulation: resource allocation*

sion of resources from the consumption sector into applied R&D. After these sudden shifts in resource allocation in output and in the growth rate, resources are slowly transferred back into consumption as productivity grows in that sector. Once again, this slows the growth rate, which, in the absence of a new GPT, asymptotically approaches zero.

This two-sector version of the model illustrates the rejuvenating power of GPTs. In the absence of the arrival of a new GPT, the diminishing returns to resources in all lines of activity cause the growth rate to converge to zero asymptotically so that the system approaches a steady state equilibrium. However, the arrival of a new GPT encourages further applied R&D and rejuvenates growth.

III.   THE THREE-SECTOR BASELINE MODEL

We now endogenize productivity growth in the applied R&D sector by adding a pure research sector that engages in R&D directed at the invention of new GPTs. These emerge as a result of conscious effort; they differ from one another, and they can affect the economy in different ways.

Conceptual Issues and Assumptions

Historical Increasing Returns

In Chapter 12, we argued that new GPTs often introduce scale effects in the sense that the most efficient scales of operations of the new technologies (the GPT and its many derivative technologies) are sometimes larger and sometimes smaller than the most efficient scale of operations of the challenged technology. The cost-reducing effects of these scale changes only enter the system as capital equipment embodying the new efficient scale replaces the old equipment when it is no longer economically valuable. This process is drawn out over time. For example, it took thirty to forty years for new electrically powered factories to replace the old steam-powered factories after the former proved their superiority over the latter. Once the transition is complete, however, the scale economies are exhausted and further expansions in output occur at constant or diminishing returns. As we have observed earlier, the structure of a single aggregate production function cannot capture these scale effects that, although transient, recur with many GPTs. We model them as a jump in the efficiency of some new GPTs relative to the incumbent, a jump that happens with some GPTs but not with others. Jumps of this sort are shown by the transition from GPT-A to either GPT-B at t_1 or to GPT-C at t_2 in Figure 13.2 on page 437. Ideally, this increase should be spread over Phase 1 of the GPT's evolution, which would be closer to reality and would remove the spikes that occur when some new GPTs are introduced. But this is a modification for future work and, in the mean time, we accept the slight unrealism of an immediate spike rather than an increase, which is spread over the early part of the new GPT's existence.

Spillovers

At the outset, we must decide how to handle the spillover effects between applied R&D and the other two sectors. There is an obvious complementarity between applied R&D and the consumption sector because applied knowledge increases the productivity of the consumption sector directly by shifting its production function. The spillover from applied to pure research is well attested by many of the studies that we have discussed earlier in this book.[21] There are two basic ways in which we could model it. We could assume that the whole stock of applied knowledge was useful in the consumption sector, while some fraction of it spilled over as an externality to increase the efficiency of pure research. We do this in a later model, but here we choose another way, which is to assume that the stock of applied knowledge is *divided* between the consumption sector and the pure research sector. This division ensures that we do not introduce any permanent increasing returns to accumulating knowledge, nor any externalities. This has two advantages. First, it allows us to produce a model of sustained endogenous growth without some of the

---

[21] The spillovers from applied to pure research are discussed more fully in Chapter 4 and several examples are found in Rosenberg (1982: ch. 7).

characteristics that are needed to sustain growth in some models of endogenous growth. Second, it creates a model suited to studying the relation between technological change and measures of changes in TFP, most of which assume constant returns to scale.

The Objective Function

To solve this model, we maintain the earlier assumption that the objective is to maximize consumption. But we must now make a further assumption about how agents form expectations of the consumption pay-off from resources devoted to pure research. Since agents cannot anticipate surprises, we assume that they make decisions on the assumption that the expected value of the surprises is zero. We also assume that they estimate the pay-off on the assumption that pure knowledge is immediately useful in the applied R&D sector, rather than being useful only after a new GPT is discovered. This is equivalent to assuming that they have a zero time discount. As a result of these two assumptions, there is the same type of intersectoral trade-off as in the two-sector model, but there is no intertemporal trade-off. The difference between this and the previous model is that the trade-off is now across three sectors and based on expectations.

We needed to make some assumption about how agents grope into an uncertain future and the above seemed as good as any. Resources are allocated so as to maximize consumption output in each current period by equating the expected marginal increase in consumption from a unit of resources allocated to each of the three sectors, but with their productivities taken as given. We could assume that a social planner makes the entire allocation over all three sectors. Alternatively, we could assume that the allocation is made by private price-taking agents in the consumption and applied research sectors[22] and by a government that taxes agents in these two sectors to pay for pure research, which has the assumed pay-off just described. The model is flexible enough to accommodate many other assumptions and we examine one of these in Chapter 15. However, it becomes more cumbersome to programme when there are time discounts on expected future returns to R&D.

Relation Between Successive GPTs

To complete our model, we need to deal with the relation between the incumbent GPT and a new GPT that challenges it. This is something the other authors of the GPT models that we discussed in Chapter 11 did not need to consider because all their models concentrated on the life cycle of a single GPT. Neither did we need to worry about this issue in Carlaw and Lipsey (2001, 2006, forthcoming) because, although we did deal with a succession of GPTs, each new arrival always had both a higher productivity level and a higher rate of productivity growth than the incumbent. This was because the full productivity impact of the new GPT was released instantaneously into the applied R&D sector. In contrast to these models, one of the

---

[22] As was stated in an earlier note, Dixit–Stiglitz-style monopolistic competition can be introduced into these two sectors with an increase in complexity and no change in qualitative behaviour.

refinements in our current treatment is modelling the productivity impact of a new GPT on the applied R&D sector as a logistic diffusion process rather than the instantaneous fully fledged arrival. Logistic diffusion creates the possibility that the level and/or the initial rate of change of a new challenger's productivity may be less than that of the incumbent. This suggests the need for rules governing the adoption or rejection of a new challenger.

We consider three possible criteria to determine whether or not a new GPT will displace the incumbent that it challenges. First, the challenger may displace the incumbent whatever the state of either. This is the simplest and most unrealistic criterion. Second, the challenger may displace the incumbent if the initial *level* of its efficiency exceeds the current level of the challenger. Third, the challenger may displace the incumbent if its current level of efficiency is at least equal to that of the incumbent and if it has a higher *rate of change* of productivity over the near future. In practice, we only look one period ahead when making these rate-of-change comparisons, but any amount of foresight can be allowed for. In all these cases, the efficiency of a GPT is determined by the amount of accumulated, currently useful, pure knowledge that it embodies, G_t.

The application of these criteria raises the issue of what happens to the challenger if it fails whatever test is applied, so that the incumbent remains in place. Here we consider two possibilities: either the unsuccessful challenger is discarded and further research directed towards inventing a new GPT or the unsuccessful challenger is returned to the pure research sector to be developed further. These two cases model the observation that some attempts at developing a major new technology are failures and the experiment is abandoned, while in other cases, a technology may take longer than expected to reach a commercially viable level of efficiency, but development work continues on it until the technology finally does become competitive. The possibilities may now be summarized.

Transition criterion 1. There is no comparison between the two GPTs; the challenger replaces the incumbent GPT, whatever the characteristics of each. Any one of the transitions from the logistic curve A to the logistic curves B, C, or D, illustrated in Figure 13.3, is possible under this criterion.

Transition criteria 2 and 3. The challenger replaces the incumbent if the level of its productivity is higher than that of the incumbent. If the challenger fails this test, it is discarded under criterion 2, while it is returned to the pure research sector for further development under criterion 3. The transitions from logistic curve A to curves B and C in Figure 13.3 illustrate cases in which the new GPT is adopted on these criteria.

Transition criteria 4 and 5. The challenger replaces the incumbent if the level of its productivity is at least as high as that of the incumbent and its expected near future rate of growth is higher. If the challenger fails this test, it is discarded under criterion 4, while it is returned to the pure research sector for further development under criterion 5. The transition from logistic curve A to curve C in Figure 13.3 illustrates a transition where the new GPT is adopted on these criteria.

Transition criterion 1 is interesting only for purposes of comparison, as it is hard to think of any private profit-seeking behaviour that would mirror it. However, public sector agents motivated by a search for political or national prestige who push projects to completion even when evidence accumulates that they will be losers could be cases in point.[23] Transition criteria 2 and 3 are more myopic than 4 and 5 since only the current rate of productivity is considered. Transition criteria 4 and 5 are less myopic in that the expected growth rate in the immediate future is also taken into account. These criteria can be made as forward-looking as one wishes by altering the period over which comparisons of rates of productivity growth are made. However, looking forward for even one period turns out to be a more powerful discriminating test than just comparing current productivity levels.

Modelling Issues

The two alternatives for dealing with an unsuccessful challenger present some interesting modelling issues. In the first alternative, the rejected GPT is returned to the pure research sector for further development. The amount by which its efficiency increases in each subsequent period is a function of the amount of resources devoted to pure research and a random variable, θ, that models uncertainty about the results of pure research. We then assume that a comparison is made with the incumbent in each subsequent period. Sooner or later, the challenger will be chosen over the incumbent because the incumbent must eventually progress into the later stages of its logistic curve in which its productivity growth asymptotically approaches zero.

In the second alternative, the unsuccessful challenger is abandoned. We must then decide what happens to the accumulated stock of pure knowledge that went into the development of the abandoned GPT. As we have modelled it, this stock of pure knowledge is maintained and added to by all subsequent research. Thus, the only difference between the case in which the rejected GPT is abandoned and the one in which it is sent back to the drawing board for further development is in the timing of the next challenge to the incumbent GPT. When the failed challenger is discarded, a further comparison must await the discovery of a wholly new GPT. When it is sent back for further development, comparison with the incumbent is made in every subsequent period. In a more specific analysis, it would be desirable to have some part of pure knowledge discarded when the unsuccessful GPT is abandoned. This would model the fact that some of the research would have been specific to that technology and of little value elsewhere. The modelling procedure would then be to reduce the stock of potentially useful knowledge by some random obsolescence factor at the time the unsuccessful challenger was discarded.

The next modelling issue is when to apply the random variables ϖ and ϑ that determine the effectiveness of the new GPT to assist the applied research sector. We have more to say about the definition and working of these random variables when

---

[23] Lipsey and Carlaw (1996) document several such cases in their evaluation of a number of technology policies.

we discuss the model in the next subsection. Here we lay out the intuition of what these variables model. The randomness that they introduce models the fact that one can never be sure how a technology that looks good on the drawing board or in small prototype applications will work in practice. In our models, we compare the efficiency of the challenger with that of the incumbent *after* we have applied this randomness. But in some cases it may be more interesting to make the comparison of the two GPTs *before* the effect of the randomness is known. The potential of the challenger is then compared with the incumbent before it is known how well the new GPT will work in practice. This sequence could model experiences such as those who installed computers in offices and workshops and found that they resulted in an unexpected fall in productivity. Eventually, the changeover proved its worth, but the impact effects were often disappointingly small, sometimes even negative.

We believe that such experience is not uncommon with major new technologies. (Fortunately our transition criterion 1 can mimic what would happen with criteria 2 and 3 when the randomness is applied after the selection criterion because with criterion 1, those GPTs that initially lower productivity are selected.) The logistic evolution ensures that eventually the new GPT will do better than the replaced one would have done but, with the random variables applied after the new GPT is accepted, it may do better or worse in the short run. In cases where the random effect lowers the challenger's initial productivity below that of the GPT it displaces, there will be a temporary slowdown in productivity growth, possibly even negative growth for a time. Of course, if the random variable turns out to make the GPT perform much better than was predicted when the comparison was made, there may be an unexpected productivity bonus at the outset.

When we want to compare the results that follow from these five selection criteria, we cannot just do five independent runs. Instead, we do a run using one of the transition criteria and then repeat the runs for the other transition cases, imposing the same realized values for all the random variables each time, thus providing a genuine comparative dynamics exercise. In most of what follows in this and the next chapter, we calculated such results for all the five transition criteria in the manner just described. But in this book we are interested mainly in concepts rather than specific detailed applications. At that level, we found that the qualitative results were broadly similar, so we reproduce the graphs for only one of the cases. This gives the general idea of what is happening. In more detailed applications, however, the differences really do matter—but that is another story awaiting applications of our model to specific situations.

The Model and Its Workings

The new equations of the three-sector model are laid out in Box 14.3. There are now three sectors to which resources must be allocated (equation 14.1'), while the equations governing the consumption and applied R&D sections still apply (equations 14.2 and 14.3). The pure research sector produces a flow of knowledge, g_t, according to the production function shown in equation (14.5). This flow depends on two influences. The first is the resources allocated to it. $r_{c,t}$, which are subject to

Box 14.3. The Three-Sector Model

The consumption goods and the applied R&D sectors are the same as in the two-sector model (equations 14.2 and 14.3). The resource constraint is:

$$R_t = r_{c,t} + r_{a,t} + r_{g,t} \tag{14.1$'$}$$

$r_{c,t}$ and $r_{a,t}$ are already defined, and $r_{g,t}$ is resources in the pure knowledge sector.

The flow of new pure knowledge, g_t, is generated by:

$$g_t = [(1 - \mu)A_{t-1}]^{\sigma_1}(\theta_t r_{g,t})^{\sigma_2}, \quad 0 < \sigma_i \leq 1, \ i = (1, 2), \text{ and } \sigma_2 < 1 \tag{14.5}$$

The restrictions on σ_i ensure diminishing returns to resources producing pure knowledge, $r_{g,t}$, and either constant or diminishing returns to the applied knowledge, A_t, used in the pure knowledge sector. We assume $G_1 = 1$ in our baseline model. θ_t, a random variable distributed uniformly with support [0.8, 1.2], mean 1, and variance $(0.4)^2/12$ models the uncertainty about how much knowledge will be generated by a given effort. The first part of the production function, $[(1 - \mu)A_{t-1}]^{\sigma_1}$, allocates a proportion of the stock of knowledge to the consumption sector to act as the productivity coefficient in that sector.

The current stock of potentially useful pure knowledge, G_t^p, is the last period's stock, G_{t-1}^p, suitably depreciated by δ plus the flow produced this in period, g_t:

$$G_t^p = g_t + (1 - \delta)G_{t-1}^p \tag{14.6}$$

Actually useful pure knowledge enters the system as G_t when a new GPT is discovered, that is, when the realization of the random variable λ_t surpasses a threshold value λ^*. The model is calibrated by setting the parameters ν and η (defined below) so that this realization occurs infrequently.

$$G_t = \varpi_{t_z} G_{t_z-1} + \left(\frac{e^{\tau+\gamma(t-t_z)}}{1 + a^{\tau+\gamma(t-t_z)}} \right)(G_t^h - G_{t_z-1}) \tag{14.7}$$

$$\text{where } G_t^{\prime h} = \left\{ \begin{array}{c} G_{t-1}^h + \vartheta\left(G_t^p - G_{t-1}^h\right) \text{ if } \lambda \geq \lambda^* \\ G_{t-1}^h \text{ otherwise} \end{array} \right\} \tag{14.8}$$

t_z in equation (14.7) is the arrival date of the zth GPT and γ and τ are calibration parameters controlling the rate of diffusion. The only term that evolves in equation (14.7) from the date of the GPT's arrival is the logistic diffusion function in the parentheses.

ϖ, which shifts the logistic curve, is a variable drawn from a beta distribution and weighted so that it can take on values from 0 up to 1.5, the distribution parameters are calibrated so that ϖ only occasionally takes on values less than 1. ϑ is a random number that takes on only positive values (many of which can be fractions). It shifts the upper asymptote of the logistic diffusion curve and, together with ϑ determines the productivity of emerging GPTs. Both λ and ϑ are derived from beta distributions, where each distribution is defined as $\beta(x|\nu, \eta) = \frac{x^{(\nu-1)}x^{(\eta-1)}}{\beta(\nu, \eta)}$ with support [0, 1], mean $(\nu/(\nu + \eta))$ and variance $\frac{\nu\eta}{(\nu+\eta)^2(\nu+\eta+1)}$. $\beta(\nu, \eta)$ is the beta function, and ν and η are parameters that take on positive integer values.

Box 14.3. (continued)

The evolution of actually useful pure knowledge shown in equation (14.7) can most simply be seen as follows. Assume that the potential of the existing GPT has been fully exploited so that $G_t^h = G_{t-1}$. Now let a new GPT be discovered ($\lambda_t > \lambda^*$). Initially the productivity of the new GPT is equal to that of the incumbent, modified by a random drawing on ϖ. However, there is a discrete jump in the accounting of the increment of pure knowledge $\vartheta(G_t^p - G_{t-1}^h)$ in equation (14.8) and this amount slowly diffuses through each period of the GPT's existence into actually useful pure knowledge according to the logistic diffusion coefficient $\left(\frac{e^{\tau + \gamma(t-t_z)}}{1 + e^{\tau + \gamma(t-t_z)}}\right)$ in equation (14.7). When another GPT arrives, there is a further discrete jump in G_t^h and the diffusion process begins again.

---

decreasing returns. The knowledge output of these resources is altered each period by a random variable, ϑ, that models the observation that one is never sure how much knowledge will be generated by a given amount of R&D. The second influence is the productivity parameter $(1 - \mu)A_{t-1}$, which divides the total stock of applied knowledge, A, between the proportion that is useful in the consumption goods sector, μ, and the proportion that is useful in the pure research sector, $1 - \mu$.

The current stock of potentially useful pure knowledge, G_t^p, which is shown in equation (14.6), is calculated as this period's flow of pure knowledge, g_t, plus the stock of last period's knowledge, G_{t-1}^p, reduced by an obsolescence factor, δ.[24] This stock of potentially useful pure knowledge only becomes actually useful after a new GPT is discovered. This occurs at a time that is determined randomly—whenever the drawing made each period of a random arrival, variable, λ (defined in Box 14.3), exceeds some threshold value λ^*. The model is calibrated so that such discoveries occur infrequently.

If the full potential value of the GPT became available immediately, the stock of actually useful pure knowledge would jump immediately every time a new GPT was discovered and then remain constant until the advent of the next GPT (as it did in our original model). Instead, we model the usefulness of the GPT as evolving according to the logistic curve for productivity shown in Figure 13.1 (where the upper asymptote represents the full potential productivity of the new GPT). We do this through an accounting variable, G^h, which only changes when a new GPT is invented (equation 14.8).[25] The amount of the increase depends on two influences: first, the amount of potentially useful pure knowledge that has accumulated since the last GPT arrived ($G_t^p - G_{t-1}^h$ in equation 14.8); and second, a random variable, ϑ,

---

[24] For now, the process that renders this knowledge obsolete is treated as exogenous. A more sophisticated version of the model would make obsolescence endogenous based on agents' decisions about the adoption of new technologies. Howitt (1999) provides a dynamic model that illustrates how increases in the arrival rate of technology can cause increases in the rate of obsolescence. Carlaw (2000) provides a choice theoretic model where agents faced with unanticipated improvements in technology optimally choose to render old technology obsolete by writing off the old and investing in the new. Such models could be the starting point for endogenizing obsolescence in our framework.

[25] This accounting variable increases with the invention of each new GPT, whether the challenger displaces the incumbent or is rejected.

which models the fact that the applied potential of GPTs varies in ways that cannot be predicted when they are originally being developed. This randomness alters the upper asymptote of the logistic diffusion curve and so models the uncertainty about how long a GPT will take to reach the final stages of its development and how much productivity will have been increased along the way.

The accounting variable is then used in the logistic diffusion equation (14.7). To see how this diffusion process works, note that when the new GPT is first discovered, the value of the diffusion coefficient in equation (14.7) is effectively zero (actually a very small positive number). Thus, the productivity of the new GPT is equal to that of the previous GPT, $G_{t_{z-1}}$, multiplied by another random number, ϖ, which alters the lower asymptote of the logistic curve. Thus ϖ shifts the whole curve either upwards or downwards, but with a higher likelihood of producing small upward shifts. It models the possibility of historical increasing returns that exist at the early stages of a new GPT but are exhausted once the new technology is fully embodied, plus surprises that affect how the new GPT looks in practice rather than on the drawing board. Next assume that the diffusion process is complete so that the value of the diffusion coefficient is effectively unity. Then, the new GPTs productivity is equal to the productivity of the previous GPT, $G_{t_{z-1}}$, in equation (14.7) (as altered somewhat by the random variable ϖ) plus the full increment to useful pure knowledge conferred by the existing GPT, that is $(G_t^h - G_{t_{z-1}})$ in equation (14.7). Between these two dates, the diffusion process logistically feeds the potential productivity of the new GPT into its actual productivity.

When another GPT arrives, there is a further discrete jump in the accounting variable and the logistic diffusion process begins again. There is an implicit assumption here that all previous knowledge net of obsolescence is used in each subsequent GPT.[26]

The parameterization for the three-sector model is shown in Box 14.4. The values are chosen to meet the criteria of ensuring diminishing returns to resources, an average annual growth rate of approximately 2 per cent, and constant returns to the accumulating factor, knowledge (in line with the discussion in Chapter 13, which has already been referred to). GPTs arrive on average every thirty-five years, but with a large variance.

The behaviour that drives the simulation, which is laid out formally in Box 14.5, now proceeds as follows. Based on expectations of their pay-offs, resources are allocated to each of the three sectors to maximize the objective function in each period (equation 14.9). The actual outputs that flow out of the applied R&D and pure knowledge sectors are then fed into the appropriate stock of knowledge and the maximization exercise with respect to resources is repeated in the next period, and so on.

Results

Our choice of the transition criteria that determine whether and when a new GPT will replace the incumbent affects the timing of the sequence of GPTs. Criterion 1 has

---

[26] It would be a simple matter to relax this implicit assumption by allowing a temporary acceleration of obsolescence on the old GPT when the new one arrives.

Box 14.4. Numerical Simulation in a Three-Sector Model

These are the parameter values used to simulate the results of the three-sector model as reported in the text and shown in Figures 14.1–14.4:

$\alpha_1 = 1$	$\alpha_2 = 0.34$	$\beta_1 = 1$	$\beta_2 = 0.34$
$\sigma_1 = 1$	$\sigma_2 = 0.34$	$\nu = 0.1$	$A_0 = 1$
$G_0 = 1$	$R = r_{c,t} + r_{a,t} + r_{g,t} = 1{,}000$	$\varepsilon = 0.01$	$\delta = 0.01$
$\gamma = 0.06$	$\tau = -6$	$\mu = 0.5$	

In cases where ϑ is endogenized $\kappa = 1$ and $\omega = 0.02$. For λ we choose $\nu = 5$ and $\eta = 10$. For ϑ we choose $\nu = 10$ and $\eta = 5$. For ϖ we choose $\nu = 12$ and $\eta = 5$ and multiply all values of x_t by 1.5.

Box 14.5. Maximization in the Three-Sector Model

The Bellman equation for the three-sector model is:

$$V(A_t, G_t, t) = \max_{\{r_{c,t},\, r_{a,t},\, r_{g,t}\}} c_t + \rho E[V(A_{t+1}, G_{t+1}, t+1)] + \rho^2 E[V(A_{t+2}, G_{t+2}, t+2)]$$

s.t.

$(14.1) - (14.3)$,

$$\bar{g}_t = \nu((1-\mu)A_{t-1})^{\beta_1} r_{g,t}^{\beta_2}$$

$$\bar{G}_t = \bar{g}_t + (1-\varepsilon)G_{t-1}$$

where the upper bars indicate expected rather than the actual values of g_t and G_t. This is a complicated problem in two dimensions of state variables. We simplify by allowing the stocks of applied and pure knowledge to have immediate impact in the production functions for consumption, applied R&D, and pure knowledge as follows:

$$c_t = (\mu A_t)^{\alpha_1} r_{c,t}^{\alpha_2} \quad \text{with} \quad \alpha_i \in (0, 1], \ i = (1, 2), \text{ and } \alpha_2 < 1 \qquad (14.2')$$

$$a_t = \nu(\bar{G}_t)^{\beta_1} r_{a,t}^{\beta_2} \quad \text{with} \ \beta_i \in (0, 1], \ i = (1, 2), \text{ and } \beta_2 < 1 \qquad (14.3')$$

$$g_t(r_{g,t}) = ((1-\mu)A_t)^{\sigma_1}\theta_t(r_{g,t})^{\sigma_2} \quad \text{with} \ \sigma_i \in (0, 1] i = (1, 2), \text{ and } \sigma_2 < 1 \qquad (14.5')$$

Note that equation $(14.3')$ has been altered to include the expected rather than the actual stock of pure knowledge in the present period instead of the actual stock in the previous period. These results permit an easier expression of the maximization problem without affecting any of the qualitative results.

Recursive substitution of the constraints into the objective function yields the following reduced form:

$$c_t = \left\{ \mu \left[\nu((1-\mu)E[A_t])^{\sigma_1}(r_{g,t})^{\sigma_2} + (1-\delta)G_{t-1} \right]^{\beta_1}(r_{a,t})^{\beta_2} + (1-\varepsilon)A_{t-1} \right\}^{\alpha_1}(r_{c,t})^{\alpha_2}$$

The expectations operator is applied to the stock of applied knowledge in this equation because there is a problem of simultaneous determination. We adopt the simplest assumption of expectations by setting $E[A_t] = A_{t-1}$.

Maximization problem is:

$$\max_{\{r_{c,t},\, r_{a,t},\, r_{g,t}\}} c_t = (\mu A_t)^{\alpha_1} (r_{c,t})^{\alpha_2}$$

s.t.

$$R_t = r_{c,t} + r_{a,t} + r_{g,t}$$

$$A_t = a_t + (1 - \varepsilon)A_{t-1}$$

$$a_t = \nu(\bar{G}_t)^{\beta_1} r_{a,t}^{\beta_2}$$

$$\bar{G}_t = \bar{g}_t + (1 - \delta)G_{t-1}$$

$$\bar{g}_t = [(1 - \mu)A_t]^{\sigma_1} r_{g,t}^{\sigma_2} \qquad (14.9)$$

the most frequent replacement of one GPT by another because all new GPTs succeed in replacing the incumbent, including those that would have been rejected by any of the other criteria. As already noted, this can mimic the results of criteria 2 and 3 when the two random variables that influence the transference of potential into actual knowledge are applied after, rather than before, the selection criterion is applied. Criteria 2 and 3 produce more frequent GPTs than criteria 4 and 5. The reason is that with criteria 2 and 3 the challenger succeeds as long as it does better than the incumbent at the outset, whatever stage the incumbent is at on its logistic evolutionary path, while in Cases 4 and 5, a comparison of growth rates, even over one future period, rules out all the cases in which the incumbent has not yet encountered a productivity slowdown. Because the challenger must begin in its Phase 1, with a low growth rate of its productivity it will succeed with criteria 4 and 5 only if the incumbent also has a low productivity growth rate. This implies that the incumbent must be in the last stage of its evolution.

The growth rate of consumption output is not, however, uniquely determined across all five transitional criteria. Indeed, experiments show that, depending on the parameter values that we choose, any one of the five criteria is capable of producing faster growth than all the others. For example, if the occurrence of new GPTs is so spread out that each incumbent has virtually finished its evolution when the new GPT is discovered, all the various criteria produce the same result. At the other extreme if there is a sequence of GPTs coming quickly one after the other, criteria 2 and 3 will accept some of these while criteria 4 and 5 will reject them all, provided only that the incumbent is sufficiently far along its early development path to have a rate of productivity growth higher than that of a new GPT. Which of these two sequences produces the higher consumption path depends on the values of the parameters and random variables.

One might think that the results based on criteria 2 and 3 would always dominate those based on criterion 1, since criterion 1 includes the negative realizations on the new GPT's initial productivity that are excluded by criteria 2 and 3. But, surprisingly, this is not so. For example, if a GPT with a ϖ less than one is developed while the incumbent is in the early part of its Phase 4, the challenger will be rejected by criteria 2–5 but accepted by criterion 1. Now assume that there is an even longer gap before the next GPT is invented. The path of consumption under the new GPT that is selected under criterion 1 will initially be below the path produced by the existing GPT that has been left in place by criteria 2–5. But before long, the new GPT will enter its Phases 2 and 3, causing its path to rise above the path produced by the GPT left in place by the other criteria as the survivor progresses through the later stages of its Phase 4. Variations in the intervals between GPTs and variations in the random shocks that make the new GPT's initial productivity level rise above or fall below that of the existing GPT give rise to many different consumption paths and can make any one of these criteria produce results that are superior to the others. Thus there are no general results that are true for all GPT sequences at all times. The devil is in the details. Specific circumstances matter in every case.

Similarly, there is no unique outcome with respect to the effect of a new GPT on productivity. Since the new GPT enters in its Phase 1, initially it always has a low rate of productivity growth. If under criteria 2 and 3, the displaced GPT were well into its Phase 4, its contribution to the rate of productivity growth in applied R&D would have been low and the displacement might immediately raise the growth rate of productivity in applied R&D. But if the displaced GPT were in Phase 3, its contribution to the rate of productivity growth in applied R&D would have been high and the displacement of the old by the new might lower the rate of productivity growth. The transition from path *A* to *B* in Figure 13.3 illustrates a case of this sort, where a GPT that would have been rejected by criteria 4 and 5 but is accepted by criteria 2 and 3 produces results over an intermediate period that are inferior to what the dismissed incumbent would have produced. Of course, if the new GPT has its development cut off by the early arrival of yet another GPT, the growth rate may remain low. It may seem improbable that a series of potential GPTs could be cut off early in their potential lifespans by the arrival of new GPTs, but no one can tell how many technologies that might have grown into GPTs were cut off in their early stages of development when they were crude, single-purpose technologies. The potential of new technologies can seldom be known except by developing them through decades of use. Nonetheless, even in the unlikely event of a quick succession of several GPTs and a resulting prolonged low growth rate, the rate must eventually become higher than it would have been if the original GPT had never been replaced. This is because the original GPT must eventually progress through its Phase 4 where its rate of productivity growth asymptotically approaches zero. This is the sense in which the new GPT rejuvenates the growth process, although its transitional effects may be to lower the growth rate.

One of the main differences between criteria 4 and 5 on the one hand and 2 and 3 on the other is that under 4 and 5 the growth of pure knowledge is smoother and the productivity of an existing GPT is more fully exploited, giving it a longer life because it cannot be truncated in phase 3 by the arrival of a new GPT. Also, it is not possible to have a prolonged period of slow growth due to a series of GPTs being closely bunched together in their arrival times.

Some readers may be disturbed by lack of general results reported in this section. We are not, because we accept the importance of historical specificity. We do not expect to find results of this sort that hold for all circumstances in the real world and hence for all parameter values in our models. This is particularly so because technological innovation is a non-ergodic process in which small initial differences can be magnified, and what are apparently two very similar starting points can often evolve along radically different paths. There is thus a profound sense in which our models differ from all the first-generation GPT models, in which GPTs always evolve in the same way. We have repeatedly argued in previous chapters that this characteristic of the earlier models is misleading because we expect the experience of successive GPTs to differ. The differences will depend on a host of circumstances outlined in Chapter 13—although GPTs do display some similarities at a high level of abstraction, as also outlined in Chapter 13. We were thus pleased to discover that our model displays the diversity of behaviour that our earlier appreciative theorizing led us to expect.

Figure 14.3 shows the resource allocations and Figure 14.4 shows the growth rates of consumption and the stocks of applied and pure knowledge. The first two of these coincide because the latter primarily determines the former.

Sustained Growth

As in the simple two-sector model, growth in the three-sector model would peter out in the absence of the arrival of new GPTs. Having a pure knowledge sector that occasionally produces GPTs is a necessary condition for achieving sustained growth in our model. But it is not sufficient. Growth is sustained with GPTs because, in line with the analysis in Chapter 13, we assume that new knowledge impacts with a non-decreasing effect on the productivity of the activities that it influences. (This is done by setting α_1 in equation 14.2, β_1 in equation 14.3, and υ_1 in equation 14.5 all at unity.) Because new GPTs always arrive sooner or later, and because the knowledge embodied in them has a non-decreasing impact, growth is sustained.[27]

Now let us consider what might sustain growth even if the stocks of knowledge did encounter decreasing returns in all lines of production. In this case, even with GPTs arriving periodically, growth would peter out because resources in each of the knowledge-producing sectors would grow less productive over time due to diminishing returns to knowledge. As a result, resources would continuously migrate into the consumption sector, which would eventually employ all the resources, thus bringing growth to a halt.

Given decreasing returns to resources allocated to current production in all three sectors and our new assumption of decreasing returns to knowledge, is there anything that can sustain growth in our model? One possibility that is of particular interest, given what we know about technological change, is the existence of

---

[27] The most straightforward way to show that the model's growth can be thus sustained is to eliminate uncertainty in every period. This is equivalent to turning the model into an endogenous growth model with a balanced growth solution. When we run the simulation, the system converges to a constant growth rate where consumption, stocks of applied R&D, and pure knowledge are all growing at the same rate.

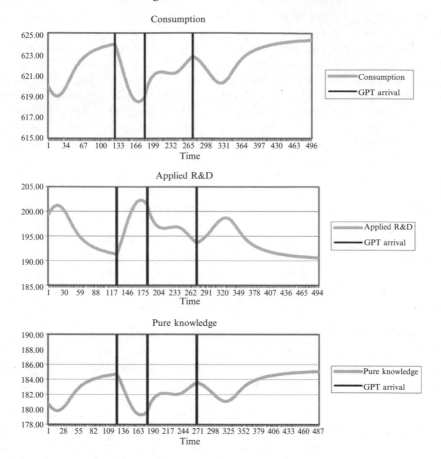

Figure 14.3. *Resource allocations (transition criterion 4)*
Note: When the first and the third GPTs arrive, resources are drawn in to the applied R&D sector from the other two sectors and this continues during the early phases of the new GPT's logistic diffusion. When the stock of applied knowledge has become large enough to make resources more productive in the other sectors, the migration of resources is reversed. The second GPT arrives when the incumbent is still in its Phase 3. As a result, productivity falls in applied R&D, causing resources to move out of that sector into consumption and pure research. This opposite process occurs in spite of the increased productivity in applied R&D because the relative trade-off in productivity among the sectors determines the resource allocation.

knowledge spillovers. Such spillovers have been observed many times in the history of technology, when discoveries by applied researchers have had profound effects on pure research. In Chapter 4, we discussed many cases of this phenomenon.

To model these feedbacks, we start by altering the assumption of constant returns to knowledge that we have so far used to produce sustained growth. We first introduce diminishing returns to applied knowledge by making the coefficient $0 < \alpha_1 < 1$ in equation (14.2 in Box 14.1). This is sufficient to cause the whole system to display

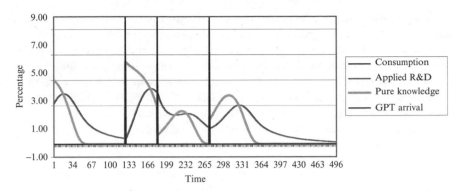

Figure 14.4. *Growth rates (transition criterion 4)*
Note: The arrival of the first and third new GPTs (at periods 129 and 280) occurs in the later stages of the evolution of the incumbent in which pure knowledge production has reached a low level. The second GPT arrives when the incumbent is still evolving rapidly and, as a result, pure knowledge production is reduced.

diminishing returns to knowledge, in which case growth will peter out in spite of the arrival of a succession of new GPTs.[28]

We now consider two ways in which the spillover running from applied R&D to pure research can reintroduce sustained growth. First, we model a technological complementarity between old and new pure knowledge by making the random weight, ϑ, that partially determines the productivity of a new GPT in the applied R&D sector an increasing function of the existing stock of pure knowledge (see equation 14.10 in Box 14.6).[29] With this assumption in place, the model produces sustained growth for certain calibrations of the parameters, even though the existing stocks of knowledge that enter all lines of production exhibit diminishing returns. The net effect, given the calibration we use, is slightly increasing returns in the system. When the model's uncertainty is turned off, this is manifested as increasing growth rates in all three sectors.[30] This is because the diminishing returns are offset by the technological complementarity by which the accumulation of pure knowledge increases the productivity of new GPTs. This is nothing more startling than saying, for example, that the computer software helps in discovering fundamental new knowledge in biotechnology and nanotechnology, or that the ability to design things on computers has greatly reduced the amount of costly learning by using, which older methods of design made necessary—and which was studied in detail by Rosenberg (1982: ch. 6).

---

[28] Equation 14.10 derives the reduced recursive form of the objective function. From inspection of the equation it is clear that setting the exponent on applied knowledge in the consumption sector to a fraction such that the whole function exhibits diminishing returns is sufficient to produce diminishing returns to all stocks of knowledge in the system.

[29] The spillover from past to future GPT models is the sort of technological complementarity described in Carlaw and Lipsey (2002) by which GPTs open up *possibilities* for further discoveries while not guaranteeing that further discoveries will be made, or that they will pay off significantly.

[30] With a different calibration, growth rates can be made constant or even decreasing.

To see another way in which the externality might operate, we alter the production functions for the consumption and pure knowledge sectors to allow applied knowledge to generate positive spillovers in the whole system. In our baseline model, we divided the stock of applied knowledge between the consumption and the pure knowledge sectors. Now we allocate the whole stock of applied knowledge to the consumption sector and allow a part of the stock to spillover to influence the pure knowledge sector. The alteration is also shown in Box 14.6.

In the previous case, sustained growth was generated by accumulated pure knowledge and the spillover was to the productivity of new GPTs. In the present

---

Box 14.6. Spillovers from Applied Knowledge

Two types of spillovers are modelled.

I. Accumulated Knowledge Makes GPTS More Powerful

The equations that turn potential knowledge into useful knowledge are repeated below from Box 14.3:

$$G_t = \varpi_{t_z} G_{t_{z-1}} + \left(\frac{e^{\tau + \gamma(t - t_z)}}{1 + e^{\tau + \gamma(t - t_z)}} \right) \left(G_t^h - G_{t_{z-1}} \right) \tag{14.7}$$

$$\text{where } G_t^h = \left\{ \begin{array}{c} G_{t-1}^h + \vartheta \left(G_t^p - G_{t-1}^h \right) \text{ if } \lambda \geq \lambda^* \\ G_{t-1}^h \text{ otherwise} \end{array} \right\} \tag{14.8}$$

In our baseline model, the distribution that determines ϑ is fixed. We now make it endogenous and a function of accumulated knowledge:

$$\vartheta = (s_t)(x_t), \text{ where } s = \kappa (G_t)^\omega \text{ and } \omega \in (0, 1] \tag{14.10}$$

where x_t is the draw from the beta distribution each period. This has the effect of increasing the expected value of the upper asymptote of the logistic diffusion curve for new GPTs. This increases the maximum effect a new GPT will have on the productivity of the whole system if the GPT's life extends well into Phase 4.

II. Applied Knowledge Spills Over to Affect Pure Research

We make the entire stock of pure knowledge useful in the consumption sector and add an externality that makes some of it also useful in the pure research sector. The production function for the consumption sector is altered to give constant returns to the entire stock of applied knowledge, A_t, implying that all the applications of GPTs developed in the applied R&D sector are useful in the consumption sector:

$$c_t = A_t r_{c,t}^\alpha \text{ with } \alpha \in (0, 1) \tag{14.2''}$$

A fraction μ of the stock of applied knowledge also enters as an externality into the production function for pure knowledge with an exponent $\sigma_1 \in (0, 1]$.

$$g_t(r_{g,t}) = (\mu A_t)^{\sigma_1} \theta_t r_{g,t}^{\sigma_2}, \sigma_i \in (0, 1], i = (1, 2), \sigma_2 < 1, \text{ and } \mu \in (0, 1] \tag{14.5''}$$

This externality sustains growth by increasing the productivity of pure research over time.

case, sustained growth is generated by the applied R&D sector. This sector produces two effects: a positive effect, which is directly useful to, and is paid for by, the consumption sector, and a spillover effect to the pure knowledge sector. As with the first case, under certain calibrations of the parameters, the spillovers overcome the diminishing returns to knowledge in the consumption sector, and lead to *accelerating* growth rates when the model's uncertainty is turned off. However, when the uncertainty is operational, the same parameter values generate increasing returns to knowledge and *sustained but non-accelerating* growth on average over the very long run. Over shorter time spans this growth may, however, display decreasing, constant, or increasing returns, depending on the historical pattern of uncertain arrival dates, the magnitudes of the GPTs, and the start and end points of the time period under examination. Thus, spillovers are modelled without requiring the empirically unsupported global increasing returns that lead to continuously accelerating growth in some endogenous growth models.

IV. SUMMARY AND CONCLUSION

One of the main reasons why we are able to extend the existing models of GPTs from their current state in the literature is our use of a non-stationary equilibrium concept. This technique is unpopular in many quarters because it does not lead to neat analytical solutions. We maintain, however, that the evidence of real growth processes shows that they are uneven. Since that characteristic cannot be mirrored by any model that produces a stationary growth equilibrium, we accept the messy simulations as the price of obtaining a model that reflects this reality.

Most standard growth models have flat technology, either in the form of a single scalar multiple to an aggregate production function, changes in which cause Hicks neutral growth, or in the form of an efficiency coefficient on labour, so that labour-enhancing technological change (plus capital accumulation) causes Harrod neutral growth. To make our baseline model tractable, we use a flat technology in each sector, described by each sector's single production function. The complex structure of technology is thus found in the relations among the sectors. Research generates the knowledge that develops into a GPT once a lucky strike occurs. Its potential efficiency depends on the amount of research that went into it and a random disturbance. This potential raises the efficiency of applied R&D through a logistic diffusion process. The output of applied knowledge then raises efficiency in the consumption and the pure research sectors.

The step increase in efficiency that occurs in those cases in which the new GPT is significantly more efficient than the incumbent represents historical increasing returns. These raise efficiency during the early stages of the new GPT's life, but then their effects peter out as their potential is fully exploited, as argued in more detail in Chapter 12. These scale effects are achieved in spite of the model showing decreasing returns to the accumulation of factors for given technology at any one time. Such transitory bursts of scale effects, commonly observed in the real growth experience, cannot be captured in any model that uses a single aggregate production function because that function must display either increasing, constant, or diminishing returns at all times.

We argued in earlier chapters that because of fixed factors such as land, carrying capacity of the environment, good harbour sites, and easily available minerals, we should expect diminishing returns to the accumulation of factors under conditions of constant technological knowledge. Our resource, R, does encounter diminishing returns whenever more of it is allocated to any one use, and it would encounter global diminishing returns if we allowed it to accumulate at the macro level. In our model, the arrival of new GPTs under conditions of constant returns to knowledge (or decreasing returns combined with sufficiently large externalities) produces a sustained rate of growth but one that that varies over the lifetime of each GPT, and on average from one GPT to another, as well as sometimes displaying growth slowdowns and at other times accelerations when new GPTs displace incumbents.

Thus our models generate all the commonly accepted stylized facts concerning growth, including sustained growth at a varying rate that shows no long-term trend to acceleration or deceleration, a constant ratio of knowledge stock to output, a falling ratio of labour to output, non-stationarity in growth rates over time (and across countries when multicountry models are used), absence of any inevitable tendency for the growth rate to accelerate over the long term, and no strong long-term, positive relation between the amount of applied R&D and the rate of economic growth over the long term.[31] We do this while having universal decreasing returns to the allocated factor and decreasing returns to the knowledge that is accumulated within the lifetime of any one GPT.

We also incorporate into our baseline model many more of the stylized facts concerning GPTs than any previous GPT-driven growth model, including a succession of GPTs with different characteristics and different effects on the growth rate, decisions taken under uncertainty and a resulting groping forward in a profit-oriented manner instead of maximization over a long-term horizon, the possibility but not the inevitability of slowdowns, historical increasing returns that exist in the changeover period from one GPT to another but do not exist indefinitely and so are not brought into any of the production functions as permanent scale effects. Subsequent models described in Chapter 15 extend the number of empirically relevant characteristics that we incorporate.

A Postscript on Applicability

With all theorizing there is a clear trade-off between generality and explanatory power: the more general a theoretical formulation, the less it is able to explain events for which specific local conditions matter. This is the issue of historical specificity that we first encountered in Chapter 1.

---

[31] We use a Tornquist aggregator to produce the knowledge stock and compare this to consumption output as our version of the captial-output ratio. We treat our resources as being the counterpart to labour when we construct our labour-output ratio, which implicitly assumes that labour force is not growing and so it is obvious that the ratio of labour to output will be falling as long as growth is occurring.

Growth theory is no exception to this general rule. Indeed, we have argued in several places in this book that growth theories purporting to apply at all times and all places have to be so general as to have only limited explanatory power. Although growth has some universal characteristics, which must be shared by any theory, it is also influenced by specific characteristics that vary over time and space. Furthermore, although technology does have some general characteristics, it is far too complex for all of its important influences to be caught by alterations in a single scalar multiple on an aggregate production function.

In earlier chapters, we have argued that the emergence of sustained growth in the West was a contingent process that cannot be explained by any existing formal growth model. Once the West's growth had become sustained, however, we believe that the models in this chapter are useful tools for analysing the subsequent process of sustained, GPT-driven growth. To capture the importance of GPTs, technology has to be modelled in a much more structured manner than in models based on a single aggregate production function.

Both the explicit characteristics and the implicit assumptions of these models alter the trade-off towards less generality and more specificity. Our models implicitly assume the institutional circumstances that underpin modern market economies, such as private property, limited liability, and the rule of law. They also assume the specific institutions involved in the West's invention of how to invent. As discussed towards the end of Chapter 7, these made the West's growth process self-sustaining—equations (14.3) and (14.5) depend on the existence of these institutions.

The models also implicitly assume low rates of population growth so that extensive and intensive growth are highly correlated. Because of their structure, they apply only to countries whose growth depends to a significant extent on developing from their own resources new technologies, both fundamental and derivative. Thus, they are not meant to apply to countries whose growth processes are more or less completely driven by the diffusion of technologies developed elsewhere. Nor are they meant to apply to those whose GDPs are currently static and who seek conditions that would allow them to enter a period of sustained growth.

All these qualifications illustrate once again the issue of historical specificity: the richer the explanatory power of a theory and the more predictions that it makes, the more restricted is its range of applicability in both time and space. Finally, we observe that there is no single 'correct' way to make the historical specificity trade-off. All growth processes have things in common, and to deal with these, very general theories are helpful. But all growth processes also have many aspects that are more specific in time and place. To deal with these, and, therefore, to get to deeper levels of explanation requires less generality and more specificity.

15

Formal Models of GPT-Driven Sustained Growth: Extensions and Applications

In this chapter, we consider a number of alterations to our baseline model—alterations that begin our research programme of augmenting our initial highly aggregated treatment to bring it progressively closer to a micro-evolutionary approach. We simulate some of our amended models, but in other cases, we must be content with showing how the effect being considered can be modelled by revising our equations, but not going further. Doing so each time would require a treatment extending well beyond the scope of this book.

In the course of making these extensions, we are able to generate some interesting results. We show that in some cases rational and myopic expectations give nearly identical results, while in other cases, myopic expectations generate results that are superior to those that follow from rational expectations. When we model our facilitating structure, even in a crude form, we can generate productivity slowdowns and bonuses associated with some new GPTs but not others. This happens in ways that mimic some of what is observed with the introduction of real GPTs. It suggests the possibility of deriving predictions about the circumstances in which new GPTs will and will not be associated with such phenomena. We also use Monte Carlo methods to show that not only do changes in TFP not closely follow changes in technology in many situations but also that technology can be changing while TFP is constant in some cases.

I.   RATIONAL VERSUS ADAPTIVE EXPECTATIONS

Thus far, we have dealt with expectations in a fairly simplistic way in order to focus on other details of the model. Introducing more complicated assumptions allows us to use the model to determine under what conditions different behavioural and informational assumptions cause different outcomes. For the starkest contrast with our model of adaptive expectations in which agents cannot anticipate changes in the current values of the variables, we make the forward-looking, perfect-information assumption used in most standard aggregate growth models. Agents now know the distributions from which the random variables are being drawn and can form forward-looking expectations about the pay-offs from allocating resources to each line of activity based on the means of these distributions. In other words, they can formulate stationary long-run resource allocation rules.[1] Although we have argued that it is impossible in practice for agents to obtain such full information when GPTs are evolving under uncertainty, making the assumption that they can do so produces some revealing comparisons.

The Model

We model forward-looking behaviour in three steps:

Step 1: we simulate our baseline model using in each period the means of all the random variables rather than realized drawings from each of the distributions. The equilibrium, after making sufficient iterations to remove the influence of the initial conditions, has constant resource allocations across all sectors. This replicates the stationary, balanced growth equilibrium that would exist in the absence of uncertainty in the model.

Step 2: we repeat the simulation, imposing in each period the forward-looking, constant resource allocation rule derived from step 1, although the realizations of the random variables are now drawn from their respective distributions (i.e. the realized values are not forced to be the mean value in every period).

Step 3: we do a comparative dynamics exercise to compare the growth history under rational expectations with the results generated by using our simple adaptive behavioural rule that allocates resources based on the current period's marginal products. To do this, the model is seeded with identical initial conditions and influenced by the same set of realizations for the random variables as emerged in step 2. The simulation is then allowed to iterate for enough periods to remove any effects of the initial conditions. This was done for each of our five transition criteria outlined in Chapter 14.

Results

The result is that the long-run average growth rates are virtually identical under rational and adaptive expectations and for all transition criteria. The growth histories vary slightly when each new GPT is introduced but in the long run their average growth behaviour is almost identical. In one of our comparisons, the average per period growth rates over 500 periods were identical at 2.95 per cent. We made several more comparison runs with virtually identical results.

It may seem rather surprising that foresighted behaviour and behaviour that can look no further than the current period should produce outcomes that are essentially the same. Each GPT arrives at the same date and with the same random effect on its magnitude. The only difference is that the allocation of resources is constant in the rational expectations model, while in the non-foresighted model, resources move into applied R&D when the GPT first arrives and then slowly back to the other two sectors. This affects the values of the variables period by period within the lifespan of one GPT. But on average over its whole lifetime, there is virtually no

---

[1] The random variables of the three-sector model that we use here, and the first two moments of the relevant distributions, are defined in Box 14.3.

difference between the behaviour of the two models. Our conclusion is that there are plausible growth processes in which the most myopic possible assumption about expectations produces results, which are for all intents and purposes, identical to those produced by fully rational expectations. The reason is that the system is ergotic in the sense that short-run differences in behaviour with respect to the allocation of resources do not push it onto different growth trajectories.

In contrast, short-term differences with respect to resource allocations will cause long-run growth trajectories to diverge if the differences alter some of the processes that influence the pattern of growth. One interesting possibility is that the differences may affect the arrival rate of GPTs. Indeed, the history of GPTs suggests that the more the effort that is put into making a breakthrough in the development of pure knowledge, the faster such a breakthrough will be realized on average—although there will still be many surprises along the way. The research done to achieve the atom bomb, controlled atomic power, and the first flight to the moon are examples.

To model this possibility, we allow the arrival of new GPTs to be positively influenced by the accumulated amount of resources devoted to the pure knowledge sector so that the larger this amount, the shorter will be the time interval between GPTs. (The modification to the model is shown in equation 14.8$'$.)

Box 15.1. Endogenous Arrival and Diffusion Rates for New GPTs

An endogenous arrival rate

To make accumulated knowledge affect the arrival rate of GPTs, we modify the expression for the threshold value of λ^* to allow it to be a decreasing function of the accumulated resources allocated to the pure knowledge sector since the arrival of the last GPT. This implies we must modify equation (14.8) in Box 14.3 as follows:

$$G_t^h = \begin{cases} G_{t-1}^h + \vartheta\left(G_t^p - G_{t-1}^h\right) & \text{if } \lambda \geq \dfrac{(\lambda^*)}{\varphi \sum_{t_z}^{t} r_{g,t}} \\ G_{t-1}^h & \text{otherwise} \end{cases} \tag{14.8$'$}$$

where φ is a calibration parameter and t_z is defined in Box 14.3 as the arrival date of the zth GPT.

An endogenous diffusion rate

To allow resource allocations to influence the diffusion rate, we modify the logistic diffusion process so that the rate of diffusion of a new GPT is an increasing function of the accumulated resources devoted to applied R&D since the time of the GPTs arrival. We do this by modifying equation (14.7) in Box 14.3 as follows:

$$G_t = \varpi_{t_z} G_{t_z-1} + \left(\frac{e^{\gamma \overline{\sum_{t_z}^{t}} r_{a,t} + \gamma(t - t_z)}}{1 + e^{\gamma \sum_{t_z}^{t} r_{a,t} + \gamma(t - t_z)}} \right) \left(G_t^h - G_{t_z-1} \right) \tag{14.7$'$}$$

where γ is a calibration parameter and t_z is defined as in Box 14.3.

With foresighted behaviour, the resource allocations in all three sectors, including the production of pure knowledge, once again remain constant throughout the lifetimes of a succession of GPTs. Under adaptive behaviour some of the resources devoted to consumption and pure knowledge once again move into the applied R&D sector when the GPT first arrives. Then we also see the usual pattern that, as the GPT matures through its phases of development, resources slowly migrate out of applied R&D back into consumption and pure knowledge. Given our assumed parameter values, this occurs under all five of our transition criteria. These resource allocation patterns are shown in Figure 15.1, which is based on transition criterion one.[2] So far, all of this is qualitatively the same as in our first comparison of the two expectations formation rules. But this time the different time paths of research have lasting effects.[3]

Allowing the resources devoted to the pure knowledge sector to influence the arrival rate of new GPTs causes the consumption paths to differ significantly between the two expectations assumptions. Adaptive behaviour generates a higher long-run consumption trajectory and slightly lower rate of growth of consumption than does foresighted behaviour. In these two models, the case with the higher long-run average growth rate[4] generates the lower consumption path through time. Figure 15.2 plots a new run over four successive GPTs showing consumption levels for the two types of behaviour under transition criterion 1(described on page 452). The graphs of the consumption behaviour for these two types of expectations formation look coincident on Figure 15.2 because, in the early stages of their growth, they are sufficiently close for the differences not to show up even though they are there from period one. Later, the two paths diverge dramatically. The paths look relatively smooth in spite of a difference in resource allocation patterns between adaptive and foresighted behaviour because the differences in resource allocation between the two types of behaviour are relatively small.[5]

The difference between the ordering of the growth rates of consumption and the path of its level may seem counterintuitive to those used to working with models that have stationary equilibria, in which the average growth rate is also the period-by-period growth rate and changes in the time pattern of the level of consumption must reflect the average rate of change. In contrast, our model is non-stationary and therefore its variances matter as well as its means. Under the non-stationary process, the extreme random realizations of the system play an important role because of the system's path dependence. The more productive a new GPT is, the more resources

---

[2] The comparison for adaptive and foresighted expectations was done for all the selection criteria with similar results.

[3] In all cases, our simulation starts well before the first period shown and with a GPT in place. The observations are not interesting until the arrival of the first new GPT, which is at period 90 in Figure 15.1.

[4] The long-run average growth rate of consumption is calculated as an average over the 500-period horizon of the simulation under the two behavioural assumptions for each of the four transition criteria.

[5] Adaptive behaviour varies around the constant foresighted allocation of resources in a range of about plus or minus 5 units of the resource, which is small given that the total amount of resources is set to 1,000 and each sector uses at least 200 units in all periods.

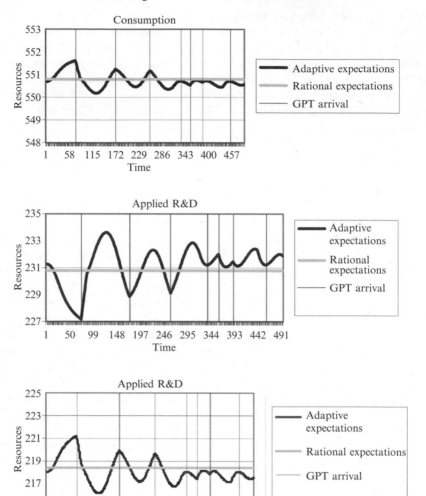

Figure 15.1. *Resource allocations under rational and adaptive expectations (transition criterion 1)*

Note: In all cases, rational expectations lead to an allocation of resources that is constant over time while adaptive expectations lead to a variable allocation. In this case the pattern is the usual one. If the incumbent GPT has matured through its Phase 4, the arrival of a new GPT causes resources to move from consumption and pure research into applied R&D. Then as the new GPT matures, resources move back into pure knowledge and consumption out of applied R&D. However, if a GPT is still in Phase 2 or 3 when the new GPT arrives, as occurs twice in periods 365 and 396, the reverse migration occurs. In these cases the new GPT enters and cuts off a more productive GPT in the applied R&D sector.

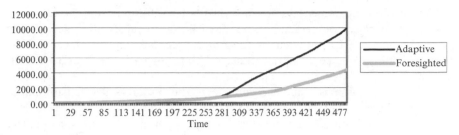

Figure 15.2. *Consumption paths under rational and adaptive expectations*
Note: The path of consumption under adaptive expectations is everywhere above the path of consumption under rational expectations.

are pulled out of consumption and pure research into applied research, and hence the longer is the expected interval until the arrival of the next GPT (since the interval is now influenced positively by the amount of resources devoted to pure research). Under rational expectations, this does not happen and the allocation of resources stays at the long-term average. Thus the longer interval between GPTs allows each GPT a longer period of maturing through its Phases 3 and 4, thus allowing it to generate a larger effect on the level of consumption. So the growth path of consumption is more likely to reflect a series of nearly complete logistic curves grafted one on the other than a series of curves that are often cut off in the earlier stages of their trajectories. All of this has the effect of making the average growth rate higher under rational rather than under adaptive expectations. But adaptive expectations produce a higher level of consumption output through time. When the random draws produce extreme values of the power of new GPTs, there is an upward ratcheting effect on the accumulation of applied knowledge under adaptive expectations, and this pushes the system onto a higher consumption trajectory than that produced by rational expectations.[6]

We have not articulated an explicit social utility function to determine which of the trajectories is more desirable. But since the model acts to maximize consumption in each period, higher consumption growth is implicitly the desired outcome of the behavioural decisions.

Finally, we note that the consumption trajectories reported here are conditional on the parameterization of the model. In particular, the results are sensitive to the parameter values chosen for the diffusion process. For the results reported in Figure 15.2, the diffusion process is slow and therefore it takes time for the GPT to have its full productivity impact. If interrupted by new GPTs before then, the growth rate slows.

---

[6] The consumption level in any period is the integration of all the growth in history. In a system with a high variance, this integrated value can be high even though the average growth rate is low. This is the key to understanding this seemingly counterintuitive result, which goes so much against our usual training. We are used to functional forms where the growth rate is smooth and continuous and usually monotonic so that the average and the total always align. In the non-stationary environment of this model, this does not have to be the case because averages vary with the length of time (or the number of observations included).

Under alternative parameter values that yield faster diffusion rates, the results on consumption trajectories reverse because the GPTs mature sufficiently quickly for the arrival of the next GPT not to cut off the growth potential of the incumbent. Under these conditions, the consumption trajectories are higher under rational expectations.[7]

The above result raises another possibility. The resources devoted to applied knowledge between GPT arrivals might influence the diffusion rate of GPTs positively. The modification to the model is shown in equation (14.7′) in Box 15.1. This alteration produces differences in the resource allocations under the two assumptions about expectations formation. If we combine the arrival rate and diffusion assumptions, the difference in expectations formations behaviour generate very different histories of growth.

Significance

The results reported in this section suggest some interesting lessons with respect to the implications of different kinds of behaviour. First, the results are an illustration of a general point that does not seem to have received sufficient attention in the literature. When the system contains positive feedbacks, externalities, and other relations among its variables that cannot be exploited by individual action, individual decisions based on fully informed rational expectations do not necessarily lead to a result that would be preferred by everyone. If agents had full knowledge of the system's behaviour and acted collectively, they could achieve the higher consumption path, but each acting individually cannot. Thus the system's non-stationarity is similar to an externality. Even if agents know about it, they cannot exploit it by non-cooperative action, so that the best they can do is to base their behaviour on the known means of the probability distributions that are disturbing the system's behaviour.

Second, the results are relevant to the contentions of Alchian and Friedman that groping behaviour at the micro level would produce macro results that were indistinguishable from those produced by maximizing behaviour. We discussed and criticized their views in Chapter 2, making the point that in the absence of a dynamic theory, which modelled these different types of behaviour, their contentions were merely unsupported assertions. Here we see a specific example that refutes the views of these two authors, and others who continue, even today, to reference them. When the system is ergodic in the sense that random (or purposeful) deviations from the mean of rational behaviour tend to be ironed out, random groping and fully foresighted behaviour tend to be indistinguishable over the long run, just as Friedman and Alchian argued. But when the system is non-ergodic, displaying path dependency, the two forms of behaviour can produce very different results because random (or purposeful) deviations from the rational norm tend to get magnified.[8] There is then no guarantee that the two types of micro behaviour will lead to the same macro results over any period of time.

---

[7] We leave for another time the full exploration of the parameter space for the model.

[8] These considerations suggest another line of enquiry that we are pursuing in our ongoing research. There is abundant empirical evidence that, while capitalist economies are observed to have sustained growth in per capita income, growth has not been at a constant rate. Instead, the growth data are pervaded by trends.

II. TWO APPLIED R&D AND CONSUMPTION SECTORS

The historical cases discussed in Chapters 5 and 6 show that a new GPT often appears in a small number of production activities and then, as it develops, it overtakes the incumbent technologies in many other activities. This is stylized by our applications curve in Chapter 13.

To model this type of behaviour, we need more than one consumption and applied R&D sector. The increasing number of applications of a new GPT as its use spreads throughout the economy can be modelled by having it used in more and more sectors. When we model such an economy, the incumbent and the new GPT must each be given some specific relation to each of the applied sectors. To get the diversity we require, we allow these relations to differ across GPTs and across the applied R&D sectors. We deal here with the simplest case in which there are two types of consumption goods and two lines of applied R&D activity.

In Box 15.2, we lay out the required changes to our baseline model and in the text we discuss their implications. We assume two consumption and two applied R&D sectors, in addition to the sector generating pure knowledge that is specified in our baseline model. Resources must then be divided among the five production activities. The two consumption sectors each receive the stock of knowledge from their own sector-specific applied R&D activity. The pure knowledge sector is almost identical to that of our baseline three-sector model, with two exceptions. First, when the GPT arrives, it comes accompanied by two random variables that affect the productivity of the GPT differently in the two applied sectors. Second, pure knowledge production depends, as before, on the resources devoted to it, but now also on a portion of each of the two applied sectors' knowledge stocks that is useful to it.[9]

The maximization problem is altered somewhat with the move to multiple activities in consumption and applied R&D. Previously, when there was just one consumption good, we simply maximized consumption, assuming that the underlying representative utility function was monotonically increasing in total consumption. Now, with more than one consumption sector, we must make our utility function explicit. In equation (15.5), we assume a very simple additive utility function that makes the two consumption goods substitutes. This implies that there

---

In spite of many decades of research in fields like monetary theory and economic growth, economics provides little guidance about the source of such trends and even less guidance about suitable formulations for practical work. Indeed, trend formulations that appear in economic theory models are often based on mathematical convenience and/or appeal to some broadly acknowledged steady state characteristic. (Phillips 2003: 945)

It will be interesting to explore whether, and under what conditions, any of the empirical, time series tests for stationarity hold up in the data generated from our non-stationary model. If the time series tests detect stationarity, doubt will be cast about their ability to determine the kind of process by which the real data are generated.

[9] Because we do not simulate this model, it is not necessary to specify which of the five transition criteria is used when the new GPT enters the system.

Box 15.2. Two Applied R&D and Consumption Sectors

Resources are divided among five sectors: two for consumption goods, two for applied R&D, and one for pure knowledge. Each R&D sector produces results useful in its associated consumption sector.

$$R_t = \sum_{j=1}^{2} r^j_{c,t} + \sum_{j=1}^{2} r^j_{a,t} + r_{g,t} \quad \text{where} \quad j = (1, 2) \tag{15.1}$$

We simplify by making the functional forms of the production functions in two consumption sectors similar to each other so that they differ only in the amount of resources and stock of applied R&D knowledge that go into them:

$$c_{j,t} = (A_{j,t})^{\alpha_1}(r^j_{c,t})^{\alpha_2} \quad \text{with} \quad \alpha_i \in (0, 1], \ i = (1, 2) \tag{15.3}$$

There are two applied R&D activities denoted by $j = (1, 2)$ in equation (15.3).

$$a_{j,t} = \left(\nu_{j,t_z}G_t\right)^{\beta_1}(r^j_{a,t})^{\beta_2}$$
$$A_{j,t} = a_{j,t} + (1 - \varepsilon)A_{j,t-1} \quad \text{with} \quad \beta_i \in (0, 1], \ i = (1, 2) \tag{15.2}$$

$j = (1, 2)$ and $\nu_{j,t}$ is a random variable distributed uniformly with support $[0, 2]$. It determines the relative productivity effect of the GPT in the two applied R&D sectors and is determined at each t_z, which denotes the arrival date of GPTs. When the GPT arrives, it comes accompanied by a random variable, ν_j, that affects the productivity of the GPT in each of the two applied R&D sectors.

The pure knowledge production function now has three arguments (instead of two), resources, and a portion, μ, of each of the two applied sectors' knowledge stocks:

$$g_t = (\mu_1 A_{1,t})^{\sigma_1}(\mu_2 A_{2,t})^{\sigma_2}(\theta_t r_{g,t})^{\sigma_3} \text{ with } \sigma_i \in (0, 1], \ i = (1, 2, 3) \tag{15.4}$$

As in the three-sector baseline model, θ_t is distributed uniformly with support $[0.8, 1.2]$.

Potentially useful pure knowledge is the same as defined by equation (14.6). Actually useful pure knowledge is the same as defined by equations (14.7) and (14.8). The random variable, ϑ, is made partially endogenous in the same way as in equation (14.9). All of these equations are found in Box 14.3. Also, the transition criteria for the introduction of a new GPT are the same as those defined in Chapter 14 for the three-sector baseline model.

We define the objective function as a representative additive utility function, which makes the two consumption goods substitutes, and the maximization problem becomes:

$$\max_{\{r^1_{c,t}, r^2_{c,t}, r^1_{a,t}, r^2_{a,t}, r_{g,t}\}} U(c_{1,t}, c_{2,t}) = (c_{1,t})^{\chi_1} + (\eta c_{2,t})^{\chi_2}$$

$s.t$

$$R_t = \sum_{j=1}^{2} r^j_{c,t} + \sum_{j=1}^{2} r^j_{a,t} + r_{g,t}$$

$$c_{j,t} = (A_{j,t})^{\alpha_1}\left(r^j_{c,t}\right)^{\alpha_2} \tag{15.5}$$

$$A_{j,t} = a_{j,t} + (1 - \varepsilon)A_{j,t-1}$$

$$a_{j,t} = (\nu_{j,t}\bar{G}_t)^{\beta_1}\left(r^j_{a,t}\right)^{\beta_2}$$

$$\bar{G}_t = \bar{g}_t + (1 - \delta)G_{t-1}$$

$$\bar{g}_t = (\mu A_t)^{\sigma_1}r^{\sigma_2}_{g,t}$$

is a pure trade-off between the two consumption and applied R&D activities.[10] Although diversity is the theme of S-E theory, we here assume a single representative consumer because our incremental approach is first to introduce diversity on the production side. Later, we can add diversity on the consumption side but, for present purposes, we see no pay-off from the added complexity this would entail.

These revisions allow for a richer interaction between an existing and a new GPT. It is now possible for the new GPT to have a relatively high productivity contribution to one of the applied R&D sectors and a relatively low contribution to the other. The new GPT would, therefore, immediately displace the old GPT in one sequence of production and yet take a long time to displace it in the other, mirroring the kinds of sequential adoptions that we detailed in Chapters 5, 6, and 13. The older GPT will continue to make productivity contributions to the applied R&D sector in which it remains but will ultimately be replaced by the new GPT as the old one approaches the upper limit of its logistic diffusion. Given the framework developed here, it is possible to model the kinds of productivity bursts associated with the old GPT as it comes into competition with the new one in some lines of application. This would accommodate more of the observations of GPTs made in earlier chapters.

Again, we do not simulate this model because our main concern is to demonstrate the flexibility of the baseline model to accommodate much more complexity than it contains in its initial presentation in Chapter 14. By showing how to formulate these extensions, we show that, with minor formal adjustments and sufficient computational power, much interesting, but seemingly complex, behaviour can be incorporated into our framework.

III. MORE THAN ONE ACTIVE GPT

Probably the greatest limitation in all previous GPT models, and in ours up to this point, is that they contain only one GPT at any one time. Two of the major problems caused by this modelling limitation are, first, that the behaviour of the macroeconomy is predominantly determined by the behaviour of the single GPT and its related applied technologies; and second, that relations among several contemporaneous GPTs cannot be modelled.

With respect to the first limitation, it is obvious that the macro behaviour of the whole economy mirrors that of a typical GPT much more closely when there is only one GPT in operation at any one time than when there are several, each at a different stage in its development and each of which will give way to a challenger at a different time.

With respect to the second limitation, the historical cases discussed in Chapters 5 and 6 show many examples of GPTs that complement each other rather than

---

[10] A utility function such as a Cobb–Douglas, or in the extreme a Leontief, would imply complementarities among the sectors and would complicate the resource allocation trade-off unnecessarily for our present purpose of merely demonstrating how these complications can be handled.

compete. An example is the complementary relationship between electricity and electronic computers, where the former could not exist without the latter. We have also discussed the complementarity among GPTs that fit together in broader technology systems. For example, goods are packed into containers and trucked to the railhead from which trains carry them to the port, where they are transferred to cargo ships. This transportation system combines power GPTs, such as internal-combustion engines, with transportation GPTs, such as ships and cargo containers, with materials GPTs, such as iron and steel. In this example, each technology exists independently of the transportation network but, when combined, they create a valuable technology system that none of them could provide in isolation.

Relations of this type have already been partially modelled by endogenizing the coefficient that determines how much pure knowledge is actually useful in a new GPT. Doing this allows knowledge accumulated in the past to influence the impact of future GPTs. But we have not yet allowed two new GPTs to coexist. The modelling steps needed to allow for this important complication are shown in Box 15.3. They build on the model shown in Box 15.2 by expanding the production of pure knowledge to include two sectors.

The total pool of resources must now be allocated among the six sectors. The production functions for the two applied R&D activities now have three arguments, two types of GPT, and the resources allocated to each line of applied R&D activity. In each of the applied research sectors, a new GPT of, say, type 1, arrives with its own productive power, v^1, which is determined by a combination of exogenous and random variables. If it is adopted, it will also alter, v^2, the productive power of the existing type-2 GPT. Depending on the comparative degrees of complementarity between the old and the new type-1 GPTs with the type-2 GPT, the productivity parameter v^2 is either increased or decreased.

Resources must now be allocated between two types of pure knowledge research, which requires keeping track of the accumulation of pure knowledge and the arrival process of GPTs. The way in which we allow the GPTs to arrive in each line of activity is the same as in the three-sector model.[11]

The recursive maximization is also altered slightly to include the two lines of pure knowledge research. Once again, agents are unaware of the underlying and uncertain processes by which GPTs are introduced into the system and take only the expected current marginal products of resources in all lines of activity into account when allocating resources across the six sectors.

When a new GPT arrives, it encounters in each applied research sector two existing GPTs, one of its own type and one from the other line of research. We now compare two combinations: the existing type-2 GPT with either the old or the new type-1 GPT, selecting the one that leads to the higher output. Depending on the realization of the *v*s, the new GPT may have to wait for any adoptions, or it may be

---

[11] The five possible transition criteria are complicated slightly because each of the two GPTs enters each of the two applied R&D sectors and the transitions have to be considered for each.

Box 15.3. Two Active GPTs

Additional GPTs are added to the model from Box 15.2. Resources are now allocated among six sectors:

$$R_t = \sum_{j=1}^{J} r_{c,t}^j + \sum_{j=1}^{J} r_{a,t}^j + \sum_{x=1}^{X} r_{g,t}^x \qquad (15.6)$$

$j = (1,\ldots,J)$ denotes the $J = 2$ types of consumption and applied R&D production. $x = (1,\ldots,X)$ denotes the $X = 2$ types of pure knowledge production. The two consumption sectors are the same as in equation (15.2). For simplicity, we keep most of the parameters in the production functions the same across the two pure knowledge sectors.

Applied R&D will now utilize GPTs produced from each of the pure knowledge sectors so the production function for each applied R&D activity now has three arguments, two types of GPT knowledge, and resource inputs. Each GPT arrives with a set of parametric coefficients, v, a coefficient that determines its own productive potential and one that alters the productive potential of the other type of GPT.

$$a_{j,t} = \max \left\{ \left[\prod_{x=1}^{X} (v_{j,t_z}^x G_{t,z}^x)^{\beta_x} \right], \left[\prod_{x=1}^{X} (v_{j,t_{z-1}}^x G_{t,z-1}^x)^{\beta_x} \right] \right\} (r_{a,t}^j)^{\beta_{x+1}}$$

$$A_{j,t} = a_{j,t} + (1-\varepsilon)A_{j,t-1}$$

$$\beta_i \in (0,1), i = (1,\ldots,X+1).$$

$\qquad (15.7)$

Suppose a new GPT of type 1 arrives, bringing with it a new set of vs, each drawn from a beta distribution and denoted t_z. We now compare two combinations: the existing type-2 GPT with the old type-1 GPT, denoted z-1, and the existing type–2 with the new type-1 GPT, denoted z, selecting the one that leads to the higher output. Depending on the realization of the vs, the new GPT may have to wait for any adoptions, or it may be adopted in one sector immediately and in the other much later, or it may immediately eliminate its competitor everywhere. (Note once again that equation 15.7 represents the impact of the actual current stock of pure knowledge on the applied R&D sector where expectations of the current stock of pure knowledge are employed in the maximization procedure.)

Resources must now be allocated between two types of pure knowledge research, which requires keeping track of the accumulation of pure knowledge and the arrival process of GPTs from both sources of pure knowledge. GPTs arrive in each line of activity in the same way as in the three-sector model.

$$g_{x,t} = \prod_{j=1}^{J} (\mu A_{j,t})^{\sigma_j} (\theta_t r_{g,t}^x)^{\sigma_{j+1}} \text{ with } \sigma_i \in (0,1], i = 1,2,3. \qquad (15.8)$$

Potential useful knowledge in each of the x lines of pure research is accumulated according to:

$$G_{x,t}^p = g_{x,t} + (1 - \delta)G_{x,t-1}^p \tag{15.9}$$

Actually useful pure knowledge (when the GPT arrives) is:

$$G_{x,t} = \varpi_{x,t_z} G_{x,t_z-1} + \left(\frac{e^{\tau+\gamma(t-t_{z,x})}}{1 + e^{\tau+\gamma(t-t_{z,x})}}\right)(G_{x,t}^h - G_{x,t_z-1}) \tag{15.10}$$

where

$$G_{x,t}^h = \left\{\begin{array}{l} G_{x,t-1}^h + (G_{x,t}^p - G_{x,t-1}^h) \ if \lambda \geq \lambda^* \\ G_{x,t-1}^h \ otherwise \end{array}\right\} \tag{15.11}$$

and $t_{z,x}$ is the arrival date of the zth GPT in the pure knowledge sector x, while γ and τ are calibration parameters controlling the rate of diffusion. As in the previous model, θ_t is distributed uniformly with support $[0.8, 1.2]$ and λ and ϑ are drawn from beta distributions as in the three-sector model of Section III.

The maximization problem requires the redefinition of the objective function to include the two lines of pure knowledge research. Once again agents take only the current marginal products into account when allocating resources across the six sectors.

$$\max_{\{r_{c,t}^1, r_{c,t}^2, r_{a,t}^1, r_{a,t}^2, r_{g,t}^1, r_{g,t}^2\}} U(c_{j,t}) = \sum_{j=1}^{J} (c_{j,t})^{\varphi_j}$$

$s.t.$

$$R_t = \sum_{j=1}^{J} r_{c,t}^j + \sum_{j=1}^{J} r_{a,t}^j + \sum_{x=1}^{X} r_{g,t}^x$$

$$c_{j,t} = (A_{j,t})^{\alpha_1}(r_{c,t}^j)^{\alpha_2} \tag{15.12}$$

$$A_{j,t} = a_{j,t} + (1 - \varepsilon)A_{j,t-1}$$

$$a_{j,t} = \max\left\{\left[\prod_{x=1}^{X}(v_{j,t_z}^x \bar{G}_t^{x_z})^{\beta_x}\right], \left[\prod_{x=1}^{X}(v_{j,t_z-1}^x \bar{G}_t^{x_z-1})^{\beta_x}\right]\right\}(r_{a,t}^j)^{\beta_{x+1}}$$

$$\bar{G}_{x,t} = \bar{g}_{x,t} + (1 - \delta)G_{x,t-1}^a$$

$$\bar{g}_{x,t} = (\mu A_{1,t})^{\sigma_1}(\mu A_{2,t})^{\sigma_2}(r_{g,t}^x)^{\sigma_3}$$

adopted in one sector immediately and in the other much later, or it may immediately eliminate its competitor everywhere.[12]

Of course the macro behaviour of the economy is an aggregation of the different technological diffusion processes being driven by the existing GPTs, and is not necessarily dominated by a single GPT. The simplest way to view the macro behaviour in relation to the underlying GPTs is to eliminate much of the complexity

[12] We have not made two important refinements in modelling applied R&D. First, the results of R&D are uncertain in both applied and pure knowledge research. To be complete, we should model applied R&D as uncertain by allowing some or all of the uncertainty that we model in pure knowledge research to appear also in applied R&D. Second, we could allow for a lagged effect of applied R&D into consumption

associated with the relations among GPTs. To this end, we assume that each GPT enters only a single applied R&D sector and the output from each of these affects the productivity of only one consumption sector. In effect, we have two stand-alone versions of our three-sector model operating simultaneously. Box 15.4 contains the parameter values and specific assumptions for the simulation. Once again these are illustrative of a wide range of possible values that meet our assumptions and that we have tested to ensure the robustness of the qualitative results.

We aggregate over the two activities in each of these three-sector subsystems to determine the macro behaviour of the whole system. Figure 15.3 shows the aggregate growth rates for the new consumption sector and the knowledge generated by each pair of pure and applied research sectors.[13] The macro behaviour of the system is not dominated entirely by the diffusion rates of either sequence of GPTs or their respective impacts in their pure and applied R&D sectors. Depending on the period of observation, one or both GPT sequences drive the growth rate of consumption. For example, between periods 120 and 170 the growth rate of consumption is increasing, while the growth of knowledge, which is being driven by the first sequence of GPTs, is falling after period 135, and only the growth of knowledge,

---

Box 15.4. Parameter Values for the Simulation with Two GPTs

We assume that each pair of the three types of production (consumption, applied knowledge, and pure knowledge) has the same exponents on inputs (e.g. both have identical α_1 and α_2). The knowledge depreciation rates are also assumed to be the same for each pair of the applied and pure knowledge sectors. μ is assumed to be identical in each of the two pure knowledge sectors. The values are:

$$x = (1, 2) \qquad j = (1, 2)$$
$$\alpha_1 = 1 \qquad \alpha_2 = 0.34 \qquad \beta_1 = 1 \qquad \beta_2 = 0.34$$
$$\sigma_1 = 1 \qquad \sigma_2 = 0.34 \qquad \varepsilon = 0.01 \qquad \delta = 0.01$$
$$G_{1,0} = G_{2,0} = 1 \qquad A_{1,0} = A_{2,0} = 1 \qquad J = 2 \qquad X = 2$$
$$\gamma = 0.06 \qquad \tau = -6 \qquad \mu = 0.5$$

$$v_{j,t} = \begin{cases} 1 \text{ for } j = x \\ 0 \text{ for } j \neq x \end{cases}, \text{ except for a initial seed value of } v_{j,t} = 1 \text{ for } j \neq x, \text{ which eliminates many of the possibilities for complementarities.}$$

$R^j = r^j_{c,t} + r^j_{a,t} + r^j_{g,t} = 1,000$ for $j = x$, and we assume that the allocations of resources within each set of consumption, applied R&D, and pure knowledge sectors are independent of those in the other set.

For each λ_x we choose $\nu = 5$ and $\eta = 10$. For each ϑ_x we choose $\nu = 10$ and $\eta = 5$. For each ϖ_x we choose $\nu = 12$ and $\eta = 5$ and multiply all values by 1.5.

---

and pure knowledge. This could be accomplished by creating a version of the logistic diffusion process modelled in pure knowledge for applied R&D. We avoid these extra steps here because the model developed thus far captures as much of the rich historical process discussed in Part I as time and space permits. The full formal treatment of that fact set is a subject for at least another whole volume.

[13] Each pair of outputs, consumption, pure research, and applied research is aggregated using a Tornquist index.

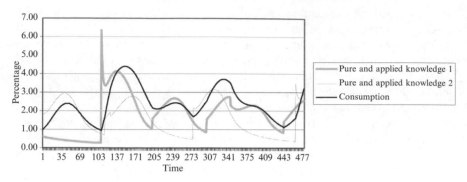

Figure 15.3. *Knowledge and consumption growth rates with simultaneous GPTs*
Note: The aggregate growth rate of consumption is not determined solely by the diffusion rate of any one sequence of GPTs. Over some periods both diffusion rates determine the growth rate of consumption while over other periods one diffusion sequence has a dominating influence over the growth rate of consumption.

driven by the second sequence of GPTs, is rising throughout the whole period. In contrast, between periods 205 and 260 increases in the growth rate of consumption are being driven solely by increases in the growth rate of knowledge generated by the first sequence of GPTs.

The development of the model thus far opens up a number of obvious possibilities to bring it closer to the observed reality of an economic system in which several GPTs are operating with many applications and many consumption goods. For example, this simple framework can be extended to many sectors simply by adding more lines of production to the three main production activities. Such an extension would allow for the integration of Grossman and Helpman's separate models (1991) of quality improvement and product expansion into a single model that has the characteristics of both the logistic applications and efficiency curves discussed in Chapter 13. Using Monte Carlo methods to track the diffusion of a given GPT across the various applications sectors would also provide insights into how such diffusion processes manifest themselves in the observed economic data produced by statistical agencies.

IV.   A SIMPLE MODEL OF FACILITATING STRUCTURE AND GPTS

We now introduce a simple, first approximation of the facilitating structure. This enables us to model a concept that is not found in any of the other macroeconomic models of economic growth, but one that is critical to our S-E theory of technology-driven growth. For ease of presentation when introducing the facilitating structure, we revert to the baseline, three-sector model.

Since a new GPT is typically not well adapted to the existing facilitating structure, real resources must be invested in altering many of the elements of that structure.[14]

---

[14] Although we do not introduce labour explicitly in the model, we note that these structural adjustment costs can be severe when the arriving GPT causes big dislocations by separating significant numbers of workers from their work because an old technology is made obsolete.

We begin with the simplifying assumption that all of the structural adjustments are accomplished by the applied R&D sector. We make this assumption for two reasons. The first is simplicity, since having the structural adjustment in one sector is sufficient to demonstrate all the qualitative outcomes of this simple formulation. The second is that many of the actual structural adjustment problems do occur in the application of the GPT to various uses, for example, the application of electricity to factories required a new organizational technology, new design of factories, and changes in industrial concentration, and in workers' skills.

Box 15.5. A Simple Model of Facilitating Structure and GPTs

Equations (14.2) and (14.5–14.10) of the baseline model are unaltered. The resource constraint is now:

$$R_t = r_{c,t} + r_{a,t} + r_{g,t} + r_{s,t} \qquad (15.13)$$

where r_s is the amount of the resource used in structural adjustment. As with the three-sector baseline model, the arrival of a new GPT increases G_t in equation (14.3″). G_t is all past accumulations of realized pure knowledge plus the current period's *expected* accumulation of pure knowledge, as originally defined in Box 14.4. However, a new GPT comes with a structural adjustment cost, SA_t, defined in equation (15.14), which reduces the immediate impact of the new GPT on productivity in the applied R&D sector:

$$
\begin{aligned}
a_t &= \nu\big((\chi\bar{G}_t)(SA_t)^{\beta_3}\big)^{\beta_1}(r_{a,t})^{\beta_2} \\
A_t &= a_t + (1-\varepsilon)A_{t-1}
\end{aligned}
\quad \text{with} \quad \beta_i \in (0, 1], \ i = (1, 2, 3), \text{ and } \beta_2 < 1 \ (14.3″)
$$

where ν, the calibration parameter, is set to unity in this model and where $\chi \in (0, 1]$ allows only a portion of realized pure knowledge to influence applied R&D. (We make this assumption to simplify the total factor productivity calculations that we make later.) SA_t is defined as follows:

$$SA_t = \frac{S_t}{SC_t} \qquad (15.14)$$

The required structural adjustment, S_t, accumulates from the point that the GPT arrives:

$$SC_t = SC_{t_z-1} + \left(\frac{e^{\tau_s + \gamma_s(t-t_z)}}{1 + e^{\tau_s + \gamma_s(t-t_z)}}\right)(SC_t^h - SC_{t_z-1}) \qquad (15.15)$$

$$SC_t^h = \psi_t\big(G_t^h - G_{t-1}^h\big)$$

SC_t is the cost of structural adjustment defined as a function of the total impact of the new GPT, which we model by taking the difference between the total value of the new GPT relative to the old and a random variable, ψ_t, drawn from a beta distribution. The structural adjustment costs are assumed to follow a logistic diffusion process similar to the GPT itself. The larger the GPT impact, the more the structural adjustment is required.

Box 15.5. (continued)

We assume that $\gamma_s > \gamma\tau_s < \tau$ making the structural adjustment occur more quickly than the productivity diffusion of the GPT.

S_t is the required effort to adapt the facilitating structure to a new GPT:

$$S_t = s_t + S_{t-1}(1 - \phi_t) \tag{15.16}$$

where

$$s_t = [(1 - \chi)G_t]r_{s,t}$$

and

$$\phi_t = \left\{ \begin{array}{ll} \varsigma & \text{if } \lambda \geq \lambda* \\ 0 & \text{otherwise} \end{array} \right\}$$

The flow of structural adjustment, s_t, depends on the resources devoted to producing adjustment, $r_{s,t}$, and a portion of the stock of useful pure knowledge, $(1 - \chi)G_t$.

The random variable, ψ_t, that conditions SC_t^h reflects the amount of new investment in structure that is required and that cannot be predicted in advance. The random variable, ϕ_t, makes obsolete some of the past investment in structure, S_t, that is not useful to the new GPT. During the life of an incumbent GPT, ϕ_t is zero and upon the arrival of the new GPT, it takes on a value, ς, chosen randomly from a uniform distribution. It is applied once and then reverts to zero.

$$\psi_t = s_c[\beta(x|\nu, \eta)], \ 0 < s_c < 2 \tag{15.17}$$

The constant s_c allows the random variable drawn from the beta distribution to take on values larger than one. This, combined with the calibration of ν and η, determines the probability that ψ_t is greater than or less than one.

The maximization problem includes the allocation of resources to structural adjustment:

$$\max_{\{r_{c,t}, r_{a,t}, r_{g,t}, r_{s,t}\}} c_t = (\mu A_t)^{\alpha_1}(r_{c,t})^{\alpha_2}$$

s.t.

$$R_t = r_{c,t} + r_{a,t} + r_{g,t} + r_{s,t}$$

$$a_t = \nu\left((\chi\bar{G}_t)(SA_t)^{\beta_3}\right)^{\beta_1}(r_{a,t})^{\beta_2} \tag{15.18}$$

$$A_t = a_t + (1 - \varepsilon)A_{t-1}$$

$$\bar{G}_t = \bar{g}_t + (1 - \delta)G_{t-1}$$

$$\bar{g}_t = ((1 - \mu)A_t)^{\sigma_1}r_{g,t}^{\sigma_2}$$

and equations (15.14–15.17)

We now modify the model to introduce structure explicitly. The alterations appear in Box 15.5, along with the additional equations needed to introduce our version of the facilitating structure. (With the exception of equations 14.1 and 14.3 all the equations of Box 14.3 are unchanged by the introduction of a facilitating structure.)

The resource constraint now allocates resources across four activities: our original three sectors—consumption, applied R&D, and pure R&D—plus a fourth sector, structural adjustment (equation 15.13). The production of applied knowledge is altered to include the possibility of allocating resources to the activity of adjusting the structure (equation 14.3" in Box 15.5).

We model the productivity in the applied research sector as being determined by two forces: first, the productivity-enhancing effect of the logistic diffusion of the current GPT (χ_t in equation 14.3"); and second, the effective structural adjustment (SA_t in equation 15.16).[15] But the effective structural adjustment itself depends on two things (as shown in equation 15.14): first, the accumulated amount of adjustment achieved by allocating resources to structural adjustment, which tends to increase effective adjustment; and second, the need for further adjustment introduced by the arrival of a new GPT, which tends to decrease current effective adjustment. The total amount of structural adjustment produced is determined by the relative productivity of resources in the activity. These are highly productive when the GPT first arrives, then, through time the resources migrate out of the structural adjustment sector as they become more productive elsewhere. Since resources in structural adjustment asymptotically approach zero as time passes after the arrival of the GPT, the amount of structural adjustment required for a given GPT is finite.

The maximization problem (equation 15.8) is altered slightly to include the allocation of resources for producing structural adjustment. The new structural adjustment sector requires that an extra marginal product be included. Resources are still allocated so as to maximize consumption output in each current period by equating the expected marginal increase in consumption from a unit of resources allocated to each of the three sectors, but with productivity taken as given. Again we could assume that a social planner makes the entire allocation over the four sectors. Alternatively we could assume that the allocation is made by private price taking agents in the consumption and applied research sectors[16] and by a government that taxes agents in the other two sectors to pay for pure research and structural adjustment, which has the assumed pay-off just described.

Box 15.6 gives the parameter values that we use to simulate this model. The results are shown in the figures. Figure 15.4 shows the resource allocations among the four lines of production. The resources devoted to structural adjustment shown in the last panel spike up when a new GPT arrives and then gradually migrate out into

---

[15] We have made an additional change by weighting the diffusion of the GPT by a fractional coefficient, χ, so that we can apportion the stock of pure knowledge into that which positively influences the production of a_t in the applied R&D sector and the proportion $(1 - \chi)$ which positively influences the production of s_t in the structural adjustment sector. As mentioned in an earlier footnote, we break this stock up to avoid increasing returns to accumulating knowledge and facilitate TFP calculations that follow.

[16] As was stated in an earlier footnote, Dixit–Stiglitz-style monopolistic competition can be introduced into these two sectors with an increase in complexity and no change in the qualitative behaviour of the model.

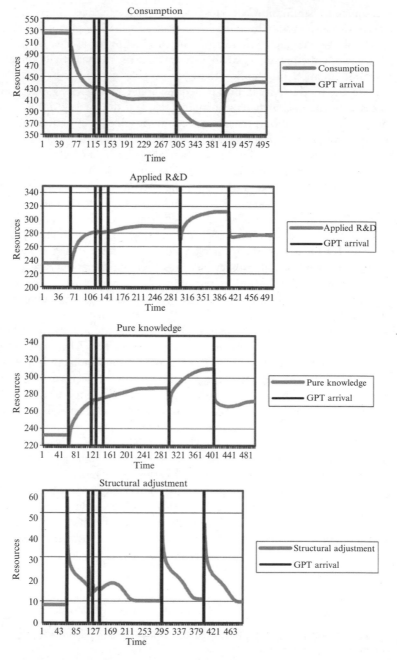

Figure 15.4. *Resource allocations with structural adjustment*

Note: The resources allocated to consumption, applied R&D, and pure knowledge respond as in the basic three-sector model when a new GPT arrives. The resources devoted to structural adjustment spike up when a new GPT arrives and then gradually migrate out into other lines of production as the GPT matures and the facilitating structure is adjusted to it.

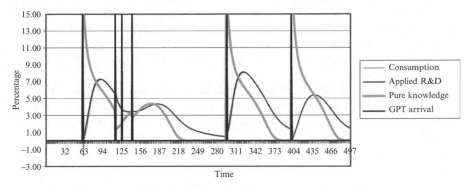

Figure 15.5. *Growth rates with structural adjustment*
Note: There is a pronounced slowdown in the growth rate of consumption due to the adjustment cost imposed on the system by the arrival of a new GPT.

other lines of production as the GPT matures and the structure adjusts to it. Figure 15.5 shows the consumption growth rate. In this case, however, the slowdowns associated with the arrival of a new GPT are more pronounced due to the extra cost of structural adjustment imposed on the system.

We have modelled the cost of adjusting the facilitating structure to a new GPT as depending on both the size of the required new investment and the amount of obsolescence that the pre-existing structure experiences. This has some interesting implications. First, structural adjustment costs are a potential source of productivity

---

Box 15.6. Simulation of the Three-Sector and Structural Adjustment Models

Baseline three-sector model

The parameter values are as follows:

$\alpha_1 = 1$	$\alpha_1 = 0.34$	$\beta_1 - 1$	$\beta_2 - 0.34$
$\sigma_1 = 1$	$\sigma_2 = 0.34$	$\nu = 1$	$A_0 = 1$
$G_0 = 1$	$R = r_{c,t} + r_{a,t} + r_{g,t} = 1,000$	$o - 0.01$	$\delta = 0.01$
$\gamma = 0.06$	$\tau = -6$	$\mu = 0.5$	

For λ we choose $\nu = 5$ and $\eta = 10$. The threshold value of $\lambda^* = 0.64$. For ϑ we choose $\nu = 10$, $\eta = 5$, and $s = 1$. For ϖ we choose $\nu = 12$ and $\eta = 5$ and multiply all values of x_t by 1.5. θ_t is a random variable distributed uniformly with support $[0.8, 1.2]$, mean 1, and variance $(0.4)^2/12$.

Structural adjustment, four-sector model

The parameterization for the model of structural adjustment is the same as the baseline model with the following additions:

$\chi = 0.8$	$R = r_{c,t} + r_{a,t} + r_{g,t} + r_{s,t} = 1,000$	$\beta_3 = 0.85$
$\gamma_s = 0.08$	$\tau_s = -8$	

For ψ_t we choose $\nu = 10$ and $\eta = 5$.

slowdowns that do not directly result from characteristics built into GPTs them-selves. We demonstrate this result in the next section when we calculate TFP for both the baseline model and this model of structural adjustment. Second, the arrival of each GPT will result in different structural adjustment costs, which mirror the historical experience.

Third, different GPTs may cause structural adjustment costs and related product-ivity slowdowns for different reasons. Structural investments of the sort that get counted at their resource costs, such as public infrastructure or policy structure adjustments, will not contribute to measured increases in productivity. If these costs are big enough, a productivity slowdown of the sort originally discussed by David (1991*b*) can result as resources are diverted to structural adjustment with no productivity pay-off. Once the structure has been adjusted to the new GPT, these resources migrate back to productivity-enhancing activities, and a temporary prod-uctivity boom may ensue. Unlike the diversion of resources to an R&D sector that occurs in other authors' GPT models as a direct consequence of the characteristics of the GPTs, but which are too small to generate empirically significant productivity slowdowns, our resource diversions into structural adjustment can be large enough to do so. Thus our theory presents an opportunity to investigate further the causes of productivity slowdowns. In this section, we model the structural adjustment costs as stochastic. In reality, the characteristics of some GPTs undoubtedly lead to high structural adjustment costs and, therefore, large productivity slowdowns, whereas others with different characteristics do not come with high structural adjustment costs and, therefore, may not generate slowdowns. Our modelling to this point allows us to demonstrate cases where productivity is sometimes slowed and some-times negatively correlated with the arrival of GPTs, the outcome depending on the structural adjustment requirements. Thus we are able to pose empirically testable hypotheses in which some GPTs cause slowdowns while others do not, where the slowdowns that do occur are of different magnitude from GPT to GPT, and where the explanation relies on quantitative diversions of resources that are realistic. What is needed is to be able to predict what circumstances will cause large adjustment costs and what will cause small ones. Our historical studies in Chapters 5 and 6 suggest many ways in which this can be done.

Fourth, introducing structure explicitly allows for the modelling of different strategies for adjusting the structure to new technologies. We have adopted a myopic behavioural assumption in which the structure is adjusted to maximize current consumption based on current marginal productivities, whereas the structure might actually be adjusted by a combination of government policies and individual actions motivated by different objectives. The modelling of these different objectives is possible within the framework we have developed and will move us towards a more complete model of evolutionary behaviour.[17]

---

[17] Although we think it a big step forward to get any form of structural adjustment into a growth model, our present formulation is crude and represents only a first step towards the full integration of such adjustment costs into our models.

V. CHANGES IN TFP THAT DO NOT TRACK CHANGES IN TECHNOLOGY

In this section, we calculate TFP growth using simulated data from our baseline and structural adjustment models and ask under what conditions, if any, changes in TFP measure technological change. These calculations illustrate our more general argument given in the Appendix to Chapter 4 and in Lipsey and Carlaw (2004) that changes in TFP do not adequately measure changes in technology.

General Considerations

In Chapter 3, we defined technology as knowledge of how to create economic value. In all of our models, technology is the stock of knowledge that is embodied in the currently used GPT (G_t in equation 14.3' in Box 14.3) plus the stock of applied knowledge (A_t in equation 14.3 in Box 14.1).[18] The stocks of pure and applied knowledge are aggregated using the standard approach of marginal product prices and a Tornquist index. When we come to calculate TFP, we need to know the form that new knowledge takes. We argued in the Appendix to Chapter 4 that most of the new technological knowledge that alters production processes is embodied in new capital goods. For simplicity here, we assume that all of it is thus embodied. So changes in G_t and A_t, pure and technological knowledge, take the form of new, more productive, capital goods.

We also need to consider scale effects in the model's individual sectors. At the macro level, the only accumulating factor is knowledge, which we assume entered the production function with a coefficient of unity. Since the economy's supply of resource inputs, R, is constant, output rises in proportion to the increase in inputs of embodied technological knowledge (capital). But when we calculate TFP, we need to consider the relation between inputs and outputs in each sector. Since resources do get reallocated among sectors, any sector that gets an increased supply of the resource, r, as well as new knowledge embodied in new, improved capital, that is, an increase in A, will encounter scale effects. Output will rise more than in proportion to inputs since the coefficients on f and A sum to more than unity. This does not violate the assumption of constant returns to scale when all factor inputs are altered in equal proportion with *unchanged technology* since the new capital embodies new technological knowledge.

TFP in the Baseline Model

We first calculate changes in TFP in our baseline, three-sector model with its three outputs of consumption, applied R&D, and pure research. The parameter values for the simulation are provided in Box 15.6 and the TFP calculations are shown in Box

---

[18] Thus it is the accumulation of the technological knowledge generated in the pure and applied knowledge sectors that is the technological change which drives growth.

Box 15.7. Measuring TFP in the Three-Sector Baseline Model

We start with an accounting identity that includes all of the inputs and outputs:

$$p_c c + p_a a + p_g b \equiv q_{rc} r_c + q_{ra} r_a + q_{rg} r_g + q_{Ac}\mu A + q_G G + q_{Ag}(1-\mu)A \quad (15.19)$$

where p_i's, $i \in \{c, a, g\}$ are output prices, and q_j's, with the subscripts $j \in \{rc, ra, rg, Ac, Ga, Ag\}$, are input prices. The first letter of the input price subscripts indicates the input and the second letter, the sector in which the input is used. For example, q_{rc} means the price of the resource input used in the consumer goods sector. We measure everything in consumption units, which requires dividing through by p_c to establish relative prices.

$$c + \frac{p_a}{p_c}a + \frac{p_g}{p_c}g \equiv \frac{q_{rc}}{p_c}r_c + \frac{q_{ra}}{p_c}r_a + \frac{q_{rg}}{p_c}r_g + \frac{q_{Ac}}{p_c}\mu A + \frac{q_G}{p_c}G + \frac{q_{Ag}}{p_c}(1-\mu)A \quad (15.19')$$

Given the assumption of competitive equilibrium in each time period (but not a stationary equilibrium over time), the price of resources must be the same in all uses. Letting this common price be q, we can write:

$$q = q_{rc} = p_c MP_{rc}$$
$$q = q_{ra} = p_a MP_{ra} \quad (15.20)$$
$$q = q_{rg} = p_g MP_{rg}$$

which implies:

$$\frac{p_a}{p_c} = \frac{MP_{rc}}{MP_{ra}}$$
$$\frac{p_g}{p_c} = \frac{MP_{rc}}{MP_{rg}}$$

Similarly we can derive input prices relative to the price of the consumption good as follows:

$$\frac{q_{rc}}{p_c} = \frac{q_{ra}}{p_c} = \frac{q_{rg}}{p_c} = \frac{p_c MP_{rc}}{p_c} = MP_{rc}$$
$$\frac{q_{Ac}}{p_c} = \frac{q_{Ag}}{p_c} = \frac{p_c MP_A}{p_c} = MP_A \quad (15.21)$$
$$\frac{q_{Ga}}{p_c} = \frac{p_a MP_G}{p_c} = \frac{MP_{rc}}{MP_{ra}}MP_G$$

Since the data generated by our model are discrete, we use a Tornquist index to calculate TFP change. We measure the rate of growth of technology directly as the rate of change of the knowledge stocks A_t and G_t, aggregated using a Tornquist index.

Letting Y_i's represent the outputs of the three sectors and X_j's represent their inputs, the Tornquist index of TFP changes is:

$$\Delta TFP_t = [\ln(Y_t) - \ln(Y_{t-1})] - [\ln(X_t) - \ln(X_{t-1})]$$
$$= \sum_i 0.5(w_{i,t}+w_{i,t-1})[\ln(Y_{i,t}) - \ln(Y_{i,t-1})] - \sum_j 0.5(\nu_{j,t}+\nu_{j,t-1})[\ln(X_{j,t}) - \ln(X_{j,t-1})]$$

$$(15.22)$$

15.7. There are three resource inputs and three knowledge inputs, which are aggregated using marginal product prices and a Tornquist index. Only the current amount of actually useful pure knowledge is included as part of knowledge inputs. We use transition criterion 1 for our calculations, although our qualitative results hold for all of the transition criteria.

Figure 15.6 plots the growth rates of aggregate TFP and aggregate knowledge through a simulation of 500 periods where the time increment can be interpreted as representing annual data. For this baseline model with no structural adjustment costs, the correlation coefficient between TFP change and aggregate knowledge growth is 0.846 over the 500 time periods shown. However, the average growth rate of technological knowledge is 1.6 per cent while that of TFP is 0.6 per cent. So clearly TFP is measuring only a fraction of the technological change that is occurring in the system.

We now conduct another simulation in which we reduce the amount of variability in the system by making the probability of the arrival of a GPT in each period equal to one. Figure 15.7 demonstrates that TFP growth is once again significantly below the growth rate of technological knowledge. TFP growth is positive only because the sum of the coefficients on r and capital (embodied knowledge) exceeds unity while the Tornquist index number aggregation method imposes share weights that sum to unity.

We illustrate this point by altering the value of the parameter on applied knowledge in the consumption sector to 0.66 so that the sum of the parameter values in that sector is unity. Figure 15.7a shows the case where the exponents on knowledge in all lines of activity are equal to one (as in the base case) while Figure 15.7b shows the case in which the exponent (α_1) on applied knowledge in consumption is 0.66. In the later case, TFP growth in consumption is close to zero but remains slightly

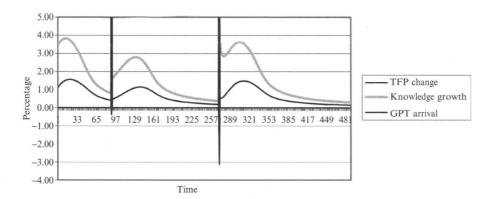

Figure 15.6. *Rate of change of knowledge and TFP*
Note: TFP change is positively correlated with, but everywhere below, the rate of knowledge growth, except when GPTs arrive when TFP change becomes negatively correlated with knowledge change.

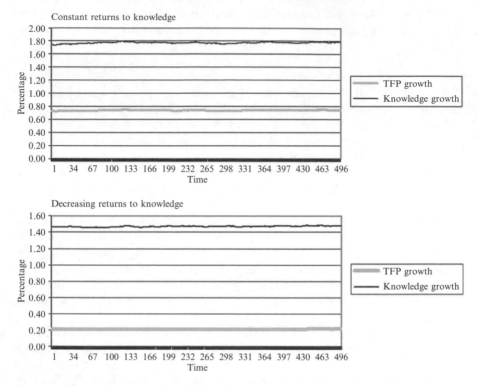

Figure 15.7. *Aggregate TFP and technological growth rates*

Note: TFP growth is lower when knowledge is subject to decreasing rather than constant returns. Where all lines of production have constant returns, and therefore decreasing returns to knowledge, TFP growth is zero while growth in technological knowledge is positive. Thus the Tornquist measure of TFP actually detects increasing returns to all inputs, including technological knowledge, not technological change.

positive due to the scale effects elsewhere in the system—the sum of the coefficients on r and knowledge exceeds unity in the other two sectors.

Finally, in simulations where the production functions in all three sectors have coefficients that sum to unity, TFP growth is zero while technological change is positive. We know that given these parameter values, growth will eventually come to a halt because of diminishing returns to knowledge. But this steady state will only be slowly approached. So over many hundreds of periods we have technological change, and rising total and per capita income (measured here as the amount of the consumption good produced per unit of the composite resource, R) while TFP is constant. Clearly, changes in technology are not being measured by changes in TFP. Furthermore, if the actual exponential parameters of the individual production functions are used to calculate TFP growth rather than the share weights of the Tornquist index, TFP growth is also zero while the growth of technological knowledge is positive.

Box 15.8. Measuring TFP in the Model of Facilitating Structure

All of the inputs and outputs of our four-sector structural adjustment model (presented in Box 15.7) are now included in the accounting identity.

$$p_c c + p_a a + p_g b + p_s s$$
$$\equiv q_{rc} r_c + q_{ra} r_a + q_{rg} r_g + q_{rs} r_s$$
$$+ q_{Ac}(\mu A) + q_{Ga}(\chi G) + q_{Gs}((1 - \chi)G) + q_{Ag}((1 - \mu)A) + q_{As} SA \qquad (15.23)$$

where once again p_i's, $i \in \{c, a, g, s\}$, are output prices and q_j's, with the subscripts $j \in \{rc, ra, rg, rs, Ac, Ga, Gs, Ag, As\}$, are input prices. Note that we include SA_t as an input rather than just S_t because it is the ratio of S_t to SC_t that matters in the production function for applied R&D. Again we divide through the identity by p_c to establish relative prices:

$$c + \frac{p_a}{p_c} a + \frac{p_g}{p_c} g + \frac{p_s}{p_c} s$$
$$\equiv \frac{q_{rc}}{p_c} r_c + \frac{q_{ra}}{p_c} r_a + \frac{q_{rg}}{p_c} r_g + \frac{q_{rs}}{p_c} rs$$
$$+ \frac{q_{Ac}}{p_c} \mu A + \frac{q_{Ga}}{p_c}(\chi G) + \frac{q_{Gs}}{p_c}((1 - \chi)G) + \frac{q_{Ag}}{p_c}(1 - \mu)A + \frac{q_s}{p_c} SA \qquad (15.23')$$

Input prices are established as in the previous case:

$$q = q_{rc} = p_c MP_{rc}$$
$$q = q_{ra} = p_a MP_{ra}$$
$$q = q_{rg} = p_g MP_{rg}$$
$$q = q_{rs} = p_s MP_{rs} \qquad (15.24)$$

which implies:

$$\frac{p_a}{p_i} = \frac{MP_{rc}}{MP_{ra}}$$
$$\frac{p_g}{p_c} = \frac{MP_{rc}}{MP_{rg}}$$
$$\frac{p_s}{p_c} = \frac{MP_{rc}}{MP_{rs}}$$

Similarly we can derive input prices relative to the price of the consumption good as follows:

$$\frac{q_{rc}}{p_c} = \frac{q_{ra}}{p_c} = \frac{q_{rg}}{p_c} = \frac{q_{rs}}{p_c} = \frac{p_c MP_{rc}}{p_c} = MP_{rc}$$
$$\frac{q_{Ac}}{p_c} = \frac{q_{Ag}}{p_c} = \frac{p_c MP_A}{p_c} = MP_A$$
$$\frac{q_{Ga}}{p_c} = \frac{p_a MP_{Ga}}{p_c} = \frac{MP_{rc}}{MP_{ra}} MP_{Ga}$$
$$\frac{q_s}{p_c} = \frac{p_s MP_s}{p_c} = \frac{MP_{rc}}{MP_{rs}} MP_s \qquad (15.25)$$

Again, we use a Tornquist index to calculate TFP and to aggregate the knowledge stocks.

TFP in the Model of the Facilitating Structure

By way of comparison to the baseline model, we now calculate TFP using the model with structural adjustment costs as shown in Box 15.6. It has four outputs, four resource inputs, four knowledge inputs, and a stock of structural adjustments. Technological knowledge, or technology, comprises the four stocks of knowledge, which are just the accumulated flows of output from the pure and applied research sectors embodied in physical capital and divided among the four production activities. Box 15.8 shows the income accounting identity and the calculations for TFP growth for this model using a Tornquist index. We assume for this illustration that the stock of accumulated structural adjustment is not included in aggregate knowledge, though it is arguable that it should be included. When we do include investment in structural adjustment as knowledge, it strengthens the result that changes in TFP are either unrelated or negatively related to the growth of technological knowledge.

Figure 15.8 plots the growth rates of aggregate TFP and technological knowledge, which are now negatively correlated with each other. In the simulation of the structural adjustment model (that has major scale effects since the coefficients on knowledge are all unity), the correlation coefficient is −0.86. When a GPT arrives, the TFP growth rate drops and in many cases becomes negative for several periods. The implication is that when new GPTs require major adjustments in the facilitating structure, changes in measured TFP will slow down even though actual technological change is accelerating over several periods. Furthermore, when the rate of technological change starts to slow, we observe TFP rising. In the cases shown, a maximum of 3.6 per cent (an average of 1.6 per cent) of the economy's total resources are allocated to structural adjustment. This small resources cost has significant implications for TFP growth rates and their interpretation as measures of technological change. A small diversion of resources out of other productive

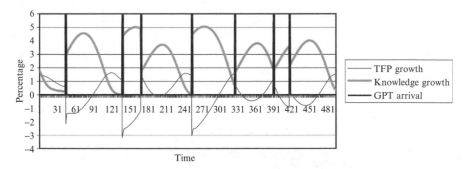

Figure 15.8. *Growth rates of knowledge and TFP with structural adjustment costs*
Note: In this model of structural adjustment, TFP is negatively correlated with knowledge growth (with a correlation coefficient of −0.86). In periods when a GPT arrives, the TFP growth rate drops and in many cases becomes negative for a short time.

activities into the activity of structural adjustment can cause productivity slow-downs of the sort documented at the beginning of the First Industrial Revolution by Crafts (1985, 2003), at the early stages of the electrification by David (1991*b*), and from the mid-1970s to the mid-1990s by most measures of productivity growth. Furthermore, our results are consistent with the kind of 'New Economy' product-ivity bonus experienced in the USA from the mid-1990s. Our theory also has the interesting prediction that the bonus period for measured TFP growth occurs when the rate of growth of technological knowledge has already slackened. These are all issues that we argued verbally in the latter parts of Chapter 4.

We have now illustrated within the context of a precise model the arguments made in Appendix 4A that TFP is not a good measure of technological change and that some GPTs generate productivity slowdowns while others do not. Furthermore, only a small diversion of resources into the activity of structural adjustment is required to generate significant slowdowns.[19]

VI. SUMMARY AND CONCLUSIONS

We have introduced additions to our model that are intended to capture an increasing amount of the rich detail contained in the historical fact set and bring our formal aggregate modelling closer to an S-E-type model of GPT-driven growth by:

- introducing a logistic diffusion of the productivity enhancing effects of GPTs on applied R&D;
- sometimes allowing an existing GPT to be cut off by a new rival GPT causing productivity slowdowns;
- sometimes allowing a GPT to arrive very late in the stage of an incumbent's evolution, thus following on from a productivity slowdown;
- imposing additional behavioural structure on the model, which explains why GPTs might have to accumulate a minimum amount of pure knowledge before entering the system;
- modelling historical scale effects, which give temporary bursts to growth but do not show up as permanent increasing returns in an aggregate production function;
- beginning the process of modelling the facilitating structure laid out in Chapter 3;

---

[19] This analysis could be extended in several interesting ways in subsequent research. TFP could be calculated for all five of our transition cases to see how TFP changes compare to technological change under different GPT adoption rules. The effect on TFP calculations of the different behaviours with respect to expectations that we model previously could also be studied. The analysis of TFP for different modelling assumptions, concerning such things as returns to scale and returns to knowledge in the production functions, could be extended beyond what we have done here—and so on for a wide range of interesting issues relating to investigating the relationship between changes in TFP and changes in technology.

- allowing for externalities that feed back from applied research results to assist pure research;
- disaggregating the model into several production lines within the three broad production sectors, allowing us to begin to model the complex interrelations of technological complementarities; and
- allowing more than one GPT to exist simultaneously in the model.

Having taken these initial steps, it is clear that further modelling possibilities are more or less unlimited. Probably the most important remaining task is to develop full models in which several GPTs coexist, some new, some long established, some cooperating, and some competing. Useful studies of conditions leading to slow-downs (and acceleration) in the macro growth rate require such a model—in contrast to models where the whole economy is dominated by the one GPT that exists at each point in time.

We also intend to extend our analysis of complementarities within the existing framework to capture more of the subtle dimensions of technological interaction. This will allow us to use the model to predict the conditions under which a particular set of complementary interactions would lead to various aggregate phenomenon. We have taken some initial steps here but more needs to be done.

Our assumption about how agents form expectations and make allocative decisions is overly simple in allowing zero foresight. A further extension, therefore, is to allow some form of limited foresight, possibly with a learning process incorporated, but with some remaining uncertainty. This could be done, for example, by allowing agents to anticipate actual results over some finite number of future periods, but when maximizing over these, to apply increasing rates of discount to reflect growing uncertainties about the accuracy of these forecasts as they are made further and further into the future.

Finally, we have shown that even our existing very basic model can produce interesting results through Monte Carlo experiments. Since we know the underlying data-generating processes, we can use the model to generate data and then check on standard estimation procedures. We have already shown, as we had earlier argued, that TFP measures do not do a good job of tracking technological change in our model and, therefore, are suspect as measures of such change in the real world. We also intend to use the generated data to study the efficacy of current procedures for using data to determine whether or not the generating mechanism is stationary.

In conclusion, we paraphrase Winston Churchill's famous quote in the context of our efforts to revive the theoretical development of GPT theory, and to extend it well beyond its existing state into the province of S-E theory and observation: Our work may not mark the beginning of the end, but we can hope that that it does mark the end of the beginning.

Part IV

Policy

In this concluding part of our book, we apply some of what we have studied in previous parts to a consideration of economic policy. In two short chapters, we cannot write a comprehensive treatise on general economic policy, or even growth policy. What we seek to do instead is to illustrate selectively some of the insights offered by S-E theory when it is focused on some important issues related to policies designed to encourage technological change. The key to understanding S-E views on policy is that agents and the opportunities and obstacles they face are heterogeneous. So that unlike the text book neoclassical view where investment opportunities are equated on the margin, S-E economists see these opportunities as having widely differing expected and actual rates of return due to the heterogeneity that is inherent in any evolving economy characterized by technological change.

We concentrate on what we call 'technology enhancement policies', policies designed to alter the amount and/or direction of invention and innovation with respect to the development of new technologies and the improvement of existing ones. Because these policies are typically directed at all technologies, ranging from the innovation of radically new GPTs to incremental improvements in existing technologies, we do not emphasize GPTs in what follows. Instead, we discuss these policies as they relate to all technologies, including GPTs.

When we refer to 'S-E economists', we mean all those whose theoretical or applied work has mainly been related to evolutionary theories of economic behaviour. Of course, this is not a homogeneous group. Although we believe that the views we ascribe to 'S-E economists' are typical of those who work in this field, we do not mean to imply that each of these economists holds all of the views that we outline.

Technology Enhancement Policies: Theory and Evidence

We consider a selection of government policies designed to influence technological change, attempting to accelerate it and/or to alter its direction. Policy can use incentives or disincentives that are either generally applied or narrowly focused. Policy can also seek to exert its influence indirectly, by altering such structural variables as the concentration of industry, the amount of foreign competition, the volume of foreign investment, the location of firms, and the education system. At different times and places, policies designed to influence technological change have been given various names and administered under different administrative structures. We cover all such policies under the generic heading 'technology enhancement policies'.

Economists' advice concerning such policies is often derived from the canonical GE version of the neoclassical model, although many of the complications that are omitted from this version have been studied at the micro level. Since the resulting advice is based on the general proposition that free markets produce an optimal allocation of resources always and everywhere, it is not context-specific. But, as we have argued extensively in earlier parts of this book, context does matter, especially when it comes to technological change.

Much policy discussion at both the domestic and international levels uses non context-specific stereotypes, some of which do not depend on the neoclassical model. For example, at the international level, 'traditionalists' argue for free trade while 'revisionists' argue that tariffs are a useful policy tool. S-E economists argue that if these propositions are stated generally, rather than in context-specific situations, both are wrong, since tariffs and other trade restrictions may be useful in some contexts and harmful in others. What really matters, they argue, is not condoning or condemning either position in general, but understanding the circumstances in which each is correct.

Here we contrast theories that provide general policy prescriptions with theories that only provide context-specific prescriptions. An understanding of the importance of context-specific advice is not unique to S-E theorists. The older generation of development economists, much of whose work was swept aside when mathematical

---

[1] Much of Chapters 15 and 16 are an amalgamation and major revision of Lipsey and Carlaw (1996, 1998*b*: ch 1 and 5). Material from Lipsey and Carlaw (1998*a*) 'Technology Policies in Neoclassical and Structuralist-Evolutionary Models' originally appeared in the *STI Review: Special Issue on 'New Rationale and Approaches in Technology and Innovation Policy'* No 22 Volume 1998 Issue 1, OECD 1998.

growth models came to dominate the growth literature, clearly understood the dangers of one-size-fits-all policy advice. Economists in the historical and institutional schools also recognized the importance of context-specificity and, as we observed in Chapter 1, they took the issue of 'historical specificity' as an important topic for study—a study that is almost totally neglected by modern economists. (See Hodgson 2002 and our discussion in Chapter 1.) Also, the newer school of economists who operate more or less within the neoclassical maximizing paradigm, but who emphasize such things as imperfect and asymmetric information and transactions costs, reject the applicability of the model of perfectly competitive optimality and the generalized policy advice that follows from it. Although they depart from some of the more restrictive assumptions of the canonical neoclassical model, they typically maintain others, such as maximizing under conditions of risk and the relevance of end state equilibrium analysis.[2]

Although S-E theorists share many of their general policy views with these other schools of thought, S-E theory provides a framework to assist the analysis that does not have obvious counterparts in the other approaches. This framework is based on a micro analysis of the process of endogenous technological change and the non-maximizing behaviour of profit-oriented firms as they grope into the uncertain future. Our concern here is to see what light our S-E theory can shed on a range of technology enhancement policies.

I. TWO GENERIC THEORIES

In Chapter 2, we discussed two generic classes of theories: the canonical neoclassical theory based on the Arrow–Debreu-style GE model, and the canonical S-E theory. We compared and contrasted some of their key defining characteristics. The critical differences between the two classes of theory that matter for technology enhancement policies are summarized in Table 16.1.

---

[2] Whether this branch of economics should be regarded as part of neoclassical economics or a different branch is a grey area. Certainly, Joseph Stiglitz, one of the recipients of the Nobel Prize in economics for his work on information theory, sees his work as having critically different implications from the sort of new classical economics (neoclassical in our definitions) that has guided much of the operations of the World Bank and the IMF.

> This work [on asymmetric information] provided the foundation for more realistic theories of labor and financial markets, explaining, for instance, why there is unemployment and why those most in need of credit often cannot get it.... The standard models that economists had used for generations argued either that markets worked perfectly... or that the only reason that unemployment existed was that wages were too high.... Information economics... provided deeper insights into unemployment... [and explained] the recessions and depressions that had marked capitalism since its beginnings. These theories have strong policy implications.... While I thought they were obvious, these policy prescriptions ran counter to those that were frequently insisted upon by the International Monetary Fund (IMF). The IMF's policies, in part based on the outworn presumption that markets, by themselves, lead to efficient outcomes, failed to allow for desirable government interventions in the market. (Stiglitz 2002: xi–xii)

Table 16.1. *Neoclassical and S-E theories compared*

Assumption type	Neoclassical	S-E
Behaviour	Maximizing under certainty or risk	Purposeful groping under uncertainty
Equilibrium	Often unique, typically optimal	Multiple and possibly *ex post* non-optimal
Role of technology	Kept behind the scenes in a 'black box'	Explicitly modelled
How technological change is observed	By its results (eg. total factor productivity)	By direct observation of an endogenous process
Competition	End-state equilibrium (static concept)	Process competition (dynamic concept)
Economic structure	None	Made explicit

We accept that neoclassical theory and risk analysis is valuable in situations for which equilibrium theory is relevant. *Indeed, for the great majority of questions that are put to economists as policy advisers, it is appropriate for them to reach for the neoclassical tool kit.*

This is not necessarily so, however, for situations in which endogenous technological change is important. Indeed, in Chapter 2 we contrasted the desirable characteristics of a market as seen by neoclassical and S-E theories and found them to be almost diametrically opposed (see pages 45–6), the differences arising from the neoclassical emphasis on static efficiency and the S-E emphasis on growth and change. This contrast is important in the present context since the object of technology enhancement policies is to influence technological change. In summary, perhaps the most important comparison between the two approaches to policy is that neoclassical policy advice is quite simple and quite general, applying to all countries whatever their circumstances–remove market imperfections wherever they are found–while S-E advice is context-dependent, there being no simple set of policy rules that apply to all countries, times, and circumstances.

Although as we observed above, and in more detail in Chapter 2, the gap between these two approaches has been narrowed somewhat by some modern theorizing, particularly concerning the implications of incomplete and asymmetric information, a gap still exists between the strong policy advice advocated by many economists on the basis of neoclassical-type models and the policy advice advocated by many S-E theorists. The gap is most obvious when one considers endogenous technological change and the uncertainties and groping behaviour that attend it, none of which are studied in the new branches of standard theory. The contrast between the policy implications of S-E and those types of theories, newer and older, that are based on the analysis of the end states achieved by agents who are maximizing under conditions of risk is no straw man as will be revealed by attendance at any debate on policies, either domestic or international, to encourage economic growth and technological change. Thus the choice between the two types of theory is not merely a matter of taste and convenience. Instead, it is a choice between two basic views of how the world works. As we will see later in this chapter, each suggests views on appropriate policies and programmes that are often, although by no means always, opposed to each other.

II. POLICY THROUGH NEOCLASSICAL LENSES

Background

Neoclassical theory presents an idealized form of all market systems. There is nothing in the general models that distinguish one economy from another such as different specific technologies, different institutions, and the different stages of development, of an economy that is catching up technologically and one that is at the technological frontier. Given all the other standard assumptions, a welfare-maximizing equilibrium exists. Departures from this equilibrium are caused by market failures, which take three general forms: externalities, imperfect information, and non-convexities. The removal of these market failures is the main object of neoclassical microeconomic policy advice, which applies to all market economies operating at all times.

The Neoclassical Justification for Technology Enhancement Policies

The neoclassical theoretical literature on technology externalities usually takes Arrow's view as its starting point.[3] On the basis of indivisibilities,[4] sunk costs, appropriability, and uncertainty, Arrow (1962a) argues that a positive externality results from any new technological knowledge. Since R&D is the source of much new knowledge, the social return to R&D exceeds the private return.

Arrow's basic insight has been employed in a number of models of production externalities.[5] In their aggregate versions, knowledge is modelled as a homogeneous stock that can be added to incrementally. This is a valid procedure within a

---

[3] In Chapter 4, we distinguished 'spillovers' from the narrower concept of 'externalities'. Spillovers refer to the non-priced effects of any economic activity that are felt by parties not directly participating in the activity. Externalities are unpaid-for effects conferred by the *continuing* and *potentially variable* actions of a set of initiating agents on a set of receiving agents who are not involved in the initiating agent's activity, and for which the receiving agents would be willing to pay. Although we showed the importance of making this distinction in some contexts, in this chapter we do not need the distinction and we refer interchangeably to externalities and spillovers as the class of 'third-party effects' that may be spread widely over time and space.

[4] Innovation is replete with non-convexities. R&D directed to a specific objective is a sunk cost that need not be repeated once that objective is achieved. Learning how to embody any piece of technology in a working piece of equipment is also a sunk cost, as is the acquisition of tacit knowledge about how to operate the equipment effectively. What is important in the present context is that the R&D and the accumulated experience do not need to be repeated to hold the technology at the existing stage of its evolution. Past R&D is thus a sunk cost of bringing the technology to its current level.

[5] Griliches (1992) surveys the literature that attempts to measure R&D spillovers at the levels of the firm, industry, and aggregate economy. He starts with Simon (1947) and progresses through Arrow (1962b) up to the present endogenous growth formulations.

neoclassical framework because maximizing under conditions of risk implies equality of the net marginal values of the expected increments in all lines of knowledge-creating activities. Knowledge externalities arise because one firm's productivity depends not only on its own R&D effort but also on the stock of general knowledge available to it. New knowledge is implicitly assumed to diffuse instantaneously and costlessly because the stock of knowledge is treated as just another input in the aggregate production function.[6]

In such models, we can imagine a perfect patent system that gives each agent a complete and enforceable property right to the knowledge that he or she creates. If we add the assumption of zero transaction costs, each creator of knowledge would act as a perfectly discriminating monopolist. Both the use of existing knowledge and the value of the resources devoted to knowledge creation would then be optimal.

In reality, property rights to knowledge are highly incomplete, leading to the prediction that knowledge-creating activities, such as R&D, will be below their optimal levels. Encouraging these activities through public policy may therefore be welfare-enhancing. Two instruments are typically recommended. The first is extending patents to cover a wider scope of creative activities and making them more enforceable, and hence to convert more of the social return into private return to inventors and innovators. The second is to give direct support to R&D in the form of subsidies and/or tax relief. Notice that in the neoclassical model, in which the expected pay-offs from all lines of R&D expenditure are equated at the margin, there is no distinction between encouraging the inputs into the advancement of technological knowledge and encouraging the output of the new technological knowledge. Increasing one increases the other. The policy prescription, therefore, does not differentiate between lowering the costs of generating new technological knowledge and raising the pay-off to that knowledge.

Because in the aggregate neoclassical formulation there is only one body of technological knowledge with one private and one social marginal product, a comparison cannot be made between policies that cover the entire economy, such as R&D tax credits, and more focused policies, such as encouragement of innovation in some specific industry. To compare these, we need to disaggregate and differentiate among the many actual types of technological knowledge. When we do so, we find that, if there are no externalities or other sources of market failure, and if all situations of less-than-perfect knowledge are risky and not uncertain, the unaided price system yields an optimum allocation of resources between all lines of activities, including the creation of new knowledge through R&D. If the only source of externalities is the non-rivalrous aspect of new knowledge, R&D will be below its optimal rate, justifying public policies to encourage these activities. If the externalities are uniform across all lines of R&D, a generalized R&D subsidy is appropriate and, in principle, can restore a first-best optimum. In contrast, more focused policies, such as protection of some local industries from foreign competition,

---

[6] Caballero and Lyons (1992) provide an example of how such a model is often employed in an attempt to measure R&D spillovers.

support for research into the next generation of long-distance passenger aircraft, or special support for R&D undertaken by small firms, are judged to be non-optimal. The reason is that such policies selectively distort the price and profit signals that are generated by perfectly competitive markets. Although such policies may sometimes yield a positive net benefit, more benefit can always be achieved by devoting the same expenditure to a non-distorting, generalized policy.

III.   POLICY THROUGH S-E LENSES[7]

Whatever theory one uses, the case for an active technology policy requires accepting the proposition that it is socially desirable to attempt to influence the pace and/or direction of technological change. We have seen that an optimal policy designed to influence the pace, but not the direction, of technological change by influencing the amount of R&D can be derived from the neoclassical model, given all of its characteristics, plus the existence of positive externalities associated with the creation of new technological knowledge. In this section, we see why S-E theory implies that an optimal R&D policy cannot be derived. The argument is given in three steps in the next three subsections.

Knowledge Externalities

S-E theorists accept that technological knowledge creates beneficial externalities. Indeed, because of the complex set of spillovers associated with new technologies, the inventor/innovator of any fundamental new technological idea is unlikely to be able to appropriate more than a tiny fraction of the total social benefits flowing from his or her idea—benefits that extend over space and time. Therefore, there is a case for encouraging R&D beyond the level that the incentives of the free market would provide.

When we pursue this line of argument at a lower level of abstraction than an aggregate production function, important complexities arise. In particular, we see that the spillovers resulting from the creation of new technological knowledge are heterogeneous, rather than being evenly spread across all lines of R&D. Research has shown that the social returns to different lines of R&D vary greatly, as do the abilities of firms to internalize those external benefits. (As noted above, the aggregate production function approach suppresses these differences by condensing all knowledge into a single measure that has only one marginal private return and one social return.) Dissaggregation thus reveals a complex second-best problem. If policymakers had full information, and there were no other market failures, an optimal policy in the neoclassical world would provide a different amount of focused support to each different line of R&D activity. The amount of support would vary directly with the magnitude of the externalities associated with each line of possible innovation. Since

---

[7] Lipsey (2000) and (2002a) discusses these policies from the points of view of developed and developing countries respectively.

this is impossible in practice, second-best theory shows that there is no general presumption in favour of equal support for all lines of activity over support that varies across activities.

No Optimal Level of R&D

The above point can be made from within the neoclassical model and requires merely that R&D be disaggregated to reveal different amounts of externalities associated with different lines of activity plus an application of second-best theory (Lipsey and Lancaster 1956). A second type of criticism goes beyond neoclassical theory to reject the proposition that the market would *necessarily* produce too little R&D, even if its externalities were equal in all lines of activity, since there is no well-defined optimum allocation of resources when technology is changing endogenously under conditions of uncertainty. S-E theories incorporating this position have the following important implication: *Because there is no optimum allocation of resources when technology is changing endogenously under conditions of uncertainty, there does not exist a set of scientifically determined, optimum public policies with respect to technological change in general and R&D in particular.* In the world described by S-E theory, dynamic efficiency is as inapplicable a concept as is static efficiency.

Even if such an optimum allocation of R&D expenditures did exist, we do not know whether agents would produce too much or too little R&D, given that they are making decisions under uncertainty about lumpy investment with lumpy potential pay-offs. The market economy encourages innovation by rewarding successful innovators, giving huge rewards to the really successful, while the unsuccessful suffer losses. There is no existing theory of choice that allows us to predict how agents would react to such uncertain and lumpy possibilities, especially when both the *ex ante* and *ex post* R&D pay-offs differ among various entrepreneurs.[8]

Policy Judgement

Accepting this conclusion has important consequences for how S-E theorists view economic policy in the area of growth and technological change: *If there are no unique optimum rates of R&D, innovation, and technological change, policy with respect to these matters must be based on a mixture of theory, measurement, and subjective judgement.*

The need for judgement does not arise simply because we have imperfect measurements of the variables that our theory shows to be important, but because of the very nature of the uncertain world in which we live. Although a radical idea with

---

[8] Romer (1993*a*, 1993*b*) also concludes that the market will not produce an optimum allocation of resources so that there can be no unique optimal level of R&D. He does this by emphasizing the non-rivalrous nature of appropriable technological knowledge. This introduces a major set of non-convexities making perfectly competitive neoclassical theory inapplicable. Romer's point is avoided in many neoclassical analyses by treating knowledge just like another rivalrous good having externalities. Lipsey (2000) compares Romer's treatment with S-E theory and argues that similar policy conclusions follow from both.

respect to microeconomic policy, the point that policy requires an unavoidable component of subjective judgement is commonly accepted with respect to monetary policy. From the mid-1950s to the mid-1970s, Milton Friedman tried to remove all judgement from the practice of central banking by making it completely rule-based. When his advice was followed by several of the world's central banks, the monetary rule proved ineffective in determining policy, as many of his critics had predicted it would. Today, the practice of central banking is no different from the practice of most economic policy: it is guided by theoretical concepts; it is enlightened by many types of empirical evidence, studied for the information that each provides; and, in the end, all of these are inputs into the judgement calls that central bankers cannot avoid making.[9]

In rejecting the neoclassical argument, we are not dismissing the possibility that it would be socially desirable to accelerate the rate of technological change or influence its direction. Most economists (the present authors included) make the judgement that innovation and economic growth improve human welfare on average, that the pure science and the R&D that lie behind innovation is therefore socially valuable, and that because of the non-rivalrous nature of knowledge, the marginal benefits of knowledge accumulation at the rate that would be provided by the unaided market greatly exceed the marginal cost. But this is a judgement call that cannot be conclusively demonstrated by comparing the actual amount of R&D to a scientific-ally derived optimal amount. It is also a judgement call that virtually all governments are revealed to make by their own choices on technology enhancement policies.

Nor are we dismissing efficiency analysis for all purposes. Because there is no unique optimal allocation of the nation's resources that can be determined scientif-ically, it does not follow that optimality is an irrelevant concept for micro studies where well-defined objectives do exist. For example, if a limited budget is available for reducing smoke pollution, alternative methods can be studied and the one that eliminates most smoke for the least cost can be predicted. In such a study, the concepts of welfare economics and maximization are critical. Furthermore, the predictions are empirically testable. What is impossible to determine is some optimal allocation of the nation's resources among all uses including current con-sumption, R&D, and pollution control.

We turn now to more specific policies. To begin with we look at that old chestnut: free trade versus protectionism. This debate is relevant to our subject matter for several reasons. First, trade restrictions are often advocated as a means of accelerat-ing the pace of technological change by influencing its direction (and hence influ-encing economic growth), particularly, but not exclusively, for developing nations.

---

[9] Many economists who were trained in neoclassical welfare economics are unwilling to accept that some microeconomic policy decisions depend on significant amounts of subjective judgement rather than on purely scientific analysis. Many prefer models that provide precise policy recommendations, even in situations in which the models are obviously inapplicable to the world of our experience. Our own view is that, rather than using neoclassical models which give precise answers that do not apply to situations in which technology is evolving endogenously, it is better to face the reality that there is no optimal policy with respect to technological change.

Second, the debate about trade policy provides us with an introduction to the issue of general versus context-specific policy advice. Third, the issues involved lead directly to a consideration of microeconomic policies designed to encourage the innovative activity and technological change that is our main focus in Part IV. It is here that our S-E decomposition is most valuable.

IV.   FREE TRADE VERSUS PROTECTIONISM

The Ricardian classical model justifying free trade, along with the neoclassical models that followed it, was based on the assumption of a given technology—an assumption that renders comparative advantage exogenous. The enormous insight that the gains from trade depend on comparative not absolute advantage has stood the test of time. However, the same universal acceptance has not been extended to the inference that to maximize world income, as well as the incomes of most, or even all, individual countries, completely free markets should be allowed to set the pattern of international specialization—although over the last hundred or so years many economists, possibly the majority, have accepted its validity.

Policy Assessment

Tariffs come in policy bundles, not as isolated measures, and they are operated within an institutional structure. A non-context-specific policy is to advocate free trade independently of what other policies and institutions are in place. In contrast, the S-E context-specific approach emphasizes that parts of the relevant context are other policies and the policy structure. For example, much evidence supports the contention that interfirm competition is a potent force in encouraging endogenous technological change, while tariffs inhibit competition among firms located in different countries. So, even if it could be established that tariffs encouraged endogenous technological change in some circumstances, it would have to be set against the probability that they will discourage such change through their effect in diminishing competition. In some contexts, the balance might be for more international competition while in other contexts, it might be for some tariff protection. In countries in early stages of development, small nascent industries can be wiped out if subjected too soon in their life cycles to stiff competition from established foreign firms, as were many in the south of Italy when the Italian nation was established in the latter part of the nineteenth century.[10] Nor is there any reason to believe that the Taiwanese electronics industry, which is discussed later in this chapter, would have arisen at all under a laissez-faire regime, let alone grow into the successful giant that it became. In other cases, too much of the wrong kind of protection has retarded development by drastically reducing the incentives for local firms to engage in the uncertain activity of innovating. The point is that much policy debate takes place as if a single policy, such as liberalizing trade, encouraging infant

---

[10]   See the discussion in Myrdal (1958).

Policy

industries, or facilitating competition, can be evaluated on its own rather than as a part of a policy package to be applied in a country-specific set of circumstances.

If the successes or failures of specific policies are context-specific, it follows that evidence of both types of outcome will be forthcoming in specific circumstances. Then, as long as trade policy debates use as evidence the results of specific policies while not taking account of their context, the two sides will continue to talk past each other. Each will be able to cite cogent evidence that any specific policy being considered has succeeded and/or failed.[11] Such debates are more fruitful when the protagonists concentrate on distinguishing the various conditions that encouraged the observed successes from those that brought on the observed failures. As Rodrik (1993: abstract) puts it:

In thinking about policy, academic economists alternate between theoretical models in which governments can design finely tuned optimal interventions and practical considerations which usually assume the government to be incompetent and hostage to special interests. I argue ... that neither of these caricatures is accurate, and that there is much to be learned by undertaking systematic, analytical studies of state capabilities—how they are generated and why they differ across countries and issue areas.

The Debate

In the nineteenth century, Rae (1905) argued that if technology were treated as endogenous rather than exogenous, the formal case for free trade no longer held.[12] Later in that century, Friedrich List urged temporary tariff protection to help the infant industries of newly industrializing countries to catch up to the industrial leaders, although he did not stress endogenous technological change. In modern times, the critique of the free trade doctrine has followed two strands: one relating to the inability to achieve the unique welfare-maximizing equilibrium in a static world and the other relating to the behaviour of endogenous technological change in a dynamic world.

As we have argued above, in a world of endogenously changing technology in which an optimum allocation of resources is not a defined concept, policy must be based on *judgement* informed by both *theory* and *evidence*. This applies to trade policy just as much as it does to technology policy. What then can we say about both the theory and the evidence needed to inform policy judgements on this issue of free trade versus protectionism?

---

[11] For example, after providing some important evidence on the effects of Japanese trade restrictions from 1964 to 1973, Lawrence and Weinstein (2001: 404) conclude: 'Our results call into question the views of both the World Bank and the revisionists and provide support for those who advocate more liberal trade policies.' Their analysis does provide support for those who argue that Japan might have gained from more liberal trade policies in that decade but it hardly supports those who advocate liberalizing trade at all times and at all places—which a literal reading of their conclusion seems to imply.

[12] Writing in *The New Palgrave* (1987: vol. 4: 40), K. H. Hennings summarizes Rae's advice as follows: 'Instead of pursuing a policy of non-intervention, the "legislator" should stimulate foreign trade and technical progress, encourage the transfer of knowledge, tax luxuries, and use tariffs to protect infant industries.'

Theory

The first critique of free trade mentioned above concerns the theory of second best and since it is not relevant to our focus on endogenous technological change, we confine its discussion to a footnote.[13] The second critique is based on two key points that apply when technology is changing endogenously. First, comparative advantage is not given exogenously. It is changed by the actions of innovating agents, and their actions can be influenced by public policy. So the policy advice 'allocate resources so as to exploit current comparative advantages' is not obviously better than the advice 'allocate resources so as to create new comparative advantages that will make use of natural advantages that are available'. Second, as we have already noted, the groping behaviour under uncertainty and the endogeneity of choice sets that results when technology is changing endogenously implies the absence of a unique, welfare-maximizing equilibrium. If such an equilibrium does not exist, there can be no unique optimal allocation of resources, even in the absence of all other 'distortions'. It follows that the allocation resulting from free trade cannot be shown to be superior to all other allocations. There is then, as we shall develop in more detail later in this chapter, a case for government policy directed at altering the amount and direction of R&D from what it would be under completely free market conditions. This may imply increasing the production and R&D of, and encouraging exports from, sectors that do not currently have a comparative advantage.

Such arguments for an interventionist trade policy posit that by influencing the direction of investment and technological change towards industries that require some protection from foreign competitors, at least initially, the pace of technological change can be accelerated. Virtually all modern arguments for public assistance to specific sectors take this form: by influencing the direction of investment and R&D, its pace, and hence the rate of growth, can be accelerated.

This second line of criticism of the case for free trade leads us to reconsider the infant industry argument for tariff protection. This argument was designed to give a theoretical underpinning to tariff policies in developing countries, and was initially

---

[13] The second-best critique applies to an economy in which a Paretian optimum allocation of resources could conceivably exist. It starts with the observation that 'distortions' that prevent the attainment of such an optimum are ubiquitous in the form of such things as oligopoly, non-market clearing, wage setting, fixed costs of both the entry of new firms and new product development, historical scale effects (as defined in Chapter 12), and the partial appropriability of non-rivalrous new knowledge. In the presence of these, the second-best theory tells us that there is no guarantee that the removal of one set of 'distortions', such as some or all tariffs, will improve the welfare of all the world's countries—or any subset of them.

It is worth noting that the second-best theory does not imply that efficiency theory is useless but only that it cannot establish a unique set of policies that is best for the entire economy. As we observed earlier in this chapter, efficiency theory is particularly useful in many specific settings in which partial equilibrium analysis is appropriate, such as predicting the relative efficiencies of alternative methods of reducing pollution. But the second-best theory demonstrates that given the inevitable impediments to establishing the conditions required for a welfare-maximizing equilibrium, free trade cannot be demonstrated to be superior to restrictions on some imports and encouragement of some exports, both in terms of production and R&D in the relevant industries.

applied to the European countries whose nineteenth-century industrial development was behind Britain's.

As it is usually presented in modern textbooks, it is a static argument that assumes
given technology. A product has a falling cost curve that has a very large MES, and
production costs are the only relevant costs. All firms face the same cost curve
wherever they are located. Established firms are at their MESs but new ones have to
start high up on their long-run cost curve and need assistance to exist long enough
to move along and down it. If the potential new entrants are in one country and the
established firms in other countries, the objective can be achieved through tariffs.
The argument clearly applies only to non-price-taking firms since with price-taking,
and many existing firms each operating at its MES, a new entrant could go all the
way to its own MES immediately.

This argument never seemed convincing to theorists. They argued that with
perfect capital markets, a new entrant could borrow enough to go to its MES
immediately. If it could not do so, they asked why some private sector agent
would not bankroll the firm to get to the MES if the firm would be viable thereafter.
Supporters claimed, among other things, that capital rationing was common in less
developed countries.

But standard industrial organization (IO) and S-E theories suggest that this
version of the infant industry defence is wide of the mark. First, IO theory shows
that in any manufactured commodity, selling, distribution, design, product quality,
after-sales servicing, maintenance, and other similar costs are at least as important as
direct production costs. Some of these are once-for-all entry costs while others
persist. The former can create powerful barriers to entry. Second, S-E theory suggests
that the technology of production is not costlessly transferable among agents. A new
start-up firm has to undergo much learning by doing and by using in order to
accumulate the requisite tacit knowledge. So it cannot go to its MES immediately.
The extra costs incurred until the learning is completed, which may last for years,
can be thought of as yet another entry cost. Third, when an industry's technology
is continually changing endogenously, a new firm does not face a given static cost
curve. The firm does not know in advance how long it will take to get to the cost level
currently achieved by those already in the industry—or if it will ever be able to do so
given local limitations. But this is not enough to guarantee success since existing
oligopolistic firms are continually engaging in competition to lower their costs and
improve their products through R&D. So the new entrants are pursuing a moving
target rather than shooting at a stationary one. Fourth, it follows from the above
points that there is much uncertainty in trying to enter a market in which costs and
products are constantly changing. Private investors may take a different, more
conservative view on accepting uncertainty than does the state, and that view may
differ among nations according to their different social values.

Thus, the simple textbook cost curve, which is assumed to be available to any new
entrant anywhere in the world, and which is the one that will be operated on when
entry is completed, is a misleading fiction. It results in a misstatement of the infant
industry problem as one of moving along a pre-existing, negatively sloped, long-run

cost curve, whereas the real problem is to develop an industry whose rate of technological progress—progress that shifts cost curves downwards and develops new products—compares favourably with those of its foreign competitors.

When technological change is endogenous, the encouragement of a successful infant industry can *shift* the local cost curve downwards as new technologies are developed that produce at lower cost than anything previously in existence. This is not an easy thing to do, as is attested by countless failures to develop such industries through public policy. But neither is it impossible, as is attested by some of the major successes reviewed below.

Another aspect of S-E theory that is relevant to infant industries concerns the dynamic path that an industry must follow as it develops through the creation and acquisition of both technologies and the related elements of the facilitating structure, including human capital. New technologies develop out of, and are placed into, the facilitating structure, creating path-dependent development trajectories that may be unique to one industry and/or one economy. Many of the benefits from creating new elements of that structure cannot be reaped by those who do the creating. There are many externalities and wider spillovers, some of which take the form of scale effects. For example, an isolated firm may find invention and innovation difficult. A growing cluster of related firms may find it much easier for several reasons: technicians can trade inside knowledge (Von Hippel 1988); a trained labour force will be evolving; and the supply of entrepreneurs will sooner or later reach some critical mass. For these and other similar reasons, creating many key elements of an emerging facilitating structure imposes net costs on the firms that begin a cluster and gives net benefits to firms that enter the cluster later. Infant industry protection, provided it is judiciously applied, conditioned on other market signals, and sunsetted, can assist in developing a structure that would not arise solely from profit-motivated actions by private firms, which create more value in the structure than they themselves can benefit from. These and other similar ideas 'flag the policy implications of a Schumpeterian approach that views industrialisation as a cascade of interlinked technological changes' (Westphal 1990: 41).

Evidence

So much for the theory. The other major input into policy judgement is evidence. In the trade policy debate there is ample evidence of the power of *appropriately used* trade restrictions and infant industry assistance. As a general observation, not a single country in the West industrialized under completely free trade. The closest was probably Britain. But that country gave key protection to its textile industry in the eighteenth century when it banned the importation of Indian cotton goods. It also placed a series of restrictions on manufacturing activity in its colonies, and forced exports from its colonies bound for anywhere in Europe to flow through English ports.[14] Virtually all other countries including Germany, France, the USA,

---

[14] A recent detailed argument that Britain's success owed much more to its mercantilist policies than is normally credited can be found in Ormrod (2003).

and the former British Dominions sheltered their emerging manufacturing industries behind trade restrictions. These were eventually reduced, and some were lifted completely, but only *after* the industries had developed for at least several decades and often for more than a century.

Many cases of the altering of comparative advantage through government policy are found in the modern growth experiences of some of the most successful non-Western countries. Here are just three examples.

One of the most spectacular examples of a successful infant industry policy concerns the Japanese automobile industry. This was discussed briefly under the subheading 'Lean Production' in Section VII of Chapter 6. If the industry had not been protected from foreign entry after the Second World War, US firms would have entered Japan. If they went on to dominate the Japanese industry, as they did in Canada, Japanese-based firms would probably have become miniature copies of US firms using US technology. It is also clear that the prohibition on foreign investment was not sufficient. The new Japanese-owned firms needed substantial tariff protection to exist at all. If tariffs had been low or non-existent, the Japanese market would have been served by imports from the USA and Europe, leaving little room for Japanese firms and no room for their R&D. The success of the Japanese firms, first in their home market and then across the world, is a prime case of endogenously created technological change. Unable to reach the MESs of US firms in the small local market, Japanese car producers, particularly Toyota, innovated until their MESs shrunk to a size that was reachable in the local market—and *quite unexpectedly* at a cost level below those of US firms operating at their larger MESs. This result was based on a new method of organizing production, a new organizational GPT, which became the model for the automobile industry throughout the world and then spread to many other industries. In this case, not only did the protected industry grow up to be successful, it also established worldwide standards for efficiency in the automobile industry and developed the new method of lean production that revolutionized many manufacturing industries other than the automotive. A more dramatic example of the potential of well-executed trade policy is hard to imagine.

A great success at creating an entire industry from scratch is Taiwanese electronics.[15] The electronics industry was created by the Taiwanese government through a three-pronged policy. The first feature was the creation of a wholly new industry through government agencies, rather than government support of private firms. Government organizations licensed foreign technologies then sublicensed them to local industry. The industry was fostered by public assistance until mature enough to be commercially viable. Much of it was then transferred to the private sector. The second feature was the specific direction given to the industry. Because the infant industry was not able to compete internationally on a wide range of products, the government ordered capacity to be built in a specialized product—custom-tailored chips. These provided many spin-offs across the emerging industry. The third

---

[15] This paragraph is based on Lipsey and Carlaw (1996), where a more detailed treatment can be found.

feature was to gain support from established multinational companies. The government persuaded Phillips to enter a joint venture with several small Taiwanese manufacturing firms that had been pulled together by the government into the Taiwan Semiconductor Manufacturing Corporation. The policy of targeting the electronics and information industry was successful. Taiwan developed the largest pool of chip design talent in Asia outside of Japan. 'Nowhere else in Asia has the personal computer revolution spun off such a frenzy of activity' (Wade 1990: 106).

In a third example, the government of Singapore, in cooperation with the local private sector and hired researchers, has more than once identified emerging technologies well before anyone else. For example, in 1978 it decided to concentrate on software and computer services at a time 'when computer software was embedded in machines and given away freely. At that time, there was almost no distinct software industry anywhere in the world' (Lipsey and Wills 1996: 579). The strategy was to attract high technology and knowledge-based industries from abroad based on three related measures: development support for new industries; export encouragement through tax relief; and development of human capital, whose lack was identified early on as an impediment to growth in these areas. The ICT industries grew at a phenomenal rate during the 1980s and the World Competitiveness Report consistently identified Singapore as top in the world with respect to the effective use of ICTs in business.[16]

There is debate about how much specific polices such as export promotion helped in the spectacular development of the newly industrialising countries (NICs). There is little debate, however, about the creation of these highly successful industries through government policy, which included both initial protection from foreign competition and substantial domestic assistance. We do not have space here to do an in-depth evaluation of the more general growth experiences of the NICs or of their detailed policy packages. We only make the one observation that by drawing conclusions about the general effectiveness of some specific policies, such as export promotion, from observations about how well or how poorly the policy performed in one specific situation, many investigators assume implicitly that such policies can be judged in general, independent of the specific circumstances in which they were initially used.

Although we do not enter the more general debate on the sources of the NICs' growth, what is clear is that these countries got onto sustained growth paths and went from poor backward countries with third-world living standards to modern industrialized countries with standards approaching those in the West within twenty to thirty years while other countries remained stagnant, and that they did so while building local industries under initial heavy protection from foreign competition and with substantial government assistance. In many of these cases, wholly new products, and sometimes wholly new industries, have grown up with initial government assistance. In other cases, existing products and industries have been given substantial assistance. In virtually none of these cases was the industry left open to unrestricted competition from foreign firms and products, although once

---

[16] See Lipsey and Wills (1996: 597) for a more detailed discussion.

established, restrictions on competition from foreign sources was reduced or eliminated.

On the debate about the effectiveness of infant industry protection, under the revised form of the theory pointed out above, Rodrik (1993: 2) observes:

> But fundamentally the trade economist's suspicions of trade policy... are more deeply rooted in a general scepticism regarding the ability of governments to act in the common good, rather than as an instrument of special interests.... Hence, the preference for laissez-faire is based fundamentally on political reasoning of a certain type, leading in turn to a special presumption about the capability of states to deliver effective policies.

Critics of active focused government policies tend to accept the above judgement as always correct. The S-E approach is to regard the potential failures as context-specific and to look for conditions in the policy structure that make such government failures more or less likely. After all, the evidence is that, although governments have often failed to deliver such effective policies, they have sometimes succeeded, and these successes have sometimes been spectacular, as with Japanese automobiles and Taiwanese electronics. Elsewhere Rodrik (1994) studied some of the conditions that led to success in South Korea and Taiwan. He (1994: 39) argued that, among other things:

> what was required was a competent, honest, and efficient bureaucracy to administer the interventions, and a clear-sighted political leadership that consistently placed high priority on economic performance. In Korea and Taiwan, unlike in so many other developing countries, these additional [and necessary] requirements were present.

The quotation points to another important type of context-specificity that influences the outcomes of technology enhancement policies, or any other type of policy for that matter—the nature of a country's government. This is a complex issue but consider just one illustration. It is not surprising that technology enhancement policies are administered differently and have different outcomes when put in place by a small fairly homogeneous country whose rulers are focused on economic growth and by a large heterogeneous country whose rulers are concerned to broker conflicting regional interests.

Proponents argue that S-E theory shows the need for focused policies—always understanding that these are in addition to, not substitutes for, the market-orienting measures. As one of us has put it elsewhere (Lipsey 2002a: 336–7):

- Accepting that new technological knowledge, whether acquired from abroad or produced by domestic R&D, has major positive externalities provides a reason to encourage technological advance with public funds.
- Accepting that technology changes endogenously provides a reason why present comparative advantage need not be accepted as immutable; it can be changed by public policy as well as by the activities of private agents.
- Accepting that technological change is highly dependent on local contexts implies that the best policies are context-specific rather than being the same for all countries at all times.

- Accepting the conclusion that there is no unique optimum allocation of resources ... has important consequences for how we view economic policy in the area of growth and technological change.... [P]olicy with respect to these matters must be based, as we have already argued, on a mixture of theory, measurement and subjective judgement.
- These ideas are both powerful and dangerous. They are powerful because they suggest ways to go beyond neoclassical generic policy advice to more context-specific advice. They are dangerous because they can easily be used to justify ignoring the market-oriented consensus, accepting only the interventionist part of the S-E policy advice (forgetting that this is meant to supplement the advice of the consensus, not to replace it).

Another aspect of the debate over the effectiveness of technology enhancement policy in the most successful of the Asian countries that is of direct relevance to us because it concerns what can be learned from total factor productivity is briefly discussed in Box 16.1.

Box 16.1. Total Factor Productivity and Technological Change in the Asian NICs

We do not have space to consider in detail the argument that the key to the success of the Asian NICs was the adoption of market-oriented policies and an investment boom, and that their more interventionist development policies contributed little or nothing. Since one argument to this effect is of particular relevance to our analysis, we do consider it briefly here.

In a series of papers, Alwyn Young has calculated that changes in TFP were minutely positive in all but one of the Asian NICs and negative in Singapore.[17] From these measurements, Young and Paul Krugman conclude:

Singapore will only be able to sustain further growth by reorienting its policies from factor accumulation toward the considerably more subtle issue of technological change. (Young 1992: 50)

A growth-accounting exercise [conducted by Young] produces the startling result that Singapore showed no technical progress at all. (Krugman 1996: 55)

This interpretation raises the question: What were the successful infant industry policies discussed in the text doing if they were not instituting technological change? The development from scratch of Taiwan's highly successful electronics industry was surely accomplished by the introduction of new technologies, as was the growth of Singapore's computer component industry. Singapore went, in the space of a few decades, from 'a labour-surplus, entrepot-trade-based, urban mercantile centre, with a rural hinterland, into a high-tech island ... attracting high-value-added, technology and knowledge-based industries such as software, computer service industries, financial services, and medical consultancy services' (Lipsey and Wills 1996: 591–2). If this were done without technological change, one must wonder just what technological change really is!

---

[17] See Young, for example, (1992, 1995) for the argument and Nelson and Pack (1997) for in-depth criticism.

Box 16.1. (continued)

Young's argument—that as the NICs industrialized and prospered, there was no technological change, just more investment—depends on the assumption that changes in TFP measure changes in technology. This has been denied by several students of technological change including Jorgenson and Griliches (1967), Hulten (2000), and Lipsey and Carlaw (2004 and also in the Appendix to Chapter 4). We concluded there that TFP is at best an imperfect measure of the gains from technological change that exceed the cost of invention and innovation. In the limit, technological change can go on while just covering its full costs, in which case there will be continued growth with zero change in TFP. Aside from all the theoretical arguments given by us elsewhere, the evidence of what happened as the Asian NICs transformed themselves technologically over the decades while TFP rose only slowly, if at all, is strong confirmation that, whatever they do measure, changes in TFP do not measure technological change. In Singapore's case, much of its technological transformation took place through capital imported by foreign multinationals. So if Singapore paid foreigners the full cost of that capital, whose price had to include the capitalized costs of developing the new technologies embodied in it, the measured amount of capital would rise as would real wages (since the quantity of capital appears in the expression for the marginal product of labour) with no necessary change in TFP.

This case study illustrates just how misleading is the general but erroneous belief that changes in TFP do measure changes in technology.[18]

V. DOMESTIC TECHNOLOGY ENHANCEMENT POLICIES

We turn now to domestic policies directed at influencing the pace and direction of technological change. The same issues as we encountered in the debate over trade policy arise concerning the efficacy of domestic policies directed at influencing R&D and technological change in whole industries or with specific products. We argued above that given the reality of endogenous technological change, there is no scientifically derivable unique set of optimal polices; instead, policies must be decided on by a combination of theory, evidence, and an irreducible element of judgement.

Theory

Although it is interesting to show that policies thought to have a scientific basis must depend partly on subjective judgement, if that were all that S-E theory accomplished, it might not be of great practical value. Fortunately, S-E decompositions also shed much light on ways of accomplishing the goal of influencing technological change. These ways sometimes supplement, and sometimes differ from, those suggested by neoclassical theory.

First, as we have noted earlier, technological interrelationships that cause positive spillovers are extremely rich, making most of them context-dependent both secto-

---

[18] See Nelson and Pack (1997) for a more in-depth criticism.

rally and temporally.[19] An S-E decomposition reinforces this view and reveals an additional set of spillovers associated with the relation between technology and the facilitating structure. Second, there is a complex relation between innovation and diffusion that complicates technology policy. Third, there are many roles for technology policy beyond internalizing spillovers. Fourth, institutional competence to administer policies and programmes becomes a much more complex issue than it is in neoclassical principal–agent analysis. These issues are considered separately in the four sections that follow.[20]

In discussing these, we adopt the usual procedure of investigating the potential for public policy that is directed at some desirable goal—in this case promoting profitable technological change. The very real possibility that government failures can (and often do) prevent the realization of the potential of such policies is accepted but postponed for a later discussion.

Specific Externalities

An important way in which S-E theories assist in motivating and directing innovation policies is by identifying a much more complex set of spillovers than is found in neoclassical theory. The classes of spillovers suggested by S-E theories that we discussed in Chapters 4 and 13 cover spillovers (*a*) between technology, facilitating structure, and performance; (*b*) within technology; and (*c*) within the facilitating structure. (Because economic performance is defined as the final outcome of economic activity, there are no relevant spillovers within performance.) A detailed knowledge of these spillovers suggests some policy opportunities that tend to be ignored by neoclassical theory. Many of the specific policy lessons that we develop in Chapter 17 are related to those spillovers that create opportunities for useful policy interventions and pitfalls for policies that ignore them.

Spillovers within technology. Developments that improve the efficiency of one technology are often useful in many other technologies. Such was the case, for example, in the nineteenth century, when improvements in machine tools used in very specific applications turned out to have wider applications to the machine tools used in other industries (Rosenberg 1976). Much of the value of these indirect effects cannot be appropriated by their initiators, thus giving rise to intertechnology spillovers. This situation creates a potential role for policy, which we consider in detail below.

Spillovers between technology and structure. A change in any element of technology typically affects the values of many elements of the structure. Spillovers arise because innovators do not usually take account of the effects that they induce in the facilitating structure. A new GPT will typically affect the values of most elements of

---

[19] Lipsey (2001) discusses in more detail the many ways in which the policy advice following from S-E theory is context-dependent.

[20] Sulzenko (1997) discusses a major restructuring within Industry Canada that is much in line with this structuralist perspective and in which he played a major part as Assistant Deputy Minister for Industry and Science Policy.

the facilitating structure, such as existing capital goods, whole firms, contracts, locations, and items of the infrastructure. Changes to the facilitating structure will in turn affect the values of many other existing technologies and R&D programmes. The potential roles for policy are obvious.

Spillovers within the facilitating structure. A change in any one of the interrelated elements of the facilitating structure affects the value and efficiency of many others. The spillovers arise because agents who change those elements of structure that are under their control typically do not take account of induced changes in the values of other elements. For example, before changes in the nature of physical capital can achieve their full potential, they often require changes in human capital, in the physical location and organization of firms, and in the infrastructure. The policy implication is that there is a potential role for government to assist the full adjustment of that structure where private incentives are lacking.

Spillovers from performance to structure and technology. Experience with the use of evolving technologies often alters the values of elements of the existing technology and/or structure. The Schumpeterian model of innovation saw technology developing in a one-way flow moving from pure science to applied work, and then to the shop floor and the salesroom. Modern research shows a two-way flow of information running among all stages of the value-added chain. For example, Von Hippel (1988) shows that some innovations are derived from the initiative of producers, some from downstream users, and some from upstream suppliers. New technologies typically have many imperfections that can be identified only through 'learning by using', causing users to face significant amounts of uncertainty (Rosenberg 1982: especially ch. 6). Spillovers occur because the experience of the new users often generates non-appropriable new knowledge that benefits producers and, through product improvements, other users. The two obvious places where policy has the potential to assist are in improving the information flows between users and producers, and in inducing users to create this knowledge.

Innovation–Diffusion Trade-Off?

Consider a simple world in which innovators introduce new stand-alone technologies, which then diffuse through the economy in unchanged form. Since invention and diffusion are then separate activities, there is a simple trade-off between more secure property rights to encourage invention and less secure property rights to encourage diffusion. As we know, however, transforming GPTs, and other major radical innovations, never enter the world in a fully developed form. Instead, they first appear in a crude embryonic state with only a few specific uses. Diffusion and improvements then occur simultaneously as the technology is made more efficient and adapted for use over an increasingly wide range of applications, many of which require the invention of additional supporting technologies. The more fundamental is the new technology, the more marked is this process of long and slow evolution from crude prototypes with narrow use to highly efficient products with a wide range of applications. This whole process is usually called 'diffusion' because an original generic idea, such as how to generate electricity, how to drive a cylinder with steam, or the integrated circuit, is diffusing throughout the economy. However, the process bears little relation to diffusion defined as the use of an unchanged piece of technology by more and more agents.

In practice, therefore, any measure that slows diffusion will also slow the rate at which related downstream innovations occur. Thus, strengthening property rights does not unambiguously accelerate invention. Because it slows *diffusion of any pre-existing set of inventions*, its effects on future inventions, many of which depend on the diffusion of existing inventions, cannot be determined in the absence of detailed, case-by-case knowledge. Thus, a judgement call is needed on the policy balance between intellectual property rights to protect *existing* technological knowledge and conditions designed to increase its diffusion (and hence the creation of new, related knowledge).

In contrast, the neoclassical theory that predicts a role for assistance to R&D because of its spillovers does not typically distinguish invention and innovation from diffusion, relying either explicitly or implicitly on the assumption that once innovated a technology becomes freely available to everyone (unless protected by patents or other created barriers). This is certainly true of the macro treatment in which knowledge is a single homogeneous commodity and it is also true of many less aggregated treatments. As a result, the trade-off between encouraging new inventions and innovations on the one hand and encouraging the inventions and innovation that accompany diffusion on the other hand often goes unanalysed, as does the relation between technology and facilitating structure.

Roles Beyond Internalizing Spillovers from Technological Knowledge

S-E theory emphasizes several features that provide scope for technology-enhancing policies in addition to those emphasized by neoclassical theory.

Assisting induced changes in structure. Changes in technological knowledge typically require accommodating changes in the facilitating and policy structures. Public policy can respond helpfully in two ways.[21] First, relevant elements of the policy structure can be altered. An example is the changes that were needed in the regulation of the telecommunications industry in response to the ICT revolution. In this case, changes often come all too slowly. Second, public policy can assist adjustments in the facilitating structure that are subject to major externalities; examples are altering the education system to produce skills required by the new technology, or altering elements in the publicly owned infrastructure to make the best use of new technologies. (Of course, policy can, and often does, respond in

---

[21] It has been argued that in a world of uncertainty there is no place for forward-looking public policy since nothing can be foreseen. This is a misunderstanding of the implications of uncertainty. As we observed in Chapter 2, agents operating under uncertainty must still look forward; they consult evidence from past behaviour; they try to anticipate future events from what they know of public policy and of the normal behaviour of the economy. But because all foresight involves an irreducible element of personal judgement, what they cannot do is to arrive at a unique probability distribution of the possible outcomes on which all rational agents agree.

unhelpful ways by slowing down the necessary adjustments to the structure. This can be done by errors of omission as well as commission.)

Making proactive changes in structure. Policies may also indirectly target technological change by altering elements of the facilitating structure. Examples of such policies include attempts to integrate some university, government, and private-sector research activities; attempts to create technology information networks; and attempts to change private-sector attitudes toward adopting new or different technologies. Furthermore, a government can attach structural conditions to funds given to firms to assist them to develop technologies that they would have developed anyway. More than one government have done this to encourage the development of long-term research facilities. All these initiatives would fail a test that looks only for direct changes in specified technologies. If successful, they would, however, pass a test that looks for structural alterations that would not have happened without government pressure. A prime example is the US military procurement policy, which to a great extent created the US software industry and then developed and imposed consistent standards on it (see Lipsey and Carlaw 1996: 311). Another is the Canadian Defence Industry Productivity Programme (DIPP), which gave government assistance but attached conditions that encouraged the building of R&D facilities in Canada. Since much of that assistance went to efforts that would have been undertaken anyway, it would not have passed the usual tests that look for direct results. But it would have passed a wider test, which also considered induced changes in the facilitating structure that could affect the amount of future R&D (see Lipsey & Carlaw 1998*b*: ch. 2).

Overcoming the disincentive of sunk costs. We have seen in earlier chapters that sunk costs and path-dependent technological trajectories play a prominent role in S-E theories. Sunk costs are important for the development of new products and processes; they are equally important for acquiring codifiable knowledge about new technologies, as well as tacit knowledge about how to operate given technologies. One major policy implication is that government bodies can efficiently disseminate technological knowledge by operating on a scale that makes the sunk costs bearable, or even trivial, where they would otherwise be prohibitively high for small firms. This is one of the objectives of the Canadian Industrial Research Assistance Programme (IRAP), which seeks, among other things, to help firms to identify existing technologies that are of potential value to them and to assist them in adapting these technologies to their own specific needs. This particular programme has been strongly criticized by neoclassical economists for distorting market signals by operating at the firm-specific level rather than generally across the whole economy.[22]

Reacting to path dependence. In Chapter 3, we argued that technologies typically evolve along path-dependent trajectories. Path dependence suggests that the encouragement of generic technologies in their early stages of development is more likely to produce socially valuable spillovers than the encouragement of highly specialized

---

[22] See, for example, Usher (1983), The Economic Council of Canada (1983), and Tarasofsky (1985); see Lipsey and Carlaw (1998*b*: ch. 4) for a more favourable evaluation.

technologies at later stages in their development. However, as Paul David has repeatedly emphasized, the early stages of many technological trajectories, when government assistance can have most impact, is the stage at which exposure to uncertainty is greatest. What looks like a sure winner, such as lighter-than-air craft, hovercraft, or atomic energy, may turn out later to have unforeseen problems that severely limit commercial success.

One important lesson is that policy opportunities vary over the course of a particular technology's development. Expectations of large spin-offs from a new generic technology must be balanced against the many uncertainties inherent in its early development. Assistance is often best applied after it becomes clear that the technology has major potential but while it is still in a relatively generic state. By this criterion, US policy was correct in not offering major support to the aircraft industry before 1914, when its potential was still unclear, and then giving substantial public assistance between the two world wars, when aircraft were evolving rapidly and coming into more general use. (The evidence from other technology support policies suggests that this advice is much easier to give than to follow.)

A cautionary lesson is suggested by the theory and evidence on competition between firms working on the same technological trajectory. Procurement decisions may lock the economy into one version of the competing technology before the relative merits of the alternatives have been seriously explored (an issue that would not matter if everything was reversible, as in neoclassical theory). Arthur (1988) gives several examples in which this appears to have happened.[23]

Institutional Competence

Of course, many economists of various persuasions who have had experience in policy situations know that particular programmes and policies are only as good as those who administer them. Nonetheless, the neoclassical model yields optimal policies that do not depend on any specific institutional structure. If the same generic policy is recommended under all circumstances, it follows that such local matters as institutional competence are not taken fully into account. As Stiglitz (2002: 34) puts it in his critique of the IMF: '[T]o the IMF the lack of detailed knowledge [of local capabilities] is of less moment, because it tends to take a "one-size-fits-all" approach.' Many economists also oppose any government attempts made anywhere to pick and back new technologies, no matter what the institutional arrangements that surround specific attempts and no matter what the track record of the country in question. (In contrast, context-specificity is suggested by the different experiences of the UK, which has been relatively unsuccessful in such attempts, and of Singapore and Taiwan, which have been successful.)

In reality, as emphasized in S-E approaches, various public-sector institutions have different institutional capabilities. The behavioural differences are based partly on constitutional differences, partly on the different power relations between various

---

[23] Although some of Arthur's specific examples have since been challenged, his general point of caution is still in order.

special interest groups, partly on the differences in the quality of recruits and the subsequent training of civil servants, and partly on differences in accumulated learning by doing in operating each country's specific policy instruments. (See Lipsey 1997 for a more detailed discussion.)[24]

The issue here is analogous to that of the difference between technological knowledge and the facilitating structure. Technological knowledge, which is the blueprint for doing things, is embodied in physical capital, which is part of the facilitating structure. Good technological knowledge may be embodied in poor physical capital if its production is beyond the capabilities of those who produce it (as it sometimes is when capital goods designed in the developed countries are produced in less developed ones). Similarly, public policies are blueprints for public-sector actions that are given effect by institutions and their bureaucracies. A policy that looks good in the abstract may work poorly in a particular country because it is beyond the competence of that country's bureaucracy to administer, or because it runs afoul of other incompatible elements in that country's facilitating or policy structures. Many factors may be to blame, including the routines of government agencies, the mindset of the delivery officers, the lending and project approval procedures, and all of the principal–agent issues analysed in public choice theory. The obvious but important lesson is that the success of a policy is not determined solely by its blueprint. Its success also depends on the specific context in which the policy is implemented. Policies that work well are those that are designed to operate within the institutional competencies of the organizations that will administer them—which is one reason why success or failure of some policy in one context cannot be uncritically assumed to provide evidence about the potential of that policy when applied in other contexts.

Evidence

There is an ongoing debate between those who see little place for the government in encouraging technological development and growth and those who see a significant place for it. The debate is strewn with clichés such as 'governments cannot pick winners' or 'significant government assistance is always needed for satisfactory development'. These seem to us to be maxims designed to prevent serious thought on the issue. The case studies, such as are found in Lipsey and Carlaw (1996) and Mowery and Nelson (1999), show that both these extreme views are untenable. Governments can and have picked winners and sometimes, as with the post-war Japanese automobile industry and the US software industry, backed spectacular winners. Thus, the important issue seems to us to be to identify the types of policies

---

[24] As we have already emphasized, such insights are not the exclusive prerogative of S-E theory. Many applied policy analysts have recognized the importance of institutional competence. Nonetheless, it is true that such considerations play no part in the neoclassical *theory* of policy, nor, to take the evidence of many of the authors cited in Chapter 17, do they play much part when neoclassical economists give actual policy advice in such situations as privatizing the Soviet economy or introducing market forces in West African countries. See Griffiths (2003) for one cautionary tale related to the African experience.

that are likely to succeed and the political and economic conditions that encourage success rather than failure—as we attempt to do in Chapter 17.

Here are just a few further examples of the evidence that governments do sometimes get it right. The US aircraft industry has long been the beneficiary of significant amounts of public assistance. From the 1920s to the 1950s the National Advisory Committee for Aeronautics (NACA) shaped early US technology policies to assist the commercial aircraft industry. It supported aviation innovation by providing assistance through its government-operated experimental facilities. It played an important supporting role by freely providing precommercial research, thus helping to equalize firms' non-appropriable technical knowledge and leaving them to compete in generating commercially viable innovations. This provision of technical knowledge reduced duplication of costly precommercial research, thus reducing exposure to uncertainty. For example, it pioneered the construction and use of large wind tunnels and provided essential test data that led to the development of such innovations as the 'NACA cowl', and demonstrated the superiority of airframes designed with a retractable landing gear.

In the period following the Second World War, US assistance policies have not usually been specifically designed to support commercial innovation. Instead, policies designed to create military innovations have produced commercial applications as spin-offs. For example, the designing of the military transport KC-135 bore a major share of the development cost for the airframe for the Boeing 707. The early lead of the British firm, De Havilland, was destroyed by the unexpected phenomenon of metal fatigue in the Comet, the world's first operational commercial jet transport—a lead that was in turn built up by defence contracts in the Second World War. Boeing was then well positioned to capture the bulk of the long haul market. De Havilland's failure with the Comet is an illustration of the uncertainties that beset attempts at major technological advances. Boeing's success with the 707, and later with the 747, are examples of US Department of Defense support, which helped in the latter case to finance the development of the aircraft's engines.

In the 1950s, the US Bureau of Standards encouraged the development of a US software industry primarily to assist in the cold war. The government intervention had two major spin-offs to the commercial sector. An infrastructure of academic experts was created largely with government funding, and high industry standards were set by the rigorous demands of the Department of Defense. Both of these were changes in the facilitating structure that greatly enhanced the opportunities for further commercial innovations.

Military procurement also supported the growth of the US semiconductor industry. In many cases, procurement provided an important incubation for innovations that were not yet commercially viable. The military also imposed rigid standards and quality controls that helped to standardize practices and diffuse technical knowledge. Procurement contracts were awarded by having firms compete to produce a prototype and then rewarding the best design with a long-term supply contract. This fostered competition in innovation for the contracts and provided a secure market for those who were successful innovators. Between 1955 and 1968, military demand accounted for between one-fourth and one-half of the semiconductor market. Firms supplying that market, often on a cost plus basis, refined their innovations and often reduced their costs sufficiently to achieve commercial viability. The policy also often provided incubation for new firms.

Another example is Airbus Industrie. Substantial government support by way of subsidies and other assistance allowed this new firm to enter an industry in which the number of firms was shrinking through mergers and bankruptcies. There was a long history of aircraft manufacture in both France and the UK that had created pools of human capital on which the new firm could draw. Nonetheless, many observers predicted that the new European producer would remain an infant, needing substantial subsidies and other forms of protection forever. Others said, when it seemed to be succeeding, that it would never create enough wealth to justify the initial government assistance. Today, the Airbus series are a viable product that challenge Boeing aircraft in all markets. The two giant firms have almost equal market shares and Airbus is as dynamic technologically as is Boeing. Although comparisons are difficult, when all assistance is taken into account, including indirect help from the US Department of Defense, it is not clear that one of these firms now secures substantially more public assistance than the other—although Airbus insists on maintaining some forms of support that might be more appropriate to an infant industry than to an established giant. Furthermore, as an important side effect, the entry of Airbus has preserved competition in the market for long-range passenger aircraft where, with the demise of other competitors, Boeing might otherwise have achieved a near monopoly.

Other successes include the French Caravelle, the first successful short- and medium-range commercial transport; the early development of the Japanese semiconductor industry, a catch-up (to the US) policy encouraged by the Japanese Ministry of International Trade and Industry; stoves in Kenya, a programme to develop alternatives to the wood-burning stoves that were fast running out of indigenous fuels; boat building in India, a private–public partnership, which developed and diffused new technologies for building plywood boats that used fewer trees per boat than the traditional technology; electricity in Nepal, a public–private sector cooperation, which succeeded in developing the technology for mini-hydroelectric mills that suited local conditions and assisted rural electrification.

On the other side of the ledger, government failures are numerous. Suffice it to mention the British Labour Government's groundnut scheme in the 1940s, an expensive failure to develop a groundnut (peanut) industry in West Africa; the Anglo-French Concorde, a technological triumph and a commercial failure; the US supersonic transport, begun in 1962 and abandoned 1970; the French attempt to build a successful micro-electronics industry, which attempted unsuccessfully to put French micro-electronics on an equal footing with US firms by backing a national flag carrier, Compagnie Internationale de l'Informatique; the British attempt to build a computer industry that would rival US firms, based on another national champion, International Computers Limited that never managed to come close to competing with US firms in quality and price; the British Advanced

Gas-Cooled Reactor to produce nuclear energy (the AGR programme), which proved to be the wrong line for developing nuclear energy; the Canadian CANDU nuclear reactor, which has achieved limited success and a few international sales but only through highly subsidized contracts (a debatable case that some would call a limited success); the British Alvey Programme, designed to meet increasing Japanese dominance in computer hardware in the early 1980s, a 'technology push' programme that failed partly because of its 'top-down' bureaucratic structure for administration; the Japanese attempt in the 1950s and 1960s to build from scratch a full commercial aircraft industry, which was 'a modest technical achievement,... [but] a commercial flop'[25] (Woronoff 1992: 183).

Conclusion

In the light of the above selected list of available evidence, the extreme view that governments can never become involved in assisting winners is clearly wrong. The list raises the important question, which we take up in Chapter 17, of why some initiatives are such spectacular successes while others are equally spectacular failures.

---

[25] All the successes and failures alluded to in this chapter are discussed in more detail by Lipsey and Carlaw (1996), who use these as case studies from which to extract the hypotheses about the conditions favouring success or failure for such government activities that we review in Chapter 17.

17

Assessing Technology Enchancement Policies

If we accept that technology enhancement policies sometimes succeed and sometimes fail, the question arises as to the conditions that favour success and lower the chance of failure.

I. JUDGING POLICY PACKAGES

We first need to distinguish among policies, programmes, and projects and then among types of policies.

Definitions

A policy is some stated objective, which may be specific, such as developing a nuclear power industry, or general, such as encouraging technological change. A *programme* defines the set of instruments and the administrative apparatus that give effect to the policy. For example, the programme to develop the Advanced Gas Reactor was intended to give effect to the policy of developing an indigenous nuclear power capability in the UK. A *project* defines a specific task that is part of a programme. An example is the construction of a specific Advanced Gas Reactor power plant.

At the level of abstraction at which much economic analysis occurs, the distinction between these three does not need to be made and the general term *policy* is used. Our analysis from here on requires that the distinctions be explicit when assessing and evaluating both design and performance.

We distinguish three major types of technology policy. The first is *framework policies*, which provide general support for one specific activity across the whole economy. In practice, they are usually single-instrument policies. They do not discriminate among firms, industries, or technologies. They do not judge the viability of recipient firms or the specific projects in which they are engaged. Instead, to be engaged in the covered activity is both a necessary and sufficient condition for obtaining benefits under the policy. Examples are patent protection for the owners of intellectual property and R&D tax credits.

The second type is *focused policies*, which are designed to encourage the development of specific technologies, such as nuclear power, specific products, such as unmanned undersea craft, and particular types of R&D, such as precommercial research. They are usually narrowly focused to make falling within the covered activity a necessary and sufficient condition for receiving benefits under the policy.

The third type is *blanket policies*, which incorporate elements of both framework and focused policies. On the one hand, they typically have broad-based objectives similar to framework policies and on the other, they typically use multiple instruments and have some form of assessment mechanism that enables the administrators to tailor the assistance they provide, at least to some degree. For example, assistance may be provided only to companies deemed financially viable or projects deemed to have a good chance of commercial success. Thus, being engaged in the covered activities is a necessary but not sufficient condition for receiving benefits under this type of policy. Sufficient conditions vary with the policy and the instrument, but must be met to gain benefits. Sometimes these conditions are laid down quite explicitly by the rules and regulations of particular programmes; and sometimes substantial discretion is left to administrators in deciding whether a firm's specific activity fulfils the sufficient conditions.

Assessment and Evaluation

In assessing any policy, programme, or project, we first need to distinguish the three stages shown in Figure 17.1.

'Design' in Figure 17.1 includes the rules of the game, the design of the delivery system, the institutional context, and the relevant characteristics of the administrators including technical and administrative expertise and mindset. Mindset is particularly important because policies that are identical in all other respects often produce different results depending on who administers them. It can matter, for example, whether a specific technology-enhancing policy is administered by a tax department, a science and technology department, a regional development department, or a human resources department.

Here is an example that illustrates the importance of context-specificity in the administration of a programme. The administrators of an R&D tax credit programme can make the two classic errors of including some activities that really are not R&D and excluding some activities that really are R&D. If the programme is administered by the tax department, concern will tend to be directed at minimizing the first type of error, at the cost of accepting quite a few errors of the second type. In contrast, if the programme is administered by an industry department, concern is more likely to be with minimizing the second type of error, at the cost of committing quite a few of the first type.

For assessment purposes, in the early stages of a new programme, design and implementation are all there is to go on. Experience of past successes and failures of

Figure 17.1. *The three stages of a programme*

other programmes can be a good guide to judging a programme at this stage. However, since policy and programme innovation is replete with uncertainties similar to those that affect technological innovation, one can never be sure how a new programme design will work until it has been implemented. Once it has been in operation for some time, the programme's performance can be directly assessed. Finally, since working well over any time period is no guarantee of working well in the future, periodic independent assessment of policies and programmes is needed.

If the judgement is accepted that it is socially desirable to have technology enhancement policies, it remains to investigate how to assess various types of policies and programmes. We consider, first, how to assess the relative advantages of framework, focused, and blanket of policies and programmes; second, how to assess the design of particular policies and programmes before they are operational; and third, how to assess their performance after they have been put in place.

Relative Advantages of Different Types of Policies and Programmes

We devote most of our discussion to how the relative advantages look from the standpoint of S-E theory because this theory suggests more complex choice criteria than does neoclassical theory.

Framework Policies and Programmes

We have seen that in the aggregate version of neoclassical theory, in which knowledge is a single, homogeneous, continuous variable producing a single positive externality, there is an optimum amount of innovation that can be achieved either by lowering the cost of the inputs to R&D or by increasing the value of the outputs (i.e. technological advances). For example, Usher (1983) argues that framework policies are superior to focused or blanket policies because, among other things, a framework policy can accomplish anything useful that a focused or blanket policy can, and less expensively. The details of our structuralist rejection of this view are given below.

In a structuralist world with uncertainty and non-convexities, the calculation that equates expected pay-offs to R&D across the economy cannot be performed. Expected values thus cannot be rationally calculated in advance and are often misassessed even after some initial breakthrough has occurred. One implication is that there is no neutral framework policy. Instead, the various programmes that give effect to framework policies will have different consequences for the amount of R&D performed, depending on both the technological and the structural contexts within which they operate. For those who think we are dealing with straw men, the neutrality debate provides a strong counter-example. Countless economists condemn policies that 'distort' price signals. To an S-E theorist 'distortions' are neither good nor bad per se, their effects being context-specific. Below are some illustrations for this pragmatic approach to 'distortions'.

There are several reasons why an across-the-board subsidy to costs will have different effects from an across-the-board increase in the security of intellectual property. First, patents only reward those who succeed, while R&D support is independent of results. Thus, a given R&D subsidy reduces R&D costs equally everywhere and is of equal benefit to all agents engaged in that activity. In contrast, because intellectual property protection is much more effective in some lines of activity than in others, and because the (unknowable) likelihood of success differs across activities, strengthening this type of protection will affect R&D differentially across a wide spectrum of activities.

Second, the ability to extract value from patents varies greatly across types of innovation. Firms in industries such as pharmaceuticals, where patents are effective, are able to internalize much of the value that they create—enough to provide strong incentives to innovate. Because patents already protect their profits, these industries gain unnecessary benefits from R&D support compared with those industries where patents are relatively ineffective.

Third, invention and diffusion are closely linked in ways that are differently affected by changes in the costs and in the pay-off from R&D. For example, if patents are used to encourage an innovation that has many potential future complementarities, the initial innovation might be accelerated but all subsequent innovation would be retarded, while an R&D subsidy would accelerate the whole trajectory of innovation. Note that we are not denying any overlap between neoclassical and S-E policy recommendations but we are arguing that a policy that aspires to 'neutrality' and condemns all 'distortions' is not necessarily the most desirable policy—partly because there can be no neutral policy and partly because even framework policies have differential effects and hence change relative signals throughout the economy.

Another important example of non-neutrality concerns the upstream–downstream complementarities of technology. As argued in more detail by Lipsey and Carlaw (1996), the inability to keep the results of precommercial research secret in some cases may lead to too little of it, while ability to keep it secret in other cases may lead to an excess of overly duplicative R&D, particularly when everyone is seeking to solve the same technological problem. An R&D subsidy in sectors where firms are hoarding, and thus duplicating, precommercial R&D efforts only aggravates what is often wasteful behaviour because it merely encourages more of whatever is already being done. A focused policy that discriminates between situations in which the free market produces too much and those in which it produces too little, precompetitive research is potentially superior. For example, where there is too little precompetitive research, both focused and blanket policies can create commitments among firms that encourage them to carry out precommercial research in which they all share but which none of them can keep secret.[1]

Not only will a framework policy cover some activities that do not need support, it will also miss some that do. For example, because in practice there is no clear distinction between innovation and diffusion, much activity that is related to the development and use of new technologies may not appear to be basic R&D. Baldwin

---

[1] In its heyday during 1960–1980, MITI often helped to create commitments that provided firms with incentives to engage in, and share, this type of precompetitive research.

and Hanel (2003) have shown that many small firms do little recognizable R&D but spend considerable time monitoring what larger firms are doing and then adapting the findings to their own uses. Other small and medium-sized enterprises engage in much informal R&D, which is difficult to separate from routine production activities. Although these activities may be just as important in advancing technology as is more formal R&D, much of it will be missed by such framework polices as R&D tax credits.

From an S-E point of view, and given sufficient knowledge, a good policy for R&D support would not be a framework policy that would give equal support to all agents engaged in R&D. Instead, it would be focused in giving each inventor/innovator a lump sum payment sufficient to provide the appropriate incentives to invent and innovate (generally much less than the social value that they create), and then to make the resulting technological knowledge freely available. This ideal public assistance would vary among agents according to the externalities that their innovations create. In turn, the externalities depend on the total social value that the innovations create and the proportion of that value that inventors/innovators can appropriate through their own unaided efforts. Assistance would thus be tied only indirectly to their R&D and their invention and innovation. Although such 'sufficient knowledge' can very probably never be obtained and it is thus unfeasible to focus public assistance precisely on the externalities created by each agent, this discussion undermines the presumption of neoclassical theory that framework policies are always superior to focused and blanket policies because they are non-distorting.[2]

We conclude that out of the feasible set of instruments, S-E theories do not preclude such framework policies as patents, R&D subsidies, and investment tax credits. Instead, they provide an explanation for the differential effects of these supposedly neutral framework policies, and a method of going beyond them.

Focused and Blanket Policies in General

Just as we earlier observed with trade policy, much of the past discussions of domestic focused and blanket policies have centred on slogans, such as 'governments cannot pick winners'. Governments, particularly in North America and Europe, have no doubt squandered vast amounts of funds on interventions in the names of both science and technology and industrial policies. Many economists, including the present authors, agree that if the choice were between no government policies in these areas and a heavy-handed picking by bureaucrats of technology winners that would then be innovated by protected national champions, the preferred choice would be no policy. But holding that view does not require one to believe that governments have had no successes in these areas.

---

[2] Of course, framework policies may be preferred to focused and blanket policies on all sorts of other grounds, such as administrative simplicity, being less liable to capture, and a relative lack of principal–agent problems. If so, the case needs to be made on these grounds, without assuming that there is a general theoretical argument in favour of 'non-distorting' framework policies independent of any context-specific considerations.

Examples of both successful and unsuccessful policies can be found in many writings such as of Lipsey and Carlaw (1996, 1998*a*), Mowery and Nelson (1999), and Lipsey (2001). We have reviewed some of these in Chapter 16. Mowery and Nelson (1999: 15) state that they have studied both successes and failures in an attempt to make the policy debate 'more nuanced and less polarized'. In view of these, and myriad other examples, Lipsey (1997: 106) concludes:

A host of S&T and innovation policies [programmes and projects] have been used in various countries. The great success of some and the massive failure of others suggest several lessons. First, there is scope for major government activity in the area of encouraging technological change. Secondly, there is also enormous scope for wasteful failure. Thirdly, the expectations are poor for big technology pushes that require massive changes in the existing facilitating structure or even the development of wholly new structures; the successes have tended to be those that accept the path dependency of technological change, going for significant advances that build on existing strengths and not trying for the great leaps in the technological dark that unfortunately seem to attract politicians. Fourthly, although no assistance is clearly better than bad assistance, good assistance is often better than none—at least in some circumstances in some countries.

Clearly, the evidence does not support either of the polar extremes that focused and blanket policies always fail or always succeed. The relevant issue is, as we have already observed, to identify the conditions that make success more or less likely. We make a beginning at such an attempt later in this chapter, but first we must look at focused and blanket policies separately.

Focused policies

Focused policies are typically embodied in single programmes or even a single project. For this reason, we use 'focused policy' as a generic term for focused programmes, projects, and policies when further distinction is unnecessary.

Neoclassical theory sees no place for focused technology-enhancing policies, since these 'distort' market signals in undesirable ways while doing nothing of value that cannot be accomplished by framework policies. In contrast, S-E theory suggests a significant role for focused policies. Given enough knowledge, they would target exactly where assistance was needed. They would discriminate among various private-sector efforts to invent and innovate, in accordance with their (guesstimated) potential to create social benefits that the firm cannot capture. They would not, however, be aimed to internalize all social benefits but only to create incentives sufficient to encourage some target level of innovative activity. While doing this, they would also be used to seek an appropriate balance between encouraging innovation and encouraging diffusion in each particular context. They would be used as well to encourage changes in the facilitating structure at rates that were appropriate to the existing pattern of technological change and/or that altered it in such a way as to encourage more technological change.

Seeing what would be done under ideal circumstances is a useful place to start one's analysis, but we also need to see what can be done in realistic circumstances. In reality, sufficient knowledge does not exist to make possible the high degree of policy 'fine-tuning' referred to in the previous paragraph. This causes problems when focused policies are relied on heavily, and still more when they are relied on exclusively. First, a mass of detailed information is required to calculate the externalities associated with each potential innovation in order to design the appropriate, context-specific focused assistance. Second, the transaction costs required to calculate externalities that can in principle be located, and to design and administer the large set of required focused policies, would be prohibitive. Third, even if such a set of policies could be designed and instituted at zero transaction cost, their administration would require a highly sophisticated bureaucracy at all levels, from head office to the field. Fourth, the more a policy or programme is focused on small groups, the easier it is for clients to capture it. Fifth, the more focused a policy is, the more likely it is to be captured by politicians who have self-interest in the projects that are accepted and rejected. Sixth, focused policies carry the risk of trade sanctions, since subsidies and other similar supports must be generally available to be exempt under WTO rules. These points show the undesirability of providing support to technological change *exclusively* with focused policies.

However, when specific needs and major externalities can be identified, and when capture and other pitfalls can be avoided, focused policies can provide effective assistance to specific technologies, industries, and even firms. Lipsey and Carlaw (1996) cite several examples. Such focused assistance can be used to complement blanket and framework policies.

Blanket Policies and Programmes

Neoclassical theory rejects the use of blanket policies for the same reasons that it rejects focused policies: they are alleged to be 'distorting'. Given the general objective of encouraging technological change and the problems that are associated with framework and focused policies, there is much in S-E theory to recommend blanket policies, which are intermediate between the other two.

First, blanket policies can be used to push a policy objective without being tied to a particular generic instrument. In contrast, framework policies are typically associated with specific instruments, such as tax credits for R&D, intellectual property protection, and broad-based subsidies. Second, blanket policies can accommodate some context-specific tailoring, which makes them less conducive to capture by their clients than focused policies because they can be made conditional on serving the general objective. Third, blanket policies can be used to induce changes in parts of the facilitating structure that are used by firms in their R&D activities, such as technology networks, establishment of public research laboratories, and business information networks. Fourth, blanket policies can sometimes be used to alter the internal structure of firms in ways such as changing attitudes toward the employment of new or leading-edge technologies, and encouraging the employment of university-trained research staff. Lipsey and Carlaw (1998a) have studied two Canadian blanket programmes, the Defence Industry Productivity Programme (DIPP) and the Industrial Research Assistance Programme

(IRAP), which seem to have worked, at least for some period of time, in many of the aspects outlined here.

The most serious problem with blanket policies compared with either of the other two types is their potential to degenerate into uncoordinated activities that support some things and not others with no clear criteria for inclusion and exclusion. Cases in point seem to be the succession of Canadian policies IRDIA, PAIT, EDP, and IRDP.[3] These policies, which are also studied in Lipsey and Carlaw (1998*a*: ch. 3), degenerated into incoherence because, among other things, the administrators were not given clear directions on such matters as precise goals, instruments, and selection criteria.

Design and Operational Criteria

We say nothing here about the design of such framework polices as R&D support and intellectual property protection since, being the preferred policies of neoclassical theory, they have been widely studied. For obvious reasons, much less attention has been paid to focused and blanket policies, so we concentrate on these two.

We suggest some design and operational criteria that are based on the observations of successes and failures of actual programmes and projects. These are derived from Lipsey and Carlaw's study (1996) of about thirty mainly focused policies drawn from around the world for which reasonably reliable indications of success or failure existed. They looked for characteristics that distinguished the successes from the failures. They fitted these into the S-E decomposition presented in Chapter 3. To do this, they classified the targeted changes in technology as either 'incremental' or 'large leap' and the required changes in the facilitating structure as small, medium, or large. Then by comparing the characteristics associated with success with those associated with failure, they developed a set of empirically generated policy lessons that refer to the design and operation of policies and programmes.

The policy lessons that follow are an elaboration of those drawn by Lipsey and Carlaw from their study. Although some of the items may sound trite, each is derived from one or more real cases, with the 'don't' items all being cautionary tales drawn from failures in real policies, programmes, or projects. Although following these lessons does not guarantee success, the authors suggest that doing so should increase the likelihood of success. The full analysis of the case studies from which the lessons are derived can be found in Lipsey and Carlaw (1996).

For our present purposes, we have grouped the lessons into four categories, which are primarily related to uncertainty; primarily concerned with design pitfalls; primarily concerned with structural relationships; and primarily related to market forces and information. We say 'primarily' because many of the lessons concern more than one category.

---

[3] IRDIA: Industrial Research and Development Incentives Act; PAIT: Programme for the Advancement of Industrial Technology; EDP: Enterprise Development Programme; IRDP: Industrial and Regional Development Programme.

Uncertainty

Large leaps are dangerous. Attempts at large technological leaps involve many exposures to uncertainties because they require many changes in the main technology and its various subtechnologies, as well as the accumulation of the tacit knowledge that is required to operate the new technology efficiently. Large leaps in technology for which the facilitating structure already exists are extremely difficult to accomplish; large leaps in technology that also require large leaps in the facilitating structure are nearly impossible to accomplish successfully. The history of focused policies is replete with failed programmes that attempted large technological leaps (of either the catch-up or leading-edge variety), which also required major accommodating changes in the facilitating structure.[4]

Successful policies and programmes often pursue incremental innovation and (where possible) aid in the acquisition of tacit knowledge. Policymakers can reduce exposure to uncertainty by pursuing incremental innovation, assisting firms to acquire tacit knowledge about established technologies and targeting niche developments. This approach parallels the incremental focus that characterizes much private-sector activity.

Pushing the development of a technology off its established trajectory is dangerous. Exploiting the potential of a technology within its established trajectory involves fewer exposures of firms to uncertainties than trying to alter the trajectory or establish a wholly new one.

Flexibility is important. In the uncertain world of technological advances, almost the only certainty is that something unexpected will happen. There are many uncertainties related to technological change as well as to the design and operation of new projects, programmes, and policies. Because coping with this kind of uncertainty requires learning from experience, policy designers and programme administrators must be able to change course or cancel any venture as unfavourable experience accumulates. Many programmes and projects have failed because their procedures and objectives could not be changed as experience accumulated about what was and was not possible. To allow for change, procedures must be put in place for reviews, amendments, and/or cancellation of projects, programmes, or even entire policies. We refer to the ability to revise the internal structure of policies and programmes as design flexibility, and the ability to change course or cut off particular projects as delivery flexibility.

Diversity is one of the best protections against uncertainty. Because technological advances are uncertain, diverse experiments are often more productive than one big push along what appears to be the most likely path at the outset.

---

[4] A good illustration comes from the aircraft industry with the transfer from propeller-driven aircraft to jets. The first round almost succeeded in the UK and did succeed in the USA and both countries had a well-developed facilitating structure to support production and innovation in the aircraft industry. In contrast, the Japanese attempt in the 1960s to develop a programme to produce full-sized passenger aircraft (YS-11) without any pre-existing, well-developed facilitating structure of the sort that existed in Europe or the USA failed.

Exposure to uncertainty can be reduced by exploiting the interrelation between users and producers. Users of a technology can provide producers with information about desired characteristics and about problems with past and present designs; they can also give some indication of market demand for innovations.

Design Pitfalls

Multiple objectives are dangerous. When policies and programmes have multiple objectives, the uncertainties involved in technological advances make it likely that the non-technological objectives will predominate, *and the prediction about the future commercial viability of the technological advance will be whatever is needed to justify the decision to proceed.* If technological objectives become mixed with political prestige, regional development, or any other policy objectives, it is likely that the technological objectives will be made subservient to other ends.[5] The history of technological programmes shows many instances where favourable technological judgements continued to be held in the face of accumulating unfavourable evidence because of fear about the employment effects, the regional impacts, or other non-technological consequences of cancellation. The implication is that, wherever possible, technology advancement policies and programmes should not be given additional non-technological objectives.

Multiple objectives may be sustainable where there are multiple tools. The lesson immediately above relates mainly to focused policies. More complex policies and programmes may successfully employ multiple objectives if they assign separate policy tools to each objective.

Multiple objectives may be sustainable if they are clearly prioritized. Since we are considering policies designed to advance technology, whenever there are multiple objectives to be served by the same instrument, priority must be given to the technological objective for the reasons outlined in the lesson 'Multiple objectives are dangerous'. There is a strong warning here, however, that prioritization is much easier to state in principle than it is to follow in practice.

National prestige should be an outcome, not an objective. Policies and programmes should not have national prestige as upfront objectives, whether stated or merely implicit. Such policies and programmes are handicapped relative to ones that are chosen for potential commercial viability. They tend to bring the opposite of international prestige when they publicly fail to produce commercially viable innovations. Furthermore, they often have serious negative spillover effects when they introduce inferior technologies that government policy requires to be widely used.

Capture should be avoided. Capture can come from three directions: the administrators, the clients, and the politicians. All policies and programmes are liable to capture by their administrators, who then run them for their own benefit and who have little desire to achieve real success. The longer a policy or programme has been

---

[5] By technological objective we mean the desire to bring about commercially successful technological change. See below: 'Commercial viability should be sought' under the subheading 'Market Forces and Information.'

in existence, the more likely it is that an entrenched bureaucracy will capture it. Capture by clients who would run the programme for their own purposes and by politicians who would use the available funds as political pork barrels is likely where a policy provides significant funded assistance to a limited number of firms. The probability of capture is increased when contributions are allocated on a discretionary basis, and when policy objectives and project selection criteria are ill defined. Political capture also becomes more likely the more publicity surrounds the creation and operation of the policy or programme, and the more political concerns are allowed to influence the selection process.

Policies and programmes need independent periodical reviews. Since there is no easy way to guard fully against all types of capture, especially internal capture by bureaucrats, it is essential that policies, programmes, and projects either be sunsetted or be subject to periodic external review by independent agents. Adopting this criterion would greatly reduce the chances of failure for future policies and programmes. Yet, this is so rarely written into the design that one has to wonder about the political will to create programmes that really do what they are supposed to do.

Structural Relationships

Attention needs to be paid to the relationship between technology and structure. Changes in either technology or the facilitating structure typically induce changes in the other. If policymakers target only one of these, there will be induced consequences in the other, which will affect the overall performance of the policy or programme, for example, by imposing unforeseen costs or by retarding the targeted developments. If policymakers target technology and structure in ignorance of the interrelations, they may target an inconsistent set of changes that will inhibit attaining their main goals. However, as pointed out in 'Large leaps are dangerous' under the subheading 'Uncertainty', policies and programmes that require large leaps in both technology and structure are prone to failure.

Policies and programmes can play a useful role in inducing and coordinating precommercial R&D efforts. Policies and programmes can assist in gathering and disseminating non-appropriable technical information. They can also provide mechanisms through which firms can credibly commit to jointly conducting precommercial R&D, thus reducing the hoarding of such knowledge and minimizing costly duplication.

Policies and programmes should seek to maximize positive spillovers. We have seen that different technological advances have different spillovers. These depend, among other things, on the current stage in the development trajectory and the number of complementarities, both within the subtechnologies of a main technology and across technology systems.

Market Forces and Information

Market forces and the market expertise of private-sector agents should be utilized wherever possible. Policymakers can successfully intervene to aid innovators provided that commercial and competitive objectives guide the intervention. This implies that market concentration and protection must be balanced against competition in innovation, and policy must respond to commercial signals reflecting viability. Policymakers and administrators are ill advised to dictate business decisions (i.e. they should avoid micro management and the suppressing or ignoring of market signals).

Information coordination and dissemination are important. Not all firms are aware of the current and evolving best-practice technologies that may be of use to them. Policies and programmes that assist in spreading existing technical knowledge can cover the discrete sunk costs of acquisition that are often too high to be taken on by individual firms, especially small ones.

Commercial viability should be sought. Technology for its own sake, commonly called 'technology push', has frequently produced technological marvels that are commercial failures.

Policies and programmes should exploit as much expertise as possible. Although this good advice is obvious, it has been ignored repeatedly in many policies and programmes in many countries. Administering any even moderately complex policy or programme requires a wide variety of expertise, including technological, commercial, financial, and administrative skills. As much as possible, these skills should be developed in-house. Where this is impossible or excessively expensive, mechanisms must be developed to tap outside expertise.

Competition-inducing mechanisms increase the chances of commercial success. Policies and programmes designed to produce interfirm competition in innovation increase the likelihood of commercial success. Such competition also induces a variety of diverse experiments by profit-seeking firms, often yielding a cluster of innovations. This approach stands in contrast to policies that suppress competition by choosing and backing a national champion in terms of a firm or a technology

Firms should have a substantial financial stake in any public-sector initiative that involves them. Those projects that involve private-sector agents but are wholly government-financed are prone to failure for obvious reasons of moral hazard.

Governments should avoid picking winners through their own bureaucratic processes. Success is much more likely when private and public sectors cooperate: both sides providing expertise, with public funds compensating for gaps caused by factors such as externalities and non-appropriability and the high fixed costs of some learning activities, while private-sector agents remain at significant risk for the consequences of failure.

Performance Criteria

We have been mainly concerned in this chapter with basic approaches to technology policy. These have led quite naturally to a discussion of the design and operational criteria outlined in the previous section. We now give only brief mention to the criteria for judging performance, since these are discussed in more detail in Lipsey and Carlaw (1998*b*).

The main test of the efficacy of policies and programmes is called incrementality in North America and additionality in Europe.[6] The neoclassical and the S-E theories differ, not in their acceptance of incrementality as a necessary condition for success, but in the policy objectives that they recognize and hence the scope of the incrementality tests that they apply.

Those using the neoclassical approach typically use what we call the 'narrow test of incrementality'. When applied to technology policy, this test requires that some thing happens to technology that would not have happened otherwise. No other changes are permitted to enter as policy objectives. The reasons are, first, that the elements of the facilitating structure are not a part of the neoclassical model and, second, that the object of neoclassical policy is to reduce the gap between the private and social marginal products of R&D (see, for example, Tarasofsky 1985, and The Economic Council of Canada 1983).

S-E theorists use what we call the 'broad test of incrementality', which requires that some technologically relevant objective be achieved, either a new or enhanced technology or a change in the facilitating structure. The broad test accepts that a policy may have beneficial incremental effects even if it causes no direct change in technology, as long as it causes a targeted change in the facilitating structure that indirectly encourages technological change. For example, an R&D subsidy may be used as the carrot to induce firms to create research laboratories or to establish closer links with government and university research laboratories, even if it does not affect the technologies currently being developed. This type of policy is not uncommon and, since it fails the narrow test of incrementality, it is often criticized by neoclassical economists.

From our S-E perspective, the distinction between the two concepts of incrementality is important because the myriad technological complementarities that manifest as spillovers and externalities often operate through the facilitating structure in ways that will not show up directly as measured performance. So the narrow definition of incrementality will miss some of the broader effects of technology policy that might push a system onto a superior technological trajectory by altering elements of the facilitating structure.

II.   AN S-E PACKAGE FOR TECHNOLOGY POLICY

In this concluding section, we summarize much of the analysis of Part IV by outlining a policy package stemming from the S-E analysis of technological change. While our focus has been technology enhancement policies for advanced countries, much of what we say is applicable with fairly obvious corrections to developing countries.

---

[6] The use of the term 'incrementality' to describe the results of some technology policy is unfortunate because the same term is used to distinguish incremental from radical technical innovations.

Justification

Because of the uncertainties associated with technological change and because of the non-rivalrous nature of knowledge that makes it unlike a normal private good, we cannot expect to be able to define an optimum policy for encouraging technological advances. Neither can we expect to have a neutral policy that increases R&D across the board without 'distorting' relative incentives from what they would be in a free market. Instead, we look for a broad spectrum of projects that can enhance techno-logical change in ways that informed judgement suggests will be beneficial.

This judgement is to be informed by S-E theory, which identifies many techno-logical complementarities that are the sources of spillovers. These differ in the amount of social benefit following from the chain of technological changes neces-sitated and/or made possible by the innovation in question; they also differ in the proportion of that benefit that can be appropriated by the innovator. In many cases, markets fail to provide what is judged to be sufficient stimulus for invention and innovation. One of the main reasons for this failure is fixed costs, both of creating and acquiring knowledge that is non-rivalrous once it is in existence, and of setting up production facilities for new products and processes. The extent of these failures vary greatly from innovation to innovation.

Objective

The objective of any technology policy or programme should be clear, unambiguous, and single-minded: *to influence the rate of growth by increasing technological change (which includes innovation and diffusion), either generally or in specific directions.* The framers of a particular technology policy may expect it to have benefits in addition to its direct impact on technology. These policy goals should not, however, be muddled by stating expected benefits as if they were explicit policy goals. For example, the framers may hope that the policy will also increase international competitiveness, lower domestic unemployment, and reduce environmental deg-radation. These and other expected indirect benefits can be proclaimed on the political platform but confusion results when they are included as a part of the policy's explicit objectives, as they often are. For example, the perceptions of programmes and projects that should be supported may differ widely among the programme's designers, administrators, and critics because they place different emphasis on the various indirect benefits that have been stated as some of the policy's multiple goals.

A policy or programme designed to pursue the single-minded objective of en-couraging some aspect of technological change may be expected to have some adverse side effects. The policy or programme may nonetheless be accepted if the social benefits are judged to be greater than the costs. Other policies may be designed to address the adverse side effects. It is important, however, that these remedies be set up as separate programmes and hence administered under separate structures. This approach protects the technology policy in question against being sidetracked by having to temper its thrust with potentially conflicting considerations. For example, retraining and relocation schemes, as well as subsidies to slow the rate of regional adjustment, should (in so far as they are desirable at all) be established as separate policies under separate programmes and administrations and not be included as secondary objectives in some regional technology enhancement programme. (This advice is all too often ignored in practice, giving rise to multiple and often conflicting objectives of an individual policy or programme.)

Policy Tools

The single objective should be achieved through a combination of framework, blanket, and focused policies, programmes, and projects, each directed at a particular means of advancing the overall objective.

Framework Policies

At one extreme, framework policies should be used to give broad encouragement to all types of technological advances. R&D tax credits and reasonable protection for intellectual property are both desirable. The level of R&D support is a difficult judgement call. There are inevitable conflicts in administering a support policy through the tax department, as may be done with refundable R&D tax credits, since this department has a strong interest in raising revenue rather than giving it away. For this reason, institutional competence needs to be watched carefully. Does the revenue department have sufficiently knowledgeable and approachable science auditors to ensure that firms obtain the credits to which they are entitled? A strong case can be made for separating the science audit, which determines whether or not a firm has done R&D within the meaning of the legislation, from the financial audit, which determines whether or not the money was really spent on the eligible categories. This suggestion highlights the importance of constantly ensuring that programmes that look good on paper are administered by departments with the correct collection of abilities, training, and mindset.

Intellectual property protection needs to be set within the limits allowed by international agreements, at levels that provide adequate incentives for technological advances while minimizing payments beyond those levels. For example, the current patent life allowed for pharmaceuticals may be too long by that criterion, as was James Watt's patent on the basic design of a steam-driven piston. Watt's patent inhibited the development of the high-pressure engines needed for steam to spread into the transportation industry, a development that happened only after his patent expired in 1800.

Focused Policies

At the other extreme, focused policies and programmes should be used where markets are working poorly or not at all, especially when these problems are localized. Focused policies may be suitable to help the development of major new technologies that will be beneficial to all but where appropriation is either impossible or, where possible, would slow development. A case in point is the US government's support for research into technologies required by the rapidly developing aerospace industry in the period 1919–39. Focused policies may also be useful where new industries need consistent standards imposed on them. The US software industry is largely a creation of US military procurement; during the industry's early stages, the military provided monetary support while imposing uniform standards that greatly benefited the industry long after it had become self-sustaining.

Focused policies may also have a role when several competing firms are seeking a particular breakthrough. In some cases, non-patentable research cannot be kept secret, and so there is too little incentive to do the research. In other cases, the non-patentable research can be kept secret and the competing firms may duplicate each other's research. (When uncertainty calls for many different experiments, 'duplication' can be an advantage, but when all firms are pushing for the same fairly well-defined breakthrough, duplication may be largely wasteful and results may be produced more slowly than when firms cooperate.) In both sets of cases, a focused policy can create commitment mechanisms that allow firms to cooperate on pre-commercial research and then start competitive commercial research with all firms on the same footing—something that MITI was particularly good at during its heyday.

Dealing with these and similar cases requires carefully focused policies. The dangers involved are many. Capture either by politicians or client firms is much easier than with broader-based policies. Mistakes can be wasteful, particularly when the policies seek to foster national prestige or other non-commercial goals. The wrong sort of administrators can easily become enamoured with technological push, creating technological wonders that have little or no commercial value. To avoid these and many of the other pitfalls, the focused policies need the clear goal of advancing technologies and making them commercially viable. They also need to be administered by staff with the appropriate institutional competence and incentives.

Blanket Policies

In between, there is some place for blanket policies. In principle, a blanket policy is required where the problem being addressed is too localized to be covered by a framework policy and too generalized to be met with a narrowly focused policy. One example is the dissemination of technological knowledge to small firms, for which the fixed cost of scanning all relevant information is often prohibitive. Government bodies can acquire and disseminate such knowledge, spreading the fixed costs over many operations—provided the administrators are well versed in the appropriate technologies as well as in the problems faced by small firms.

The biggest problem with blanket policies is that they typically do not state clear guidelines regarding objectives and selection criteria. Nor are they always given well-trained administrators, particularly when specialized technical knowledge or business experience is needed. All too easily, the programmes then become channels for handing out government largesse without clear purpose or criteria for selection.

Furthermore, poor policy design is much harder to spot in a broad-based blanket policy than in a policy narrowly focused on one specific objective.[7]

Evidence shows that if properly conceived and executed, some blanket policies can work. However, the failure of the others provides a strong cautionary tale showing the dangers inherent in most blanket policies. Perhaps the most important difference between the successes and failures is in the objectives of the different programmes. Many of the programmes fail because, in addition to all the uncertainties associated with supporting innovation projects, they lack an overriding guideline for selecting projects for support. This confusion contrasts with the single, clearly articulated, relatively narrow objectives of some of the successful programmes. Such programmes have been able to build up an internal structure that focused on a particular set of technological problems, thus being able to exploit the relationship between facilitating structure and technology. The internal structures of those that lacked focus had no coordinated connection with the technological problems they were seeking to address.

Furthermore, the single objectives of the focused programmes enabled them to recruit well-trained people of like mind in order to meet their objectives. Those that lacked clear guidelines and had multiple objectives did not discriminate in terms of the kind of personnel employed, and the end result was ambiguity about what was an appropriate project, and why. Thus, another reason why programmes need an overriding objective is to generate structural consistency, in terms of both programme design and expertise of the personnel administering it.

Design

All policies and programmes should meet the design and operational criteria laid out above. Although we do not need to repeat these here, one point needs emphasis. Capture by politicians and clients is a serious problem, which can, and should, be guarded against by good design. However, there is *no design* that can reduce to negligible proportions the threat of capture by the bureaucrats who administer the policy or programme. As time passes, the threat increases. In sharp contrast to the private sector, there is no bottom line to constrain such activities or to punish them if they seriously affect the organization's performance. It follows that compulsory sunsetting or review by independent authorities at fixed time intervals should be a part of all acceptable polices (but seldom is). Auditors General provide some protection but their brief is typically too narrow to do the whole job. Independent authorities need to review the rationale of each policy and programme and assess

---

[7] The series of Canadian programmes that started with PAIT and ended with IRDP illustrates these pitfalls. PAIT evolved a focused objective as it went through a self-revision process to correct problems it had initially experienced in meeting its objective of providing more funding to support innovation projects. With the creation of it successor, EDP, different programmes were integrated into one package and PAIT's single objective was combined with other multiple and vague objectives. This vagueness continued when EDP was succeeded by IRDP. This programme and its predecessors were unsuccessful because, in addition to all the uncertainties associated with supporting innovation projects, they lacked adequate selection criteria (see Lipsey and Carlaw 1998*b*: ch. 3).

both its internal management and its external success. Private consulting firms can sometimes do this job successfully but usually a wider-based group is needed. The group should include technical experts in the areas covered by the policy's objectives, experts in administration, economists, and other relevant experts. The reports should be made public, probably by being presented to the legislature.

If we could make one change to existing policies, programmes, and projects, it would be to adopt this recommendation. If we could make a second change, it would be to treat our design and operational criteria, suitably enlarged by the experience of others, as a required checklist to be used by parliamentary committees and others when they assess the design of proposed new technology policies and programmes.

Summary

In summary, the ideal S-E technology-enhancing policy set has a single aim but multiple policies and programmes to achieve that aim. Framework policies provide the general push. Focused policies cover particular spots where the market fails to achieve desired objectives in substantial and specific ways. A few blanket policies are cautiously applied when a relatively broad-based single need can be identified and clearly communicated to the administrators. Before such middle-range policies are used, very careful study is needed—much fuller and more careful study than has typically gone into the design of policies that have often been hastily thrown together in response to political pressures. Before millions are spent on any new blanket policy, a few tens of thousands should be spent on clearly defining its goals, selection criteria, and administrative structure. In principle, this advice is easier to follow than the neoclassical advice of searching out the optimum level of R&D and instituting neutral policies to achieve it. The advice may, however, be no less difficult to follow in practice.

Bibliography

Adams, James (1991). *Flying Buttresses, Entropy and O-Rings: The World of an Engineer.* Cambridge, MA: Harvard University Press.

Adams, Robert M. (1960). 'Early Civilizations, Subsistence, and Environment', in Carl H. Kraeling and Robert M. Adams (eds.), *City Invincible.* Chicago: University of Chicago Press.

—— (1965). *Land Behind Baghdad: A History of Settlement on the Diyala Plains.* Chicago: University of Chicago Press.

—— (1996). *Paths of Fire: An Anthropologist's Inquiry into Western Technology.* Princeton, NJ: Princeton University Press.

Adkins, Lesley and Roy Adkins (1997). *Handbook to Life in Ancient Greece.* New York: Facts on File.

Aghion, P. and P. Howitt (1992). 'A Model of Growth Through Creative Destruction', *Econometrica*, 60: 232–396.

—— —— (1998). 'On the Macroeconomic Effects of Major Technological Change', in Elhanan Helpman (ed.), *General Purpose Technologies and Economic Growth.* Cambridge, MA: MIT Press, 21–144.

Akerlof (2002). 'Behavioral Macroeconomics and Macroeconomic Behavior', *The American Economics Review*, June.

Alchian, Armen A. (1950). 'Uncertainty, Evolution and Economic Theory', *Journal of Political Economy*, 58: 211–21.

Allen, Robert C. (2001). 'The Great Divergence in European Wages and Prices from the Middle Ages to the First World War', *Explorations in Economic History*, 38(4): 411–47.

Archibald G. Christopher, B. Curtis Eaton, and Richard G. Lipsey (1986). 'Address Models of Value Theory', in J. S. Stigliz and G. F. Mathewson (eds.), *New Developments in the Analysis of Market Structure.* Cambridge, MA: MIT Press, 3–47.

Arrow, Kenneth J. (1962*a*). 'Economic Welfare and the Allocation of Resources for Innovation', in *Rate and Direction of Economic Activity.* NBER Conference series.

—— (1962*b*). 'Economic Implication of Learning by Doing', *Review of Economic Studies*, 29: 155–73.

Arthur, W. Brian (1992). 'On Learning and Adaptation in the Economy', *Santa Fe Institute Working Paper*, 92: 7–38.

—— (1994). *Increasing Returns and Path Dependence in the Economy.* Ann Arbor, MI: University of Michigan Press.

—— (1988). 'Competing Technologies: An Overview', in G. Dosi et al. (eds.), *Technical Change and Economic Theory.* London: Pinter, 590–607.

Ashton, Thomas, S. (1955). *An Economic History of England: The 18th Century.* London: Methuen & Co.

Backus, D., P. Kehoe, and T. Kehoe (1992). 'In Search of Scale Effects in Trade and Growth', *Journal of Economic Theory*, 58: 377–409.

Bailey, R. (2000). 'Petri Dish Politics', in L. Messina (ed.), *Biotechnology.* New York: The H.W. Wilson Co.

Balazs, Etienne (1964). *Chinese Civilization and Bureaucracy.* New Haven, CT: Yale University Press.

Baldwin, John and Petr Hanel (2003). *Innovation and Knowledge Creation in an Open Economy: Canadian Industry and International Implications.* Cambridge: Cambridge University Press.

Barraclough, Geoffrey (1978). *The Times Atlas of World History.* London: Times Books.

Barro, R. J. (1990). 'Government Spending in a Simple Model of Endogenous Growth', *Journal of Political Economy,* 98: 103–26.

—— (1999). 'Notes on Growth Accounting', *Journal of Economic Growth,* 4: 119–37.

Baumol, William J. (2002). *The Free-Market Innovation Machine: Analyzing the Growth Miracle of Capitalism.* Princeton, NJ: Princeton University Press.

—— Alan S. Blinder, and Edward N. Wolff (2003), *Downsizing in America: Reality, Causes and Consequences.* New York: Russell Sage Foundation Press.

Beeching, Jack (1982). *The Galleys at Lepanto.* London: Hutchinson.

Bekar, Clifford and Richard G. Lipsey (forthcoming 2005) 'Science Institutions and the Industrial Revolution', *Journal of European Economic History.*

Berman, Harold (1983). *Law and Revolution.* Cambridge, MA: Harvard University Press.

Blaine, Bradford B. (1976). 'The Enigmatic Water-Mill', in Bert S. Hall and Delno C. West (eds.), *On Pre-Modern Technology and Science: A Volume of Studies in Honor of Lynn White Jr.* Malibu: Undena Publications.

Blaug, Mark (1992) *The Methodology of Economics,* 2nd edn. Cambridge: Cambridge University Press.

—— (1997). 'Competition as an End-State and Competition as a Process', in *Trade Technology and Economics: Essays in Honour of Richard G. Lipsey.* Cheltenham, UK: Edward Elgar.

Blum, Jerome (1982). *Our Forgotten Past: Seven Centuries of Life on the Land.* London: Thames & Hudson.

Bodde, Derk (1963). 'Basic Concepts of Chinese Law: The Genesis and Evolution of Legal Thought in Traditional China', in Dorothy Borei and Charles Le Blanc (eds.), *Essays on Chinese Civilization,* 2nd edn. (1981). Princeton, NJ: Princeton University Press.

—— (1981). *Essays on Chinese Civilization.* Princeton, NJ: Princeton University Press.

Böhm-Bawerk, E. (1889). *Positive Theory of Capital.* New York: W. Smart.

Bowers, B. (1996). 'Electricity', in Ian McNeil (ed.), *An Encyclopaedia of the History of Technology.* London: Routledge.

Braudel, Fernand (1982). *Civilization & Capitalism 15th–18th Century,* 3-vol. series. New York: Harper & Row.

Bresnahan, Timothy F. and Manuel Trajtenberg (1992). 'General Purpose Technologies: Engines of Growth?' NBER Working Paper, No. 4148.

Browne, Edward G. (1962). *Arabian Medicine.* New York: Cambridge University Press.

Burnham, James (1942). *The Managerial Revolution: Or What is Happening in the World Now.* London: Putnam.

Caballero, R. and R. Lyons (1992). 'External Effects in the U.S. Procyclical Productivity', *Journal of Monetary Economics,* 29: 209–26.

Cambridge Encyclopaedia (1990). Cambridge: Cambridge University Press.

Cardwell, D. S. L. (1995). *The Norton History of Technology.* New York: Norton.

—— (1971). *From Watt to Clausius: The Rise of Thermodynamics in the Early Industrial Age.* London: Heinemann.

Carlaw, Kenneth I. (2000). *Uuncertainty and Complementarity Lead to Scale Effects in the Production of Capital*, Ph.D. dissertation. Vancouver: Simon Fraser University.

—— (2004). 'Uncertainty and Complementarity Lead to Increasing Returns to Durability', *Journal or Economic Behaviour and Organization*, 53(2): 261–82.

Carlaw, Kenneth I. and Richard G. Lipsey (2001). 'Externalities versus Technological Complementarities: A Model of GPT-driven, Sustained Growth'. Paper presented at the Conference in Honour of the 20th Anniversary of Nelson and Winter's Book *An Evolutionary Theory of Economic Change*, Aalborg, Denmark, 12–15 June 2001.

—— —— (2002). 'Externalities, Technological Complementarities and Sustained Economic Growth', *Research Policy*, 31: 1305–15.

—— —— (2003) 'Productivity, Technology and Economic Growth: What is the relationship?' *Journal of Economic Surveys*, 17(3): 457–95.

—— —— (2006, forthcoming). 'GPT-Driven Endogenous Growth', *Economic Journal*.

Carus-Wilson, E. M. (1941). 'An Industrial Revolution of the Thirteenth Century', *The Economic History Review*, 11(1): 39–60.

Chandler, Alfred, D. (1977). *The Visible Hand: The Managerial Revolution in American Business*. Cambridge, MA: Harvard University Press.

—— (1990). *Scale and Scope: The Dynamics of Industrial Capitalism*. Cambridge, MA: Belknap Press.

—— (2001). *Inventing the Electronic Century: The Epic Story of the Consumer and Computer Industries*. New York: Free Press.

Chapam, S. D. (1972). *The Cotton Industry in the Industrial Revolution*. London: Macmillan Education.

Chen, E. K. Y. (1997). 'The Total Factor Productivity Debate: Determinants of Economic Growth in East Asia', *Asian Pacific Literature*, 11: 18–38.

Christianson, Gale, E. (1984). *In the Presence of the Creator: Isaac Newton & His Times*. New York: Free Press.

Clapham, Michael (1957). 'Printing', in Charles Singer et al. (eds.), *A History of Technology*, Vol. 2: *From the Renaissance to the Industrial Revolution*. Oxford: Oxford University Press, 377–411.

Clark, Gregory (2001). 'The Second History of the Industrial Revolution', mimeo. Davis, CA: University of California.

Cohen, Joel E. (1995). *How Many People Can the Earth Support?* London: W.W. Norton.

Colander, David (2003). 'Are Institutionalists an Endangered Species?', *Journal of Economic Issues*, 37(1): 111–22.

Collins, F. and K. Jegalian (2000). 'Deciphering the Code of Life', in L. Messina (ed.), *Biotechnology*. New York: The H.W. Wilson Co.

Courant, R. (1934). *Differential and Integral Calculus*. London: Blackie & Son.

Crafts, N. F. R. (1985). *British Economic Growth During the Industrial Revolution*. Oxford: Clarendon.

—— (2003). 'Steam as a General Purpose Technology: A Growth Accounting Perspective', LSE Working Paper, 75/03.

—— and C. K. Harley (1992). 'Output Growth and the Industrial Revolution', *Economic History Review*, 45: 703–30.

Dahrendorf, Ralf (1982). *On Britain*. Chicago: University of Chicago Press.

David, Paul (1991*a*). 'The Hero and the Herd in Technological History', in P. Higonnet, D. Landes, and H. Rosovsky (eds.), *Favorites of Fortune*. Cambridge, MA: Harvard University Press.

—— (1991*b*). *Computer and Dynamo: The Modern Productivity Paradox in a Not Too Distant Mirror.* Paris: OECD.

—— (1997). 'Path Dependence and the Quest for Historical Economics: One More Chorus', Discussion Papers in Economic and Social History, No. 20. Oxford University.

Day, Lance (1996). 'Language, Writing, Printing and Graphic Arts', in Ian McNeil (ed.), *An Encyclopedia of the History of Technology.* New York: Routledge.

Dertouzos, Michael L., Richard Lester, and Robert Solow (1989). *Made in America: Regaining the Productive Edge.* London: MIT Press.

Diamond, Jared M. (1992). *The Rise and Fall of the Third Chimpanzee.* London: Vintage.

—— (1997). *Guns, Germs, and Steel: The Fates of Human Societies.* New York: W.W. Norton.

Diffie, Bailey W. and George D. Winius (1977). *Foundations of the Portuguese Empire, 1415–1580.* Minneapolis: University of Minnesota Press.

Dosi, Giovanni (1997). 'Opportunities, Incentives and the Collective Patterns of Technological Change', *The Economic Journal,* 107(444): 1530–47.

—— and L. Orsenigo (1988). 'Coordination and Transformation: An Overview of Structures, Behaviours and Change in Evolutionary Environments', in G. Dosi et al. (eds.), *Technical Change and Economic Theory.* London: Pinter.

—— Christopher Freeman, Richard Nelson, Gerald Silverberg, and Luc Soete (eds.) (1988). *Technical Change and Economic Theory.* London: Pinter.

Drews, Robert (1993). *The End of the Bronze Age: Changes in Warfare and the Catastrophe CA. 1200 BC.* Princeton, NJ: Princeton University Press.

Drexler, K. Eric (1986). *Engines of Creation, Coming of the Era of Nanotechnology.* Garden City, NY: Anchor Press/Doubleday.

Dudley, L. (1991). *The Word and The Sword: How Techniques of Information and Violence Have Shaped Our World.* Cambridge: Cambridge University Press.

Dyer, Christopher (1989). *Standards of Living in the Later Middle Ages: Social Change in England c.1200–1520,* rev. edn. Cambridge: Cambridge University Press.

Easterlin, Richard Ainley (1998). *Growth Triumphant: The Twenty-First Century in Historical Perspective.* Ann Arbor, MI: University of Michigan Press.

Eaton, B. Curtis and Richard G. Lipsey (1989). 'Product Differentiation', in R. Schmalensee and R. Willig (eds.), *Handbook of Industrial Organization.* Amsterdam: North-Holland, 725–68.

—— —— (1997). *On the Foundations of Monopolistic Competition and Economic Geography: The Selected Essays of B. Curtis Eaton and Richard G. Lipsey.* Cheltenham, UK: Edward Elgar.

Eatwell, J., M. Milgate, and P. Newman (eds.) (1987). *The New Palgrave: A Dictionary of Economics.* London: Macmillan.

Economic Council of Canada, The (1983). *The Bottom Line: Technology, Trade and Income Growth.* Ottawa: Economic Council of Canada.

Eisenstein, Elizabeth L. (1979). *The Printing Press as an Agent of Change: Communications and Cultural Transformations in Early Modern Europe.* New York: Cambridge University Press.

—— (1983). *The Printing Revolution in Early Modern Europe.* New York: Cambridge University Press.

Epstein, Richard Allen (1998). *Principles for a Free Society: Reconciling Individual Liberty with the Common Good.* Reading, MA: Perseus Books.

Evans, F. (1997). 'Roads, Railways, and Canals: Technical Choices in 19th-Century Britain', in T. Reynolds and S. Cutcliffe (eds.), *Technology and the West.* Chicago: University of Chicago Press.

Febvre, Lucien and Henri-Jean Martin (1997). *The Coming of the Book: The Impact of Printing 1450–1800*. London: Verso Books.

Feinstein, Charles (1998). 'Pessimism Perpetuated: Real Wages and the Standards of Living in Britain During and After the Industrial Revolution, *Journal of Economic History*, 58(3): 625–58.

Fletcher, R. A. (2003). *The Cross and the Crescent: Christianity and Islam from Muhammad to the Reformation*. London: Allen Lane.

Fogel Robert, William (1964). *Railroads and American Economic Growth. Essays in Econometric History*. Baltimore, MD: Johns Hopkins Press.

Forbes, R. J. (1964). *Studies in Ancient Technology*, vol. 9. Leiden: E. J. Brill.

—— (1967). 'Extracting, Smelting, and Alloying', in C. Singer, E. J. Holmyard, and A. R. Hall (eds.), *A History of Technology*. Oxford: Clarendon Press.

Frank, Robert H. and Philip J. Cook (1995). *The Winner-Take-All Society: How More and More Americans Compete for Ever Fewer and Bigger Prizes, Encouraging Economic Waste, Income Inequality, and an Impoverished Cultural Life*. New York: Free Press.

Freeman, Christopher and Francisco Louçã (2001). *As Time Goes By: From the Industrial Revolutions to the Information Revolution*. Oxford: Oxford University Press.

——and Luc Soete (eds.) (1987). *Technical Change and Full Employment*. New York: Basil Blackwell.

—— and Carlota Perez (1988). 'Structural Crises of Adjustment: Business Cycles and Investment Behaviour', in Dosi et al. (ed.), *Technical Change and Economic Theory*. London: Pinter, 38–66.

—— J. Clark, and Luc Soete (1982). *Unemployment and Technical Innovation: A study of Long Waves and Economic Development*. London: Pinter.

Friedman, Milton (1953). 'The Methodology of Positive Economics', in *Essays in Positive Economics*. Chicago: University of Chicago Press.

Galor, Oded and David N. Weil (2000). 'Population, Technology, and Growth: From Malthusian Stagnation to the Demographic Transition and Beyond', *American Economic Review*, 90(4).

Geremek, B. (1997). *Poverty: A History*. Oxford: Blackwell.

Gies, Frances and Joseph Gies (1994). *Cathedral, Forge, and Waterwheel: Technology and Invention in the Middle Ages*. New York: HarperCollins.

Gimpel, Jean (1993). *The Medieval Machine: The Industrial Revolution of the Middle Ages*. London: Plimlico.

Goldschmidt, E. P. (1967). *Gothic and Renaissance Bookbindings*. Nieuwkoop: B. de Graaf.

Goldstone, J. (2002). 'Efflorescences and Economic Growth in World History: Rethinking the "Rise of the West" and the Industrial Revolution', *Journal of World History*, 13(2): 323–90.

Gordon, Robert, J. (2000). 'Does the "New Economy" Measure up to the Great Inventions of the Past?', NBER Working Paper, 7833.

Grace, C. S. (1997). *Biotechnology Unzipped: Promises and Realities*. Toronto: Trifolium Books.

Grant, Edward (1996). *The Foundations of Modern Science in the Middle Ages: Their Religious, Intuitional, and Intellectual Contexts*. Cambridge: Cambridge University Press.

Grantham, George (1999). 'Contra Ricardo: On the Macroeconomics of Europe's Agrarian Age', *European Review of Economic History*, 3: 199–232.

Griffiths, Peter (2003). *The Economist's Tale: A Consultant Encounters Hunger and the World Bank*. New York: ZED Books.

Griliches, Z. (1992). 'The Search for R&D Spillovers', *Scandinavian Journal of Economics*, 94(suppl.): 29–47.

Grossman, Gene M. and Elhanan Helpman (1991). *Innovation and Growth in the Global Economy*. Cambridge, MA: MIT Press.

Grübler, Arnulf (1998). *Technology and Global Change*. Cambridge: Cambridge University Press.

Hanson Victor, Davis (2001). *Carnage and Culture: Landmark Battles in the Rise of Western Power*. New York: Doubleday.

Harris, Richard (1998). 'The Internet as a GPT: Factor Market', in Elhanan Helpman (ed.), *General Purpose Technologies and Economic Growth*. Cambridge, MA: MIT Press, 145–66.

Hassan, Fekri A. (1981). *Demographic Archaeology*. New York: Academic Press.

Hawke, G. R. (1970). *Railways and Economic Growth in England and Wales, 1840–1870*. Oxford: Clarendon Press.

Head, Simon (2003). *The New Ruthless Economy: Work and Power in the Digital Age*. Oxford: Oxford University Press.

Helliwell, John F. (2002). *Globalization and Well-Being*. Vancouver: UBC Press.

Helpman, Elhanan (ed.) (1998). *General Purpose Technologies and Economic Growth*. Cambridge, MA: MIT Press.

—— and M. Trajtenberg (1998*a*). 'A Time to Sow and a Time to Reap', in Elhanan Helpman (ed.), *General Purpose Technologies and Economic Growth*. Cambridge, MA: MIT Press, 55–84.

—— —— (1998*b*). 'Diffusion of General Purpose Technologies', in Elhanan Helpman (ed.), *General Purpose Technologies and Economic Growth*. Cambridge, MA: MIT Press, 85–119.

Herman, Arthur (2001). *How the Scots Invented the Modern World*. New York: Three Rivers Press.

Hirsch, Rudolf (1974). *Printing, Selling and Reading, 1450–1550*. Wiesbaden: Harrassowitz.

Hiscock, Eric C. (1965). *Cruising Under Sail*. Oxford: Oxford University Press.

Hodgson, Geoffrey M. (2002). *How Economists Forgot History: The Problem of Historical Specificity in Social Science*. London: Routledge.

Holt, Richard (1988). *The Mills of Medieval England*. Oxford: Basil Blackwell.

—— (1996). 'Medieval Technology and the Historians: The Evidence for the Mill', in Robert Fox (ed.), *Technological Change: Methods and Themes in the History of Technology*. Amsterdam: Harwood Academic.

—— (1997). 'Mechanization and the Medieval English Economy', in Elizabeth Bradford Smith and Michael Wolfe (eds.), *Technology and Resource Use in Medieval Europe: Cathedrals, Mills and Mines*. Aldershot: Ashgate Publishing.

Hourani, Albert (1991). *A History of the Arab Peoples*. Cambridge, MA: Harvard University Press.

Howell, F. Clark (1965). *Early Man*. New York: Time.

Howitt, Peter (1999). 'Steady Endogenous Growth with Population and R&D Inputs Growing', *Journal of Political Economy*, 107(4): 715–30.

—— (2006). 'Agent-Based Computational Economics', in Kenneth L. Judd and Leigh Tesfatsion (eds.), *Handbook of Computational Economics*, Vol. 2. Amsterdam: North-Holland.

Huff, Toby E. (1993). *The Rise of Early Modern Science: Islam, China and the West*. Cambridge: Cambridge University Press.

Hughes, Thomas P. (1983). *Networks of Power: Electrification in Western Society, 1880–1930*. Baltimore: Johns Hopkins University Press.

Hulten, Charles R. (1979). 'On the Importance of Productivity Change', *American Economic Review*, 65: 126–36.

—— (2000). 'Total Factor Productivity: A Short Biography', NBER Working Paper, 7471.

Hutchinson, Gillian (1994). *Medieval Ships and Shipping*. London: Leicester University Press.

Innis, H. (1972). *Empire and Communications*. Toronto: University of Toronto Press.

Jacob, Margaret C. (1997). *Scientific Culture and the Making of the Industrial West*. Oxford: Oxford University Press.

Jones, Charles I. (1995). 'R&D Based Models of Economic Growth', *Journal of Political Economy*, 103(4): 759–84.

Jones, Eric (1981). *The European Miracle: Environments, Economies and Geopolitics in the History of Europe and Asia*. Cambridge: Cambridge University Press.

—— (1988). *Growth Recurring: Economic Change in World History*. Oxford: Oxford University Press.

Jorgensen, Dale (2001). 'Information Technology in the U.S. Economy', *American Economic Review*, 91: 1–31.

—— (2002). 'American Economic Growth in the Information Age', *ISUMA* (*Canadian Journal of Policy Research*), 3(1): 24–33.

—— and Z. Griliches (1967). 'The Explanation of Productivity Change', *Review of Economic Studies*, 34: 249–83.

Kahneman, D. and A. Tversky (1979). 'Prospect Theory: An Analysis of Decision Under Risk', *Econometrica*, 47(2): 263–91.

Kaldor, Nicholas and James A. Mirrlees (1962). 'A New Model of Economic Growth', *The Review of Economic Studies*, 29(3): 174–92.

Katz, Michael L. and Carl Shapiro (1994). 'Systems Competition and Network Effects', *The Journal of Economic Perspectives*, 8(2): 93–115.

Kearney, Hugh (1971). *Science and Change, 1500–1700*. Toronto: McGraw-Hill.

Knetsch, Jack L. and J. A. Sinden (1987). 'The Perspective of Evaluation Disparities', *Quarterly Journal of Economics*, 102: 691–5.

Knight, Frank Hyneman (1921). *Risk, Uncertainty and Profit*. New York: Houghton Mifflin.

Koopmans, T. C. (1957). *Three Essays on the State of Economic Science*. New York: McGraw-Hill.

Krugman, Paul (1996). 'The Myth of Asia's Miracle', in *Pop Internationalism*. Cambridge, MA: MIT Press.

Landes, David (1969). *The Unbound Prometheus: Technological Change and Industrial Development*. London: Cambridge University Press.

—— (1983). *Revolution in Time: Clocks and the Making of the Modern World*. Cambridge, MA: Harvard University Press.

—— (1998). *The Wealth and Poverty of Nations*. New York: W.W. Norton.

Lawrence, Robert Z. and David E. Weinstein (2001). 'Trade and Growth: Import-Led or Export-Led? Evidence from Japan and Korea', in Joseph E. Stiglitz and Shahid Yusuf (eds.), *Rethinking the East Asian Miracle*. New York: Oxford University Press and the World Bank.

Leibenstein, H. (1987). *Inside the Firm: The Inefficiencies of Hierarchy*. Cambridge, MA: Harvard University Press.

Lewis, Bernard (1953). 'Some Observations on the Significance of Heresy in the History of Islam', *Studia Islamica*, 1: 43–63.

—— (1970). 'The Arabs in Eclipse', in Carlo M. Cipolla (ed.), *The Economic Decline of Empires*. London: Methuen & Co.

Lewis, Frank and Mary MacKinnon (1987). 'Government Loan Guarantees and the Failure of the Canadian Northern Railway', *The Journal of Economic History*, 47(1): 175–96.

Liebowitz, S. J. and Stephen E. Margolis (1994). 'Network Externality: An Uncommon Tragedy', *The Journal of Economic Perspectives*, 8(2): 133–50.

Lilley, Sam (1966). *Men, Machines and History: The Story of Tools and Machines in Relation to Social Progress*. New York: International Pub.

Lindberg, David C. (1992). *The Beginnings of Western Science*. Chicago: University of Chicago Press.

Lipsey, Richard G. (1994). 'Markets, Technological Change and Economic Growth', Quaid-I-Azam Invited Lecture, *The Pakistan Development Review*, 33: 327–52.

—— (1997). 'Globalization and National Government Policies: An Economists View', in John Dunning (ed.), *Governments, Globalization, and International Business*. Oxford: Oxford University Press, 73–113.

—— (2000). 'New Growth Theories and Economic Policy for the Knowledge Economy', in Kjell Rubenson and Hans G. Schuetze (eds.), *Transition to the Knowledge Society: Policies and Strategies for Individual Participation and Learning*. Vancouver, BC: University of British Columbia Press.

—— (2001). 'Successes and Failures in the Transformation of Economics', *The Journal of Economic Methodology*, 8(2): 169–201.

—— (2002a). 'Some Implications of Endogenous Technological Change for Technology Policies in Developing Countries', *Economics of Innovation and New Technology*, 11(4–5): 321–51.

—— (2002b). 'The Productivity Paradox: A Case of the Emperor's New Clothes', *ISUMA (Canadian Journal of Policy Research)*, 3(1): 120–6.

—— and C. Bekar (1995). 'A Structuralist View of Technical Change and Economic Growth', *Bell Canada Papers on Economic and Public Policy*, 3: 9–75, Kingston: John Deutsch Institute.

—— and Kenneth I. Carlaw (1996). 'A Structuralist View of Innovation Policy', in Peter Howitt (ed.), *The Implications of Knowledge-Based Growth*. Calgary: University of Calgary Press.

—— —— (1998a). 'Technology Policies in Neoclassical and Structuralist-Evolutionary Models', *OECD Science, Technology and Industry Review*, No 22, Special Issue, 31–73.

—— —— (1998b). *Structural Assessment of Technology Policies: Taking Schumpeter Seriously on Policy*. Ottawa: Industry Canada, October.

—— —— (2004). 'Total Factor Productivity and the Measurement of Technological Change', *Canadian Journal of Economics*, 37(4): 1118–50.

—— and K. Lancaster (1956). 'The General Theory of Second Best', *The Review of Economic Studies*, 24: 11–32.

—— and Russell Wills (1996). 'Science and Technology Policies in Asia-Pacific Countries: Challenges and Opportunities for Canada', in Richard Harris (ed.), *The Asia-Pacific Region in the Global Economy: A Canadian Perspective*. Calgary: University of Calgary Press, 577–612.

—— and Clifford Bekar and Kenneth I. Carlaw (1998a). 'What Requires Explanation' in Elhanan Helpman (1998), 15–54.

—— —— (1998b). 'The Consequences of Changes in GPTs', in Elhanan Helpman (1998), 194–218.

Livi-Bacci, Massimo (1997). *A Concise History of World Population*. Oxford: Blackwell.

Lucas, R. E. (1988). 'On the Mechanics of Economic Development', *Journal of Monetary Economics*, 22: 3–42.

MacFarlane, Alan (1997). *The Savage Wars of Peace: England, Japan and The Malthusian Trap.* Oxford: Blackwell.

Makdisi, George (1981). *The Rise of Colleges: Institutions of Learning in Islam and the West.* Edinburgh: Edinburgh University Press.

——(1990). *The Rise of Humanism in Classical Islam and the Christian West.* Edinburgh: Edinburgh University Press.

Malthus, T. R. (1872). *An Essay on the Principle of Population*, 7th edn. Reprinted with Introduction in 1973. Great Britain: J. M. Dent & Sons.

Mankiw, N., D. Romer, and D. N. Weil (1992). 'A Contribution to the Empirics of Economic Growth', *Quarterly Journal of Economics*, 107(2): 407–37.

Maskin, E. and J. Tirole (1987). 'A Theory of Dynamic Oligopoly, III: Cournot Competition', *European Economic Review*, 947–68.

McNeill, William (1976). *Plagues and Peoples.* Garden City, NY: Anchor Press.

—— (1982). *The Pursue of Power.* Chicago: University of Chicago Press.

Messina, L. (ed.) (2000). *Biotechnology.* New York: The H.W. Wilson Co.

Mieroop, Marc VanDe (1997). *The Ancient Mesopotamian City.* Oxford: Clarendon Press.

Minski, Marvin (1986). 'Foreword', in Eric K. Drexler (ed.), *Engines of Creation: Coming of the Era of Nanotechnology.* Garden City, NY: Anchor Press/Doubleday.

Mitch, David (1999). 'The Role of Education and Skill in the British Industrial Revolution', in Joel Mokyr (ed.), *The British Industrial Revolution: An Economic Perspective.* Oxford: Westview.

Mokyr, Joel (1990). *The Lever of Riches: Technological Creativity and Economic Progress.* New York: Oxford University Press.

—— (ed.) (1999). *The British Industrial Revolution: An Economic Perspective.* Oxford: Westview.

—— (2002). *The Gifts of Athena: Historical Origins of the Knowledge Economy.* Princeton, NJ: Princeton University Press.

Moser, Petra and Tom Nicholas (2004). 'Was Electricity a General Purpose Technology? Evidence from Historical Patent Citations', *AEA Papers and Proceedings*, 94(2): 288–394.

Mowery, David C. and Richard R. Nelson (1999). *Sources of Industrial Leadership: Studies of Seven Industries.* Cambridge: Cambridge University Press.

Muhly, J. D. (1980). 'The Bronze Age Setting', in T. A. Wertime and J. D. Muhly (eds.), *The Coming of the Age of Iron.* New Haven, CT: Yale University Press.

Musson, A. E. (1963). 'Introduction', in H. W. Dickinson (ed.), *Short History of the Steam Engine.* New York: Macmillan.

—— (1972). *Science, Technology, and Economic Growth in the Eighteenth Century.* Methuen: London.

—— (1980). 'The Engineering Industry', in R. Church (ed.), *The Dynamics of Victorian Business.* London: Allen & Unwin, 87–107.

—— and Eric Robinson (1989). *Science and Technology in the Industrial Revolution.* USA: Gordon and Breach.

Myrdal, Gunnar (1958). *Rich Lands and Poor.* New York: Harpers and Brothers.

Needham, Joseph (1954). *Science and Civilisation in China.* Cambridge: Cambridge University Press.

Nelson, Daniel (1980). *Fredrick W. Taylor and the Rise of Scientific Management*. Madison: The University of Wisconsin Press.

Nelson, R. (1964). 'Aggregate Production Function and Medium-Range Growth Projections', *American Economic Review*, 54: 575–606.

—— and H. Pack (1997). 'The Asian Miracle and Modern Growth Theory', World Bank Research Working Paper, 1881.

—— and S. Winter (1982). *An Evolutionary Theory of Economic Change*. Cambridge, MA: Harvard University Press.

New Oxford Dictionary of English, The (1999). Oxford: Oxford University Press.

North, D. C. (1981). *Structure and Change in Economic History*. New York: Norton.

—— (1990). *Institutions, Institutional Change and Economic Performance*. Cambridge: Cambridge University Press.

—— and Robert Paul Thomas (1973). *The Rise of the Western World: A New Economic History*. Cambridge: Cambridge University Press.

Nye, D. (1990). *Electrifying America: Social Meanings of a New Technology, 1880–1940*. Cambridge, MA: MIT Press.

Ormrod, David (2003). *The Rise of Commercial Empires: England and the Netherlands in the Age of Mercantilism, 1650–1770*. New York: Cambridge University Press.

Pacey, A. (1975). *The Maze of Ingenuity*. New York: Holmes and Meier.

Parkin, T. G. (1992). *Demography and Roman Society*. London: The Johns Hopkins University Press.

Perez, C. (1983). 'Structural Change and the Assimilation of New Technologies in Economic and Social Systems', *Futures*, 15(5): 357–75.

—— (1985). 'Microelectronics, Long Waves and World Structural Change', *World Development*, 13(3): 441–63.

Pfeiffer, J. E. (1978). *The Emergence of Man*. New York: Harper and Row.

Phillips, P. C. (2003). 'Challenges of Trending Time Series Econometrics', Proceeding of the Modelling and Simulation Society of Australia and New Zealand International Congress, 3. *http://mssanz.org.au/modsim03/Media/Articles/Vol%203% 20Articles/945–952.pdf*

Piore Michael, J. and Charles F. Sabel (1984). *The Second Industrial Divide: Possibilities for Prosperity*. New York: Basic Books.

Polanyi, Karl (1957). 'Marketless Trading in Hammurabi's Time', in K. Polanyi, C. M. Arensberg, and H. W. Pearson (eds.), *Trade and Markets in the Early Empires*. Chicago: Regnery.

Pomeranz, Kenneth (2000). *The Great Divergence: China, Europe and the Making of the Modern World Economy*. Princeton, NJ: Princeton University Press.

Porter, Michael E. (1990). *The Competitive Advantage of Nations*. New York: Free Press.

Pumfrey, Stephen (2002). *Latitude & the Magnetic Earth*. Cambridge: Icon Books.

Qian, Wen-yuan (1985). *The Great Inertia: Scientific Stagnation in Traditional China*. Beckenham Kent: Croom Helm.

Rae, John (1905). *The Sociological Theory of Capital*. New York: Macmillan. First published in 1834 as *Statement of Some New Principles on the Subject of Political Economy Exposing the Fallacies of the System of Free trade and of Some Other Doctrines Maintained in the Wealth of Nations*.

Ransom, P. J. G. (1996). 'Rail', in *An Encyclopedia of the History of Technology*. New York: Routledge.

Regis, E. (1995). *Nano, The Emerging Science of Nanotechnology.* New York: Little, Brown and Co.

Reynolds, Robert L. (1967). *Europe Emerges: Transition Towards an Industrial Worldwide Society, 600–1750.* Madison, WI: University of Wisconsin Press.

Riddle, J. M. (1992). *Contraception and Abortion: From the Ancient World to the Renaissance.* Cambridge, MA: Harvard University Press.

—— J. W. Estes, and J. C. Russell (1994). 'Ever since Eve: Birth Control in the Ancient World', *Archaeology,* 47: 29–35.

Roaf, Michael (1990). *Cultural Atlas of Mesopotamia and the Ancient Near East.* Oxford: Facts of File.

Roberts, J. M. (1993). *History of the World.* New York: Oxford University Press.

Rodrik, Dani (1993). 'Taking Trade Policy Seriously: Export Subsidization as a Case Study in Policy Effectiveness', NBER Working Paper, 4567.

—— (1994). 'Getting Interventions Right: How South Korea and Taiwan Grew Rich', NBER Working Paper, 4964.

Rogers, Everett (1995). *Diffusion of Innovations.* New York: Free Press.

Romer, Paul (1986). 'Increasing Returns and Long-Run Growth', *Journal of Political Economy,* October, 94(3): 1002–37.

—— (1990). 'Endogenous Technological Change', *Journal of Political Economy,* 98: S71–102.

—— (1993*a*). 'Two Strategies for Economic Development: Using Ideas and Producing Ideas', Proceedings of the World Bank Annual Research Conference 1992, Supplement to the *World Bank Economic Review,* March, 63–91.

—— (1993*b*). 'Idea Gaps and Object Gaps in Economic Development', *Journal of Monetary Economics,* 32: 543–73.

—— (1994). 'The Origins of Endogenous Growth', *Journal of Economic Perspectives,* 8(1): 3–22.

—— (2001). 'Comment on "It's Not Factor Accumulation: Stylized Facts and Growth Models" by William Easterly and Ross Levine', *World Bank Economic Review,* 15(2): 225–7.

Rose, Mark (1997). 'Ashkelon's Dead Babies', *Archaeology,* 50(2).

Rosenberg, Nathan (1963). 'Technological Change in the Machine Tool Industry, 1840–1910', *The Journal of Economic History,* 23(4): 414–43.

—— (1976). *Perspectives on Technology.* Cambridge: Cambridge University Press.

—— (1982). *Inside the Black Box: Technology and Economics.* Cambridge: Cambridge University Press.

—— (1994). *Exploring the Black Box: Technology, Economics and History.* Cambridge: Cambridge University Press.

—— (1996). 'Uncertainty and Technological Progress', in R. Landau, T. Taylor, and G. Wright (eds.), *The Mosaic of Economic Growth.* Stanford: Stanford University Press.

—— (1998). 'Chemical Engineering as a General Purpose Technology', in Elhanan Helpman (ed.), *General Purpose Technologies and Economic Growth.* Cambridge, MA: MIT Press, 167–92.

—— and L. E. Birdzell (1986). *How the West Grew Rich.* New York: Basic Books.

—— and Manuel Trajtenberg (2004). 'A General Purpose Technology at Work: The Corliss Steam Engine in the Late Nineteenth-Century United States', *The Journal of Economic History,* 64(1): 61–99.

Rosenzweig, M. R. and O. Stark (eds.) (1997). *Handbook of Population and Family Economics.* New York: North-Holland.

Rowen, Herbert H. (1960). *A History of Early Modern Europe: 1500–1815*. New York : Bobbs-Merrill.

Russell, Josiah Cox (1985). *The Control of Late Ancient and Medieval Population*. Philadelphia: The American Philosophical Society.

Rymes, Thomas K. (1971). *On Concepts of Capital and Technical Change*. Cambridge: Cambridge University Press.

Saggs, H. W. F. (1989). *Civilization Before Greece and Rome*. New Haven, CT: Yale University Press.

Sautet, F. E. (2000). *An Entrepreneurial Theory of the Firm*. Routledge: London and New York.

Scarre, Chris (1993). *Timelines of the Ancient World: A Visual Chronology from the Origins of Life to AD 1500*. New York: Dorling Kindersley.

Schick, Kathy D. and Nicholas Toth (1993). *Making Silent Stones Speak*. London: Weidenfeld & Nicolson.

Schmandt-Besserat, Denise (1992). *Before Writing: Volume 1 From Counting to Cuneiform*. Austin, TX: University of Texas.

Schmookler, J. (1966). *Invention and Economic Growth*. Cambridge, MA: Harvard University Press.

Schofield, Robert E. (1963). *The Lunar Society of Birmingham: A Social History of Provincial Science and Industry in Eighteenth-Century England*. Oxford: Clarendon Press.

Schumpeter, Joseph (1934). *The Theory of Economic Development, English Translation*. Cambridge, MA: Harvard University Press. First published in German in 1912.

—— (1943). *Capitalism, Socialism and Democracy*. London: George Allen & Unwin.

Schurr, S. H., C. C. Burwell, W. D. Devine, and S. Sonenblum (eds.) (1990). *Electricity in the American Economy: Agent of Technological Progress*. New York: Greenwood Press.

Shapin, Steven (1996). *The Scientific Revolution*. Chicago: University of Chicago Press.

Shermer, Michael (1997). *Why People Believe Weird Things: Pseudoscience, Superstition and Other Confusions of Our Time*. New York: Freeman.

Shulman, Beth (2003). *The Betrayal of Work: How Low-Wage Jobs Fail 30 Million Americans and Their Families*. New York: New Press.

Silver, Morris (1985). *Economic Structures of the Ancient Near East*. London: Groom Helm.

Silvestre, J. (1987). 'Economies and Diseconomies of Scale', in J. Eatwell et al. (eds.) *The New Palgrave: A Dictionary of Economics*. London: Macmillan.

Simon, Herbert A. (1947). *Administrative Behavior*. New York: Macmillan.

Sivin, N. (1980). 'Science in Chinas Past', in Leo A Orleans (eds.), *Science in Contemporary China*. Stanford: Stanford University Press.

Slicher Van Bath, B. H. (1963). *The Agrarian History of Western Europe*. London: Edward Arnold Publishers.

Snell, Daniel C. (1997). *Life in the Ancient Near Future*. New Haven, CT: Yale University Press.

Snodgrass, Anthony M. (1980). 'Iron and Early Metallurgy in the Mediterranean', in T. A. Wertime and J. D. Muhly (eds.), *The Coming of the Age of Iron*. New Haven, CT: Yale University Press.

Solow, R. (1957). 'Technical Change and the Aggregate Production Function', *Review of Economics and Statistics*, 39: 312–20.

Solsten, Eric (1994). *Portugal: A Country Study*. Washington, DC: Federal Research Division, Library of Congress.

Starr, Chester G. (1991). *A History of the Ancient World*. Oxford: Oxford University Press.

Steinberg, S. H. (1996). *Five Hundred Years of Printing*. London: British Library.

Stewart, Larry (1992). *The Rise of Public Science: Rhetoric, Technology, and Natural Philosophy in Newtonian Britain, 1660–1750*. Cambridge: Cambridge University Press.

Stiglitz, Joseph, E. (2002). *Globalization and Its Discontents*. New York: W. W. Norton.

Stringer, Christopher and Robin McKie (1996). *African Exodus: The Origins of Modern Humanity*. New York: Henry Holt and Co.

Sulzenko, Andrei (1997). 'Technology and Innovation Policy for a Knowledge-Based Economy: The Changing Views in Canada'. Paper presented at the OECD Conference on Technology, Vienna, manuscript.

Szostak, Rick (1991). *The Role of Transportation in the Industrial Revolution*. Montreal: McGill-Queen's University Press.

—— (2003). 'Classifying Natural and Social Scientific Theories', *Current Sociology*, 51(1): 27–49.

Tarasofsky, A. (1985). *The Subsidization of Innovation Projects by the Government of Canada*. Ottawa: Economic Council of Canada.

Taylor, F. W. (1903). 'Shop Management', in *Scientific Management*. London: Harper & Row (1964).

Testart, A. (1982). 'The Significance of Food Storage Among Hunter-Gatherers: Residence Patterns, Population Densities and Social Inequalities', *Current Anthropology*, 23(5): 523–7.

Thaler, R. H. (1980). 'Towards a Positive Theory of Consumer Choice', *Journal of Economic Behaviour and Organization*, 1: 39–60.

Thompson, Silvanus (1910). *Calculus Made Easy*. London: Macmillan.

Thurston, Robert, H. (1878). *A History of the Growth of the Steam-Engine*. New York: D. Appleton and Co.

Titmus, R. M. (1966). *Essays on the Welfare State*. London: Unwin.

Triplett, J. E. (1999) 'Economic Statistics, the New Economy, and the Productivity Slowdown', *Business Economics*, 34(2): 13–17.

Tsiang, S. C. (1984). 'Taiwan's Economic Miracle: Lessons in Economic Development', in A. C. Harberger (ed.), *World Economic Growth*. San Francisco: ICS Press.

Tversky, A. and D. Kahneman (1992). 'Advances in Prospect Theory: Cumulative Representation of Uncertainty', *Journal of Risk and Uncertainty*, 5: 291–323.

Uglow, J. S. (2002). *The Lunar Men: Five Friends Whose Curiosity Changed the World*. New York: Farrar, Straus and Giroux.

Unger, Richard W. (1980). *The Ship in the Medieval Economy, 600–1600*. Montreal: McGill-Queen's University Press.

Usher, Abbott Payson (1920). *An Introduction to the Industrial History of England*. Cambridge, MA: The Riverside Press.

—— (1988). *A History of Mechanical Inventions*. New York: Dover Publications. Originally published in 1929.

Usher, Dan (1983). *The Benefits and Cost of Firm-Specific Investment Grants: A Study of Five Federal Programs*. Discussion Paper 511, Kingston, ON: Department of Economics, Queen's University.

Vassilakis Spiros (1987). 'Increasing Returns to Scale', in J. Eatwell, M. Milgate, and P. Newman (eds.), *The New Palgrave: A Dictionary of Economics*. London: Macmillan, 761–5.

Von Hippel, Eric (1988). *The Sources of Innovation*. New York: Oxford University Press.

Von Tunzelmann, G. N. (1978). *Steam Power and British Industrialization to 1860*. Oxford: Oxford University Press.

—— (1994). *The Dynamics of Technology, Trade and Growth*. Aldershot: Edward Elgar.

Wade, Robert (1990). *Governing the Market: Economic Theory and the Role of Government in East-Asian Industrialization.* Princeton, NJ: Princeton University Press.

Waldbaum, Jane (1980). 'The First Archaeological Appearance of Iron and the Transition of the Iron Age', in T. A. Wertime and J. D. Muhly (eds.), *The Coming of the Age of Iron.* New Haven, CT: Yale University Press.

Warren, Elizabeth and Amelia Warren Tyagi (2003). *The Two-Income Trap: Why Middle-Class Mothers and Fathers are Going Broke.* New York: Basic Books.

Watson, James D. (2003). *DNA: The Secret of Life.* New York: Knopf.

Weatherford, Jack (2004). *Genghis Khan and the Making of the Modern World.* New York: Crown Publishers.

Wenke, Robert J. (1990). *Patterns in Prehistory: Humankind's First Three Million Years.* Oxford: Oxford University Press.

Wertime, T. A. and J. D. Muhly (eds.) (1980). *The Coming of the Age of Iron.* New Haven, CT: Yale University Press.

—— and S. F. Wertime (eds.) (1982). *Early Pyrotechnology: The Evolution of the First Fire-Using Industries.* Washington, DC: Smithsonian Institution Press.

Westphal, Larry E. (1990). 'Industrial Policy in an Export Propelled Economy: Lessons From South Korea's Experience', *Journal of Economic Perspectives*, 4(3), 41–59.

White, Andrew Dickinson (1896). *The Warfare of Science with Theology.* New York: D. Appleton.

White, Lynn, Jr. (1962). *Medieval Technology and Social Change.* Oxford: Oxford University Press.

—— (1969). 'The Expansion of Technology, 500–1500', in Carlo M. Cipolla (ed.), *The Fontana Economic History of Europe*, Vol. 1. London: Collins Clear-Type Press.

—— (1978). *Medieval Religion and Technology: Collected Essays.* California: University of California Press.

Wicksell, K. (1893/1954). *Value, Capital and Rent.* London: Allen & Unwin.

Williamson, Jeffrey G. (ed.) (1990). *Latin American Adjustment: How Much Has Happened?* Washington: Institute for International Economics.

—— (1996). 'Globalization, Convergence, and History', *The Journal of Economic History*, 56(2): 277–306.

Womack, James, P., Daniel T. Jones, and Danie Roos (1990). *The Machine that Changed the World.* New York: Rawson.

World Commission on Environment and Development (1987). *Our Common Future.* Gro Harlem Brundtland, Chairman, Oxford: Oxford University Press.

Woronoff, L. (1992). *Japanese Targeting: Successes, Failures, Lessons.* London: Macmillan.

Wright, Gavin (1997). 'Towards a More Historical Approach to Technological Change', *The Economic Journal*, 107(444): 1560–6.

Wrigley, E. A. and R. S. Schofield (1981). *The Population History of England, 1541–1871: A Reconstruction.* Cambridge, MA: Harvard University Press.

—— R.S. Davies, J.E. Oeppen, and R.S. Schofield (1997). *English Population History from Family Reconstitution, 1580–1837.* Cambridge: Cambridge University Press.

Young, Alwyn (1992). 'A Tale of Two Cities: Factor Accumulation and Technical Change in Hong Kong and Singapore', in *NBER Macroeconomic Annual.* Cambridge, MA: MIT Press.

—— (1995). 'The Tyranny of the Numbers', *Quarterly Journal of Economics*, 110: 641–80.

Young, Michael Dunlop and Peter Willmott (1957). *Family and Kinship in East London.* London: Routledge & Kegan Paul.

Yu-lan, Fung (1922). 'Why China Has No Science', *International Journal of Ethics*, 32(3).

Index

abandoned technologies,
    unknown potential of 80
acceleration of technological
    change 132–3, 424–5
Adams, J. 390
Adams, R. M.
    irrigation works as public goods 147 n.
    signposts 78 n.
adaptive versus rational expectations,
    modelling 468–74
additionality, 538
Advanced Gas-Cooled Reactor
    (AGR) 525, 526
age of discovery, spread of disease 143
aggregate production function 11, 22, 107,
    119–20 n, 355, 401, 503
    in calculations of TFP 12, 119, 120
    technology in the 28 n, 36
    in vintage capital models 64n.
    in conventional growth theory 20, 25, 28,
        55, 107, 111, 118, 308 n, 401–4
    limitations 403, 428, 430, 465, 467,
        495, 504
    in models of endogenous population 303,
        319, 329, 331
    neoclassical theory 8, 10, 55
    in S-E-driven growth 404–6
    and sustainability of growth 426–7
Aghion, P. and Howitt, P. 25 n.
    models of GPT-driven growth 371, 382–4,
        441 n, 442 n, 443 n.
agriculture
    application of biotechnology 212–13
    beginnings of 137–8
    domestication of plants 138–9
    medieval agricultural revolution 160–4
    Neolithic agricultural
        revolution 138–44

productivity increase, effect on
    population 325, 327–8
Airbus Industrie, government support
    524
aircraft industry
    main and sub-technologies 91
    technological convergence 91
    transfer from propeller-driven to
        jets 534 n.
    US government assistance 523, 541
Akerlof G. 26
Alchian, A. A. 27
    groping behaviour 47–8, 474
Allen, R. C., Middle Ages, living
    standards 295
alternating current (AC) 197
Alvey Programme 525
American System of Manufactures 104–5
Anatolia, first use of smelting 151
Angel, J. L. 336
Anglican Church, support for new
    science 237, 238, 241
animals
    domestication 139–40
        association with use of wheel 141
        as source of diseases 143
    selective breeding 131
Anselm, St. 226
applications curve, GPTs 436, 437–8
appreciative theories 19, 40, 62, 78, 111, 371,
    376, 384, 407, 434, 436
appreciative theorising 39, 45, 46, 65, 219,
    220, 222, 288
Aquinas, St. Thomas 233, 234
Archibald, G. et al. 87
Aristotle's teaching 236, 275
    conflict with Christianity 232–4, 235
Armenia, early development of steel 157